$3⁰⁰

THE
WHOLE

PEOPLE • MATERIALS • GUIDEL... ...CHNOLOGY

LIBRARY

OPERATIONS • FUNDING • STAFF DEVELOPMENT

HANDBOOK

ISSUES • DIVERSITY • THE INTERNET • LIBRARIANA

3

CURRENT DATA, PROFESSIONAL ADVICE, AND
CURIOSA ABOUT LIBRARIES AND LIBRARY SERVICES

COMPILED BY **George M. Eberhart**

AMERICAN LIBRARY ASSOCIATION
Chicago and London   2000

Printed on 60-pound white offset, a pH-neutral stock, and bound in 10-point C1S cover stock by McNaughton & Gunn.

The paper used in this publication meets the minimum requirements of American National Standard for Information Sciences–Permanence of Paper for Printed Library Materials, ANSI Z39.48-1992. ∞

Library of Congress Cataloging-in-Publication Data

Eberhart, George M.

    The whole library handbook 3 : current data, professional advice, and curiosa about libraries and library services / compiled by George M. Eberhart.

        p.   cm.

    Includes bibliographical references and index.

    ISBN 0-8389-0781-4

    1. Library science—United States—Handbooks, manuals, etc. 2. Libraries—United States—Handbooks, manuals, etc. I. Title: Whole library handbook three. II. Title.

Z665.2.U6 .E243 2000

020′.973—dc21   99-089307

Printed in the United States of America.

05   04   03   02   5   4   3   2

CONTENTS

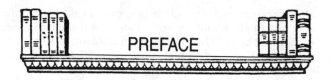

PREFACE

The Whole Library Handbook 3

George M. Eberhart

LIBRARIANSHIP is by no means static, and any reference book that tries to keep up with the profession must revitalize itself frequently. The last edition of *The Whole Library Handbook* came out in 1995 when the Web was just taking off. By 2000, the Internet has brought about the most profound changes to the art and science of information management since the invention of the card catalog. In many ways, this has made the job of compiling library-related facts, figures, and ephemera much easier; but the task of selecting the best sources from this cornucopia is formidable.

This third edition contains what I consider to be the most relevant, informative, and digestible nuggets from the literature of librarianship. About 95% of *WLH3* is completely new or substantially revised, and the book is a solid 48 pages thicker than the last one. Those earlier editions are not obsolete; you may still consult them to find out, for example, the status of comic books in society or how to keep a dictionary on its stand. But in *WLH3* you will discover such new features as the oldest and largest national libraries, what to put in your resumé, what they didn't tell you in library school, secrets of the Freedom of Information Act, the protohistory of information retrieval, how to provide library service to the poor, how to cultivate donors, how to repair compact discs, how to be an ethical archivist, and plentiful facts on library cats, library postcards, and library ghosts.

There are several reasons why a printed handbook like this can stay above water in a cyberspace sea:

(1) Not everything is on the Web.

(2) Back issues of magazines are not always available for consultation.

(3) Computers and connections can go down instantly, leaving information-seekers virtually stranded.

(4) A handbook is quicker to browse for serendipitous discoveries than surfing the Web. The feel of one's thumb flipping through physical pages is also more satisfying and natural than link hopping or exploring Yahoo.

(5) Having a wide range of relevant information stuffed into a compact package is the classic hallmark of a useful reference source. The Internet, though wide-ranging, is rarely compact and often irrelevant and misleading. If the text in this edition looks crowded, that's because the fact density is high.

(6) Though the articles are written by many different authors, an invisible editorial hand can unify and augment their features and transform them from a ragtag mob of vagabonds into a precision marching band. In some instances, I have had fun rearranging traditional data and giving it a new spin. And by seeking a comfortable mix of the whimsical with the practical, I can make palatable the driest and most distasteful of data.

In short, perhaps the *Whole Library Handbook* can trick you into reading some professional literature that you might otherwise not have known or cared about, whether you are a student, a library director, a trustee, an information broker, or someone who just wants to know more about what librarians do. As Dorothy Sayers once wrote, "Detail delights me. Ramifications enchant me. Distance no object." I've tried to present some tidbits for everyone interested in the future of libraries and knowledge.

As in earlier editions, please keep in mind that many of the selections are only extracts of longer books or articles. The originals in their full glory are almost always worth seeking out.

If I have, through ignorance or unconscious editorial preference, neglected to cover a topic or reprint a particularly splendid checklist, let me know and I will consider it for a future edition. Send ideas to me c/o *American Libraries*, 50 E. Huron St., Chicago, IL 60611, or e-mail geberhart@ala.org.

Finally, I would like to thank the many people who contributed their time and talents to this project. Some who made a special effort to provide information and data include: Mary Jo Lynch, Norman Stevens, Godfrey Oswald, Barbara Semonche, John Y. Cole, Marjorie Warmkessel, Gary Roma, Marty Raish, and Larry Nix. Also, my deepest appreciation goes to Art Plotnik, who helped craft the content and scope of the first two books; ALA Editions production editor Dianne Rooney for fine-tuning the layout; proofreader Sara Guth; indexer Janet Russell; my wife and occasional collaborator Jennifer Henderson; our two own library cats, Andy and the late, lamented Noodles; and all of you who purchased earlier editions of the handbook—may you find even more helpful and humorous information in these pages.

LIBRARIES
CHAPTER ONE

"How is it, though, that libraries are shrines of such austere calm? If books are as provocative as you suggest, one would expect every librarian to utter the shrill screams of a hierophant, to clash ecstatic castanets in his silent alcoves!"

—Christopher Morley, *The Haunted Bookshop* (1919)

Some basic figures

by Mary Jo Lynch

MANY OF THE FIGURES given here are from surveys published by the National Center for Education Statistics (NCES): *Academic Libraries, 1994* (1998), *Public Libraries in the United States, 1996* (1999); and *School Library Media Centers, 1993–1994* (1998). Additional sources are cited where appropriate.

How many libraries are there?

Libraries of various types exist in all parts of the United States, and there is no official source that counts them all every year. The following count is based on the surveys cited above for academic, public, and school libraries. Figures for special libraries, armed forces libraries, and government libraries come from the 1998–1999 *American Library Directory* compiled by the R. R. Bowker Company.

Libraries in the United States		
College and university libraries		3,303
Public libraries		*8,946
Centrals*	8,923	
Branches	7,124	
Buildings	16,047	
School library media centers		98,169
Public schools	77,218	
Private schools	20,951	
Special libraries		9,898
Armed forces libraries		363
Government libraries		1,897
TOTAL		**122,576**

* The number of central buildings is different from the number of public libraries because some public library systems have no central building and some have more than one.

These libraries are often involved in cooperative organizations through which they share collections, technology, and staff expertise. The most recent national survey found that approximately 760 networks and cooperatives existed in the United States at that time (*Survey of Library Networks and Cooperative Library Organizations, 1985–1986*, NCES, 1987). Most college, university, and public libraries and many school libraries belong to at least one and many participate in more than one.

Another important factor in library services is the state library agency in each of the 50 states. The agency may have a library or may contract with a public or academic library to act as a resource or reference/information center. But all 50 states are involved in electronic network development, facilitating access to the Internet, and distribution of funds received under the Library Services and Technology Act (LSTA).

How much are they used?

The 3,303 **college and university libraries** submitting "gate count" figures to NCES for 1993–1994 reported that more than 17,830,800 people visited these libraries in a typical week. During 1993–1994, more than 183,123,000 items circulated from academic libraries. Another 48,380,000 were used in reserve collections.

The 1996 NCES report on **public libraries** shows 1,013,798,000 "visits" in that year, an increase of 3.2% over the figure in the 1995 report. In 1996, the average circulation for public libraries was 6.5 items per capita. The total number of items circulated nationally from public libraries in 1996 was over 1,642,625,000, an increase of 2% more than the figure reported in 1995.

The 1993–1994 NCES survey estimated that for the 77,218 **public school library media centers** in the United States:

- more than 32.5 million students visited the libraries per week;
- each student averaged 1.2 visits to the library per week.

During the 1993–1994 school year, all public school libraries in the United States:

- circulated a total of more than 41,748,000 items per week;
- circulated an average of 538 items per school per week.

Almost all public schools have library media centers, but many **private schools** have small enrollments and are less likely to have a library. The 1993–1994 NCES survey estimated that:

- of the 16,050 private schools with less than 300 students, 76% had libraries;
- of the 4,901 private schools with 300 or more students, 97% had libraries.

The same survey showed that for the 20,951 private school library media centers in the United States:

- more than 3.4 million students visited all libraries per week;
- each student averaged 1.2 visits to the library per week.

Who uses public libraries?

It is fairly obvious who uses college and university libraries and who uses school library media centers—students and faculty associated with those institutions. But who uses public libraries? See pp. 19–21 for an article on the 1996 National Household Education Survey sponsored by NCES. It reports on household use of public libraries by families with or without children and on use by households of different racial/ethnic groups. Another perspective on public libraries comes from a national survey conducted by the Gallup Organization for the American Library Association. In May 1998, Gallup surveyed a random sample of adults over 18 and found that:

- 64% said they had a library card;
- 66% said they used a public library at least once in the last year (in person, by phone, or by computer).

Most (64%) visited the library in person, and the frequency of those visits varied as follows:

1–5 times	31%
6–10 times	11%
11–25 times	11%
More than 25 times	11%
Not at all	36%

People do many different things in public libraries. Gallup asked about seven different activities and respondents answered as shown below:

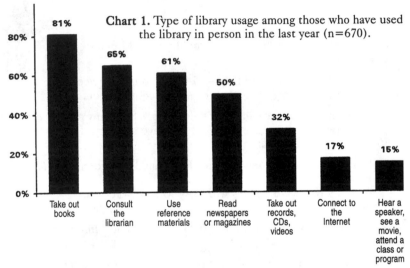

Chart 1. Type of library usage among those who have used the library in person in the last year (n=670).

When people access the library by phone or by computer, they do different things as shown below:

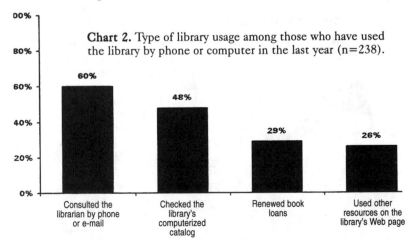

Chart 2. Type of library usage among those who have used the library by phone or computer in the last year (n=238).

Three in 10 respondents said they used a computer in the library. Ninety percent said they believe libraries will continue to be a necessary service despite the growing availability of information through computers.

Public libraries are well regarded as government services. When asked to rank the benefits of public libraries as compared to the benefits of other tax-supported services, respondents rated them somewhat differently depending on their age, but few rated them low (see Chart 3).

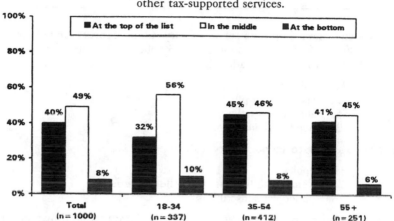

Chart 3. Perceived value of public libraries compared to other tax-supported services.

The traditional library

Ownership. For many years, librarians have acquired, organized, and helped people use collections of printed materials, primarily books and serials (i.e., magazines, journals, newspapers). Audiovisual materials and microforms were added in the 20th century. Although electronic resources are revolutionizing library service today, collections of print, audiovisual, and microform material are still the bedrock of library service.

The 3,303 **college & university libraries** reporting to NCES in the fall of 1994 held a total of 776,447,422 volumes of books, bound serials, and government documents. Collections ranged in size from 237 libraries with less than 5,000 volumes to 157 with 1,000,000 or more. The 3,303 academic libraries held 6,212,000 serial subscriptions and material in several other formats including:

- 929,248,000   microform units
- 34,900,000   cartographic items
- 9,292,000   sound recordings
- 3,392,000   film and video titles

Of the 8,946 **public libraries** in the United States included in the 1996 NCES report, slightly more than half had collections of less than 25,000, but 170 had collections of 500,000 or more. These libraries held a total of 771,013,000 book and serial volumes and received 1,857,000 serial subscriptions. These libraries also hold material in many nonprint formats including:

- 25,164,000   audio titles
- 13,094,000   video titles

Libraries in Canada	
College and university libraries	487
Public libraries	1,633
Special libraries	1,422
Government libraries	389
TOTAL	**3,931**

SOURCE: *American Library Directory*, 51st ed. (New York: R. R. Bowker, 1999).

Book collections in **public school library media centers** range from less than 2,000 in 6% of schools to more than 30,000 in 1%. The average public school library in 1993–1994 had:

- 9,722 volumes
- 26 volumes per pupil
- 652 audiovisual titles
- 30 periodical subscriptions

The average **private school library** had:

- 6,430 books
- 295 items of audiovisual and other materials
- 14 periodical subscriptions

Access. For many years, libraries of all types have borrowed materials for their clients from other libraries through a cooperative arrangement known as interlibrary loan. Guidelines and forms devised by ALA facilitate this service. During the academic year 1993–1994, **academic libraries** in the United States:

- provided more than 8,761,000 items to other libraries;
- received more than 6,344,000 items from other libraries.

In 1996 the 8,946 **public libraries** in the United States:

- provided more than 10,531,000 items to other libraries
- received more than 10,968,000 items from other libraries.

In the figures above, the number of items provided is not equal to the number received for each type of library. This is due to several factors such as lending across library types (including types for which no statistics are available).

In recent years, there have been many changes in interlibrary loan services. Photocopying technology, telefacsimile technology, and the development of commercial document delivery services have had major impacts on the volume and speed of traffic. Other factors are the increasing cost of serial publications and the increasing availability of electronic indexes to those publications. A recent study of interlibrary loan in 76 of the largest research libraries in the United States and Canada found that 60% of filled transactions were for nonreturnable copies rather than original items.

Answers to questions

Librarians find answers to questions or help library users do so. During 1996, **public libraries** in the United States answered more than 284,513,000 reference questions. The 3,303 **academic libraries** reporting in the fall of 1990 answered a total of 2,147,000 reference questions in a typical week.

The automated library

Between 1970 and 1990, library automation became widespread in the United States. Single-function systems came first, using computers to manage cataloging, circulation, acquisitions, or serials. In the 1980s, integrated systems were developed, using a single bibliographic database to support multiple library operations, including online public access catalogs (OPACs). In 1997, 20 different server-based systems and 9 microcomputer-based systems were available.

The annual *Library Journal* article on the automated system marketplace estimates that revenues in 1998 for the 27 vendors surveyed was $475,000,000. They sold a total of 20,001 systems in the United States and 2,835 outside of the United States. Installations and upgrades in 1998 that could be assigned to a specific type of library and type of platform were as follows:

Academic Libraries		*School Libraries*	
Microcomputers	594	Microcomputers	12,640
Servers	480	Servers	234
Public Libraries		*Special Libraries*	
Microcomputers	3,570	Microcomputers	679
Servers	323	Servers	358

The electronic library

Automating library functions has changed the traditional library, particularly for those who staff it. But for those who use libraries, a much more profound change occurred in the 1990s with the increasing use of computer and telecommunications technologies to provide access to information. The rapid growth of the Internet, especially the World Wide Web, has had a profound effect on libraries in the 1990s.

Academic libraries were first to connect to the Internet in large numbers, probably because the Internet started in academic institutions. A 1996 ALA study showed that all four-year college and university libraries offered Internet access to staff, and almost all offered Internet access to users. For two-year college libraries the numbers offering access were smaller. Indications are that Internet access in all academic libraries has expanded since 1996.

A 1998 study sponsored by ALA's Office for Information Technology Policy found that 83.6% of **public library** outlets were connected to the Internet and 73.3% of the outlets offered public Internet access. A 1997 study by MCI found that 35% of Americans over 16 searched the Internet in 1997 and 15% of them searched from someplace other than their home, school, or work. The public library was the most popular of those other sites, used by 45% of those who searched the Internet but not from home, school, or work. A 1998 NCES survey of **public schools** indicates that 51% of "instructional rooms" (classrooms, computer labs, library media centers) are connected to the Internet.

Online bibliographic databases were a first step toward the electronic library, with searches of remote sources available in many libraries since the early 1980s. Today, almost all databases are available on the Web. Many are also available in several other forms for use on local computers. According to the September 1998 edition of the two-volume *Gale Directory of Databases*, there are approximately 5,500 online databases made available by the producer or by an online service.

In 1997, *Library Journal* started running an annual article on the database marketplace, analyzing information gathered from the almost 30 companies that sell electronic databases to libraries. Some of these companies also sell database access directly to individuals. But the more common pattern is to sell to libraries, who may then make the databases available to their constituents from outside the library as well as in the library itself. Some of their vendors offer the same database in CD-ROM, on the Web, or online, either locally or remote. The result is a confusing and volatile situation but one in which a large number of libraries are participating.

A 1996 ALA study found that electronic reference databases (e.g., indexing and abstracting services) were offered by all four-year **college and university libraries** and almost all two-year college libraries. A Public Library Association survey in 1998 found that 59% of **public libraries** serving populations of 100,000 or more offer these databases through their online public access catalogs.

Libraries subscribe to periodicals of all types (magazines, journals, etc.) in electronic editions available on the Internet. The January 1999 edition of *Fulltext Sources Online* lists over 7,000 general-interest titles, while the 1998 edition of a similar directory from the Association of Research Libraries lists 1,456 scholarly periodical titles. Most are electronic editions of paper titles but some are available only in electronic form.

Librarians are answering an increasing number of questions using Web resources. They are also providing content to the Web by digitizing unique resources and providing Web access. The Library of Congress's American Memory project is a prime example of this activity (see memory.loc.gov/ammem/ amabout.html). American Memory is a multimedia collection of digitized documents, photographs, recorded sound, moving pictures, and text from LC's Americana collections. The Digital Library Federation is a group of 20 other libraries involved in substantial digitization projects (www.clir.org/diglib/ diglib.html).

SOURCE: Mary Jo Lynch, ALA Office for Research and Statistics.

Libraries: An American value

LIBRARIES IN AMERICA are cornerstones of the communities they serve. Free access to the books, ideas, resources, and information in America's libraries is imperative for education, employment, enjoyment, and self-government.

Libraries are a legacy to each generation, offering the heritage of the past and the promise of the future. To ensure that libraries flourish and have the freedom to promote and protect the public good in the 21st century, we believe certain principles must be guaranteed.

To that end, we affirm this contract with the people we serve:

We defend the constitutional rights of all individuals, including children and teenagers, to use the library's resources and services;

We value our nation's diversity and strive to reflect that diversity by providing a full spectrum of resources and services to the communities we serve;

We affirm the responsibility and the right of all parents and guardians to guide their own children's use of the library and its resources and services;

We connect people and ideas by helping each person select from and effectively use the library's resources;

We protect each individual's privacy and confidentiality in the use of library resources and services;

We protect the rights of individuals to express their opinions about library resources and services;

We celebrate and preserve our democratic society by making available the widest possible range of viewpoints, opinions and ideas, so that all individuals have the opportunity to become lifelong learners—informed, literate, educated, and culturally enriched.

Change is constant; but these principles transcend change and endure in a dynamic technological, social, and political environment.

By embracing these principles, libraries in the United States can contribute to a future that values and protects freedom of speech, in a world that celebrates both our similarities and our differences, respects individuals and their beliefs, and holds all persons truly equal and free.

SOURCE: Adopted by the American Library Association Council, February 3, 1999.

12 ways libraries are good for the country

MOST AMERICANS KNOW what they can expect from a library. And librarians know what it takes to provide comprehensive access to every recorded detail of human existence. It takes support.

Libraries are ready when they are needed, ready to enrich our minds and defend our right to know, just as other institutions protect our safety and property. Without sound minds, however, the American dream of safe streets and secure homes will never be fulfilled.

Libraries safeguard our freedom and keep democracy healthy. To library advocates everywhere—Friends, trustees, board members, patrons, and volunteers—*American Libraries* offers this gift of 12 ideals toward which we strive. It will take all of us, in a spirit of pride and freedom, to maintain libraries as a living reality in a free nation into the 21st century.

1.   Libraries inform citizens. Democracy vests supreme power in the people. Libraries make democracy work by providing access to information so that citizens can make the decisions necessary to govern themselves. The public library is the only institution in American society whose purpose is to guard against the tyrannies of ignorance and conformity, and its existence indicates the extent to which a democratic society values knowledge, truth, justice, books, and culture.

2. Libraries break down boundaries. Libraries provide free family literacy programs for low-literate, illiterate, and non-English-speaking people. In addition, hundreds of librarians across America lead outreach programs that teach citizenship and develop multilingual and multicultural materials for their patrons. Libraries serve the homebound elderly, prisoners, and other institutionalized individuals, the homeless, and the blind and hearing-impaired.

3. Libraries level the playing field. Economists have cited a growing income inequity in America, with the gap between the richest and poorest citizens becoming wider year by year. By making all its resources equally available to all members of its community, regardless of income, class, or other factors, the library levels the playing field. Once users have access to the library's materials, they have the opportunity to level the playing field outside the library by learning to read, gaining employment, or starting a business.

4. Libraries value the individual. Library doors swing open for independent thinking without prejudgment. Libraries offer alternatives to the manipulations of commercialism, from the excellence of public-television productions to the freethinking of renegade publishers and the vision of poets and artists outside the mainstream business of art and literature.

5. Libraries nourish creativity. In the library we are all children. By stimulating curiosity—parent to the twin forces of creativity and imagination—even the most focused and specialized library serves the purpose of lifting the mind beyond its horizons. Libraries store ideas that may no longer work but can serve as the raw material that, cross-fertilized in the innovative mind, may produce answers to questions not yet asked.

6. Libraries open kids' minds. Bringing children into a library can transport them from the commonplace to the extraordinary. From story hours for preschoolers to career planning for high schoolers, children's librarians make a difference because they care about the unique developmental needs of every individual who comes to them for help. Children get a handle on personal responsibility by holding a library card of their own, a card that gives them access to new worlds in books, videos, audiotapes, computers, games, toys, and more.

7. Libraries return high dividends. What do Gallo wines, the I Can't Believe It's Yogurt chain, and billboard-sign giant Metromedia have in common? Libraries made millionaires out of each of these companies' grateful owners by providing crucial start-up information when they were no more than wannabe business titans. Libraries are there to help people with more personal goals, too. The seed money expended for these and other success stories? Less than $20 per capita per year in tax dollars.

8. Libraries build communities. No narrow definition of community will work in a library. Each community has its libraries and its special collections. Libraries validate and unify; they save lives, literally and by preserving the record of those lives. Community-building means libraries link people with information. Librarians have become experts at helping others navigate the Internet. Before there was talk of cyberspace, there were libraries, paving the way for the superhighway.

9. Libraries make families friendlier. The American family's best friend, the library, offers services guaranteed to hone coping skills. Homework centers, literacy training, parenting materials, after-school activities, summer reading programs, outreach—like the families they serve, libraries everywhere are adapting to meet new challenges.

10. Libraries offend everyone. Children's librarian Dorothy Broderick contends that every library in the country ought to have a sign on the door reading: "This library has something offensive to everyone. If you are not offended by something we own, please complain." This willingness and duty to offend connotes a tolerance and a willingness to look at all sides of an issue that would be good for the nation in any context; it is particularly valuable when combined with the egalitarianism and openness that characterize libraries.

11. Libraries offer sanctuary. Like synagogues, churches, mosques, and other sacred spaces, libraries can create a physical reaction, a feeling of peace, respect, humility, and honor that throws the mind wide open and suffuses the body with a near-spiritual pleasure. But why? Perhaps it is because in the library we are answerable to no one; alone with our private thoughts, fantasies, and hopes, we are free to nourish what is most precious to us with the silent companionship of others we do not know.

12. Libraries preserve the past. Libraries preserve the record; a nation, a culture, a community that does not understand its own past is mired in its own mistakes. Libraries enable us to communicate through distance and time with the living and the dead. It is a miracle kept available by the meticulous sorting, storing, indexing, and preservation that still characterizes library work—work that will carry, in the electronic environment, challenges and a price tag yet unknown.

SOURCE: "12 Ways Libraries Are Good for the Country," *American Libraries* 26 (December 1995): 1113–19.

ACADEMIC LIBRARIES

The largest university
research libraries, 1998

THE FOLLOWING FIGURES are based on an index developed by the Association of Research Libraries (ARL) to measure the relative size of its university library members. The five categories used in the rankings were determined by factor analysis of 22 categories of quantitative data and represent the elements in which ARL university libraries most resemble one another. The index does not attempt to measure a library's services, quality of collections, or success in meeting the needs of users.

The five data elements are: number of volumes held, number of volumes added (gross), number of current serials received, total operating expenditures, and number of professional and support staff.

This rank order table is only for 111 university library members of ARL, which has 11 nonuniversity library members. Nonuniversity libraries are not gauged by the same index formula as the universities, and are sufficiently different that it would be misleading to incorporate them into the table.

ARL does not claim that this ranking incorporates all the factors necessary to give a complete picture of research library quality. However, it is a measuring device that has proven reliable over the years for specific internal and comparative purposes.

Volumes in library does not include microforms, manuscripts, audiovisual and computer resources, maps, or certain other items central to research library collections and services. It includes government documents in some (but not all) cases. It is thus not a complete indicator of library resources.

Total staff includes professionals, nonprofessionals, and student assistants; however, only the first two groups are used to calculate the rank score.

Total expenditures include money spent on materials purchases, salaries, and general operations, but does not include capital expenditures for buildings, expenditures for plant maintenance, and some kinds of computing and administrative services; these are often part of the main university budget and not directly allocated to the library. However, such additional expenditures are crucial to an effective library and reflect the total commitment of an institution to providing and preserving research information.

	Rank	Volumes in library	Volumes added	Current serials	Total staff	Total expenditures[1]
Harvard University	1	13,892,429	310,016	105,449	1,188	$75,814,280
Yale University	2	10,108,371	180,953	54,933	611	42,109,000
University of California/ Los Angeles	3	7,212,229	210,975	94,748	617	37,077,594
University of Toronto	4	8,605,956	238,027	49,876	652	36,094,797
University of California/ Berkeley	5	8,792,009	155,007	79,125	634	35,962,762
Stanford University	6	6,997,003	212,558	44,504	601	47,568,884
University of Illinois/ Urbana-Champaign	7	9,171,693	153,293	90,801	543	26,206,794
Columbia University	8	7,018,408	218,519	66,780	516	30,743,348
University of Michigan	9	7,071,842	141,359	69,280	594	34,747,186
Cornell University	10	6,260,779	219,195	61,941	562	29,516,909
University of Texas	11	7,648,678	157,659	52,515	574	28,744,448
University of Washington	12	5,820,229	138,298	50,245	502	26,605,188
Pennsylvania State University	13	4,260,519	148,733	35,789	575	32,119,520
Indiana University	14	6,043,233	149,845	42,293	499	24,185,658
University of Minnesota	15	5,613,171	141,753	46,989	431	28,489,796
University of Wisconsin	16	5,902,197	106,311	42,518	501	29,186,521
University of North Carolina	17	4,928,026	125,561	44,023	431	24,345,333
Princeton University	18	5,637,901	125,382	34,348	370	27,018,275
University of Chicago	19	6,271,045	159,852	35,693	336	21,284,860
University of Pennsylvania	20	4,672,777	131,606	34,276	393	28,838,071
Duke University	21	4,764,033	125,512	34,872	359	23,919,245
University of Virginia	22	4,513,843	103,172	47,479	363	22,854,406
Ohio State University	23	5,177,386	115,405	36,020	438	22,474,700
New York University	24	3,731,910	127,522	29,776	418	26,703,405
University of Iowa	25	3,926,853	131,943	46,786	298	20,095,042
Rutgers University	26	3,703,052	83,009	28,934	457	25,122,306
Arizona State University	27	3,372,529	98,570	36,621	363	20,794,434
University of Georgia	28	3,539,483	91,885	42,323	360	18,825,259
University of Alberta	29	5,275,697	104,980	27,886	316	15,492,145
Northwestern University	30	3,954,204	89,659	40,008	351	18,420,379

1. Figures for Canadian libraries are expressed in U.S. dollars.

	Rank	Volumes in library	Volumes added	Current serials	Total staff	Total expenditures
University of Arizona	31	4,528,588	94,185	25,274	358	$20,353,655
University of Florida	32	3,401,279	97,160	25,213	415	20,791,059
University of Pittsburgh	33	3,911,168	108,209	24,375	379	19,264,332
University of Southern California	34	3,480,853	93,399	28,534	339	23,974,666
University of British Columbia	35	3,913,833	76,830	21,888	394	19,865,433
Texas A&M University	36	2,549,470	99,183	29,671	401	20,530,310
North Carolina State University	37	2,713,146	103,907	35,194	310	17,210,758
University of California/ Davis	38	3,014,490	78,267	43,334	287	16,111,444
Michigan State University	39	4,188,141	108,288	27,311	273	16,595,981
Johns Hopkins University	40	3,275,082	57,311	21,337	316	21,774,961
Emory University	41	2,442,504	79,666	23,711	297	22,089,001
University of Kansas	42	3,607,522	76,583	33,090	282	15,329,371
University of California/ San Diego	43	2,577,641	91,648	23,456	315	18,166,088
Washington University (Mo.)	44	3,296,358	77,570	18,626	287	20,248,164
University of Maryland	45	2,699,919	79,208	27,137	329	15,891,946
University of Utah	46	2,684,321	82,485	16,433	381	19,713,669
Georgetown University	47	2,363,799	76,214	27,379	262	17,563,059
University of Colorado	48	2,789,579	85,388	25,263	239	16,005,275
University of Kentucky	49	2,719,088	50,850	28,535	362	17,418,260
Wayne State University	50	3,045,681	64,239	24,200	279	16,049,894
Vanderbilt University	51	2,512,072	75,672	21,608	291	15,945,583
University of South Carolina	52	3,067,457	72,653	18,933	277	15,231,693
Notre Dame University	53	2,644,486	68,452	24,106	237	15,032,442
University of New Mexico	54	2,244,315	74,117	17,788	392	17,498,083
State University of New York at Buffalo	55	3,106,748	73,917	21,262	261	14,732,765
University of Connecticut	56	2,885,664	71,893	17,173	261	17,134,042
McGill University	57	3,059,524	72,993	16,787	268	13,103,008
University of Cincinnati	58	2,524,410	64,237	21,556	285	16,522,529
Boston University	59	2,129,423	52,447	28,172	289	13,573,720
University of Oklahoma	60	4,066,129	91,258	16,890	182	10,886,028
University of California/ Santa Barbara	61	2,503,741	110,296	18,100	217	11,461,583
University of Hawaii	62	2,991,974	73,882	20,871	222	10,488,805
University of Missouri	63	2,856,649	45,666	23,522	246	11,425,853
University of Nebraska	64	2,501,014	60,527	23,231	214	11,486,317
Louisiana State University	65	3,006,356	74,682	17,975	203	10,813,226
Brown University	66	2,978,970	52,232	13,640	241	15,084,997
University of Tennessee	67	2,276,004	50,041	17,433	253	12,540,216
University of Illinois/ Chicago	68	1,989,739	52,278	15,538	273	14,446,345
Purdue University	69	2,280,681	43,830	19,025	264	13,336,543
University of Miami	70	2,165,040	56,190	18,987	221	13,489,740
Massachusetts Institute of Technology	71	2,532,175	47,427	18,359	217	12,371,940
Texas Tech University	72	2,079,888	53,832	23,888	245	12,469,706
Laval University	73	2,326,630	75,193	11,566	223	11,209,980
University of California/ Irvine	74	2,030,624	58,761	18,187	249	14,487,141

	Rank	Volumes in library	Volumes added	Current serials	Total staff	Total expenditures
Ohio University	75	2,174,674	65,863	29,065	201	$10,658,273
Iowa State University	76	2,167,294	48,314	22,455	213	13,886,724
Temple University	77	2,391,914	51,820	16,755	225	11,961,824
University of Western Ontario	78	2,292,285	61,212	14,572	203	10,734,174
Florida State University	79	2,263,257	53,631	15,511	247	11,183,790
University of Massachusetts	80	2,882,541	56,909	15,835	194	11,154,585
University of Oregon	81	2,306,007	62,385	14,984	220	12,676,918
Syracuse University	82	2,733,382	37,565	16,298	268	10,586,245
Dartmouth College	83	2,261,911	46,816	20,043	186	11,925,052
Washington State University	84	1,963,546	41,662	27,377	201	11,916,822
George Washington University	85	1,848,636	44,958	15,023	246	13,743,095
University of Rochester	86	2,992,304	50,936	11,254	214	12,185,856
Brigham Young University	87	2,500,849	39,029	16,029	304	13,834,157
York University (Ontario)	88	2,250,952	53,497	14,359	225	11,160,395
University of Delaware	89	2,358,006	50,502	12,220	214	11,955,644
Virginia Polytechnic Institute and State University	90	2,004,684	58,031	18,518	197	11,113,142
Howard University	91	2,372,112	40,331	14,368	188	14,860,026
Kent State University	92	2,392,571	56,811	12,953	235	10,503,985
Oklahoma State University	93	2,038,952	78,331	17,552	183	9,145,786
Southern Illinois University	94	2,359,797	42,126	16,445	229	11,097,444
University of Houston	95	1,986,642	48,815	18,103	204	11,049,227
Auburn University	96	2,504,557	47,814	18,739	159	9,266,646
University of Alabama	97	2,136,423	46,620	18,042	193	10,019,101
Rice University	98	2,019,068	69,096	14,282	130	10,416,047
Tulane University	99	2,148,660	40,723	14,986	203	11,086,198
Colorado State University	100	1,752,704	50,449	21,255	189	9,782,499
University of Manitoba	101	1,784,395	46,918	9,249	225	9,675,616
State University of New York at Albany	102	1,900,626	46,358	16,077	164	9,356,792
Case Western Reserve University	103	1,996,479	35,499	14,042	172	10,781,317
Georgia Institute of Technology	104	2,022,141	59,169	14,407	112	9,017,104
University of Saskatchewan	105	1,736,771	52,923	13,087	167	8,354,725
Queen's University	106	2,175,352	38,988	10,825	184	8,890,007
University of California/ Riverside	107	1,896,960	48,732	12,565	167	9,330,020
McMaster University	108	1,823,724	44,691	11,232	163	8,412,818
State University of New York at Stony Brook	109	2,025,373	34,890	10,506	172	10,599,668
University of Waterloo	110	1,873,863	34,291	13,228	160	8,076,487
University of Guelph	111	2,125,779	29,459	8,156	126	7,103,082

SOURCE: Association of Research Libraries, *ARL Statistics 1997–1998* (Washington, D.C.: ARL, 1999).

Data from non-ARL libraries, 1998

THE FOLLOWING STATISTICS are from more than 1,000 of all types of North American academic libraries. Those shown here are for the 35 largest institutions that do not appear in the Association of Research Libraries statistics. Institutions are arranged by number of volumes in the library and not by a ranking similar to the ARL list, although the same measures have been used.

	Volumes in library	Volumes added	Current serials	Total staff	Total expenditures
Southern Methodist University	2,410,087	57,542	11,216	156	$ 8,140,829
Miami University	2,275,562	57,496	10,314	162	7,342,492
Bowling Green State University	2,204,330	78,729	4,520	168	5,982,421
Baylor University	2,163,456	653,987	9,117	161	7,760,207
Wheelock College	2,099,515	52,447	29,162	289	13,573,720
College of William & Mary	1,941,943	40,559	11,757	104	7,901,896
Boston College	1,737,880	67,852	20,910	218	13,983,570
Fordham University	1,730,390	56,597	13,456	156	8,650,100
Saint Louis University	1,701,519	—	—	145	8,910,356
Northern Illinois University	1,632,343	39,103	17,000	177	8,585,806
State University of New York at Binghamton	1,632,194	35,778	7,265	153	8,217,223
University of South Florida	1,588,761	36,662	9,159	221	10,666,482
Wake Forest University	1,575,455	47,921	16,125	156	9,657,348
Concordia University	1,567,535	34,012	5,805	166	6,512,497
University of Arkansas	1,509,345	34,811	15,431	152	6,746,017
University of Wisconsin/ Milwaukee	1,506,172	32,172	7,582	144	7,113,501
University of North Dakota	1,483,586	23,636	5,910	90	4,360,036
University of Louisville	1,431,279	50,018	13,333	181	12,363,694
California State University/ Long Beach	1,426,652	20,969	5,660	120	5,315,418
Utah State University	1,417,185	44,663	14,863	122	6,420,792
Kansas State University	1,410,709	31,312	12,967	134	7,119,754
University of North Texas	1,402,087	58,913	12,243	165	6,589,032
West Virginia University	1,381,431	16,591	7,653	218	6,459,927
Loyola University of Chicago	1,372,300	61,023	—	—	—
Simon Fraser University	1,359,906	40,051	—	138	8,931,571
Oregon State University	1,359,610	25,907	11,605	108	7,357,517
Georgia State University	1,356,601	47,272	11,792	173	9,107,786
Florida International University	1,310,825	70,624	8,896	150	9,067,258
Virginia Commonwealth Univ.	1,277,310	51,497	10,743	104	9,015,797
Catholic University	1,271,144	15,268	5,452	96	3,606,818
Indiana State University	1,248,860	27,080	5,109	98	4,219,494
Texas Christian University	1,248,680	28,755	5,374	71	3,806,419
Indiana University–Purdue University Indianapolis	1,248,311	55,568	18,875	317	10,148,547
University of California/ Santa Cruz	1,233,773	40,461	8,604	138	8,252,822
Smith College	1,225,078	23,587	5,036	97	4,516,129

SOURCE: ALA Association of College and Research Libraries, Academic Library Trends and Statistics Project, 1999.

The oldest academic libraries

by Godfrey Oswald

ARISTOTLE'S PERIPATETIC SCHOOL LIBRARY was set up about 380 B.C. in Athens, Greece. It was used by such famous Romans as Cicero. Most pre-Renaissance European university libraries were run by theological librarians, and it is sometimes difficult to differentiate a library set up purely for religious studies and one for academic studies that included theology.

The five oldest university libraries in the world are all in the Middle East:
1. **Al-Qarawiyin University Library,** Fès, Morocco. Founded ca. 870. (Not to be confused with the nearby Al-Akhawayn University in Ifrane).
2. **Al-Azhar University Library,** Cairo, Egypt. Founded ca. 985.
3. **Istanbul Üniversitesi Kütüphane,** Turkey. Founded ca. 1059 during the Byzantine era. It was reestablished in 1455 just after Constantinople fell to the Ottoman empire. (www.istanbul.edu.tr/library/index.htm)
4. **Al-Nizamiya University Library,** Baghdad, Iraq. Founded ca. 1070.
5. **Hacettepe Üniversitesi Kütüphane,** Ankara, Turkey. 1210. (www.library.hacettepe.edu.tr)

The ten oldest university libraries in Europe are:
1. **Università di Bologna Biblioteca,** Italy. Founded ca. 1095. (www.cib.unibo.it/eng/) (Two other strong candidates are the libraries of the universities of Salerno, ca. 1093, and Parma, ca. 1098, in Italy.)
2. **Università di Modena Biblioteca,** Italy. Founded ca. 1223. (www.casa.unimo.it/new/)
3. **Università di Padova Biblioteca,** Italy. 1225. (www.unipd.it/main/strutt.html)
4. **Universidad de Salamanca Library,** Spain. 1240.
5. **Università di Perugia Biblioteca,** Italy. 1243. (www.unipg.it/ricerche-bib.html)
6. **Università di Siena Biblioteca,** Italy. 1245. (www.unisi.it/sbs/biblio.html)
7. **Université de Paris 1 (Panthéon-Sorbonne) Bibliothèque (de la Sorbonne),** France. 1258. (panoramix.univ-paris1.fr/biblis.html)
8. **Università di Napoli "Federico II" Biblioteca,** Italy. 1260. (sab.unina.it/biblio.html)
9. **Universidade de Coimbra Biblioteca,** Portugal. 1290. (www.uc.pt/BGUC/)
10. **Université de Toulouse Bibliothèque,** France. 1292. (www.biu-toulouse.fr)

The two oldest university libraries in England:
1. **Cambridge University Library.** ca.1400. (www.lib.cam.ac.uk)
2. **Bodleian Library, Oxford University.** 1580. (www.bodley.ox.ac.uk)

The oldest Asian university library:
Ryukoku University Library, Kyoto, Japan. 1642. (opac.lib.ryukoku.ac.jp/e-index.html)

The four oldest university libraries in the Americas:
1. **Universidad Nacional Autonóma Biblioteca,** Mexico City. 1580.
2. **Universidad Nacional Mayor de San Marcos,** Lima, Peru. 1587. (www.unmsm.edu.pe*)*
3. **Universidad de Santo Domingo Biblioteca,** Dominican Republic. 1598.
4. **Universidad Nacional de Córdoba Biblioteca,** Argentina. 1620.

SOURCE: Godfrey Oswald, InfoConnect (www.kush.dircon.co.uk/Page1.htm).

Public library records

Most bookmobiles	St. Louis County (Mo.) Library: 18
Most branches	Toronto (Ont.) PL: 97
Most on-site public parking spaces	Marin County (Calif.) Library: 1,081
Highest director's salary	Cleveland (Ohio) PL: $146,426
Highest entry-level salary	San Francisco PL: $44,005
Most reference transactions (including branches)	Brooklyn (N.Y.) PL: 10,358,068
Most reference transactions (central library)	Brooklyn (N.Y.) PL: 2,082,522
Most interlibrary loans to others	Madison (Wisc.) PL: 259,312
Most interlibrary loans from others	Madison (Wisc.) PL: 273,686
Highest expenditures per capita	Cutchogue (N.Y.) Free Library: $199.20
Highest materials expenditures per capita	Worthington (Ohio) PL: $21.65
Highest registrations as a percentage of population served	Randolph (N.Y.) PL: 175.2%
Highest circulation per registered borrower	New Hanover County (N.C.) PL: 103.6%

SOURCE: Statistical Report 1999: Public Library Data Service (Chicago: ALA Public Library Association, 1999).

The 20 largest public libraries

THE NUMBER OF VOLUMES a library owns is not a measure of the quality of library service. But as the late Herman Fussler noted in 1949, "Yet the reverence for size continues. The library that has the most books is likely to be regarded as ipso facto, the best." Volume counts do have a certain fascination. The following are the largest public libraries in North America, according to 1999 data in the annual *Public Library Data Service Statistical Report,* which surveyed 790 libraries.

New York (N.Y.) Public Library (The Research Libraries)	10,483,628
Queens Borough (N.Y.) Public Library	9,510,814

Public Library of Cincinnati and Hamilton County (Ohio)	9,271,068
Chicago (Ill.) Public Library	9,222,449
Toronto (Ont.) PL	8,718,431
Free Library of Philadelphia (Pa.)	7,968,978
Boston (Mass.) Public Library	7,261,323
County of Los Angeles (Calif.) Public Library	6,883,210
Carnegie Library of Pittsburgh (Pa.)	6,632,303
Los Angeles (Calif.) Public Library	5,739,540
Brooklyn (N.Y.) Public Library	5,129,468
Houston (Tex.) Public Library	4,913,944
Cleveland (Ohio) Public Library	4,413,248
Miami-Dade (Fla.) Public Library System	3,882,275
King County (Wash.) Library System	3,717,247
Buffalo & Erie County (N.Y.) Public Library	3,524,297
Minneapolis (Minn.) Public Library	3,263,250
St. Louis (Mo.) County Library District	3,138,143
Hawaii State Public Library System	3,127,247
Dallas (Tex.) Public Library	3,098,091

SOURCE: Statistical Report 1999: Public Library Data Service (Chicago: ALA Public Library Association, 1999).

How the states rank, 1996

DATA ON PUBLIC LIBRARY expenditures and operations are given for FY 1996. The rankings were compiled by the National Data Resource Center of the National Center for Education Statistics (NCES) using data submitted through the Federal-State Cooperative System (FSCS) for public library data. States are ranked by expenses per capita. Other measures are for local income, circulation transactions, reference transactions, and total staff expenditures per capita.

State	Number of PLs	1996 Operating Expenditures	Expenses Per Capita	Rank	Rank Local Income	Rank Circ. Trans.	Rank Ref. Trans.	Rank Total Staff $
N.Y.	740	$ 637,005,000	$ 38.19	1	2	23	3	2
Ohio	250	415,859,000	37.22	2	47	1	5	3
D.C.*	1	19,854,000	36.56	3	1	51	1	1
Ind.	238	171,236,000	33.75	4	4	2	4	9
Alaska	85	19,897,000	32.74	5	6	29	35	7
Conn.	195	105,215,000	32.13	6	8	13	12	4
N.J.	307	251,495,000	32.11	7	5	32	20	5
Ill.	617	328,832,000	31.47	8	7	16	6	6
Wash.	69	160,600,000	30.21	9	3	3	N/A	8
Colo.	108	107,063,000	28.01	10	9	12	7	15
Md.	24	136,173,000	27.08	11	18	9	10	10
Mass.	370	154,270,000	25.54	12	14	22	N/A	12
Minn.	130	116,340,000	25.46	13	11	6	9	13
R.I.	50	24,940,000	24.85	14	19	26	26	11
Ore.	124	71,886,000	24.25	15	10	4	32	17
Wis.	381	123,552,000	24.02	16	12	8	13	14
Kans.	324	48,634,000	23.17	17	16	5	8	18

State	Number of PLs	1996 Operating Expenditures	Expenses Per Capita	Rank	Rank Local Income	Rank Circ. Trans.	Rank Ref. Trans.	Rank Total Staff $
Wyo.	23	$ 11,108,000	$23.01	18	13	18	14	16
Nev.	23	34,116,000	21.56	19	15	38	33	22
Va.	90	139,132,000	21.32	20	25	20	17	20
N.H.	229	24,504,000	21.09	21	23	21	31	19
Mich.	383	194,121,000	20.91	22	22	36	25	21
Mo.	148	102,561,000	20.67	23	17	14	19	31
Nebr.	230	28,563,000	20.45	24	21	19	38	28
Utah	70	38,889,000	20.38	25	24	7	11	23
Me.	268	19,951,000	19.30	26	33	17	N/A	26
S.Dak.	112	10,259,000	19.14	27	20	10	N/A	24
Ariz.	40	77,898,000	18.96	28	26	27	16	30
Iowa	529	52,782,000	18.57	29	27	11	N/A	29
Fla.	98	252,306,000	18.03	30	29	35	2	34
Calif.	171	577,227,000	17.98	31	28	39	15	27
Idaho	106	17,737,000	17.83	32	32	15	23	32
Vt.	197	9,456,000	17.81	33	36	25	N/A	33
Hawaii	1	19,854,000	17.40	34	51	30	39	25
N.Mex.	72	22,802,000	16.98	35	30	34	28	35
Pa.	460	188,837,000	16.24	36	44	41	40	37
La.	65	69,241,000	15.92	37	31	45	37	40
Dela.	30	10,333,000	15.51	38	37	40	41	36
Ky.	116	55,508,000	15.20	39	40	37	43	46
Okla.	114	37,538,000	14.63	40	34	28	34	39
N.C.	75	103,784,000	14.43	41	38	33	24	41
Ga.	55	103,188,000	14.31	42	45	43	30	38
S.C.	40	49,899,000	13.58	43	39	44	18	43
Mont.	82	10,723,000	13.04	44	35	31	36	45
Ala.	205	49,831,000	12.78	45	42	49	42	44
N.Dak.	79	6,918,000	12.68	46	43	24	29	47
Tex.	500	214,128,000	12.60	47	41	46	22	42
Tenn.	141	58,409,000	11.29	48	48	48	27	48
Ark.	37	25,030,000	11.05	49	46	47	44	50
W.Va.	97	19,775,000	11.03	50	50	42	21	49
Miss.	47	25,411,000	9.42	51	49	50	45	51

* NCES includes data for the District of Columbia to be comprehensive, but the Public Library of the District of Columbia might more legitimately be compared to other large cities.

SOURCE: *Public Libraries in the U.S.: FY 1996* (Washington, D.C.: National Center for Education Statistics, February 1999).

Using public libraries: What makes a difference?

by Mary Jo Lynch

FOR MANY YEARS, the National Center for Education Statistics (NCES) has produced summary statistics about education in the United States by collecting data from the schools themselves. In the late 1980s NCES began something very different—gathering data from individuals and households through the National Household Education Survey (NHES). Library use by individuals was one of the topics included in the 1991 NHES; Jim Scheppke described those results very effectively in an article in *Library Journal* (Oct. 15, 1994).

More recently, the 1996 survey measured a different dimension of library use—library use by the whole household surveyed. The results are presented here in terms of two factors: the presence of children in the home and the race/ethnicity of persons in the household.

The 1996 National Education Survey was conducted for NCES, by Westat, a survey research firm based in Rockford, Maryland. Data collection took place from January through April 1996. The sample (over 55,000 households) was selected using list-assisted, random-digit-dialing methods and is nationally representative of all civilian households in the 50 states and the District of Columbia. Because 5% of U.S. households do not have telephones, a special procedure was followed to reduce the bias caused by that lack. Survey data was collected using computer-assisted telephone interviewing technology.

Table 1. Use of Public Libraries by Presence of Children

Period of use	All households	Households with children under 18	Households without children under 18
Past month	44%	61%	35%
Past year	65%	82%	54%

Basic results were presented in a 12-page report, "Use of Public Library Services by Households in the United States. 1996," published in the February 1997 issue of *Statistics in Brief* (NCES 97-446). Table 1, based on that report, shows that public library use was more common in households with children under 18 than in households without children. Whereas 61% of households with children used public library services in the past month, only 35% of households without children did so. When the entire past year is taken into account, households with children again show substantially higher rates of use than households without children (82% versus 54%).

The results shown in Table 1 are not a surprise. It is well known that households with children use public libraries heavily. But other data gathered in the 1996 NHES enable us to explore another dimension of public library use that is less obvious—use by persons in different racial/ethnic groups. Although the published report cited above does not display those results, they were tabulated at ALA's request by the National Education Data Resource Center and used to create Tables 2 and 3. Note that the race/ethnicity of the oldest per-

Table 2. Percentage of Households in Which Any Member Used a Public Library

	White	Black	Hispanic	Asian/ Pacific	Am. Indian/ Nat. Alaskan	Other race
Estimated number of households (in thousands)	79,641	9,375	6,881	1,763	677	751
Percentage of all households	80%	9%	7%	2%	1%	1%
Used a public library in past month	44%	45%	41%	53%	46%	51%
Used a public library in past year (including past month)	65%	63%	58%	72%	65%	66%

Table 3. Percentage of Households in Which Any Member
Used a Public Library for Selected Purposes in the Past Month

	White	Black	Hispanic	Asian/ Pacific	Am. Indian/ Nat. Alaskan	Other race
Estimated number of households (in thousands)	79,641	9,375	6,881	1,763	677	751
Percentage of all households	80%	9%	7%	2%	1%	1%
For enjoyment or hobbies, including to borrow books or tapes or to attend activities	32%	30%	28%	38%	33%	38%
To get information for personal use such as consumer or health issues, investments, and so on	20%	19%	15%	25%	21%	29%
For a school or class assignment	17%	26%	24%	28%	20%	24%
For a work assignment or to keep up-to-date at work	8%	11%	9%	16%	11%	10%
To get information to help find a job	4%	8%	5%	10%	5%	9%
For a program or activity designed for children ages 6–12	3%	7%	6%	7%	4%	6%
For an activity for children under 6, such as story hour	3%	6%	6%	6%	3%	4%
To work with a tutor or take a class to learn to read	1%	3%	3%	5%	1%	3%

son in the household was used as an indicator of the entire household; that factor should be considered in estimating the validity of the data.

Table 2 shows that households headed by someone who is an Asian-Pacific Islander are most likely to use the public library (53% last month, 72% last year), whereas households headed by a Hispanic person are least likely (41% in last month, 58% in last year). The other three groups have very similar rates of use, which fall between the two extremes. The 1991 study of individuals described by Scheppke shows use in past year by only three groups—white, black, Hispanic. In all three cases the percentage of household use is higher in the 1996 survey.

Table 3 displays results for a question regarding the purposes for which people use libraries. Respondents were asked if any member of the household used a public library for one or more of eight different purposes. For all five standard racial/ethnic groups the purpose most often named was "for enjoyment or hobbies, including to borrow books or tapes or to attend activities." Second for whites and for American Indian or Alaskan natives was "to get information for personal use such as consumer or health issues, investments, and so on." For the three other groups, the second most mentioned was "for a school class or assignment." The least-often mentioned of all purposes was "to work with a tutor or take a class to learn to read."

Table 3 should be used with caution because only one person in a household was asked about the purposes of the whole household. It seems quite unlikely that one person would be aware of *all* the purposes for which each member of the household used a public library.

SOURCE: Mary Jo Lynch, "Using Public Libraries: What Makes a Difference?" *American Libraries* 28 (November 1997): 64–66.

Unserved Americans

by Keith Curry Lance

ACCORDING TO 1996 DATA from the National Center for Education Statistics (with some corrections from a few state library agencies), 6,908,844 Americans in 24 states live beyond the legal service area of any public library—roughly the equivalent of the entire Washington, D.C., or San Francisco metropolitan areas. These individuals are "unserved," as there is no public library legally responsible for meeting their needs for reading matter, information, and access to the "information superhighway." Reasons for this situation include, but are not limited to, the following:

- In many U.S. counties, there are only municipal libraries and no provision is made for countywide service that covers residents of unincorporated areas.
- Some units of government (e.g., counties, cities, towns, townships) that are not part of larger units of service (e.g., library districts, county library systems) cannot afford to support libraries.
- A few local governments have even closed public libraries due to fiscal problems.
- Beyond such circumstances, which explain the actual absence of any public library service, some public libraries are so inadequate in terms of local support, staffing, hours of service, or the like, that they are not recognized by the state library agency as a public library.

A close look at NCES data on 1996 state population estimates, the population living within library service areas (excluding overlaps), the difference between those two figures, and that difference both as a percent of the state population estimate and as a percent of the national difference reveals the following highlights:

- Two states, Texas and New York, account for 40% of unserved Americans. Each state reports over 1.3 million unserved residents.
- Six states—South Dakota, New Mexico, Oklahoma, Maine, Idaho, and North Dakota—report 18–30% of their state populations as unserved. At the extremes of this group, three out of 10 South Dakotans and one out of five North Dakotans live outside public library service areas.
- Seven states—Indiana, Vermont, Texas, Missouri, New York, Alabama, and Oregon—report 5–10% of their state populations as unserved. At the extremes of this group, about one of every ten Indianans and one of every 17 Oregonians live outside public library service areas.
- Another seven states—Washington, Florida, Pennsylvania, Colorado, New Jersey, Kentucky, and California—report 1–5% of their state populations as unserved. At the extremes of this group, one of every 25 Washingtonians and one of every 100 Californians live outside public library service areas.
- Four states—Virginia, Michigan, Massachusetts, and Kansas—report negligible unserved populations—less than one percent of each state's population.
- Typically, among states with unserved populations, the number of unserved individuals ranges between 100,000 and 300,000. (The

median is about 200,000.) Such figures approximate the populations of metropolitan areas, such as Boulder, Colo.; Galveston, Tex.; Manchester, N.H.; Racine, Wis.; and Santa Cruz, Calif.

The good news is:

- The remaining 27 states report no unserved populations.
- In many of the states that reported unserved populations, there are statewide reciprocal borrowing programs (e.g., the Colorado Library Card) as well as other formal and informal arrangements that provide some kind of access to library services to the unserved.

Still, these findings should serve as a wake-up call to those who erroneously believe that the now defunct Library Services and Construction Act (LSCA) brought all Americans into the public library fold. While an even greater number of Americans are "underserved" by public libraries that lack adequate resources, the unserved are still with us. Such individuals should be counted among the many eligible to be labeled under the new Library Services and Technology Act (LSTA) as "persons who have difficulty using libraries."

SOURCE: *Fast Facts: Recent Statistics from the Library Research Service* (Colorado State Library, Library Research Service), September 1, 1998. Reprinted with permission.

SCHOOL LIBRARIES

The school library media program

THE SCHOOL LIBRARY MEDIA PROGRAM is an integral part of the school curriculum and provides a wide range of resources and information that satisfies the educational needs and interests of students. Materials are selected to meet the wide range of students' individual learning styles. The school library media center is a place where students may explore more fully classroom subjects that interest them, expand their imagination, delve into areas of personal interest, and develop the ability to think clearly, critically, and creatively about the resources they have chosen to read, hear, or view.

The school library media center provides a setting where students develop skills they will need as adults to locate, analyze, evaluate, interpret, and communicate information and ideas in an information-rich world. Students are encouraged to realize their potential as informed citizens who think critically and solve problems, to observe rights and responsibilities relating to the generation and flow of information and ideas, and to appreciate the value of literature in an educated society.

The school library media program serves *all* of the students of the community—not only the children of the most powerful, the most vocal, or even the majority, but all of the students who attend the school. The collection includes materials to meet the needs of all learners, including the gifted; the reluctant readers; the mentally, physically, and emotionally impaired; and those from a diversity of backgrounds. The school library media program strives to maintain a diverse collection that represents various points of view on current and historical issues, as well as a wide variety of areas of interest to all students served. Though one parent or member of the school community may feel a particular title in the school library media center's collection is inappropriate, others will feel the title is not only appropriate but desirable.

The school library media center is the symbol to students of our most cherished freedom—the freedom to speak our minds and hear what others have to say. School boards are urged to reaffirm the importance and value of the freedom to read, view, and listen. Students have the right to develop the ability to think clearly, critically, and creatively about their choices—rather than allow others to do this for them.

SOURCE: Statement on the Role of the School Library Media Program (Chicago: ALA American Association of School Librarians, 1994), www.ala.org/aasl/positions/PS_roleschool.html.

School libraries: A global view

PRINCIPLE 7 OF THE UNITED NATIONS Declaration on the Rights of the Child (1959) states: "The child is entitled to receive education which shall be free and compulsory, at least in the elementary stages.

He shall be given an education which will promote his general culture, and enable him on a basis of equal opportunity to develop his abilities, his individual judgment, and his moral sense of social responsibility, and to become a useful member of society."

The existence and utilization of the school library are a vital part of this free and compulsory education. UNESCO sees the school library as essential to "the development of the human personality as well as the spiritual, moral, social, cultural and economic progress of the community."

The school library is central to the fulfillment of the instructional goals and objectives of the school and promotes this through a planned program of acquisition and organization of information technology and dissemination of materials to expand the learning environment of all students. A planned program of teaching information skills in partnership with classroom teachers and other educators is an essential part of the school library program.

The school library provides a wide range of resources, both print and nonprint, including electronic media, and access to data which promotes an awareness of the child's own cultural heritage, and provides the basis for an understanding of the diversity of other cultures.

Functions

The school library functions as a vital instrument in the educational process, not as a separate entity isolated from the total school program, but involved in the teaching and learning process. Its goals could be expressed through the following functions:

- **Informational**—to provide for reliable information, rapid access, re-

trieval, and transfer of information. The school library should be part
of regional and national information networks.

- **Educational**—to provide continuous, lifelong education through provision of the facilities and atmosphere for learning; guidance in location, selection, and use of material; training in information skills through integration with classroom teaching; and promotion of intellectual freedom.
- **Cultural**—to improve the quality of life through the presentation and support of the aesthetic experience; guidance in appreciation of arts; encouragement of creativity; and development of positive human relations.
- **Recreational**—to support and enhance a balanced and enriched life and encourage meaningful use of leisure time through provision of recreational information, materials, programs of recreational value, and guidance in the use of leisure time.

Materials

"Appropriateness" implies:

- an awareness of the total range of information and communication technology;
- variety concerning many fields of knowledge and recreational activities;
- material designed to serve children within the range of their cognitive, effective, and psychomotor skills;
- relevance to the school's teaching/learning program;
- appeal to children's interests;
- use of the student's primary language;
- reflection of the cultural interests valued by the children's families;
- application of the economic environment.

Facilities

All school libraries, from basic preschool through secondary level, need adequate space in which to exploit the technology available for preparation, processing, and storage of all library materials, as well as space to enable students and teachers to utilize fully these materials through reading, viewing, listening, and information retrieval and processing skills. The plans should fit functionally into the general architectural design of the school, located near natural centers of traffic with easy accessibility for all users including the disabled and handicapped. Consideration might also be given to the use of the library outside normal school hours. There is a need for flexibility and scope for future expansion and rearrangement of space and use with adequate provision of electrical outlets to allow this. Attention must be given to lighting, acoustical treatment of doors and ceilings, control of temperature and humidity, and furniture and shelving suitable to the age of the users.

Personnel

Establishment of the school library requires that all persons who use it learn how it could be used effectively and efficiently. Administrators provide the leadership for such use. Preparation for administrators, as for all teachers, should include information about the role of the school library in the learning process and in the planning and implementation of teaching activities. The administrator should be aware of the unique librarianship skills which the school librarian needs, in addition to professional training as a teacher, to effectively coordinate the role of the library program in the school, including the preparation of the budget and arranging for a flexible school schedule so the students can make greater use of the library materials and facilities. The administrator should be aware of the educational benefits of a cooperative planning and teaching program within the school.

The International Association of School Librarianship advocates that school librarians be qualified teachers who have, in addition, completed professional studies in librarianship. This type of preparation ensures that teachers receive assistance from, and cooperatively teach with, professional personnel who have an understanding of the principles and practices of effective teaching, the educational program, and practices of the child's school. This cooperation with teachers may concern: development of the curriculum, the educational activities offered by the school to the child, short- and long-term planning concerning the uses of materials, information technology and equipment, and development of information skills for the child's education.

Lifelong education, skills, literacy development

The skills learned by the student through the school library provide the child with the means of adapting to a wide variety of situations, and enable education to be continued throughout life, even in adverse conditions. The school library promotes literacy through the development and encouragement of reading for instruction and recreation. Reading, viewing, and listening activities all stimulate and reinforce the child's interest in reading.

In addition, the student is provided with an insight into the full range of information and communication technology as it is available, and is provided with instruction in the utilization of this technology in order to locate and evaluate information to answer educational and recreational needs and interests, thus being able to construct visual, recorded, audiovisual, and electronic messages as appropriate for purposes of communication. These skills promote lifelong learning. Acquiring these skills enables the child to continue independent learning even where education is interrupted by natural disasters and social unrest.

All education systems should also be encouraged to extend the learning environment beyond textbook and teacher into the school library. School librarians should cooperate with staff in public libraries and other community information centers to enable sharing of the community's information resources.

Government and public support

The establishment of good school libraries can demonstrate that public authorities are fulfilling their responsibilities to implement education that will enable children to become useful members of the global society and develop each child's individual potential. A good school library with a qualified school librarian is a major factor in developing quality education.

The school library may provide materials as sources of information for parents and social agencies to use in serving the needs of children in the home, preschool, school, and after-school environments.

For societies and public authorities endeavoring to promote the education of the child, one of the measurable achievements that can be observed is the provision of the tools for education. The society that invests in school libraries for its children invests in its own future.

SOURCE: IASL Policy Statement on School Libraries (Seattle: International Association of School Librarianship, 1994); www.hi.is/~anne/policysl.html. Reprinted with permission.

After hours in the school library

by Keith Curry Lance

IN 1997, COLORADO'S Library Research Service conducted a survey of the state's library media centers (LMCs) to see how many stayed open after regular school hours. Fifty-six questionnaires were completed and returned.

It should come as no surprise that, for those schools with extended hours, more than 90% of the regular media center staff are working both normal school hours and after school, even volunteering their time occasionally.

* 54% are library media aides;
* 45% are Colorado Department of Education–endorsed school library media specialists; and
* 29% are librarians with an MLS.

Circulation accounts for the highest level of school use, followed closely by study (i.e., on-site use of library media resources by students). In a typical week, responding libraries reported checking out an average of 32 items and enabling an average of 26 students to study.

Total annual circulation for Colorado's LMCs in 1997 topped 1.1 million. Based on typical-week estimates, after-school circulation accounted for more than 68,000 of those transactions (6%). Information skills instruction contacts totaled approximately 278,000 statewide—about 30,000 of which (11%) occurred during after-school hours.

Two out of three school districts pay after-school staff. Nine out of ten pay staff to work after school at the school day rate. One out of seven pays after-school staff at a higher overtime rate.

SOURCE: Fast Facts: Recent Statistics from the Library Research Service (Colorado State Library, Library Research Service), April 30, 1998. Reprinted with permission.

Basic rules for working with school administrators

by Richard C. Pearson and Kaye Y. Turner

THE FOLLOWING ARE SOME BASIC RULES that every librarian should incorporate into her relationship with school administrators. It is worthwhile for both the principal and the librarian to be aware of them.

It is very important to contact the administrator frequently when there are positive aspects of the library's program to show and tell them. Invite them to come to the library often and acquaint them with the many valuable services and accomplishments of the library. The librarian should be viewed as a positive source of information.

Principals seldom have strong library backgrounds. They are usually former classroom teachers, not librarians. The best thing a school librarian can do  when faced with a library problem that needs the principal's help is to have several possible solutions in mind. This creates two positive situations. One, the principal appreciates a professional's input and is not left "hanging alone." Two, library problems are often unique to the library and need a library perspective to solve them. Weeding the collection and volunteer help in the library are examples that come to mind.

Keep the principal informed so she is always knowledgeable concerning the library and its programs. Setting up an annual professional goals conference for the library and the librarian is imperative. In districts where the principals read weekly classroom-teacher lesson plans, the principal should do the same for the librarian's flexible scheduling, library skills classes, and classroom curricula tie-ins.

Ask for advice in those situations where there is no clear policy.

Establish the librarian and the library as an indispensable cog in the school's educational picture. The following are some proven methods that will contribute to this goal.

Teach library skills to students. Be willing to do so in the classrooms if necessary. Have librarian, will travel.

Involve students in building the library's collection. Ask for their input in book selection. The materials they request will be heavily used.

Include faculty and administration whenever possible in library events, programs, and services.

Work closely with faculty to order library materials in their subject areas and other areas of interest. Why other areas of interest? Because faculty will often teach or refer to these interests in their classrooms. This is "strength teaching," and it should always be encouraged.

Use faculty as subject area specialists and as resource people whenever possible.

The librarian should be active in curriculum decision making throughout the school, both as to (1) supporting curricula in the school with library resources, and (2) helping to relate and teach curricula with interested faculty members.

Be familiar with school policy, i.e., the school's approach to discipline, educational mission, statement of philosophy, etc.

Be personally visible. Attend faculty meetings, conferences, and workshops. Be an active participant in the educational process.

If possible, provide library services to the community in which the school is located.

SOURCE: © Richard C. Pearson and Kaye Y. Turner, *The School Library Media Specialist's Tool Kit* (Fort Atkinson, Wis.: Highsmith Press, 1999), pp. 20–21. Reprinted with permission.

SPECIAL LIBRARIES

1

Special libraries

by Barbara P. Semonche

IT HAS BEEN SAID THAT the Library of Congress is the United States' first special library. Certainly it met the major criteria for such a designation: a special, rare, and (at first) private collection of books and materials that came to be managed by skilled information professionals for a select group of clients, namely the U.S. Congress. Over the centuries the collection, scope, and services of the Library of Congress increased far beyond its early beginnings and has become a worldwide symbol for the entire library profession.

What are special libraries?

In 1904, Newark (N.J.) public librarian John Cotton Dana created a new business branch of the Free Public Library. As far as we know, he did it largely on his own. This branch was developed to attract corporate executives into the library and make it easy for them to make use of its reference and research services. This new concept was enhanced with skilled staff on hand to help guide these executives.

Then in 1909, Sarah Ball, in charge of the Newark collection, attended a joint conference of the New Jersey Library Association and the Pennsylvania Library Club in Atlantic City. There she met Anna B. Sears, librarian of the Merchants' Association of New York. Together, they explored the idea of close cooperation between their libraries and the librarians in the New York Metropolitan area. This pair of "change agents" allied themselves with Dana.

Dana delivered a paper at the ALA meeting that year titled "Municipal, Legislative Reference, Commercial, Technical, and Public Welfare Libraries." He then extended an invitation to interested librarians at that meeting to join him in Bretton Woods, New Hampshire. This meeting was later to become known as the "Veranda Conference." A group of 26 adventurous librarians accepted his invitation and soon they were breaking completely new ground. They felt they had everything to gain by forming a working group to tackle their problems and serve their collective specialized interests. They recognized early on that this was not a one-person job. Consequently, the Special Libraries Association (SLA) was formed on July 2, 1909, with Dana as its first president, and the term "special library" was born.

Special librarians emerged in an era responsible for, at that time, the most spectacular scientific and industrial developments the world had ever known. The very year of SLA's founding was the year that Henry Ford set up the first assembly line to produce his revolutionary Model-T automobile. The decades that followed saw the birth and development of aviation, motion pictures, radio, and television. An industrial age was born that produced, among other things, the material to win two world wars, split the atom, discover the polio vaccine, and land a man on the moon. But in reality, rapid scientific discoveries and technological expansion gave rise to as many, if not more, questions than they addressed.

The information produced from these monumental developments led to an overwhelming flood of knowledge. Access to this data became as vital to industrial and scientific success as inventive machinery, new materials, and inspired management. And it was talented, knowledgeable, specialized librarians who brought access and structure to this vast, ever-growing information. Catalogers, indexers, abstracters, bibliographers, collection developers, and reference librarians were all in high demand. In short, putting knowledge to work required librarians with special skills. As noted author Robert A. Heinlein observed:

> Library Science is the key to all science, just as mathematics is its language—and civilization will rise or fall, depending on how well librarians do their jobs.

Then the Industrial Age evolved into the Information Age. Online public-access catalogs emerged. Electronic journals made their debut. Full-text databases appeared. Competitive intelligence, digital copyright, image database design, Dublin Core metatags, and much more took center stage in this scenario. Had special librarianship gone as far as it could go?

Changing roles

Technological changes have had a significant impact on the role of special librarians. As more and more end-users acquire desktop access to information in an intuitive search environment, librarians are reexamining their traditional roles. Most special librarians see their roles evolving into information consultants and knowledge managers who collect, store, retrieve, and evaluate data. They are are deeply involved in state-of-the-art delivery mechanisms such as corporate intranets, competitive intelligence, and in-house employee-profiling systems. These "knowledge engineers" are central to the management of their companies' intellectual resources. They are part of corporate strategic-planning teams on a global scale as their corporations transcend geographic boundaries.

This changing role implies a different skill set. The emphasis will shift from technical search and retrieval skills in the library toward more sophisticated communication and management skills. Marketing skills are highly valued, as well as the ability to communicate and partner successfully with diverse groups of corporate managers. The ability to demonstrate a high level of understanding of computing and network architecture is becoming vital as well. Special libraries are transforming into virtual libraries with foot traffic being replaced by remote access (possibly halfway around the world), access to full-text library resources. The future promises even more of this global reach and delivery. Evaluating new products and assessing cost benefits of information services will occupy more and more of the future information professional's time. Quality and accountability are critical.

What's in a name?

In a very short time, special librarians and information specialists have morphed into database designers, Web architects, knowledge engineers, Internet coaches, data marketers, product developers, copyright specialists, contract/

licensing negotiators, and independent information consultants. Job titles change in rapid succession along with job descriptions. We evolved from the Information Age into the information economy, bringing permanent new challenges to the skills and ethics of special librarians. We can only imagine what future corporate special librarians will be called. As baseball philosopher Yogi Berra once observed, "Prediction is very hard, especially when it's about the future."

The term "librarian" is not necessarily the best descriptor for this new type of knowledge manager. Does this mean that the term "special librarian" will become extinct? Probably not, but the term is targeted for redefinition. For example, at least one-third of the members of SLA are not employed in corporate libraries or research centers. Are they candidates for the job title "knowledge manager"? Perhaps. However, changing job titles in other work environments is not as simple as in the fast-paced corporate world.

Who are special librarians?

Special librarians are a diverse group; nearly 15,000 of them are members of SLA. They are employed most frequently by large knowledge-based firms, but are often associated with service organizations, public and private businesses, state and federal government agencies, museums, public and private colleges and universities, hospitals and health centers, trade associations, research institutes, information management consulting firms, and dozens of other fields. There are special libraries in organizations with staffs of 50 or more; others are managed by a single librarian. Knowledge managers can be found not only in the United States and Canada, but in multinational organizations in Europe, Asia, Mexico, Latin and South America, and the Pacific Rim.

Special librarians' subject expertise ranges from advertising and marketing to science and engineering, from environmental management to library management, from chemistry to agriculture and nutrition, from insurance and employee benefits to petroleum and energy reserves, from social science to metals and materials science, from information technology to pharmaceutical and health technology, from geography and maps to transportation, from law to news, from military to physics, astronomy and math, from education to communication, and from national sports to international business and finance. Special librarians come equipped with not only their graduate degrees in library and information science but with advanced degrees in their subject specialties.

Today's special librarians do far more than locate and collect data; they add value to information and they do this by authenticating, synthesizing, and distributing it to employees across the hall, across applications, and across the world. Using the Internet and other current technologies, they also evaluate, analyze, organize, package, and present information in a way that maximizes its usefulness.

SOURCE: Special report by Barbara P. Semonche for *The Whole Library Handbook 3.*

NATIONAL LIBRARIES

National libraries
by Godfrey Oswald

NATIONAL LIBRARIES are those that serve as copyright depositories, compile current and retrospective national bibliographies, maintain central catalogs, and serve as national centers for bibliographic information.

The International Federation of Library Associations and Institutions Web site maintains current links to national library sites at www.ifla.org/II/natlibs. htm. More library superlatives can be found at the InfoConnect site at www.kush.dircon.co.uk/Page16.htm.

Oldest

This list includes all national libraries with a founding date prior to 1800. National libraries that were founded by states that are no longer sovereign, such as Florence and Scotland, are also represented.

1366—Narodni Knihovna, Prague, **Bohemia.** Holy Roman Emperor Charles IV donated a set of codices to Prague's university, which became the Jesuit Klementinum college in 1566. After nationalization and several name changes, it was reorganized in 1990 as the Narodni Knihovna. (www.nkp.cz)

1368—Österreichische Nationalbibliothek, Vienna, **Austria.** Founded by Duke Albrecht III. The library claims the oldest card catalog in the world, invented in the 1780s by Gottfried van Swieten. (www.onb.ac.at/english.htm)

1468—Biblioteca Nazionale Marciana, Venice, **Venetian Republic.** (marciana. venezia.sbn.it)

1480—Bibliothèque Nationale de France, Paris, **France.** A royal library was established in 1368 by King Charles V "the Wise," but collections were sometimes dispersed at the death of each king; by 1483 King Louis XI had established its permanence as the Bibliothèque du Roi. Legal status was obtained in 1617, and the library opened to the public in 1735. The Bibliothèque Nationale reorganized in 1994 and gained a new building (La Bibliothèque François-Mitterrand) in Tolbiac that opened in December 1996. (www.bnf.fr)

1555—National Library, Valetta, **Malta.** By magisterial decree, the books of deceased knights of the Order of St. John of Jerusalem were to be preserved for the use of its members. A library building to house them was begun in 1649.

1558—Bayerische Staatsbibliothek, München, **Bavaria.** (www.bsb.badw-muenchen.de/index2.htm)

1559—Bibliothèque Royale Albert 1ᵉʳ, Brussels, **Belgium.** (www.kbr.be/eng)

1606—National and University Library, Zagreb, **Croatia.** (www.nsk.hr)

1640—Helsinki University Library/Finnish National Library, Helsinki, **Finland.** (linnea.helsinki.fi/hyk/hul/)

1653—Det Kongelige Bibliotek, Copenhagen, **Denmark.** Founded by King Frederik III, with three major collections acquired by 1664. (www.kb.bib.dk/index-en.htm)

1661—Kungliga Bibliotcket, Stockholm, **Sweden.** (www.kb.se)

1661—Staatsbibliothek zu Berlin / Preussischer Kulturbesitz, Berlin, **Prussia.** Founded by Friedrich Wilhelm, Elector of Brandenburg. (www.sbb.spk-berlin.de)

1682—National Library of Scotland, Edinburgh, **Scotland.** Founded as the Library of the Faculty of the Advocates, it was formally constituted as the National Library of Scotland in 1925. (www.nls.uk)

1712—Biblioteca Nacional, Madrid, **Spain.** Founded by King Philip V as the Biblioteca Real. (www.bne.es)

1720—Biblioteca Nazionale Universitaria di Torino, University of Turin, **Savoy.**

1747—Biblioteca Nazionale Centrale, Florence, **Tuscany.** (www.bncf.firenze.sbn.it)

1753—British Library at St. Pancras, London, **England.** Parliament purchased the collection of Sir Hans Sloane and created a new museum to house it along with the collections of Sir Robert Cotton and Robert and Edward Harley. Opened to the public in 1759, the British Museum was a de facto national library until 1973 when it was incorporated into the reorganized British Library system. The British Library moved to new quarters near the St. Pancras Railway Station in 1998. (portico.bl.uk)

1774—National and University Library, Ljubljana, **Slovenia.** (www.nuk.uni-lj.si)

1777—Biblioteca Nacional de Colombia, Bogota, **Colombia.**

1782—Biblioteca Centrale della Regione Siciliana, Palermo, **Sicily.**

1786—Biblioteca Nazionale Braidense, Milan, **Lombardy.**

1792—Biblioteca Nacional, Quito, **Ecuador.**

1795—National Library of Russia, St Petersburg, **Russia.** Formerly the M.E. Saltykov-Shchcdrin State Public Library. Founded by Empress Catherine the Great.

1796—Biblioteca Nacional, Lisbon, **Portugal.** (www.ibl.pt)

1798—Koninklijke Bibliotheek, The Hague, **Netherlands.** (www.konbib.nl/home-fe.html)

Largest

NORTH AMERICA AND THE WORLD. Library of Congress, Washington, D.C. 30 million+ volumes. Founded 1800. (lcweb.loc.gov)

EUROPE. The five largest in Europe are:
1. The British Library, London. 18 million+ volumes. (portico.bl.uk)
2. Die Deutsche Bibliothek, Germany. 15.5 million volumes. Founded in 1990 following the merger of the Deutsche Bücherei Leipzig (founded in 1912) and the Deutsche Bibliothck Frankfurt am Main (founded in 1947). (www.ddb.de)
3. The Russian State Library, Moscow. 15 million volumes. Founded in 1918 as the Lenin State Library. (www.rsl.ru)
4. The Bibliothèque Nationale de France, Paris. 11 million volumes. (www.bnf.fr)
5. National Library of Russia, St. Petersburg. 10.8 million volumes.

ASIA. The three largest in Asia are:
1. National Library of China, Beijing. 16.7 million volumes. The main

building is claimed to be the largest single library building in the world, with 140,000 square meters of floor space. (www.lib.tsinghua.edu.cn/english/beitu)

2. National Diet Library, Tokyo. 9 million volumes. Founded 1948. (www.ndl.go.jp/index-e.html)

3. National Library of India, Calcutta. 4.5 million volumes.

LATIN AMERICA. The three largest in Latin America are:

1. Biblioteca Nacional de la República Argentina, Buenos Aires. 3 million volumes. Founded in 1810. (www.bibnal.edu.ar)

2. Biblioteca Nacional de Mexico, Mexico City. 2.4 million volumes. (biblional.bibliog.unam.mx/bib01.html)

3. Biblioteca Nacional "José Marti," Havana, Cuba. 2 million volumes.

MIDDLE EAST. The three largest in the Middle East are:

1. Jewish National and University Library, Jerusalem. 3.8 million volumes. (sites.huji.ac.il/jnul/)

2. National Library of Egypt, Cairo. 2.6 million books. Also Africa's largest national library.

3. Millî Kütüphane, Ankara, Turkey. 1.2 million books. (www.mkutup.gov.tr)

AUSTRALASIA. National Library of New Zealand, Wellington. 5.2 million volumes. (www.natlib.govt.nz)

SOURCE: Godfrey Oswald, InfoConnect (www.kush.dircon.co.uk/Page16.htm), special for *The Whole Library Handbook 3.*

Library of Congress 1998 fact sheet

IN FISCAL YEAR 1998, the Library of Congress—

Welcomed nearly 2 million on-site visitors.
Responded to reference inquiries from 548,763 readers who visited the library in person.
Held a total of 115,505,695 items in the collections, including:

> 17,772,400 cataloged books in the Library of Congress classification system.
> 9,379,391 books in large type and raised characters, incunabula (books printed before 1501), monographs and serials, music, bound newspapers, pamphlets, technical reports, and other printed material.
> 88,353,904 items in the nonclassed (special) collections. These included:

>> 2,374,011 audio materials, such as disks, tapes, talking books, and other recorded formats.
>> 50,682,161 total manuscripts.
>> 4,481,334 maps.
>> 12,171,496 microforms.
>> 13,218,544 visual materials. This total included 772,104 moving images, 11,908,937 photographs, 82,628 posters, and 393,044 prints and drawings.

Registered 558,645 claims to copyright.
Completed 560,000 research assignments for Congress through the Congressional Research Service.

Circulated 22,500,000 disk, cassette, and braille items to a readership of 769,000 blind and physically handicapped patrons.

Averaged 60 million transactions a month on all the library's public electronic systems, including 8 million on the Thomas legislative information system and 9 million on the American Memory Web site. At year's end, the library's American Memory online historical collections contained 1.4 million digital files.

Employed a permanent staff of 4,213 employees.

Operated with a total 1998 fiscal appropriation of $377,207,000.

SOURCE: Library of Congress.

The newly renovated Reading Room in the Thomas Jefferson Building of the Library of Congress.

The National Library of China

by Sharon Chien Lin

CURRENTLY THERE IS ONLY ONE national library in mainland China, namely, the National Library of China (NLC), known domestically as Beijing or Peking Library. Under the jurisdiction of the Ministry of Culture (MOC), NLC is the Chinese counterpart of the Library of Congress. It serves both as depository and comprehensive research library for the nation's publications. It also provides cataloging to other libraries through cards, floppy disks, magnetic tapes, and CD-ROMs. NLC plays a pivotal role in the promotion and development of standardization, automation, and networking in Chinese libraries.

The library has grown considerably in the 1980s. Though the original Wenjin Street building was enlarged several times after 1949, the available space still failed to keep pace with the growth of the collections. A new building was completed in 1987, which covers an area of 7.42 hectares with a floor space of 140,000 square meters and shelving capacity of 20 million volumes. The old building on Wenjin Street is now a branch library. The new library has more than 30 reading rooms offering 3,000 reading seats and the capacity of receiving 7,000 to 8,000 readers daily. NLC now has a collection of 16.7 million volumes and a staff of 1,700. It is equipped with various automatic systems, modem installations, and equipment. The structure is earthquake resistant and features a symmetrical design consisting of towers, gardens, and courtyards.

Organization and staff

The NLC is a government organization under the jurisdiction of the MOC. It is headed by a director and several deputy directors. Aside from various administrative offices, the library has 11 core departments plus a committee for acquisitions, a branch library, a staff training and education center, a publishing house, the China Center of the International Serials Data System, and other profit-generating services. Its core departments include acquisitions, Chinese-language cataloging, foreign-language cataloging, reference, reading rooms, collection and circulation, rare books and special collections, serials and newspapers, automation development, electronic information service, and technical services. Library services are offered in the reading rooms, each of which is responsible for its own reference and circulation activities. Of the 1,700 staff, 74% hold postsecondary degrees, 29% are trained in library science, and 85% are professionally trained in one of 200 subject specialties.

Collection development

The NLC's collection is characterized by its comprehensiveness and rarity. As of the end of 1991, the library's total collection amounted to 1.7 million volumes (items), ranking it fifth among the libraries of the world. Forty percent of the collection is in Chinese, and the rest is in various foreign languages. Annually, it receives 26,000 volumes of monographs and nearly 8,000 periodical titles. Its collections date back to the Southern Song dynasty (1127–1279). It inherited part of the collections of Qixidian, the Imperial Library of the Southern Song dynasty, and Wenyuange, the Imperial Library of the Ming dynasty. After its founding in 1912, it also took over the collections of the Cabinet Grand Library, the imperial academy, and the Southern School of the Imperial College of the Qing dynasty (1644–1911). Gradually, it acquired priceless woodblock-printed books and such handwritten volumes as the Wenjin edition of the *Si ku quan shu (Complete Collection of the Four Branches of Literature),* which was originally preserved in the Rehe Provisional Palace; it also holds the manuscripts from the Dunhuang Caves.

The library's 291,700-volume rare book collection is the largest in the country. It is the sole holder of many rare items from the Southern Song, Ming, and Qing dynasties, and also includes 35,000 tortoise-shell and animal-bone scripts of the Yin-Shang dynasty (approximately 1100 B.C.). The collection has a large number of rubbings, ancient maps, and atlases, as well as documents of Chinese minorities. Furthermore, the NLC holds the world-renowned Dunhuang Buddhist manuscripts; the collection of Buddhist scriptures preserved in Zhaocheng, Shanxi; and the monumental *Yongle Encyclopedia.*

In addition to the rare book collection, NLC possesses approximately 2 million volumes of traditional thread-bound books, all of which are regarded as unique copies. It also emphasizes the collection of historical documents produced in revolutionary times, such as the Chinese version of the Communist Manifesto and a large number of publications published in the Liberated and Revolutionary Areas before 1949. A special collection of manuscripts was also established in 1954 for scripts of well-known writers and scholars as well as authors in communism.

Since 1916, the NLC has been receiving deposit copies of domestic publications. In order to guarantee its comprehensive collection of national publications, the State Council, MOC, State Press, and Publishing Administration have all stressed the importance of implementing the legal deposit regulations. The NLC also collects newly compiled local chronicles, census records, and Chinese doctoral theses. In recent years, the library has spared no effort in collecting conference proceedings and documents and statistical materials, as well as the official publications of the American government, the United Nations, and other international organizations and institutions, through international publication exchange.

Moreover, the NLC has acquired a sizable collection of foreign materials, consisting of more than 2.5 million monographs, about 36,000 serial titles, and 1,400 newspapers in 115 languages (mostly English, Russian, Japanese, French, and German). At present, the annual acquisition of foreign materials includes over 60,000 new monographs, 13,000 current serials, and 400 newspapers. The administration stresses both the preservation and the circulation of its collection. The freezing method and chemicals are used to preserve books. Presently, the NLC is converting some of its collection from the traditional paper format into microform or digital format. It also began acquiring audiovisual materials in 1987, and it has a collection of more than 10,000, items, including audio- and videocassettes, high-density videodisks, laser videodisks, and compact disks. In order to keep abreast with developments in science and technology, sci-tech material has become the fastest growing category in the collection. Numerous types of information-retrieval media, including CD-ROM databases, were introduced to facilitate information retrieval.

Reader services

The NLC offers modern multichanneled services for readers at different levels. Library collections as well as reference works, lending, microphotocopying, photocopying, and audio and video services are available in the reading rooms. The NLC also organizes exhibitions and academic lectures. These services are described in the following sections.

Reading rooms constitute the most direct service to readers. Within the library there are over 30 reading rooms that offer open access to collections. Among them are reading rooms for foreign books, Chinese books, current foreign periodicals, and current Chinese periodicals. Readers may also borrow from the collections in the basic stacks and other closed stacks. In addition, the library has set up several specialized, subject oriented reading rooms. They include reading rooms for Marxist-Leninist research materials, newspapers, library science, Taiwanese and Hong Kong books, rare books and special collections, fine art materials, and Chinese minority materials. The abstract and index reading room offers database searching on CD-ROM.

Service hours for most reading rooms are 8:00 a.m. to 5:00 p.m., Monday through Friday and Sunday (a few reading rooms are open till 7:00 p.m. in the evening). The library is not open to the public on Saturdays or national holidays.

Reference service is provided in person, by telephone, or by mail. Reference librarians also compile subject bibliographies, union catalogs, and indexes. In recent years, the library has been providing selective dissemination of information (SDI) and online retrieval services. Additionally, upon request, the reference desk will prepare subject bibliographies and indexes, and provide photocopying, training, and translation services.

Lending. The library acts as a national interlibrary service center. Users outside the Beijing area may borrow books from the library through their local, provincial, municipal, county, or university libraries. The library also works actively to expand its cooperation with libraries abroad. Presently, the NLC maintains interlibrary loan services with 30 countries. Individual borrowing cards are only issued to researchers and faculty members with senior professional titles and to senior officials of the party, government, army, and other organizations.

Microphotocopying and audiovisual materials. Photocopies may be requested in person or by mail and are available in either paper or microfilm. The library also utilizes modern equipment including computers, cameras, television sets, optical disks, and recording facilities.

International activities and academic exchange

As the national library, the NLC is responsible for execution of the book exchange program in accordance with the cultural agreements signed by the Chinese and foreign governments. As of 1991, the library has had an exchange relationship with more than 1,000 libraries and institutions in approximately 100 countries and an interlibrary loan service with about 260 libraries in more than 30 countries. Moreover, the NLC has developed a librarian exchange program and holds regular meetings with a number of university libraries abroad. Furthermore, it organizes and sponsors lectures and seminars in library science, which serve as a medium for intellectual exchange between domestic and international librarians. The library also sends its staff abroad to participate in international library conferences and visit foreign libraries. The NLC has been a member of the International Federation of Library Associations and Institutions (IFLA) since 1981, and it has been actively involved in IFLA-sponsored activities, including hosting the 1996 IFLA meeting in Beijing. As a matter of fact, China was one of the founding members of IFLA, in 1927.

SOURCE: © Sharon Chien Lin, *Libraries and Librarianship in China* (Westport, Conn.: Greenwood Press, 1998), pp. 57–67. Reprinted with permission.

Presidential libraries

THROUGH THE PRESIDENTIAL LIBRARIES, which are located at sites selected by the presidents and built with private funds, the National Archives and Records Administration preserves and makes available the records and personal papers of a particular president's administration. In addition to providing reference services on presidential documents, each library prepares documentary and descriptive publications and operates a museum to exhibit documents, historic objects, and other memorabilia of interest to the public.

The records of each president since Herbert Hoover are administered by the agency. Once considered personal papers, all presidential records created on or after January 20, 1981, are declared by law to be owned and controlled by the United States and are required to be transferred to the National Archives at the end of the administration.

Herbert Hoover Library, 211 Parkside Drive, P.O. Box 488, West Branch, IA 52358-0488; (319) 643-5301 (hoover.nara.gov).

Franklin D. Roosevelt Library, 511 Albany Post Road, Hyde Park, NY 12538-1999; (914) 229-8114; (www.fdrlibrary.marist.edu/).

Eleanor Roosevelt (left), opening Franklin D. Roosevelt papers at Franklin D. Roosevelt Library in Hyde Park, New York, March 17, 1950. (www.academic. marist.edu/fdr/)

Harry S. Truman Library, 500 W. U.S. Hwy 24, Independence, MO 64050-1798; (816) 833-1400; (www.trumanlibrary.org).

Dwight D. Eisenhower Library, 200 SE 4th Street, Abilene, KS 67410-2900; (785) 263-4751; (redbud.lbjlib.utexas.edu/eisenhower/ddehp.htm).

John Fitzgerald Kennedy Library, Columbia Point, Boston, MA 02125-3398; (617) 929-4500; (www.cs.umb.edu/jfklibrary/).

Lyndon Baines Johnson Library, 2313 Red River Street, Austin, TX 78705-5702; (512) 916-5137; (www.lbjlib.utexas.edu).

Richard Nixon Presidential Materials Project, National Archives, 8601 Adelphi Road, College Park, MD 20740-6001; (301) 713-6950;(metalab.unc.edu/lia/president/nixon.html).

Gerald R. Ford Library, 1000 Beal Ave., Ann Arbor, MI 49504-5353; (734) 741-2218; (www.lbjlib.utexas.edu/ford/index.html).

Gerald R. Ford Museum, 303 Pearl Street N.W., Grand Rapids, MI 49504-5353; (616) 451-9263; (www.lbjlib.utexas.edu/ford/index.html).

Jimmy Carter Library, 441 Freedom Parkway, Atlanta, GA 30307-1498; (404) 331-3942; (carterlibrary.galileo.peachnet.edu).

Ronald Reagan Library, 40 Presidential Drive, Simi Valley, CA 93065-0666; (805) 522-8444; (www.reagan.utexas.edu).

George Bush Library, 1000 George Bush Drive West, College Station, TX 77843; (409) 260-9554; (csdl.tamu.edu/bushlib/).

William Jefferson Clinton Library, to be built in Little Rock, Arkansas.

Presidential libraries not administered by the National Archives and Records Administration are:

National First Ladies' Library, The Saxton McKinley House, 331 S. Market Avenue, Canton, OH 44702; (330) 452-0876; (www.firstladies.org).

David R. Atchison Presidential Library, Atchison County Historical Museum, 200 S. 10th St., Atchison, KS 66002; (913) 367-6238. Atchison was president for 24 hours between Polk and Taylor.

An **Abraham Lincoln Presidential Library** is under consideration in Springfield, Illinois.

Jefferson Davis Presidential Library, Beauvoir, 2244 Beach Blvd., Biloxi, MS 39531; (228) 388-9074; (www.beauvoir.org/prezlib.html).

Rutherford B. Hayes Memorial Museum and Library, Spiegel Grove, 1337 Hayes Ave., Fremont, OH 43420; (419) 332-2081; (www.rbhayes.org/library.htm).

James A. Garfield National Historical Site Memorial Library, 8095 Mentor Ave., Mentor, OH 44060; (440) 255-8722; (www.nps.gov/jaga/).

William Howard Taft National Historic Site, 2038 Auburn Ave., Cincinnati, OH 45219; (513) 684-3627; (www.nps.gov/wiho/).

Library and Archives of New Hampshire's Political Tradition, 20 Park St., Concord, NH 03301; (603) 271-2081; (www.nhprimary.nhsl.lib.nh.us).

Richard Nixon Library and Birthplace, 18001 Yorba Linda Boulevard, Yorba Linda, CA 92886; (714) 993-3393; (www.nixonfoundation.org).

STATE LIBRARIES

What state library agencies do

A STATE LIBRARY AGENCY is the official agency of a state charged by the law of that state with the extension and development of public library services throughout the state, which has adequate authority under law to administer state plans in accordance with the provisions of the Library Services and Construction Act [since 1997 the Library Services and Technology Act]. Beyond these two essential roles, these agencies vary greatly.

Presented here are the highlights of a 1997 survey of the library agencies in the 50 states and the District of Columbia.

Governance

Nearly all state library agencies (48 states and the District of Columbia) are located in the executive branch of government. Of these, over 65% are part of a larger agency, the most common being the state department of education. In two states, Arizona and Michigan, the agency reports to the legislature.

Allied and other special operations

A total of 16 state library agencies reported having one or more allied operations. Allied operations most frequently linked with a state library agency are the state archives (10 states) and the state records management service (11 states). Fifteen state agencies contract with public or academic libraries in their states to serve as resource or reference/ information service centers. Eighteen state agencies operate a state Center for the Book.

Electronic network development

In all 50 states, the state library agency plans or monitors electronic network development; 42 states operate such networks; and 46 states develop network content.

All state library agencies are involved in facilitating library access to the Internet in one or more of the following ways: training library staff or consulting in the use of the Internet; providing a subsidy for Internet participation; providing equipment needed to access the Internet; providing access to directories, databases, or online catalogs; or managing gopher/Web sites, file servers, bulletin boards, or electronic discussion lists.

Library development services

Services to public libraries. Every state library agency provides these types of services to public libraries: administration of LSCA [LSTA] grants, collection of library statistics, and library planning, evaluation, and research. Nearly every state library association provides consulting services and continuing education programs.

Services to public libraries provided by at least three-quarters of state agencies include administration of state aid, interlibrary loan referral services, library legislation preparation or review, literacy program support, reference referral services, state standards or guidelines, summer reading program support, and union list development.

Over three-fifths of state agencies provide Online Computer Library Center (OCLC) Group Access Capability to public libraries and statewide public relations or library promotion campaigns. Less common services to public libraries include accreditation of libraries, certification of librarians, cooperative purchasing of library materials, preservation/conservation services, and retrospective conversion of bibliographic records.

Services to academic libraries. At least two-thirds of state library agencies report the following services to the academic library sector: administration of LSCA [LSTA] grants, continuing education, interlibrary loan referral services, reference referral services, and union list development.

Less common services to academic libraries include cooperative purchasing of library materials, literacy program support, preservation/conservation, retrospective conversion, and state standards or guidelines. No state agency accredits academic libraries; only Washington state certifies academic librarians.

Services to school library media centers. At least two-thirds of all state library agencies provide continuing education, interlibrary loan referral services, and reference referral services to school library media centers (LMCs). Services to LMCs provided by at least half of all state agencies include administration of LSCA [LSTA] grants, consulting services, and union list development.

Less common services to LMCs include administration of state aid, cooperative purchasing of library materials, and retrospective conversion. No state agency accredits LMCs or certifies LMC librarians.

Services to special libraries. Over two-thirds of state agencies serve special libraries through administration of LSCA [LSTA] grants, consulting services, continuing education, interlibrary loan referral, reference referral, and union list development.

Less common services to special libraries include administration of state aid, cooperative purchasing of library materials, and summer reading program support. Only Nebraska accredits special libraries and only Washington state certifies librarians of special libraries.

Services to systems. At least three-fifths of state agencies serve library systems through administration of LSCA [LSTA] grants, consulting services, continuing education, interlibrary loan referral, library legislation preparation or review, reference referral, and library planning, evaluation, and research.

Accreditation of systems is provided by only six states, and certification of librarians by only seven states.

Service outlets

State library agencies reported a total of 153 service outlets. Main or central outlets and other outlets (excluding bookmobiles) each accounted for 47.1%, and bookmobiles represented 5.9% of the total.

Collections

The number of books and serial volumes held by state library agencies totaled 22.4 million, with New York accounting for the largest collection (2.4 million). Five state agencies had book and serial volumes of over one million. In other states, these collections ranged from 500,000 to one million (12 states); 200,000 to 499,999 (10 states); 100,000 to 199,999 (10 states); 50,000 to 99,999 (six states); and 50,000 or less (six states). The state library agency in Maryland does not maintain a collection, and the District of Columbia does not maintain a collection in its function as a state library agency.

The number of serial subscriptions held by state library agencies totaled over 84,000, with New York holding the largest number (over 14,300). Ten state agencies reported serial subscriptions of over 2,000. In other states, these collections ranged from 1,000 to 1,999 (six states), 500 to 999 (18 states), 100 to 499 (13 states), and under 100 (one state).

Staff

The total number of budgeted full-time equivalent (FTE) positions in state library agencies was 3,762. Librarians with ALA-accredited MLS degrees accounted for 1,206 of these positions, or 32.1% of total FTE positions. Rhode Island reported the largest percentage (57.1%) of librarians, and Virginia reported the lowest (16.3%).

Income

State library agencies reported a total income of $847.1 million in FY 97 (83.1% came from state sources, 15.4% from federal, and 1.5% from other sources).

Of state library agency income received from state sources, nearly $477 million (67.8%) was designated for state aid to libraries. Eight states had over 75% of their income from state sources set aside for state aid. Georgia had the largest percentage of state library agency income set aside for state aid (97.4%). Six states and the District of Columbia targeted no state funds for aid to libraries. Hawaii, Iowa, South Dakota, Vermont, Washington, and D.C. had all of their state income set aside for operation of the state agency.

Expenditures

State library agencies reported total expenditures of over $822.2 million. The largest percentage (83.6%) was from state funds, followed by federal funds (15.3%), and other funds (1.1%).

In five states, over 90% of total expenditures were from state sources. These states were Georgia (94.7%), Massachusetts (93.5%), Illinois (92.4%), New York (92.0%), and Maryland (91.9%). Utah had the lowest percentage of expenditures from state sources (59.2%).

Almost 70% of total state library expenditures were for financial assistance to libraries, with the largest percentages expended on individual public libraries (53.1%) and public library systems (16.4%). Most of the expenditures for financial assistance to libraries were from state sources (86.2%), while 13.6% were from federal sources.

Fifteen state library agencies reported expenditures for allied operations. These expenditures totaled over $24.0 million and represented 2.9% of total expenditures by state library agencies. Of states reporting such expenditures, Texas had the highest expenditure ($3.3 million) and Vermont the lowest ($398,000).

Twenty-seven state library agencies reported a total of over $16.7 million in grants and contracts expenditures to assist public libraries with state education reform initiatives or the National Education Goals. The area of adult literacy accounted for the largest proportion of such expenditures (47.7%), followed by the areas of lifelong learning (34.9%), and readiness for school (17.4%). Three state agencies (Nebraska, Oregon, and Pennsylvania) focused such expenditures exclusively on readiness for school projects, and five state agencies (Georgia, Kansas, New Jersey, Oklahoma, and Utah) focused their expenditures exclusively on adult literacy projects. In four state agencies (Connecticut, Indiana, Michigan, and South Carolina), over two-thirds of such expenditures were for lifelong learning projects.

SOURCE: *State Library Agencies, Fiscal Year 1997* (Washington, D.C.: National Center for Education Statistics, March 1999), pp. iii–viii.

SMALL LIBRARIES

Flying solo

by Judith A. Siess

WHAT IS A SOLO LIBRARIAN? One who flies an airplane alone? Not exactly, but there are similarities.

Martha Rhine, founder of the Solo Librarians Division of the Special Libraries Association (SLA), defined a "solo" as "an isolated librarian or information collector/provider who has no professional peers within the immediate organization." Other names for solo librarian are "one-man band" (in the U.K.), "sole-charge librarian" (sometimes used in Australia and New Zealand), and "one-person librarian" (used most everywhere else). Many solo members of the American Library Association call themselves "independent librarians" and join the Independent Librarians' Exchange, a section of the Association of Specialized and Cooperative Library Agencies.

How many solos are there and where do they work? SLA estimates that a third to a half of its 14,000+ members are in solo positions. That's 5,000–7,000 solos in special libraries alone.

Solos work mostly in corporate libraries, but they are also found in museums, schools, churches or synagogues, prisons, law firms, and hospitals. The presence of solo librarians is growing rapidly in nontraditional jobs or nonlibrary settings such as information brokers, sales for library-related firms, publishing, and infopreneurs.

In addition, U.S. Department of Education figures show that the vast majority of public libraries employ only one professional librarian; often this is true of branches of larger library systems. In addition, nearly 80% of public libraries serving populations under 25,000 are staffed by only one professional.

The solo is most likely found in a small library without extensive holdings or resources. Solos are expected to do it all—ordering, cataloging, reference, bibliographic instruction, online searching, filing, budgeting—everything. They may have a part-time assistant, volunteers, or if they are lucky, some full-time clerical assistance. But the solo is the only trained librarian on the staff. In addition, the solo has no one in the organization doing the same job to go to for advice or a shoulder to cry on. Finally, solos probably work for a nonlibrarian—a boss who does not really understand what they do or how they do it.

Do you want to be captain or just a crew member?

Why would anyone want to be a solo librarian? The three most common reasons are independence, variety, and an enhanced feeling of self-worth.

Cathy Wright of the Albany Research Center in Oregon said she relishes being in charge. "I call the shots—I can do things my way; I don't have to deal with other coworkers' attitudes, problems, baggage, whatever; I set the priorities, etc. That's pretty nice."

Former solo Frances Drone-Silvers of Champaign, Illinois, said "One of the best things about being a solo is that 'Small Can Be Beautiful'—the library's reputation is yours to make and maintain!"

Linda Appel of Tektronix in Wilsonville, Oregon, said that her interns (school librarians) were surprised at the speed at which she worked and the variety of topics she was asked to search on. "They didn't seem to be used to having to get answers *now* and always having work waiting. They were also surprised at how limited my resources were. I think they expected that an industrial library would have the latest, greatest systems, be fully automated, and have all other business accoutrements as well as plush quarters and lots of space. Welcome to the real world!"

The "ideal" solo is flexible, creative, well organized, able to think analytically and independently, and confident in her ability to make good decisions. She is a team player who specializes in working alone. She should possess a high frustration tolerance, an entrepreneurial attitude, and the ability to juggle multiple clients and priorities.

Jane Bomberger's story best sums up why someone would want to become a solo. After she graduated, she had to decide between two job offers. One company had a library that ran like the machine the firm manufactured. It had 20 professional librarians on staff, apparently unlimited resources, and established services and resources. "I would have worked with these great professionals every day, picking up new skills on an hourly basis, and I would have had a fairly clear career path," Bomberger said.

The second job was a solo position in a company that didn't even have a library, "just a room with books strewn all over the floor and magazines that were extras dumped there from the mailroom." Bomberger, now with the Silicon Valley software company Inprise Corporate, explained why she chose to work virtually by herself in an unproven library: "I would rather be Captain Janeway on the small spaceship *Voyager* than, say, an entry-level engineer on the powerful flagship *Enterprise*."

The captain's headaches

The solo life, however, is not a bed of roses. Solos face unique problems:

Professional isolation. Cathy Wright pointed out: "Solos lack the existence of peer support and interaction. I sometimes miss the shared goals, the we're-all-in-this-together attitude."

Lack of clerical support. There never seems to be enough time to get everything done. Filing, reading, public relations, and professional development fall victim to too little time.

Reporting to a nonlibrarian. Often we tire under the strain of constantly having to explain ourselves and our work to managers who do not understand us. If you are the type who needs constant reinforcement, this is not the job for you.

Low pay. A 1998 survey done for the SLA Solo Librarians Division by Ailya Rose of Varian Associates Corporate Library showed 15% of solos earning less than $30,000 and 81% under $50,000. In addition, 11% of the libraries had no annual budget and 50% had a budget of less than $30,000.

Lack of job security. Downsizing is always around the corner and for a solo, downsizing means you.

Frustration at not being able to "do it all." Not being able to serve your patrons at the high level you would like.

Inadequate preparation for the job. Once on the job, solos wish they had learned more in library school about financial matters, management, corporate culture, computer skills, assertiveness, time management, public relations, and negotiation skills, and had gotten more practical experience.

On common ground

No matter how different solos may seem, they are still librarians. They deal with information, patrons, cataloging, reference, reshelving, acquisitions, and all the other issues that the profession faces.

Most solos could not serve their patrons without the resources of the larger libraries and are very appreciative of their telephone reference, interlibrary loan, and specialized collections.

Many solos are members of OCLC or its member networks and use its cataloging and interlibrary loan services. Solos also are active members of library consortia, bringing their specialized collections and knowledge to other libraries.

"Public libraries really do help us do our job because we need the general reference materials they provide," said Elizabeth Meylor, library manager with the architectural and engineering firm of Hammel, Green, and Abrahamson in Minneapolis. "For my particular library, the question range is a mile wide and an inch deep. We want to know something about a topic but we don't special-

Linda Appel at Tektronix helps attorneys with patent searches.

ize in just one topic like some other special/solo libraries do. So I sometimes feel like a public library without all the resources. Consequently I use my public and university libraries a lot."

Barbara McCall of Allison Transmission in Indianapolis has found many similarities. "I worked as a librarian for 10 years in two different public library systems before I became a corporate solo. The company is a microcosm of the world: I get a variety of questions; I have assisted parents with their children's homework; everyone wants his or her information now and everyone wants access to the Internet."

It is almost certain that in the future there will be more solos in corporate and other institutional settings, and probably even in public and academic settings.

"Management will find that they get more value for their money by employing one highly skilled and effective librarian/information specialist instead of a team—however small—of generalists who are not as skilled," wrote Guy St. Clair, creator of the newsletter *The One-Person Library.*

How do solos go about preparing for the future? Just like every other good librarian, they join professional organizations such as ALA, the Medical Library Association, the American Association of Law Libraries, SLA, the Church and Synagogue Library Association, and so forth. Although they have a bit more trouble getting away to attend conferences and continuing education workshops, they go when they can. Solos also rely on e-mail, lists, and Web sites to stay in touch. Many participate in formal or informal mentoring programs.

"The most important thing for helping us do our jobs better is networking, networking, networking," said Jennifer McCready, information resource specialist at Hudson's Bay Company in Toronto. "I must, for reasons of sanity and job completion, keep in touch with others in the field. This forces us to go outside our organizations to find peers and colleagues. Rather than making me feel lonely, I believe this has made me feel more a part of the librarian/information specialist profession. I consider those librarians I have visited or from whom I have sought advice, to be my work mates as much as the people I see every day."

Cathy Wright noted that the various library Internet discussion lists "ameliorate the feelings of isolation that I have experienced as a solo." She also advocates attending a conference or two a year, joining various library groups, and finding training sessions to keep up-to-date on new techniques and technology.

Solo librarians are here to stay. Although solo organizing and support activities have centered primarily on special libraries, there are many in the public and academic library world. You might even consider going solo yourself!

SOURCE: Judith A. Siess, "Flying Solo: Librarian, Manage Thyself," *American Libraries* 30 (February 1999): 32–34.

FACILITIES

1

Planning for a new library

by Jeannette Woodward

WHILE YOU'RE BUSY planning for a new building, a number of annoying little details may escape your attention. Begin making a list of such irritating but important puzzle pieces early in the process and keep adding to it throughout the planning and construction phases. Many librarians say that they keep a small notebook with them at all times until their project is complete. They even place it on their bedside tables at night in case they wake up at 3 a.m. with either an inspiration or a frightening premonition.

Here is a conglomeration of last-minute thoughts I've assembled from the many suggestions of librarians around the country:

- Provide a safe, dry place for daily newspaper delivery. It's no fun to have them disappear or become wet, sodden masses.
- Don't forget literature racks, both wall-mounted and revolving-floor models. Begin preparing the bookmarks, brochures, and information sheets that will soon fill them.
- Make sure the employee entrance is well-lighted and protected from the elements. Imagine staff members fumbling for keys in the dark or struggling to swipe access cards while being pelted by rain.
- Locate outside book drops where the staff can easily get to them. Remember that they will be wheeling loaded book trucks over uneven sidewalks and negotiating steps or curbs only with difficulty.
- If your geographic area gets a lot of snow, be sure to include enough snow guards for the roof. You don't want heavy snow to melt and slide onto people's heads or nearby vehicles.
- Since even high-performance acoustical partitions won't entirely conceal the sound of power-flush commercial toilets, locate rest rooms away from offices and reading areas. On the other hand, position them close enough to high-traffic areas so that patrons don't wander around for 15 minutes trying to find one.
- Estimate stack dimensions and aisle widths early in the project so you don't find yourself forced to narrow aisles to accommodate the required number of stack units. Wider aisles are not only needed for ADA compliance, but they facilitate browsing and reshelving.
- Have complete plans for any buried conduit: These plans tend to disappear shortly after the building is completed. You don't want workers digging up your parking lots looking for buried cable.
- Make sure that the architect has planned for the cleaning of skylights and clerestory windows, both inside and outside. Too often, relatively new buildings have dirty windows because the regular window cleaners have concluded they are too difficult or dangerous to reach.

- Take precautions against children turning task lights on and off and see that switches are sufficiently tough to accommodate heavy usage.
- Consider installing a buzzer at the circulation and reference desks that notifies staff that they are needed.
- Provide free in-library phones so patrons on the second or 10th floor can speak with a reference librarian. Make sure that the phones are solidly attached to the wall, since otherwise they will quickly disappear.
- Select workstations that permit easy installation of cable into panels (ones in which electricians are able to separate and store cables by function) and that don't require wiring to be accessed from behind panel base plates so the workstation doesn't have to be disassembled during changes or repairs.
- Provide desk-height access to electrical, voice, and data outlets.
- Encourage electricians to store "goof loops" (extra wire) in workstations to avoid rewiring when changes are made or equipment added. Running cables through the panels protects them.
- Allow five feet of space in computer-equipped study carrels for books, equipment, data ports, power outlets, and locks where appropriate. Multipurpose tables should also be spacious, with data and power provided at every seat.

SOURCE: Jeannette Woodward, *Countdown to a New Library: Managing the Building Project* (Chicago: American Library Association, 2000).

ADA accessibility compliance: Parking
by William W. Sannwald

COMPLETE CHECKLISTS for compliance with the federal Americans with Disabilities Act (ADA) are found in the author's *Checklist of Library Building Design Considerations.* In addition, consult state and local codes.—*GME.*

1. Are there safe and accessible parking spaces located on the shortest accessible route of travel to an accessible entrance?
2. Do accessible parking spaces have a designated sign showing the symbol of accessibility?
3. Are the accessible parking spaces at least eight feet wide and 20 feet long?
4. Is one in every eight accessible parking spaces, but not less than one overall, served by an access aisle 96 inches in width with signage that indicates "Van Accessible" under the accessibility symbol?
5. Are access aisles between van parking spaces five feet in width, striped, and part of an accessible route? (Two accessible parking spaces can share a common access aisle.)
6. Does the van-accessible parking space clear vertically to at least nine feet, six inches high?
7. If the library has a passenger loading zone, does the zone have an access aisle five feet wide and 20 feet long, adjacent and parallel to vehicle pull-up space?

8. Are there any curbs between the access aisle and the vehicle pull-up space? If so, are there cuts or curb ramps?

9. Are the accessible parking lot spaces and aisles level so that wheelchairs will not roll if left unattended while transferring persons to their vehicle?

10. If the pavement is not level, is the slope no more than 2% in all directions?

11. Does the facility observe the following requirements for parking spaces?

No. of spaces	Minimum accessible spaces
1–100	1 for each 1–25 spaces
101–200	4 + 1 for each 1–50 spaces
201–500	6 + 1 for each 1–100 spaces
501–1000	2% of total spaces
+1001	20 + 1 for each 1–100 over 1000

12. Are there curb cuts or curb ramps at all curbs and walks on accessible routes to accessible entrances?

13. Do the curb cuts or curb ramps provide drainage so that water will not be trapped after a storm?

14. Do curb cuts or curb ramps have a slope of 1:12 or less and flared sides with a slope of 1:10?

15. If there are curb ramps, are they built so they do not extend into vehicle traffic lanes?

16. Are curb cuts or curb ramps 36 inches wide excluding the flared sides?

17. Is the slope of all exterior walkways 1:12 or less?

18. Do the ramps have a minimum clear width of 36 inches? have level landings at the top and bottom, at least as wide as the ramp? have landings at least 60 inches in length?

THE SYMBOL OF ACCESS

Indicates ACCESS for the DISABLED

PLEASE HELP ELIMINATE ARCHITECTURAL BARRIERS

19. If the ramp changes direction, is the landing at least 60 inches by 60 inches?

20. If the slope of the ramp is between 1:12 and 1:16, does the ramp have level landings 60 inches in length at 30-foot intervals? If between 1:16 and 1:20, does the ramp have level landings 60 inches in length at 40-foot intervals?

21. Is the cross slope of all ramps and walks 1:50 or less?

22. If the ramp has a rise (a height of six inches or more), does it have handrails on both sides? If the ramp is six feet or more in length, does the ramp have handrails on both sides?

23. Are stairs at least 36 inches in width?

24. Are all the steps on any given flight of stairs uniform in height and depth?

25. Are stair depths no less than 11 inches?

26. Are the nosings (end of the steps) rounded or curved?

27. Do the nosings project no more than 1.5 inches past the riser of the steps?

28. Do stairways have handrails on both sides?

29. Is the diameter or width of the gripping surface of the handrail 1.25 inches to 1.5 inches?

30. If the handrail is located adjacent to a wall, is the space between the handrail and wall at least 1.5 inches?

31. If the ramp or stairs has a change of direction, is the inside handrail continuous?

32. Does the handrail extend at least 12 inches beyond the top for stairs, and 12 inches beyond the top and bottom for ramps?

33. Are the extended sections parallel to the surface of the landing for ramps and floor for the top step of stairs?

34. Does the handrail extend the depth of one tread plus 12 inches past the bottom step for stairs?

35. Does the handrail extension for stairs slope with the bottom step for the distance of one tread and is the 12-inch extension parallel to the floor?

36. Is the top of the handrail gripping surface between 34 inches and 38 inches above the ramps or steps?

37. Are the ends of handrails for ramps and stairs rounded or returning smoothly to the floor or landing?

38. If there is an outside book return, is it accessible to the disabled?

SOURCE: William W. Sannwald, *Checklist of Library Building Design Considerations* (Chicago: American Library Association, 1997).

Academic library buildings in 1850

by David Kaser

UNTIL THE LATTER HALF OF THE 19TH CENTURY, American academic library buildings could be small and simple because the colleges themselves were small and simple. In 1840, the average enrollment in the colleges of New England, which were then the largest in the nation, was only 166, whereas in the Trans-Allegheny West, where colleges were smallest, average enrollment was a meager 72. Almost until the time of the Civil War, all study in the nation was at the undergraduate level and was available only to men. Curricula were severely restricted and were intended only to build upon the instruction given in the Latin schools of the land. The only mode of learning was the continuing and largely sterile cycle of lecture and recitation. Overworked and underpaid professors were drawn predominantly from the clergy rather than from fields of productive scholarship. Except for the very few wealthier institutions, the entire college operation tended to be largely a shabby, impoverished, hand-to-mouth affair. In retrospect, it seems remarkable indeed that this lugubrious state of affairs nonetheless resulted somehow in producing the leaders needed to bring the nation through one of its most vigorous periods of growth.

Given this very circumscribed purpose of American higher education at the time, it is not surprising that college libraries were of very limited importance and consequently of very infrequent use. Again, in 1840 the average sizes of college-owned library book collections were 8,002 volumes in New England, 4,023 in the Middle Atlantic states, 3,477 in the South, and only 2,516 above the Ohio River. In most cases these libraries operated totally without book funds—the University of North Carolina appears not to have purchased a single library book for 35 years following 1824—but rather they accreted only occasional gifts of charity to their meager collections. Administered uniformly by a lone professor assigned part-time to be library custodian, unheated and unlighted library rooms were usually open only one or two hours a week for use by members of the college community. The table shows the sizes of the college-owned book collections, as well as the number of hours weekly that the libraries were open, at the nine institutions that erected separate library buildings prior to the Civil War. Operated under the most restrictive of policies, these libraries were even less stimulating of intellectual vigor than were their parent institutions.

Antebellum college library buildings, 1862			
Name of institution	Year opened	Volumes	Hours open weekly
South Carolina	1840	25,000	20
Harvard	1841	74,000	28
Yale	1846	36,000	30
Williams	1847	7,200	2
North Carolina	1851	3,500	5
Amherst	1853	12,000	3
Charleston	1856	7,000	—
Ohio Wesleyan	1856	6,300	—
Centre	1862	5,100	2

Understandably, libraries with such limited obligations could operate in very small amounts of space laid out in very simple designs. Almost the sole function of college libraries prior to the Civil War was to house and protect the books owned by the college. Then as now, the library was usually also the repository of the college's "nonbook media," in the 19th century comprising collections of portraiture, globes, and marble statuary, of which there always seemed to be some. Busts of Classical-period authors and philosophers were usually conveniently situated at the inner ends of stack ranges, and portraits of past presidents of the college or bishops in the church were hung on the gallery front, both sometimes serving as location symbols for the books in the adjacent ranges.

Sometimes, but not always, a few tables and chairs were provided in case someone wished to consult a reference on-site, but more often so that the librarian would have a place to sit while he (and they were always men) inscribed new acquisitions into the manuscript catalogue of the library's holdings or added a name to its donor list. But those few tables and chairs, if indeed they were needed at all, could be fitted in almost anywhere, most easily into the aisle alcoves or in the nave. The infrequency of their use meant that they did not require any particular location or configuration. Rather, the single function of providing most effective book storage dictated the simple arrangement of space within all library buildings of the time.

Although there was little disagreement as to the appropriate interior layout of American library buildings when they first began to appear in 1840, preference regarding exterior design treatment was about equally divided between two styles, largely determined by the region of the country. In the Southland, popular taste still favored the severe, restrained lines of Classical Revival architecture that had been rediscovered and adapted by Palladio in the 16th century and had flourished so long in harmony with the spirits of both the Renaissance and the Enlightenment. Elsewhere in the Union, however, especially in New England, the Romantic movement was in full sway, bringing with it a growing partiality for the more effusive and elaborate motifs of Gothic Revival buildings. This was the pedagogical and bibliothecal environment in the United States when the first separate college library building was built at the beginning of the fourth decade of the 19th century.

SOURCE: David Kaser, *The Evolution of the American Academic Library Building* (Lanham, Md.: Scarecrow, 1997), pp. 8–11. Reprinted with permission.

Do's and don'ts for moving a small academic library

by Joanna M. Burkhardt

PLANNING AND MOVING into a new library can either be a nightmare with long-range ramifications, or a sweet dream of perfect coordination and timing.

The University of Rhode Island (URI) College of Continuing Education, including the library for that campus, moved into a new building in January 1996. This small academic library has four full-time staff members and about 50,000 volumes supporting the widely varied curriculum of the college and the research needs of several other university or state departments, an alternative high school, and a day care center.

We eventually ended up with a beautiful and functional space. Many things went right simply because I did some reading, talked to library professionals with moving experience, followed my intuition and training, and insisted on having my own way. For the sanity and well-being of others who may be facing a move, I have compiled a list of suggested do's and don'ts.

1. Make your own plan for the new facility. Think about the services you want to offer both now and in the future. Submit your plan to the architect, space planner, or project manager.

Often space is designed for visual impact rather than practical use. Without the guidance of a library professional, an architect cannot be expected to understand why sight lines from the circulation desk to the microfilm machines might be important, or why leaving an open doorway into work areas might be a problem. The specific needs of your library should be discussed

with those in charge of the layout so that practical concerns can be considered. Submit your own plan, even if you are not invited to do so. Any reputable architect will at least ponder the differences between your plans and their own. A 30-minute discussion in the planning stages can save everyone time and money.

2. Allow your staff to be part of the planning process. Ask what they need or want to see as top priorities.

People are interested in their workspaces. Those on the front lines know how the current arrangement could be made better. I drew up the initial plans for the library and amended them several times, asking my staff for input at each revision. Their responses gave me valuable information about what they wanted and needed in a new work environment.

The top priorities they listed gave me guidelines about what to emphasize to the architect. For example, a top priority for my staff was a space where they could work on assignments undisturbed. When the architect tried to talk me out of the private offices, I knew what my staff wanted. Cooperation can be expected from staff members whose wishes have been considered.

3. Make your own plan for computers and what they will access. Find out how much connectivity you need and where to put it. Meet with the computer experts, electricians, and/or architects to discuss the present and future needs for your library. Don't assume they know what your specialized needs are.

Talk to the people who can translate library services into electricity, outlets, modular plugs, data lines, surge protectors, and other related paraphernalia. Combining professional knowledge in libraries and computers will optimize the eventual outcome and possibly avoid expensive changes later on.

4. Visit the new site frequently while it is under construction. In construction projects, things happen very quickly. One day it's all I-beams and concrete, the next day the walls are in place. Adjustments frequently have to be made to accommodate changes and unforeseen circumstances. Economies may be needed, which will affect your space. It may be that you will have fewer electrical outlets, or that a quiet study room has to be eliminated. If too much time goes by between visits to the new site, economies may be achieved without your knowledge or approval.

5. Plan the move for the season most likely to provide good weather and avoid weather-related illness. Many factors have to be considered when scheduling a move. Higher powers may prevail when setting the moving schedule. Your timetable may or may not be given priority. However, if given the opportunity, opt for a dry season with moderate temperatures. Plan for a time when you have a maximum work crew available, and when the traffic between the old site and the new site is the lightest.

6. Start packing early. Think about packing earlier than that. Do as much sorting, weeding, and discarding as possible before you move. Don't move anything you plan to throw away when you get there.

Close your eyes and try to imagine packing up all your belongings, transporting them across the city, and putting them down in a new place over a 10-day period. What would you move first? What will you need on hand until the very last minute? What will be the first thing you need at the new site? What will you need in the middle? What is the best way to pack things so that you only have to handle them once at the other end? It's good to have thought about this. It's better to have written it down.

Office files and supplies were packed early in the process. We weeded files and packed as much as possible during the fall semester. Slowly the pile of boxes grew with the pile of paper to be discarded. Old forms, stationery, and invoices disappeared into the dumpster. Every piece of equipment was examined. If it was not in working order and had not been used during the last year, it was left behind.

7. Allow a flexible time frame and provide sufficient funds for the materials needed for moving. Schedule the move, including plenty of room for delays. Pack the collection in boxes and transport it all at the same time or in as few trips as possible. Do your packing with efficient unpacking in mind.

We moved the monographic collections on fully loaded book trucks, which were wheeled onto a large moving van, driven to the new location, wheeled off the moving van, and rolled into the library. The book trucks were unloaded directly onto the shelves, then sent back to the old location for reloading. In theory, this scheme should have worked.

However, in reality, fully loaded book trucks do not move well in snow and ice, nor do they easily roll up and down the loading tailgates of the moving trucks. The wheels of fully loaded three-shelf book trucks buckled under the weight of the books. The book trucks were dented and otherwise damaged in the rigors of moving through the snow and ice on the uneven city streets.

8. Hire movers with library experience. Hire literate movers who speak the same language you do. Train your movers in the basics of library organization. Have a "moving drill."

This is not a jab at multiculturalism. Communication is closely linked to efficiency and accuracy in moving. If you hire movers who cannot understand your instructions or cannot read the labels on the boxes, the move becomes much more complicated.

9. Limit the number of different companies and contractors involved in various installations. Schedule contractors for firm dates in the order they will be needed. Schedule delivery of equipment and furnishings—stagger their arrival. Be on hand when the contractors assemble and place shelving and furniture.

As opening day approached, we still had huge bundles of wires lying on the floor where the computers were supposed to be. Furniture could not be installed until the wiring was finished. The contractors could not agree on who had to do what with the wires. Where did Company A's responsibility end and Company B's responsibility start? Our security system took months to install, because there was no one to cut a hole in the circulation desk.

The library stacks went up the week before we moved without supervision by the library staff. The shelves were fully loaded when the building inspectors arrived and suggested that there might be a problem with the width of the aisles for emergency exit routes. Supervision of all library installations by a library staff member would have been a good idea.

During a move it is very important to schedule deliveries at the loading dock so progress does not come to a standstill. Our library move was delayed because the trucks simply could not get to the loading dock. There was no prioritization of need, and there was no plan in place when several semis arrived at the same time. The bad weather added nothing helpful to the mix.

10. Measure and mark out the areas for collections ahead of time. A good deal of time was spent measuring the collection and marking out how and where it would fit on the new shelving. This time was well spent. Preplanning gave some concrete view of how much room I had to work with, how much I could leave for growth, where the various parts of the collection could be housed, and how to fit equipment and furniture around the collection.

11. Give communication a high priority. Make sure the people at the old site can communicate with the people at the new site. Maintain the phone, e-mail, and fax at the old site until the move has been completed. Hook up the same at the new location as soon as possible.

It took us a week to find out what our new fax number was. It was also several weeks before our e-mail connection was back in service. The computers joined the library network in March. It was April before the telephones all worked properly and were located in appropriate spots. Preplanning and on-site supervision at the time of installation could have decreased these delays.

12. Make a punch list of items that need the contractor's attention. Interact with the project manager. During the actual construction process, details, repairs, and corrections are deferred until another time. To remind the contractor of what still needs to be accomplished, you must compile and submit a punch list to the project manager. Walk around your library. Look up and down, over and under, being as detailed as possible in describing what needs to be accomplished.

I prioritized my list, putting the items that most drastically affected operations at the top. The top priorities all received attention, if not a permanent fix, before the end of our first semester in residence. The old adage about the squeaky wheel applies here. Be creative in how you squeak.

13. Document your move. Share your experiences with others. One of the things that I did, which was actually fun, was to videotape the old library as it looked while we were working there, while we were packing, and while we were leaving. I also videotaped the new library as it emerged from the rubble, took shape, filled up, and got organized. I took still pictures as well, from hard-hat days to the finished product in the new library. I have written the process of planning, revising, moving, and settling in for my own benefit, and I have tried to share some sense of how it all happened with interested parties. The pictures and the story are now part of the history of the URI Libraries.

14. Blow your own horn. Say thank you. Celebrate. Celebrate your victory. The chance to say "good job" and "we did it" is not something that should be passed up. Many people worked very hard to make our move happen. Saying thank you is a small thing, but it can mean a great deal to those on the receiving end.

Many things can go wrong when planning and moving into a new library. The time spent in preparation for a move is closely related to its success or failure, but no amount of planning can guarantee a perfect move. It is possible to avoid some of the pitfalls by using the experience of others in combination with strategic planning, communication, and on-site presence.

SOURCE: Joanna M. Burkhardt, "Do's and Don'ts for Moving a Small Academic Library: Fourteen Helpful Tips," *College & Research Libraries News* 59 (July/August 1998): 499–503.

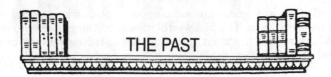

THE PAST

The Renaissance librarian

COURT REGULATIONS of the Duke of Urbino in 15th-century Italy offered the equivalent of a job description for the contemporary special collections librarian.

> The librarian should be learned, of good presence, temper, and manners; correct and ready of speech. He must get from the gardrobe an inventory of the books, and keep them arranged and easily accessible, whether Latin, Greek, Hebrew, or others, maintaining also the rooms in good condition. He must preserve the books from damp and vermin, as well as from the hands of trifling, ignorant, dirty, and tasteless persons. To those of authority and learning, he ought himself to exhibit them with all facility, courteously explaining their beauty and remarkable characteristics, the handwriting and miniatures, but observant that such abstract no leaves. When ignorant or merely curious persons wish to see them, a glance is sufficient, if it be not some one of considerable influence. When any lock or other requisite is needed, he must take care that it be promptly provided. He must let no book be taken away but by the Duke's orders, and if lent must get a written receipt, and see to its being returned. When a number of visitors come in, he must be specially watchful that none be stolen. All which is duly seen to by the present courteous and attentive librarian, Messer Agabito.

SOURCE: James Dennistoun, *Memoirs of the Dukes of Urbino, Illustrating the Arms, Arts and Literature of Italy, 1440–1630* (London: John Lane, 1909), Vol. 1, pp. 167–68.

Development of the municipal library

by Frederick G. Kilgour

THE MOST IMPORTANT DEVELOPMENT in the 19th-century literary world was the invention of an entirely new kind of library—the municipal library, whose collection was freely available to all the citizens of a community This event occurred simultaneously at midcentury in the United States and Britain and a decade later in France. Prior to the 1850s the phrase "public library" meant a library that was a private library available to a few but not to all; after 1850 it came to mean a library financially supported by taxation whose book collection was available free of charge. In general, it was the increasing desire for information, particularly information for self-improvement, that brought the public library into being, just as it had brought the mechanics and mercantile libraries into being earlier in the century. There can be no doubt that the economic crisis of 1847–1848, following so soon after that of 1837–1842, triggered the legislative action in Massachusetts (1848 and 1851), in New Hampshire (1849), and in Great Britain (1850) that authorized the use of tax money to support public libraries. The same kind of need that caused the establishment of public libraries propelled the soaring use of them during the Great Depression of the 1930s.

The public library in Manchester, England, opened in 1852, and that in Boston, Massachusetts, in 1854. Four years later, when it possessed 100,000 volumes, the Boston Library moved into its own building. Two decades later it had nearly 300,000 volumes and was circulating more than a million volumes a year—more than three books per inhabitant per year. At the century's end it had more than a million volumes. This growth of a million volumes in 50 years exemplifies the remarkable new market for books that came into being in just the last half of the century. The vast majority of the library users who borrowed those million volumes yearly were unable themselves to purchase the books they used.

Academic libraries had a growth history similar to that of the new public libraries. Until shortly after the enactment of the Copyright Law of 1870, which provided the Library of Congress with large numbers of free new books, Harvard possessed the largest library in the United States. From 1849 to 1876 Harvard added books at an average rate of 5,926 volumes per year; from 1876 to 1900, the average rate was 34,000 volumes a year—nearly six times as great as in the previous quarter century. This accelerated growth was due to the introduction of German research techniques into American institutions in the 1870s and the simultaneous shift in instruction from a single textbook to assignments in multiple works. Indeed, it was the Harvard College Library that, in the 1890s, first introduced the reserved-book procedure that made multiple copies of multiple books available to many students.

Britain and the United States were in the forefront of developing municipal and academic librarianship and furthering its professionalism and education. The American Library Association was founded in 1876, and Great Britain's Library Association was founded in the following year. Melvil Dewey established the world's first university library school at Columbia University in New York City in 1887. He transferred the school to Albany two years later because the Columbia trustees would not permit him to teach women students; 17 of his first class of 20 had been women.

Denmark, Norway, and Sweden developed public libraries on a par with those in Britain and the United States. Notably, Denmark, with its dense population, has been able since the Second World War to bring library service—directly from a library, or by book truck, or by mail—in reach of every citizen, a major and unique achievement. France and Germany achieved networks of municipal libraries; however, German libraries suffered two disasters. First, the Nazi government after 1933 exercised control and censorship of public libraries: Acquisition of foreign books by Jews was prohibited, and "communist" authors' books were removed and often burned. Subsequently a half-dozen years of air raids destroyed and severely damaged many German libraries. In Italy and Spain, library service had not advanced as far as it had in northern Europe by 1940; at that time only three percent of Spanish municipalities had public library service.

Although it is likely that some library users could have purchased some of the books they borrowed from libraries, very few, if any, could have purchased all. By and large, public libraries stimulated a demand for books and increased their sales.

SOURCE: © Frederick G. Kilgour, *The Evolution of the Book* (New York: Oxford University, 1998), pp. 130–32. Reprinted with permission.

The Carnegie heritage
by Theodore Jones

IN 1898, A U.S. BOARD OF EDUCATION SURVEY found only 637 public libraries across the United States, most on the East Coast and many hidden away in odd corners for want of independent buildings on prime sites. But in the following 30 years, public libraries were built at such an astounding rate as to become woven into the fabric of civic life—as cornerstones of the educational system, as social centers, and as architectural landmarks in young clapboard cities and towns across the country.

This change began in the small community of Fairfield in the rolling hills of southern Iowa, where, like Grovers Corners in Thornton Wilder's *Our Town*, "nothing much ever seemed to happen." Except on November 28, 1893, when Fairfield dedicated its new library, an impressive Romanesque Revival building. It was a properly dignified ceremony. Miss Mae Spielman and Mrs. Frank Howlett played a piano duet; a U.S. senator, a minister, a judge, a college president, and others gave speeches; and witnesses came from as far away as Des Moines, a day's train journey away. Everyone in town chipped in on the library effort, and they were all there, including Mrs. Rachel Hampson, who gave a fancy $700 Chickering piano for the library's 300-seat auditorium; Dr. J. M. Shaffer, who provided an entire set of mounted birds and other animals of Iowa for display; and a local day-laborer, who anted up $43 to upgrade the building's gutters to copper, a project never completed. And everyone remembered to thank the man who had made the library possible: Andrew Carnegie, the East Coast steel tycoon who had donated $40,000 to build the library even though he had never even passed through town.

It was a big event in a small town, but it was a ceremony with far broader meaning than local folks knew. The Fairfield library was the first typical building funded by Andrew Carnegie. Over the next 30 years, a period considered the golden age of the American public library, Carnegie paid for the construction of 1,689 public library buildings throughout the country in large cities and tiny crossroads alike. At the time of his last grant in 1919, 3,500 public libraries stood across the nation, and Carnegie had paid for half of them. His buildings served an estimated patronage of 35 million people. More than any other individual, Carnegie was responsible for dispersing these public institutions of learning and entertainment and making them a key landmark on the American landscape.

The Carnegie public library program, which never had a formal name, constructed buildings in large cities, such as New York, San Francisco, Los Angeles, Saint Louis, and Detroit, with the majority, about 70%, built for under $20,000 in small towns with populations of 10,000 or less. In all of these communities, Carnegie libraries played a formative role in education, as well as civic politics, finance, and artistic and social developments. Many American

Dedication ceremony for the Carnegie Library
in Dawson, Yukon Territory, Canada, 1905.

women cast their first ballot on the issue of whether their communities should accept a Carnegie library building—years before the passage of the 19th Amendment in 1920 gave them equal voting rights. Carnegie's grant stipulations fostered the now-unquestioned concept that it is a governmental duty to provide tax monies to support public libraries, as well as other major public works projects. In many towns, Carnegie libraries were the only large public buildings in town, and they became hubs of social activities like concerts, lectures, and meetings and did double duty as museums and community storehouses. They also served as city halls, hospitals, churches, and schools—and a few, though the funds had been accepted in good faith, never served as libraries at all.

Carnegie provided the construction funds for these landmarks, but left book-club presidents, mayors, clerks, and big-city committees in charge of design, which resulted in the construction of hundreds of classically influenced libraries. By sheer number, these Classical Revival libraries, along with a few other institutional structures, such as banks, helped to establish the idea that an important civic building must feature columns supporting a pediment—an architectural image yet to be displaced a century later. Over time, these buildings became architectural landmarks for surrounding townships and counties and today are often the first buildings restored in their communities. At least 377 have been nominated to the National Register of Historic Places. By function and funding, they are the largest group of buildings so honored.

For the fledgling discipline of library science, the impact was immense: Carnegie's efforts provided not only library buildings but also the impetus for initial library services at a time when America was changing. In the 10 years following the Fairfield library dedication, the Wright Brothers flew their self-propelled plane near Kitty Hawk, Henry Ford experimented with his horseless carriage, and Edwin S. Porter directed *The Great Train Robbery* and

The Life of the American Fireman, which introduced the basic tools of storytelling and film editing to the most important art form of the 20th century. If people wanted to read about these revolutionary changes, or even see a Porter film, the new Carnegie library was just down the street, around the corner, or in the next town.

The cost of all the Carnegie public libraries in the United States was $41,478,689, about $800 million in 1996 dollars. In addition, Carnegie paid for 830 public library buildings in other English-speaking nations around the world, as well as academic and specialized libraries, library schools, and professional and scholarly organizations. All told, the entire cost of the Carnegie library project was $68,333,973.

SOURCE: © Theodore Jones, *Carnegie Libraries Across America: A Public Legacy* (New York: John Wiley & Sons, 1997), pp. 2–3. Reprinted with permission.

Libraries in the 1940s

by Bernard Berelson

THE PUBLIC LIBRARY INQUIRY was the first national assessment of the status of public libraries and librarians in American society. Initiated by ALA and the Carnegie Corporation in 1947, and carried out by the Social Science Research Council under the leadership of University of Chicago political scientist Robert D. Leigh, this series of surveys examined public library operations, management, governance, services, and technology. The following excerpt is taken from one of the resulting reports, written by Bernard Berelson, dean of the University of Chicago Graduate Library School, who analyzed library use studies conducted before 1949.—*GME.*

The rationale of the public library has always assumed a wide popular use, but there are certain groups in the community which are not reached by library service. For example, the public library often asserts as an important objective its interest in improving the citizenship of the community by enlightening people on political affairs. Yet the groups who are least enlightened, as indicated in the report for the Inquiry on civic enlightenment, are precisely the groups which make least use of the public library. To the extent that the library does reach people with political materials, it reaches those who are already interested and informed. The others—those who "need it most"—are the ones who have not been and probably cannot be attracted to the public library for this purpose. If they are to become politically enlightened, it will be through other channels of communication, not the public library.

The question arises whether the public library is the appropriate distribution agency for readers of "light fiction." Should material of this kind be distributed through a professedly educational institution supported by public funds to achieve socially valuable ends? Librarians are continuously arguing this question in discussion of public library objectives, standards for book selection, and the philosophy of public librarianship. One argument is that the people pay for the library and should get what they want; another is that the public library should not supply light fiction and similar material of little or no literary distinction which is available elsewhere in the community. If the latter argument prevails and recent widely publicized novels of little literary merit are discontinued as staples of library circulation, the public library may lose a portion of its clientele. The public library can be in the position of compensating for the loss of clientele by improving the quality of its service to those who remain its users.

The relationship of the public library to the commercial media of mass communication in this country must also be considered. To a greater extent than ever before, people read newspapers and magazines, see films, and listen to the radio. These media provide recreation, information, and education to a greater or a lesser degree; and they thus represent, in a special sense, competitors of the public library. In the field of recreation and entertainment they compete quite effectively. In other respects, however, these media do not, and by their nature cannot, compete. They cannot present the range and depth of serious communication materials held by even the most modest public library. The public library is the only communication agency within the community which makes permanent accessibility of reading materials an objective. The public library does not need to depend upon immediate popular support so much as the commercial media. It is thus freer of the topical or fortuitous shifts in popular taste and more able to apply sounder criteria for its activities.

The public library has, therefore, a unique and distinctive place in the community as, among other things, a continuing storehouse of communication material. It might leave the field of popular entertainment to the commercial media (including the rental library) and devote itself to the serious communication needs of the community. For if, as another report in this Inquiry series suggests, the book industry in this country is becoming increasingly commercialized, with an attendant lowering of critical standards, this definition of the public library function becomes all the more appropriate. By so doing the public library might well take upon itself a distinctive role in the community's pattern of communication. . . .

The several publics of the library are the several distinctive groups which make distinctive demands for library materials. There is a public of high school students who mainly want from the public library what their school libraries cannot adequately supply. There is a public mainly composed of housewives and white-collar workers who want "some light reading." There is a public of business representatives who want specific and isolated pieces of information from the library files. There is a public of ambitious young people who hope to use the library in their drive for occupational mobility. There is a public of serious-minded people concerned with serious-minded materials on a variety of topics who find in the library what they cannot get elsewhere. There is a public of miscellaneous people

Riverside (Calif.) Public Library, 1940s.

with leisure and "nothing else to do." There are other publics.

The library's problem is a problem of optimum allocation of resources. Like the economy as a whole, the public library is limited in facilities, time, money, and staff. Since it cannot be all things to all men, it must decide what things it will be to whom. The present distribution of resources may be as much the result of traditional growth as of rational decision. Professional integrity and responsibility require self-inquiry and experimentation, against library objectives. Librarians have the problem of designating the library's publics to whom more and less consideration will be given. It is a matter of ranking the library's actual and potential publics in a value hierarchy.

In this connection, some historical perspective on the library's role in the community is desirable. There are two social trends which will affect the evolution of the public library in the coming years which are relevant to any consideration of library objectives and programs. One is often termed "the communication revolution." Among other things, this revolution has enormously extended audiences for relatively standardized communication content. The revolution is by no means over; technological advances are rapidly being made in the field of print, radio, and motion pictures. These developments will bring increased competition to the public library in the recreational area of communication, but will probably do little to compete with the public library in its provision of serious and permanent materials. There is also a second and in a sense a contrary trend—the steady rise in the educational level of the population resulting from the extended period of formal schooling. These developments mean two things for the public library: more clients and more use of better materials.

Thus, the public library in this country for the next few years and for the long pull may be presented with a first-rate opportunity for greater service to its community by defining its service with reference to some qualitative standards. It will still have to operate, as it always has, within the general level of American culture. The public library cannot outdistance the intellectual climate in which it finds itself. But given its appropriate share of resources, administered to exploit its own unique strength within the community's system of communication, the public library over the years can make an effective contribution to the development and the enrichment of that cultural climate. And that is its proper task.

SOURCE: Bernard Berelson, *The Library's Public* (New York: Columbia University, 1949), pp. 131–35. Reprinted with permission of the publisher via Copyright Clearance Center.

The five laws of library science

by S. R. Ranganathan

1. Books are for use.
2. Every person his or her book.
3. Every book, its reader.
4. Save the time of the reader.
5. A library is a growing organism.

SOURCE: S. R. Ranganathan, *The Five Laws of Library Science* (1st ed., Madras, India: Madras Library Association, 1931).

THE FUTURE

1

Five new laws of librarianship

by Michael Gorman

MORE THAN 60 YEARS AGO, the great Indian librarian S. R. Ranganathan published his Five Laws of Library Science (see p. 62). These brief statements remain as valid—in substance if not in expression—today as when they were promulgated.

Looking beyond the language of 1931, one can see truths in these laws that are as applicable to the practice of librarianship today as they will be to the librarianship of tomorrow. In the process of coauthoring a book and thinking about the issues it addresses, I have had the temerity to formulate Five New Laws of Librarianship—a reinterpretation of Ranganathan's truths in the context of the library of today and its likely futures. I offer these laws in all humility, standing on the shoulders of this giant of our profession.

Libraries serve humanity

The dominant ethic of librarianship is service to the individual, community, and society as a whole. By "service" I mean both individual acts of help and the furtherance of the higher aspirations of humankind. Beyond that, service in librarianship implies an attention to quality, a desire to live up to and to surpass the expectations of library users. The question "How will this change make the service that this library gives better?" is an analytical tool of great effectiveness.

The psychological urge to serve is at the root of successful careers in librarianship and its psychic rewards are many. In the words of library educator Lee Finks: "It is, we should admit, a noble urge, this altruism of ours, one that seems both morally and psychologically good" (*American Libraries*, April 1989, pp. 352–56). Another aspect of this law is its emphasis on humanity—our mission is both to the individual seeker of truth and to the wider goals and aspirations of the culture.

Respect all forms by which knowledge is communicated

Many myths have arisen from the use of electronic technology—the "death of the book," "the paperless society," and other dreams and nightmares. The truth lies in respecting all forms of communication for the strengths that each brings to the conquest of space and time; in acknowledging that the library of the future will use all kinds of carriers of knowledge and information; and in studying the realities of each means of communication in the light of the history of innovation in communication.

Each new means of communication enhances and supplements the strengths of all previous means. This appears to be an ineluctable process despite the fact that each new means is greeted with predictions that it will eliminate previous forms of communication. There is no reason to cling to print on paper, images on film, or grooves on disks in cases when it can be demonstrated clearly that technology offers a cost-beneficial alternative. What is the point, however, in replacing print on paper, etc., when new technology is less effective, more costly, or has other disadvantages? The best approach to the future of libraries lies in this utilitarianism.

Use technology intelligently to enhance service

Technology has created a false dichotomy in the minds of many librarians. It is almost as though one has to pick between two sides, each of which is violently opposed to the other. In reality, one does not have to choose between being a Luddite or a soulless technocrat.

The history of progress in librarianship has been a story of the successful integration of new technologies and new means of communication into existing programs and services. Librarians have, if anything, been sometimes over-eager in the embrace of the new. The intelligent use of technology involves seeking answers to problems rather than seeking applications of interesting new technology; weighing the cost-effectiveness, cost-benefit, and, above all, impact on service of any proposed innovation; and rethinking the program, service, or workflow that is being automated rather than automating what one has.

Online catalogs are demonstrably superior to card and microform catalogs. Networked indexing and abstracting services are demonstrably superior to their print forerunners. It goes without saying that modern libraries should have electronic circulation and acquisition/serial control systems and should provide access, by one means or another, to the world of digitized data and facts of all kinds (numeric, bibliographic, image-based, and textual).

Looked at objectively, the relative roles of electronic communication and nonelectronic communication (print, sound recordings, film, video, etc.) become clear. Electronic methods are best for "housekeeping" and for giving access to data and small, discrete packets of textual, numeric, and visual information (such as those found in many reference works). Each of the other media has areas in which it is the best. In particular, print on paper is and will be the preeminent medium for the communication of cumulative knowledge by means of sustained reading.

Protect free access to knowledge

Two of the professional values advanced by Lee Finks are stewardship and democratic values. The former calls upon us to "take responsibility for the library as an institution." People of the future will only know that which we preserve. This is a weighty responsibility and one that should be in the minds of all librarians. Our praiseworthy pursuit of the preservation of intellectual freedom for today's materials should, of course, be continued. It should be noted, however, that allowing the records of the past to disappear is a kind of censorship. Libraries are the collective archive of human achievement and the knowledge of the ages. This important role must be at the forefront of any consideration of technological change.

Libraries are central to freedom—social, political, and intellectual. A truly free society without libraries freely available to all is an oxymoron. A society without uncensored libraries is a society open to tyranny. For this reason, libraries must preserve all records of all societies and communities and make those records available to all. Putting an emphasis on the speedy delivery of ephemeral information to the detriment of knowledge would be a betrayal of that trust.

Honor the past and create the future

We live in a historical age. The little that is known about the past is not used to inform the actions of the present. Anyone can see the bad effects on society, politics, and daily life of ignoring George Santayana's famous dictum, "Those who cannot remember the past are condemned to repeat it." No one should cling to old things just because they are old, nor should anyone discard old things just because they are old.

The library of tomorrow must be one that retains not only the best of the past but also a sense of the history of libraries and of human communication. Without those, the library will be purely reactive, a thing of the moment, sometimes useful and sometimes not but never central to human society.

With a sense of history and a knowledge of enduring values and the continuity of our mission, the library can never be destroyed. Along with this sense of time future being contained in time past there must be the acceptance of the challenge of innovation. It is neither the easiest of prescriptions nor the most fashionable, but libraries need to combine the past and the future in a rational, clear-headed, unsentimental manner.

SOURCE: Michael Gorman, "Five New Laws of Librarianship," *American Libraries* 26 (September 1995): 784–85.

What is the future of the public library?

by Fred Lerner

IN DEVELOPED COUNTRIES, there are increasingly many rivals to the book as a source of entertainment and information. What were once mass media are increasingly personal. Videocassettes, compact disks, and CD-ROMs allow the individual to see a movie, listen to music, or interact with a multimedia resource at a time and place of his own choosing. This is eroding the traditional advantage of the book over other methods of packaging information and education. But the book is far from dead. Unlike videotapes and CD-ROMs, books do not require an expensive display apparatus before they can be used. Nor do their display systems tend to become obsolete quickly. So long as literacy is widespread, the printed book is capable of benefiting a much wider portion of the community than the newer media.

Although many public libraries have added materials in these new media to their collections, the library is far from being the only source for them. People have become accustomed to renting videotapes from commercial enterprises, and an increasing number of outlets are now renting books on audiotape. Some observers wonder, now that the public has become used to paying for the privilege of borrowing its home entertainment, for how much longer will they see a reason for providing one form of home entertainment—

ALA's Goal 2000

In 1995, the American Library Association envisioned that by the year 2000 ALA would have achieved the following:

1. ALA will have been accepted by the public as a voice and the source of support for the participation of people of all ages and circumstances in a free and open information society.

2. ALA will have become an active formal participant in the various national arenas discussing and deciding aspects of the information society affecting libraries and their publics.

3. ALA will have identified and will already be in collaboration with other organizations and groups working for broader public participation in the development of information society issues.

4. ALA will have created a vision statement for broad distribution defining its position and role within the emerging information environment.

5. ALA will have an expanded Washington Office, a major organizational entity devoted to serving as an advocate for the public's intellectual participation. It will have greatly increased its ability to learn about, analyze, share information about, and effect important national information issues as they occur, in addition to tracking traditional library issues.

6. ALA will have completed a five-year thematic cycle that has framed the advancement of these issues and coordinated the support of all areas of the Association in preparation for the 21st century.

7. ALA will have provided training and support to library professionals and members of the public in order to create an awareness of the variety of social and technical issues related to the information society, providing the necessary background for promoting further dialogue at more local levels.

8. ALA will have reviewed and adjusted its internal operations as a means of assisting all divisions and units in carrying out the new focus as appropriate to their sphere.

9. ALA will have redefined library information education and provided five years of training for professionals to update their skills for the new Information Age.

SOURCE: American Library Association Council, January 1995.

the book—at the taxpayers' expense? What will be the justification for providing the public with recreational reading free of charge, while expecting users of other recreational media to pay for them?

In those communities where there is a substantial number of people who read for pleasure, a market may develop for private subscription libraries such as the London Library or the Boston Atheneum. Perhaps the commercial circulating library will make a comeback, prompted by the commercial success of firms that rent audiotapes largely to people who listen to them while driving or using public transport.

If the continued existence of the free public library is to be justified, it will have to be as an educational rather than a recreational institution. The public library collection will have to reflect the long-term needs of the society it supports rather than the transitory desires of that small portion of the public that reads books for amusement. This will fit in with the increasing need that an information-based society will have for lifelong continuing education.

The public library of the future, then, will in many ways represent a return to the original concept of the free library: a people's university, whose serious purpose justifies its public support. In the developing countries, where a rapidly increasing population will strain the limited resources for formal education, the public library's role as an educational agency will be even stronger.

As an adjunct to its basic educational role, the public library will increasingly serve as an access point to the resources of other libraries as well as to nonlibrary sources of publicly available information. In those societies that place an importance upon a freely informed citizenry, libraries and librarians wishing to expand their role in equipping and supporting their public in the art and science of information gathering will be able to create such a role for themselves. Those without this desire will find themselves relegated to the status of antiquarians, whose maintenance will be seen as a luxury easily forsaken in hard times.

Until utopia is realized, there will still be societies whose rulers will attempt to control access to information. They will have to balance this desire with the realization that technological progress and economic development require extensive access to information resources. In these societies, the public library can serve (as it did in Nazi Germany and Soviet Russia) as a carefully controlled gateway to the world's information resources.

The future will certainly bring substantial changes in the ways in which information is produced, transmitted, and preserved. The continuing advance of computer technology will increase the flexibility of access to, and use of, recorded information. This will render readers increasingly independent of the library and the librarian, at least with regard to obtaining information. But paradoxically it will also increase the importance of such traditional library functions as cataloging and reader guidance. The ease and economy of producing documents in electronic form will transform the economic structure of publishing and the library's role in the selection and preservation of texts.

The functions of the librarian have always been to select the material that his constituents will require; to catalog it so that those who would use it can know what is available and where it is kept; and to preserve it so that both contemporary readers and those who will follow will be able to use it. With the opening of libraries to a wider public, another task fell to the librarian, that of helping the patron to choose the library materials most appropriate to his needs.

None of these tasks will disappear with the emergence of the electronic library. Somebody will have to perform them: if not the librarian, then his replacement. The anarchy of the Internet may be daunting for the neophyte, but it differs little from the bibliographical chaos that is the result of five and a half centuries of the printing press. The same science that produced the *Anglo-American Cataloguing Rules* and the Universal Decimal Classification can be applied to the World Wide Web. The same cooperative spirit that has informed interlibrary loan and cooperative acquisitions programs can ensure the establishment and maintenance of digital archives. And the expertise in bibliographic instruction and reader guidance acquired by generations of librarians can be as well applied to electronic media as to printed publications.

So long as human beings continue to use the knowledge they have inherited from their ancestors and learned from their contemporaries, so long as human ingenuity and creativity increase the store of information, there will be a need for persons and institutions to collect, to catalog, to preserve, and to guide. Books, and libraries, have changed over the thousands of years since the invention of writing. The pace of change accelerated with the invention of printing, and again in the age of the computer. But the essential task of the librarian has remained the same: to collect and preserve the record of human accomplishment and imagination, and to put this record in the hands of those who would use it.

SOURCE: Fred Lerner, *The Story of Libraries from the Invention of Writing to the Computer Age* (New York: Continuum, 1998), pp. 209–11. Reprinted with permission.

Our singular strengths

by Michael Gorman

WHAT WILL BE THE FUTURE of libraries and of learning? The same people who call for literacy and lament that "Johnny can't read" (try cuts in public and school libraries as part of that problem!) also preach the "death of the book" and say that all that matters is information. According to them, we are moving into a postliterate society dominated by the image. In their future, the global village turns out to be populated by illiterates who have rejected learning and are lulled by 1,000-channel TV and other anti-intellectual sensory gratifications. Such populations are malleable and readily manipulated politically, financially, and socially.

Would it not be the ultimate irony if the postliterate society were to come to pass and the records of humankind came full circle? The journey from the few people of the Aurignacian-Perigordian Epoch in 18,000 B.C., who left the graphic images of their lives on the walls of the Lascaux Cave, to billions of modern humans, solitary and sedated by flickering transitory images, will have taken a long time but could scarcely be accounted an advance.

What is it to be? Enhanced and flourishing libraries combining the best of all kinds of recorded knowledge and information on the one hand, or a global Lascaux Cave on the other? A new golden age of literacy and learning, or the end of the text? For myself, I would prefer to live in a reality informed by dreams and possibilities than to cyber-surf into oblivion as a member of the largest and loneliest crowd in all human history.

SOURCE: Michael Gorman, *Our Singular Strengths* (Chicago: American Library Association, 1998).

PEOPLE
CHAPTER TWO

"You see, I don't believe that libraries should be drab places where people sit in silence, and that's been the main reason for our policy of employing wild animals as librarians."

—Monty Python's Flying Circus (1969)

How many people work in libraries?

by Mary Jo Lynch

THE LIBRARY WORKFORCE includes librarians and other professionals, paraprofessionals, clerical and technical personnel. Statistics are not available for each category of personnel in each type of library. This is a summary of the most recent statistics on the two major categories—librarians and other professionals, and other paid staff—in the three types of libraries for which reliable national figures are available from the National Center for Education Statistics (NCES).

Figures for public librarians are from *Public Libraries in the United States, 1996* (1999); those for academic librarians from *Academic Libraries, 1994* (1998); and those for school library media specialists are from *School Library Media Centers, 1993–94* (1998).

Each source uses a different definition of "librarian." The report on public libraries distinguishes the 27,353 persons with master's degrees from programs of library and information studies accredited by ALA—ALA's definition of librarian—from 11,742 staff who have the title of librarian but not an ALA/ MLS. The report on academic libraries gives a figure for "librarians and other professionals." We have reason to believe that the majority of these persons do have an ALA/MLS. The figure for school libraries includes only state-certified library media specialists.

	Librarians	Other Paid Staff	Total Staff
Academic Libraries	26,726	69,117	95,843
Public Libraries	27,353	78,717	117,812
School Libraries	72,160	92,483	164,643
Total	126,239	240,317	378,298

Comparable figures for employment in special libraries (e.g., libraries serving businesses, scientific and government agencies, and nonprofit organizations) are not available. However, the Special Libraries Association counts among its personal members almost 12,000 who work in such libraries. The total figure for all persons who work in special libraries is higher. A 1982 study of the library workforce (*Library Human Resources: A Study of Supply and Demand*) prepared for NCES found that total paid staff in special libraries was 47,410 with 18,600 identified as "librarians" and 28,819 identified either as other professionals, or technical, clerical, and other support staff. Those figures still seem reasonable.

SOURCE: Mary Jo Lynch, ALA Office for Research and Statistics.

The Bold Librarian

Oh, some, they like the sailor man
When he comes back to shore,
And some they like the beggar man
That begs from door to door,
And some, they like the soldier man
With his musket and his can,
But my delight can read and write,
He's the bold librarian.

—chorus from *The Bold Librarian* ©1976 Joy Rutherford

Recruitment for the future

by Margaret Myers

GROUPS AND INDI-VIDUALS within the library profession have been exploring human-resources needs as well as the knowledge, skills, and abilities needed for the changing information environment. Although the economy has hampered most professions and occupations, there are long-term needs  as retirements take place and information needs grow. A profession-wide consensus has not been reached on what mix of knowledge, skills, and abilities are needed in the future. Strong interpersonal and communication skills, ease with technology, and problem-solving ability are often cited as desirable. The need to recruit the "best and the brightest" continues.

At the 1992 ALA Annual Conference, the Recruitment Assembly participants outlined desirable qualifications for recruits to the profession. These included:

Service oriented	Curious
Communication skills (oral, written, interpersonal)	Able to deal with people of diverse backgrounds
Leadership skills	Entrepreneurial
Takes risks	Proactive
Enthusiastic	Shows initiative
Committed	Bright
Creative	Reads
Analytical	Articulate
Open-minded	Academically gifted
Humanistic	Specific skill knowledge in subject areas
Passionate	
Ethical	Technologically oriented
Knows foreign languages	Marketing oriented
Listens	Assertive
Detail oriented	Solves problems
Flexible	Caring
Technically competent	Self-confident
Broad thinker/systems thinking	

Although it was acknowledged that some of the skills listed above could be taught in library and information studies programs, many are attributes that should already be evident in prospective students. Additionally the Assembly identified priority target groups for recruitment efforts, namely, young persons, support staff, people of diverse racial and cultural backgrounds, and those who are differently abled.

The need for a multicultural workforce to serve in the multicultural society of the future has often been cited in the library literature. A 1989 study by the ALA Office for Library Personnel Resources showed that students with ethnic backgrounds from the traditionally underrepresented racial/ethnic groups (i.e., African Americans, American Indians and Alaskan Natives, Asian Americans, Hispanics) were more apt to be attracted by the opportunities for high-tech application and management than Caucasian students. Where will these interests appear in the inventories? Currently, only about 10% of MLS students and librarians in the field are people of color.

SOURCE: Margaret Myers, "Recruitment Implications, Issues, and Future Action," in Mary Jane Scherdin, ed., *Discovering Librarians: Profiles of a Profession* (Chicago: ALA Association of College & Research Libraries, 1994), pp. 201–2.

JOB SEARCHING

Guide to library placement sources

General sources of library jobs

CLASSIFIED ADS are regularly found in *American Libraries, Chronicle of Higher Education, College & Research Libraries News, Library Journal,* and *Library Hotline*. State and regional library association newsletters, state library journals, and foreign library periodicals are other sources. Members of associations can sometimes list "position wanted" ads free of charge in their membership publications.

The *New York Times* Sunday "Week in Review" section carries a special section of ads for librarian jobs in addition to the regular classifieds. Local newspapers, particularly the larger city Sunday editions, such as the *Washington Post, Los Angeles Times,* and *Chicago Tribune,* often carry job vacancy listings in libraries for both professional and support staff. A few newspapers have classifieds in their online versions.

The many library-related electronic discussion lists on the Internet often post library job vacancies interspersed with other news and discussion items. A growing number of general online job-search bulletin boards exist; these may include information-related job notices along with other types of jobs:

Sources for Job Ads (www.uic.edu/~aerobin/libjob/libads.html); Finding Library Jobs on the WWW (toltec.lib.utk.edu/~tla/nmrt/libjobs.html); Career and Job Information (www.peachnet.edu/galileo/internet/jobs/jobsmenu.html); Job Opportunities—Librarians and Library Science Net Links (librarians. miningco.com/msubjobs.htm); the Librarian's Job Search Source (www.lisjobs. com); Library Jobs on the Net (wings.buffalo.edu/scils/alas/usamap.html); the Networked Librarian Job Search Guide (pw2.netcom.com/~feridun/nlintro. htm); and Sarah Nesbeitt's "Library Job Postings on the Internet" (topcat. bridgew.edu/~snesbeitt/libraryjobs.htm).

See also the listing of telephone joblines on pp. 78–79.

Specialized library associations and groups

Other organizations assist library job seekers with advertisements or placement services. Only a short listing with address and phone number is found here; further information may be obtained from the organization itself.

Academic Position Network, 1655 124th Lane NE, Blaine, MN 55449; (612)767-5949; fax (612) 767-5852; info@apnjobs.com; (www.apnjobs.com). Customized searching.

Access: Networking in the Public Interest, 1001 Connecticut Ave., N.W., Suite 838, Washington, DC 20036; (202) 785-4233; fax (202) 785-4212; accesscntr@aol.com; some jobs listed on their Web site (www.communityjobs. org/jobs.html). The site serves as a resource to nonprofit organizations on recruitment, diversity, and staff development.

Advanced Information Management, 444 Castro St., Suite 320, Mountain View, CA 94041; (650) 965-7900; fax (650) 965-7907; aimno.aimusa@ juno.com. Placement agency that specializes in library and information personnel. They offer work on a temporary, permanent, and contract basis for both professional and support staff in special, public, and academic libraries in California. There is no fee to register. Brief job openings for registrants are listed on their Web site (www.aimusa.com/hotjobs.html). Southern California office: 900 Wilshire Blvd., Suite 1424, Los Angeles, CA 90017; (213) 489-9800; fax (213) 489-9802.

Affirmative Action Register, 8356 Olive Blvd., St. Louis, MO 63132; (314) 991-1335, (800) 537-0655; fax (314) 997-1788; aareeo@concentric.net. A national EEO recruitment publication directed to females, minorities, veterans, and disabled persons, as well as to all employment candidates. Positions are listed by employer, state, and type (www.aar-eeo.com).

American Association of Law Libraries, 53 W. Jackson Blvd., Suite 940, Chicago, IL 60604; (312) 939-4764; aallhq@aall.org; career hotline on their Web site (www.aallnet.org/services/hotline.asp). Interested employers should contact the AALL placement assistant at membership@aall.org or (312) 939-4764 to inquire about current fees.

American Indian Library Association Newsletter, c/o Joan Howland, Law Library, University of Minnesota, 229 19th Ave. South, Minneapolis, MN 55455. Quarterly. Contains some job listings. To place an ad, e-mail rtaylor@slis.lib. uoknor.edu.

American Libraries, "Career LEADS," 50 E. Huron St., Chicago, IL 60611; (312) 280-4211; e-mail jkartman@ala.org. Classified job listings are published in each monthly issue of *American Libraries* and on the ALA Web page (www.ala. org/education/).

American Libraries, "Career LEADS Express," c/o Georgia Okotete, 50 E. Huron St., Chicago, IL 60611-2795; gokotete@ala.org. Advance notice of classified job listings to be published in the next issue of *American Libraries.* Sent about the 17th of each month. For each month, send a $1.00 check made out to "AL Express" and enclose a 4 × 9″ SASE with 55 cents postage.

ALA/Office for Library Personnel Resources, 50 E. Huron St., Chicago, IL 60611; (312) 280-4281; (www.ala.org/olpr/). A placement service is provided at each ALA Annual Conference and Midwinter Meeting; (www.ala.org/ olpr/placemnt.html). Request job-seeker or employer registration forms prior to each conference. The office also provides handouts on interviewing, preparing a resume, and other job search information.

American Society for Information Science, 8720 Georgia Ave., #501, Silver Spring, MD 20910-3602; (301) 495-0900; fax (301) 495-0810; asis@ asis.org. An active placement service is operated at ASIS annual meetings. All attendees are eligible to use the service to list or find jobs. Current job openings are provided in *ASIS Jobline,* a monthly publication sent to all members, and available to nonmembers on request.

Art Libraries Society/North America, c/o Executive Director, 4101 Lake Boone Trail, Suite 201, Raleigh, NC 27607-7506; (800) 892-7547; (919) 787-5181; fax (919) 787-4916; arlisna@olsonmgmt.com. Art information and visual resources curator jobs are listed six times a year in the *ARLIS/NA Update,* and a job registry is maintained at the society's headquarters. The ARLIS/NA JobNet (www.lib.duke.edu/lilly/arlis/jobs.html) lists vacancy announcements for art librarians, visual resources professionals, and related positions. The postings come from ARLIS-L, VRA-L, and other discussion lists or have been submitted to the Webmaster.

Asian/Pacific American Libraries Newsletter, Katherine Wong, Cataloging Department, University of Oklahoma Libraries, 401 W. Brooks, Norman, OK 73019-0528. Quarterly. Free to APALA members. Includes some job ads. Job announcements are also posted on the listserv at APALA-L@listserv.uic.edu.

Association for Educational Communications and Technology, Placement and Referral Service, 1025 Vermont Ave., N.W., Suite 820, Washington, DC 20005-3516; (202) 347-7834; fax (202) 347-7839; aect@aect.org. AECT maintains a placement listing on its Web site (www.aect.org/Employment/Employment.htm) and at its annual conference.

Association for Library and Information Science Education, Sharon J. Rogers, Executive Director, ALISE, P.O. Box 7640, Arlington, VA 22207; (703) 243-8040; fax (703) 243-4551; sroger7@ibm.net; (www.alise.org). Provides placement service at its annual conference for library and information science faculty and administrative positions.

Association of Research Libraries, 21 Dupont Circle, N.W., Washington, DC 20036; (202) 296-2296. Job openings at ARL member libraries are on their Web site (db.arl.org/careers/index.html).

Black Caucus Newsletter, c/o George C. Grant, Editor, Rollins College, 1000 Holt Ave., #2654, Winter Park, FL 32789; (407) 646-2677; fax (407) 646-2546; bcnews@rollins.edu. Lists paid ads. Free to members, $10 per year for others. Bimonthly. Ads also on Web at (www.bcala.org/jobannouncements.htm).

British Columbia Library Association, 900 Howe St., #150, Vancouver, BC, V6Z 2M4, Canada; fax (604) 609-0707; (www.interchg.ubc.ca/bcla/job/jobpage.htm).

C. Berger Group, Inc., P.O. Box 274, Wheaton, IL 60189; (630) 653-1115, (800) 382-4CBC; fax (630) 653-1691; cberger@cberger.com; (www.cberger.com). This company conducts nationwide executive searches to fill permanent positions in libraries, information centers, and related businesses at the management, supervisory, and director levels. Professionals and clerks are also available from the company as temporary workers or contract personnel for short- and long-term assignments in special, academic, and public libraries in Illinois, Indiana, Georgia, Pennsylvania, Texas, and Wisconsin.

California Library Association, 717 K Street, Suite 300, Sacramento, CA 95814-3477; (916) 447-8541; fax (916) 447-8394; info@cla-net.org; (www.cla-net.org/txtfiles/jobline.txt).

Canadian Association of Special Libraries and Information Services,

c/o CASLIS Job Bank Coordinator, 266 Sherwood Dr., Ottawa, Ontario, Canada K1Y 3W4; (613) 728-9982; (www.yukia.yk.net/caslis/).

Catholic Library World, Catholic Library Association, 9009 Carter St., Allen Park, MI 48101; cla@vgernet.net. Personal and institutional members of CLA are given up to 35 words to list job openings in their quarterly magazine.

Chinese-American Librarians Association Newsletter, c/o Jian Liu, Reference Department, Indiana University, Bloomington, IN 47405; (812) 855-8028; fax (812) 855-1624; jiliu@indiana.edu. Free to members.

Cleveland Area Metropolitan Library System, 20600 Chagrin Blvd., Suite 500, Shaker Heights, OH 44122-5334; (216) 921-3900; fax (216) 921-7220; camls@oplin.lib.oh.us; (www.camls.org). Northern Ohio only.

Chronicle of Higher Education, 1255 23d St., N.W., Suite 700, Washington, DC 20037; (202) 466-1000; fax (202) 296-2691; careers@chronicle.com. The Web site (chronicle.com/jobs/) has job listings; the most recent ones require a password furnished to subscribers of the print version. Job seekers can also register (chronicle.com/jobs/notify.htm) for weekly e-mailings.

College & Research Libraries News, ALA/Association of College & Research Libraries, 50 E. Huron St., Chicago, IL 60611-2795; (312) 280-2513. Classified advertising appears in each monthly issue. Ads also appear in "C&RL News Net," an abridged electronic edition (www.ala.org/acrl/advert3.html).

Colorado State Library, 201 E. Colfax Ave., #309, Denver, CO 80203-1704; fax (303) 866-6940; sagee_k@cdc.state.co.us; (jobline.aclin.org). Paper printouts are available by sending your name, address, and a supply of 1st-class postage stamps to the address above.

Council for International Exchange of Scholars, 3007 Tilden St., N.W., Suite 5L, Washington, DC 20008-3009; (202) 686-7877; scholars@cies.iie.org; (iserver.iie.org/cies/). Administers the Fulbright Scholar Program.

Drexel University College of Information Science and Technology, Placement Office, Drexel University, Philadelphia, PA 19104; (215) 895-2478; fax (215) 895-2494; placement@cis.drexel.edu; (www.cis.drexel.edu/placement/placement.html).

Feliciter, Canadian Library Association, 200 Elgin St., Suite 602, Ottawa, Ontario, Canada K2P 1L5; (613) 232-9625, ext. 301; gkneen@cla.ca; (www.cla.amllbs.ca/feliciter.htm).

Florida Division of Library and Information Services, 500 S. Bronough Street, Tallahassee, FL 32399-0250; (850) 487-2651; fax (850) 488-2746; rstephens@mail.dos.state.fl.us; (dlis.dos.state.fl.us/flibjobs/Jobs.html).

Georgia Public Library Services, 1800 Century Place, N.E., #150, Atlanta, GA 30345-4304; (www.gpls.public.lib.ga.us/pls/job-bank/).

Gossage Regan Associates, Inc., 25 W. 43d St., Suite 812, New York, NY 10036; (212) 869-3348; fax (212) 997-1127; wgossage@hotmail.com; (www.wwa.com/~dsager/gossage.htm). An executive search firm specializing in the recruitment of library directors and other top management. Salary limitation: $60,000 and up.

Illinois Library Association, 33 W. Grand Ave., Suite 301, Chicago, IL 60610-4306; (312) 644-1896; (www.ila.org/jobs.html).

Independent Educational Services, 1101 King St., Suite 305, Alexandria, VA 22314; (800) 257-5102, (703) 548-9700; fax (703) 548-7171; info@ies-search.org; (www.ies-search.org). IES is a nonprofit faculty and administrative placement agency for independent elementary and secondary schools across the country.

Indiana Statewide Library Jobline, Library Development Office, Indiana State Library, 140 N. Senate Ave., Indianapolis, IN 46204-2296; (800) 451-6028 (Indiana only); (317) 232-3697; ehubbard@statelib.lib.in.us; (www. statelib.lib.in.us/www/ldo/posop16.html).

Institutional Library Mail Jobline, c/o Gloria Spooner, State Library of Louisiana, P.O. Box 131, Baton Rouge, LA 70821-0131; (504) 342-4931; fax (504) 342-3547; gspooner@pelican.state.lib.la.us. Compilation of job openings in institutional libraries throughout the United States. Send SASE for current list. Openings appear for one month unless resubmitted.

Iowa Library Joblist, c/o Annette Wetteland, State Library of Iowa, E. 12th and Grand, Des Moines, IA 50319; (515) 281-4105; awettel@mail.lib.state. ia.us; (www.silo.lib.ia.us). Send SASE for current listing.

Kansas Library Association, Brig C. McCoy, c/o Southeast Kansas Library System, 218 E. Madison St., Iola, KS 66749; (316) 365-5136; fax (316) 365-5137; brigc@world.std.com; (skyways.lib.ks.us/kansas/KLA/helpwanted/).

Kentucky Job Hotline, Dept. for Libraries and Archives, P.O.Box 537, Frankfort, KY 40602; (502) 564-8300; fax (502) 564-5773; (www.kdla.state. ky.us/libserv/jobline.htm).

Labat-Anderson, Inc., 8000 Westpark Dr., Suite 400, McLean, VA 22101; (703) 506-9600; fax (703) 506-4646; (www.labat.com). One of the largest providers of library and records management services to the federal government.

LIBEX, the Bureau for International Library Staff Exchange, Thomas Parry Library, University of Wales Aberystwyth, Llanbadarn Fawr, Aberystwyth, Ceredigion SY23 3AS, Wales UK; +44 (1970) 622417; fax +44 (1970) 622190; (www.aber.ac.uk/~tplwww/libex.html).

The Library Co-Op, Inc., 3840 Park Ave., Suite 107, Edison, NJ 08820; (732) 906-1777, (800) 654-6275; fax (732) 906-3562; librco@compuserve.com. The company acts as both a temporary and permanent employment agency.

Library Journal, 245 W. 17th St., New York, NY 10011; (212) 463-6819; fax (212) 463-6734. To place a classified ad in LJ Digital, contact Nicole Sette, (212) 337-7059. Ads are online (www.libraryjournal.com/classifieds/).

Library Management Systems, Corporate Pointe, Suite 755, Culver City, CA 90230; (310) 216-6436, (800) 567-4669; fax (310) 649-6388; lms@ix. netcom.com. Also, Three Bethesda Metro Center, Suite 700, Bethesda, MD 20814; (301) 961-1984; fax (301) 309-8992; lmsdc@ix.netcom.com. Provides library staffing, recruitment, and consulting to public and special libraries and businesses.

Library Mosaics, P.O. Box 5171, Culver City, CA 90231; (310) 410-1573; emartine@admin.elcamino.cc.ca.us. Bimonthly magazine accepts listings for library/media support staff positions.

LITA Jobs in Library and Information Technology, ALA Library and Information Technology Association, 50 E. Huron St., Chicago, IL 60611-2795; (800) 545-2433, ext. 4270; (www.lita.org/jobs/postings.html).

Michigan Library Association, 6810 S. Cedar, #6, Lansing, MI 48911; (517) 694-6615; fax (517) 694-4330; (www.mla.lib.mi.us/jobline.html).

MLA News, Medical Library Association, 65 E. Wacker Pl., Suite 1900, Chicago, IL 60601-7298; (312) 419-9094; fax (312) 419-8950. *MLA News* (10 issues per year) lists positions wanted and positions available. MLA also offers a placement service at its annual conference in the spring. Ads appear on the MLA Web site (www.mlanet.org/jobs/).

Music Library Association, c/o Paul Orkiszewski, MLA Placement Officer, P.O. Box 980278, Houston, TX 77098-0278; (713) 527-4832; fax: (713)

285-5258; orkis@rice.edu. Monthly job listing (www.musiclibraryassoc.org/se_job.htm). To subscribe, contact Business Office, Music Library Association, P.O. Box 487, Canton, MA 02021-0487; (781) 828-8450; fax (781) 828-8915; acadsvc@aol.com.

Nebraska Library Commission, 1200 N St., #120, Lincoln, NE 68508-2023; (www.nlc.state.ne.us/libjob/adjobs.html).

New Hampshire State Library, 20 Park Street, Concord, NH 03301; (603) 271-2144; fax (603) 271-2205; (www.state.nh.us/nhsl/ljob/).

New Jersey Library Association, P.O. Box 1534, Trenton, NJ 08607; fax (609) 394-8164; (www.burlco.lib.nj.us/njla/hotline/jobs.shtml).

New York Library Association, 252 Hudson Ave., Albany, NY 12210-1802; (518) 432-6952, (800) 252-6952 (N.Y. only); nyla.membership@pobox.com; (www.nyla.org/pac/JobInformationCenter.html). Job listings published twice a month; subscribers are charged a fee; no charge to employers.

North Carolina Jobline, State Library Building, 109 E. Jones St., Raleigh, NC 27601-2807; (919) 733-2570; fax (919) 733-8748; (statelibrary.dcr.state.nc.us/jobs/jobs.htm).

Oklahoma Department of Libraries, 200 N.E. 18th St., Oklahoma City, OK 73105-3298; (405) 521-2502; fax (405) 525-7804; bpetrie@oltn.odl.state.ok.us; (www.odl.state.ok.us/fyi/jobline.htm).

Oregon State Library, 350 Winter St., N.E., Salem, OR 97310; (503) 378-4243, ext. 221; (www.olaweb.org/jobline.shtml).

Pacific Northwest Library Association, (www.pnla.org/jobs/joblist.htm). To subscribe to the PNLA electronic list, e-mail listproc@wln.com (nothing in subject line, "SUBSCRIBE PNLA-L" first name last name).

Pro Libra Associates, Inc., 6 Inwood Place, Maplewood, NJ 07040; (973) 762-0070, (800) 262-0070; fax (973) 763-6500; prolibra-2@mail.idt.net. A multiservice agency, Pro Libra specializes in consulting, personnel, and project support for libraries and information centers.

Reforma, National Association to Promote Library Services to the Spanish Speaking. Job ads are posted on the Web (latino.sscnet.ucla.edu/library/reforma/refoempl.htm).

Society of American Archivists, 527 S. Wells, 5th Floor, Chicago, IL 60607; (312) 922-0140; fax (312) 347-1452; info@archivists.org. The bimonthly *Archival Outlook* and the bimonthly *SAA Employment Bulletin* contain information on professional opportunities. Jobs are also listed on their Web site (www.archivists.org/restricted/Default.html) and updated every Friday.

Special Libraries Association, 1700 18th St., N.W., Washington, DC 20009-2514; (202) 234-4700, ext. 627; fax (202) 265-9317. Most SLA chapters have employment chairpersons who refer employers and job seekers. SLA's monthly magazine, *Information Outlook,* carries classified ads. SLA offers an employment clearinghouse and career advisory service during annual conference in June. Job postings (www.sla.org/professional/jobs/index.shtml) are only accessible by password.

TeleSec Corestaff, 11160 Veirs Mill Rd., Suite 414, Wheaton, MD 20902-2538; (301) 949-4097; fax (301) 949-8729; moreinfo@corestaff.com; (www.telesec.com/about/telesec.html). Offers many opportunities to get started in the metropolitan Washington, D.C., library job market.

Texas Library Association, 3355 Bee Cave Rd., Suite 401, Austin, TX 78746-6763; (512) 328-1518, (800) 580-2852; fax (512) 328-8852; tla@txla.org; (www.txla.org/jobline/jobline.txt). Texas listings only.

Texas State Library and Archives Commission, P.O. Box 12927, Austin, TX 78711-2927; (512) 463-5448; fax (512) 463-8800; mae.murray@tsl.state. tx.us; (www.tsl.state.tx.us/LD/Pubs/Jobline/jobline.html).

Tuft & Associates, Inc., 1209 Astor St., Chicago, IL 60610; (312) 642-8889; fax (312) 642-8883. Specialists in nationwide executive searches.

University of South Carolina College of Library and Information Science, Placement Coordinator, USC-CLIS, Columbia, SC 29208; (www.libsci. sc.edu/career/job.htm).

Virginia Library Association Jobline, P.O. Box 8277, Norfolk, VA 23503-0277; (757) 583-0041; hahne@bellatlantic.net; (www.vla.org).

Washington, D.C., Metropolitan Council of Governments, 777 N. Capitol St., N.E., Suite 300, Washington, DC 20002-4239; (202) 962-3200; fax (202) 962-3201; (www.mwcog.org/ic/libjobs.html).

Wisconsin Library Association, 5250 East Terrace Drive, Suite A, Madison, WI 53718-8345; (608) 245-3640; fax (608) 245-3646; ponufrak@esls. lib.wi.us; (www.wla.lib.wi.us/wlajob.htm).

Occupational outlook, 1996–2006

TOTAL EMPLOYMENT is projected to increase by 18.6 million jobs over the 1996–2006 period, rising from 132.4 million to 150.9 million, according to a 1997 projection of the Bureau of Labor Statistics. The projected 14% increase in employment is less than the 19% increase achieved in 1986–1996, when the economy added 21 million jobs.

Here are the projections for library-related jobs, with some others for comparison.

Category	1996	2006	±%
Computer support specialists	212,000	461,000	117.8
Curators and archivists	20,000	23,000	14.7
Librarians	154,000	162,000	4.8
Library assistants and bookmobile drivers	125,000	145,000	15.4
Library technical assistants	78,000	100,000	28.0
Parking lot attendants	68,000	86,000	26.2
Proofreaders and copy editors	26,000	16,000	−10.0
Receptionists	1,074,000	1,392,000	30.0
Special ed teachers	407,000	648,000	59.0
Writers and editors, including technical writers	286,000	347,000	21.2

SOURCE: George T. Silvestri, "Occupational Employment Projections to 2006," *Monthly Labor Review,* November 1997, pp. 58–83.

Library joblines

LIBRARY JOBLINES PROVIDE recorded telephone messages of job openings. Though Web sites have replaced many, a few still exist and are useful. Most tapes are changed once a week, although individual listings may be repeated. The majority are for professional jobs only.

Jobline sponsor	**Job seekers call**	
Arizona Dept. of Library, Archives & Public Records	(602) 275-2325	(Arizona only)
British Columbia Library Association	(604) 683-5354	(B.C. only)
California Library Association	(916) 447-5627	
California School Library Association	(650) 697-8832	
Florida State Library	(850) 488-5232	(Fla. only)
Illinois Library Association	(312) 409-5986	
Kentucky Job Hotline	(502) 564-3008	
Long Island Library Resources Council	(516) 632-6658	(L.I. only)
Maryland Library Association	(410) 685-5760	
Missouri Library Association	(573) 442-6590	
Mountain Plains Library Association	(800) 356-7820	(regional only)
	(605) 677-5757	
Nebraska Library Commission	(800) 307-2665	(in Nebr.)
	(402) 471-4016	
New England Library Jobline	(617) 521-2815	
New Jersey Library Association	(609) 695-2121	
North Carolina Jobline	(919) 733-6410	(N.C. only)
Ohio Library Council	(614) 225-6999	
Pennsylvania Cooperative Job Hotline	(717) 234-4646	
Pratt Institute	(718) 636-3742	
Special Libraries Association, N.Y. Chapter	(212) 439-7290	(regional only)
Special Libraries Association, San Andreas- San Francisco Bay Chapter	(650) 528-7766	
University of South Carolina College of Library & Information Science	(803) 777-8443	
Washington (D.C.) Metropolitan Council of Governments Library	(202) 962-3712	

What to put in your résumé

by Kay Womack and Tyler Goldberg

AN OCTOBER 1996 SURVEY of recent library appointees ranked 46 elements that might be put on a résumé when applying for a position in an academic library from very important (4) to unimportant (1). Consider this list if you are having difficulty fitting everything onto one or two pages.—*GMF.*

Previous experience in librarianship	3.95
Telephone number	3.73
Brief description of duties in previous positions	3.71
Colleges and universities attended	3.65
Current address	3.58
List of references (names, addresses, phone numbers)	3.47
Subject field of degrees (undergraduate and/or advanced)	3.44
Dates of employment in previous positions	3.42
Offices held in professional organizations	3.27
Committee service (work and/or professional)	3.23
Membership in professional organizations	3.23

Permanent address	3.18
Foreign language skills	3.10
Complete list of applicant's publications	3.03
Awards, honors, and scholarships	3.00
Tenure in previous positions	2.99
Previous experience in other occupations	2.95
Years degrees awarded	2.92
Continuing education and conference attendance	2.92
Research interests	2.66
Full chronological accounting for time after completion of education	2.61
Memberships in honorary societies	2.52
Specialization in library school	2.50
Career objectives	2.47
Names of previous supervisors	2.15
Memberships and involvement in community or social organizations	1.87
Citizenship	1.73
Salary requirements	1.72
Transcripts from other institutions	1.69
Grade point average	1.68
Transcript from library school	1.60
Physical limitations	1.56
Military experience	1.56
Hobbies, leisure interests	1.46
Class standing	1.39
State of health	1.34
Social security number	1.27
Age or date of birth	1.16
Sex	1.12
Race	1.11
Height and weight	1.06
Spouse's occupation	1.06
Photograph	1.05
Religion	1.05
Marital status	1.03
Number of dependents	1.02

The authors conclude that there are common elements that applicants consider important to include in a résumé. The minimum elements in a model résumé are information that identifies the applicant and his or her educational and employment history.

Identifying information includes the applicant's:
    Name
    Current mailing address
    Current phone number

Educational information includes:
    Names and locations of colleges and universities attended
    Subject field of degrees received
    Years degrees awarded

Employment information includes:

Previous experience in librarianship, including names of organizations and job titles of positions held

Dates of employment in previous positions

Brief description of duties

Full chronological accounting for time after completion of education

Professional information can also be important as a component of a resumé and includes:

List of references

Professional memberships, including offices held and community service

List of publications

Additional technological items that did not appear in the survey are:

Computer skills

E-mail address

URLs created

SOURCE: Kay Womack and Tyler Goldberg, "Résumé Content: Applicants' Perceptions," *College & Research Libraries* 58 (November 1997): 540–49.

Job-hunting tips for new librarians

by Philip C. Howze

HAVING SERVED ON MANY SEARCH COMMITTEES and applied for numerous jobs in academic librarianship, my experiences have led me to believe that there are certain rules that prospective job seekers, new MLS graduates in particular, should take care to observe. While following these suggestions will not guarantee you a position, they can help you avoid having your application placed in the out-basket prematurely. The longer an applicant remains viable, the better the chances of getting an interview and, hopefully, a job. Here are ten rules to follow.

1. **"What's in it for me?"** is probably the most important rule, because it is the single issue that both the applying and hiring parties have in common. Knowing what's in it for you makes it easier to answer what is usually the first question asked by a search committee, "What interested you in this position?" Many applicants do not understand that a job notice in librarianship begins with the library's belief that spending money to provide, maintain, or enhance a service is an important and worthwhile expression of its mission. Applicants who become candidates should ask for a copy of the library's mission statement.

The library gets a talented, skilled, trainable (or at least somewhat adaptable) librarian who graduated from an institution accredited by ALA; the opportunity to help keep the library profession alive by training new librarians to become valued experts in the storage, retrieval, and use of information; and relatively inexpensive labor that is likely to increase in quality over time.

The applicant gets dough-re-mi with which to begin paying back student loans; the opportunity to begin a career, build a reputation, and establish relationships with other professionals familiar with the quality of his or her work and character; and on-the-job training, as well as access to continuing higher education.

2. One rarely gets a second chance to make a good first impression. The cover letter and resume are the means by which the applicant makes his or her first, and sometimes last, impression.

Cover letters. The purpose of the cover letter is to provide the reader with a sample of your writing ability, as well as to introduce yourself. (Remember, many librarians were English majors, and chances are at least one will be on the search committee.)

(1) The cover letter should be no more than 1–2 pages, word processed, on clean paper (mustard stains rarely go unnoticed). Preferred paper colors for the cover letter, as well as the resume, are whites, grays, and light shades of blue. Avoid such hues as electric pink or neon-emerald green.

(2) Personalize the letter. There is nothing worse than sending a letter to one institution that was meant for another. It is preferable to type out the full name of the library and position title for which you are applying; avoid the appearance of a form letter.

(3) Write only to the job announcement. (Tailor the thing, because the words in the job announcement were not written with everyone in mind except you.)

(4) Highlight what you have that the library wants. Choose your words carefully, and introduce yourself in the best possible light. Avoid typos and misspelled words. Yes, white-out is considered a typo.

Résumés. The résumé has but one overriding purpose: to get the applicant an interview. Not a job, but an interview. The idea is to tell the reader enough about yourself to make the person want to know more. The search committee member has not been born who, after reading a hundred résumés, did not come to appreciate brevity.

(1) The résumé should be no more than three pages if possible, word processed, on clean paper. Why a maximum of three pages? It takes about ten years to build a fluff-free resume. Even if you bring to librarianship extraordinary talents from a previous career, it doesn't take much space to indicate that you are a Nobel laureate or a former president of the United States.

(2) Use a good résumé-writing guide. Recommended is Tom Jackson's *The New Perfect Résumé* (1996).

(3) Write the résumé yourself, if possible; avoid the appearance of "professionally done" vitae.

(4) Avoid fabrication.

(5) Do not be afraid to toot your own horn.

(6) Avoid telling your life's story; it defeats the purpose of the résumé. If you submit your résumé "by the pound" (and I have been guilty of this from time to time), there is no point meeting you to hear it all again.

(7) Always number your pages if more than one, and never write on the verso. Remember, you've been to library school!

(8) Do not be afraid to use white space. The reader will be grateful (unless you are a Nobel laureate or a former president of the United States).

(9) Never fold a résumé. Appearance is also a matter of how you look in the pile. Now, what happens next?

Step 1. After the personnel officer determines that all materials for all candidates are in order, they are forwarded to the search committee. Just as a judge instructs a jury on outcomes of guilt or innocence, the personnel officer instructs the search committee on matters of decision making, including affirmative-action mechanisms. The instructions usually come directly from the job description.

Step 2. Some form of nominal group technique is employed to allow each member of the committee to rate your fitness for the position. The ratings of each member are usually compiled, averaged, and ranked. All those found to be unanimously unfit for the position will be notified by the personnel officer.

Step 3. Some form of active group technique is employed to further shorten the list. It is at this point that your advocate (yes, by now you have a friend on the committee) argues for your continuance in the pool. If your candidacy complies with the personnel officer's instructions (remember the job description), your advocate has a good chance of keeping you in the pool. If not, then your candidacy is discontinued. All persons meeting minimum job requirements continue in the pool, and nominal group technique probably begins again to further shorten the list.

Step 4. During the second round of nominal group, candidates are rated for quality, meaning the relative strength of their applications to the fit of the position. It is at this point that preferred qualifications are often considered, and a new ranking is established for the pool.

Step 5. Group activity begins again for two purposes: last arguments by advocates for their candidates, and to decide which candidates will enter into the next phase of the search, checking references.

References. The search committee seeks references to avoid risk, by asking your references whether you are all you appear to be in your résumé. There are no ALA-accredited library schools in Transylvania, for example, but if you list the Count as a reference, it is bloody likely he'll be called. Risk avoidance includes identifying your behavior in stressful situations, interpersonal transactions, job performance, and creative, independent environments. References offer informed opinions about your ability or potential to do the work desired by the hiring agency, as well as how well you work with others. The bottom line is that there is an active exchange about you, your accomplishments, and your character.

Telephone interviews. The telephone interview is given to shorten a short list, based on the irrational criteria of how you sound over the phone. It is sometimes given before references are checked, or not given at all.

Actual interviews. The actual interview does two things: It tests your stamina, and gives you the opportunity to continue building advocates for your appointment. Librarians often decide whether or not you should be hired based on the most irrational of reasons: because they like you. How long does it take interviewers to decide if they like you? Usually, about five minutes.

The rest of the rules are for the applicant who has been invited to campus for an interview. Note that the steps mentioned above do not necessarily occur in the order presented; still, most processes are variations on this theme.

3. Lunch is not lunch, it's an interview with food. Some more tips.

(1) If given the opportunity, ask to be seated at a round table so that everyone can see you.

(2) Do not feel free to smoke or order alcoholic beverages, even if your hosts do so.

(3) Do not feel free to order first. Also, do not feel free to order the last supper. After all, it's a job interview, not a crucifixion.

(4) Mind your manners. Emily Post or Letitia Baldrige may be watching.

(5) Small talk is an art not to be taken lightly.

4. Be willing to travel. The wider the net, the more likely the catch. Remember to do your homework. Check uniform crime reports, cost of living indexes, *Places Rated Almanac*—you know the drill.

5. Be flexible. A not-so-positive experience with the AACR2 in library school does not necessarily render an applicant permanently unfit for a cataloging position. As a reference librarian, however, I might wonder about the applicant who cannot hold his or her own in a game of Trivial Pursuit. Apply anyway. Do not limit your applications to directorships, particularly in the first year.

6. Smile, though your head is aching; smile, even though you're quaking. Remember these maxims:

"A kind word and a gun will get you farther than just a kind word."—*Al Capone.*

"A good résumé and a pleasant disposition will get you farther than just a résumé, even if that résumé is Herbert S. White's."—*Phil Howze.*

A positive attitude is worth its weight in gold. Know when to smile and not to smile. A newly graduated MLS-holder who, during an interview, is asked by some sadist to explain the history of the relationship between GPO and NTIS, and smiles through the clearly forthcoming bout of incontinence would definitely arouse suspicion.

7. Be teachable. It is not uncommon, in the Sea of Irrationality, for an interviewer to advocate for a new librarian because he or she thinks that training such a person will be easier than training, say, a Rottweiler or an experienced librarian.

8. It never hurts to rehearse being natural. Fear comes naturally; confidence often does not. To appear naturally confident, practice interviewing with another person. If a presentation is required, practice before you make your presentation, even if it's on the plane. So what if the flight attendant refuses to serve you any more drinks? Rest soberly assured that reading word-for-word from a prepared paper rarely benefits one's candidacy.

9. Exercise extreme caution when asked to technospeak. There are three reasons for this rule:

(1) There is always someone who can do it better than you.

(2) There is always someone who actually understands it better than you.

(3) Running into either, during an interview, is only a matter of time.

10. Network your little heart out. How? Join ALA. Join ALA's New Members Round Table. Who knows? You may meet your future employer.

SOURCE: Philip C. Howze, "10 Job-Hunting Tips for New Librarians," *College & Research Libraries News* 58 (July/August 1997): 490–92.

How to interview job candidates

by Stacey Kimmel and Scott R. DiMarco

JOB INTERVIEWS INVOLVE considerable planning and preparation on the part of both the interviewer and the interviewee. There is a sizable body of literature for job applicants who want advice on making a good impression during an interview. In contrast, there is comparatively little information for organizations on how to make a good impression on the candidate. Most of us have heard the adage that the interview is a two-way street—while we assess the candidate, the candidate assesses us. Because of the tight job market, competition for qualified candidates is keen. Top candidates may receive several job offers from prestigious institutions. Both library and management literature address the importance of recruitment and interview practices in attracting candidates. While the position, salary, and professional opportunities are important considerations, a candidate's perception of the coworkers, the work environment, and the surrounding community are also factored into a job decision. By tailoring the interview experience to candidate interests and needs, the library can increase the likelihood that the candidate will say yes to a job offer.

The red carpet treatment

A well-executed interview combines the art of public relations, rules of etiquette, and rituals of courtship. Planning an exceptional interview experience takes extra time and painstaking attention to detail. Why should a library roll out the red carpet for its candidates? The interview is an example of a small-scale project that the library has undertaken. A well-run interview suggests a well-run library. The treatment of the candidate during the interview reflects the library's attitude toward its staff and the value it places on the position. Word-of-mouth can have a powerful and far-reaching impact. A good or bad interview experience may circulate widely and affect future applicant pools.

What do candidates want?

In the recruiting literature, Sara Rynes asserts that the recruiting representative, administrative practices, and interview procedures can be important influences on job seeker attitudes and behaviors (*Personnel Psychology* 33 (Autumn 1980): 529–42). Fink, Bauer, and Campion surveyed MBA graduates on their reactions to the on-site interview (*Journal of Career Planning and Employment* 54 (March 1994): 32–34). The candidates rated highly the chance to meet formally and informally with coworkers, tours of the community and housing, and tours of the work environment. Negative ratings resulted from repetition of interview questions, poor travel arrangements and accommodations, a rushed or hectic schedule, and unexpected changes in the itinerary. As for the overall rating of the position, Mick Donahue reported (*Focus* 70 (July 1993): 32–34) that candidates look primarily at the company, the management, the work environment, and the salary when evaluating a job offer. Of these four considerations, three are perceptions gleaned primarily from the on-site visit. These studies suggest that a well-planned interview experience can assist in the recruiting effort.

The suggestions presented below are based on a review of library and management literature, interviews with job seekers, and responses to a posting to the LIBADMIN electronic discussion list. These suggestions are especially applicable to candidates who are inexperienced at on-site interviews. For a detailed discussion on planning an interview, we suggest *Managing the Interview* by Susan Carol Curzon (Neal-Schuman, 1995) and the ACRL "Model Statement for the Screening and Appointment of Academic Librarians Using a Search Committee" (1992) (www.ala.org/acrl/guides/scrnappt.html). Finally, this article is not intended as a substitute for knowledge of federal and state laws regarding interviewing and hiring practices.

Planning

Before contacting the candidate. Assess strengths and weaknesses in the job and the organization. Use this information in recruiting efforts. (If the salary is low, stress the strong benefits package or generous professional travel funding.) Know your institution's internal travel/reimbursement policy and procedures.

Interview arrangements. Provide an overview of the search process and timeline for completion. If possible, give the candidate a choice of interview dates. Encourage the candidate to bring questions and concerns to your attention. Provide an e-mail address for making travel arrangements. E-mail is suitable for informal communications and cuts down on long-distance calls. Tell the candidate about travel reimbursement policy at your institution. Mail the information packet promptly. If travel involves an overnight stay, invite the candidate to dinner the night before or the evening after the interview. If the interview is early or late in the week, give the candidate the option of staying over the weekend. Weekend air travel is much less expensive than a one-night stay and gives candidates time to explore the surrounding community. Arrange airport pickup for air travelers if possible. Otherwise, provide approximate costs and recommendations for cabs and shuttles. Distribute résumés to staff well in advance of the interview date. This will allow them to review qualifications and prepare for the visit.

What to put in your interview packet

Library mission statement.
Interview agenda and participants.
Library annual reports, newsletters, and statistics.
Library governance information.
Benefits and personnel documents.
Community information (local newspaper, housing, tourist information).
Visitor parking sticker, if appropriate.
Maps.
Hotel phone, location, and reservation information.
Reimbursement instructions.
Presentation instructions, if any.
Work and home phone of contact (in case of travel delay, other problems).
Library or institutional brochures.

Phone interviews. When arranging the date and time of a phone interview, designate the time zone if appropriate. Provide the names and positions of participating staff in advance, and test the conferencing feature prior to the call. Call from a private office and avoid interruptions. Before starting the interview, have participants introduce themselves. Do not attempt to hold an interview over a noisy line.

Candidate presentations. If possible, give the candidate latitude in choosing the presentation topic. Suggesting a general topic or range of topics is less constraining and gives insight into the candidate's interests. Ask about equipment needs and preferences. Have technical support available before and during the presentation. Provide complete information about facilities (size of room, equipment, power, etc.). If the room is large, provide a microphone. Make sure no construction, fire drills, network/power outages, or other disruptions are scheduled for that time. Make sure all candidates have access to the same facilities.

Planning the schedule. Begin the day with a review of the schedule and note any changes. For interview sessions, designate a host who makes staff introductions and reserves time for candidate questions.

Over mealtimes, pace questioning and make sure the candidate has a chance to eat. Don't overschedule the candidate; provide short breaks between interviews. Schedule the presentation (if any) early in the day. The presentation provides a basis for future discussions and lets the candidate speak while he or she is fresh. Allow 10 minutes prior to a presentation for room setup and preparation. Provide ample time with supervisor and coworkers. Schedule a wrap-up meeting with the search committee (or committee chair) late in the day. Schedule a meeting with the personnel officer to review benefits and personnel information. Provide the candidate a stamped, addressed envelope for sending receipts for reimbursement.

Internal candidates. Plan ahead to avoid awkward encounters with an internal candidate. If a staff member is acting in the position the candidate has applied for, inform the candidate. This will permit open discussion of projects and activities related to the position. Assure candidates that the selection process is fair and unbiased. Caution library staff against discussing other candidates with the visiting candidate.

The day before

Arrival. If you are meeting the candidate at the airport, arrive promptly. Carry a sign to help the candidate find you. If the candidate arrives by car, phone to touch base and review the next day's activities. Alternatively, leave a message with home and work phone numbers. Arrange for staff to have dinner and/or breakfast with the candidate.

Interview day

General. Designate a locked, secure place for the candidate to put any of his or her personal belongings. Use neutral phrasing in discussing the job (e.g., if you were in this position . . .). Provide frequent rest room breaks. Have water available during interview sessions. Participating staff should dress professionally. Solicit the candidate's perceptions of the job and correct misunderstandings.

Interview time averages

Based on a survey of 62 MBA graduates and their interview schedules for entry-level positions:

Number of interviews in a day	4.67
Length of individual sessions	50 minutes
Time with supervisor	2 hours, 45 minutes
Time with coworkers	2 hours, 20 minutes
Time with human resources staff	2 hours
Time completing paperwork	10 minutes

SOURCE: Laurence S. Fink, Talya N. Bauer, and Michael Campion, "Job Candidates' Views of Site Visits," *Journal of Career Planning and Employment* 54 (March 1994): 32–34.

Tours. Provide a tour of the work environment and the surrounding community. Gear the tour to the candidate's position and interests. Do not rush the tour. Show the candidate the office and equipment designated for the position. Limit the amount of walking required for the tour and use elevators when available.

Exit interview. Solicit applicant's perceptions and concerns regarding the position. Provide a timeline for the selection decision and tell the candidate how he or she will be contacted. Provide a contact person for the candidate to call with questions or for an update. Escort the candidate to the library entrance or to the hotel.

Contacting the candidates

Making an offer. Be cautious in making promises to the candidate. After negotiations are over, accept refusal gracefully. Try to ascertain the reason for refusal. End with a gesture of goodwill.

When a candidate accepts. Offer to assist with moving, housing, and other arrangements. Describe the university appointment process and provide a timeline for the formal (written) offer. Secure equipment, furniture, and office space in time for the new staff member's arrival. As soon as the acceptance is confirmed, contact other applicants regarding their status.

Contacting other candidates. Contact those who interviewed promptly and personally. Be brief and positive. Recognize/acknowledge the candidate's qualifications. If the pool was exceptionally large or exceptionally strong, share this with the candidate. Avoid comparisons of candidates ("We hired someone with stronger leadership skills"). Provide qualifications of the candidate hired if they are exceptional and can be stated objectively ("We hired someone with more than 20 years of experience"). Do not give the name of the person hired or share information that could be used to identify him or her. End with a gesture of goodwill.

The on-site interview should seek to recruit as well as select the best candidate. Candidates will appreciate small courtesies, attention to personal comfort, and activities that address their interests and concerns. Organizations that create exceptional interview experiences will increase the likelihood of hiring the best candidate for the job.

SOURCE: Stacey Kimmel and Scott R. DiMarco, "Planning an Interview: What Do Candidates Want?" *College & Research Libraries News* 58 (April 1997): 239–53.

First-day decorum

by Will Manley

OKAY, YOU'VE FOLLOWED THE ADVICE I've given you recently. You've picked out the right job ad, prepared a serviceable résumé, aced the interview, and gotten the job you've always wanted. Tomorrow you are scheduled to show up for your first day of work. Don't blow it now. Remember what Pee Wee Herman used to say: "First impressions last a lifetime." Here are my five friendly pointers for avoiding a first-day fiasco:

1. Do not hang your library school diploma on the wall above your desk. It's a common mistake for newly stamped MLS ticket holders to greatly exaggerate the weight of their degree and the value of their library school education. People who work in libraries (especially now) do not put much stock in library school.

Colleagues who already have the degree are fully aware of the fact that there is very little relationship between what you learn in the average library-school class and what you do in the real world of library work. They will, therefore, not be impressed by your academic credentials.

Colleagues who do not have the degree will resent you for having it—especially if you flaunt it. They are just as important to the library as you are, and if you put on airs around them they will throw darts at your photograph during happy hour.

Therefore, if you see a stray book lying on the floor, don't refuse to pick it up because "you did not go to library school to shelve books." Also, if you want to make a point in a staff meeting, you're better off quoting Dennis Rodman than your favorite library-school professor. Very few people know less about what goes on in a library than library-school faculty members. If, however, you have credentials in other areas such as software design, accounting, law, foreign languages, auto repair, or plumbing, tell everyone about it. These are skills that are in great demand in the average library. Expertise in these areas will garner you great respect.

2. Keep your politics, religion, and sexual orientation to yourself. Nothing will turn off your new colleagues more than discussing your most private and personal thoughts right off the bat. Despite the enthusiasm that some Americans have for going on afternoon TV talk shows to chat about their sexual relationships with their fathers, the first day of work is not the time to bare your soul. When, therefore, you are introduced to your colleagues at a staff meeting and asked to tell a little bit about yourself, resist the temptation to share the innermost secrets of your private life.

Avoid too the desire you might have to turn your work area into a shrine to your religious faith. A new hire that I worked with spent a good part of her first day setting up a little temple to Christianity. Not only did this strike me as inappropriate, but the glow-in-the-dark Jesus with the pivoting eyes scared the night janitor to the point where he asked for a transfer to a different branch.

3. Do not replace the furniture in your work area with beanbag chairs. A new supervisor I worked for had all the furniture removed from her office and replaced with beanbag chairs. "This will send out a clear message from day one that I am a nonstructured person who invites honest communication between myself and those who work for me," she pontificated. Call me overly structured, but personally I avoided this woman at all costs because I could think of nothing more unpleasant than discussing authority control with her while sitting on a giant beanbag that was leaking little Styrofoam balls. Beanbag furniture ranks with polyester clothing as the two most unpleasant inventions of the 20th century.

4. Do not prate on about how great things were in your last library. Without a doubt, this is the biggest mistake new employees make. They feel compelled to praise the merits of their last library. Avoid these phrases at all costs: (a) "At Oakdale Public we didn't have an authority control problem"; (b) "We did it a different way at Oakdale"; and (c) "For our next staff meeting we all ought to visit Oakdale Public to see what a real library looks like." If you really want to endear yourself to your new colleagues, you should tear down Oakdale Public every chance you get. Librarians take pleasure in the fact that things are actually more miserable in some other library.

5. Do not play the role of a Christ figure. Another common mistake occurs when the new employee makes the assumption that he or she has been brought on board to be the savior who will lead the library into a messianic future. Consider this comment from a new reference librarian I worked with some years ago. On his first day of work he said: "The only difference between this library and the *Titanic* is that the *Titanic* had a band. But don't worry; I was hired to resurrect this place." Several years later another reference librarian showed up for work with this nameplate for his desk: "Dick Jones—Change Agent."

The bottom line is that in the average library, a little modesty goes a long way on your first day.

SOURCE: Will Manley, "First-day Decorum," *American Libraries* 28 (March 1997): 120.

LIBRARIANS

Librarians: A quick tour

THE TRADITIONAL CONCEPT OF A LIBRARY is being redefined, from a place to access paper records or books, to one which also houses the most advanced media, including CD-ROMs, the Internet, virtual libraries, and remote  access to a wide range of resources. Consequently, librarians are increasingly combining traditional duties with tasks involving quickly changing technology. Librarians assist people in finding information and using it effectively in their personal and professional lives. They must have knowledge of a wide variety of scholarly and public information sources, and follow trends related to publishing, computers, and the media to effectively oversee the selection and organization of library materials. Librarians manage staff and develop and direct information programs and systems for the public, to ensure information is organized to meet users' needs.

There are generally three aspects of library work—user services, technical services, and administrative services; most librarian positions incorporate all three aspects. Even librarians specializing in one of these areas may perform other responsibilities.

Librarians in user services, such as reference and children's librarians, work with the public to help them find the information they need. This may involve analyzing users' needs to determine what information is appropriate, and searching for, acquiring, and providing information. It also includes an instructional role, such as showing users how to access information. For example, librarians commonly help users navigate the Internet, showing them how to most efficiently search for relevant information.

Librarians in technical services, such as acquisitions and cataloging, acquire and prepare materials for use and may not deal directly with the public.

Librarians in administrative services oversee the management and planning of libraries; negotiate contracts for services, materials, and equipment; supervise library employees; perform public relations and fundraising duties; prepare budgets; and direct activities to ensure that everything functions properly.

In small libraries or information centers, librarians generally handle all aspects of the work. They read book reviews, publishers' announcements, and catalogs to keep up with current literature and other available resources, and select and purchase materials from publishers, wholesalers, and distributors. Librarians prepare new materials for use by classifying them by subject matter, and describe books and other library materials in a way that users can easily find them. They supervise assistants who prepare cards, computer records, or other access tools that direct users to resources. In large libraries, librarians may specialize in a single area, such as acquisitions, cataloging, bibliography, reference, special collections, or administration. Teamwork is increasingly important to ensure quality service to the public.

Librarians also compile lists of books, periodicals, articles, and audiovisual materials on particular subjects, analyze collections, and recommend materials to be acquired. They may collect and organize books, pamphlets, manuscripts, and other materials in a specific field, such as rare books, genealogy, or music. In addition, they coordinate programs such as storytelling for children, and literacy skills and book talks for adults; conduct classes on Internet use and other topics; publicize services; provide reference help; supervise staff; prepare budgets; write grants; and oversee other administrative matters.

Librarians may be classified according to the type of library in which they work—public libraries, school library media centers, academic libraries, and special libraries. They may work with specific groups, such as children, young adults, adults, or the disadvantaged. In school library media centers, librarians help teachers develop curricula, acquire materials for classroom instruction, and sometimes team teach.

Librarians may also work in information centers or libraries maintained by government agencies, corporations, law firms, advertising agencies, museums, professional associations, medical centers, hospitals, religious organizations, and research laboratories. They build and arrange the organization's information resources, usually limited to subjects of special interest to the organization. These special librarians can provide vital information services by preparing abstracts and indexes of current periodicals, organizing bibliographies, or analyzing background information and preparing reports on areas of particular interest. For instance, a special librarian working for a corporation may provide the sales department with information on competitors or new developments affecting their field.

Many libraries have access to remote databases, as well as maintaining their own computerized databases. The widespread use of automation in libraries makes database searching skills important to librarians. Librarians develop and index databases and act as trainers to help users develop searching skills to obtain the information they need. Some libraries are forming consortia with other libraries through electronic mail (e-mail). This allows patrons to submit information requests to several libraries at once. Use of the Internet and other worldwide computer systems is also expanding the amount of available reference information. Librarians must be aware of how to use these resources to locate information.

Librarians with appropriate computer and information-systems skills may work as automated systems librarians, planning and operating computer systems; or information science librarians, designing information storage and retrieval systems and developing procedures for collecting, organizing, interpreting, and classifying information. These librarians may analyze and plan for future information needs. The increased use of automated information systems enables librarians to focus on administrative and budgeting responsibilities, grant writing, and specialized research requests, while delegating more technical and user services responsibilities to technicians.

Increasingly, librarians apply their information management and research skills to arenas outside of libraries—for example, database development, reference tool development, information systems, publishing, Internet coordination, marketing, and training of database users. Entrepreneurial librarians may start their own consulting practices, acting as freelance librarians or information brokers and providing services to other libraries, businesses, or government agencies.

SOURCE: 1998–99 Occupational Outlook Handbook (Washington, D.C.: Bureau of Labor Statistics, 1998).

Librarian salaries in 1998

by Mary Jo Lynch

BETWEEN 1997 AND 1998, the average salary for librarians increased 3.31%—much lower than the increase for comparable occupations reported by the U.S. Bureau of Labor Statistics in the June 1998 *Monthly Labor Review*, which shows that civilian workers—in private industry, state and local government—received an average 3.7% increase over the previous year.

Table 1 shows the percent change in mean of salaries paid to librarians in six different positions in 1997–1998. After a healthy increase in 1996–1997, the percent change in mean of salaries paid is disappointingly low. Tables 2–5 show salaries for various types of librarians.

Table 1. Rank order of position title by mean salary, 1997–1998

Title	1998 Salary	1997 Salary	%1997–98	%1996–97
Director	$63,965	$61,607	+3.8	+5.7
Deputy/Associate/Assistant Director	56,636	54,289	+4.3	+3.1
Department Head/Branch Head	45,144	44,285	+1.9	+3.6
Reference/Information Librarian	38,651	37,437	+3.2	+4.6
Cataloger or Classifier	39,005	38,182	+2.1	+4.3
Children's/Young Adult Services Librarian	38,437	36,809	+4.4	+6.5

SOURCE: Mary Jo Lynch, *ALA Survey of Librarian Salaries 1998* (Chicago: American Library Association, 1998).

Table 2. Median salaries for academic library positions, 1997–1998

Dean, Library and Information Services	$88,683
Director, Library Services	59,112
Director, Educational/Media Services Center	45,760
Director, Learning Resources Center	44,356
Chief Public Services Librarian	44,293
Chief Technical Services Librarian	42,900
Acquisitions Librarian	41,000
Reference Librarian	38,028
Catalog Librarian	37,900

SOURCE: College and University Personnel Association.

Table 3. Annual salaries for beginning public librarians, 1999

Public libraries serving	High	Low	Mean
over 1,000,000	$39,929	$21,403	$29,209
500,000 to 999,999	44,005	20,729	30,177
250,000 to 499,999	36,608	18,888	28,126
100,000 to 249,999	47,892	16,379	28,392
50,000 to 99,999	52,292	16,182	28,547
25,000 to 49,999	39,520	13,500	27,633
10,000 to 24,999	39,738	7,280	26,111
5,000 to 9,999	30,639	15,000	25,365
under 5,000	28,000	3,536	21,481

SOURCE: *Statistical Report '99: Public Library Data Service* (Chicago: ALA Public Library Association, 1999), p. 40.

Table 4. Salary trends in ARL university libraries, 1984–1999

Fiscal year	Median salary	Median beginning salary	Adjusted CPI
1998–99	$45,775	$30,000	156.9
1997–98	44,534	28,500	154.3
1996–97	43,170	27,687	151.0
1995–96	41,901	27,000	146.7
1992–93	39,265	25,000	134.9
1989–90	34,629	22,000	119.3
1984–85	26,100	16,500	100.0

SOURCE: *ARL Annual Salary Survey, 1997–98* (Washington, D.C.: Association of Research Libraries, 1999). Consumer Price Index adjusted to July 1984 as the base.

Table 5. Median salaries of special librarians by region, 1997–1998

Census Division	1997 Salary	1998 Salary	% change
Canada*	$49,007	$49,920	1.86
Middle Atlantic	52,000	53,800	3.46
Pacific	46,800	48,100	2.78
New England	45,500	50,000	9.89
South Atlantic	45,000	47,944	6.54
East North Central	43,449	44,171	1.66
Mountain	42,000	40,733	–3.02
East South Central	40,500	42,300	4.44
West North Central	40,500	45,950	13.46
West South Central	40,040	41,000	2.40

SOURCE: SLA Annual Salary Survey, 1998 (Washington, D.C.: Special Libraries Association, 1998).
*All Canadian salaries are reported in Canadian dollars.

Librarians: Racial and ethnic diversity

by Mary Jo Lynch

PEOPLE OFTEN ASK ALA, "What is the current racial/ethnic makeup of the librarian workforce?" Data became available in 1998 to answer that question about academic, public, and school librarians. The table below shows percentages by racial/ethnic category and by sex. To put this data in context, it is essential to describe the way it was gathered.

Data on academic and public librarians was collected in a "supplementary question" included on the questionnaire for the *ALA Survey of Librarian Salaries 1998.* That supplementary question asked the respondent to complete a table showing the five basic racial/ethnic categories as defined by the Equal Employment Opportunity Commission (EEOC). Respondents were asked to report on full-time staff with master's degrees from programs in library and information studies accredited by ALA. The questionnaire went to a national sample of 1,267 public and academic libraries, but there were restrictions on the universe from which the sample was drawn. Public libraries serving populations of less than 25,000 were not included; nor were libraries in either category who have fewer than two professionals.

The data for school librarians in that table comes from a totally different

Percent of Librarians by EEOC Category and by Sex			
	Academic 1998	Public 1998	School 1994
American Indian/Alaskan Native	0.57	0.25	1
Asian/Pacific Islander	4.98	3.93	1
Black	5.87	6.33	6
Hispanic	1.80	2.95	2
White	86.78	86.55	90
TOTALS			
Female	67.99	78.91	92
Male	32.01	21.09	8

source. This data was collected from a national sample of schools by the National Center for Education Statistics (NCES) in 1993–1994 as part of the NCES School and Staffing Survey (SASS). Because of the way this survey was done, the term "librarian" is much less well-defined. In the larger table on which this data is based, the term "librarian" included both full-time and part-time staff, as well as persons with and without state certification, and persons with and without master's degrees from programs accredited by ALA or the National Council for the Accreditation of Teacher Education.

Looking backward

Can we compare this data to any older data in order to determine if the field is changing? The short answer is "no." NCES has never collected this type of data on school librarians before. ALA did conduct sample surveys of public and academic librarians in 1985 and again in 1991, but results of these surveys cannot legitimately be compared to the results in the 1998 salary for two reasons: The earlier surveys included both full-time and part-time employees and the earlier surveys did not specify the master's degree from programs in library and information studies accredited by ALA.

Looking forward

What about the future? Will these data be collected again? It seems likely that both ALA and NCES will collect this type of data again in a few years. But there is a problem with future data collection: the Office of Management and Budget has revised the "Standards for the Classification of Federal Data on Race and Ethnicity" (www.whitehouse.gov/WH/EOP/OMB/html/fedreg/Ombdir15.html).

The new standards are being used in the 2000 decennial census and all federal agencies must follow them not later than January 1, 2003. By that time, most nonfederal agencies will follow suit. The new standards are different in two ways: The categories are different and respondents will have the option of selecting more than one. The new categories are: American Indian or Alaskan Native, Asian, Black or African American, Hispanic or Latino, Native Hawaiian or Other Pacific Islander, and White.

It seems likely that the next time ALA or anyone else collects data on the race and ethnicity of librarians, the new categories will be used. Future reports on this topic may look different. But this table is the best we can do to describe the current workforce.

SOURCE: Mary Jo Lynch, "Librarians' Salaries: Smaller Increases This Year," *American Libraries* 29 (November 1998): 66–70.

Tips for part-time librarians

THREE MEMBERS of the Association of Part-Time Librarians—Kathleen Quinlivan, Linda Herman, and Anne Huberman—have put together the following list of features that they feel an ideal position for a part-time professional librarian should have.

Pro-rated pay. The pay for part-time librarians should be proportionate to the pay received by full-time librarians having the same qualifications and performing the same work.

Health insurance. If full health benefits are not possible, then employers should contribute proportionately toward the premiums, or at the very least allow part-timers to purchase health insurance at the group rates.

Sick leave and vacation time. These benefits should be prorated for part-time librarians.

Training and orientation. It is in the best interests of libraries to offer thorough training and orientation to newly hired librarians. Often, part-time librarians work night and weekend hours when no other professionals are on duty. They may not have the luxury of asking more experienced librarians for help during their working hours, and they need to be totally familiar with the library procedures for which they are responsible and with the collections they are using.

Communication. Changes in procedures, policies, resources, and programs often take part-time librarians by surprise because they are not around to hear about these changes when they are discussed by the full-time staff. Further, they may miss out on valuable hints about the current "difficult questions" patrons are asking if full-time librarians don't use an effective means of communication. Inclusion of part-timers in staff meetings, use of e-mail, and use of a reference-desk notebook can improve communication.

Professional development. Library administrations should encourage part-time librarians to attend conferences and workshops and make it financially possible for them to do so.

Flexibility. Part-time librarians often work during night and weekend hours when important family and social events are likely to occur. Allowing part-timers to trade hours and rearrange their schedules for important events can make the difficulties of working unpopular hours much more manageable.

Retirement plan. Part-time librarians should have the same access to retirement plans as full-time librarians, and employer contributions should be made in proportion to the hours they work.

Professional recognition. Administrators and colleagues should recognize part-time librarians professionally by assigning them meaningful responsibilities that expand their skills and develop new ones, by listening to their ideas and opinions, by providing feedback on the quality of their work, by providing them with adequate facilities (e.g., office space; use of a computer, telephone, and e-mail), and by avoiding assigning them nonprofessional duties.

Job security. A renewable contract for a specified period of time can give a part-time librarian the kind of job security that few now have.

SOURCE: Association of Part-Time Librarians, www.canisius.edu/~huberman/aptl.html.

John Cotton Dana's Rules

1. Read.
2. Read.
3. Read some more.
4. Read anything.
5. Read about everything.
6. Read enjoyable things.
7. Read things you yourself enjoy.
8. Read, and talk about it.
9. Read very carefully, some things.
10. Read on the run, most things.
11. Don't think about reading, but
12. Just read.

Special librarians in the new century

by Barbara P. Semonche

TODAY'S SPECIAL LIBRARIANS do far more than locate and collect data; they add value to information and they do this by authenticating, synthesizing, and distributing it to employees across the hall, across applications, and across the world. Using the Internet and other current technologies, they also evaluate, analyze, organize, package, and present information in a way that maximizes its usefulness. A few examples of the diverse services that special librarians may perform include:

- preparing research reports and data analyses;
- gathering competitive intelligence;
- digitizing/indexing corporate 3-D models, images, and design data;
- verifying and evaluating quality of data;
- creating databases/intranets for an organization's intellectual capital;
- participating in organizational strategic planning;
- evaluating product (software and hardware) information;
- training other staff in use of wide variety of research resources; and
- marketing information products and services.

The value of information provided by special libraries was demonstrated dramatically in a study conducted by José-Marie Giffiths and Donald W. King, *Special Libraries: Increasing the Information Edge* (SLA, 1993). Four out of five of the surveyed executives felt that the information provided by their special librarians helped them decide upon a course of action. And three-quarters of them felt the information helped them avoid making a poor business decision.

In a 1997 study commissioned by SLA, Frank Portugal, a researcher for Cabtech, found that corporate libraries are essential if a company wants to maintain a competitive edge. The study, *Exploring Outsourcing: Case Studies of Corporate Libraries*, found that using outside sources to research or retrieve information is not cost-effective. One reason outsourcing corporate library services does not always pay off is because there are barriers to doing the research, such as ready access to existing internal reports, memos, and other key documents, as well as staff expertise. Companies are discovering that technology alone will not solve their intellectual-capital problems; competitive companies know that a skilled knowledge-management leader is critical to its near, and long-term, success.

What is the real value of corporate libraries or research centers? Joanne G. Marshall in *The Impact of the Special Library on Corporate Decision-making* (SLA, 1993) reports that organizations spend 7.2 times more not to have a corporate library than they do to have one. Further, it is 2.9 times more expensive for professionals to obtain information from outside sources than it costs to run a company library. There is a positive correlation between a company's information-related expenditures and its profit and productivity. Finally, Marshall's research reveals that with corporate libraries, 84% of management reported better-informed decision making, with 33% indicating that the change was of considerable or great importance to the organization.

What special skills are needed?

Special librarians require two main types of competencies:

Professional competencies relate to the special librarian's knowledge of information resources, information access, technology, management, and research, and the ability to use it as a basis for providing library and information services.

Personal competencies represent a set of skills, attitudes, and values that enable librarians to work efficiently; be good communicators; focus on continuing learning throughout their careers; demonstrate the value-added nature of their contributions; and survive in the new world of work.

The major competencies of special librarians are detailed at www.sla.org/professional/comp.html.

SOURCE: Special report by Barbara P. Semonche for *The Whole Library Handbook 3.*

American Library Association presidents

Justin Winsor	1876–1885	Herbert Putnam	1903–1904
William Frederick Poole	1885–1887	Ernest Cushing Richardson	1904–1905
Charles Ammi Cutter	1887–1889	Frank Pierce Hill	1905–1906
Frederick Morgan Crunden	1889–1890	Clement Walker Andrews	1906–1907
Melvil Dewey	1890–July 1891	Arthur Elmore Bostwick	1907–1908
Samuel Swett Green	July–Nov. 1891	Charles Henry Gould	1908–1909
William Isaac Fletcher	1891–1892	Nathaniel Hodges	1909–1910
Melvil Dewey	1892–1893	James Ingersoll Wyer	1910–1911
Josephus Nelson Larned	1893–1894	Theresa West Elmendorf	1911–1912
Henry Munson Utley	1894–1895	Henry Eduard Legler	1912–1913
John Cotton Dana	1895–1896	Edwin Hatfield Anderson	1913–1914
William Howard Breft	1896–1897	Hiller Crowell Wellman	1914–1915
Justin Winsor	July–Oct. 1897	Mary Wright Plummer	1915–1916
Herbert Putnam	Jan.–Aug. 1898	Walter Lewis Brown	1916–1917
William Coolidge Lane	1898–1899	Thomas Lynch Montgomery	1917–1918
Reuben Gold Thwaites	1899–1900	William Warner Bishop	1918–1919
Henry James Carr	1900–1901	Chalmers Hadley	1919–1920
John Shaw Billings	1901–1902	Alice S. Tyler	1920–1921
James Kendall Hosmer	1902–1903	Azariah Smith Root	1921–1922

Justin Winsor   William F. Poole   Melvil Dewey   Mary V. Gaver

The American Library Association (ALA) was founded in Philadelphia in 1876 by Justin Winsor, William Frederick Poole, and Melvil Dewey.

Roger McDonough

Betty Stone

E. J. Josey

Regina Minudri

2

George Burwell Utley	1922–1923	Charles Harvey Brown	1941–1942
Judson Toll Jennings	1923–1924	Keyes D. Metcalf	1942–1943
Herman H. B. Meyer	1924–1925	Althea H. Warren	1943–1944
Charles F. D. Belden	1925–1926	Carl Vitz	1944–1945
George H. Locke	1926–1927	Ralph A. Ulveling	1945–1946
Carl B. Roden	1927–1928	Mary U. Rothrock	1946–1947
Linda A. Eastman	1928–1929	Paul North Rice	1947–1948
Andrew Keogh	1929–1930	Errett Weir McDiarmid	1948–1949
Adam Strohm	1930–1931	Milton E. Lord	1949–1950
Josephine Adams Rathbone	1931–1932	Clarence R. Graham	1950–1951
Harry Miller Lydenberg	1932–1933	Loleta Dawson Fyan	1951–1952
Gratia A. Countryman	1933–1934	Robert Bingham Downs	1952–1953
Charles H. Compton	1934–1935	Flora Belle Ludington	1953–1954
Louis Round Wilson	1935–1936	L. Quincy Mumford	1954–1955
Malcolm Glenn Wyer	1936–1937	John S. Richards	1955–1956
Harrison Warwick Craver	1937–1938	Ralph R. Shaw	1956–1957
Milton James Ferguson	1938–1939	Lucile M. Morsch	1957–1958
Ralph Munn	1939–1940	Emerson Greenaway	1958–1959
Essae Martha Culver	1940–1941	Benjamin E. Powell	1959–1960
		Frances Lander Spain	1960–1961
		Florrinell F. Morton	1961–1962
		James E. Bryan	1962–1963
		Frederick H. Wagman	1963–1964
		Edwin Castagna	1964–1965
		Robert Vosper	1965–1966
		Mary V. Gaver	1966–1967
		Foster E. Mohrhardt	1967–1968
		Roger McDonough	1968–1969
		William S. Dix	1969–1970
		Lillian M. Bradshaw	1970–1971
		Keith Doms	1971–1972
		Katherine Laich	1972–1973
		Jean E. Lowrie	1973–1974
		Edward G. Holley	1974–1975
		Aille Beth Martin	1975–April 1976
		Clara Stanton Jones	July 1976–1977
		Eric Moon	1977–1978
		Russell Shank	1978–1979
		Thomas J. Galvin	1979–1980
		Peggy A. Sullivan	1980–1981
		Elizabeth W. (Betty) Stone	1981–1982
		Carol A. Nemeyer	1982–1983

𝕬 𝕷 𝕬

1876

Sketch of the room where ALA
first met in 1876.

Brooke E. Sheldon	1983–1984	Marilyn L. Miller	1992–1993
E. J. Josey	1984–1985	Hardy R. Franklin	1993–1994
Beverly P. Lynch	1985–1986	Arthur Curley	1994–1995
Regina Minudri	1986–1987	Betty J. Turock	1995–1996
Margaret E. Chisholm	1987–1988	Mary R. Somerville	1996–1997
F. William Summers	1988–1989	Barbara J. Ford	1997–1998
Patricia Wilson Berger	1989–1990	Ann K. Symons	1998–1999
Richard M. Dougherty	1990–1991	Sarah A. Long	1999–2000
Patricia G. Schuman	1991–1992	Nancy Kranich	2000–2001

ALA executive secretaries

Melvil Dewey	1879–1890	(Edward C. Hovey, executive officer)	
William E. Parker and			1905–1907
Mary Salome Cutler	1890–July 1891	Chalmers Hadley	1909–1911
Frank Pierce Hill	1891–1895	George Burwell Utley	1911–1920
Henry Livingston Elmendorf	1895–1896	Carl H. Milam	1920–1948
Rutherford Plan Hayes	1896–1897	Harold F. Brigham (interim)	
Melvil Dewey	1897–1898		July–Aug. 1948
Henry James Carr	1898–1900	John MacKenzie Cory	1948–1951
Frederick Winthrop Faxon	1900–1902	David H. Clift	1951–1958
James Ingersoll Wyer	1902–1909		

ALA executive directors

David H. Clift	1958–1972	Peggy Sullivan	1992–1994
Robert Wedgeworth	1972–1985	Elizabeth Martinez	1994–1997
Thomas J. Galvin	1985–1989	Mary W. Ghikas (acting)	1997–1998
Linda F. Crismond	1989–1992	William Gordon	1998–

Special Libraries Association presidents

John Cotton Dana	1909–1911	Howard L. Stebbins	1935–1937
Robert H. Whitten	1911–1912	William F. Jacob	1937–1938
Daniel N. Handy	1912–1914	Alma C. Mitchill	1938–1940
Richard H. Johnson	1914–1915	Laura A. Woodward	1940–1942
Andrew Linn Bostwick	1915–1916	Eleanor S. Cavanaugh	1942–1944
Frederick H. Morton	1916	Walter Hausdorfer	1944–1945
Charles C. Williamson	1916–1918	Herman H. Henkle	1945–1946
Guy Elwood Marion	1918–1919	Betty Joe Cole	1946–1947
Maude A. Carabin Mann	1919–1920	Irene M. Strieby Shreve	1947–1948
Dorsey W. Hyde Jr.	1920–1922	Rose L. Vormelker	1948–1949
Rebecca B. Rankin	1922–1923	Ruth H. Hooker	1949–1950
Edward H. Redstone	1923–1924	Elizabeth W. Owens	1950–1951
Daniel N. Handy	1924–1926	Grieg Aspnes	1951–1952
Francis E. Cady	1926–1929	Elizabeth Ferguson	1952–1953
William Alcott	1929–1930	Lucile L. Keck	1953–1954
Margaret Reynolds	1930–1931	Gretchen D. Little	1954–1955
Alta B. Chaflin	1931–1932	Chester M. Lewis	1955–1956
Mary Louise Alexander	1932–1934	Katharine L. Kinder	1956–1957
Ruth Savord	1934–1935	Alberta L. Brown	1957–1958

Margaret H. Fuller	1958–1959	James B. Dodd	1980–1981
Burton W. Adkinson	1959–1960	George H. Ginader	1981–1982
Winifred Sewell	1960–1961	Janet M. Rigney	1982–1983
Eugene B. Jackson	1961–1962	Pat Molholt	1983–1984
Ethel S. Klahre	1962–1963	Vivian J. Arterbery	1984–1985
Mildred H. Brode	1963–1964	H. Robert Malinowsky	1985–1986
William S. Budington	1964–1965	Frank H. Spaulding	1986–1987
Alleen Thompson	1965–1966	Emily R. Mobley	1987–1988
Frank E. McKenna	1966–1967	Joe Ann Clifton	1988–1989
Elizabeth R. Usher	1967–1968	Muriel Regan	1989–1990
Herbert S. White	1968–1969	Ruth K. Seidman	1990–1991
Robert W. Gibson Jr.	1969–1970	Guy St. Clair	1991–1992
Florine A. Oltman	1970–1971	Catherine "Kitty" Scott	1992–1993
Efren W. Gonzalez	1971–1972	Miriam A. Drake	1993–1994
Edward G. Strable	1972–1973	Didi Pancake	1994–1995
Gilles Frappier	1973–1974	Jane Dysart	1995–1996
Edythe Moore	1974–1975	Sylvia E. A. Piggott	1996–1997
Miriam H. Tees	1975–1976	Judith Field	1997–1998
Mark H. Baer	1976–1977	Suzi Hayes	1998–1999
Shirley Echelman	1977–1978	Susan DiMattia	1999–2000
Vivian D. Hewitt	1978–1979	Donna Scheeder	2000–2001
Joseph M. Dagnese	1979–1980		

Tips for new academic librarians

by Priscilla K. Shontz and Jeffrey S. Bullington

IF YOU ARE JUST BEGINNING a tenure track position, you may be wondering, "Where do I begin?" How do you plan your work and pursue activities that will help you pass a tenure review several years down the road? Although tenure requirements vary by institution, most reviews will focus on three areas: librarianship, service (professional involvement), and scholarship (publication). As novice librarians, we offer the following tips for making the most of your first year on the job).

Familiarize yourself with the tenure process. Ask your supervisor and colleagues to explain your institution's tenure process. What are the expectations? What criteria will be used to evaluate your progress and qualifications for receiving tenure? Expectations can differ from place to place. Publication may outweigh service to the profession. Active professional involvement or the pursuit of an additional degree may replace publication expectations. Do nonrefereed journal or newsletter articles, coauthored articles, or book and product reviews count? Are you expected to be active in the ALA, or does other professional involvement count as heavily? Ask about librarians who have been denied tenure in the past. Are there pitfalls to avoid? Are there periodic reviews throughout the process or a single review at the end of the process?

Read your institution's policy statement outlining the tenure process. Does the campus-wide tenure policy differ from the library's? In the tenure process, you will be evaluated not only by colleagues in the library but also by a college or campus-wide

committee. Talk to teaching faculty about their expectations and experiences. Attend informational meetings to learn more about the process.

Maintain a calendar of your accomplishments and events. From day one, start a tenure file. Include a copy of the tenure policy, your own notes, and any supporting documents such as user aids, policy statements, memos, procedures, Web sites, etc. Keep thank-you notes that people send for things you do in your job.

Even if you do not use all the documents you keep, you will be glad you have them when you prepare your tenure documentation. Save e-mail or electronic files; print them out to place in your tenure folder. Having all of this information in one place will make it much easier for you to put together your dossier.

Learn your job well. Your first priority, naturally, will be to learn the new job—your daily routines and responsibilities. It often takes a year or more to feel comfortable in your new surroundings. You may feel overwhelmed by the variety or amount of work. Try setting a schedule to learn different duties. For example, a new reference librarian might focus on learning collection development responsibilities one week and library instruction duties the next. Ask colleagues to orient you to their areas of responsibility. Do not forget to ask classified staff to explain procedures or give background information.

Becoming proficient at your new job is your single most important ongoing task. If you are not doing your job well or pulling your own weight, no amount of publication or service will impress your colleagues at your tenure review.

Learn your organizational culture. Every workplace has a unique culture. Learn how to function effectively in your new environment. Watch how other librarians interact with each other, the library director, the teaching faculty, and the administration. How do classified staff members interact with librarians and the director? Is it a bureaucratic organization with a strict hierarchy, or is it more egalitarian? Watch how meetings are run and, more importantly, how decisions are made. Do tenured librarians and library administrators treat you as a peer? Are you able to speak out in meetings, or are new librarians expected to observe? Are you given freedom to change procedures and try new ideas, or should you submit all ideas to a supervisor for approval?

Use your first year to evaluate the work environment and decide how you fit into your new library. Being aware of the library and campus political environments can help you get things done and maintain good relationships with colleagues. Tenure is a political process. If your colleagues do not like your work style, they might be less inclined to evaluate you favorably.

Discuss your performance and progress with your supervisor. Talk with your supervisor regularly to keep him or her informed of your activities and to discuss problems or ideas. Even if your institution does not require a formal annual evaluation, set up a specific time with your supervisor to discuss your performance and progress toward tenure.

Ask tenured colleagues to assess your progress. Provide your reviewer with a summary of your accomplishments for the past year; it is virtually impossible for your reviewer to know about all of your work activities. Do not be afraid to ask for guidance and feedback. Request clarification of review comments, suggestions for improvement, and an assessment of your progress toward tenure.

Seek out mentors. Seek guidance from experienced librarians or professionals. You could use a formal mentoring program such as the ALA New Members Round Table's Mentoring Program. An NMRT mentor will meet with you at the ALA Annual Conference, show you how to get the most from the conference, and may introduce you to other experienced librarians.

You may choose a less formal route for mentoring. Is there someone in your organization with whom you "connect?" Someone who gets things done? A mentor might be a library school professor, a supervisor, a colleague, someone at another library, or a faculty member at your institution. Find people who will encourage you and guide you. Talk with them when you have questions, ask them for their opinions, and thank them for their help. Maintain regular contact with them (without becoming a nuisance). Throughout your career you will need mentors, although those mentors will change with time. Remember to mentor others as you progress through your career.

Start networking. It is never too early to start making contacts with other library professionals, even while still in library school. Your fellow students, professors, and work supervisors will soon become your professional peers; keep in touch with these people. Visit local libraries to meet librarians, attend local, regional, or state conferences and go to conference social events. Carry business cards to hand out when appropriate. Volunteer for organizational activities. Contact authors of articles that particularly interest you. Keep track of your contacts and work at remembering names and faces. The library world is smaller than you think, and chances are good that you will meet that person again. Who knows? He or she may be the key to a publication, a committee appointment, a great job lead, or a friendship.

Join professional, campus, and community organizations. You are expected to take part in professional organizations, campus committees, and community service activities. In addition to joining organizations, you must also demonstrate active involvement. Although it can be expensive, it is a good idea to join professional organizations such as the ALA, your state library organization, or special organizations such as the North American Serials Interest Group (NASIG). Some institutions value national professional service above local, university, or community service. Ask your colleagues what types of service count most heavily toward tenure, but do choose activities that interest you.

Getting committee appointments can sometimes feel like job hunting all over again. Volunteer for anything that interests you—it doesn't hurt to try. Because appointments can be competitive, describe your interest in that particular committee when you volunteer. This gives the appointing member more information about your qualifications for an appointment. In a large organization such as the ALA, consider a division, section, or round table committee—there are many committees at these levels, all engaged in different missions. The ALA Web site (www.ala.org) has links to many division, section, and round table home pages. Use this information to identify committees you would enjoy.

An ALA New Members Round Table committee or state NMRT committee can be a fun, effective way to begin professional involvement. As ALA NMRT's mission is to help new ALA members develop leadership skills, NMRT guarantees a committee appointment to any volunteer. Chairing NMRT committees gives you leadership experience and contacts that can help you get onto other ALA division or section committees. Remember our networking advice? Being known as "someone who gets things done" can be a great way to get the committee appointment of your dreams.

On your campus, find out what university committees are available and volunteer to serve. This helps you meet people on campus and gives you the opportunity to promote a positive image of your library to the rest of the institution. Volunteer to help out with a pledge drive, graduation activities, and other events. Getting involved in student activities or organizations can increase your visibility. Identify community service opportunities by asking your colleagues what activities they engage in or by contacting your local United Way chapter, public broadcasting stations, or local churches.

Keep up with professional literature and discussion lists. Set up a system to monitor trends in librarianship. Whether you browse the current journals, read certain journals from cover to cover, or research specific subjects, it's important to keep up with the current literature. In addition to reading literature about your specific job or interests, consider reading *The Chronicle of Higher Education* to keep up with general developments in higher education.

For electronic communications, subscribe to discussion lists that appeal to you. Look at ALA's list of discussion lists (www.ala.org/lists.html) and ask colleagues and other librarians what lists they monitor. Discussion lists can keep you informed about hot topics and in touch with fellow librarians who share your interests. Posting messages on a discussion list may also increase your name recognition.

Develop research interests. During your first year, you may be too busy to write. Nevertheless, begin thinking about ideas for publication Can you expand on a research idea from library school? Articles and lists you read or problems you notice may generate ideas. Consider researching one topic in depth to become an expert in that area. Discuss ideas with colleagues, mentors, and supervisors. They may provide helpful ideas or feedback. You may even find someone to coauthor an article with you. Once you have written an article for submission, let trusted colleagues proofread it. Ask them to suggest journals to which you could submit your article. Seek opportunities to present papers or poster sessions at professional meetings.

Plan or write articles for nonrefereed publications. One way to begin publishing is to write a short article for a newsletter or a nonrefereed journal. Investigate opportunities to cover ALA conference meetings, programs, or events for *Cognotes* or for section or roundtable newsletters. Offer to write book reviews for journals. Compile bibliographies as you begin your research. Such publications help get your name into print and give you a publication to list on your resume. Some begin working on a specific topic in this way, and later develop the same topic into a more in-depth article for a refereed journal. Others may use this opportunity to refresh their research and writing abilities as they begin thinking about publication.

Make the most of your first year. Don't let the tenure review process overwhelm you. Use this time to plan and start your progress toward your final tenure review. Learning your new job, beginning your professional involvement, and planning your publication ideas will put you well on your way toward a successful tenure track career.

SOURCE: Priscilla K. Shontz and Jeffrey S. Bullington, "Tips for New Librarians: What to Know in the First Year of a Tenure-Track Position," *College & Research Libraries News* 59 (February 1998): 85–88.

Myers-Briggs profiles for librarians

by Mary Jane Scherdin

IN 1992, THE AUTHOR DISTRIBUTED the Expanded Analysis Report (EAR) version of the Myers-Briggs Type Indicator (MBTI®) to a random sample of American Library Association (ALA) and Special Libraries Association (SLA) members as part of a survey sponsored by ALA's Association of College and Research Libraries (ACRL). Unlike the commonly used 94-question form, the EAR is composed of 131 questions. Results of the EAR include scores on 20 subscales which add a depth of understanding regarding similarities and differences within types. The sample group used for analysis was 1,600 satisfied librarians with master's degrees in library science or library and information science who completed the Strong Interest Inventory, the demographic questionnaire, and the MBTI. For more information on the MBTI, refer to Isabel Briggs Myers and Mary H. McCaulley, *Manual: A Guide to the Use of the Myers-Briggs Type Indicator* (Palo Alto, Calif.: Consulting Psychologists Press, 1985).

Librarians and the general population

A comparison of librarians with the general population as reported by Isabel Myers in 1985 reveals dramatic differences. Librarians are the opposite of the general population on Introversion (I) and Intuition (N), and women librarians are almost twice as likely as other women to have the Thinking (T) preference. A partial explanation for these differences lies in the fact that while Introverted Intuitive types are relatively infrequent in the general population, their numbers are more frequent at higher educational levels. A preference for Intuition indicates a theoretical orientation that is associated with interest and comfort in college and university settings. Since librarians are among the most highly educated people in the population, their placement in this category seems appropriate.

Comparison of librarians and the general population

Preferences of Librarians	ACRL Study Population	General Population
Extraversion (E)	37% E	65% E
Introversion (I)	63% I	35% I
Sensing (S)	41% S	68% S
Intuition (N)	59% N	32% N
Thinking (T)	69% men T	61% men T
	58% women T	32% women T
Feeling (F)	31% men F	39% men F
	42% women F	68% women F
Judging (J)	66% J	55% J
Perceiving (P)	34% P	45% P

This data shows that library and information professionals are distinctly different from the general population. Significant differences were found on 14 of the 16 four-letter types. Only ISFJ (Introverted Sensing Feeling Judging) and ENTP (Extraverted Intuitive Thinking Perceiving) do not have significant differences. Twelve of the 14 are highly significant (.001 level).

ISTJ (Introverted Sensing Thinking Judging) and INTJ (Introverted Intuitive Thinking Judging) are clearly the two types most often found in the ACRL study. While the majority of librarians are Introverted (I), Intuitive (N), Thinking (T) and Judging (J), the greatest frequency for a given four-letter type is ISTJ (16.5%), followed by INTJ (11.5%).

Two most frequent types

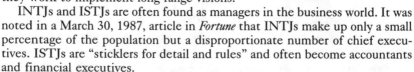

Since three of the four preferences are identical (Intuitive, Thinking and Judging), there are many similarities between the two types, such as being decisive, logical, productive, and reflective. The important difference is on the Sensing/Intuitive (S/N) scale. Interestingly, the S/N preference is thought to have the most influence on occupational choice in general. Sensing types are drawn to occupations that let them use their practical skills, where they can deal with facts. Intuitives like situations in which they look at possibilities, think independently, and problem-solve at a systems level. This contrast, then, may influence the direction taken within the profession. Both Sensing and Intuitive types are needed in a library. The visionary Intuitive is needed to look at broad ramifications of problems and to generate ideas for fresh alternatives. The dependable, consistent, precise Sensing person makes others aware of pertinent facts.

ISTJs are quite dedicated to getting the job done, do so without fanfare, and pride themselves on being accountable. They may have trouble saying no and thus become overloaded. Since they are perfectionists, it may be difficult for them to delegate unless they have confidence in their subordinates. They communicate a message of reliability and stability, which often makes them excellent supervisors. Since ISTJs are organized, thorough, factual, and careful in managing details, it seems likely that persons with this type would function well in structured tasks, such as those in technical services where consistency and accuracy are crucial.

In contrast, INTJs are confident, independent, ingenious, visionary, systems-minded, and like to plan and create. With their focus on efficiency, INTJs are single-minded in their work toward achieving a goal. They like to make things work, but when the task becomes routine, they prefer to move on to something else. They can develop strategies to solve complex problems or implement change, and they have an uncanny ability to project far into the future. These qualities seem appropriate for managers and leaders as they work to implement long-range visions.

INTJs and ISTJs are often found as managers in the business world. It was noted in a March 30, 1987, article in *Fortune* that INTJs make up only a small percentage of the population but a disproportionate number of chief executives. ISTJs are "sticklers for detail and rules" and often become accountants and financial executives.

It is interesting to note that ISTJ and INTJ were also the most frequent types found in studies of computer professionals in 1982–1984. When compared with librarians, there were slightly more Introverts (67%), slightly fewer Intuitives (54%), more Thinking types (81%), and exactly the same percentage of Judging types (66%). Of the 1,229 computer specialists who took the MBTI at that time, 73% were male.

Specialties within the profession

The ACRL study verified that there were significant differences among the specialties within the library profession. Of the five specialties studied—technical services, adult public services, children's public services, administration, and automation—the adult public services group is closest to being representative of the entire sample.

There were significantly more Extraverts among administrators than in the rest of the sample. However, despite this difference, more than half (57%) of the administrators are Introverted rather than Extraverted. In contrast, 75% of technical services librarians and 73% of automation librarians are Introverted.

There are a greater number of Sensing types among technical services librarians, while there are more Intuitives among administrators. Percentages of Intuitives in the two groups are 63% administrators and 47% technical services. Administrators would be able to make use of the insight and visionary qualities of Intuition. Those in technical services need the sensing qualities of precision and patience with detail.

Significant differences were found on the Thinking/Feeling scale, with more children's librarians having the Feeling preference (56%). Feeling types tend to be tuned into the mood or climate in the workplace and tend to make decisions compassionately based on personal or social values. They have a need for affiliation, a capacity for warmth, and a desire for harmony. Feeling types are attracted to working closely with people and are concerned with the human as opposed to the technical aspects of problems. In contrast, more administrators and automation librarians have the Thinking preference (67% and 66%, respectively). Thinking types rely on principles of cause and effect and tend to be more impersonal when making decisions. They are objective, analytical, and concerned with principles of justice and fairness.

A separate analysis based on percentage of time spent on daily activities showed that those who said they spent over 50% of their time on reference (N=277) were significantly higher on the Feeling scale. However, still less than half (45%) were Feeling types as opposed to 39% for the entire sample. Since they have a strong belief in the values involved with helping people, Feeling types would most likely be happier in public service work.

There is also a difference on the Judging/Perceiving scale. More administrators showed a preference for Perceiving, although that percentage is still only 37%. When people are using their Perceiving preference, they are spontaneous, curious, open to new events and changes, and they aim to miss nothing. Administrators with the Perceiving preference may postpone making decisions while they search for options.

In contrast, 73% of the technical services librarians have the Judging preference. When using this preference, people are concerned with seeking closure, planning and organizing activities. When analyzing the data by type of activity, it was found that those who spend more than 50% of their time on cataloging activities ($N=87$) were significantly higher on both Introversion (76%) and Judging (80%) than the rest of the sample. These two preferences would serve catalogers well, since they need to focus in and be systematic in making decisions within the parameters of cataloging rules.

Type of library

Differences were also found when comparing participants by the type of library in which they worked. Special librarians, including those who work in profit and nonprofit organizations, had no significant differences from the sample group as a whole. This was also true for the group called "other," which includes librarians from state library agencies, the federal government (including armed forces), and network/bibliographic utilities.

Similar to the children's public services librarians described above, school library media specialists were significantly higher on the Feeling preference than the total sample (52% vs. 39%). In contrast, more academic librarians were Thinking types (64% vs. 61%). Academic librarians were also significantly higher on Perceiving than the entire sample (37% vs. 34%). (Since there were no significant differences between the two- and four-year academic institutions, they were grouped together for this analysis.)

Conclusion

The fact that 63% of librarians have Introverted preferences has importance for the profession. While Extraverts show their first or best function to the outside world, Introverts save their best function for the inner world of ideas.

Although a well-developed Introvert can deal ably with the Extraverted world when necessary, he/she works best, most easily, and most enjoyably with the reflective world of ideas. It follows, therefore, that Introverts are more likely to be underestimated in casual contacts.

In addition, Introverts are not as apt to initiate contact with others or to promote themselves. While Introverted public services librarians may have no problem approaching a patron to offer help, they may hesitate to originate contact with others either within or outside of the organization they serve, e.g., faculty in an academic institution. Most Introverts prefer personal, one-on-one interactions. Medium- to large-size groups, such as book discussions, are not as comfortable. Considering that the majority of the population is Extraverted, it may be easy for the general public to think of librarians as timid, lacking vigor, initiative, and self-confidence, since they are less comfortable with marketing themselves. Using the academic library example, librarians could take the opportunity to meet and greet as many faculty as possible on an individual basis and make a conscious effort to become involved in campus activities, such as working on small committees. Since Introverts need time to reflect before speaking, it is helpful to them to study the agenda prior to a meeting.

The profession is also affected by the fact that 66% of librarians have the Judging preference. Those with the Perceiving preferences need to be welcomed for the flexibility they bring to their work. Their curiosity and ability to see opportunities for change can be valuable assets to a library staff.

The survival of the library profession depends on diversity. As computers take over more of the custodial tasks of the library world, librarians are able to spend more time taking a leadership role in conceiving and creating ways to meet the information needs of tomorrow. They need to be capable of critical judgment in discerning patterns of future change.

The profession needs those who are accurate and good with detail (Sensing) as well as those with a holistic approach (Intuitive), those who get things done on schedule (Judging) and those who are open to new possibilities (Perceiving), those who plunge quickly into new opportunities (Extravert) and those with a more cautious approach but follow projects over a long period of time (Introvert), those who make an impersonal analysis of cause and effect (Thinking) as well as those who take into consideration how people are affected by plans and decisions (Feeling).

Knowledge of MBTI types can be useful to help direct librarians to a good job match, where they will be able to exercise their preferences and be happy in their work. It is believed that the Sensing/Intuition and Thinking/Feeling preferences exert more influence over which occupation is chosen, while Extraversion/Introversion and Judging/Perceiving affect the kind of working environment chosen, once a field has been selected. Thus, if a librarian likes the academic setting but is unhappy in a large university library, he/she might be very happy in a small college setting.

In addition, if librarians are aware of the various types and how to work with them, they can help each other with problem solving. People may be uncomfortable working with those with different preferences, but the differences often are essential for a good balance.

If a librarian finds him/herself in a circumstance where his/her type is underrepresented, e.g., an Extravert in a group of Introverts, he/she needs to find or create a special role within the situation, such as offering to lead book discussions, teach classes in the library, or represent the library to an outside agency. He/she might also seek out other Extraverts on the staff, or seek out Introverts who have two other preferences similar to his/her own.

We need to create a climate where our differences are seen as interesting and valuable rather than problematic. Tasks that call on our strengths and preferences require less effort for better performance and give more satisfaction. Let's celebrate *la différence* that keeps us both satisfied with our profession and contributing to a diverse and complementary environment.

SOURCE: Mary Jane Scherdin, "Vive la différence: Exploring Librarian Personality Types Using the MBTI," in Mary Jane Scherdin, ed., *Discovering Librarians* (Chicago: ALA Association of College & Research Libraries, 1994), pp. 125–56.

MANAGERS

Personal qualities of good managers
by David A. Baldwin

LIBRARIANS USUALLY DON'T CHOOSE librarianship in order to manage people. Management preparation is sparse, there are many things employees don't like about their managers, and managers make a variety of mistakes in managing. So what are the personal qualities of good managers?

1. Energy and good health. Managing is a demanding activity and requires that individuals not only be able to handle a variety of activities but be physically and emotionally up to the task.

2. Leadership potential. Managerial responsibilities require the ability to get people to work for and with the manager to accomplish the objectives of the unit.

3. Ability to get along with people. One of the most important qualities library administrators look for in a manager is the ability to get along with others. Getting others to carry out their responsibilities depends greatly on their feelings toward their manager.

4. Job know-how and technical competence. The manager must know the job to be effective in training and problem solving. Managers in libraries usually have their own job duties and responsibilities in addition to supervision, and must be proficient in those duties.

5. Initiative. The manager needs to be able to recognize when adjustments must be made in the work flow or changes made to improve procedures. Initiative is required to recognize when potential problems loom and to deal with problems when they occur.

6. Dedication and dependability. Workers who sense that their manager is not dedicated to the job and the employer may display the same attitude. For example, a manager who is absent regularly will find that employees will also be absent regularly.

7. Positive attitude toward the library administration. Workers will mirror the feelings of the manager toward the library administration.

Types of persons who should not be managers

Certain types of persons should not assume managerial positions. These include the negative employee, the rigid employee, the unproductive employee, and the disgruntled employee. The attitude of a negative employee will be contagious. The rigid employee will be unable to deal effectively with employees. The unproductive employee will find it difficult to get others to work hard. The disgruntled employee simply spreads unhappiness.

Manager attitudes

Attitude is extremely important to good supervision. Managers have the proper attitude if they agree with the following statements:

Managers must:

1. manage with a high degree of integrity and lead by example;
2. keep their word to employees;
3. earn the respect, trust, and confidence of employees;
4. strive to help employees develop to their full potential;
5. give credit to employees who do a good job;
6. accept higher-level decisions and directives and demonstrate this to employees;
7. refrain from discussing personal feelings about library administration with employees;
8. discuss disagreements with library administration privately;
9. be responsible for the performance of their employees;
10. be objective in judging the actions of employees;
11. decide matters involving employees on the basis of facts and circumstances, not personal sympathies;
12. accept the responsibility for rehabilitating rather than punishing employees whenever possible;
13. be prepared to support employees in cases where they are in the right;
14. allow employees to have as much control over their own work as possible;
15. work to maintain a workplace climate that allows employees to express their feelings and concerns openly without fear of reprisal.

The library manager

Individuals charged with the responsibility of supervising one volunteer or 25 librarians need essentially the same basic supervisory skills. It is easy to underestimate the value and impact of volunteer supervision. On the one hand, it can provide valuable supervisory experience, which, if done well, can prepare one for higher-level supervision. On the other hand, if done poorly, it can have a negative effect on volunteers, for many of whom this is a first volunteer experience. Libraries must recognize that assigning supervisory responsibilities to an individual carries with it the obligation to help him or her learn and develop the skills needed to do the job right.

SOURCE: David A. Baldwin, *Public Librarian's Human Resources Handbook* (Englewood, Colo.: Libraries Unlimited, 1998), pp. 164–66. Reprinted with permission.

Taking charge of micromanagers
by Larry Corbus

LIBRARY DIRECTORS CAN DRIVE THEMSELVES to immediate distraction if they even suspect that their board members are trying to wrest the day-to-day management of their libraries from them. For many directors—the lucky ones—this worry is but a fleeting thought, the farthest thing from reality. But for those less fortunate, being micromanaged has become a way of professional life.

What are the factors that cause one group of trustees to preempt every decision its director makes when another does not? What can library directors do to stave off unwelcome meddling? And is trustees' attention to administrative minutiae necessarily a bad thing?

Essentially there are two managerial styles among public library directors—head librarian and chief executive officer. Those who prefer to play the head librarian "role" tend to invite more hands-on attention from their boards.

What's the difference between the two? A head librarian takes responsibility for the traditional duties of collection development, reference, and adult and children's services, often deferring to the board on questions not directly related to the provision of services. CEO types, on the other hand, may delegate some professional responsibilities but nonetheless see the entire library operation as their domain.

At libraries run by a head librarian, the buck invariably stops with the board. At libraries with a CEO at the helm, most decisions are made by the director because he or she feels empowered to make things happen in a way that trustees would approve.

Many directors fall into a continuum somewhere between these two extremes. However, a board almost takes it as an invitation to peer over a director's shoulder when he or she accepts less than full responsibility for a library's business operations. And once their managerial authority is relinquished, head librarians have enormous difficulty regaining it.

Problem director behaviors

Of course, there are other factors that contribute to a library director's inadvertently "sending an invitation" to be second-guessed, among them:

Not getting enough respect. Every public library director needs the confidence of at least three constituencies—the board, the staff, and the public. Most directors who excel have the confidence of all three; with the backing of two (one of which must be the board), some directors can succeed, although usually under great strain. No one with the confidence of just one constituency will be successful for long, and anyone lacking the trust of all three should be sending out resumes.

When trustees lack confidence in a library director, they may feel obligated as custodians of the public trust to second-guess his or her decisions. On the other hand, board members who trust their managers' judgment have been known to authorize the expenditure of millions of dollars without any misgivings.

Lacking the vision thing. Most boards expect directors to articulate a vision of the library's future. Directors who try to manage without one soon find that the board as a whole, or individual trustees, are imposing their own. On the other hand, trustees view just as skeptically a director who has been unable to "sell" his or her dreams for the library.

Dropping the reins. If nature abhors a vacuum, does a lack of leadership on the part of a director invite micromanagement by the library board? Most definitely yes. In fact, it might not even be a board member who steps in; sometimes another administrative department or a strong-willed staffer dons the leadership role.

No organization is successful unless someone takes charge. Library directors are expected to be leaders, but not all directors are natural leaders.

Playing prima donna. It is wise for today's library director to develop a consensus among trustees on difficult decisions. Failure to shape and crystallize the opinions of the decision-making body will maximize the board's tendency to second-guess.

Not passing the hat. Who is responsible for developing adequate funding for public libraries? If your answer is the board, you are inviting micromanagement. Operations and funding go hand in hand.

If funding falls short, trustees will question more and more of the overall operation. When the money is there, most boards have an attitude of "Let's do it"; if it's not there, they start to question more and more. Library directors today must take responsibility for fundraising and alert trustees to opportunities from traditional and nontraditional sources of income.

Contracting-out labor relations. Whenever a library is unionized, it can cause a severe reaction by the director. In fact, many directors do not take part in labor negotiations, nor do they designate another senior manager to participate in the process. This sometimes leads to either trustees or board-hired attorneys writing the contracts that greatly impact day-to-day library operations. The results can be disastrous.

Playing favorites. If trustees perceive a director as making decisions that favor library workers over patrons, they may feel the need to intervene as protectors of the public interest.

Directors must always weigh the interests of the library's service population against those of staff. One tool that may aid in such deliberations is the managerial grid Robert R. Blake and Jane S. Mouton developed in the 1960s for analyzing what they deemed "public impact" decisions (*The Managerial Grid,* Gulf Publishing, 1994). In this process, any management decision can be plotted as being more or less beneficial to one's clientele or employees.

Not pressing enough flesh. Many directors are uncomfortable with politics and defer to their trustees in handling the elected keepers of the library purse strings. Actually, this is one area in which a great deal of board involvement might be perceived as good.

While it's advisable to involve the board, though, this sometimes opens the door to board interference when the director fails to be as assertive with local authorities as is necessary. Examples are difficult to provide since each political issue is unique. However, directors must assess political situations and be prepared to navigate stormy waters when necessary.

Trustee maladies

Of course, sometimes the micromanagement thorn can be traced to the Achilles heel of one or more clay-footed trustees, who occasionally suffer from such maladies as:

Private-sector worship. A great fallacy among many a trustee who works in the business or nonprofit sphere is that the public sector is always less efficient. Operating under this misperception, some board members assume they can devise a better way to accomplish a given library goal. Although this is simply untrue, this perception will persist as long as there are so few library directors with private-sector management experience. This phenomenon is not unique to libraries—school-district operations often seem to be judged by people adhering to this same belief.

Gender bashing. It's bunk, but it happens: Some trustees still believe that there are certain things men handle better than women, not only in libraries but society in general. It has happened that boards have assumed control of certain management issues precisely because the director was a woman.

Ego building. So many people, including trustees, fancy themselves architectural experts in one or more aspects of a building project that there may be no single management issue that invites board micromanagement more than a capital construction project. I have witnessed boards bypass directors entirely so they can work directly with the architect or building consultant.

Automation reflex. Some board members perceive their library's director (and staff, for that matter) as technologically naive and behind the times. Of course, directors do not necessarily have to be technology whizzes, but it is important for them—or a trusted staff member—to be conversant with automation issues. When such familiarity is lacking, board members tend to usurp the responsibility for selecting technology. This is not to be confused with the need to inform board members or to seek their input.

Danger signals

Then, there are the no-fault situations that seem to attract take-charge types:

Falling into the limelight. Whether triggered by a censorship challenge, an employee dismissal, or another high-profile controversy, increased public scrutiny also invites micromanagement. Boards take seriously their role in protecting the public trust. When that trust breaks down, a board often feels compelled to delve into issues it once considered the domain of the director.

Electing to serve. Whether a board is elected or appointed can influence the degree of its participation in library management. Some elected trustees feel a greater need for involvement because they have a more direct constituency to serve. Generally this is a minimal factor, except perhaps when the chair or president takes on the role of spokesperson for not only the board but the entire library operation.

Force of habit. Some library boards have traditionally involved themselves in day-to-day management details, particularly in smaller libraries. When these libraries expand or switch from a head librarian–style manager to a CEO type, longtime trustees have difficulty relinquishing power.

Success in 10 steps

So with all these potential reasons for a board to interfere in the direct management of the library, what's a director to do to prevent intrusion? The best-run libraries have a balance of power between staff and trustees. The board, the director, and staff members all have roles, but no one is more pivotal to maintaining the equilibrium of the group dynamic than the library director. Success in 10 steps:

1. Realize that the head librarian/CEO paradigm exists. Decide which type of library director you are, and determine which type your board expects. If you're a "head librarian," get used to trustees looking over your shoulder.

2. Select the right job. Be cognizant of the necessity for finding the right match, and pick a job that meets your skills. If you are the CEO type and you

suspect that your new board may be accustomed to a hands-on approach, clearly define lines of authority—in writing—before accepting a job offer. And keep in mind that there are some jobs not worth taking.

3. Develop annual goals. The director should facilitate a consensus-building process with the board that results in setting measurable goals whose attainments can be evaluated at the end of the year. This also affords the opportunity to assign responsibilities.

4. Create trust. From time to time micromanagement will happen to even the best director. When it happens to you, use your political capital wisely in reminding board members of their roles—and trust that they want to do the right thing.

5. Don't sit on the fence. Directors need to take positions on difficult issues. Don't abdicate decision making to trustees because you're unwilling to be unpopular.

6. Insist on an annual performance review as a means of redefining everyone's role and area of responsibility.

7. Be assertive. Let your board know when they are venturing onto your turf. Be diplomatic, but firm. Be equally respectful of their areas of authority and understand nuances and shades of gray.

8. Accept blame when its due. Be accountable. If you have made a mistake, take responsibility for it.

9. Be aware of the need to hone your managerial skills. just as librarians in the 1990s have focused on refining their technology skills, so too must library leaders actively pursue managerial development. Workshops, MPA/MBA programs, and selective reading of managerial resources all help to challenge conventional thinking. Also, speak to successful colleagues from other organizations about techniques that work.

10. Communicate. Let trustees know what you are doing, and anticipate what the board wants to know. If you tell them what you are doing, they won't have to ask.

SOURCE: Larry Corbus, "Taking Charge of Micromanagers," *American Libraries* 30 (February 1999): 26–28.

Field guide to library managers

by Art A. Lichtenstein

PROVEN FIELD GUIDES ALREADY EXIST on a wonderful variety of useful subjects. Handy titles like *How to Know the Nongilled Fleshy Fungi; Tracks, Scats, and Other Traces,* and *Bottled Gas Manual: A Text Book and Field Guide* are all readily available. But, surprisingly, a careful search of the literature reveals that there is no field guide to the identification of library managers.

Theoretical models of library managers are easy to find. Most come to us from business management, some from behavioral psychology, others from organizational behavior. For example, in *Library and Information Center Management* (Libraries Unlimited, 1993), Robert Stueart explains "country club," "authority compliance," and "middle of the road" managers. Joanne Euster, in *The Academic Library Director* (Greenwood, 1987), profiles "energizer," "sustainer," and "politician" type managers. In *Behavior in Organizations* (R. D. Irwin, 1979), James Lau presents "great man," "organization man," and "retired but still on the job" managers. Theoretical models like these are useful. They help us step away from our hectic routines, put our emotions on hold, and look at the behavior of our managers with objectivity and cool reason.

Writing in 1934, Roger Tory Peterson prefaced his now famous *Field Guide to Birds* with a tale about a young boy named Yan. This was a lad who, though he studied with great concentration his stuffed duck specimens, could not identify ducks in the wild. They moved too fast, flew away too quickly, and could not be measured and weighed. Prior to Peterson's work, there was no guide for identifying live birds, on the wing, in their natural habitat.

Anyone who works with contemporary library managers can readily understand young Yan's problem. No matter how carefully we study the theoretical models, no matter with what scrutiny we examine the stuffed specimens, it is virtually impossible to identify live library managers as they go about their daily managing. They move too quickly, are erratic in their behavior, and, like all creatures subject to frequent attack, they have developed sophisticated methods of concealment and evasion.

To assist in the correct field identification of library managers, the following brief guide is offered. Please read it with a critical eye. It is the author's hope that it will lead to a more comprehensive work covering all regions of the United States and all types of libraries. Comments, corrections, additions, and suggestions are welcome.

Pinstriped common traveler (scooter). Readily identifiable; a good type for beginners; definitive marking is overnight bag clutched under the arm. Wide-ranging; migrates frequently all over the continental United States. Rarely spotted in home nest. Often sighted en route to any national conference held in close proximity to luxury hotels and first-class eateries. Often heard singing, "Yes, soon as I'm back next week, we'll work on that. Sorry, gotta go!"

Elbow-patched therapist thrasher. Known for its incessant call, "Yes, I understand your feelings on this," the therapist manager is a nonindigenous species imported from the human-relations movement of the 1970s. Its well-meaning but misguided adherents believed that the purpose of good management was to make everyone feel better. Unique in silhouette; always perched in an easy chair, leaning forward with hand under chin; listens attentively. Not known for conflict resolution or problem solving; nevertheless, a very congenial bird. Coloration of plumage always soothing—earthy browns, tans, and rich reds.

Pastureland committee former. Characteristic behavior pattern is to encourage the formation of small, quarrelsome flocks consisting of four to a dozen specimens. Rarely, if ever, spotted alone, this bird thrives on detailed agendas and exhaustive reports. Known for its ability to sit on its rump for long periods of time. Call is a strident "Let's meet, let's meet, let's meet." Displays an impressive propensity to turn molehills into mountains. Firmly believes that any issue, no matter how trite, merits endless group discussion. Widely admired for its ability to make time stand still. Caution: Though outwardly pleasant, this manager type is capable of great ferocity if it perceives a threat to its next meeting date.

Waxy-throated fast talker. Easy to spot in good weather; uncanny in its ability to disappear at the first hint of storm clouds, this manger type could convince goldfish to purchase mittens. Distinctively marked, with garish plumage and a huge, plump beak. Capable of producing extensive variety of melodious, meaningless calls. Convinced that all problems are "situations" and all situations may be solved through the application of the hearty handshake and the unctuous smile. A comical bird, fun to watch, always well-groomed and ready to "do lunch."

Dart-flinging ladder-backed stabber. A bird of prey; best left undisturbed. Long-tailed, sneaky, sinuous in flight; full plumage with oily, iridescent sheen. Hooked beak; hooded eyes; powerful talons. On mature specimens, talons are stained red from frequent contact with blood. A nasty, wily bird possessed of a low, cunning intelligence; very dangerous. Not a recommended manager type for beginners. Invariably perched in the shadows and known for its ability to ambush subordinates. Fortunately, a rare type but definitely not a bird to be taken lightly. Close study best left to experienced field researchers.

Greater upland retired-on-the-jobber. A small, rufous bird; distinctive call is a melodious "That won't work, that won't work, that won't work," alternating with "It's been tried, it's been tried, it's been tried." This type of manager enjoys history and serves as the flock's unofficial historian; a staunch conservative. Often heard reminding other birds that any new ideas they may wish to explore were undoubtedly tried out in the 19th century and failed miserably.

Buffle-headed lesser witless coot. A large, ungainly, almost flightless manager type, the only bird you are likely to spot crashing into trees; look for the crumpled feathers and dazed expression. Unable to sing; may be heard emitting low, painful croaks. Fascinating to observe; often overpaid; bumbles around its environment alternately amusing and enraging subordinates. Often mistakenly identified in the field as Old World dodo.

Field notes and suggestions

Do not forget that library managers have their own field guides and, while you are studying them, they are probably studying you. Always carry something into the field, maybe a clipboard or book. Preferred equipage for the 1990s is a stack of computer paper and a couple of floppy disks. These items provide excellent camouflage.

As tempting as it may be to stroll slowly over the terrain, pausing quietly from time to time so you can focus on your subject, try to move along at a steady pace. If you must pause to identify a particular field mark, make it a short pause and seek cover. Fortunately, library terrain is full of good cover: Book trucks, study tables, old mainframes, display cases, and members of the public all do nicely.

Keep a life list, preferably annotated and cross-referenced. At a minimum, you will want to note species type, location, date of sighting, and the distinctive markings that helped you make a positive identification. Such a list is satisfying to build on and, as your career progresses, will prove invaluable as an aid to evaluating new territory. Photos or sketches greatly enhance the value (and collectibility) of any life list. Resist the temptation to purchase notes and preserved specimens from commercial supply houses.

SOURCE: Art A. Lichtenstein, "Field Guide to Library Managers," *College & Research Libraries News* 60 (April 1999): 274–76.

The school library supervisor

TODAY'S SCHOOLS DEMAND the presence of quality library media programs in order to meet the needs of students in gaining the competencies needed to manage the vast amount of knowledge in our rapidly changing, technologically oriented world. Superior instruction requires the use of multiple instructional resources in the educational process. To satisfy these needs, the quality school library media program is led by a library media supervisor and staffed by qualified library media professionals and competent library media support personnel. The responsibilities of a supervisor encompass many areas but can be classified as those of administrator, communicator, teacher, facilitator, and leader.

Administrator: The library media supervisor directs and administers the library media program based on a plan of action that is based on the district's mission statement, goals, and objectives. The supervisor is responsible for evaluating and making recommendations for the improvement of the library media program, developing, and administering the budget, and administering district policies and procedures. Additional responsibilities include administering policies regarding materials selection, the handling of challenged materials, and copyright issues. Personnel responsibilities include selection, supervision, and evaluation of the district media office staff, and, along with principals, selection and evaluation of building library media staff. Closely related activities are the development of job descriptions and the recruitment of school library media personnel. In a consulting capacity, the supervisor is actively involved in specifications for remodeling or new construction of library media centers.

Communicator: The supervisor must know and be able to explain the district's goals and objectives, administrative and educational policies, and philosophy. The supervisor conveys information to library media specialists, teachers, administrators, parents, and students through the development of newsletters, manuals, handbooks, presentations, and bulletins. Reports and studies pertaining to library media are provided as needed to the district, the state, or other agencies. The interpretation and promotion of library media programs are important functions of the supervisor. Serving as a spokesperson for school library media programs, the supervisor represents the district in government, private agencies, and professional organizations. The supervisor provides information on educational studies, research, standards, legislation, and growth opportunities to library media staff, administrators, and other teachers.

Teacher: The supervisor serves as a teacher in developing and coordinating an integrated program of library/information skills instruction, and as a resource person to administrators, teachers, library media specialists, and students. The supervisor provides staff development in the use of instructional resources and technology innovations for school district personnel.

Facilitator: The supervisor coordinates the operation of a district-wide library media program that encompasses all aspects of instructional resources. The major goal is to provide access to information through a variety of sources at each building and throughout the district. The supervisor serves as a member of curriculum development teams, and as a planner and implementor of the K 12 instructional program.

Leader: The supervisor is alert to new ideas, keeps abreast of innovative teaching methods, and applies research principles to the development and advancement of library media programs. The supervisor assesses needs and develops long-range plans for the district and building-level library media programs. The supervisor gives direction to the district in implementing the objectives of the school library media program.

Scenarios

The library media supervisor as administrator. There is an opening for a library media specialist in one school. The library media supervisor screens the applications to select qualified applicants. The supervisor reviews the job description with the interview team and drafts interview questions based on input from team members. As chairperson of the interview team, the supervisor directs the questioning of the candidate by team members and leads the team in arriving at consensus on the candidate to be hired.

The library media supervisor as communicator. The library media supervisor writes a monthly one-page newsletter for all building and district-level administrators. The newsletter contains short articles on what is happening in the library media centers in the district and explains some of the state and national trends and how these trends might impact the district. The trends have been identified by reading journals in the education and library media fields and by attending workshops and conferences. Building-level library media specialists receive copies of the newsletter so they may share items of interest with others in their buildings.

The library media supervisor as teacher. After a discussion with the building-level librarian and the school administrator, the library media supervisor presents a series of seminars for the faculty on the impact of collaborative planning and flexibly scheduled access to library media centers on teaching and learning.

The library media specialist as facilitator. During the revision of the information-literacy curriculum, the library media supervisor acts as chairperson of the committee. To focus the committee's work on incorporating the information retrieval and use skills into units of instruction, the supervisor brings copies of the national standards and examples of exemplary curricula and relates them to the curricular goals of the district.

The library media specialist as leader. After reviewing the district's policy on copyright, the library media supervisor alerts the superintendent to the need for a policy revision, especially in the area of new and emerging technologies. At the superintendent's request, the library media supervisor forms a committee of library media specialists, teachers, principals, students, and community members to revise the policy. The library media supervisor is available to interpret the new policy when it is presented to the school board for adoption.

SOURCE: Position Statement on the School Library Media Supervisor (Chicago: ALA American Association of School Librarians, 1994).

Outcomes-based education

THE LIBRARY MEDIA SPECIALIST has an essential role in curriculum development. Outcomes-based education is a curriculum practice which establishes clearly defined learner outcomes based on the premise that all students can be successful learners. High-expectation outcomes, which are essential for success after graduation, require carefully aligned curricula, instructional strategies, and performance-based assessment. In their unique roles as information specialist, teacher, and instructional consultant, library media specialists actively participate in both the planning and implementation of outcomes-based education.

As information specialist, the library media specialist working collaboratively with teachers, administrators, and parents:

- provides knowledge of availability and suitability of information resources to support curriculum initiatives;
- engages in the developmental process with the planning team, using knowledge of school curriculum and professional resources;
- facilitates the use of presentation tools in print, technology, and media for dissemination efforts;
- serves as an expert in organizing, synthesizing, and communicating information.

As teacher:

- determines learning outcomes, including those in information literacy, for all students in the school and/or system;
- plans, implements, and evaluates resource-based learning;
- integrates information literacy into all curriculum outcomes;
- develops ongoing performance-based assessments for determining the achievement of outcomes.

As instructional consultant:

- facilitates development of teachers' understanding and implementation of outcomes-based education;

- plans for learning environments supportive of curriculum integration;
- previews and selects resources and technology to accommodate the learning styles and multiple intelligence of students;
- designs and implements a variety of instructional strategies and experiences that engage each student in successful learning.

Information Power: Building Partnerships for Learning (AASL, 1998) states that the mission of the library media program is to ensure that students and staff are effective users of ideas and information. The school library media specialist is a powerful partner in providing an integrative curriculum that prepares students for success in the 21st century.

Scenarios

Library media specialists actively participate in the planning and implementation of outcomes-based education as information specialists, teachers, and instructional consultants. In the following scenarios, library media specialists demonstrate these essential roles.

Information specialist

Scenario 1. A library media specialist, recently appointed to the school district's new Outcomes-Based Committee, returns to the library media center and goes online to locate information sources on this new curriculum initiative. After assessing the suitability of accumulated resources, the library media specialist selects three full-text articles to copy for the committee members and prepares an annotated bibliography of additional resources.

Scenario 2. A library media specialist and two other members of the Outcomes-Based Education Committee are working together to prepare a presentation for a public hearing on the outcomes proposed by the committee. After some discussion, the group decides to use a variety of media to communicate their outcomes proposal. The library media specialist has assembled a number of resources, which can be used for the presentation. Working together, the three teachers select appropriate text, audio, and visuals for their multimedia presentation.

Teacher

Scenario 1. A library media specialist, as a member of the K–8 science curriculum writing team, is meeting with the group to identify the information literacy outcomes that will become part of the science curriculum. After reviewing the learning outcomes of the library media department, the team decides to integrate information literacy skills into the study of an estuary. The team asks the library media specialist to work with other team members to prepare suitable examples to be incorporated into the curriculum document.

Scenario 2. A library media specialist and an English teacher are meeting with a class of high school students to evaluate video projects recently completed by the class under the guidance of the library media specialist. The videos are being used as a part of the assessment of an extensive research project on contemporary American authors. Later, the two teachers will meet to discuss and evaluate the process the students used to complete their projects.

Instructional consultant

Scenario 1. A library media specialist is meeting with the middle-school social studies department to determine the resources needed for their recently developed outcomes curriculum. Suggestions are given for the use of primary sources in several units, and a variety of multimedia programs that fit and demonstrate the desired outcomes. Annotated bibliographies of other available resources and examples of assessment products are provided.

Scenario 2. A library media specialist, after reviewing the new curriculum documents and soliciting input from the faculty, meets with the school administrator to discuss the need to provide a wider variety of learning environments within the library media center. A tentative long-range plan has been prepared that would add additional resources, in a wide variety of formats, to the library media collection. In addition, a floor plan providing more space for production of materials needed for assessment is presented. The administrator, while agreeing in principle with the plan, expresses concern about fiscal constraints; both agree to investigate grant possibilities.

SOURCE: Position Statement on the Role of the Library Media Specialist in Outcomes-Based Education (Chicago: ALA American Association of School Librarians, 1994).

State certification agencies

SCHOOL LIBRARY MEDIA SPECIALISTS must meet certain state standards to work in public schools. The following list identifies the agencies with certification oversight. A good summary of the requirements is found in Patsy H. Perritt's "The Knowledge You Need," *School Library Journal* 44 (June 1998): 36–56.

Alabama Dept. of Education, Teacher Education & Certification Office, 5201 Gordon Persons Building, P.O. Box 302101, Montgomery, AL 36130-2101; (334) 242-9977; (www.alsde.edu/tcert/tcert.htm).

Alaska Dept. of Education, Teacher Education & Certification, 801 West 10th St., Suite 100, Juneau, AK 99801-1894; (907) 465-2831; (www.educ.state. ak.us/TeacherCertification/DIGEST.html).

Arizona Dept. of Education, Certification Unit, P.O. Box 6490, Phoenix, AZ 85005-6490; (602) 542-4367; (www.ade.state.az.us/prodev/certification/ general.html).

Arkansas Dept. of Education, Office of Professional Licensure, 4 Capitol Mall, Little Rock, AR 72201-1071; (501) 682-4342; (arkedu.state.ar.us/t.htm).

California Commission on Teacher Credentialing, Division of Certification, Assignment, & Waivers, 1900 Capitol Ave., Sacramento, CA 95814-4213; (916) 445-7256; (www.ctc.ca.gov).

Colorado Dept. of Education, Educator Licensing Unit, 201 E. Colfax Ave., Denver, CO 80203; (303) 866-6628; (www.cde.state.co.us/index_license.htm).

Connecticut Dept. of Education, Bureau of Certification & Teacher Preparation, P.O. Box 150471, Room 243, Hartford, CT 06115-0471; (860) 566-5201; (www.state.ct.us/sde/cert/index.htm).

Delaware Dept. of Education, Professional Standards & Certification, P.O. Box 1402, Dover, DE 19903-1402; (302) 739-4686; (www.doe.state.de.us/certification/dpi_home.htm).

District of Columbia Public Schools, Teacher Education & Certification, 825 North Capitol Street, 6th Floor, N.E.,Washington, D.C. 20002; (202) 442-5377.

Florida Dept. of Education, Bureau of Teacher Certification, 325 W. Gaines St., #201, Tallahassee, FL 32399-0400; (850) 488-2317; (www.firn.edu/doe/menu/t2.htm).

Georgia Professional Standards Commission, Certification Section, 1452 Twin Towers East, Atlanta, GA 30334; (404) 657-9000; (www.gapsc.com).

Hawaii Office of Personnel Services, Teacher Recruitment Unit, P.O. Box 2360, Honolulu, HI 96804; (808) 586-3420; (www.k12.hi.us/~personnl/license.html).

Idaho Dept. of Education, Office of Teacher Certification, P.O. Box 83720, Boise, ID 83720-0027; (208) 332-6880; (www.sde.state.id.us/certification/default.htm).

Illinois State Board of Education, Teacher Education & Certification, 100 N. First St., Springfield, IL 62777-0001; (800) 845-8749; (www.isbe.state.il.us).

Indiana Professional Standards Board, 251 E. Ohio St., Suite 201, Indianapolis, IN 46204-2133; (317) 232-9010; (www.state.in.us/psb/).

Iowa Dept. of Education, Board of Educational Examiners, Grimes State Office Building, Des Moines, IA 50319-0146; (515) 281-5849; (www.state.ia.us/educate/programs/boee/).

Kansas Dept of Education, Certification & Teacher Education, Kansas State Education Building, 120 S.E. 10th Ave., Topeka, KS 66612-1182; (785) 296-2288; (www.ksbe.state.ks.us/cert/cert.html).

Kentucky Dept. of Education, Office of Teacher Education and Certification, 1024 Capital Center Dr., Frankfort, KY 40601; (502) 573-4606; (www.kde.state.ky.us/default.asp?m=45).

Louisiana Dept. of Education, Division of Teacher Standards, Assessment, and Certification, P.O. Box 94064, Baton Rouge, LA 70802-9064; (225) 342-3490; (www.doe.state.la.us/DOE/asps/home.asp).

Maine Dept. of Education, Certification & Placement, 23 State House Station, Augusta, ME 04333-0023; (207) 287-5944; (janus.state.me.us/education/cert/cert.htm).

Maryland State Dept. of Education, Division of Certification and Accreditation, 200 W. Baltimore St., Baltimore, MD 21201-2595; (410) 767-0406; (www.msde.state.md.us/divisions/ca.html).

Massachusetts Dept. of Education, Office of Certification, 350 Main St., Malden, MA 02148-5023; (617) 388-3300; (www.doe.mass.edu).

Michigan Dept. of Education, Office of Professional Preparation and Certification Services, P.O. Box 30008, Lansing, MI 48909; (517) 373-3310; (www.state.mi.us/mde/off/ppc/office.htm).

Minnesota Dept. of Children, Families, & Learning, Personnel Licensing Section, 1500 Highway 36 West, Roseville, MN 55113; (651) 582-8691; (www.educ.state.mn.us/licen/license.htm).

Mississippi Dept. of Education, Office of Educator Licensure, Central High School Building, 359 N. West St., Jackson, MS 39205-0771; (601) 359-3483; (mdek12.state.ms.us/OVTE/License/license.htm).

Missouri Dept. of Elementary & Secondary Education, Teacher Certification, P.O. Box 480, Jefferson City, MO 65102-0480; (573) 751-3486; (services.dese.state.mo.us/divurbteached/teachcert/).

Montana Office of Public Instruction, Certification Division, P.O. Box 202501, Helena, MT 59620-2501; (406) 444-3150; (www.metnet.state.mt.us/main.html).

Nebraska Dept. of Education, Teacher Certification Office, 301 Centennial Mall South, P.O. Box 94987, Lincoln, NE 68509-4987; (402) 471-0739; (nde4.nde.state.ne.us/TCERT/TCERT.html).

Nevada Dept. of Education, Teacher Licensure, 1820 East Sahara Avenue, Suite 205, Las Vegas, NV 89104; (702) 486-6458; (www.nsn.k12.nv.us/nvdoe/).

New Hampshire Dept. of Education, Bureau of Credentialing, 101 Pleasant St., Concord, NH 03301-3860; (603) 271-2407; (www.state.nh.us/doe/credenti.htm).

New Jersey Dept. of Education, Office of Licensing and Credentials, P.O. Box 500, Trenton, NJ 08625-0500; (609) 292-2045; (www.state.nj.us/njded/educators/license/).

New Mexico State Dept. of Education, Professional Licensure Unit, 300 Don Gaspar St., Santa Fe, NM 87501-2786; (505) 827-6587; (sde.state.nm.us/divisions/ais/licensure/).

New York State Education Dept., Education Building, Albany, NY 12234; (518) 474-3901; (www.nysed.gov/tcert/homepage.htm).

North Carolina Dept. of Public Instruction, Licensure Section, 301 N. Wilmington St., Raleigh, NC 27601-2825; (919)733-4125; (www.dpi.state.nc.us/HumanRsrcs/).

North Dakota Dept. of Public Instruction, Approval & Accreditation, 600 East Boulevard Ave., Bismarck, ND 58505-0080; (701) 328-2295; (www.dpi.state.nd.us/dpi/approve/).

Ohio Dept. of Education, Division of Professional Development & Licensure, 65 S. Front St., Room 412, Columbus, OH 43215-4183; (614) 466-3593; (www.ODE.Ohio.Gov/www/tc/teacher.html).

Oklahoma State Dept. of Education, Professional Standards Section, 2500 N. Lincoln Blvd., Oklahoma City, OK 73105-4599; (405) 521-3337; (sde.state.ok.us/pro/tcert/tchrcert.htm).

Oregon Teacher Standards & Practices Commission, 255 Capitol St. NE, Suite105, Salem, OR 97310-1332; (503) 373-3586; (www.ode.state.or.us/tspc).

Pennsylvania Dept. of Education, Bureau of Teacher Certification & Preparation, 333 Market St., Harrisburg, PA 17126-0333; (717) 787-3356; (www.pde.psu.edu/certification/teachcert.html).

Rhode Island Dept. of Education, Office of Teacher Education & Certification, Shepard Building, 255 Westminster St., Providence, RI 02903-3400; (401) 222-2675; (instruct.ride.ri.net/RIDE1/list.html).

South Carolina State Dept. of Education, Office of Teacher Education, Certification, and Evaluation, 1600 Gervais St., Columbia, SC 29201; (803) 734-8466; (www.state.sc.us/sde/educator/certqa.htm).

South Dakota Dept. of Education & Cultural Affairs, Office of Policy and Accountability, 700 Governors Dr., Pierre, SD 57501-2291; (605) 773-3553; (www.state.sd.us/state/executive/deca/account/edcert.htm).

Tennessee Dept. of Education, Office of Teacher Licensing, Andrew Johnson Tower, 5th Floor, 710 James Robertson Parkway, Nashville, TN 37243-0377; (615) 532-4885; (www.state.tn.us/education/lic_home.htm).

Texas Education Agency, State Board for Educator Certification, 1001 Trinity, Austin, TX 78701-2603; (888) 863-5880; (204.65.110.2/sbec_depts/account/cert/index.htm).

Utah State Office of Education, Teacher Certification, 250 East 500 South, Salt Lake City, UT 84111; (801) 538-7753; (www.usoe.k12.ut.us/cert/require/reqs.htm).

Vermont Dept. of Education, Licensing & Professional Standards, 120 State St., Montpelier, VT 05620-2501; (802) 828-2445; (www.state.vt.us/educ/stndards.htm).

Virginia Dept. of Education, Division of Teacher Education and Licensure, P.O. Box 2120, Richmond, VA 23218-2120; (804) 225-2022; (www.pen.k12.va.us/go/VDOE/Compliance/home.html).

Washington Superintendent of Public Instruction, Professional Education and Certification, Old Capitol Building, P.O. Box 47200, Olympia, WA 98504-7200; (360) 753-6773; (www.k12.wa.us/cert/).

West Virginia Dept. of Education, Office of Professional Preparation, 1900 Kanawha Blvd. East, Bldg. 6, Rm. 252, Charleston, WV 25305-0330; (800) 982-2378; (wvde.state.wv.us/certification/).

Wisconsin, Dept. of Public Instruction, Teacher Education & Licensing, 125 S. Webster St., P.O. Box 7841, Madison, WI 53707-7841; (800) 441-4563; (www.dpi.state.wi.us/dpi/dlsis/tcl/licguide.html).

Wyoming Dept. of Education, Professional Teaching Standards Board, Hathaway Building, 2nd Floor, 2300 Capitol Ave., Cheyenne, WY 82002-0050; (307) 777-7291; (www.k12.wy.us/ptsb/).

TRUSTEES

Who are trustees?

by Mary Jo Lynch

IT IS A WELL-KNOWN FACT that most of the nation's 8,946 public libraries have boards of trustees that have a lot to say about how public libraries operate. Trustees are important enough to public library development that most state library agencies maintain lists of the trustees in their states. And they are important enough to ALA that the association has a separate division for them, the Association of Library Trustees and Advocates (ALTA). But what do we know about the demographic characteristics of trustees? If they represent the public interest—a prime function of trustees of public agencies—how close do they come to representing the characteristics of the public?

These were among the questions that prompted ALTA and the ALA executive director to jointly fund a national survey of public library trustees in the summer of 1997. ALTA members and staff worked with the ALA Office for Research and Statistics to draft a questionnaire, 35 state library agencies provided computerized files of trustee names and addresses, and the University of Illinois Library Research Center selected a random sample of 1,200 trustees stratified by the size of population served by the trustees' libraries.

The response rate was over 63%, and the returns represented adequately the distribution of public libraries by region of the United States and by ranges of population served. Therefore, the results can be said to provide a reasonably accurate picture of trustees nationwide

Earlier studies

The first national research on the demographics of public library trustees was done in 1935 and published as part of Carlton Joeckel's *The Government of the American Public Library* (University of Chicago Press, 1935). Summarizing Joeckel in *The Public Library Trustee* (Scarecrow, 1973), Ann Prentice noted that "the 1935 trustee was most apt to be a man, over 50 years of age, well educated, and a member of a profession such as law." In her review of subsequent studies, Prentice found that they tended to support Joeckel's findings. Prentice's own study came to the same conclusion about the 1970 trustee. There has been little done on this topic since.

Context

Before asking about demographics, the ALTA survey asked several questions about how boards operate.
- Are members of your local library board elected or appointed?
- Does your board have legal responsibility for the library or are its powers advisory only?
- What is the official length of your current term as a local library board member?
- How many people are on your board?

The overwhelming majority of board members are appointed (74%) and the rest were elected (25%) with only a few boards (1%) having some of both. Most boards have legal responsibility for the library (64%) while a sizable number are advisory only (36%). Almost all respondents (93%) reported board terms of eight years or less, the most frequent response being three years (39%). Nearly all respondents (95%) reported boards of 12 members or less; the most common number reported was seven (33%).

Demographics

The ALTA questionnaire asked about the following characteristics: gender, race, age, education, income. Results for the first two are easy to summarize:
- 65% of trustees are female;
- 96% of trustees are white.

The first statement is a marked contrast from the Joeckel study, which found that 78% of trustees were men. The Joeckel study did not even mention race; the Prentice study in the 1970s found that 97% were white. For the other three variables, the ALTA questionnaire deliberately used language that would enable results to be compared to government data about the population of the United States as reported in the 1996 *Statistical Abstract.*

Results for age show that trustees today are similar in age to trustees in Joeckel's day—most over 50—whereas the majority of the population of the

United States is under 35. Again in education the similarity to trustees in Joeckel's day is clear: Most have at least an undergraduate degree, whereas the majority of the U.S. population has, at most, a high-school diploma. Joeckel did not mention household income, but the ALTA data shows that the majority of trustees have incomes of $50,000 or greater, while the majority of the population at large makes over $25,000.

The ALTA questionnaire asked if respondents were employed and requested them to list their occupation "as you report it to the IRS." As might be expected from the age data reported above, 41% were not employed and 14% were employed only part-time. Occupation was reported by trustees; over half (51%) could be categorized as professional, echoing Joeckel, although the number of teachers far outnumbered the number of lawyers.

What conclusions can be drawn from this data? Clearly the characteristics of library trustees today are very similar to those of trustees in 1935 and somewhat different from the characteristics of the current U.S. population. Whether that is good or bad is not a question that can be answered with data. But the data adds an important dimension to what is known about public libraries at the end of the 20th century.

SOURCE: Mary Jo Lynch, "Who Are These People?" *American Libraries* 29 (August 1998): 100–101.

Trustees: The most important people
by Will Manley

WHEN I REFLECT BACK on all the people I have met in the public-library arena, the most valuable individuals I have worked with were not reference librarians or catalogers or children's librarians or even administrators. No, it has always been my experience that the people who are most important to the future of the public library are trustees. Actually, I should qualify that to read "good trustees," because other than a rude reference librarian or a children's librarian who hates children it's hard to think of anyone more destructive to the library cause than a bad trustee.

This is an important distinction to make because there are only two types of trustees—good ones and bad ones. Bad trustees are easy to spot because they have gotten on the board for any of the following reasons:

   1. To get fine-free status.

2. To pad their resumes.

3. To get their friends or relatives on the library payroll.

4. To get the circ clerk who was rude to them fired.

5. To get the library to subscribe to an obscure but expensive periodical that only they will read.

6. To be in a better position to date the head librarian.

7. To cut taxes.

8. To have *Daddy's Roommate* removed from the shelves.

9. To satisfy some vague sense of civic responsibility in the most painless and controversy-free way possible.

I have worked with many bad trustees, and, yes, some of these people have been real jerks who have selfish ulterior motives (like reasons 1–6); but for the most part bad trustees are not bad people. Even the tax cutters and the moral crusaders (7 and 8) have the best of intentions, and at least they have some passion for the library, even if it is misdirected.

The real enemies of the public library movement are the passionless people who come under reason number 9. Like Dante's *Inferno,* there is a special ring in the lower, hotter regions of Library Hell reserved for those trustees who are indifferent to their cause. Many number-niners are nice, polite people. In fact, they are too nice and too polite. The problem with them is that they have no fire in their bellies. They are simply lukewarm bodies sitting in chairs at the board table that could be occupied by hot-blooded warrior trustees who are willing to fight for every nickel and dime that the library needs.

What is a good trustee? This is a person who possesses three qualities: 1) a strong and unshakable belief in the importance of libraries in a democratic society, 2) the time and desire to fight for quality library services, and 3) the chutzpah to get things done in the rough-and-tumble world of the local political arena. Anyone who sits on a library board and does not have all three of these qualities is a bad trustee who should vacate his or her post to someone who does. Public libraries are too important and too fragile to be left in the hands of well-intentioned wimps.

But well-intentioned wimps, ironically enough, are just the type of trustees that many library directors prefer. Check out the bar late at night during your next state library conference, and I guarantee you'll find library directors clumped together and crying in their beers about problem trustees who do not know their "place." Many directors who feel threatened by strong-willed trustees truly believe that the role of the library board is largely ceremonial— to make speeches and cut ribbons when new buildings open.

The irony of course is that new buildings don't get built in library systems that are governed by ceremonial trustees. Libraries grow and prosper when trustees and directors both understand that when it comes to political clout, one trustee is more powerful than a thousand directors. That's because when a city council member, county commissioner, or state legislator sees a trustee championing the library cause, he or she sees voters. The library director, on the other hand, is looked at as just one more public administrator who is trying to advance a personal agenda.

Ultimately, then, the future of the public library in these uncertain times of technological change is dependent not upon librarians but upon library trustees. Are your trustees up to the task?

SOURCE: Will Manley, "The Most Important People in the Library Profession," *American Libraries* 29 (February 1998): 108.

FRIENDS

Organizing an academic Friends group

2

1. Obtain support of the library administration, the development office, and the administration of the parent institution.

2. Establish a liaison position in the library with a specific time designated for Friends activities.

3. Select a steering committee of concerned people from the alumni, faculty, student body, and local community. Include a liaison with the development office. It is important to have access to the institution's lawyer, PR and advertising talent, and high-profile leaders.

4. Define your dues structure, membership categories, and prerequisites.

5. Clarify tax status of *Friends groups or of the parent institution so* that when you collect dues they will be deductible by *the member.*

6. Define the mission to be fulfilled by the Friends, and develop a constitution and bylaws reflecting this mission.

7. Decide on a membership brochure, artwork, and how you will reproduce and distribute the brochure.

8. Begin your publicity campaign. Be sure to involve university public relations and development offices, the alumni office, and the local media.

9. Decide on a tentative schedule for the first year to involve new members on committees as soon as they join.

10. Set a date for an opening meeting. Plan the program carefully. Have a *brief* agenda for first annual meeting.

11. Develop a long-range plan for Friends. Reevaluate it periodically. When fundraising becomes feasible, develop a campaign and set goals.

SOURCE: Friends of Libraries U.S.A. (www.folusa.com).

Using the Web to find E-Friends

by Adam Corson-Finnerty and Laura Blanchard

AN IMPORTANT GOAL of the University of Pennsylvania Library is to build its Friends organization—what others might call their "membership." To do this, we have several tasks in mind for our Web site (www.library.upenn. edu/friends/):

1. We want the site to keep our Friends informed of library news, as well as programs and events.

2. We want the site to recognize and celebrate the contributions that Friends make to the library.

University of Pennsylvania Library Friends, 1996–1997.

3. We want the site to gather new Friends.

The library's Friends are a very important constituency, but not primarily because they pay annual dues or respond to our annual appeal. The amount of money that we raise or hope to raise from annual Friends group gifts is minor ($50,000 to $100,000) compared to our overall fundraising goals ($2 million to $5 million each year).

The Friends are important because many of our major gift donors will come from among the Friends. In addition, many Friends are reunion-class leaders, and these classes have made millions of dollars in gifts to the library. Also a significant number of important collection (book and manuscript) gifts have come from card-carrying Friends. Finally, the Friends provide us with consistent feedback, and link the library with the wider community.

Click and join

So the more Friends the merrier, and the easier it is to become a Friend, the better. With this in mind, we have created a new membership category called the "E-Friend." E-Friends can join online and are not asked to pay a membership fee. A special button was created and sprinkled throughout our pages, saying "I want to be an E-Friend."

Click on the button and you are taken to an online form for joining. Fill it out, click "send," and you are part of our wired membership.

Generally, we respond by e-mail immediately, so the membership is cheap, painless, and fast. From then on you receive alerts to library events, word of cool new library cyberservices, bulletins about library gifts, Web postcards—and who knows what else we will think up?

It is also possible to join the regular Friends online. In this case, the visitor clicks on a "Join the Friends" link and is given a form that also allows him or her to indicate a desired level of membership. We do not currently allow online credit card payments, but instead simply bill the new member for dues.

We have seen many sites that invite the prospective member to print out the form, fill it out by hand, and mail it in with their check. This seems foolish to us. If the person is at your site, and wants to join, let them join then and there, even if you have to bill them. For most of us the membership fee is secondary, anyway. The highest priority is in gathering the new Friend, who can then become an active source of support for many years to come.

We plan to experiment with the E-Friend concept over the next several years. Our university has a very widespread alumni base—literally, it is worldwide. Our traditional Friends organization has relied upon geographical proximity to the campus. However, our E-Friends program can reach out to every corner of the planet.

The new possibilities presented by electronic membership may be even more promising for organizations such as the Sierra Club, the National Organization for Women, or the Christian Coalition. For the library, we can imagine many future directions for our E-Friend effort, including:

- book reviews and Web site reviews, prepared by library staff or Friends and communicated to the entire list;

- a "question & answer" Web site, where Friends' queries can be answered by library staff;
- a "bulletin board" site, where E-Friends can post comments and questions, and where other E-Friends can reply. This could be similar to an Internet "news" site;
- an E-Friends "listserv," where postings are automatically sent to all E-Friends (this is both more intrusive and more engaging than a bulletin board);
- a "Friends forum," where E-Friends can periodically engage in live Internet exchanges with library leaders, authors, and professors;
- and a "Friends chat room," where any E-Friend can engage with any other E-Friend in real time, while others watch or jump in and add their two cents worth. Such chat capabilities have been popular with Internet service providers like America Online.

We have placed the Friends calendar online. Many of the events have live links to a more detailed description of the undertaking. In the case of the calendar entry for the Illustrated Books exhibit, for example, viewers could also click on a link to the online virtual version of the exhibit.

We also have created "RSVP" buttons at each upcoming event. This allows Friends to let us know if they plan to attend a particular event. (Most Friends events are free to members; the reason we ask for responses is to get an estimated count for refreshments and room arrangements.)

A Friends and/or members site can be a very full and interactive site, limited only by your time and imagination. Ideas which we are considering include a list of the Friends leaders, perhaps with their pictures and e-mail addresses, and a "message from the Friends' president" page, where updated news can be placed. We are currently putting the Friends newsletter online, along with an archive of past issues (www.library.upenn.edu/friends/news/).

Met's Net bet

Most organizations that take the trouble of establishing a Web site will want to consider some form of online membership. Why not? Such new friends are wonderful prospects for fundraising!

The Metropolitan Museum of Art (www.metmuseum.org) obviously feels that gathering new friends, and even new acquaintances, is of value.

The primary emphasis of the Met's Web strategy appears to be to use its site to gather members, or at least to capture the e-mail addresses of visitors. Note the clickable option, in large print, is to become a "Met net member."

Click on "Membership" and the visitor is given a choice of Become a Member, Events for Members, Corporate Entertaining, and Travel. Click on "Become a Member" and a "special announcement" appears, describing a new category of membership created for online visitors and listing the perks that go with it, all for the low price of $50. Other membership categories are listed, from Student ($35) all the way up to Patron Circle at $7,000. Next to each level of membership is an "order here" button which takes the visitor through the museum shop to "purchase" a membership using a credit card.

One option on the Met's home page is to visit the museum gift shop. Another clickable option is to get "instructions" on how to access net member benefits. Only after a section on education does the visitor have the chance to see the collections or check the exhibits calendar. Before seeing the collections, the new visitor is invited to "register" before entering the museum. This registration is nice and simple, consisting of a brief form which allows you to leave your name and e-mail address. No doubt the Met has promotional plans for this list, which is likely to grow very quickly.

SOURCE: Adam Corson-Finnerty and Laura Blanchard, *Fundraising and Friend-Raising on the Web* (Chicago: American Library Association, 1998), pp. 44–49.

Organizing a teen
Friends of the library group

1. First, decide on the library's goals for having the group. These could include getting advice on planning buildings, interior design, services, and collections with appeal to teens; having teens participate directly in library programs and services; having teens help publicize library services among their peers; or a combination of these things. Second, the teens must choose their own goals for the organization as well. A staff member or a volunteer will usually be the facilitator for the group and the liaison with the library.

2. Target age range: grades 7–12. Because teens change so rapidly, it may be desirable to target only early adolescents, or to have separate groups for younger and older teens.

3. Decide on the source(s) of funding: library budget, adult Friends group, dues, fundraising, etc.

4. Recruit members both formally through schools and other youth-serving organizations and through advertising and word-of-mouth from other teens. Hold an organizational meeting and have a staff member facilitate the group's choice of goals and activities. Set up a steering committee to help the teens decide how much structure they need to achieve their goals and help them create bylaws. Provide examples they can work from (available from FOLUSA).

5. The structure and bylaws will have established what kinds of officers or committees are needed. Assist the group in filling those positions.

6. Potential projects for Teen Friends include: book discussion groups, program planning and performing, tutoring or story telling for younger children, creating teen-oriented displays, creating a library newsletter, helping adult Friends with book sales, serving as Internet advisors/trainers, serving as library advocates, creating Web pages, participating in Internet book discussions, and assisting with a variety of short-term projects in the library.

7. Always keep business portion of meetings brief.

8. Keep work and fun projects in balance.

9. Try whenever possible to have food available at meetings/projects. Teens always seem to work better and longer when food is available.

10. Do not let adults assume responsibility for planning. Teens will make decisions with the assistance of an adult facilitator, who can keep teens aware of available resources and limitations.

SOURCE: Friends of Libraries U.S.A. (www.folusa.com).

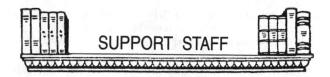

SUPPORT STAFF

"Paraprofessional and proud of it"

by Betty Cook

WHAT A STATEMENT! I say it to myself on a regular basis, and not long ago I said it as the introduction to a talk I gave at a South Carolina Library Association (SCLA) Paraprofessional Round Table workshop.

One afternoon, Shirley Davidson, the Round Table chair at the time, called me about participating in a panel discussion on the decision-making process that one goes through on whether or not to attend library school. I decided her call must be a form of divine intervention. I had been struggling with the idea of whether to attend library school for at least five years. One minute I was convinced—yes it was a good idea and I could do it. The next day or week something would happen and I would be convinced no, the time was not right. Now I really had to think about how I could come to some conclusion.

What I came up with is a 10-step plan that worked for me. I sincerely hope it works for you or at least gets you thinking about your career in library science and where you want to be two, five, or 10 years from now.

1. Talk to people who are librarians. It sounds obvious, I know, but in your daily routine it may not occur to you to have a one-on-one conversation with a coworker who may be able to shed some light on this area. Invite a librarian to have lunch and have a friendly chat about how he or she made the decision to attend graduate school. Choose someone whose background matches your own, if possible. Discuss the pros and cons and how he or she handled them. Get a snapshot of what to expect. For example, how difficult is it to work and attend school part-time? Has it been worth it? What does the future hold for librarians? Would this person be willing to be a mentor to you?

2. Visit a library school to get a more complete picture. I attended an information session at a metropolitan public library sponsored by the School of Library and Information Science at the University of South Carolina. It was informative and eye-opening. I was comfortable with all the information presented, until the speaker came to the cost for a three-credit-hour course. With two daughters in college for another two years, I realized it would be a considerable additional cost. I could have stopped there or kept on researching. I kept on going.

3. Read library journals. I enjoy reading *American Libraries* and *College and Research Libraries News,* and, of course, *Library Mosaics.* They all contain articles that pertain to my job as well as contain job opportunities. It was in these journals I learned that with an MLS from an ALA-accredited institution and 13 years of library experience I could probably earn between $5,000 and $10,000 more than I earn now (if they count my paraprofessional experience as experience for a *professional* position).

4. Visit other libraries. When I am on vacation, I try to visit a library of some kind. It's fun to see what other libraries offer their patrons. Often I pick up brochures and handouts to bring back for samples. It is interesting to browse the reference section to see what sources they own and observe any exhibits. I am especially interested in what technology is available and how user-friendly it is for patrons.

5. Get involved in a library organization. For me, membership in SCLA has made a big difference in how I view librarianship. I work in an academic library. It was not until I joined SCLA and eventually started the Paraprofessional Round Table that I met so many people from public, corporate, special, and school libraries. Then I realized that although each one is different, there are many common experiences, especially with the introduction of technology. As a whole, we are an empathetic group and willing to listen and help each other when the opportunity presents itself. Involvement also enhances my daily work. For the last two years I have also belonged to the Southeastern Library Association and recently joined the Council on Library/Media Technology (COLT).

6. Develop a good network with other paraprofessionals within your library and with people in positions like yours in other libraries. The Clemson University Libraries Classified Staff Council was established 10 years ago to be a means of communication between the classified staff (nonlibrarians) and the administration. The chair is a member of the Libraries' Administrative Council. As manager of the Interlibrary Loan Office, I developed a good working relationship with other ILL managers. This is extremely helpful as a means of sharing information.

7. Talk to your family. See how they feel about your returning to school. Discuss the ups and downs of trying to juggle family responsibilities, holding a job, attending class, and doing homework, housework, and yard work. I went to school from September 1981 to May 1989 to earn an associate's degree from our local junior college and then a bachelor's degree in English from Clemson University. It was rough at times. When I graduated, I needed a break and so did my family. Although I took the Graduate Record Exam, I let my scores lapse because I just could not make up my mind about returning to school and the homework, tests, and stress. It is definitely a commitment.

8. Mention to your friends that you are thinking about returning to school. See what their reaction is. Most of my friends have said, "That's great! You would make an excellent librarian!" That type of reinforcement works wonders. If you can get your employer to pay for part of your education, that's even better.

9. Stop talking about doing it and just do it. Fill out the library-school application form. Get your references to write letters of recommendation. Take the GRE or Miller Analogies Test. Write your check and mail the forms to the library school of your choice. If you sit and think about it for too long, you could talk yourself out of doing it. "I'm too old. I don't have the money. I'm not smart enough. I can't manage my time. The kids are too young. My husband or wife will not adjust well. I'm too tired." Phooey! You can do it.

10. Make your decision and move forward. For me, I know that I can do it. But I just don't want to do it right now. The time is still not right. I will probably do it in the future, but until then . . . I am a library paraprofessional and proud of it.

SOURCE: Betty Cook, "I Am a Library Paraprofessional and Proud of It!" *Library Mosaics* 8 (September/October 1997): 22.

Making federal work-study work

by Sherry E. Young

THE FEDERAL WORK-STUDY PROGRAM provides funds to pay for work done by college students who meet certain financial aid qualifications. Campus financial aid personnel use a need-analysis formula, as defined by program guidelines, to calculate student eligibility for participation. Institutions then use their own individualized methods to put eligible students to work. Many of these students go to work in the library to help fill the never-ending needs for student employees.

Scholars frequently criticize the work-study program for some of its outcomes. They argue that the system of federal funding for student jobs fosters discrimination against students who are ineligible for program participation. Discrimination occurs when departments, in efforts to conserve money, hire students based upon the sources of their paychecks as opposed to their job qualifications. Employers may thus discriminate against well-qualified students who seek part-time campus jobs by hiring less qualified work-study award recipients to avoid departmental funding of student positions.

Critics of the work-study program also charge that its participants often do substandard work. Observers blame this problem on the fact that the system encourages supervisors to employ poorly qualified students who do not possess the abilities to learn properly their jobs.

According to this argument, departments may hire unqualified or poorly motivated individuals for work-study positions in the event that no qualified applicant applies. When supervisors select underqualified students for jobs that require immediate and specific skills, those students will likely fail to successfully perform their jobs. Similar problems occur when work-study students possess the ability to master the skills they need to do their 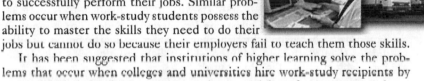 jobs but cannot do so because their employers fail to teach them those skills.

It has been suggested that institutions of higher learning solve the problems that occur when colleges and universities hire work-study recipients by restricting their employment to areas where poor job performance cannot hamper an institution in its quest to fulfill its mission, and that colleges and universities should ban such students from library work.

It is possible for librarians to utilize the federal work-study program to maintain or improve library service. They can accomplish this goal by familiarizing themselves with program guidelines, by understanding the problems associated with their implementation, and by working to avoid those problems. By adhering to a few basic guidelines, librarians can eliminate poor student employee performance and make the work-study program work as envisioned by its creators.

Create jobs that matter

Critics of the work-study program often complain that the program encourages colleges to design make-work jobs to ensure that the maximum number of eligible students receive aid from the federal government. Administrators who create jobs where no need exists may end up with a bored and apathetic workforce. Similar problems occur when supervisors, who lack the time to adequately train and supervise students to do complex work, assign them simple, repetitious, and boring tasks. Departments that hire students to do unchallenging tasks will face problems associated with poorly motivated workers. Such employees may make careless errors that detrimentally impact a library's ability to fulfill its mission. Thus, librarians should consider carefully both their library's need for student assistance and the availability of supervisors who can adequately train and manage student workers. Administrators may avoid the problems that poorly challenged workers cause by requesting only that number of work-study positions for which genuine need and adequate supervision exists.

Fortunately for librarians who wish to take advantage of the work-study program, the nature of library work encourages the design of substantive student jobs. Library student assistants can do work that is both short- and long-term. They may process and shelve materials or complete special projects. The variety of possible tasks makes it possible for librarians to create jobs with meaningful duties that challenge students to work at their full potential.

Select applicants with care

Librarians who successfully design substantive work-study positions then face the challenge of hiring only those students who possess the qualifications needed to do the jobs. When hiring work-study awardees for library work, librarians should follow standard procedures designed to gather information needed to make appropriate hiring decisions. They may use completed application forms to check the applicants' ability and desire to follow written directions and to answer questions completely and accurately. Those in charge of making the hiring decisions should schedule face-to-face interviews with candidates who submit acceptable applications. Interviewers may ask open-ended and fact-finding questions designed to provide information about each candidate's behavior. Librarians may consider asking the better qualified candidates to return for second interviews designed to identify students who are especially interested in library work.

It is unfortunate that some aspects of the work-study program may serve to discourage librarians from following their normal hiring practices. When a limited number of students apply for various campus jobs, supervisors feel pressured into hiring some applicants before considering them in relation to the total group of applicants or before checking references. Prospective student employees may arrive at the library carrying a slip of paper that requires only a departmental supervisor's signature for approval to hire, thus tempting supervisors to hire work-study applicants before adequately considering their interview results. Hasty hiring decisions may also be made by librarians who believe that rejection of applicants will anger financial aid officers.

Those who employ work-study students can prevent the problems that sometimes occur from hiring students whose employment must be coordinated with an outside department. Librarians who seek well-qualified and motivated student workers should make it policy not to hire work-study applicants on the spot. Supervisors should instead interview applicants, check references, and consider each applicant in relation to the total group of applicants who applies during any one hiring period. It is true that, by the time the library supervisor completes this process, some of these students will have found jobs elsewhere on campus. If enough applicants accept other jobs, such an outcome may leave the library short-handed. But this situation is preferable to hiring workers who harm library service by performing their jobs poorly.

Plan for job training that works

Once the hiring process is complete, the important and time-consuming work of training and supervising begins. It is essential that library supervisors adequately train students for their jobs. To become effective employees, students must know what is expected of them, both in terms of general employment guidelines and in relation to specific job duties. Librarians should make certain that each student has meaningful access to the information he or she needs to succeed as a library student assistant.

Because the lack of adequate training may lead to substandard performance, librarians need to plan the nature and composition of student assistant job training. Many college students have held few jobs and have no library experience, and supervisors need to train such students from the basics upward.

Because work-study students usually obtain their aid and apply for jobs at the beginning of the school year, supervisors may find themselves faced with the seemingly overwhelming job of training several new student workers simultaneously. Librarians can meet this challenge by planning for on-the-job training designed to cause as little disruption as possible to daily operations. Supervisors can help work-study students become focused on their jobs by meeting with each one. This is a good time to discuss the library's mission and to familiarize new student workers with such general matters as time and attendance guidelines. The librarian may take this opportunity to put students at ease by describing the library as an enjoyable place to work and gain job experience. A brief meeting between supervisor and supervised can help workers identify their personal work goals and the library's.

Full-time staff members are often responsible for supervising student assistants. Librarians do well to select carefully those employees who train new student workers. Trainers should be masters of the work they teach to others, have good communication skills, and take the challenge of teaching seriously. It is important that full-time staff members assigned the duty of training new work-study students have the time to do so. It is illogical to expect those who lack good communication skills, have full daily work schedules, or are unfamiliar with the work that students will do, to succeed in teaching job duties to new student employees.

Treat all students fairly

Departmental supervisors should employ the same disciplinary procedures for all student employees. The fear that financial aid officers will look unfavorably upon departments whose supervisors correct the mistakes of work-study employees is not a valid reason for exempting such students from adhering to normal rules of work conduct. Librarians may wish to make financial aid officers aware of any disciplinary actions the library takes regarding its work-study students so that the officers understand the reasons for the actions. Supervisors cannot afford to overlook the mistakes of any student worker, which, if continued, will compromise library service. Because of its unpleasant nature, many supervisors tend to avoid the task of correcting employee mistakes. Although it may be tempting for these individuals to cite fear of complaints to financial aid officers as an excuse not to discipline work-study students, library supervisors should exercise fairness in their supervision of all employees. By doing so, and by keeping open lines of communication with the financial aid office, they prevent complaints from occurring and make those that do occur understandable to others.

Conclusion

Some of the criticism that scholars direct against the outcome of the work-study program is legitimate. Well-qualified and motivated college students may miss on-campus employment opportunities because they fail to meet the financial aid criteria. And, because the federal government pays the wages of work-study students, students may end up with make-work jobs designed to put them to work in the absence of any real need to do so. It is also true that supervisors sometimes hire poorly motivated or unqualified individuals who desire financial aid but have no real interest in working.

In spite of these potential problems, it is by following the common-sense principles of job design and personnel management that librarians can make the program work as intended. Librarians who follow these commonly accepted principles will provide their departments with student help at little or no cost to the library's budget.

These principles include the creation of meaningful jobs and the practice of appropriate hiring, training, and supervisory techniques. In this time of financial hardships for institutions of higher learning, librarians should view the successful employment of work-study students in libraries as a challenge worth meeting.

SOURCE: Sherry E. Young, "Making Federal Work-Study Work," *College & Research Libraries News* 59 (July/August 1998): 490–92, 525.

THE PROFESSION
CHAPTER THREE

"I think it is time for librarians to differentiate between the poetry of the profession and the prose of tools and technology. Many librarians feel they enhance their image with their use of technology. This I doubt. All of us use banks and ATM machines, but no one marvels at a bank teller's use of technology."

—Jack Allen Hicks

EVENTS

Calendar to 2005

2000

June

8–10	Laubach Literacy International	Orlando, Fla.
10–15	Special Libraries Assoc.	Philadelphia, Pa.
21–25	Canadian Library Assoc.	Edmonton, Alb.

July

| 6–13 | American Library Assoc. (Annual) | Chicago, Ill. |
| 15–20 | American Assoc. of Law Libraries | Philadelphia, Pa. |

August

3–6	Reforma	Tucson, Ariz.
13–18	International Federation of Library Associations and Institutions	Jerusalem, Israel
28–Sep. 3	Society of American Archivists	Denver, Colo.

September

14–19	Colorado Library Assoc.	Snowmass, Colo.
21–23	North Dakota Library Assoc.	Dickinson, N. Dak.
24–27	Pennsylvania Library Assoc.	Lancaster, Pa.

October

1–3	New England Library Assoc.	Worcester, Mass.
2–5	South Dakota Library Assoc.	Rapid City, S. Dak.
3–6	Michigan Library Assoc.	Detroit, Mich.
4–6	Idaho Library Assoc.	Lewiston, Ida.
5–7	Nevada Library Assoc.	Reno, Nev.
10–15	Oral History Assoc.	Durham, N.C.
11–13	Minnesota Library Assoc.	Minneapolis, Minn.
13–16	Wyoming Library Assoc.	Cheyenne, Wyo.
16–19	Global 2000 on Special Librarianship	Brighton, England
18–20	Iowa Library Assoc.	Ames, Ia.
18–20	Mississippi Library Assoc.	Jackson, Miss.
23–27	LC National Libraries conference	Washington, D.C.
25–27	Nebraska/Mountain Plains L. Assoc. (joint)	Omaha, Nebr.
25–29	Virginia Library Assoc.	Williamsburg, Va.
31–Nov. 3	Wisconsin Library Assoc.	Green Bay, Wis.

November

| 8–10 | Ohio Library Council | Columbus, O. |

2001

January

| 9–12 | Assoc. for Library & Info Science Education | Washington, D.C. |
| 12–17 | American Library Assoc. (Midwinter) | Washington, D.C |

February

| 21–25 | Music Library Assoc. | New York, N.Y. |

March

6–10	Council of Planning Librarians	New Orleans, La.
15–18	ALA Assoc. of College & Research Libs.	Denver, Colo.
26–30	Texas Library Assoc.	San Antonio, Tex.

April

1–7	National Library Week	
4–6	Kansas Library Assoc.	Topeka, Kan.
4–6	Washington Library Assoc.	Tacoma, Wash.
25–28	Montana Library Assoc.	Kalispell, Mont.

May

| 25–31 | Medical Library Association | Orlando, Fla. |

June

9–14	Special Libraries Assoc.	San Antonio, Tex.
13–17	Canadian Library Assoc.	Winnipeg, Man.
14–20	American Library Assoc. (Annual)	San Francisco

August

| 16–25 | International Federation of Library Associations and Institutions | Boston, Mass. |
| 27–Sep. 2 | Society of American Archivists | Washington, D.C. |

September

| 27–29 | North Dakota Library Assoc. | Williston, N. Dak. |
| 30–Oct. 2 | New England Library Assoc. | Burlington, Vt. |

October

2–5	North Carolina Library Assoc.	Winston-Salem, N.C.
3–6	Idaho Library Assoc.	Pocatello, Ida.
10–12	Iowa Library Assoc.	Davenport, Ia.
14–17	Pennsylvania Library Assoc.	Philadelphia, Pa.
23–26	Wisconsin Library Assoc.	Appleton, Wis.

November

| 6–9 | Michigan Library Assoc. | Lansing, Mich. |

2002

January

15–18	Assoc. for Library & Info Science Education	New Orleans, La.
18–23	American Library Assoc. (Midwinter)	New Orleans, La.

April

8–13	Texas Library Assoc.	Austin, Tex.
10–12	Kansas Library Assoc.	Wichita, Kan.
12–17	Council of Planning Librarians	Chicago, Ill.
14–20	National Library Week	
17–19	Washington and Oregon L. Assoc. (joint)	Jantzen Beach, Ore.
24–27	Montana Library Assoc.	Great Falls, Mont.

May

17–23	Medical Library Assoc.	Dallas, Tex.

June

8–13	Special Libraries Assoc.	Los Angeles
13–19	American Library Assoc. (Annual)	Atlanta, Ga.

August

19–25	Society of American Archivists	Birmingham, Ala.

September

26–28	Mountain Plains/N. Dakota/S. Dakota	Fargo, N.Dak.

October

2–5	Idaho Library Assoc.	Boise, Ida.
29–Nov. 1	Wisconsin Library Assoc.	Middleton, Wis.
29–Nov. 1	Michigan Library Assoc.	Grand Rapids, Mich.

2003

January

24–29	American Library Assoc. (Midwinter)	Philadelphia, Pa.

March

29–Apr. 2	Council of Planning Librarians	Denver, Colo.
31–Apr. 4	Texas Library Assoc.	Houston, Tex.

April

6–12	National Library Week	
8–15	Assoc. of College & Research Libraries	Charlotte, N.C.
9–11	Kansas Library Assoc.	Salina, Kan.
10–11	Washington Library Assoc.	Yakima, Wash.

May

| 16–21 | Medical Library Assoc. | San Diego, Calif. |

June

| 7–12 | Special Libraries Assoc. | New York, N.Y. |
| 19–25 | American Library Assoc. (Annual) | Toronto, Ont. |

September

| 23–26 | North Carolina Library Assoc. | Raleigh, N.C. |
| 25–27 | North Dakota Library Assoc. | Minot, N. Dak. |

October

| 28–31 | Michigan Library Assoc. | Lansing, Mich. |

2004

January

| 9–14 | American Library Assoc. (Midwinter) | San Diego, Calif. |

March

| 15–20 | Texas Library Assoc. | Houston, Tex. |

April

| 18–24 | National Library Week | |
| 24–28 | Council of Planning Librarians | Washington, D.C. |

June

| 5–10 | Special Libraries Assoc. | Nashville, Tenn. |
| 24–30 | American Library Assoc. (Annual) | Orlando, Fla. |

October

| 26–29 | Michigan Library Assoc. | Grand Traverse, Mich. |

2005

April

| 11–16 | Texas Library Assoc. | Dallas, Tex. |

June

| 4–9 | Special Libraries Assoc. | Toronto, Ont. |
| 23–29 | American Library Assoc. (Annual) | Chicago, Ill. |

September

| 20–23 | North Carolina Library Assoc. | Winston-Salem, N.C. |

October

25–28	Michigan Library Assoc.	Grand Rapids, Mich.

SOURCE: For up-to-date meeting information, see the *American Libraries* datebook at www.ala.org/alonline/datebook/datebook.html.

Past ALA annual conferences

A LIST OF ALL ALA annual conference dates and locations, with attendance figures, contrasted with total ALA membership (from 1900).

Date	Place	Attendance	Membership
1876, Oct. 4–6	Philadelphia	103	[N/A
1877, Sept. 4–6	New York	66	for
1877, Oct. 2–5	London, England*	21	1876–
1878	[No meeting]		1899]
1879, June 30–July 2	Boston	162	
1880	[No meeting]		
1881, Feb. 9–12	Washington, D.C.	70	
1882, May 24–27	Cincinnati	47	
1883, Aug. 14–17	Buffalo, N.Y.	72	
1884	[No meeting]		
1885, Sept, 8–11	Lake George, N.Y.	87	
1886, July 7–10	Milwaukee, Wis.	133	
1887, Aug. 30–Sept. 2	Thousand Islands, N.Y.	186	
1888, Sept. 25–28	Catskill Mountains, N.Y.	32	
1889, May 8–11	St. Louis, Mo.	106	
1890, Sept. 9–13	Fabyans (White Mts.), N.H.	242	
1891, Oct. 12–16	San Francisco	83	
1892, May 16–21	Lakewood, N.Y., Baltimore, Washington	260	
1893, July 13–22	Chicago	311	
1894, Sept. 17–22	Lake Placid, N.Y.	205	
1895, Aug. 13–21	Denver & Colorado Springs	147	
1896, Sept. 1–8	Cleveland	363	
1897, June 21–25	Philadelphia	315	
1897, July 13–16	London, England*	94	
1898, July 5–9	Lakewood, N.Y.	494	
1899, May 9–13	Atlanta	215	
1900, June 6–12	Montreal, Quebec	452	874
1901, July 3–10	Waukesha, Wis.	460	980
1902, June 14–20	Boston & Magnolia, Mass.	1,018	1,152
1903, June 22–27	Niagara Falls, N.Y.	684	1,200
1904, Oct. 17–22	St. Louis, Mo.	577	1,228
1905, July 4–8	Portland, Me.	359	1,253
1906, June 29–July 6	Narragansett Pier, R.I.	891	1,844
1907, May 23–29	Asheville, N.C.	478	1,808

* U.S. attendance.

Date	Place	Attendance	Membership
1908, June 22–27	Lake Minnetonka, Minn.	658	1,907
1909, June 28–July 3	Bretton Woods, N.H.	620	1,835
1910, June 30–July 6	Mackinac Island, Mich.	533	2,005
1910, Aug. 28–31	Brussels, Belgium*	46	
1911, May 18–24	Pasadena, Calif.	582	2,046
1912, June 26–July 2	Ottawa, Ontario	704	2,365
1913, June 23–28	Kaaterskill, N.Y.	892	2,563
1914, May 25–29	Washington, D.C.	1,366	2,905
1915, June 3–9	Berkeley, Calif.	779	3,024
1916, June 26–July 1	Asbury Park, N.J.	1,386	3,188
1917, June 21–27	Louisville, Ky.	824	3,346
1918, July 1 6	Saratoga Springs, N.Y.	620	3,380
1919, June 23–27	Asbury Park, N.J.	1,168	4,178
1920, June 2–7	Colorado Springs	553	4,464
1921, June 20–25	Swampscott, Mass.	1,899	5,307
1922, June 26–July 1	Detroit	1,839	5,684
1923, April 23–28	Hot Springs, Ark.	693	5,669
1924, June 30–July 5	Saratoga Springs, N.Y.	1,188	6,055
1925, July 6–11	Seattle, Wash.	1,066	6,745
1926, Oct. 4–9	Atlantic City, N.J.	2,224	8,848
1927, June 20–27	Toronto, Ontario	1,964	10,056
1927, Sept. 26–Oct. 1	Edinburgh, Scotland*	82	
1928, May 28–June 2	West Baden, Ind.	1,204	10,526
1929, May 13–18	Washington, D.C.	2,743	11,833
1929, June 15–30	Rome and Venice, Italy*	70	
1930, June 23–28	Los Angeles	2,023	12,713
1931, June 22–27	New Haven, Conn.	3,241	14,815
1932, April 25–30	New Orleans	1,306	13,021
1933, Oct. 16–21	Chicago	2,986	11,880
1934, June 25–30	Montreal, Quebec	1,904	11,731
1935, May 20–30	Madrid, Seville, & Barcelona, Spain*	42	
1935, June 24–29	Denver	1,503	12,241
1936, May 11–16	Richmond, Va.	2,834	13,057
1937, June 21–26	New York	5,312	14,204
1938, June 13–18	Kansas City, Mo.	1,900	14,626
1939, June 18–24	San Francisco	2,869	15,568
1940, May 26–June 1	Cincinnati	3,056	15,808
1941, June 19–25	Boston	4,266	16,015
1942, June 22–27	Milwaukee, Wis.	2,342	15,328
1943	[No meeting]		14,546
1944	[No meeting]		14,799
1945	[No meeting]		15,118
1946, June 16–22	Buffalo, N.Y.	2,327	15,800
1947, June 29–July 5	San Francisco	2,534	17,107
1948, June 13–19	Atlantic City, N.J.	3,752	18,283
1949:	Regional conferences [not recorded]		19,324
Aug. 22–25	(Far West) Vancouver, B.C.		
Sept. 2–5	(Trans-Miss.) Fort Collins, Colo.		

Date	Place	Attendance	Membership
Oct. 3–6	(Middle Atlantic) Atlantic City, N.J.		
Oct. 12–15	(New England) Swampscott, Mass.		
Oct. 26–29	(Southeastern) Miami Beach, Fla.		
Nov. 9–12	(Midwest) Grand Rapids, Mich.		
Nov. 20–23	(Southwestern) Fort Worth, Tex.		
1950, July 16–22	Cleveland	3,436	19,689
1951, July 8–14	Chicago	3,612	19,701
1952, June 29–July 5	New York	5,212	18,925
1953, June 21–27	Los Angeles	3,258	19,551
1954, June 20–26	Minneapolis	3,230	20,177
1955, July 3–9	Philadelphia	4,412	20,293
1956, June 17–23	Miami Beach, Fla.	2,866	20,285
1957, June 23–30	Kansas City, Mo.	2,953	20,326
1958, July 13–19	San Francisco	4,400	21,716
1959, June 21–27	Washington, D.C.	5,346	23,230
1960, June 19–24	Montreal, Quebec	4,648	24,690
1961, July 9–15	Cleveland	4,757	25,860
1962, June 17–23	Miami Beach, Fla.	3,527	24,879
1963, July 14–20	Chicago	5,753	25,502
1964, June 28–July 4	St. Louis	4,623	26,015
1965, July 3–10	Detroit	5,818	27,526
1966, July 10–16	New York	9,342	31,885
1967, June 25–July I	San Francisco	8,116	35,289
1968, June 23–29	Kansas City, Mo.	6,849	35,666
1969, June 22–28	Atlantic City, N.J.	10,399	36,865
1970, June 28–July 4	Detroit	8,965	30,394
1971, June 20–26	Dallas	8,087	29,740
1972, June 24–30	Chicago	9,700	29,610
1973, June 24–30	Las Vegas	8,539	30,172
1974, July 5–13	New York	14,382	34,010
1975, June 29–July 5	San Francisco	11,606	33,208
1976, July 18–24	Chicago (Centennial)	12,015	33,560
1977, June 17–23	Detroit	9,667	33,767
1978, June 25–30	Chicago	11,768	35,096
1979, June 24–30	Dallas	10,650	35,524
1980, June 29–July 4	New York	14,566	35,257
1981, June 26–July 2	San Francisco	12,555	37,954
1982, July 10–15	Philadelphia	12,819	38,050
1983, June 25–30	Los Angeles	11,005	38,862
1984, June 23–28	Dallas	11,443	39,290
1985, July 6–11	Chicago	14,160	40,761
1986, June 26–July 3	New York	16,530	42,361
1987, June 27–July 2	San Francisco	17,844	45,145
1988, July 9–14	New Orleans	16,530	47,249
1989, June 24–29	Dallas	17,592	49,483
1990, June 23–28	Chicago	19,982	50,509
1991, June 29–July 4	Atlanta	17,764	52,893
1992, June 25–July 2	San Francisco	19,261	54,735
1993, June 24–July 1	New Orleans	17,165	55,836

Date	Place	Attendance	Membership
1994, June 23–30	Miami Beach	12,627	55,356
1995, June 24–28	Chicago	19,146	56,444
1996, July 4–10	New York	18,027	56,688
1997, June 26–July 3	San Francisco	19,339	55,919
1998, June 25–July 1	Washington	24,884	55,573
1999, June 24–30	New Orleans	22,482	57,413

What will happen to you if you don't plan for Annual Conference

by Will Manley

A. YOU WILL WAIT 45 MINUTES in line at the coffee shop in your hotel for the privilege of paying $10 so that you can eat significantly over-cooked (or possibly undercooked) eggs for breakfast.

B. You will wait 20 minutes in line at the shuttle bus stop in front of your hotel for the privilege of cramming yourself into a hot, dirty bus with 75 other people to take a five-minute ride to the convention center.

C. You will wait 15 minutes in line at the hot dog stand outside the convention center for the privilege of paying $4 so that you can eat a significantly undercooked (or possibly overcooked) hot dog for your lunch.

D. You will spend two hours aimlessly wandering around the exhibit hall desperate to find someone you know who will be a decent dinner companion (i.e., someone who will not embarrass you by pulling out a calculator to figure out who owes what when the bill arrives).

E. You will finally latch on to a group of reference librarians you vaguely knew from a committee you once served on and go with them to Interstices, a trendy restaurant recommended by *Library Journal*, where you will find a line of 57 people, most of whom are holding Baker & Taylor shopping bags.

F. After waiting 45 minutes and progressing to 26th in line, you decide to bail out and grab a cab and head for the McDonald's located down the street from your hotel.

G. After waiting 20 minutes for a cab, you finally throw caution to the four winds and decide to walk. After all, you ask yourself, what's the difference between dying of hunger and being mugged?

H. After being followed for four blocks by a man with a scar on his right cheek, you duck into a hotel lobby where the desk clerk asks, "How many hours will you need a room?"

I. You get back into the street and are relieved to know that the man with the scar on his right cheek is gone, but 20 minutes later, guess what? You find yourself back in front of Interstices and, guess what? Your party of reference librarians is now first in line.

J. You nonchalantly rejoin them ("Goodness, it took forever to get into that bathroom") and five minutes later you're seated at a table next to another table where four people are talking about interlibrary-loan fill rates.

K. After waiting for 52 minutes, your meal, veal Oscar, arrives and it's overcooked, which you tolerate because you're so hungry that you'd eat it even if someone told you that what you are about to eat is a dog named Oscar. Also, the piece of meat they've given you is so small that whether it's undercooked or overcooked is completely academic.

L. Unfortunately not everyone in your party is as tolerant. Two of your dinner mates send their meals back. As a consequence, dinner takes an extra 45 minutes, and now you find yourself talking about interlibrary-loan fill rates.

M. It takes 27 minutes to get a taxi and at 11:00 you find yourself back in front of your hotel, but instead of going up to your room you walk down the street to the McDonald's to get some real food. It's closed.

N. On the way up to your room you run into Kim, who just has to buy you a drink and talk about old times.

O. After three drinks, Kim wanders off to the bathroom and never comes back.

P. The waitress comes up to you and says "Last call," and you say, "What the hey, how about a double vodka on the rocks."

Q. The bar tab ($57.23) arrives and you say, "What the hey, charge it to my room."

R. The guy at the piano starts playing "Stormy Weather" and it makes you cry because you realize you are not happy.

S. After everyone else in the lounge has left, you go around to each table and start emptying bowls of pretzels into your pockets.

T. You begin the long trek up to your room but on the way you stop at the front desk where you say, "I need a 7 a.m. wake-up call. I have a Social Responsibilities Round Table meeting at 8." The desk clerk says "okay" but looks at you like you're an alien.

U. You make it up to your room and instinctively turn on the television because you're lonely. The movie channel is on. It's that absorbing, frenetic, and awful thing about the life and death of Jim Morrison. Somehow you connect this madness to your own life and you sit on the edge of the bed eating pretzels and watching it for two hours. It is now 4 a.m.

V. While trying to make up your mind about whether or not to take a shower, you fall asleep.

W. At 7 a.m. the phone rings.

X. No problem about making that SRRT meeting. You're already dressed.

Y. You go down to the coffee shop and wait in line for 45 minutes for the privilege of paying $10 so that you can eat significantly overcooked (or possibly undercooked) eggs for breakfast.

Z. You wait 20 minutes in line at the shuttle bus stop for the privilege of cramming yourself into a hot, dirty bus with 75 other people to take a five-minute ride to the convention center.

SOURCE: © Will Manley, *The Manley Art of Librarianship* (Jefferson, N.C.: McFarland, 1993), pp. 154–56. Reprinted with permission.

MANY OPPORTUNITIES EXIST in the field of library and information science for its practitioners to obtain assistance for their research and to gain recognition for their achievements. The following list provides information on grants, scholarships, and awards given by ALA and other national associations. Not all of them can be applied for, although most have some procedure by which others can be nominated. Though 2000–2001 deadlines are given, most of these programs are ongoing.

The arrangement is topical under two major headings: **grants and scholarships** (money awarded for things you are going to do); and **awards** (honors and honoraria for things you have already done). Considered topically, this list can be also be viewed as a measure of what we value most in our profession.

Under grants and scholarships, the subheads are:

for education (pp. 149–53);
for programs (pp. 153–55); and
for publications, research, and travel (pp. 155–60).

Under awards, the subheads are:

for intellectual freedom (p. 160);
for professional achievement (pp. 161–65);
for publications and research (pp. 165–71);
for distinguished service (pp. 171–73);
for service to children and young adults (pp. 173–75);
for service to special populations (pp. 175–76);
for social responsibility (p. 176);
for special libraries (pp. 176–79);
for archives (pp. 179–80); and
for technology (pp. 180–81).

Grants and scholarships

For education

AALL Scholarships and Grants. Scholarships in support of library degrees for both law school graduates and non-law school graduates, minority stipends, and law degrees for library school graduates. *For more information:* American Association of Law Libraries, 53 W. Jackson Blvd., Suite 940, Chicago, IL 60604. *Deadline for applications:* April 1, 2001.

AJL Association of Jewish Libraries Scholarship. A $500 scholarship to a library school student who has taken Judaic/Hebraic courses. *For more information:* Association of Jewish Libraries, 15 E. 26th Street, Room 1034, New York, NY 10010. *Deadline for applications:* April 15, 2001.

ALA David H. Clift Scholarship. A $3,000 scholarship to an individual pursuing a master's degree in library science from an ALA-accredited program. *For more information:* ALA Office for Library Personnel Resources, 50 E. Huron St., Chicago, IL 60611-2795. *Deadline for applications:* April 1, 2001. *Previous winner:* Michael Lambert (1999).

ALA Marshall Cavendish Scholarship. A $3,000 scholarship to an individual pursuing a master's degree in library science from an ALA-accredited program. *For more* *information:* ALA Office for Library Personnel Resources, 50 E. Huron St., Chicago, IL 60611-2795. *Deadline for applications:* April 1, 2001. *Previous winner:* Michelle Simmons (1999).

ALA Mary V. Gaver Scholarship. A $3,000 scholarship to an individual specializing in youth services who is pursuing a master's degree in library science. *For more information:* ALA Office for Library Personnel Resources, 50 E. Huron St., Chicago, IL 60611-2795. *Deadline for applications:* April 1, 2001. *Previous winner:* Jennifer Lindsey (1999).

ALA Miriam L. Hornback Scholarship. A $3,000 award given to an ALA or library support staff person to support studies toward a master's degree in library and information studies. *For more information:* ALA Office for Library Personnel Resources, 50 E. Huron St., Chicago, IL 60611-2795. *Deadline for applications:* April 1, 2001. *Previous winner:* Deborah Robertson (1999).

ALA Spectrum Initiative Scholarships. Provides 50 annual scholarships of $5,000 each to minority students representing African-American, Asian-Pacific Islander, Latino/Hispanic, and Native American populations to encourage admission to graduation from an ALA recognized master's degree program in library and information studies. *For more information:* ALA Spectrum Initiative, 50 E. Huron St., Chicago, IL 60611-2795. *Deadline for applications:* April 1, 2001.

ALA Tom and Roberta Drewes Scholarship. Scholarship of $3,000 to a library support staff person currently working in a library, pursuing a master's degree in library science. *For more information:* ALA Office for Library Personnel Resources, 50 E. Huron St., Chicago, IL 60611-2795. *Deadline for applications:* April 1, 2001. *Previous winner:* Ami Chitwood (1999).

ALA Tony B. Leisner Scholarship. A $3,000 award to a library support staff person currently working in a library, pursuing a master's degree in library science. *For more information:* ALA Office for Library Personnel Resources, 50 E. Huron St., Chicago, IL 60611-2795. *Deadline for applications:* April 1, 2001. *Previous winner:* Sharon Bernard (1999).

ALA Women's National Book Association/Ann Heidbreder Eastman Grant. A $500–$1,000 grant for a librarian to take a course or participate in an institute devoted to aspects of publishing as a profession or to provide reimbursement for such study completed within the past year. *For more information:* ALA Awards, 50 E. Huron St., Chicago, IL 60611-2795. *Deadline for applications:* December 1, 2000. *Previous winner:* Carolyn Gutierrez (1998).

ALA/AASL Information Plus Continuing Education Scholarship. A $500 scholarship awarded to a school library media specialist, supervisor, or educator for attendance at an ALA or AASL continuing education event. *For more information:* ALA American Association of School Librarians, 50 E. Huron St., Chicago, IL 60611-2795. *Deadline for applications:* February 1, 2001. *Previous winner:* Betty K. Brackin (1999).

ALA/AASL School Librarians' Workshop Scholarship. A scholarship of $2,500 to a full-time student preparing to become a school library media specialist at the preschool, elementary, or secondary level. *For more information:* ALA American Association of School Librarians, 50 E. Huron St., Chicago, IL 60611-2795. *Deadline for applications:* February 1, 2001. *Previous winner:* Marie Granthe (1999).

ALA/ACRL Doctoral Dissertation Fellowship. An annual award of $1,500 presented to assist a doctoral student in academic librarianship whose research has a potential significance in the field. *For more information:* ALA Association of College and Research Libraries, 50 E. Huron St., Chicago, IL 60611-2795. *Deadline for applications:* December 1, 2000. *Previous winner:* Alenka Sauperl (1999).

ALA/ALSC Bound to Stay Bound Books Scholarship. Two $6,000 awards to assist individuals who wish to work in the field of library service to children. *For more information:* ALA Association for Library Service to Children, 50 E. Huron St., Chicago, IL 60611-2795. *Deadline for applications:* March 1, 2000. *Previous winners:* Lisa Marie Gilgenbach, Helen M. Moore (1998).

ALA/ALSC Frederic G. Melcher Scholarships. Two annual $6,000 scholarships established to encourage and assist people who wish to enter the field of library service to children. *For more information:* ALA Association for Library Service to Children, 50 E. Huron St., Chicago, IL 60611-2795. *Deadline for applications:* March 1, 2000. *Previous winners:* Karla Schmit-Benedict, Lisa Lintner-Sizemore (1998).

ALA/ERT Christopher J. Hoy Scholarship. A $3,000 award to an individual pursuing a master's degree in library science. *For more information:* ALA Office for Library Personnel Resources, 50 E. Huron St., Chicago, IL 60611-2795. *Deadline for applications:* April 1, 2001. *Previous winner:* Holly Wissink (1999).

ALA/GODORT David Rozkuszka Scholarship. A $3,000 award for financial assistance to an individual currently working with government documents in a library and working on a master's degree in library science. *For more information:* ALA Government Documents Round Table, 50 E. Huron St., Chicago, IL 60611-2795. *Deadline for applications:* December 1, 2000. *Previous winner:* Amanda Wakaruk (1999).

ALA/LITA Christian (Chris) Larew Memorial Scholarship. A $3,000 scholarship for qualified persons who plan to follow a career in library and information technology, and who demonstrate academic excellence, leadership, and vision. *For more information:* ALA Library and Information Technology Association, 50 E. Huron St., Chicago, IL 60611-2795. *Deadline for applications:* April 1, 2001. *Previous winner:* Avi Janssen (1999).

ALA/LITA GEAC Scholarship in Library and Information Technology. A $2,500 scholarship for qualified persons who plan to follow a career in automated systems in libraries, and who demonstrate a strong commitment to their use. *For more information:* ALA Library and Information Technology Association, 50 E. Huron St., Chicago, IL 60611-2795. *Deadline for applications:* April 1, 2001. *Previous winner:* Clinton Chamberlain (1999).

ALA/LITA Library Systems and Services Minority Scholarship in Library and Information Technology. A $2,500 scholarship for qualified persons who plan to follow a career in library automation, who demonstrate a strong commitment to their use, and who are members of a principal minority group. *For more information:* ALA Library and Information Technology Association, 50 E. Huron St., Chicago, IL 60611-2795. *Deadline for applications:* April 1, 2001. *Previous winner:* Ting Yin (1999).

ALA/LITA OCLC Minority Scholarship in Library and Information Technology. A $2,500 scholarship for qualified persons who plan to follow a career in library automation, who demonstrate a strong commitment to their use, and who are members of a principal minority group. *For more information:* ALA Library and Information Technology Association, 50 E. Huron St., Chicago, IL 60611-2795. *Deadline for applications:* April 1, 2001. *Previous winner:* Carrie Hurst (1999).

ALA/NMRT Ebsco Scholarship. A cash award of $1,000 for the following academic year. Applicants must enroll in an ALA-accredited library school and plan to begin graduate studies the following fall. *For more information:* ALA New Members Round Table, 50 E. Huron St., Chicago, IL 60611-2795. *Deadline for applications:* December 1, 2000. *Previous winner:* Caitlin B Augusta (1999)

ALISE Doctoral Students' Dissertation Awards. Up to two awards in the amount of $400 to defray travel expenses, conference registration, and personal ALISE membership for one year. *For more information:* Association for Library and Information Science Education, P.O. Box 7640, Arlington, VA 22207. *Deadline for applications:* July 1, 2000. *Previous winner:* Hong Xie (1999).

ASIS ISI Information Science Doctoral Dissertation Proposal Scholarship. An award of $1,500 to foster research in information science by assisting doctoral students in the field with their dissertation research. *For more information:* American Society for Information Science, 8720 Georgia Avenue, Suite 501, Silver Spring, MD 20910. *Deadline for applications:* July 1, 2000. *Previous winner:* Karla Hahn (1998).

BCALA E. J. Josey Scholarship Award. Two unrestricted grants of $2,000 awarded annually to African American students enrolled in or accepted by ALA-accredited programs. Applicants are judged on the basis of application essays of 1,000 to 1,200 words discussing issues, problems, or challenges facing library service to minority populations such as African Americans. *For more information:* Black Caucus of the ALA, c/o Office for Literacy and Outreach Services, 50 E. Huron St., Chicago, IL 60611-2795. *Previous winners:* Danielle M. Green, Roland Lemonius, Patricia M. Richard (1998).

Beta Phi Mu Blanche E. Woolls Scholarship. Award of $1,000 to a student beginning library and information studies at an ALA-accredited school with the intention of pursuing a career in school library media service. *For more information:* Beta Phi Mu, Florida State University SIS, Tallahassee, FL 32306-2100. *Deadline for applications:* March 15, 2001. *Previous winner:* Diana L. Saylor-Evans (1998).

Beta Phi Mu Doctoral Dissertation Scholarship. For doctoral students who have completed their coursework, this $1,500 award offers funding to complete the degree. *For more information:* Beta Phi Mu, Florida State University SIS, Tallahassee, FL 32306-2100. *Deadline for applications:* March 15, 2001.

Beta Phi Mu Eugene Garfield Doctoral Dissertation Fellowship. Six awards of $500 to library and information science students working on doctoral dissertations. *For more information:* Beta Phi Mu, Florida State University SIS, Tallahassee, FL 32306-2100. *Deadline for applications:* June 1, 2001.

Beta Phi Mu Frank B. Sessa Scholarship. Award of $750 for continuing education of a Beta Phi Mu member. *For more information:* Beta Phi Mu, Florida State University SIS, Tallahassee, FL 32306-2100. *Deadline for applications:* March 15, 2001.

Beta Phi Mu Harold Lancour Scholarship. Award of $1,000 for graduate study in a foreign country related to the applicant's work or schooling. *For more information:* Beta Phi Mu, Florida State University SIS, Tallahassee, FL 32306-2100. *Deadline for applications:* March 15, 2001. *Previous winner:* Loss Pequeno Glazier.

Beta Phi Mu Sarah Rebecca Reed Scholarship. Award of $1,500 for study at an ALA-accredited library school. *For more information:* Beta Phi Mu, Florida State University SIS, Tallahassee, FL 32306-2100. *Deadline for applications:* March 15, 2001. *Previous winner:* Ann Hemmens (1998).

CALA Sheila Suen Lai Scholarship. An award of $500 for students of Chinese heritage in a doctoral program in library and information science. *For more information:* Chinese American Librarians Association, Ling Hwey Jeng, lhjeng00@ukcc.uky.edu. *Deadline for applications:* March 1, 2001. *Previous winner:* Jin Zhang (1999).

CLA Dafoe Scholarship. An award of $1,750 (Can.) for a Canadian citizen or landed immigrant to attend an accredited Canadian library school. *For more information:* Canadian Library Association, 200 Elgin St., Ottawa, Ontario K2P 1L5, Canada. *Deadline for applications:* May 1, 2001. *Previous winner:* Theresa Yun Hee Lee (1999).

CLA H. W. Wilson Company Scholarship. An award of $2,000 (Can.) for a Canadian citizen or landed immigrant to pursue studies at an accredited Canadian library school. *For more information:* Canadian Library Association, 200 Elgin St., Ottawa, Ontario K2P 1L5, Canada. *Deadline for applications:* May 1, 2001. *Previous winner:* Claire Lauzon (1999).

CLA Howard V. Phalin–World Book Graduate Scholarship in Library Science. An award of $2,500 (Can.) for a Canadian citizen or landed immigrant to pursue studies at an accredited Canadian library school. *For more information:* Canadian Library Association, 200 Elgin St., Ottawa, Ontario K2P 1L5, Canada. *Deadline for applications:* May 1, 2001. *Previous winner:* Paulette Rothbauer (1999).

CLA Rev. Andrew L. Bouwhuis Scholarship. A $1,500 scholarship for graduate study toward a master's degree in library science. *For more information:* Catholic Library Association, 100 North St., Suite 224, Pittsfield, MA 01201-5109. *Previous winner:* Caitlin B. Augusta (1999).

CLA World Book Award. A $1,500 grant for up to three CLA members to attend continuing education in school or children's librarianship. *For more information:* Catholic Library Association, 100 North St., Suite 224, Pittsfield, MA 01201-5109. *Previous winner:* Chrys Rudnik (1999).

MLA Continuing Education Grants. Awards of $100–$500 to develop MLA members' knowledge of the theoretical, administrative, or technical aspects of librarianship. *For more information:* Medical Library Association, 65 East Wacker Place, Suite 1900, Chicago, IL 60601-7298. *Deadline for applications:* December 1, 2000. *Previous winner:* Katherine J. Vargo (1998).

MLA ISI Doctoral Fellowship. A fellowship given every two years in the amount of $2,000 to encourage superior students to conduct doctoral work in an area of health sciences librarianship or information sciences and to provide support to individuals who have been admitted to candidacy. *For more information:* Medical Library Association, 65 East Wacker Place, Suite 1900, Chicago, IL 60601-7298. *Deadline for applications:* December 1, 2000. *Previous winner:* Sharon Dezel Jenkins (1998).

MLA Scholarship. A scholarship in the amount of $2,000 for a student who is entering an ALA-accredited library school. *For more information:* Medical Library Association, 65 East Wacker Place, Suite 1900, Chicago, IL 60601-7298. *Deadline for applications:* December 1, 2000. *Previous winner:* Cynthia Lynn Ammons (1999).

MLA Scholarship for Minority Students. A scholarship in the amount of $2,000 for a minority student who is entering an ALA-accredited library school. *For more information:* Medical Library Association, 65 East Wacker Place, Suite 1900, Chicago, IL 60601-7298. *Deadline for applications:* December 1, 2000. *Previous winner:* Tomeka Oubichon (1999).

NASIG Fritz Schwartz Serials Education Scholarship. A $2,500 scholarship to a library science graduate student who demonstrates excellence in scholarship and the potential for accomplishment in a serials career. *For more information:* North American Serials Interest Group, info@nasig.org. *Deadline for applications:* February 16, 2001.

NASIG Student Grants. Encourage participation at NASIG conferences by funding students enrolled in an ALA-accredited school who are interested in pursuing some aspect of serials work upon completion of their professional degrees. *For more information:* North American Serials Interest Group, info@nasig.org. *Deadline for applications:* February 16, 2001.

SLA Affirmative Action Scholarship. One $6,000 grant to a minority student for graduate study in librarianship leading to a master's degree at a recognized school of library or information science. *For more information:* Special Libraries Association, 1700 Eighteenth Street, N.W., Washington, DC 20009. *Deadline for applications:* October 31, 2000. *Previous winner:* Salvador Covarrubias (1999).

SLA ISI Scholarship. A $1,000 grant for beginning graduate study leading to a Ph.D. from a recognized program in library science, information science, or related fields of study. *For more information:* Special Libraries Association, 1700 Eighteenth Street, N.W., Washington, DC 20009. *Deadline for applications:* October 31, 2000.

SLA Mary Adeline Connor Professional Development Scholarship. One or more scholarships, not to exceed $6,000 in total, granted for post-MLS certificate or degree programs in any subject area, technological skill, or managerial expertise relevant to the applicant's career needs and goals in special librarianship. *For more information:* Special Libraries Association, 1700 Eighteenth Street, N.W., Washington, DC 20009. *Deadline for applications:* October 31, 2000.

SLA Plenum Scholarship. A $1,000 grant for beginning graduate study leading to a Ph.D. from a recognized program in library science, information science, or related fields of study. *For more information:* Special Libraries Association, 1700 Eighteenth Street, N.W., Washington, DC 20009. *Deadline for applications:* October 31, 2000.

SLA Scholarships. Up to three $6,000 grants for graduate study in librarianship leading to a master's degree at a recognized school of library or information science. *For more information:* Special Libraries Association, 1700 Eighteenth Street, N.W., Washington, DC 20009. *Deadline for applications:* October 31, 2000. *Previous winners:* Kim Herzig, Felicia Fay Pope, Ken Randles (1999).

For programs

ALA Grolier National Library Week Grant. A $4,000 grant awarded to a library or library association for the best proposal for a local or statewide public awareness campaign that supports the theme and goals of National Library Week. *For more information:* ALA Public Information Office, 50 East Huron St., Chicago, IL 60611-2795. *Deadline for applications:* October 15, 2000. *Previous winner:* Detroit Public Library (1999).

ALA H. W. Wilson Library Staff Development Grant. $3,500 and 24k gold-framed citation to a library organization for a program to further its staff development goals and objectives. *For more information:* ALA Awards, 50 E. Huron St., Chicago, IL

60611-2795. *Deadline for applications:* December 1, 2000. *Previous winner:* Topeka and Shawnee County (Kan.) Public Library (1999).

ALA Loleta D. Fyan Public Library Research Grant. One or more grants up to $10,000 to a library, library school, association, unit or chapter of ALA, or an individual for the development and improvement of public libraries and the services they provide. *For more information:* ALA Office of Research and Statistics, 50 E. Huron St., Chicago, IL 60611-2795. *Deadline for applications:* December 15, 2000. *Previous winners:* Dean K. Jue, Christine M. Koontz (1999).

ALA SIRSI Leader in Library Technology Grant. A $10,000 grant to a library for a project that makes creative or groundbreaking use of technology to deliver exceptional services to its community. *For more information:* ALA Awards, 50 E. Huron St., Chicago, IL 60611-2795. *Deadline for applications:* December 1, 2000.

ALA World Book–ALA Goal Award. An award of $10,000 to ALA units for the advancement of public, academic, or school library service and librarianship through support of programs that implement the goals and priorities of ALA. *For more information:* ALA Awards, 50 E. Huron St., Chicago, IL 60611-2795. *Deadline for applications:* March 1, 2001. *Previous winners:* "Stop Talking and Start Doing! Recruitment of People of Color to Librarianship" (ALA Chapter Relations Committee and Florida Library Association) (1999).

ALA/AASL ABC-Clio Leadership Grant. Up to $1,750 for planning and implementing leadership programs at the state, regional, or local level to be given to school library associations that are affiliates of AASL. *For more information:* ALA American Association of School Librarians, 50 E. Huron St., Chicago, IL 60611-2795. *Deadline for applications:* Feb. 1, 2001. *Previous winner:* Hawaii Association of School Librarians (1999).

ALA/ALSC Book Wholesalers Summer Reading Program Grant. A grant of $3,000 to an ALSC member to implement an outstanding public library summer reading program for children. *For more information:* ALA Association for Library Service to Children, 50 E. Huron St., Chicago, IL 60611-2795. *Deadline for applications:* December 1, 2000. *Previous winner:* Karen M. Allen (1999).

ALA/ALSC May Hill Arbuthnot Lecture. An invitation to an individual of distinction to prepare and present a paper that will be a significant contribution to the field of children's literature and subsequently to be published in *Journal of Youth Services in Libraries. For more information:* ALA Association for Library Service to Children, 50 E. Huron St., Chicago, IL 60611-2795. *Deadline for applications:* May 15, 2000. *Previous winner:* Hazel Rochman (2000).

ALA/LAMA Cultural Diversity Grant. Up to $1,000 to support the creation and dissemination of resources that will assist library administrators in developing a vision and commitment to diversity. *For more information:* ALA Library Administration and Management Association, 50 E. Huron St., Chicago, IL 60611-2795. *Deadline for applications:* December 1, 2000. *Previous winner:* Fullerton (Calif.) Public Library (1999).

ALA/PLA Demco Creative Merchandising Grant. Provides cash and supplies to a public library proposing a project for the creative display and merchandising of materials either in the library or in the community. The grant consists of $1,000 cash and $2,000 worth of display furniture or supplies ordered through Demco, Inc. in conjunction with the grant project. *For more information:* ALA Public Library Association, 50 E. Huron St., Chicago, IL 60611-2795. *Deadline for applications:* December 1, 2000. *Previous winner:* Middle Country (N.Y.) Public Library (1999).

ALA/PLA NTC/Contemporary Publishing Career Materials Resource Grant. Provides cash and supplies to a public library proposing a project for the development of a career resources collection and program for a target audience either in the library or in the community. The grant consists of $500 cash and $2,000 worth of materials ordered from the NTC/Contemporary Publishing in conjunction with the grant project. *For more information:* ALA Public Library Association, 50 E. Huron St., Chicago, IL 60611-2795. *Deadline for applications:* December 1, 2000. *Previous winner:* Carnegie Library of Homestead, Pa. (1999).

ALA/RUSA Facts on File Grant. A $2,000 grant given to a library for imaginative programming that makes current affairs more meaningful to an adult audience. *For more information:* ALA Reference and User Services Association, 50 E. Huron St.,

Chicago, IL 60611-2795. *Deadline for applications:* December 15, 2000. *Previous winner:* New Mexico State University Library, Las Cruces (1999).

ALA/YALSA Book Wholesalers Collection Development Grant. Up to two $1,000 grants for collection development materials to YALSA members who represent a public library and work directly with young adults. *For more information:* ALA Young Adult Library Services Association, 50 E. Huron St., Chicago, IL 60611-2795. *Deadline for applications:* December 1, 2000. *Previous winners:* Elizabeth S. Gallaway, Karen Hultz (1999).

ALA/YALSA Frances Henne Voice of Youth Advocates Research Grant. An annual grant of $500 to provide seed money to an individual, institution, or group for small-scale projects to encourage research on library service to young adults. *For more information:* ALA Young Adult Library Services Association, 50 E. Huron St., Chicago, IL 60611-2795. *Deadline for applications:* December 1, 2000. *Previous winners:* Sheila B. Anderson and John P. Bradford (1999).

IAMSLIC Grants. Supports projects related to the recording, retrieval, and dissemination of knowledge and information in all aspects of aquatic and marine science and their allied disciplines through small grants ($200–$2,000) to IAMSLIC regional groups and members. *For more information:* International Association of Aquatic and Marine Science Libraries and Information Centers, Kristen L. Metzger, Librarian, Harbor Branch Oceanographic Institution, 5600 U.S. 1 North, Ft. Pierce, FL 34946. *Deadline for applications:* March 30, 2001. *Previous winner:* SAIL Regional Group.

MLA Janet Doe Lectureship. $250 awarded for a unique perspective on the history or philosophy of medical librarianship. The selected lecture is presented at the MLA annual meeting and published in the *Bulletin of the Medical Library Association. For more information.* Medical Library Association, 65 East Wacker Place, Suite 1900, Chicago, IL 60601-7298. *Deadline for applications:* November 1, 2000. *Previous winner:* Sherrilynne Fuller (1999).

MLA John P. McGovern Award Lectureship. For a significant national or international figure to speak on a topic of importance to health science librarianship at the MLA annual meeting. *For more information:* Medical Library Association, 65 East Wacker Place, Suite 1900, Chicago, IL 60601-7298. *Previous winners:* Laurie Garrett, Kenneth M. Ludmerer (1998).

MLA NLM Joseph Leiter Lectureship. For a lecture on biomedical communications. *For more information:* Medical Library Association, 65 East Wacker Place, Suite 1900, Chicago, IL 60601-7298. *Previous winner:* Jean-Claude Guedon (1998).

For publications, research, and travel

AALL Grants. To cover registration costs at association-sponsored educational activities. *For more information:* American Association of Law Libraries, 53 W. Jackson Blvd., Suite 940, Chicago, IL 60604. *Deadline for applications:* April 1, 2001.

AJL Doris Ornstein Memorial Award. Awards to new members who are planning to attend their first AJL conference. *For more information:* Association of Jewish Libraries, 15 E. 26th Street, Room 1034, New York, NY 10010.

AJL Travel Stipend. To subsidize the cost of attending the AJL conference. *For more information:* Association of Jewish Libraries, 15 E. 26th Street, Room 1034, New York, NY 10010.

ALA Bogle International Library Travel Fund. A $500 award to assist ALA members to attend their first international library conference. *For more information:* ALA International Relations Office, 50 E. Huron St., Chicago, IL 60611-2795. *Deadline for applications:* January 1, 2001. *Previous winner:* Wendy Miller (1999).

ALA Carroll Preston Baber Research Grant. Up to $7,500 for innovative research that could lead to an improvement in library services to any specified group(s) of people. *For more information:* ALA Library and Research Center, 50 E. Huron St., Chicago, IL 60611-2795. *Deadline for applications:* December 15, 2000. *Previous winner:* Lynn Westbrook (1997).

ALA Ebsco Conference Sponsorship. Ten awards allowing librarians to attend ALA Annual Conference. An essay of no more than 250 words addressing, "How will attending this ALA Conference contribute to your professional development?" is required. *For more information:* ALA Awards, 50 E. Huron St., Chicago, IL 60611-2795. *Deadline for applications:* December 1, 2000. *Previous winners:* Jenifer Weil Arns, Jenna Freedman, Dorothy Glew, Alice B. Haldeman, Dona J. Helmer, Leslie Lomers, Muzhgan Nazarova, Gay Helen Perkins, Leroy D. Smith, Holly Williams (1999).

ALA/AASL Frances Henne Award. A grant of $1,250 to a school library media specialist with less than 5 years in the profession, to attend an AASL national conference or ALA Conference for the first time. *For more information:* ALA American Association of School Librarians, 50 E. Huron St., Chicago, IL 60611-2795. *Deadline for applications:* February 1, 2001. *Previous winner:* Marsha Trentham Hunter (1999).

ALA/AASL Highsmith Research Grant. Two grants totaling $5,000 to conduct innovative research aimed at measuring and evaluating the impact of school library media programs on learning and education. *For more information:* ALA American Association of School Librarians, 50 E. Huron St., Chicago, IL 60611-2795. *Deadline for applications:* February 1, 2001. *Previous winners:* Violet H. Harada, Claire Sato, Joan Yoshima (1999).

ALA/ACRL Samuel Lazerow Fellowship for Research in Acquisitions or Technical Services. An annual award of $1,000 to foster advances in acquisitions or technical services by providing librarians a fellowship for travel or writing in those fields. *For more information:* ALA Association of College and Research Libraries, 50 E. Huron St., Chicago, IL 60611-2795. *Deadline for applications:* December 1, 2000. *Previous winner:* Dilys E. Morris (1998).

ALA/ACRL WESS Martinus Nijhoff International West European Specialist Study Grant. An annual grant for an ALA member to study some aspect of Western European studies, librarianship, or the book trade. The grant covers air travel to and from Europe, transportation in Europe, and lodging and board for no more than 14 consecutive days. A maximum amount of 10,000 Dutch guilders is awarded. *For more information:* ALA Association of College and Research Libraries, 50 E. Huron St., Chicago, IL 60611-2795. *Deadline for applications:* December 1, 2000. *Previous winner:* Richard Hacken (1999).

ALA/ALCTS Serial Section First Step Award/Wiley Professional Development Grant. A $1,000 award to provide librarians new to the serials field to attend an ALA Annual Conference for the first time. *For more information:* ALA Association for Library Collections and Technical Services, 50 E. Huron St., Chicago, IL 60611-2795. *Deadline for applications:* December 1, 2000. *Previous winner:* Charity K. Stokes (1999).

ALA/ALSC Louise Seaman Bechtel Fellowship Award. Three grants of $3,750 each for ALSC members with 12 or more years professional work in children's library collections, to read and study at the Baldwin Library/George Smathers Libraries, University of Florida. *For more information:* ALA Association for Library Service to Children, 50 E. Huron St., Chicago, IL 60611-2795. *Deadline for applications:* December 31, 2000. *Previous winner:* Julia Massie (1999).

ALA/ALSC Penguin Putnam Books for Young Readers Awards. $600 awards to children's librarians in school or public libraries with 10 or fewer years of experience to attend ALA Annual Conference. *For more information:* ALA Association for Library Service to Children, 50 E. Huron St., Chicago, IL 60611-2795. *Deadline for applications:* December 1, 2000. *Previous winners:* Deborah J. DeVita, Virginia Hoover, Mary Jo Peltier, Susan Seitner (1999).

ALA/ALTA Gale Outstanding Trustee Conference Grant. Two awards of $750 each, to ALTA members currently serving on a local public library board, for first attendance at an ALA Annual Conference. *For more information:* ALA Association of Library Trustees and Advocates, 50 E. Huron St., Chicago, IL 60611-2795. *Deadline for applications:* December 1, 2001. *Previous winner:* Joseph M. Mueller (1999).

ALA/ASCLA Research Grant. A citation and a $1,000 research stipend given to stimulate researchers to look at such areas as state library services, interlibrary cooperation, networking, and services to special populations as valid areas of research interest. *For more information:* ALA Association of Specialized and Cooperative Library Agencies, 50 E. Huron St., Chicago, IL 60611-2795. *Deadline for applications:* December 15, 2000. *Previous winner:* Nancy Everhart (1998).

3

ALA/FLRT Adelaide del Frate Conference Sponsorship. For attendance at ALA Annual Conference, to encourage library school students to become familiar with federal librarianship and ultimately seek work in federal libraries. *For more information:* ALA Federal Librarians Round Table, Washington Office, 1301 Pennsylvania Avenue, N.W., Suite 403, Washington, DC 20004-1701. *Deadline for applications:* December 15, 2000. *Previous winner:* Charlotte Houtchens (1999).

ALA/GODORT Readex Catharine J. Reynolds Grant. A grant of $2,000 to document's librarians for travel and/or study in the field of documents librarianship. *For more information:* ALA Government Documents Round Table, 50 E. Huron St., Chicago, IL 60611-2795. *Deadline for applications:* December 1, 2000. *Previous winner:* Melissa Lamont (1997).

ALA/LAMA Yankee Book Peddler Student Writing and Development Award. A travel grant of up to $1,000 to attend an ALA Annual Conference to honor the best article on a topic in the area of library administration and management written by a student enrolled in a library and information studies graduate program. *For more information:* ALA Library Administration and Management Association, 50 E. Huron St., Chicago, IL 60611-2795. *Deadline for applications:* March 31, 2001. *Previous winner:* Barbara J. Kemmis (1998).

ALA/NMRT 3M Professional Development Grant. A cash award to attend ALA Conference for NMRT members to encourage professional development and participation in national ALA and NMRT activities. *For more information:* ALA New Members Round Table. *Deadline for applications:* December 15, 2000. *Previous winners:* Janet Foster, Margaret Hughes, Janella Zauha (1999).

ALA/NMRT Shirley Olofson Memorial Award. A $500 award to an NMRT member to help defray costs of attending ALA Annual Conference. *For more information:* ALA New Members Round Table, 50 E. Huron St., Chicago, IL 60611-2795. *Deadline for applications:* December 15, 2000. *Previous winner:* Marilyn W. Tsirigotis (1999).

ALA/PLA New Leaders Travel Grant. Awards of up to $1,500 each, designed to enhance professional development and improve the expertise of public librarians new to the field by making possible their attendance at major professional development activities. *For more information:* ALA Public Library Association, 50 E. Huron St., Chicago, IL 60611-2795. *Deadline for applications:* December 1, 2000. *Previous winners:* Jeffrey Gifford, Leah Sparks (1999).

ALA/RUSA Disclosure Student Travel Award. An annual travel award of $1,000 that will enable a student enrolled in an ALA accredited master's degree program to attend ALA conference, including a one-year membership in the Business Reference and Services Section. *For more information:* ALA Reference and User Services Association, 50 E. Huron St., Chicago, IL 60611-2795. *Deadline for applications:* December 15, 2000. *Previous winner:* Christina Mehta Prendiville (1999).

ALA/YALSA Baker & Taylor Conference Grants. Two annual grants of $1,000 each awarded to young adult librarians in public or school libraries to attend an ALA Annual Conference for the first time. *For more information:* ALA Young Adult Library Services Association, 50 E. Huron St., Chicago, IL 60611-2795. *Deadline for applications:* December 1, 2000. *Previous winners:* Reed Williams and Patricia McHugh (1999).

ALISE Research Grant Awards. One or more grants totaling $5,000 to support research broadly related to education for library and information science. *For more information:* Association for Library and Information Science Education, P.O. Box 7640, Arlington, VA 22207. *Deadline for applications:* September 15, 2000. *Previous winners:* Karen E. Pettigrew, Lynne McKechnie, Christopher Brown-Syed (1999).

ARLIS/NA Andrew Cahan Photography Award. An award of $500 for information professionals in the field of photography to attend the ARLIS/NA conference. *For more information:* Art Libraries Society of North America, 4104 Lake Boone Trail, Suite 201, Raleigh, NC 27607-7506. *Deadline for applications:* November 17, 2000. *Previous winner:* Barbara Mathé (1999).

ARLIS/NA David Mirvish Books/Books on Art Award. An award of $500 (Can.) for a Canadian library professional to attend ARLIS/NA conference. *For more information:* Art Libraries Society of North America, 4104 Lake Boone Trail, Suite 201, Raleigh, NC 27607-7506. *Deadline for applications:* November 17, 2000. *Previous winner:* Andrea Retfalvi (1999).

ARLIS/NA G. K. Hall Conference Attendance Award. An award of $500 for committee members, chapter officers, and moderators to attend the ARLIS/NA conference. *For more information:* Art Libraries Society of North America, 4104 Lake Boone Trail, Suite 201, Raleigh, NC 27607-7506. *Deadline for applications:* November 17, 2000. *Previous winner:* Susan Wyngaard (1999).

ARLIS/NA Howard and Beverly Joy Karno Award. An award of $1,000 for art librarians in Latin America to attend the ARLIS/NA conference. *For more information:* Art Libraries Society of North America, 4104 Lake Boone Trail, Suite 201, Raleigh, NC 27607-7506. *Deadline for applications:* November 17, 2000. *Previous winner:* Carlos Acuna Ramos (1999).

ARLIS/NA H. W. Wilson Foundation Research Award. Up to $2,000 to support research activities by ARLIS/NA members in the fields of librarianship, visual resources curatorship, and the arts. *For more information:* Art Libraries Society of North America, 4104 Lake Boone Trail, Suite 201, Raleigh, NC 27607-7506. *Deadline for applications:* October 1, 2000. *Previous winner:* Claire Hills-Nova (1999).

ARLIS/NA Puvill Libros Award. An award of $1,000 for art librarians in Europe to attend the ARLIS/NA conference. *For more information:* Art Libraries Society of North America, 4104 Lake Boone Trail, Suite 201, Raleigh, NC 27607-7506. *Deadline for applications:* November 17, 2000. *Previous winner:* Anja Lollesgaard (1999).

ARLIS/NA Research Libraries Group Award. An award of $1,000 to help finance attendance at the ARLIS/NA conference for someone who has never attended. *For more information:* Art Libraries Society of North America, 4104 Lake Boone Trail, Suite 201, Raleigh, NC 27607-7506. *Deadline for applications:* November 17, 2000. *Previous winner:* Mikel Breitenstein (1999).

ASIS ISI Citation Analysis Research Grant. An award of $3,000 to support research based on citation analysis. *For more information:* American Society for Information Science, 8720 Georgia Avenue, Suite 501, Silver Spring, MD 20910. *Deadline for applications:* June 1, 2001. *Previous winner:* David Dubin (1998).

ASIS UMI Doctoral Dissertation Award. An award of $1,000 and up to $500 in travel support to recognize outstanding recent doctoral candidates whose research contributes significantly to an understanding of some aspect of information science. The award provides a forum for presenting their research and assists them with some travel support. *For more information:* American Society for Information Science, 8720 Georgia Avenue, Suite 501, Silver Spring, MD 20910. *Deadline for applications:* June 1, 2001. *Previous winner:* Tomas A. Lipinski (1998).

BSA Fellowships. A stipend of up to $1,500 per month (for up to two months) in support of travel, living, and research expenses to support bibliographical inquiry as well as research in the history of the book trades and in publishing history. *For more information:* Bibliographical Society of America, P.O. Box 1537, Lenox Hill Station, New York, NY 10021. *Deadline for applications:* December 1, 2000.

CALA C. C. Seetoo Travel Scholarship. A $500 award for students of Chinese heritage in a graduate program in library and information science to provide mentoring and networking opportunities at ALA Annual Conference. *For more information:* Chinese American Librarians Association, Ling Hwey Jeng, lhjeng00@ukcc.uky.edu. *Deadline for applications:* March 1, 2001. *Previous winner:* Janet Tom (1999).

CLA Research and Development Grants. One or more grants totaling $1,000 awarded annually to personal members of the Canadian Library Association, in support of theoretical and applied research in library and information science. *For more information:* Canadian Library Association, 200 Elgin St., Ottawa, Ontario K2P 1L5, Canada. *Deadline for applications:* April 30, 2001. *Previous winner:* Judith Saltman (1998).

IASL Jean E. Lowrie Leadership Development Grant. $1,000 and conference fees for school librarians in developing countries to attend an IASL conference. *For more information:* International Association of School Librarianship, Suite 300, Box 34069, Seattle, WA 98124-1069. *Deadline for applications:* March 1, 2001. *Previous winner:* Suzie Gamba (1998).

IASL Takeshi Murofushi Research Award. A maximum of $1,000 to encourage research in school librarianship. *For more information:* International Association of School Librarianship, Suite 300, Box 34069, Seattle, WA 98124-1069. *Deadline for applications:* March 1, 2001. *Previous winner:* Joy McGregor (1998).

MLA Cunningham Memorial International Fellowship. A four-month fellowship for health sciences librarians from countries outside the United States and Canada. The award, which provides for observation and supervised work in one or more medical libraries in the United States or Canada, is in the amount of $6,000, with up to $2,000 additional for travel within these two countries. *For more information:* Medical Library Association, 65 East Wacker Place, Suite 1900, Chicago, IL 60601-7298. *Deadline for applications:* December 1, 2000. *Previous winner:* Timothy Shola Abolarinwa, Nigeria (1999).

MLA Ebsco Annual Meeting Grant. Awards of up to $1,000 for travel and conference-related expenses to two health science librarians to attend the MLA meeting. *For more information:* Medical Library Association, 65 East Wacker Place, Suite 1900, Chicago, IL 60601-7298. *Deadline for applications:* December 1, 2000. *Previous winner:* Shirley Brooke (1999).

MLA Research, Development, and Demonstration Projects Grants. To provide support for projects that will help to promote excellence in the field of health sciences librarianship and information sciences. Grants range from $100 to $1000. *For more information:* Medical Library Association, 65 East Wacker Place, Suite 1900, Chicago, IL 60601-7298. *Deadline for applications:* December 1, 2000. *Previous winner:* Catherine Graber (1999).

MLA/HLS Professional Development Grants. Given twice a year, this award provides librarians working in hospital and similar clinical settings with the support needed for educational or research activities. *For more information:* Medical Library Association, 65 East Wacker Place, Suite 1900, Chicago, IL 60601-7298. *Deadline for applications:* August 1 and December 1, 2000. *Previous winner:* Metro Detroit MLG-Research Committee (1999).

MLA/MIS Career Development Grant. This award provides up to two individuals $1,000 to support a career development activity that will contribute to advancement in the field of medical informatics. *For more information:* Medical Library Association, 65 East Wacker Place, Suite 1900, Chicago, IL 60601-7298. *Deadline for applications:* December 1, 2000. *Previous winners:* Ruth Riley, Gang "Wendy" Wu (1999).

MLA Dena Epstein Award. Awarded to support research in archives or libraries internationally on any aspect of American music. *For more information:* Music Library Association, P.O. Box 487, Canton, MA 02021. *Previous winner:* Sally Bick, Svetlana Sigida (1999).

MLA Kevin Freeman Travel Grant. Conference registration fee and a cash award of up to $750 to support travel and hotel expenses to attend the MLA annual meeting. *For more information:* Music Library Association, P.O. Box 487, Canton, MA 02021. *Previous winners:* Sara Adams, Gail Culler, Elisa Paul (1999).

MLA Walter Gerboth Award. A cash award of $500 made to MLA-member music librarians in the first five years of their professional careers, to assist research in progress. *For more information:* Music Library Association, P.O. Box 487, Canton, MA 02021. *Previous winner:* Mary Dumont (1999).

NASIG Horizon Award. Provides funding to attend NASIG annual conference for a practicing serials librarian. *For more information:* North American Serials Interest Group, info@nasig.org. *Deadline for applications:* February 16, 2001.

NASIG Marcia Tuttle International Grant. Provides funding for a NASIG member working in serials to foster international communication and education, through overseas activities such as research, collaborative projects, job exchanges, and presentation of papers at conferences. *For more information:* North American Serials Interest Group, info@nasig.org. *Deadline for applications:* April 30, 2001.

SAA Colonial Dames Scholarship. Covers up to $1,200 of the tuition, travel, and housing expenses at two annual Modern Archives Institutes for newcomers to the archival profession, who work in repositories with holdings in the period predating 1825. *For more information:* Society of American Archivists, 527 S. Wells, 5th Floor, Chicago, IL 60607. *Deadline for applications:* November 1, 2000; February 28, 2001.

SAA Harold T. Pinkett Minority Student Award. Certificate and a cash prize supporting full registration and related expenses of hotel and travel to attend the SAA annual meeting. Awarded to a minority student who manifests an interest in becoming a professional archivist. *For more information:* Society of American Archivists,

527 S. Wells, 5th Floor, Chicago, IL 60607. *Deadline for applications:* February 28, 2001. *Previous winner:* Kathryn M. Neal.

SAA Oliver Wendell Holmes Award. Assists overseas archivists already in the United States or Canada for training, to travel to or attend the SAA annual meeting. *For more information:* Society of American Archivists, 527 S. Wells, 5th Floor, Chicago, IL 60607. *Deadline for applications:* February 28, 2001. *Previous winner:* Ann Pederson.

SALALM Enlace Award. Awards of 80% of travel costs for a Latin American library or information professional to present a paper at a SALALM conference. *For more information:* Seminar on the Acquisition of Latin American Library Materials, cpuerto@mail.sdsu.edu. *Deadline for applications:* January 15, 2001.

Awards

For intellectual freedom

AALL Public Access to Government Information Award. Honors the achievements of those who have championed public access. *For more information:* American Association of Law Libraries, 53 W. Jackson Blvd., Suite 940, Chicago, IL 60604. *Deadline for applications:* February 1, 2001.

ALA/AASL SIRS Intellectual Freedom Award. A $2,000 award to a school library media specialist who has upheld the principles of intellectual freedom. An award of $1,000 goes to a media center of the recipient's choice. *For more information:* ALA American Association of School Librarians, 50 E. Huron St., Chicago, IL 60611-2795. *Deadline for applications:* February 1, 2001. *Previous winner:* Ginny Moore Kruse (1997).

ALA/IFRT Eli M. Oboler Memorial Award. $1,500 awarded biennially to an author of a published work in English, or in English translation, dealing with issues, events, questions, or controversies in the area of intellectual freedom. *For more information:* ALA Office for Intellectual Freedom, 50 E. Huron St., Chicago, IL 60611-2795. *Deadline for applications:* December 1, 2000. *Previous winner:* David Rabban, *Free Speech in Its Forgotten Years* (1998).

ALA/IFRT John Phillip Immroth Memorial Award for Intellectual Freedom. $500 and a citation for notable contributions to intellectual freedom fueled by personal courage. *For more information:* ALA Office for Intellectual Freedom, 50 E. Huron St., Chicago, IL 60611-2795. *Deadline for applications:* December 1, 2000. *Previous winner:* Mainstream Loudoun (Va.) (1999).

ALA/IFRT SIRS State and Regional Achievement Award. $1,000 and a citation to the intellectual freedom committee of a state library, state library media association, or a state/regional coalition for the most successful and creative project during the calendar year. *For more information:* ALA Office for Intellectual Freedom, 50 E. Huron St., Chicago, IL 60611-2795. *Deadline for applications:* December 1, 2000. *Previous winner:* Oregon Coalition for Free Expression (1999).

CLA Award for the Advancement of Intellectual Freedom in Canada. *For more information:* Canadian Library Association, 200 Elgin St., Ottawa, Ontario K2P 1L5, Canada. *Previous winner:* Greater Victoria (B.C.) Public Library Board and staff (1999).

COGI James Madison Award. To honor those who have championed, protected, and promoted public access to government information and the public's right to know. *For more information:* Coalition on Government Information, c/o ALA Washington Office, 1301 Pennsylvania Avenue, N.W., Suite 403, Washington, DC 20004-1701. *Previous winner:* President John F. Kennedy Assassination Records Review Board (1999).

FTRF Roll of Honor Award. Recognizes the unwavering support of intellectual freedom, the freedom to read, and opposition to censorship. *For more information:* ALA Freedom to Read Foundation, 50 E. Huron St., Chicago, IL 60611-2795. *Previous winner:* Charles L. Levendosky (1999).

For professional achievement

ALA Elizabeth Futas Catalyst for Change Award. A $1,000 award to honor a librarian who invests time and talent to make positive change in the profession of librarianship. *For more information:* ALA Awards, 50 E. Huron St., Chicago, IL 60611-2795. *Deadline for applications:* December 1, 2000. *Previous winner:* Maureen Sullivan (1999).

ALA Gale Research Company Financial Development Award. $2,500 to a library organization that exhibited meritorious achievement in carrying out a library financial development project to secure new funding resources for a public or academic library. *For more information:* ALA Awards, 50 E. Huron St., Chicago, IL 60611-2795. *Deadline for applications:* December 1, 2000. *Previous winner:* Deschutes (Oreg.) Public Library District (1999).

ALA Hugh C. Atkinson Memorial Award. An annual $2,000 award to recognize outstanding achievement (including risk-taking) by academic librarians that has contributed significantly to improvements in library automation, management, and/or development and research. Jointly administered by ALA's ACRL, LAMA, LITA, and ALCTS divisions. *For more information:* ALA Association of College and Research Libraries, 50 E. Huron St., Chicago, IL 60611-2795. *Deadline for applications:* December 1, 2000. *Previous winner:* Susan Nutter (1999).

ALA John Ames Humphry/OCLC/Forest Press Award. The $1,000 award is made to a librarian or other person who has made significant contributions to international librarianship. *For more information:* ALA International Relations Office, 50 E. Huron St., Chicago, IL 60611-2795. *Deadline for applications:* December 1, 2000. *Previous winner:* Ron Chepesiuk (1999).

ALA Melvil Dewey Medal. A citation presented to an individual or a group for recent creative professional achievement of a high order, particularly in those fields in which Melvil Dewey was interested, notably: library management, library training, cataloging and classification, and the tools and techniques of librarianship. *For more information:* ALA Awards, 50 E. Huron St., Chicago, IL 60611-2795. *Deadline for applications:* December 1, 2000. *Previous winner:* Helen Moeller (1999).

ALA Virginia and Herbert White Award for Promoting Librarianship. A citation and a $1,000 award to honor an individual for contributing significantly to the public recognition and appreciation of librarianship through professional performance, teaching, and/or writing. *For more information:* ALA Awards, 50 E. Huron St., Chicago, IL 60611-2795. *Deadline for applications:* December 1, 2000. *Previous winner:* Marilyn Gell Mason (1999).

ALA/ACRL Academic or Research Librarian of the Year Award. A $3,000 award for outstanding contribution to academic and research librarianship and library development. *For more information:* ALA Association of College and Research Libraries, 50 E. Huron St., Chicago, IL 60611-2795. *Deadline for applications:* December 1, 2000. *Previous winner:* Hannelore B. Rader (1999).

ALA/ACRL Distinguished Education and Behavioral Sciences Librarian Award. This award honors a distinguished academic librarian who has made an outstanding contribution as an education and/or behavioral sciences librarian. *For more information:* ALA Association of College and Research Libraries, 50 E. Huron St., Chicago, IL 60611-2795. *Deadline for applications:* December 1, 2000. *Previous winner:* Jo Ann Carr (1999).

ALA/ACRL Ebsco Community College Learning Resources/Library Achievement Awards. Two awards of $500 to individuals, groups, or institutions to recognize significant achievement in the areas of programs and leadership. *For more information:* ALA Association of College and Research Libraries, 50 E. Huron St., Chicago, IL 60611-2795. *Deadline for applications:* December 1, 2000. *Previous winners:* Wanda Johnston Bahde, Richland College (1999).

ALA/ACRL Innovation in Instruction Award. A citation recognizing and honoring librarians who have developed and implemented innovative approaches to instruction within their institutions in the preceding two years. *For more information:* ALA Association of College and Research Libraries, 50 E. Huron St., Chicago, IL 60611-2795. *Deadline for applications:* December 1, 2000. *Previous winner:* Education Project Team, University of Arizona (1999).

ALA/ACRL Miriam Dudley Bibliographic Instruction Librarian Award. A $1,000 award for contribution to the advancement of bibliographic instruction in a college or research institution. *For more information:* ALA Association of College and Research Libraries, 50 E. Huron St., Chicago, IL 60611-2795. *Deadline for applications:* December 1, 2000. *Previous winner:* Mary Reichel (1999).

ALA/ALCTS Bowker/Ulrich's Serials Librarianship Award. A $1,500 award for demonstrated leadership in serials-related activities through participation in professional associations and/or library education programs, contributions to the body of serials literature, research in the area of serials, or development of tools or methods to enhance access to or management of serials. *For more information:* ALA Association for Library Collections and Technical Services, 50 E. Huron St., Chicago, IL 60611-2795. *Deadline for applications:* December 1, 2000. *Previous winner:* Regina Romano Reynolds (1999).

ALA/ALCTS Esther J. Piercy Award. An annual $1,500 award to recognize contributions by a librarian in technical services with not more than 10 years professional experience. *For more information:* ALA Association for Library Collections and Technical Services, 50 E. Huron St., Chicago, IL 60611-2795. *Deadline for applications:* December 1, 2000. *Previous winner:* Judith R. Ahronheim (1998).

ALA/ALCTS Leadership in Library Acquisitions Award. This award of $1,500 is given to recognize the contributions by and outstanding leadership of an individual in the field of acquisitions librarianship. *For more information:* ALA Association for Library Collections and Technical Services, 50 E. Huron St., Chicago, IL 60611-2795. *Deadline for applications:* December 1, 2000. *Previous winner:* Carol Pitts Diedrichs (1999).

ALA/ALCTS Margaret Mann Citation. An annual citation for outstanding professional achievement in cataloging or classification through publication, participation, or contributions over the past 5 years. *For more information:* ALA Association for Library Collections and Technical Services, 50 E. Huron St., Chicago, IL 60611-2795. *Deadline for applications:* December 1, 2000. *Previous winner:* Nancy B. Olson (1999).

ALA/ASCLA Leadership Achievement Award. A citation for leadership in consulting, multitype library cooperation, and state library development. *For more information:* ALA Association of Specialized and Cooperative Library Agencies, 50 E. Huron St., Chicago, IL 60611-2795. *Deadline for applications:* December 15, 2000. *Previous winner:* Jan Beck Ison (1999).

ALA/ASCLA Professional Achievement Award. A citation presented to one or more ASCLA members for professional achievement in the areas of consulting, networking, statewide services, and programs. *For more information:* ALA Association of Specialized and Cooperative Library Agencies, 50 E. Huron St., Chicago, IL 60611-2795. *Deadline for applications:* December 15, 2000. *Previous winner:* Bridget L. Lamont (1999).

ALA/ERT Kohlstedt Exhibit Award. A citation awarded to companies or organizations for the best single, multiple, and island booth displays at the Annual Conference. *For more information:* ALA Conference Services, 50 E. Huron St., Chicago, IL 60611-2795. *Previous winners:* Apple Books, Demco, Bell & Howell (1999).

ALA/GODORT CIS "Documents to the People" Award. $2,000 to an individual, library, organization, or noncommercial group that most effectively encourages or enhances the use of government documents in library services. *For more information:* ALA Government Documents Round Table, 50 E. Huron St., Chicago, IL 60611-2795. *Deadline for applications:* December 1, 2000. *Previous winner:* Donna Koepp (1999).

ALA/LAMA AIA Library Buildings Award Program. A biennial award presented by the American Institute of Architects and the ALA Library Administration and Management Association to encourage excellence in the architectural design and planning of libraries. Citations are presented to the winning architectural firms and to libraries. *For more information:* ALA Library Administration and Management Association, 50 E. Huron St., Chicago, IL 60611-2795. *Deadline for applications:* December 18, 2000. *Previous winners:* Thomas Jefferson Building, Library of Congress; Main Reading Room, New York Public Library's Humanities and Social Sciences Library; School of Law Center, Quinnipiac College, Hamden, Conn.; Biomedical Research

Library, Vanderbilt University Medical Center, Nashville; Carmel Mountain Ranch Library, San Diego; Queens Borough Public Library, Flushing Branch (1999).

ALA/LAMA John Cotton Dana Public Relations Awards. An annual citation made to libraries or library organizations of all types for public relations programs or special projects. *For more information:* ALA Library Administration and Management Association, 50 E. Huron St., Chicago, IL 60611-2795. H. W. Wilson Company. *Deadline for applications:* January 12, 2001. *Previous winners:* Enoch Pratt Free Library, Baltimore; Milton S. Eisenhower Library, Johns Hopkins University, Baltimore; Chardon (Ohio) Library, Geauga County Public Library System; Ela Area Public Library, Lake Zurich, Ill.; Northbrook (Ill.) Public Library; Timberland Regional Library System, Olympia, Wash.; State Library of North Carolina, Raleigh; Richmond (Va.) Public Library; San Antonio (Tex.) Public Library; North Suburban Library Foundation of Illinois (1999).

ALA/LAMA Swap and Shop "Best of Show" Award. To recognize the best individual pieces of public relations materials produced by libraries in the previous year. Many different categories and winners. *For more information:* ALA Library Administration and Management Association, 50 E. Huron St., Chicago, IL 60611-2795. *Deadline for applications:* May 1, 2001.

ALA/MAGERT Honors Award. Cash award and a citation to recognize outstanding contributions by a Map and Geography Round Table personal member to map librarianship, MAGERT, and/or a specific MAGERT project. *For more information:* ALA Map and Geography Round Table, 50 E. Huron St., Chicago, IL 60611-2795. *Deadline for applications:* December 1, 2000. *Previous winner:* Vi Moorhouse (1999).

ALA/NMRT/ERT Friendly Booth Award. A citation awarded to companies or organizations for friendliest booth displays at the Annual Conference. *For more information:* ALA Conference Services, 50 E. Huron St., Chicago, IL 60611-2795. *Previous winners:* Hooked on Phonics, Pleasant Co., Facts on File (1998).

ALA/PLA Charlie Robinson Award. A $1,000 award to a library director who, over a period of at least 7 years, has been a risk-taker, innovator, and/or change agent in a public library. *For more information:* ALA Public Library Association, 50 E. Huron St., Chicago, IL 60611-2795. *Deadline for applications:* December 1, 2000. *Previous winner:* Ginnie Cooper (1999).

ALA/RUSA Gale Research Award for Excellence in Business Librarianship. A citation and $1,000 cash award to an individual who has made a significant contribution to business librarianship. *For more information:* ALA Reference and User Services Association, 50 E. Huron St., Chicago, IL 60611-2795. *Deadline for applications:* December 15, 2000. *Previous winner:* Priscilla Cheng Geahigan (1999).

ALA/RUSA Isadore Gilbert Mudge–R. R. Bowker Award. An annual award of $1,500 and a citation to an individual who has made a distinguished contribution to reference librarianship. *For more information:* ALA Reference and User Services Association, 50 E. Huron St., Chicago, IL 60611-2795. *Deadline for applications:* December 15, 2000. *Previous winner:* Virginia Massey-Burzio (1999).

ALA/RUSA Virginia Boucher OCLC Distinguished ILL Librarian Award. An award of $2,000 to an individual for outstanding professional achievement and contributions to interlibrary loan and document delivery. *For more information:* ALA Reference and User Services Association, 50 E. Huron St., Chicago, IL 60611-2795. *Deadline for applications:* December 1, 2000.

ALISE Award for Outstanding Professional Contributions to Library and Information Science Education. For service that promotes and strengthens the broad areas of library/information science education through the holding of appropriate offices and positions within the profession. *For more information:* Association for Library and Information Science Education, P.O. Box 7640, Arlington, VA 22207. *Deadline for applications:* September 15, 2000. *Previous winner:* Marilyn L. Miller (1999).

ALISE Award for Teaching Excellence in the Field of Library and Information Science Education. For regular and sustained excellence in teaching library and information science. *For more information:* Association for Library and Information Science Education, P.O. Box 7640, Arlington, VA 22207. *Deadline for applications:* September 15, 2000. *Previous winners:* Linda C. Smith, Herman Totten (1999).

ASIS Award of Merit. To recognize that individual deemed to have made noteworthy contributions to the field of information science. *For more information:* American

Society for Information Science, 8720 Georgia Avenue, Suite 501, Silver Spring, MD 20910. *Deadline for applications:* July 1, 2000. *Previous winner:* Henry Small (1998).

ASIS ISI Outstanding Information Science Teacher Award. An award of $1,000 to recognize the unique teaching contribution of an individual as a teacher of information science. *For more information:* American Society for Information Science, 8720 Georgia Avenue, Suite 501, Silver Spring, MD 20910. *Deadline for applications:* July 1, 2000. *Previous winner:* Elisabeth Logan (1998).

ASIS Special Award. To recognize a public figure (a government or industry leader) for long-term contributions to the advancement of information science and technology which have resulted in increased public awareness of the field and its benefits to society. *For more information:* American Society for Information Science, 8720 Georgia Avenue, Suite 501, Silver Spring, MD 20910. *Deadline for applications:* April 15, 2001. *Previous winner:* Herbert A. Simon (1998).

CLA Faxon Marketing Award. Expense-paid trip to CLA Conference for excellent public relations and marketing initiatives from all types of libraries. *For more information:* Canadian Library Association, 200 Elgin St., Ottawa, Ontario K2P 1L5, Canada. *Deadline for applications:* March 31, 2001. *Previous winner:* Richmond (B.C.) Public Library.

CLA/CACUL Community and Technical College Libraries Award of Merit. This award is presented annually to a Canadian library or librarian who has made a significant contribution to the design or delivery of library service, or to the profile of library issues, in a college or technical institute. *For more information:* CLA Canadian Association of College and University Libraries, 200 Elgin St., Ottawa, Ontario K2P 1L5, Canada. *Deadline for applications:* January 31, 2001. *Previous winner:* Frieda Wiebe (1999).

CLA/CACUL Innovation Achievement Award. To recognize Canadian academic libraries which, through innovation in ongoing programs/services or in a special event/project, have contributed to academic librarianship and library development. *For more information:* CLA Canadian Association of College and University Libraries, 200 Elgin St., Ottawa, Ontario K2P 1L5, Canada. *Deadline for applications:* January 31, 2001. *Previous winners:* Simon Fraser University, COPPUL, University of Manitoba (1999).

CLA/CACUL Outstanding Academic Librarian Award. Presented to an individual member of CACUL who has made an outstanding national or international contribution to academic librarianship and library development. *For more information:* CLA Canadian Association of College and University Libraries, 200 Elgin St., Ottawa, Ontario K2P 1L5, Canada. *Deadline for applications:* January 31, 2001. *Previous winner:* Richard Ellis (1999).

CLA/TSIG Award for Achievement in Technical Services. To recognize achievement in technical services by any unit whose library has an institutional membership in the Canadian Library Association. *For more information:* CLA Technical Services Interest Group, 200 Elgin St., Ottawa, Ontario K2P 1L5, Canada. *Deadline for applications:* April 1, 2001. *Previous winner:* Advanced Education Media Acquisitions Centre, Langara College, Vancouver, B.C. (1999).

MLA Estelle Brodman Award for Academic Medical Librarian of the Year. A cash award of $500 that recognizes an academic medical librarian at mid-career level who demonstrates significant achievement, the potential for leadership, and continuing excellence. *For more information:* Medical Library Association, 65 East Wacker Place, Suite 1900, Chicago, IL 60601-7298. *Deadline for applications:* November 1, 2000. *Previous winner:* E. Diane Johnson (1999).

MLA Louise Darling Medal. Presented annually to recognize distinguished achievement in collection development in the health sciences. *For more information:* Medical Library Association, 65 East Wacker Place, Suite 1900, Chicago, IL 60601-7298. *Deadline for applications:* November 1, 2000. *Previous winner:* Jonathan Eldredge (1999).

MLA Marcia G. Noyes Award. Recognizes a career that has resulted in lasting, outstanding contributions to health sciences librarianship. *For more information:* Medical Library Association, 65 East Wacker Place, Suite 1900, Chicago, IL 60601-7298. *Deadline for applications:* November 1, 2000. *Previous winner:* T. Mark Hodges (1999).

MLA Special Achievement Award. An award recognizing extraordinary service to the profession of music librarianship over a relatively short period of time. *For more information:* Music Library Association, P.O. Box 487, Canton, MA 02021. *Previous winner:* Sherry Vellucci (1998).

ULC Highsmith Award of Excellence. A $1,000 honorarium that recognizes a ULC member library for the creation or adaptation of a service that meets an urban area's need, can be replicated easily, is not costly, and has proven results. *For more information:* Urban Libraries Council, 1603 Orrington Avenue, Suite1080, Evanston, IL 60201. *Deadline for applications:* December 1, 2000. *Previous winner:* Denver Public Library.

For publications and research

AALL Joseph L. Andrews Bibliographical Award. For significant contribution to legal bibliographical literature. *For more information:* American Association of Law Libraries, 53 W. Jackson Blvd., Suite 940, Chicago, IL 60604. *Deadline for applications:* February 1, 2001. *Previous winner:* Kendall F. Svengalis (1998).

AALL *Law Library Journal* Article of the Year. For outstanding achievement in research and writing published in *Law Library Journal. For more information:* American Association of Law Libraries, 53 W. Jackson Blvd., Suite 940, Chicago, IL 60604. *Previous winner:* Janis L. Johnston (1998).

AALL Law Library Publications Award. Honors achievement in creating in-house, user-oriented library materials that are outstanding in quality and significance. *For more information:* American Association of Law Libraries, 53 W. Jackson Blvd., Suite 940, Chicago, IL 60604. *Deadline for applications:* February 1, 2001. *Previous winners:* Cadwalader, Wickersham & Taft Library; Cornell Law Library (1998).

AALL Matthew Bender Call for Papers Awards. To promote scholarship and provide an outlet for creativity. *For more information:* American Association of Law Libraries, 53 W. Jackson Blvd., Suite 940, Chicago, IL 60604. *Deadline for applications:* February 1, 2001. *Previous winners:* Karen S. Beck, Richard A. Danner, Wendy R. Brown (1998).

AJL Bibliography and Reference Awards. $500 for works in Judaica. *For more information.* Association of Jewish Libraries, 15 E. 26th Street, Room 1034, New York, NY 10010. *Previous winners:* Sharona R. Wachs, *American Jewish Liturgies;* Paula E. Hyman and Deborah Dash Moore, *Jewish Women in America: An Historical Encyclopedia* (1997).

AJL Sydney Taylor Body of Work Award. An award of $1,000 for a lifetime of publications in the field of Jewish children's books. *For more information:* Association of Jewish Libraries, 15 E. 26th Street, Room 1034, New York, NY 10010. *Previous winner:* Barbara Diamond Goldin (1997).

AJL Sydney Taylor Children's Book Awards. Awards of $500 each for the best Jewish children's books. *For more information:* Association of Jewish Libraries, 15 E. 26th Street, Room 1034, New York, NY 10010. *Previous winners:* Marci Stillerman, *Nine Spoons* (HaChai); Donna Jo Napoli, *Stones in Water* (Dutton) (1998).

AJL Sydney Taylor Manuscript Award. An award of $1,000 for a Jewish children's book (either fiction or nonfiction) by a first-time author. *For more information:* Association of Jewish Libraries, 15 E. 26th Street, Room 1034, New York, NY 10010. *Previous winner:* June E. Nislick, *Zayda Was a Cowboy* (1999).

ALA bill boyd Literary Award. $10,000 to an author for a military novel that honors the service of American veterans during a time of war, 1861–1865, 1914–1918, 1939–1945. *For more information:* ALA Awards, 50 E. Huron St., Chicago, IL 60611-2795. *Deadline for applications:* December 1, 2000. *Previous winner:* Donald McCaig, for *Jacob's Ladder* (1999).

ALA Highsmith Library Literature Award. A $500 award presented to one author and/or coauthor who make an outstanding contribution to library literature. *For more information:* ALA Awards, 50 E. Huron St., Chicago, IL 60611-2795. *Deadline for applications:* December 1, 2000. *Previous winners:* Peter Hernon and Ellen Altman, *Assessing Service Quality: Satisfying the Expectations of Library Customers* (1999).

ALA/ACRL Instruction Section Publication Award. This award recognizes an outstanding publication related to instruction in a library environment published in the preceding two years. *For more information:* ALA Association of College and Research Libraries, 50 E. Huron St., Chicago, IL 60611-2795. *Deadline for applications:* December 1, 2000. *Previous winner:* Christine S. Bruce (1999).

ALA/ACRL K. G. Saur Award for Best *C&RL* Article. An annual award of $500 presented to an author of an outstanding article published in *College & Research Libraries* during the preceding volume year. *For more information:* ALA Association of College and Research Libraries, 50 E. Huron St., Chicago, IL 60611-2795. *Deadline for applications:* December 1, 2000. *Previous winner:* Bonnie Gratch Lindauer (1999).

ALA/ACRL Katharine Keyes Leab and Daniel J. Leab American Book Prices Current Exhibition Catalogue Awards. Three awards for the best catalogue published by American or Canadian institutions in conjunction with exhibitions of books and/or manuscripts. *For more information:* ALA Association of College and Research Libraries, 50 E. Huron St., Chicago, IL 60611-2795. *Deadline for applications:* September 30, 2000. *Previous winners:* Houghton Library, John Carter Brown Library, University of Toronto, University of Virginia (1999).

ALA/ACRL Oberly Award for Bibliography in the Agricultural Sciences. A biennial award consisting of a citation and cash award presented to an American citizen for the best English-language bibliography in the field of agriculture or a related science in the preceding two-year period. *For more information:* ALA Association of College and Research Libraries, 50 E. Huron St., Chicago, IL 60611-2795. *Deadline for applications:* December 1, 2000. *Previous winner:* Eli MacLaren (1999).

ALA/ACRL *Rare Books & Manuscripts Librarianship* Award. A biennial award of $1,000 to recognize articles of superior quality published in ACRL's *Rare Books & Manuscripts Librarianship*. *For more information:* ALA Association of College and Research Libraries, 50 E. Huron St., Chicago, IL 60611-2795. *Deadline for applications:* December 1, 2000. *Previous winner:* Robert A. Gross (1999).

ALA/ALCTS Best of *LRTS* Award. Annual citation given to the author(s) of the best paper published in *Library Resources and Technical Services*. *For more information:* ALA Association for Library Collections and Technical Services, 50 E. Huron St., Chicago, IL 60611-2795. *Deadline for applications:* December 1, 2000. *Previous winners:* Lois Mai Chan and Diane Vizine-Goetz (1999).

ALA/ALCTS Blackwell's Scholarship Award. A $2,000 scholarship to a U.S. or Canadian library school to honor the author(s) of the year's outstanding monograph, article, or original paper in the field of acquisitions, collection development, and related areas of resource development. *For more information:* ALA Association for Library Collections and Technical Services, 50 E. Huron St., Chicago, IL 60611-2795. *Deadline for applications:* December 1, 2000. *Previous winner:* Ross Atkinson (1999).

ALA/ALSC Andrew Carnegie Medal. A medal presented annually to an American producer for outstanding video production for children issued in the United States in the previous calendar year. *For more information:* ALA Association for Library Service to Children, 50 E. Huron St., Chicago, IL 60611-2795. *Deadline for applications:* December 31, 2000. *Previous winner:* Frank Moynihan, for *The First Christmas* (1999).

ALA/ALSC John Newbery Medal. A medal presented annually to the author of the most distinguished contribution to American literature for children published in the United States in the preceding year. *For more information:* ALA Association for Library Service to Children, 50 E. Huron St., Chicago, IL 60611-2795. *Deadline for applications:* December 31, 2000. *Previous winner:* Louis Sachar, *Holes* (1999).

ALA/ALSC Laura Ingalls Wilder Medal. A medal presented to an author or illustrator whose books, published in the United States, have over a period of years made a substantial and lasting contribution to children's literature. Presented every three years. *For more information:* ALA Association for Library Service to Children, 50 E. Huron St., Chicago, IL 60611-2795. *Deadline for applications:* December 1, 2000. *Previous winner:* Russell Freedman (1998).

ALA/ALSC Mildred L. Batchelder Award. A citation presented to an American publisher for a children's book considered to be the most outstanding of those books originally published in a foreign language in a foreign country and subsequently published in English in the United States during the preceding year. *For more infor-*

mation: ALA Association for Library Service to Children, 50 E. Huron St., Chicago, IL 60611-2795. *Deadline for applications:* December 31, 2000. *Previous winner:* Dial Books for Young Readers, for *Thanks to My Mother,* by Schoschana Rabinovici (1999).

ALA/ALSC Randolph Caldecott Medal. A medal presented annually to the illustrator of the most distinguished American picture book for children published in the United States in the previous year. *For more information:* ALA Association for Library Service to Children, 50 E. Huron St., Chicago, IL 60611-2795. *Deadline for applications:* December 31, 2000. *Previous winner:* Mary Azarian, *Snowflake Bentley* (Houghton Mifflin) (1999).

ALA/ALSC Reforma Pura Belpré Award. Biannual award to a Latino/Latina author or illustrator for an outstanding original children's book published in the United States or Puerto Rico that portrays, affirms, and celebrates the Latino/Latina cultural experience. *For more information:* ALA Association for Library Service to Children, 50 E. Huron St., Chicago, IL 60611-2795. *Deadline for applications:* December 31, 2000. *Previous winners:* Victor Martinez, for *Parrot in the Oven: Mi vida* (Joanna Cotler); Stephanie Garcia, for *Snapshots from the Wedding* (G.P. Putnam) (1998).

ALA/LHRT Justin Winsor Prize Essay. An award of $500 to an author of an outstanding essay embodying original historical research on a significant subject of library history. The essay will be published in *Libraries and Culture. For more information:* ALA Library History Round Table, 50 E. Huron St., Chicago, IL 60611-2795. *Deadline for applications:* November 1, 2000. *Previous winner:* Christine Pawley (1999).

ALA/LHRT Phyllis Dain Library History Dissertation Award. A biennial award of $500 to outstanding dissertations treating the history of books, libraries, librarianship, or information science. *For more information:* ALA Library History Round Table, 50 E. Huron St., Chicago, IL 60611-2795. *Deadline for applications:* November 1, 2000. *Previous winner:* P. Toby Graham (1999).

ALA/LRRT Jesse H. Shera Awards for Research. Two prizes of $500 each for outstanding and original published research or doctoral research related to libraries *For more information:* ALA Office for Research and Statistics, 50 E. Huron St., Chicago, IL 60611-2795. *Deadline for applications:* February 15, 2001. *Previous winners:* Christine Pawley, Pamela Spence Richards (1999).

ALA/RUSA Dartmouth Medal. A medal presented to honor achievement in creating reference works outstanding in quality and significance. *For more information:* ALA Reference and User Services Association, 50 E. Huron St., Chicago, IL 60611-2795. *Dartmouth College. Deadline for applications:* December 15, 2000. *Previous winners:* John A. Garraty and Mark C. Carnes, eds., *American National Biography* (Oxford) (1999).

ALA/RUSA Denali Press Award. A plaque and $500 cash award presented to an individual author(s) or corporate author to recognize the creation of a U.S. ethnic and minority reference work of outstanding quality and significance. *For more information:* ALA Reference and User Services Association, 50 E. Huron St., Chicago, IL 60611-2795. *Deadline for applications:* December 15, 2000. *Previous winners:* Ronald Fernandez, Serafine Mendez, and Gail Cueto (1999).

ALA/RUSA Gale Research Award for Excellence in Reference and Adult Library Services. A citation and $1,000 cash award to a library for development of an imaginative resource to meet patrons' reference needs. Resources may include a bibliography, guide to literature of a specific subject, directory, database, or other reference service. *For more information:* ALA Reference and User Services Association, 50 E. Huron St., Chicago, IL 60611-2795. *Deadline for applications:* December 15, 2000. *Previous winner:* New Orleans Public Library (1999).

ALA/RUSA Genealogical Publishing Company Award. A citation and $1,000 cash award to a librarian, library, or publisher to encourage professional achievement in historical reference and research librarianship. *For more information:* ALA Reference and User Services Association, 50 E. Huron St., Chicago, IL 60611-2795. *Deadline for applications:* December 15, 2000. *Previous winner:* Thomas J. Muth (1999).

ALA/RUSA Louis Shores–Oryx Press Award. A citation and $1,000 cash award to an individual reviewer, group, editor, review medium, or organization to recognize excellence in book reviewing and other media for libraries. *For more information:* ALA

Reference and User Services Association, 50 E. Huron St., Chicago, IL 60611-2795. *Deadline for applications:* December 15, 2000. *Previous winners:* Brian E. Coutts, John B. Richard (1999).

ALA/RUSA Reference Service Press Award. $1,000 award presented to recognize the most outstanding article published in *RQ* during the preceding two-volume year. *For more information:* ALA Reference and User Services Association, 50 E. Huron St., Chicago, IL 60611-2795. *Deadline for applications:* December 15, 2000. *Previous winner:* Jennifer Mendelsohn (1999).

ALA/SRRT Coretta Scott King Award. Award(s) given to an African-American author and to an African-American illustrator for an outstandingly inspirational and educational contribution. The awards consist of a plaque and $250 to the author and $250 to the illustrator. Sets of encyclopedias are also donated. *For more information:* ALA Social Responsibilities Round Table, 50 E. Huron St., Chicago, IL 60611-2795. *Deadline for applications:* December 1, 2000. *Previous winners:* Angela Johnson, *Heaven* (Simon & Schuster); Michele Wood, *i see the rhythm* (Children's Book Press) (1999).

ALA/SRRT Coretta Scott King/John Steptoe Award for New Talent. Citation for an outstanding book designed to bring visibility to a black writer or artist at the beginning of his/her career as a published book creator. *For more information:* ALA Social Responsibilities Round Table, 50 E. Huron St., Chicago, IL 60611-2795. *Deadline for applications:* December 1, 2000. *Previous winners:* Debbie Chocolate, *The Piano Man* (Walker); Sharon Flake, *The Skin I'm In* (Jump in the Sun/Hyperion) (1999).

ALA/SRRT Gay/Lesbian/Bisexual Book Award. A cash award to authors of fiction and nonfiction book(s) of exceptional merit relating to the gay/lesbian experience. *For more information:* ALA Social Responsibilities Round Table, 50 E. Huron St., Chicago, IL 60611-2795. *Deadline for applications:* November 30, 2000. *Previous winners:* Michael Cunningham, *The Hours* (Farrar Straus Giroux); Sarah Schulman, *Stagestruck: Theatre, AIDS, and the Marketing of Gay America* (Duke University) (1999).

ALA/YALSA Alex Awards. Citations to 10 authors of adult books that appeal to young adults. *For more information:* ALA Young Adult Library Services Association, 50 E. Huron St., Chicago, IL 60611-2795. *Deadline for applications:* April 9–15, 2001. *Previous winners:* Esmeralda Santiago, *Almost a Woman* (Perseus/Merloyd Lawrence); Kim Stanley Robinson, *Antarctica* (Bantam); others (1999).

ALA/YALSA Margaret A. Edwards Award. A $1,000 award given to an author or coauthor whose book(s) over a period of time have been accepted by young adults as an authentic voice that continues to illuminate their experiences and emotions. *For more information:* ALA Young Adult Library Services Association, 50 E. Huron St., Chicago, IL 60611-2795. *Deadline for applications:* January 9, 2001. *Previous winner:* Anne McCaffrey (1999).

ALA/YALSA Michael L. Printz Award. Honors the highest literary achievement in books for young adults. *For more information:* ALA Young Adult Library Services Association, 50 E. Huron St., Chicago, IL 60611-2795. *Deadline for applications:* December 1, 2000.

ALISE Methodology Paper Competition. A $500 honorarium for papers that address a methodology, related issues, and/or a particular technique. *For more information:* Association for Library and Information Science Education, P.O. Box 7640, Arlington, VA 22207. *Deadline for applications:* September 15, 2000. *Previous winner:* Yin Zhang (1999).

ALISE Research Paper Competition. A $500 honorarium for research papers concerning any aspect of librarianship or information science. *For more information:* Association for Library and Information Science Education, P.O. Box 7640, Arlington, VA 22207. *Deadline for applications:* September 15, 2000. *Previous winner:* Caroline Haythornthwaite (1999).

ARLIS/NA George Wittenborn Memorial Book Award. Annual award for outstanding publications in the visual arts and architecture. *For more information:* Art Libraries Society of North America, 4104 Lake Boone Trail, Suite 201, Raleigh, NC 27607-7506. *Deadline for applications:* December 31, 2000. *Previous winners:* David Anfam, *Mark Rothko: The Works on Canvas* (Yale University); Harriet K. Stratis and Martha

Tedeschi, eds., *The Lithographs of James McNeill Whistler* (Art Institute of Chicago) (1999).

ARLIS/NA Gerd Muehsam Memorial Award. $200 cash and $300 in travel expenses to the ARLIS/NA conference to a graduate library student for a paper or project on a topic relevant to art librarianship. *For more information:* Art Libraries Society of North America, 4104 Lake Boone Trail, Suite 201, Raleigh, NC 27607-7506. *Deadline for applications:* December 10, 2000. *Previous winner:* Lena Stebley (1999).

ARLIS/NA John Benjamins Award. Up to $2,000 to recognize research and publication in the study and critical analysis of periodicals in the fields of the fine arts, literature, and cross-disciplinary studies. *For more information:* Art Libraries Society of North America, 4104 Lake Boone Trail, Suite 201, Raleigh, NC 27607-7506. *Deadline for applications:* October 1, 2000. *Previous winner:* Tara Tappert (1999).

ARLIS/NA Melva J. Dwyer Award. Citation given to the creators of exceptional reference or research tools relating to Canadian art and architecture. *For more information:* Art Libraries Society of North America, 4104 Lake Boone Trail, Suite 201, Raleigh, NC 27607-7506. *Deadline for applications:* December 31, 2000. *Previous winner:* David Milne Jr. and David P. Silcox, *David B. Milne: Catalogue Raisonné of the Paintings* (University of Toronto) (1999).

ARLIS/NA Worldwide Books Publication Awards. To recognize outstanding publications by ARLIS/NA members. *For more information:* Art Libraries Society of North America, 4104 Lake Boone Trail, Suite 201, Raleigh, NC 27607-7506. *Deadline for applications:* October 1, 2000. *Previous winners:* James A. Findlay, Laura Graveline, Susan A. Lewis, Helene E. Roberts, Edward H. Teague (1999).

ASI H. W. Wilson Company Indexing Award. A citation and $1,000 for the indexer, and a citation for the publisher to honor excellence in indexing of an English-language monograph or other nonserial publication published during the previous calendar year. *For more information:* American Society of Indexers, P.O. Box 39366, Phoenix, AZ 85069-9366. *Deadline for applications:* April 1, 2001. *Previous winner:* Laura Moss Gottlieb, for *Dead Wrong*, by Michael A. Mello (University of Wisconsin Press) (1998).

ASIS Award for Research in Information Science. To recognize an individual or individuals for an outstanding research contribution in the field of information science. *For more information:* American Society for Information Science, 8720 Georgia Avenue, Suite 501, Silver Spring, MD 20910. *Deadline for applications:* June 1, 2001. *Previous winner:* Marcia Bates (1998).

ASIS Best Information Science Book. To recognize the outstanding book in information science published during the preceding calendar year. *For more information:* American Society for Information Science, 8720 Georgia Avenue, Suite 501, Silver Spring, MD 20910. *Deadline for applications:* June 5, 2000. *Previous winner:* Robert R. Korfhage, *Information Storage and Retrieval* (John Wiley) (1998).

ASIS John Wiley & Sons Best JASIS Paper Award. A $1,500 cash award to recognize the best refereed paper published in the volume year of the *Journal of the American Society for Information Science* preceding the ASIS annual meeting. *For more information:* American Society for Information Science, 8720 Georgia Avenue, Suite 501, Silver Spring, MD 20910. *Deadline for applications:* August 2001. *Previous winners:* Howard D. White and Katherine W. McCain (1998).

ASIS Pratt-Severn Best Student Research Paper. Up to $500 for travel expenses and full registration for the ASIS annual meeting for research and writing in the field of information science. *For more information:* American Society for Information Science, 8720 Georgia Avenue, Suite 501, Silver Spring, MD 20910. *Deadline for applications:* June 15, 2001. *Previous winner:* Melinda Axel (1997).

BCALA Literary Awards. The two annual BCALA Literary Awards (fiction and nonfiction) of $500 each recognize outstanding works by African-American authors depicting the cultural, historical, or sociopolitical aspects of the African Diaspora. *For more information:* Black Caucus of the ALA, c/o Office for Literacy and Outreach, 50 E. Huron St., Chicago, IL 60611-2795. *Deadline for applications:* December 31, 2000. *Previous winners:* Gayl Jones, *The Healing* (Beacon); Carolyn Mazloomi, *Spirits of the Cloth* (Clarkson Potter) (1999).

CLA Student Article Contest. An honorarium of $150 (Can.) and publication in

Feliciter for articles by students in Canadian library schools. *For more information:* Canadian Library Association, 200 Elgin St., Ottawa, Ontario K2P 1L5, Canada. *Deadline for applications:* March 15, 2001. *Previous winner:* Gayle Bushell (1999).

CLA/CACL Amelia Frances Howard-Gibbon Medal. For an illustrator of an outstanding children's book published in Canada the previous year. *For more information:* CLA Canadian Association of Children's' Librarians, 200 Elgin St., Ottawa, Ontario K2P 1L5, Canada. *Deadline for applications:* January 1, 2001. *Previous winner:* Kady MacDonald Denton, for *A Child's Treasury of Nursery Rhymes* (1999).

CLA/CACL Book of the Year for Children Award. For an outstanding children's book the previous year by a Canadian author. *For more information:* CLA Canadian Association of Children's Librarians, 200 Elgin St., Ottawa, Ontario K2P 1L5, Canada. *Deadline for applications:* January 1, 2001. *Previous winner:* Tim Wynne-Jones, *Stephen Fair* (1999).

CLA/YASIG Young Adult Canadian Book Award. Recognizes an author of an outstanding English-language Canadian book appealing to young adults. *For more information:* CLA Young Adult Services Interest Group, 200 Elgin St., Ottawa, Ontario K2P 1L5, Canada. *Deadline for applications:* January 1, 2001. *Previous winner:* Gayle Friesen, *Janey's Girl* (1999).

CLA John Brubaker Memorial Award. For the best article in *Catholic Library World* in the previous year. For *more information:* Catholic Library Association, 100 North St., Suite 224, Pittsfield, MA 01201-5109. *Previous winner:* Patrick A. Metress (1999).

CLA Regina Medal. A silver medal awarded to an author or illustrator for a lifetime contribution to children's books. *For more information:* Catholic Library Association, 100 North St., Suite 224, Pittsfield, MA 01201-5109. *Previous winner:* Eric Carle (1999).

CLA/ALS Jerome Award. Presented annually for excellence in Catholic scholarship. *For more information:* Catholic Library Association, 100 North St., Suite 224, Pittsfield, MA 01201-5109. *Previous winner:* Walter J. Burghardt (1999).

CSLA Helen Keating Ott Award for Outstanding Contribution to Children's Literature. A person or organization selected and honored for significant contribution in promoting high moral and ethical values through children's literature. *For more information:* Church and Synagogue Library Association, P.O. Box 19357, Portland, OR 97280-0357. *Deadline for applications:* April 15, 2001.

MLA Ida and George Eliot Prize. $200 award presented annually for a work published in the preceding calendar year that has been judged most effective in furthering medical librarianship. *For more information:* Medical Library Association, 65 East Wacker Place, Suite 1900, Chicago, IL 60601-7298. *Deadline for applications:* November 1, 2000. *Previous winners:* Barbara Schloman, Judith Burnham, Linda Slater, Eileen M. Wakiji (1999).

MLA Murray Gottlieb Prize. $100 awarded annually for the best unpublished essay on the history of medicine and allied sciences written by a health sciences librarian. *For more information:* Medical Library Association, 65 East Wacker Place, Suite 1900, Chicago, IL 60601-7298. *Deadline for applications:* November 1, 2000. *Previous winners:* Godfrey S. Belleh and Eric von der Luft (1999).

MLA Rittenhouse Award. Given for the best unpublished paper (bibliographical, issue or topic based, or report of research results) on health sciences librarianship or medical informatics written by a student in an ALA-accredited school of library science or a trainee in an internship. *For more information:* Medical Library Association, 65 East Wacker Place, Suite 1900, Chicago, IL 60601-7298. *Deadline for applications:* November 1, 2000. *Previous winner:* Charles G. Warrick (1998).

MLA Eva Judd O'Meara Award. An annual award for the best review published in *Notes. For more information:* Music Library Association, P.O. Box 487, Canton, MA 02021. *Previous winner:* Lynne Rogers (1999).

MLA Richard S. Hill Award. An annual award for the best article on music librarianship or article of a music-bibliographic nature. *For more information:* Music Library Association, P.O. Box 487, Canton, MA 02021. *Previous winner:* Laurent Guillo (1999).

MLA Vincent H. Duckles Award. Annual award for the best book-length bibliography or other research tool in music. *For more information:* Music Library Association,

P.O. Box 487, Canton, MA 02021. *Previous winner:* Paul Bryan, *Johann Wanhal, Viennese Symphonist* (Pendragon Press) (1999).

SLA H. W. Wilson Company Award. A $500 cash award to the author(s) of an outstanding article published in *Information Outlook* during the publication year. *For more information:* Special Libraries Association, 1700 Eighteenth Street, N.W., Washington, DC 20009. *Deadline for applications:* December 4, 2000. *Previous winners:* Deborah Grealy, Barbara Greenman (1999).

SLA Public Relations Media Award. Recognizes a journalist who published an outstanding feature on the profession of special librarianship, preferably in a general circulation publication or radio or television production. *For more information:* Special Libraries Association, 1700 Eighteenth Street, N.W., Washington, DC 20009. *Deadline for applications:* December 4, 2000. *Previous winner:* Leigh Buchanan, *Inc.* magazine (1999).

TLA Awards. For excellence in writing books about film, TV, or radio. *For more information:* Theatre Library Association, Shubert Archive, 149 West 45th St., New York, NY 10036. *Deadline for applications:* February 15, 2001. *Previous winner:* Cari Beauchamp, *Without Lying Down: Frances Marion and the Powerful Women of Early Hollywood* (Charles Scribners' Sons) (1997).

TLA George Freedley Award. A cash award of $250 for excellence in writing books about the theatre. *For more information:* Theatre Library Association, Shubert Archive, 149 West 45th St., New York, NY 10036. *Deadline for applications:* February 15, 2001. *Previous winner:* Gary Jay Williams, *Our Moonlight Revels: "A Midsummer Night's Dream" in the Theatre* (1997).

For distinguished service

AECT Distinguished Service Award. Granted to a person who has shown outstanding leadership in advancing the theory and/or practice of educational communications and technology over a substantial period of time. *For more information:* Association for Educational Communications and Technology, 1025 Vermont Avenue, N.W., Suite 820, Washington, DC 20005. *Deadline for applications:* January 1, 2001.

ALA Beta Phi Mu Award. A $500 award presented to a library school faculty member or an individual for distinguished service to education in librarianship. *For more information:* ALA Awards, 50 E. Huron St., Chicago, IL 60611-2795. *Deadline for applications:* December 1, 2000. *Previous winner:* D. W. Krummel (1999).

ALA Joseph W. Lippincott Award. A $1,000 award to a librarian for distinguished service to the profession, to include outstanding participation in professional library activities, notable published professional writing, or other significant activities on behalf of the profession. *For more information:* ALA Awards, 50 E. Huron St., Chicago, IL 60611-2795. *Deadline for applications:* December 1, 2000. *Previous winner:* Peggy Barber (1999).

ALA Paul Howard Award for Courage. $1,000 awarded every two years to a librarian, library board, library group, or an individual who has exhibited unusual courage for the benefit of library programs or services. *For more information:* ALA Awards, 50 E. Huron St., Chicago, IL 60611-2795. *Deadline for applications:* December 1, 2000. *Previous winner:* Jane Rustin (1999).

ALA/ACRL Marta Lange/CQ Award. This $1,000 award recognizes an academic or law librarian for contributions to bibliography and information service in law or political science. *For more information:* ALA Association of College and Research Libraries, 50 E. Huron St., Chicago, IL 60611-2795. *Deadline for applications:* December 1, 2000. *Previous winner:* Jolande E. Goldberg (1999).

ALA/ALTA Major Benefactors Honor Award. Citation to individuals, families, or corporate bodies who have made major benefactions to public libraries. *For more information:* ALA Association of Library Trustees and Advocates, 50 E. Huron St., Chicago, IL 60611-2795. *Deadline for applications:* December 1, 2000. *Previous winners:* Lynn and Charles Schustermann, Mr. & Mrs. Marv Patmos (1999).

ALA/ALTA Trustee Citations. A citation presented to each of two outstanding public library trustees for distinguished service to library development on the local, state, regional, or national level. *For more information:* ALA Association of Library

Trustees and Advocates, 50 E. Huron St., Chicago, IL 60611-2795. *Deadline for applications:* December 1, 2000. *Previous winners:* Sharon Saulmon, Patricia Fitchett Turner (1999).

ALA/ASCLA Service Award. A citation presented to recognize an ASCLA member for outstanding service and leadership to the division. *For more information:* ALA Association of Specialized and Cooperative Library Agencies, 50 E. Huron St., Chicago, IL 60611-2795. *Deadline for applications:* December 15, 2000. *Previous winner:* Barbara T. Mates (1999).

ALA/FLRT Distinguished Service Award. A citation to recognize outstanding, innovative, or sustained contributions to FLRT. *For more information:* ALA Federal Librarians Round Table, 50 E. Huron St., Chicago, IL 60611-2795. *Previous winner:* Shirley Loo (1999).

ALA/LAMA Certificate of Achievement. A citation to honor an individual LAMA member for outstanding contributions to the goals of the division. *For more information:* ALA Library Administration and Management Association, 50 E. Huron St., Chicago, IL 60611-2795. *Deadline for applications:* December 1, 2000. *Previous winner:* Robert A. Dougherty (1998).

ALA/LAMA President's Award. A citation to recognize extraordinary contributions to the goals of LAMA by outside organizations or by individuals who are not LAMA members. *For more information:* ALA Library Administration and Management Association, 50 E. Huron St., Chicago, IL 60611-2795. *Deadline for applications:* December 1, 2000. *Previous winner:* H. W. Wilson Company.

ALA/LAMA Recognition of Group Achievement Award. A citation to honor groups or committees that provide outstanding service in support of the division's goals. *For more information:* ALA Library Administration and Management Association, 50 E. Huron St., Chicago, IL 60611-2795. *Deadline for applications:* December 1, 2000.

ALA/PLA Allie Beth Martin Award. An award of $3,000 to a librarian who, in a public library setting, has demonstrated extraordinary range and depth of knowledge about books or other library materials and has distinguished ability to share that knowledge. *For more information:* ALA Public Library Association, 50 E. Huron St., Chicago, IL 60611-2795. *Deadline for applications:* December 1, 2000. *Previous winner:* Grove Koger (1999).

ALA/PLA Excellence in Small and/or Rural Public Library Service Award. This $1,000 award honors a public library serving a population of 10,000 or less that demonstrates excellence of service to its community as exemplified by an overall service program or a special program of significant accomplishment. *For more information:* ALA Public Library Association, 50 E. Huron St., Chicago, IL 60611-2795. *Deadline for applications:* December 1, 2000. *Previous winner:* Little Boston Branch of the Kitsap (Wash.) Regional Library (1999).

ALA/RUSA Margaret E. Monroe Library Adult Services Award. A citation to honor a librarian who has made significant contributions to library adult services. *For more information:* ALA Reference and User Services Association, 50 E. Huron St., Chicago, IL 60611-2795. *Deadline for applications:* December 15, 2000. *Previous winner:* Jane P. Kleiner (1998).

ALISE Service Award. Regular and sustained service to ALISE through the holding of various offices and positions within the organization or accomplishing specific responsibilities for the organization. *For more information:* Association for Library and Information Science Education, P.O. Box 7640, Arlington, VA 22207. *Deadline for applications:* September 15, 2000. *Previous winner:* June Lester (1999).

ASIS James M. Cretsos Leadership Award. To recognize a new ASIS member who has demonstrated outstanding leadership qualities in ASIS activities. *For more information:* American Society for Information Science, 8720 Georgia Avenue, Suite 501, Silver Spring, MD 20910. *Deadline for applications:* July 15, 2000. *Previous winner:* Michael Leach (1998).

ASIS Watson Davis Award. To recognize an ASIS member who has shown continuous dedicated service to the membership through active participation in and support of ASIS programs. *For more information:* American Society for Information Science, 8720 Georgia Avenue, Suite 501, Silver Spring, MD 20910. *Deadline for applications:* July 15, 2000. *Previous winner:* Judy Watson (1998).

BCALA Trailblazer's Award. Presented once every five years in recognition of an individual whose pioneering contributions have been outstanding and unique, and whose efforts have "blazed a trail" in the profession. *For more information:* Black Caucus of the ALA, c/o Office for Literacy and Outreach Services, 50 E. Huron St., Chicago, IL 60611-2795. *Previous winner:* Lucille Cole Thomas (1995).

CLA Outstanding Service to Librarianship. An award for distinguished service in the field of Canadian librarianship. *For more information:* Canadian Library Association, 200 Elgin St., Ottawa, Ontario K2P 1L5, Canada. *Deadline for applications:* January 31, 2001. *Previous winner:* Frances Schwenger (1999).

CLA/CAPL Outstanding Public Library Service Award. For outstanding service in the field of Canadian public librarianship. *For more information:* CLA Canadian Association of Public Libraries, 200 Elgin St., Ottawa, Ontario K2P 1L5, Canada. *Deadline for applications:* February 28, 2001. *Previous winner:* Jocelyn LeBel (1999).

CLA/CLTA Merit Award for Distinguished Service as a Library Trustee. Presented annually to a library trustee who has demonstrated outstanding leadership in the advancement of trusteeship and public library service in Canada. *For more information:* CLA Canadian Library Trustees' Association, 200 Elgin St., Ottawa, Ontario K2P 1L5, Canada. *Previous winner:* Neil Williams (1999).

COLT Outstanding Support Staff of the Year Award. Presented annually for noteworthy service by a library support staff member. *For more information:* Council on Library/Media Technicians, P.O. Box 951, Oxon Hill, MD 20750. *Deadline for applications:* December 31, 2000. *Previous winner:* Merulyn Meadows (1999).

COLT Outstanding Supporter of Support Staff of the Year Award. Presented annually for outstanding service to library support staff. *For more information:* Council on Library/Media Technicians, P.O. Box 951, Oxon Hill, MD 20750. *Deadline for applications:* December 31, 2000. *Previous winner:* Edward T. Gillen (1999).

FOLUSA Baker & Taylor Awards for Outstanding Friends of the Library. $6,000 in awards in six categories. *For more information:* Friends of Libraries U.S.A., 1420 Walnut St., Suite 450, Philadelphia, PA 19102-4017. *Previous winners:* Friends of the Phoenix (Ariz.) Public Library; Friends of the Handley Regional Library, Winchester, Va.; Friends of Libraries in Oklahoma; Friends of Northern Illinois University Libraries, DeKalb; Rodney Borstad; Dorothy Kee.

FOLUSA HarperCollins Barbara Kingsolver Award. An award of $10,000 for book purchases to a small, public-library Friends group for outstanding community and volunteer involvement. *For more information:* Friends of Libraries U.S.A., 1420 Walnut St., Suite 450, Philadelphia, PA 19102-4017. *Previous winner:* Friends of the Crook County Library, Prineville, Oregon.

IMLS National Award for Library Service. The award celebrates outstanding American libraries that make significant and exceptional contributions to their communities. *For more information:* Institute of Museum and Library Services, 1100 Pennsylvania Avenue, N.W., Washington, DC 20506. *Deadline for applications:* November 20, 2000.

MLA Distinguished Public Service Award. Presented to honor persons whose exemplary actions have served to advance the health, welfare, and intellectual freedom of the public. *For more information:* Medical Library Association, 65 East Wacker Place, Suite 1900, Chicago, IL 60601-7298. *Previous winner:* Rep. Henry Bonilla, Texas (1998).

MLA President's Award. For a notable or important contribution to medical librarianship in the past year. *For more information:* Medical Library Association, 65 East Wacker Place, Suite 1900, Chicago, IL 60601-7298. *Previous winner:* June H. Fulton (1999).

For service to children and young adults

ALA Grolier Foundation Award. A $1,000 award to a librarian whose contribution to the stimulation and guidance of reading by children and young people exemplifies outstanding achievement in the profession. *For more information:* ALA Awards, 50 E. Huron St., Chicago, IL 60611-2795. *Deadline for applications:* December 1, 2000. *Previous winner:* Elizabeth Huntoon (1999).

ALA/AASL Baker & Taylor Distinguished Service Award. A $3,000 award for outstanding contribution to school librarianship and school library development. *For more information:* ALA American Association of School Librarians, 50 E. Huron St., Chicago, IL 60611-2795. *Deadline for applications:* February 1, 2001. *Previous winner:* Jacqueline C. Mancall (1999).

ALA/AASL National School Library Media Program of the Year Award. Three awards of $6,000 each to school districts (large and small) and a single school, for excellence and innovation in outstanding library media programs. *For more information:* ALA American Association of School Librarians, 50 E. Huron St., Chicago, IL 60611-2795. *Deadline for applications:* February 1, 2001. *Previous winner:* Lincoln (Nebr.) Public Schools (1999).

ALA/AASL SIRS Distinguished School Administrators Award. A $2,000 grant for expanding the role of the library in elementary or secondary school education. *For more information:* ALA American Association of School Librarians, 50 E. Huron St., Chicago, IL 60611-2795. *Deadline for applications:* February 1, 2001. *Previous winner:* Eugene J. Sudol (1999).

ALA/ALSC Distinguished Service Award. $1,000 to honor an ALSC member who has made significant contributions to library service to children and/or ALSC. *For more information:* ALA Association for Library Service to Children, 50 E. Huron St., Chicago, IL 60611-2795. *Deadline for applications:* December 1, 2000. *Previous winner:* Lillian Gerhardt (1999).

ALA/ALSC Econo-Clad Literature Program Award. One annual $1,000 award to an ALSC member for development and implementation of an outstanding library program for children, involving reading and the use of literature. *For more information:* ALA Association for Library Service to Children, 50 E. Huron St., Chicago, IL 60611-2795. *Deadline for applications:* December 1, 2000. *Previous winner:* Martha Simpson (1999).

ALA/YALSA Econo-Clad Young Adult Reading or Literature Program Award. $1,000 to a YALSA member for development and implementation of an outstanding library program for young adults, involving reading and the use of literature. For more information: ALA Young Adult Library Services Association, 50 E. Huron St., Chicago, IL 60611-2795. *Deadline for applications:* December 1, 2000. *Previous winner:* Donna McMillen (1999).

ALA/YALSA Great Book Giveaway. Each year the YALSA office receives approximately 1,200 newly published children's, young adult, and adult books, videos, CDs and audiocassettes. YALSA and the cooperating publishers are offering one year's worth of review materials as a contribution to a library in need through this application process. *For more information:* ALA Young Adult Library Services Association, 50 E. Huron St., Chicago, IL 60611-2795. *Deadline for applications:* December 1, 2000. *Previous winner:* Willow Springs (Mo.) High School (1998).

CLA/CSLA Margaret B. Scott Award of Merit. For development of school libraries at the national level in Canada. *For more information:* CLA Canadian School Library Association, 200 Elgin St., Ottawa, Ontario K2P 1L5, Canada. *Deadline for applications:* February 28, 2001. *Previous winner:* Rose Dotten (1999).

CLA/CSLA National Book Service Teacher–Librarian of the Year Award. To a school-based teacher or librarian who has made an outstanding contribution to school librarianship in Canada. *For more information:* CLA Canadian School Library Association, 200 Elgin St., Ottawa, Ontario K2P 1L5, Canada. *Deadline for applications:* February 28, 2001. *Previous winner:* Barbara Poustie (1999).

CLA/HSLS Certificate of Merit. For an outstanding contribution to high school librarianship. *For more information:* Catholic Library Association, 100 North St., Suite 224, Pittsfield, MA 01201-5109.

IASL SIRS Commendation Award. A $500 award for outstanding and innovative projects, plans, publications, or programs that could serve as models for replication by individuals or associations. *For more information:* International Association of School Librarianship, Suite 300, Box 34069, Seattle, WA 98124-1069. *Deadline for applications:* March 1, 2001. *Previous winners:* James Henri, Lyn Hay, Lyn Rushby (1997).

IASL Winnebago Progressive School Library Media Awards. Two awards (one for developing and one for developed nations) for the implementation of innovative ideas by librarian(s)/media specialist(s) to enhance the lifelong learning skills of students. *For more information:* International Association of School Librarianship, Suite 300, Box 34069, Seattle, WA 98124-1069. *Deadline for applications:* March 1, 2001. *Previous winners:* Inna Groudkaya, Peter Genco (1998).

For service to special populations

AALL/SCC-CIS O. James Werner Award for Distinctive Service to Persons with Disabilities. To honor a member who has made a significant contribution to serving directly or for arranging services to be provided to persons with disabilities. *For more information:* American Association of Law Libraries, 53 W. Jackson Blvd., Suite 940, Chicago, IL 60604. *Deadline for applications:* February 1, 2001. *Previous winner:* Pamela J. Gregory.

ALA/ASCLA Exceptional Service Award. A citation presented to recognize exceptional service to patients, to the homebound, to medical, nursing, and other professional staff in hospitals, and to inmates, as well as to recognize professional leadership, effective interpretation of programs, pioneering activity, and significant research of experimental projects. *For more information:* ALA Association of Specialized and Cooperative Library Agencies, 50 E. Huron St., Chicago, IL 60611-2795. *Deadline for applications:* December 15, 2000. *Previous winner:* Rangashri Kishore (1999).

ALA/ASCLA Francis Joseph Campbell Award. A citation and a medal presented to a person who has made an outstanding contribution to the advancement of library service for the blind and physically handicapped. *For more information:* ALA Association of Specialized and Cooperative Library Agencies, 50 E. Huron St., Chicago, IL 60611-2795. *Deadline for applications:* December 15, 2000. *Previous winner:* Donald John Weber (1999).

ALA/ASCLA National Organization on Disability Award. A $1,000 award to an institution or organization that has made the library's total service more accessible through changing physical and/or additional barriers. *For more information:* ALA Association of Specialized and Cooperative Library Agencies, 50 E. Huron St., Chicago, IL 60611-2795. *Deadline for applications:* December 15, 2000. *Previous winner:* Disabilities Resources Inc. (1999).

ALA/EMIERT Gale Research Multicultural Award. $1,000 and citation in recognition of outstanding achievement and leadership in serving the multicultural/multiethnic community with significant collection building, public, and outreach services to culturally diverse populations and creative materials and programs. *For more information:* ALA Office for Library Outreach Services, 50 E. Huron St., Chicago, IL 60611-2795. *Deadline for applications:* December 1, 2000. *Previous winner:* Schaffer Library of Union College (1999).

ALA/PLA Leonard Wertheimer Multilingual Award. A $1,000 award presented to a person, group, or organization for work that enhances and promotes multilingual public library service. *For more information:* ALA Public Library Association, 50 E. Huron St., Chicago, IL 60611-2795. *Deadline for applications:* December 1, 2000. *Previous winner:* Toni Bissessar and the staff of the Multicultural Center of the Brooklyn (N.Y.) Public Library (1999).

ALA/RUSA Bessie Boehm Moore Thorndike Press Award. A $1,000 award to recognize a library organization that has developed an outstanding program for library service to the aging. *For more information:* ALA Reference and User Services Association, 50 E. Huron St., Chicago, IL 60611-2795. *Deadline for applications:* December 15, 2000.

ALA/RUSA John Sessions Memorial Award. A plaque given to a library or library system to honor significant work with the labor community and to recognize the history and contributions of the labor movement toward the development of this country. *For more information:* ALA Reference and User Services Association, 50 E. Huron St., Chicago, IL 60611-2795. *Deadline for applications:* December 15, 2000. *Previous winner:* Libraries for the Future (1999).

APALA Distinguished Service Award. For significant contributions to Asian/Pacific society in the field of library and information science. *For more information:* Asian/Pacific American Library Association, rama@uic.edu.

BCALA Demco Award for Excellence in Librarianship. An annual award of $500 presented to the librarian who has made significant contributions to promoting the status of African Americans in the library profession. *For more information:* Black Caucus of the ALA, c/o ALA Office for Literacy and Outreach, 50 E. Huron St., Chicago, IL 60611-2795. *Previous winner:* Samuel F. Morrison (1997).

CALA Distinguished Service Award. To a CALA member. *For more information:* Chinese American Librarians Association, Ling Hwey Jeng, lhjeng00@ukcc.uky.edu. *Previous winner:* Priscilla Chang Yu (1999).

Reforma Librarian of the Year Award. $400 to recognize distinguished achievement in library work that improves and promotes library services to Spanish-speaking residents of the United States. *For more information:* Reforma, P.O. Box 832, Anaheim, CA 92815-0832. *Previous winner:* Benjamin O. Ocon (1999).

For social responsibility

ALA Equality Award. $500 to an individual or group for an outstanding contribution that promotes the equality of women and men in the library profession. *For more information:* ALA Awards, 50 E. Huron St., Chicago, IL 60611-2795. *Deadline for applications:* December 1, 2000. *Previous winner:* Kansas City (Mo.) Public Library (1999).

ALA/ALTA Literacy Award. Citation to a library trustee or an individual who, in a volunteer capacity, has made a significant contribution to addressing the illiteracy problem in the United States. *For more information:* ALA Association of Library Trustees and Advocates, 50 E. Huron St., Chicago, IL 60611-2795. *Deadline for applications:* December 1, 2000. *Previous winners:* Rebecca B. Schroeder, Otissey Denton (1999).

ALA/PLA Advancement of Literacy Award. This award honors a publisher, bookseller, hardware or software dealer, foundation, or similar group (not individuals) for making a significant contribution to the advancement of adult literacy. *For more information:* ALA Public Library Association, 50 E. Huron St., Chicago, IL 60611-2795. *Deadline for applications:* December 1, 2000. *Previous winners:* Lila Wallace-Reader's Digest Fund and the Mount Clemens (Mich.) Rotary Club (1999).

ALA/SRRT Jackie Eubanks Award. An award of $500 and a certificate to honor outstanding achievement in promoting the acquisition and use of alternative media in libraries. *For more information:* ALA Social Responsibilities Round Table, 50 E. Huron St., Chicago, IL 60611-2795. *Deadline for applications:* December 1, 2000. *Previous winners:* Ed Weber, Julie Herrada (1999).

CLA/CLTA Achievement in Literacy Award. Presented annually to a public library board that has initiated an innovative program that is contributing significantly to the advancement of literacy in its community. *For more information:* CLA Canadian Library Trustees' Association, 200 Elgin St., Ottawa, Ontario K2P 1L5, Canada. *Previous winner:* High River (Alta.) Centennial Library Board (1999).

For special libraries

AALL Marian Gould Gallagher Distinguished Service Award. Recognizes extended and sustained service to law librarianship, for exemplary service to AALL, or for contributions to the professional literature. *For more information:* American Association of Law Libraries, 53 W. Jackson Blvd., Suite 940, Chicago, IL 60604. *Deadline for applications:* February 1, 2001. *Previous winners:* Richard L. Beer, Bardie C. Wolf Jr. (1998).

AALL/PRC Excellence in Marketing Awards. Honors outstanding achievement in public relations activities by an individual, group of individuals, or a library affiliated with AALL. *For more information:* American Association of Law Libraries, 53 W. Jackson Blvd., Suite 940, Chicago, IL 60604. *Deadline for applications:* February 1, 2001. *Previous winners:* Law Library of Montgomery County, Pa.; Elizabeth D. Kenney & Kenneth J. Withers; Boston College Law Library; Chicago Association of Law Libraries; U.S. Court of Appeals 5th Circuit Library System (1998).

AALL/TS-SIS Renee D. Chapman Memorial Award for Outstanding Contributions in Technical Services Law Librarianship. Recognizes extended and sustained distinguished service to technical services law librarianship. *For more information:* American Association of Law Libraries, 53 W. Jackson Blvd., Suite 940, Chicago, IL 60604. *Deadline for applications:* February 1, 2001. *Previous winner:* Peter Enyingi (1998).

AASLH Albert B. Corey Award. Recognizes primarily volunteer-operated historical organizations that best display the qualities of vigor, scholarship, and imagination in their work. *For more information:* American Association for State and Local History, 1717 Church Street, Nashville, TN 37203-2991. *Previous winner:* Chinese Historical and Cultural Project, Santa Clara County, Calif. (1998).

ACL Emily Russel Award. Honors outstanding contributions to Christian librarianship. *For more information:* Association of Christian Librarians, P.O. Box 4, Cedarville, OH 45314. *Previous winners:* Eva Kiewitt, Lois Lehman (1997).

ALA/AFLRT Armed Forces Library Achievement Citation. Citation presented to a member of the Armed Forces Libraries Round Table for significant contributions to the development of armed forces library services and to organizations encouraging an interest in libraries and reading. *For more information:* ALA Armed Forces Library Round Table, 50 E. Huron St., Chicago, IL 60611-2795. *Deadline for applications:* March 1, 2001. *Previous winner:* Deon Grinnell (1999).

ALA/AFLRT Armed Forces Library Certificate of Merit. Certificate presented to an individual or group in recognition of special contributions to armed forces libraries. Recipients need not be librarians or members of the association. *For more information:* ALA Armed Forces Library Round Table, 50 E. Huron St., Chicago, IL 60611-2795. *Deadline for applications:* March 1, 2001. *Previous winner:* Larry Osborne (1999).

ALA/AFLRT Armed Forces Library NewsBank Scholarship Award. An award of $1,000 to the school of the recipient's choice and certificate to a member of the Armed Forces Libraries Round Table who has given exemplary service in the area of library support for off-duty education programs in the armed forces. *For more information:* ALA Armed Forces Library Round Table, 50 E. Huron St., Chicago, IL 60611-2795. *Deadline for applications:* March 1, 2001. *Previous winner:* Katherine Gillen (1999).

ALA/FLRT Federal Librarians Achievement Award. Annual citation and gift for leadership in the promotion of library and information science in the federal community. *For more information:* ALA Federal Librarians Round Table, Washington Office, 1301 Pennsylvania Avenue, N.W., Suite 403, Washington, DC 20004-1701. *Deadline for applications:* December 31, 2000. *Previous winner:* Milton H. McGee (1999).

CLA/CASLIS Award for Special Librarianship in Canada. For an outstanding contribution to special librarianship in Canada through publication, research, teaching, or any other noteworthy activity of benefit to the profession. *For more information:* CLA Canadian Association of Special Libraries and Information Services, 200 Elgin St., Ottawa, Ontario K2P 1L5, Canada. *Deadline for applications:* December 5, 2000. *Previous winner:* Maggie Weaver (1999).

CLA/PCLS Aggiornamento Award. For an outstanding contribution to parish librarianship. *For more information:* Catholic Library Association, 100 North St., Suite 224, Pittsfield, MA 01201-5109. *Previous winner:* Liguori Publications (1999).

CSLA Award for Outstanding Congregational Librarian. Recognizes a church or synagogue librarian who exhibits distinguished service to his/her congregation and/or community through devotion to the ministry of congregational librarianship. *For more information:* Church and Synagogue Library Association, P.O. Box 19357, Portland, OR 97280-0357. *Deadline for applications:* April 15, 2001. *Previous winner:* Mary Jane Conger (1999).

CSLA Award for Outstanding Congregational Library. Honors a church or synagogue library that has responded in creative and innovative ways to the library's mission of reaching and serving members of the congregation and/or wider community. *For more information:* Church and Synagogue Library Association, P.O. Box 19357, Portland, OR 97280-0357. *Previous winner:* St. Paul's United Methodist Church, Kerrville, Texas (1999).

CSLA Award for Outstanding Contribution to Congregational Libraries. Given to a person or institution who has provided inspiration, guidance, leadership, or resources to enrich the field of church or synagogue libraries. *For more information:* Church and Synagogue Library Association, P.O. Box 19357, Portland, OR 97280-0357. *Previous winner:* Louise Swartz (1999).

CSLA Pat Tabler Memorial Scholarship Award. Recognizes a librarian who has shown initiative and creativity in starting or renewing a congregational library. *For more information:* Church and Synagogue Library Association, P.O. Box 19357, Portland, OR 97280-0357. *Previous winner:* Shirley McCartney (1999).

FLICC Federal Librarian of the Year. This award recognizes and commends outstanding, innovative, and sustained professional achievements of a practicing librarian or information professional in a federal library or information center. *For more information:* Federal Library and Information Center Committee, c/o Library of Congress, 101 Independence Avenue, S.E., Washington, DC 20540-4930. *Deadline for applications:* November 15, 2000. *Previous winner:* Joan Buntzen (1998).

FLICC Federal Library Technician of the Year. This award recognizes and commends outstanding, innovative, and sustained professional achievements of a practicing paraprofessional or library technician in a federal library or information center. *For more information:* Federal Library and Information Center Committee, c/o Library of Congress, 101 Independence Avenue, S.E., Washington, DC 20540-4930. *Deadline for applications:* November 15, 2000. *Previous winner:* Connie Clarkston (1998).

MLA Lois Ann Colaianni Award for Excellence and Achievement in Hospital Librarianship. Given to an MLA member who has made significant contributions to the profession through overall distinction or leadership in hospital library administration or service, production of a definitive publication related to hospital librarianship, teaching, research, advocacy, or the development or application of innovative technology to hospital librarianship. *For more information:* Medical Library Association, 65 East Wacker Place, Suite 1900, Chicago, IL 60601-7298. *Deadline for applications:* November 1, 2000. *Previous winner:* Jacqueline D. Bastille (1999).

SAA Sister M. Claude Lane Award. Certificate and cash prize that recognizes individuals who have made a significant contribution to the field of religious archives. *For more information:* Society of American Archivists, 527 S. Wells, 5th Floor, Chicago, IL 60607. *Deadline for applications:* February 28, 2001. *Previous winner:* Sr. Mary Linus Bax.

SLA Dow Jones Leadership Award–21st Century Competencies in Action. A $2,000 award presented annually to an individual SLA member who exemplifies leadership as a special librarian through examples of personal and professional competencies. *For more information:* Special Libraries Association, 1700 Eighteenth Street, N.W., Washington, DC 20009. *Deadline for applications:* December 4, 2000. *Previous winner:* Lucy Lettis (1999).

SLA Fellows. Bestowed to individual SLA members in recognition of leadership in the field of special librarianship and for outstanding contributions and expected future service. *For more information:* Special Libraries Association, 1700 Eighteenth Street, N.W., Washington, DC 20009. *Deadline for applications:* December 4, 2000. *Previous winners:* Bob Bellanti, Susan Klopper, Barbara Spiegelman, Gloria Zamora (1999).

SLA Hall of Fame Award. Granted to an SLA member at or near the end of an active professional career for an extended and sustained period of distinguished service. *For more information:* Special Libraries Association, 1700 Eighteenth Street, N.W., Washington, DC 20009. *Deadline for applications:* December 4, 2000. *Previous winners:* Ellen Mimnaugh, Angela Pollis (1999).

SLA John Cotton Dana Award. Conferred upon an individual member(s) in recognition of exceptional service to special librarianship. *For more information:* Special Libraries Association, 1700 Eighteenth Street, N.W., Washington, DC 20009. *Deadline for applications:* December 4, 2000. *Previous winner:* Fred Roper (1999).

SLA President's Award. Awarded to an individual SLA member(s) for a notable or important contribution during the past Association year. *For more information:* Special Libraries Association, 1700 Eighteenth Street, N.W., Washington, DC 20009. *Deadline for applications:* December 4, 2000. *Previous winner:* Susan A. Merry (1998).

SLA Professional Award. Given to an individual or group in recognition of a specific significant contribution to the field of librarianship or information science. *For more information:* Special Libraries Association, 1700 Eighteenth Street, N.W., Washington, DC 20009. *Deadline for applications:* December 4, 2000.

SLA Public Relations Member Achievement Award. Presented to an individual SLA member for outstanding contributions by raising visibility, public awareness, and appreciation of the profession or SLA. *For more information:* Special Libraries Association, 1700 Eighteenth Street, N.W., Washington, DC 20009. *Deadline for applications:* December 4, 2000. *Previous winner:* Lisa Guedea Carreño (1999).

SLA Rose L. Vormelker Award. Given to an individual SLA member in recognition of exceptional services to the profession of special librarianship in the area of mentoring students and/or practicing professionals in the field. *For more information:* Special Libraries Association, 1700 Eighteenth Street, N.W., Washington, DC 20009. *Deadline for applications:* December 4, 2000. *Previous winner:* Lynn Tinsley (1999).

TLA Distinguished Librarian Award. Given to individuals who have made extraordinary contributions to theatre librarianship. *For more information:* Theatre Library Association, Shubert Archive, 149 West 45th St., New York, NY 10036. *Previous winner:* Dorothy Swerdlove (1996).

For archives

ALA/GODORT Bernardine Abbott Hoduski Founders Award. Plaque given to recognize documents librarians who may not be known at the national level but who have made significant contributions to the field of state, international, local, or federal documents. *For more information:* ALA Government Documents Round Table, 50 E. Huron St., Chicago, IL 60611-2795. *Deadline for applications:* December 1, 2000. *Previous winners:* Barbie Selby, Bette L. Siegel (1999).

ALA/GODORT James Bennett Childs Award. An annual award presented to an individual for distinguished contributions to documents librarianship. *For more information:* ALA Government Documents Round Table, 50 E. Huron St., Chicago, IL 60611-2795. *Deadline for applications:* December 1, 2000. *Previous winner:* Virginia F. Saunders (1999).

FLICC Federal Library/Information Center of the Year. This award recognizes and commends outstanding, innovative, and sustained achievements by a federal library or information center. *For more information:* Federal Library and Information Center Committee, c/o Library of Congress, 101 Independence Avenue, S.E., Washington, DC 20540-4930. *Deadline for applications:* November 15, 2000. *Previous winners:* National Institutes of Health Library, Defense Technical Information Center (1998).

SAA C. F. W. Coker Award for Description. Certificate and cash award for finding aids, finding aid systems, projects that involve innovative development in archival description, or descriptive tools that enable archivists to produce more effective finding aids. *For more information:* Society of American Archivists, 527 S. Wells, 5th Floor, Chicago, IL 60607. *Deadline for applications:* February 28, 2001. *Previous winner:* Robert M. Kvasnicka, *The Trans-Mississippi West, 1804–1912.*

SAA Distinguished Service Award. Recognizes a North American archival institution, organization, education program, or nonprofit or governmental organization that has given outstanding service to its public and has made an exemplary contribution to the archival profession. *For more information:* Society of American Archivists, 527 S. Wells, 5th Floor, Chicago, IL 60607. *Deadline for applications:* February 28, 2001. *Previous winner:* Arthur and Elizabeth Schlesinger Library.

SAA Fellows' Ernst Posner Award. Certificate and cash award that recognizes the author(s) of an outstanding article dealing with some facet of archival administration, history, theory, and/or methodology that was published during the preceding year in the *American Archivist. For more information:* Society of American Archivists, 527 S. Wells, 5th Floor, Chicago, IL 60607. *Previous winner:* James M. O'Toole.

SAA J. Franklin Jameson Archival Advocacy Award. Honors an individual, institution, or organization not directly involved in archival work that promotes greater public awareness, appreciation, or support of archival activities or programs. *For more information:* Society of American Archivists, 527 S. Wells, 5th Floor, Chicago,

IL 60607. *Deadline for applications:* February 28, 2001. *Previous winner:* Former Sen. Thomas F. Eagleton.

SAA Philip M. Hamer–Elizabeth Hamer Kegan Award. Certificate and cash award that recognizes an archivist, editor, group of individuals, or institution that has increased public awareness of a specific body of documents through compilation, transcription, exhibition, or public presentation. *For more information:* Society of American Archivists, 527 S. Wells, 5th Floor, Chicago, IL 60607. *Deadline for applications:* February 28, 2001. *Previous winners:* Julie Daniels, Judy Hohmann, and Jean West.

SAA Preservation Publication Award. Recognizes the author(s) or editor(s) of an outstanding published work (audiovisual, electronic, or print; article, report, chapter, monograph) related to archives preservation published in North America during the preceding year. *For more information:* Society of American Archivists, 527 S. Wells, 5th Floor, Chicago, IL 60607. *Deadline for applications:* February 28, 2001. *Previous winner:* Mary Lynn Ritzenthaler, *Preserving Archives and Manuscripts.*

SAA Theodore Calvin Pease Award. Certificate and cash prize of $100 that recognizes superior writing achievements by students of archival administration. *For more information:* Society of American Archivists, 527 S. Wells, 5th Floor, Chicago, IL 60607. *Deadline for applications:* May 1, 2001. *Previous winner:* Shauna McRanor.

SAA Waldo Gifford Leland Award. Certificate and cash prize that encourages and rewards writing of superior excellence and usefulness in the field of archival history, theory, or practice. Monographs, finding aids, and documentary publications published in North America during the preceding year are eligible. *For more information:* Society of American Archivists, 527 S. Wells, 5th Floor, Chicago, IL 60607. *Deadline for applications:* February 28, 2001. *Previous winners:* Thomas Wilsted and William M. Nolte, *Managing Archival and Manuscript Repositories.*

For technology

AECT Annual Achievement Award. Honors the individual who during the past year has made the most significant contribution to the advancement of educational communications and technology. *For more information:* Association for Educational Communications and Technology, 1025 Vermont Avenue, N.W., Suite 820, Washington, DC 20005. *Deadline for applications:* January 1, 2001.

ALA Information Today Library of the Future Award. An award of $2,500 to honor a library, library consortium, group of librarians, or support organization for innovative development of patron training programs about information technology in a library setting. *For more information:* ALA Awards, 50 E. Huron St., Chicago, IL 60611-2795. *Deadline for applications:* December 1, 2000. *Previous winner:* Queens Borough (N.Y.) Public Library (1999).

ALA/AASL ICONnect ICPrize for Collaboration through Technology. $1,000 to be used toward the purchase of technology for use in the library media center or to support travel to attend a state or national conference. *For more information:* ALA, American Association of School Librarians, 50 E. Huron St., Chicago, IL 60611-2795. *Deadline for applications:* November 1, 2000. *Previous winners:* Northwest High School, Cincinnati; Wayne (N.J.) Valley High School; Eduardo Villarreal Elementary School, San Antonio, Tex.; Mt. Laurel (N.J.) Hartford School; Plymouth River School, Hingham, Mass.; Maxwell Hill Gifted Center, Beckley, W.Va.; Potter Road Elementary School, Framingham, Mass.; Cathedral School in New York City (1999).

ALA/AASL Information Technology Pathfinder Award. Awards of $1,000 to elementary and secondary library media specialists for demonstrating vision and leadership through the use of information technology to build lifelong learners. An additional $500 goes to each library, and the winners receive travel expenses to ALA Annual Conference. *For more information:* ALA, American Association of School Librarians, 50 E. Huron St., Chicago, IL 60611-2795. *Deadline for applications:* February 1, 2001. *Previous winners:* Sharlene Miller-Ballas, Betty K. Bracken (1999).

ALA/LITA Frederick G. Kilgour Award for Research in Library and Information Technology. $2,000 for research relevant to the development of information technologies, especially work which shows promise of having a positive and substantive impact on any aspect of the publication, storage, retrieval, and dissemination of information, or the processes by which information and data are manipulated and managed. *For more information:* ALA Library and Information Technology Association, 50 E. Huron St., Chicago, IL 60611-2795. *Deadline for applications:* April 1, 2001. *Previous winner:* Dean K. Jue (1999).

ALA/LITA Gaylord Award for Achievement in Library and Information Technology. Citation and $1,000 given to a practicing or retired librarian, an individual, or a small group of individuals working in collaboration. *For more information:* ALA Library and Information Technology Association, 50 E. Huron St., Chicago, IL 60611-2795. *Deadline for applications:* April 1, 2001. *Previous winner:* Sheila Creth (1999).

ALA/LITA Library Hi Tech Award. An award of $1,000 to recognize outstanding achievement in communication in continuing education within the field of library and information technology. *For more information:* ALA Library and Information Technology Association, 50 E. Huron St., Chicago, IL 60611-2795. *Deadline for applications:* April 1, 2001. *Previous winner:* Ann S. Okerson (1999).

ALA/PLA Baker & Taylor Entertainment CD-ROM Grant. Designed to promote the development of a circulating CD-ROM collection in public libraries and increase the exposure of the CD-ROM format within the community, the grant consists of $2,500 worth of CD-ROM titles to a public library. *For more information:* ALA Public Library Association, 50 E. Huron St., Chicago, IL 60611-2795. *Deadline for applications:* December 1, 2000. *Previous winners:* Orcas Island (Wash.) Public Library (1998), Hamburg Township (Mich.) Library (1999).

ALA/PLA Highsmith Library Innovation Award. This $2,000 award recognizes a public library's innovative achievement in planning and implementing a creative program or service using technology. *For more information:* ALA Public Library Association, 50 E. Huron St., Chicago, IL 60611-2795. *Deadline for applications:* December 1, 2000. *Previous winner:* Richmond (B.C.) Public Library (1999).

ALISE Pratt-Severn Faculty Innovation Award. A $2,000 award to identify innovation by full-time faculty members in incorporating evolving information technologies in the curricula of accredited library schools. *For more information:* Association for Library and Information Science Education, P.O. Box 7640, Arlington, VA 22207. *Deadline for applications:* September 15, 2000. *Previous winner:* Gretchen Whitney (1999).

CLA Information Today Award for Innovative Technology. $500 (Can.) given annually to honor a member or members of the Canadian Library Association for innovative use and application of technology in a Canadian library setting. *For more information:* Canadian Library Association, 200 Elgin St., Ottawa, Ontario K2P 1L5, Canada. *Deadline for applications:* March 1, 2001. *Previous winners:* B.C. College and Institute Library Services, Université Laval Library (1999).

CLA OCLC Award for Promoting Technology in Libraries. This $1,000 (Can.) award recognizes and honors a recent library graduate who invests time and talent in researching, developing, and /or implementing new information technologies. *For more information:* Canadian Library Association, 200 Elgin St., Ottawa, Ontario K2P 1L5, Canada. *Deadline for applications:* December 1, 2000. *Previous winner:* Angela Horne (1998).

MLA ISI Frank Bradway Rogers Information Advancement Award. Presented annually in recognition of outstanding contributions for the application of technology to the delivery of health science information, to the science of information, or to the facilitation of the delivery of health science information. *For more information:* Medical Library Association, 65 East Wacker Place, Suite 1900, Chicago, IL 60601-7298. *Deadline for applications:* November 1, 2000. *Previous winners:* BioSites, Beryl Glitz, Anne Swedenberg Prussing, Brian Warling, Melissa Just, Mary Buttner, Greg Williamson (1999).

SLA Innovations in Technology Award. $1,000 award granted to an individual SLA member for innovative use and application of technology in a special library. *For more information:* Special Libraries Association, 1700 Eighteenth Street, N.W., Washington, DC 20009. *Deadline for applications:* December 4, 2000. *Previous winner:* Andrew G. Breeding (1998).

LIBRARY EDUCATION

Accredited library programs

THE FOLLOWING GRADUATE LIBRARY and information studies programs are accredited (as of summer 1999) by the American Library Association under its *Standards for Accreditation*. All programs offer a master's-level degree; those marked with an asterisk(*) offer a doctorate or post-master's specialist or certificate program.

*Catholic University of America, School of Library and Information Science, Washington, DC 20064; (202) 319-5085; (www.cua.edu/www/lsc/). Peter Liebscher, dean.

Most expensive library schools, 1997

In-state tuition and fees for a full ALA-accredited master's degree:

Catholic University of America	$24,682
Drexel University	24,360
Pratt Institute	21,760
Simmons College	20,247
St. John's University	19,800
University of Michigan	19,264
Syracuse University	19,044
Long Island University	16,452
Dominican University	16,020
Clark Atlanta University	13,752
University of Pittsburgh	12,128
University of Maryland	10,378

Library schools with the largest faculties, 1997

	FTE
University of Pittsburgh	35.0
Indiana University	30.5
Syracuse University	26.4
University of Illinois	24.0
University of Texas at Austin	20.5
San Jose State University	19.5
University of Michigan	19.07
University of North Carolina-Chapel Hill	17.0
University of North Texas	16.75
Florida State University	16.0
Rutgers University	15.0
University of South Carolina	14.0

SOURCE: Evelyn H. Daniel and Jerry D. Saye, *Library and Information Science Education Statistical Report 1998* (Washington, D.C.: Association for Library and Information Science Education, 1998), pp. 304, 306.

*Clarion University of Pennsylvania, Department of Library Science, 840 Wood St., Clarion, PA 16214-1232; (814) 226-2271; (www.clarion.edu/ libsci). James T. Maccaferri, chairperson.

*Clark Atlanta University, School of Library and Information Studies, 300 Trevor Arnett Hall, 223 James P. Brawley Drive, Atlanta, GA 30314; (404) 880-8697; Arthur C. Gunn, dean.

Dalhousie University, School of Library and Information Studies, Faculty of Management, Halifax, NS, Canada B3H 3J5; (902) 494-3656; (www.mgmt. dal.ca/slis/). Bertrum H. MacDonald, director.

*Dominican University, Graduate School of Library and Information Science, 7900 West Division Street, River Forest, IL 60305; (708) 524-6845; (www.dom.edu/academic/gslishome.html). Prudence W. Dalrymple, dean.

*Drexel University, College of Information Science and Technology, 3141 Chestnut Street, Philadelphia, PA 19104-2875; (215) 895-2474; (www.cis. drexel.edu). David E. Fenske, dean.

*Emporia State University, School of Library and Information Management, P.O. Box 4025, Emporia, KS 66801; (316) 341-5203; (www.slim.emporia. edu). Robert Grover, dean.

*Florida State University, School of Information Studies, Tallahassee, FL 32306-2100; (850) 644-5775; (www.fsu.edu/~lis/). Jane B. Robbins, dean.

*Indiana University, School of Library and Information Science, 10th Street and Jordan Avenue, Bloomington, IN 47405-1801; (812) 855-2018; (www.slis.indiana.edu). Blaise Cronin, dean.

*Kent State University, School of Library and Information Science, Room 314 Library, P.O. Box 5190, Kent, OH 44242-0001; (330) 672-2782;(web.slis. kent.edu). Danny P. Wallace, director.

*Long Island University, Palmer School of Library and Information Science, C. W. Post Campus, 720 Northern Boulevard, Brookville, NY 11548-1300; (516) 299-2866; (www.liu.edu/palmer/). Michael Koenig, dean.

*Louisiana State University, School of Library and Information Science, 267 Coates Hall, Baton Rouge, LA 70803; (225) 388-3158; (adam.slis.lsu.edu). Bert R. Boyce, dean.

*McGill University, Graduate School of Library and Information Studies, 3459 McTavish Street, Montreal, QB, Canada H3A 1Y1; (514) 398-4204,(www.gslis.mcgill.ca). Jamshid Beheshti, director.

North Carolina Central University, School of Library and Information Sciences, P.O. Box 19586, Durham, NC 27707; (919) 560-6485; (www.slis. nccu.edu/). Benjamin F. Speller Jr., dean.

*Pratt Institute, School of Information and Library Science, Information Science Center, 200 Willoughby Avenue, Brooklyn, NY 11205; (718) 636-3702; (sils.pratt.edu). Larry Kroah, acting dean.

*Queens College, City University of New York, Graduate School of Library and Information Studies, 65-30 Kissena Boulevard, Flushing, NY 11367; (718) 997-3790; (www.qc.edu/GSLIS). Marianne Cooper, director.

*Rutgers University, School of Communication, Information and Library Studies, 4 Huntington Street, New Brunswick, NJ 08901-1071; (732) 932-7917; (www.scils.rutgers.edu/lis/). Gustav W. Friedrich, dean.

*St. John's University, Division of Library and Information Science, 8000 Utopia Parkway, Jamaica, NY 11439; (718) 990-6200; (www.stjohns.edu/ academics/sjc/depts/dlis/). James A. Benson, director.

San Jose State University, School of Library and Information Science, One

Washington Square, San Jose, CA 95192-0029; (408) 924-2490; (witloof. sjsu.edu). Blanche Woolls, director.

*Simmons College, Graduate School of Library and Information Science, 300 The Fenway, Boston, MA 02115-5898; (617) 521-2800; (www.simmons. edu/graduate/gslis/). James M. Matarazzo, dean and professor.

*Southern Connecticut State University, School of Communication, Information and Library Science, Department of Library Science and Instructional Technology, 501 Crescent Street, New Haven, CT 06515; (203) 392-5781; Edward C. Harris, dean.

*Syracuse University, School of Information Studies, 4-206 Center for Science and Technology, Syracuse, NY 13244-4100; (315) 443-2911; (istweb. syr.edu). Raymond F. von Dran, dean.

*Texas Woman's University, School of Library and Information Studies, P.O. Box 425438, Denton, TX 76204-5438; (940) 898-2602; (www.twu.edu/slis). Keith Swigger, dean.

*Université de Montréal, Ecole de bibliothéconomie et des sciences de l'information, C.P. 6128, Succursale Centre-Ville, Montréal, Québec, Canada H3C 3J7; (514) 343-6044; (www.fas.umontreal.ca/EBSI/). Gilles Deschatelets, director.

*University at Albany, State University of New York, School of Information Science and Policy, 135 Western Avenue, Draper 113, Albany, NY 12222; (518) 442-5110; (www.albany.edu/sisp/). Philip B. Eppard, dean.

*University at Buffalo, State University of New York, School of Information Studies, 534 Baldy Hall, Buffalo, NY 14260-1020; (716) 645-2412; (www.sils.buffalo.edu). Thomas L. Jacobson, interim dean.

*University of Alabama, School of Library and Information Studies, Box 870252, Tuscaloosa, AL 35487-0252; (205) 348-4610; (www.slis.ua.edu). Joan L. Atkinson, director.

University of Alberta, School of Library and Information Studies, 3-20 Rutherford South, Edmonton, AB, Canada T6G 2J4; (403) 492-4578; (www.slis. ualberta.ca/nuhome/slis.htm). Alvin Schrader, director.

*University of Arizona (under appeal), School of Information Resources and Library Science, 1515 East First Street, Tucson, AZ 85719; (520) 621-3565; (www.sir.arizona.edu). Carla Stoffle, acting director.

*University of British Columbia, School of Library, Archival and Information Studies, 1956 Main Mall, Rm. 831, Vancouver, BC, Canada V6T 1Z1; (604) 822-2404; (www.slais.ubc.ca). Ken Haycock, director.

*University of California, Los Angeles, Department of Library and Information Science, Graduate School of Education & Information Studies, 2320 Moore Hall, Mailbox 951521, Los Angeles, CA 90095-1521; (310) 825-8799; (dlis.gseis.ucla.edu). Michèle V. Cloonan, chair.

*University of Hawaii, Library and Information Science Program, 2550 The Mall, Honolulu, HI 96822; (808) 956-7321; (www.hawaii.edu/slis/).Violet H. Harada, program chair.

*University of Illinois at Urbana-Champaign, Graduate School of Library and Information Science, Library and Information Science Building, 501 East Daniel Street, Champaign, IL 61820; (217) 333-3280; (alexia.lis.uiuc. edu). Leigh S. Estabrook, dean.

University of Iowa, School of Library and Information Science, 3087 Library, University of Iowa, Iowa City, IA 52242-1420; (319) 335-5707; (www. uiowa.edu/~libsci/). Padmini Srinivasan, director.

University of Kentucky, College of Communications and Information Studies, School of Library and Information Science, 502 King Library Building S, Lexington, KY 40506-0039; (606) 257-8876; (www.uky.edu/CommInfoStudies/SLIS/). Timothy W. Sineath, director.

***University of Maryland,** College of Library and Information Services, 4105 Hornbake Library Building, College Park, MD 20742-4345; (301) 405-2033; (www.clis.umd.edu). Ann E. Prentice, dean.

***University of Michigan,** School of Information, 304 West Hall Building, 550 East University Avenue, Ann Arbor, MI 48109-1092; (734) 763-2285; (www.si.umich.edu). Gary M. Olson, interim dean.

University of Missouri-Columbia, School of Information Science and Learning Technologies, 217 Townsend Hall, Columbia, MO 65211; (573) 882-4546; (tiger.coe.missouri.edu/~sislt/). John Wedman, director

***University of North Carolina at Chapel Hill,** School of Information and Library Science, CB #3360 100 Manning Hall, Chapel Hill, NC 27599-3360; (919) 962-8366; (www.ils.unc.edu). JoAnne G. Marshall, dean.

University of North Carolina at Greensboro, Department of Library and Information Studies, School of Education, P.O. Box 26171, Greensboro, NC 27402-6171; (336) 334-3477; (www.uncg.edu/lis/). Kieth Wright, chair.

***University of North Texas,** School of Library and Information Sciences, P.O. Box 311068, NT Station, Denton, TX 76203-1068; (940) 565-2445; (www.unt.edu/slis/). Philip M. Turner, dean.

***University of Oklahoma,** School of Library and Information Studies, 401 West Brooks, Room 120, Norman, OK 73019-6032; (405) 325-3921; (www.ou.edu/cas/slis/). June Lester, director.

***University of Pittsburgh,** School of Information Sciences, 505 IS Building, Pittsburgh, PA 15260; (412) 624-5230; (www.sis.pitt.edu). Toni Carbo, dean and professor.

University of Puerto Rico, Graduate School of Library and Information Science, P.O. Box 21906, San Juan, PR 00931-1906; (787) 763-6199. Consuelo Figueras, director.

University of Rhode Island, Graduate School of Library and Information Studies, Rodman Hall, Kingston, RI 02881; (401) 874-2947; (www.uri.edu). W. Michael Havener, director.

***University of South Carolina,** College of Library and Information Science, Davis College, Columbia, SC 29208; (803) 777-3858, (www.libsci.sc.edu). Fred W. Roper, dean.

University of South Florida, School of Library and Information Science, 4202 East Fowler Avenue, CIS 1040, Tampa, FL 33620-7800; (813) 974-3520; (www.cas.usf.edu/lis/). Vicki L. Gregory, director.

University of Southern Mississippi, School of Library and Information Science, Box 5146, Hattiesburg, MS 39406-5146; (601) 266-4228; (www-dept.usm.edu/~slis/). Thomas Walker, director.

***University of Tennessee,** School of Information Sciences, 804 Volunteer Boulevard, Knoxville, TN 37996-4330; (423) 974-2148; (www.sis.utk.edu). Elizabeth Aversa, director.

***University of Texas at Austin,** Graduate School of Library and Information Science, Austin, TX 78712-1276; (512) 471-3821; (www.gslis.utexas.edu). Roberta I. Shaffer, dean.

***University of Toronto,** Faculty of Information Studies, 140 St. George Street, Toronto, ON, Canada M5S 3G6; (416) 978-8589; (www.fis.utoronto.ca). Lynne C. Howarth, dean.

University of Washington, School of Library and Information Science, 328 EEB, Box 352930, Seattle, WA 98195-2930; (206) 543-1794; (depts. washington.edu/~slis/). Michael B. Eisenberg, director.

*University of Western Ontario, Graduate Programs in Library and In-formation Science, Faculty of Information and Media Studies, Middlesex College, London, ON, Canada N6A 5B7; (519) 661-3542. Manjunath Pendakur, professor and dean.

*University of Wisconsin-Madison, School of Library and Information Studies, Helen C. White Hall, 600 North Park Street, Madison, WI 53706; (608) 263-2900; (polyglot.lss.wisc.edu/slis/). Louise S. Robbins, director.

*University of Wisconsin-Milwaukee, School of Library and Information Science, Enderis Hall 1110, 2400 East Hartford Avenue, Milwaukee, WI 53201; (414) 229-4707; (www.slis.uwm.edu). Mohammed M. Aman, dean.

Wayne State University, Library and Information Science Program, 106 Kresge Library, Detroit, MI 48202; (313) 577-1825; (www.lisp.wayne.edu). Ronald R. Powell, interim director.

SOURCE: ALA Office for Accreditation, September 1999.

Courses to take in library school

by Will Manley

WHAT IS THE BEST ADVICE that you can give someone who has made the decision to enroll in a graduate school of library science?

Grover C. Littleman, in an article entitled "I Survived Library School and You Can Too," claims that the key to making library school a positive experience is choosing the right professors. He says there are two types of professors. The first type of professor is Professor God. According to Littleman, "it is easy to understand why many professors develop a God complex. When you have complete control over a bunch of people who write down your every thought it is easy to think of yourself in terms of the Godly attributes of omnipotence and omniscience." The second type of professor is Professor Pal. This person is not much happier about being in library school than the student is and so he or she tries to be reasonable, thoughtful, and, yes, even friendly.

Before choosing a professor, Littleman recommends that students find out as much as possible about the various faculty members, and he offers the following specific points of advice:

Do not take any courses from a library science professor who:

1. Wears a white lab coat to class because he thinks he's a scientist.

2. Does not speak English fluently unless it is a cataloging course and then it doesn't matter because you'll be asleep most of the time.

3. Wrote a doctoral dissertation entitled "The Issues Underlying the Use of Hyphens in Online Cataloging."

4. Claims to have been a close personal friend of Melvil Dewey and collects old catalog cards as a hobby.

5. Served on the committee that wrote AACR2.

6. Expects you to read anything written by the following authors: Ranganathan, Mudge, and Spofford, or published by the following publishers: Haworth, Greenwood, and the U.S. Government Printing Office.

7. Has a sign on his or her office door that says "Office Hours—6:00 a.m. to 6:05 a.m."

8. Gives both a midterm and final exam and takes class attendance every day.

9. Gets satisfaction out of making students cry.

10. Brags about giving out only five "A's" in 28 years of teaching.

Do take a course from a professor who:

1. Uses the photography of Robert Mapplethorpe, the writings of Anaïs Nin, the pictures of Madonna, and the videos of Annie Sprinkle to illustrate the subtle differences between art, eroticism, pornography, and smut.

2. Is actively involved in an ALA committee. (This professor is always gone and rarely holds class.)

3. Has a doctorate in something other than library science.

4. Believes that tests and grades are bureaucratic nonsense and therefore gives everyone an "A."

5. Takes 30 minute breaks during a 60-minute class.

6. Has been quoted as saying that "Cataloging is for candyasses."

7. Holds classes in his or her home and serves everybody chocolate chip cookies.

8. Likes to be called by his or her first name.

9. Writes glowing letters of recommendation for anyone who asks.

10. Throws kegger parties at the end of the year.

SOURCE: © Will Manley, *The Manley Art of Librarianship* (Jefferson, N.C.: McFarland, 1993), pp. 184–85. Reprinted with permission.

You never told us what to do when the roof leaks

by Charles Curran and Laura Kelley

"YOU NEVER TOLD US what to do when the roof leaks," complained the ex-student. The comment stuck in the professor's psyche. Has library and information science education neglected to cover some essentials?

Apparently so, for 200 post-1990 graduates from 30 ALA-accredited programs willingly responded to this recent request: "Please give an example of a situation or event for which your LIS education did not prepare you." Their answers may startle LIS educators into plugging some serious leaks in their syllabi.

Shingle maintenance

"My roof *does* leak and my training did not prepare me for that or for the blue tarp our crack public works team slung over the roof instead of fixing the damn thing," said one respondent.

Another librarian was not prepared for ants. During story hour thousands of them came through the wall of her children's room, distracting her group of 3rd graders and threatening to carry several of them off. Maintenance dispatched an idle school-bus driver armed with Ant-Be-Gone spray. Ant-Be-Gone looks like whipped cream. Ants on Ant-Be-Gone look like chocolate sprinkles to 3rd graders. Then the town manager

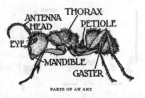

PARTS OF AN ANT

sent an exterminator who gave a lecture on carpenter ants, main nests, satellite areas, and the most important thing of all: "Nailing the queen."

There was no Bad Smells 101. So when he encountered a particularly nauseating odor in the library conference room, another librarian was prepared to blame a hygienically challenged board member. But the board member was zestfully innocent. The offender was a very dead rat who had apparently achieved final exit in the airspace under the floor.

When a toilet imitates Old Faithful and spreads a foot of water on the floor, turn the water off. If the shut-off valve comes off in your hand, with your free dry hand, dial the plumber.

Courses should cover air conditioners that drip on the heads of technical service employees and warn about systems people who whimsically shut down systems. Include copy machines that require therapy, transplants, and liposuction. Add lectures on clogged toilets, power outages, and sewers that spill out over your new shoes. Mention boiler repair and the squirrel who ate the 630s before a janitor's trap ended the rodent's voracious appetite for information.

Remedies and potions

Bizarre questions can overpower MLS remedies and potions:

- Do you mind if I kiss you?
- Do you have the *Amityville Whorehouse?*
- Do you have tax forms for people who work at Hardees?
- I need information on the Culpepper Plantation. I lived there in another life.
- What is the meaning of life? And please don't send me to any books, just tell me.
- I'm trying to think of a word. It's a common legal word, but I can not remember what it is or what it means. Can you help me?

One 1st grader regularly moons story-hour audiences, regardless of the theme of the tale. A three-year-old pulls up her shirt and nurses her doll. Other clients improvise—when comfort stations are just plain too far to walk. One well-dressed gentleman used the 100s, appropriately, to do number one. Four times in the recent past children have selected the *same spot* on a new carpet to wet themselves.

One librarian wishes he had been taught what to do about the patron who enjoys crawling under tables and licking people's legs. A media specialist speculates that *compromising* must be the current topic in her school's Advanced Placement program, for she found two AP students practicing that position in the stacks.

Another media specialist invited to dinner by a fellow teacher noticed four unchecked-out library books on the teacher's bookshelf. She snatched the fugitive books from the shelf, placed them under the dining-room table, and later sneaked them out of the house and back into the library. Their relationship remains cordial.

Some respondents indicate that in school they did not "see themselves" as managers. So they avoided management and "people skills" courses, only to discover that their jobs require them to manage themselves and others.

Public relations

What about "gifts" of 189 Reader's Digest Condensed Books, dusty attic refugees donated by a friend of the president of the library board, *at the suggestion of that president?* Does "board-approved gift policy" ring a bell?

The book club donated most of the collection for the formation of the library, reported one librarian. Then they wanted space in the library for club mementos. Their stuff has been multiplying lately and the club wants the librarian to be responsible for it. One club member spotted a cracked club curio; another discovered a precious scrapbook mysteriously scorched. They blamed the librarian. We obviously need a course that teaches librarians not to let people put their stuff in the library!

Trees

If "only God can make a tree," then librarians better not cut them down. One librarian who wanted to remove an old, overgrown, and sick sycamore from the side lawn was met by furious protesters who picketed the library and demanded that the tree be spared.

Do not, as one respondent did, use chain saws and backhoes to remove trees in which swallows nest, especially if local bird watchers are watching. The nesting birds will leave town, and you will be blamed. Then you will fault your LIS training, as this respondent did, for not offering a course in bird behavior.

"You never told us how to write condolences when donated memorial trees die, especially if we killed them." One librarian had gratefully accepted two expensive ornamental trees from the town tree board, and a trusted member of the board told the librarian to "give the trees plenty of water." The librarian figured that a running hose would provide "plenty of water." It did. But "plenty of water" is a relative term that can mean different things to different people and trees. Two weeks after the trees were planted, the librarian noticed that they were looking unwell. Three weeks after the trees were planted care instructions arrived in the mail. "Never leave a hose running on the trees—you may over-water." Four weeks after the trees were planted, the librarian struggled with the condolence note to the tree board about two trees she had killed. At least there had been no swallows in them.

LIS training shortchanges facilities placement. In one library the book drop is placed directly over the staff's porcelain convenience. Staff must remember to lower seat and/or lid after each use, for soggy books are the penalty for absent-mindedness. Too frequently staff must be admonished to refrain from screaming when books drop in their laps, for this startles patrons who return books in the drop.

Struggling with the beer drop

While one library struggles with the book drop, another contends with the *beer drop*. The librarian noticed students carrying cups. He then discovered a hose coming from outside. It stretched from a keg, through a window, and into the philosophy section. Aquinas and Old Milwaukee on tap. Fellas, it doesn't get any better than this.

A librarian was handed a plane ticket and told to fly to Italy and catalog 10,000 books in two weeks. We can't figure what she is complaining about.

At a budget hearing a medical librarian was not prepared to answer the question: "Why do you want this money?"

Other truly important things we never told anybody were how to negotiate a contract, how to write a grant, how to pack and move a library over a weekend, and how to give book talks on TV.

Librarians conducting an oral history project were chagrined to discover that their expensive recorder made the speakers sound as if they were gargling with molasses. When they complained, the manufacturer's rep suggested flipping the speed switch.

One respondent faulted LIS educators for not telling them how to deal with clerks who know more about automation than the librarians.

Library training failed to teach another librarian to retrospectively convert a collection cataloged by a predecessor who despised Dewey and had therefore refused to use his system, opting instead to *color-code* the entire library.

Now, listen. That off-key chorus you hear is the massed choir of LIS educators doing their hit single, "But in My Course I Told Them 100 Times . . ." Listen for a dean's solo on the "none of those responses came from our grads" refrain. She is probably wrong.

SOURCE: Charles Curran and Laura Kelley, "You Never Told Us What to Do When the Roof Leaks," *American Libraries* 27 (September 1996): 62–64.

RESEARCH / WRITING

Useful addresses

YOUR UNANSWERED QUESTIONS on library matters might be directed to one of the following organizations. See also other lists of addresses and telephone numbers on pp. 38–40 (presidential libraries), 72–78 (job placement sources), 122–25 (state certification agencies), 182–86 (accredited library school programs), 228–33 (federal regional depository libraries and archives), and 357 (disaster preparedness agencies).

American Association for Higher Education, 1 Dupont Circle, N.W., Suite 360, Washington, DC 20036-1110; (202) 293-6440; info@aahe.org; (www.aahe.org).

American Association of Law Libraries, 53 W. Jackson Blvd., Suite 940, Chicago, IL 60604; (312) 939-4764; aallhq@aall.org; (www.aallnet.org/index.asp).

American Association for State and Local History, 1717 Church St., Nashville, TN 37203-2991; (615) 320-3203; history@aaslh.org; (www.aaslh.org).

American Booksellers Association, 828 S. Broadway, Tarrytown, NY 10591; (914) 591-2665, (800) 637-0037; info@members.bookweb.org; (www.bookweb.org).

American Council of Learned Societies, 228 E. 45th St., New York, NY 10017-3398; (212) 697-1505; (www.acls.org/jshome.htm).

American Council on Education, 1 Dupont Circle, N.W., Suite 800, Washington, DC 20036; (202) 939-9300; web@ace.nche.edu; (www.ACENET.edu).

American Indian Library Association, c/o Lisa A. Mitten, 207 Hillman Library, University of Pittsburgh, Pittsburgh, PA 15260; (412) 648-7723; lmitten@vms.cis.pitt.edu; (www3.pitt.edu/~lmitten/aila.html).

American Institute of Architects, 1735 New York Ave., N.W., Washington, DC 20006; (202) 626-7300; aiaonline@aiamail.aia.org; (www.aiaonline.com).

American Libraries Online, 50 E. Huron St., Chicago, IL 60611-2795; (800) 545-2433, ext. 4216; americanlibraries@ala.org; (www.ala.org/alonline/).

American Library Association, 50 E. Huron St., Chicago, IL 60611-2795; (800) 545-2433; ala@ala.org; (www.ala.org).

American Library Association, Washington Office, 1301 Pennsylvania Ave., N.W., Suite 403, Washington, DC 20004; (202) 628-8410, (800) 941-8478; alawash@alawash.org; (www.ala.org/washoff/).

American Merchant Marine Library Association, c/o United Seaman's Service, 1 World Trade Center, Suite 2161, New York, NY 10048; (212) 775-1038; (www.uss-ammla.com).

American National Standards Institute, 11 W. 42nd St., 13th Floor, New York, NY 10036; (212) 642-4900; sbose@ansi.org; (web.ansi.org).

American Printing History Association, P.O. Box 4922, Grand Central Station, New York, NY 10163-4922; (212) 673-8770; (wally.rit.edu/cary/apha.html).

American Society for Information Science, 8720 Georgia Ave., Suite 501, Silver Spring, MD 20910-3602; (301) 495-0900; asis@asis.org; (www.asis.org).

American Society of Indexers, P.O. Box 39366, Phoenix, AZ 85069-9366; (602) 979-5514; info@asindexing.org; (www.asindexing.org).

American Theological Library Association, 820 Church St., Suite 400, Evanston, IL 60201-5613; (888) 665-2852; atla@atla.com; (www.atla.com).

Amigos Library Services, 14400 Midway Rd., Dallas, TX 75244-3509; (972) 851-8000, (800) 843-8482; amigos@amigos.org; (www.amigos.org).

Antiquarian Booksellers Association of America, 20 W. 44th St., New York, NY 10035-6604; (212) 944-8291; abaa@panix.com; (abaa.org).

Art Libraries Society of North America, 4101 Lake Boone Trail, Suite 201, Raleigh, NC 27607-7506; (919) 787-5181, (800) 892-7547; arlisna@olsonmgmt.com; (www.lib.duke.edu/lilly/arlis/).

Asian/Pacific American Librarians Association, c/o Rama Vishwanatham, Library of the Health Sciences, University of Illinois at Chicago, 1750 W. Polk, Chicago, IL 60612; (312) 996-8993; rama@uic.edu; (www.uic.edu/depts/lib/apala/).

Aslib, the Association for Information Management, Staple Hall, Stone House Court, 87-90 Houndsditch, London EC3A 7PB, United Kingdom; +44 (207) 903-0000; aslib@aslib.co.uk; (www.aslib.co.uk/aslib/).

Asociacion Mexicana de Bibliotecarios, c/o Nahúm Pérez Paz, Av. Ticomán 645, Col. Sta. María Ticomán, C.P. 07330 México, D.F.; +52 (5) 752-7455; ambac@solar.sar.net; (www.ambac.org.mx).

Association Bibliothécaires Français, 31, rue de Chabrol, 75010 Paris, France; +33 (1) 55 33 10 30; abf@wanadoo.fr; (www.abf.asso.fr).

Association for Educational Communications and Technology, 1025 Vermont Ave., N.W., Suite 820, Washington, DC 20005-3516; (202) 347-7834; (www.aect.org).

Association for Information and Image Management International, 1100 Wayne Ave., Suite 1100, Silver Spring, MD 20910-5603; (301) 587-8202; (888) 839-3165; (www.aiim.org).

Association for Library and Information Science Education, P.O. Box 7640, Arlington, VA 22207; (703) 243-8040; sroger7@ibm.net; (www.alise.org).

Association for Recorded Sound Collections, P.O. Box 543, Annapolis, MD 21404-0543; peters@umd5.umd.edu; (www.arsc-audio.org).

Association of American Colleges and Universities, 1818 R Street, N.W., Washington, DC 20009; (202) 884-7403; info@aacu.nw.dc.us; (www.aacu-edu.org).

Association of American Publishers, 71 Fifth Ave., New York, NY 10003-3004; (212) 255-0200, ext. 264; mwalling@publishers.org; (www.publishers.org/home/).

Association of Architectural Librarians, c/o Wayne Kent, 1749B S. Hayes St., Arlington, VA 22202; (703) 685-5275; aalmail@aol.com.

Association of Book Group Readers and Leaders, P.O. Box 885, Highland Park, IL 60035; (847) 266-0431; (lcweb.loc.gov/loc/cfbook/coborg/abgrl.html).

Association of Canadian Archivists, P.O. Box 2596, Station D, Ottawa, Ontario, K1P 5W6; (613) 443-0251, (888) 443-2243; (www.archives.ca/aca).

Association of Canadian Map Libraries and Archives, c/o Visual and Sound Archives Division, National Archives of Canada, 395 Wellington Street, Ottawa, Ontario, K1A 0N3; (613) 996-7620; pmcintyre@archives.ca; (www.sscl.uwo.ca/assoc/acml/acmla.html).

Association of Christian Librarians, P.O. Box 4, Cedarville, OH 45314; (937) 675-3799; info@acl.org; (www.acl.org).

Association of Independent Information Professionals, 10290 Monroe, Suite 208, Dallas, TX 75229-5718; (609) 730-8759; aiipinfo@aiip.org; (www.aiip.org).

Association of Jewish Libraries, 15 E. 26th Street, Room 1034, New York, NY 10010; (212) 725-5359; (aleph.lib.ohio-state.edu/www/ajl.html).

Association of Mental Health Librarians, c/o Susan Heffner, Director, APA Library, 1400 K St., N.W., Washington, DC 20005; (202) 682-6057.

Association of Part-time Librarians, Anne Huberman, Andrew L. Bouwhuis Library, Canisius College, 2001 Main Street, Buffalo, NY 14208; (716) 888-2900; huberman@canisius.edu; (www.canisius.edu/~huberman/aptl.html).

Association of Records Managers and Administrators International, 4200 Somerset Dr., Suite 215, Prairie Village, KS 66208; (913) 341-3808, (800) 422-2762; hq@arma.org; (www.arma.org).

Association of Research Libraries, 21 Dupont Circle, N.W., Suite 800, Washington, DC 20036; (202) 296-2296; arlhq@arl.org; (www.arl.org).

Associazione italiana biblioteche, c/o Biblioteca nazionale centrale, Viale Castro Pretorio 105, 00185 Roma, Italy; +39 (6) 4463532; aib@aib.it; (www.aib.it).

Australian Library and Information Association, P.O. Box E441, Kingston ACT 2604, Australia; +61 (2) 6285 1877; enquiry@alia.org.au; (www.alia.org.au).

Barbara Bush Foundation for Family Literacy, 1112 16th St., N.W., Suite 340, Washington, DC 20036; (202) 955-6183; sooc@erols.com; (www.barbarabushfoundation.com).

Beta Phi Mu International Library Science Honor Society, Beta Phi Mu National Headquarters, School of Information Studies, Florida State University, Tallahassee, FL 32306-2100; (850) 644-3907; beta_phi_mu@lis.fsu.edu; (www.cas.usf.edu/lis/bpm/).

Bibliographical Society (London), c/o The Library, Wellcome Institute for the History of Medicine, 183 Euston Road, London, England NW1 2BE; (speke.ukc.ac.uk/secl/bibsoc/).

Bibliographical Society of America, P.O. Box 1537, Lenox Hill Station, New York, NY 10021; (212) 452-2710; bsa@bibsocamer.org; (www.bibsocamer.org).

Bibliographical Society of Australia and New Zealand, c/o Ros Follett, Manager, Fryer Library, University of Queensland, Australia 4072; +61 (7) 3365 6205; r.follett@library.uq.edu.au; (www.uq.edu.au/~enctiffi/bsanz.htm).

Black Caucus of the American Library Association, P.O. Box 2228, Winter Park, FL 32790-2228; (330) 672-3045, ext. 44; gladysb@lms.kent.edu; (www.bcala.org).

Booklist, 50 E. Huron St., Chicago, IL 60611; bott@ala.org; (www.ala.org/booklist/).

British Association of Picture Libraries and Agencies, 18 Vine Hill, London EC1R 5DX, England; +44 (171) 713-1780; enquiries@bapla.org.uk; (www.bapla.org.uk).

Canadian Health Libraries Association, P.O. Box 94038, Yonge St., Toronto, Ontario, Canada M4N 3R1; (416) 485-0377; chla@inforamp.net; (www.med.mun.ca/chla/).

Canadian Library Association, 200 Elgin St., Suite 602, Ottawa, Ontario, Canada K2P 1L5; (613) 232-9625; mkim@cla.ca; (209.217.90.93).

Catholic Library Association, 100 North Street, Suite 224, Pittsfield, MA 01201-5109; (413) 443-2252; cla@vgernet.net; (www.cathla.org).

Center for Applied Linguistics, 4646 40th Street, N.W., Washington, DC 20016-1859; (202) 362-0700; info@cal.org; (www.cal.org).

Center for Book Arts, 626 Broadway, 5th floor, New York, NY 10012; (212) 460-9768; bookarts@pipeline.com; (www.colophon.com/gallery/cba.html).

Center for Children's Books, University of Illinois, GSLIS, 51 E. Armory Ave., Champaign, IL 61820; (217) 244-0324; ccb@alexia.lis.uiuc.edu; (edfu.lis.uiuc.edu/puboff/bccb/center.html).

Center for the Book, Library of Congress, 101 Independence Ave., S.E., Washington, DC 20540-4920; (202) 707-5221; cfbook@loc.gov; (lcweb.loc.gov/loc/cfbook/).

Center for the History of Print Culture in Modern America, School of Library and Information Studies, University of Wisconsin-Madison, 60 N. Park St., Madison, WI 53706; (608) 263-2914; printcul@macc.wisc.edu; (slisweb.lis.wisc.edu/printcul/).

Center for the Study of Reading, University of Illinois, 174 Children's Research Center, 51 Gerty Drive, Champaign, IL 61820; (217) 333-2552; (lcweb.loc.gov/loc/cfbook/coborg/csr.html).

Chicago Book Clinic, 825 Green Bay Road, Suite 270, Wilmette, IL 60091; (847) 256-8448; kgboyer@ix.netcom.com; (www.chicagobookclinic.org).

Chief Officers of State Library Agencies, 167 W. Main Street, Suite 600, Lexington, KY 40507; (606) 231-1925; jviens@amrinc.net; (www.cosla.org).

Children's Literacy Initiative, 2314 Market St., 4th Floor, Philadelphia, PA 19103; (215) 561-4676; clibooks@aol.com; (lcweb.loc.gov/loc/cfbook/coborg/cli.html).

Chinese-American Librarians Association, c/o Sally C. Tseng, 49 Gillman St., Irvine, CA 92612; (949) 552-5615; sctseng@uci.edu; (library.fgcu.edu/cala/).

Choice, 100 Riverview Center, Middletown, CT 06457; (860) 347-6933; choicemag@ala-choice.org; (www.ala.org/acrl/choice/home.html).

Church and Synagogue Library Association, P.O. Box 19357, Portland, OR 97280-0357; (503) 244-6919, (800) 452-2752; csla@worldaccessnet.com; (worldaccessnet.com/~csla/).

Coalition for Networked Information, 21 Dupont Circle, N.W., Suite 800, Washington, DC 20036-1109; (202) 296-5098; (www.cni.org).

College and University Personnel Association, 1233 20th Street, N.W., Suite 301, Washington, DC 20036-1250; (202) 429-0311; sjurow@cupa.org; (www.cupa.org).

Copyright Clearance Center, 222 Rosewood Drive, Danvers, MA 01923; (978) 750-8400; info@copyright.com; (www.copyright.com).

Council of Planning Librarians, 101 N. Wacker Dr., Suite CM-190, Chicago, IL 60606; (312) 409-3349; p-yu2@uiuc.edu; (www.west.asu.edu/mmyers/cpl/).

Council on Botanical and Horticultural Libraries, c/o Jane P. Gates, Secretary, CBHL, National Agricultural Library, USDA, Beltsville, MD 20705-2351; (301) 504-5724; jgates@nalusda.gov; (huntbot.andrew.cmu.edu/CBHL/CBHL.html).

Council on East Asian Libraries, Tai-loi Ma, East Asian Library, 1100 E. 57th St., University of Chicago, Chicago, IL 60637-1502; (773) 702-8436; m108@midway.uchicago.edu; (darkwing.uoregon.edu/~felsing/ceal/welcome.html).

Council on Library/Media Technicians, P.O. Box 951, Oxon Hill, MD 20750; (202) 434-6242; dwelsh@aarp.org; (library.ucr.edu/COLT/).

Council on Library and Information Resources, 1755 Massachusetts Ave., N.W., Suite 500, Washington, DC 20036; (202) 939-4750; info@clir.org; (www.clir.org).

Electronic Frontier Foundation, 1550 Bryant Street, Suite 725, San Francisco, CA 94103-4832; (415) 436-9333; ask@eff.org; (www.eff.org).

Electronic Privacy Information Center, 666 Pennsylvania Ave., S.E., Suite 301, Washington, DC 20003; (202) 544-9240; info@epic.org; (www.epic.org).

Equal Employment Opportunity Commission, 1801 L Street, N.W., Washington, DC 20507; (202) 663-4900, (800) 669-4000; (www.eeoc.gov).

European Commission on Preservation and Access, P.O. Box 19121, 1000 GC Amsterdam, The Netherlands; +31 (20) 5510839; ecpa@bureau.knaw.nl; (www.knaw.nl/ecpa/ecpatex/).

Federal Library and Information Center Committee, Library of Congress, Washington, DC 20540-4930, (202) 707-4800; flicc@loc.gov; (lcweb. loc.gov/flicc/).

Freedom to Read Foundation, 50 E. Huron St., Chicago, IL 60611-2795; (312) 280-4226; ftrf@ala.org; (www.ftrf.org).

Friends of Libraries U.S.A., 1420 Walnut St., Suite 450, Philadelphia, PA 19102-4017; (215) 790-1674; folusa@libertynet.org; (www.folusa.com).

Great Books Foundation, 35 E. Wacker Dr., Suite 2300, Chicago, IL 60601-2298; (800) 222-5870; gbf@enteract.com; (www.greatbooks.org).

Indexing and Abstracting Society of Canada, P.O. Box 744, Station F, Toronto, Ontario, Canada, M4Y 2N6; (tornade.ere.umontreal.ca/~turner/iasc/home.html).

Institute for Bibliography and Editing, 1118 Main Library, Kent State University, Kent, OH 44242-0001; (330) 672-2092; editing@kent.edu; (www.library.kent.edu/speccoll/ibeloc.html).

Institute for the Study of Adult Literacy, Pennsylvania State University, 102 Rackley Building, University Park, PA 16801-3202; (814) 863-3777; isal@psu.edu; (www.ed.psu.edu/isal/).

Institute of Museum and Library Services, 1100 Pennsylvania Ave., N.W., Washington, DC 20506; (202) 606-8536; imlsinfo@imls.fed.us; (www.imls.fed.us).

Institute of Paper Conservation, Leigh Lodge, Leigh, Worcester WR6 5LB, United Kingdom; +44 (1886) 832323; clare@ipc.org.uk; (palimpsest.stanford.edu/ipc/).

International Association of Aquatic and Marine Science Libraries and Information Centers, c/o Library, Harbor Branch Oceanographic Institution, 5600 U.S. 1 North, Fort Pierce, FL 34946; (561) 465-2400, ext. 201; harbornet@class.org; (siolibrary.ucsd.edu/iamslic/).

International Association of Law Libraries, P.O. Box 5709, Washington, DC 20016-1309; (202) 707-9866; mber@loc.gov; (www.geocities.com/~ialawlib/).

International Association of School Librarianship, Suite 300, Box 34069, Seattle, WA 98124-0266; iasl@rockland.com; (www.hi.is/~anne/iasl.html).

International Council of Library Association Executives, c/o Ann Hanning, Ohio Educational Library Media Association, 1631 Northwest Professional Plaza, Columbus, OH 43220; (614) 326-1460; oelma@mecdc.org.

International Federation of Library Associations and Institutions, POB 95312, 2509 CH The Hague, Netherlands; +31 (70) 314-0884; ifla@ifla.org; (www.ifla.org).

International Organization for Standardization (ISO), 1, rue de Varembé, Case postale 56, CH-1211 Genève 20, Switzerland; +41 (22) 749 01 11; central@iso.ch; (www.iso.ch).

International Reading Association, 800 Barksdale Road, P.O. Box 8139, Newark, DE 19714-8139; (302) 731-1600; pubinfo@reading.org; (www.reading.org).

Internet Library Association, regel@epix.net; (www-org.usm.edu/~ila/).

ISBN Agency, 121 Chanlon Rd., New Providence, NJ 07974; (908) 665-6770; isbn-san@bowker.com; (www.bowker.com/standards/home/isbn/us/isbnus.html).

ISSN Agency, National Serials Data Program, Library of Congress, Washington, DC 20540-4160; (202) 707-6452; issn@loc.gov; (www.loc.gov/issn/).

Laubach Literacy, P.O. Box 131, Syracuse, NY 13210; (315) 422-9121; (888) 528-2224; info@laubach.org; (www.laubach.org).

Libraries for the Future, 121 W. 27th St., Suite 1102, New York, NY 10001; (212) 352-2330, (800) 542-1918; lff@lff.org; (www.lff.org).

Library and Information Association of New Zealand Aotearoa, Level 6, Old Wool House, 139-141 Featherston St., P.O. Box 12 212, Wellington, New Zealand; +64 (4) 473 5834; office@lianza.org.nz; (www.lianza.org.nz).

Library Association, 7 Ridgmount St., London, England WC1E 7AE; +44 (171) 636 7543; info@la-hq.org.uk; (www.la-hq.org.uk).

Library Association of Ireland, 53 Upper Mount St., Dublin 2, Ireland; +353 (1)0 6619000; lai@iol.ie; (ireland.iol.ie/~lai/).

Library Journal, 245 W. 17th St., New York, NY 10011; (212) 463-6819; ljfeedback@bookwire.com; (www.libraryjournal.com).

Library of Congress, 101 Independence Ave., S.E., Washington, DC 20540; (202) 707-5000; Copyright Office, (202) 707-3000; lcweb@loc.gov; (www.loc.gov).

Libri Foundation, P.O. Box 10246, Eugene, OR 97440; (541) 747-9655; librifdn@teleport.com; (www.teleport.com/~librifdn/).

Literacy Volunteers of America, 635 James St., Syracuse, NY 13203-2214; (315) 472-0001; info@literacyvolunteers.org; (www.literacyvolunteers.org).

Lutheran Church Library Association, 122 W. Franklin Ave., Minneapolis, MN 55404-2474; (612) 870-3623; lclahq@aol.com.

Medical Library Association, 65 E. Wacker Place, Suite 1900, Chicago, IL 60601-7298; (312) 419-9094; mlasa1@mlahq.org; (www.mlanet.org).

Middle East Librarians Association, c/o Janet Heineck, University of Washington Libraries, Box 352900, Seattle, WA 98195-2900; (206) 543-8407; janeth@u.washington.edu; (depts.washington.edu/wsx9/melahp.html).

Modern Language Association of America, 10 Astor Place, 5th Floor, New York, NY 10003-6981; (212) 475-9500; info@mla.org; (www.mla.org).

Music Library Association, P.O. Box 487, Canton, MA 02021-0487; (781) 828-8450; acadsvc@aol.com; (www.musiclibraryassoc.org/contents.htm).

National Association for the Education of Young Children, 1509 16th Street, N.W., Washington, DC 20036-1426; (202) 232-8777, (800) 424-2460; naeyc@naeyc.org; (www.naeyc.org).

National Association of Government Archives and Records Administrators, 48 Howard St., Albany, NY 12207; (518) 463-8644; nagara@caphill.com; (www.nagara.org).

National Center for Education Statistics, 555 New Jersey Ave., N.W., Washington, DC 20208-5574; (202) 219-1828; (nces.ed.gov).

National Center for Family Literacy, 325 W. Main St., Suite 200, Louisville, KY 40202-4251; (502) 584-1133; ncfl@famlit.org; (www.famlit.org).

National Center on Adult Literacy, University of Pennsylvania, 3910 Chestnut St., Philadelphia, PA 19104-3111; (215) 898-2100; ncal@literacy.upenn.edu; (www.literacyonline.org).

National Coalition Against Censorship, 275 7th Ave., 20th Floor, New York, NY 10001; (212) 807-6222; ncac@ncac.org; (www.ncac.org).

National Coalition of Independent Scholars, Box 5743, Berkeley, CA 94705; margaret@teleport.com; (www.ncis.org).

National Commission on Libraries and Information Science, 1110 Vermont Ave., N.W., Suite 820, Washington, DC 20005-3552; (202) 606-9200; info@nclis.gov; (www.nclis.gov).

National Committee on Pay Equity, 1126 16th St., N.W., Room 411, Washington, DC 20036; (202) 331-7343; fairpay@aol.com; (www.feminist.com/ fairpay.htm).

National Council for History Education, 26915 Westwood Rd., Suite B2, Westlake, OH 44145-4657; (440) 835-1776; nche19@mail.idt.net; (www. history.org/nche/).

National Council for the Accreditation of Teacher Education, 2010 Massachusetts Ave., N.W., Suite 500, Washington, DC 20036-1023; (202) 466-7496; ncate@ncate.org; (www.ncate.org).

National Council of Teachers of English, 1111 W. Kenyon Rd., Urbana, IL 61801; (217) 328-3870, (800) 369-6283; membership@ncte.org; (www. ncte.org).

National Council of Teachers of Mathematics, 1906 Association Dr., Reston, VA 20191-1593; (703) 620-9840; infocentral@nctm.org; (www.nctm.org).

National Council on Public History, 327 Cavanaugh Hall-IUPUI, 425 University Boulevard, Indianapolis, IN 46202-5140; (317) 274-2716; ncph@ iupui.edu; (www.iupui.edu/~ncph/home.html).

National Endowment for the Arts, 1100 Pennsylvania Ave., N.W., Washington, DC 20506; (202) 682-5400; (arts.endow.gov).

National Endowment for the Humanities, 1100 Pennsylvania Ave., N.W., Washington, DC 20506; (202) 606-8400; (800) 634-1121; info@neh.gov; (www.neh.gov).

National Federation of Indexing and Abstracting Services, 1518 Walnut St., Suite 307, Philadelphia, PA 19102-3403; (215) 893-1561; nfais@nfais. org; (www.pa.utulsa.edu/nfais.html).

National Film Preservation Foundation, 870 Market St., Suite 765, San Francisco, CA 94102; (415) 392-7291; info@filmpreservation.org; (www. filmpreservation.org).

National Historical Publications and Records Commission, National Archives and Records Administration, 700 Pennsylvania Avenue, N.W., Room 111, Washington, DC 20408-0001; (202) 501-5610; nhprc@arch1.nara.gov; (www.nara.gov/nhprc/).

National Information Standards Organization, 4733 Bethesda Ave., Suite 300, Bethesda, MD 20814, (301) 654-2512; nisohq@niso.org; (www.niso. org).

National Institute for Literacy, 800 Connecticut Ave., N.W., Suite 200, Washington, DC 20006-2712; (202) 632-1500; webmaster@nifl.gov; (www.nifl.gov/nifl/ProgIndex.htm).

National Science Teachers Association, 1840 Wilson Blvd., Arlington, VA 22201-3000; (703) 243-7100; (www.nsta.org).

National Security Archive, Gelman Library, George Washington University, 2130 H Street, N.W., Suite 701, Washington, DC 20037; (202) 994-7000; nsarchiv@gwu.edu; (www.gwu.edu/~nsarchiv/).

National Storytelling Membership Association, 116½ W. Main St., Jonesborough, TN 37659-0309; (423) 913-8201, (800) 525-4514; mwhited@naxs.com; (storynet.org).

National Technical Information Service, U.S. Department of Commerce, Springfield, VA 22161; (703) 605-6000; info@ntis.fedworld.gov; (www.ntis. gov).

National Trust for Historic Preservation, 1785 Massachusetts Ave., N.W., Washington, DC 20036; (202) 588-6000, (800) 944-6847; members@nthp. org; (www.nthp.org).

North American Cartographic Information Society, American Geographic

Society Collection, P.O. Box 399, Milwaukee, WI 53201; (414) 229-6282, (800) 558-8993; cmb@csd.uwm.edu; (www.nacis.org).

North American Serials Interest Group, Geraldine Williams, NASIG Treasurer, P.O. Box 54362, Cincinnati, OH 45254-0362; info@nasig.org; (www.nasig.org).

Northeast Document Conservation Center, 100 Brickstone Square, Andover, MA 01810-1494; (978) 470-1010; nedcc@nedcc.org; (www.nedcc.org).

OCLC, Inc., 6565 Frantz Road, Dublin, OH 43017-3395; (614) 764-6000, (800) 848-5878; oclc@oclc.org; (www.oclc.org/oclc/menu/home1.htm).

Online Audiovisual Catalogers, c/o Richard Baumgarten, Johnson County Library, Box 2901, Shawnee Mission, KS 66201-1301; (913) 495-2454; neumeist@acsu.buffalo.edu; (ublib.buffalo.edu/libraries/units/cts/olac/).

Oral History Association, Dickinson College, P.O. Box 1773, Carlisle, PA 17013; (717) 245-1036; oha@dickinson.edu; (omega.dickinson.edu/organizations/oha/).

Patent and Trademark Depository Library Association, c/o Carol Giles, President, St. Louis Public Library, 1301 Olive Street, St. Louis, MO 63103; crawford@rice.edu; (riceinfo.rice.edu/Fondren/Gov_docs/ptdla/).

PEN American Center, 568 Broadway, New York, NY 10012-3225; (212) 334-1660; pen@pen.org; (www.pen.org).

Popular Culture Association/American Culture Association, Popular Press, Bowling Green State University, Bowling Green, OH 43403; (419) 372-7867; abrowne@bgnet.bgsu.edu; (www.h-net.msu.edu/~pcaaca/).

Program for Cooperative Cataloging, Library of Congress, Washington, DC 20549-4382; fax (202) 707-2824; acri@loc.gov; (lcweb.loc.gov/catdir/pcc/).

Public Record Office, Ruskin Avenue, Kew, Richmond, Surrey, England TW9 4DU; +44 (181) 392 5200; enquiry@pro.gov.uk; (www.pro.gov.uk).

Push Literacy Action Now, 1337 Pennsylvania Ave., S.E., Washington, DC 20003; (202) 547-8903; (lcweb.loc.gov/loc/cfbook/coborg/pla.html).

Reading Is Fundamental, 600 Maryland Ave., S.W., Suite 600, Washington, DC 20024; (877) 743-7323; (www.rif.org).

Reforma: National Association to Promote Library Services to the Spanish Speaking, P.O. Box 832, Anaheim, CA 92815-0832; (714) 765-3626; alex@anaheim.lib.ca.us; (latino.sscnet.ucla.edu/library/reforma/).

Research Libraries Group, 1200 Villa St., Mountain View, CA 94041-1100; (800) 537-7546; bl.ric@rlg.org; (www.rlg.org/toc.html).

Rocky Mountain Conservation Center, University of Denver, 2420 South University Boulevard, Denver, CO 80208; (303) 733-2712; lmellon@du.edu; (www.du.edu/rmcc/).

Scottish Library Association, 1 John Street, Hamilton, Scotland ML3 7EW; +44 (1698) 252526; sctlb@leapfrog.almac.co.uk; (www.slainte.org.uk).

Seminar on the Acquisition of Latin American Library Materials, Benson Latin American Collection, Sid Richardson Hall 1.109, University of Texas, Austin, TX 78713; (505) 277-5102; (latino.lib.cornell.edu/salalmhome.html).

Sociedad de Bibliotecarios de Puerto Rico, attn: Prof. Carmen Santos Corrada, Presidenta del Comité de Socios, P.O. Box 22898, San Juan, PR 00931-2898; (787) 758-2525, ext. 1345, 1369; ca_santos@rcmaca.upr.clu.edu; (www.usc.clu.edu/sbpr/).

Society of American Archivists, 527 S. Wells, 5th Floor, Chicago, IL 60607; (312) 922-0140; info@archivists.org; (www.archivists.org).

Society of School Librarians International, 275 McLoud Drive, Fort Lee, NJ 07024; (201) 947-5149; sbssteve@aol.com; (falcon.jmu.edu/~ramseyil/sslihome.htm).

Software and Information Industry Association, 1730 M Street, N.W., Suite 700, Washington, DC 20036-4510; (202) 452-1600; pr@siia.net; (www.siia.net).

Special Libraries Association, 1700 18th St., N.W., Washington, DC 20009-2514; (202) 234-4700; sla@sla.org; (www.sla.org).

Substance Abuse Librarians and Information Specialists, P.O. Box 9513, Berkeley, CA 94709-0513; (510) 642-5208; salis@arg.org; (salis.org).

Theatre Library Association, c/o Schubert Archive, 149 W. 45th St., New York, NY 10036; susan.brady@yale.edu; (www.brown.edu/Facilities/University_Library/beyond/TLA/TLA.html).

United States Board on Books for Young People, P.O. Box 8139, Newark, DE 19714-8139; (302) 731-1600, ext. 275; acutts@reading.org; (www.usbby.org).

Urban Libraries Council, 1603 Orrington Avenue, Suite 1080, Evanston, IL 60201; (847) 866-9999; ulc@gpl.glenview.lib.il.us; (www.clpgh.org/ulc/).

Virtual Library Association, vla2000@yahoo.com; (www.angelfire.com/biz/vla2000/).

Welsh Library Association, c/o Department of Information and Library Studies, University of Wales Aberystwyth, Llanbadarn Fawr, Aberystwyth, Ceredigion, Wales SY23 3AS; hle@aber.ac.uk; (www.llgc.org.uk/wla/).

Western Association of Map Libraries, Muriel Strickland, 2465 Baja Cerro Circle, San Diego, CA 92019; (619) 274-0613; 103251.1605@compuserve.com; (gort.ucsd.edu/mw/waml/waml.html).

How to convert a speech into an article

by Jerry Di Vecchio

SUNSET MAGAZINE is the largest how-to, food, home, travel, and garden magazine in the western United States. As the senior editor responsible for food, wine, and entertainment, I, along with my staff, gather a huge amount of data from a variety of sources including telephone contacts, interviews, and personal observations. This primarily oral information is then recreated for publication. In this domain, the success of our endeavors may be easily measured since, for example, it can mean the difference between preparing a great meal and a disappointing meal. We are constantly aware of the differences between oral and written presentation of information and have a great deal of practical experience in transforming an oral presentation into a piece suitable for publication.

It is important to understand that the dynamics of oral and written presentations differ greatly. Being aware of these differences and using the strengths of each will greatly increase the chances of effective communication.

A good way to begin is to review the characteristics of an oral presentation and compare and contrast them to the requirements for a written work.

Oral presentation

An oral presentation is generally a one on-one interaction and has the potential to be two-way, even in cases of a large audience. It is helpful if the presentation proceeds in a linear fashion, but it's not necessarily a problem if the speaker backs up, skips over sections, repeats information, or spontaneously answers questions to clarify points. If mistakes are made orally they can be corrected immediately and without creating confusion. In an oral presentation, all the senses may be involved: hearing, for the emotional nuances that may be translated, even subliminally; sight, because seeing is believing; touch, literally to get the feel of things; smell, a very powerful stimulant; and taste, because "the proof is in the pudding."

Written presentation

A print product also exists in a one-on-one environment, but the conversation is generally one-directional as there is no opportunity for direct or immediate interaction between the author and the reader. In a written presentation, a linear format in which information is presented as concisely as possible, is very important, for there is no suitable mechanism for correcting errors or clarifying ambiguous statements. An interesting style helps readers understand the information, keeps their attention, and compensates for the lack of sensory stimuli.

In a written presentation, increasing the visual impact of the presentation through layout and design, judicious use of white space, and overall format of the material make it easier for the reader's eye to travel the page without causing confusion or misunderstanding. Carefully engineered use of paragraphing, type size, boldface and italics, bullets, and other visual aids enhance the overall look of the printed page. Graphs, charts, diagrams, photos, and illustrations help to break up dense copy, enhance communication, and facilitate comprehension. When visual aids are used, they should be placed strategically and labeled clearly so the reader knows exactly what to look at in order to understand a crucial point. Frequently a simple sketch is more effective than a paragraph of text, no matter how brilliant the words seem to be.

Preparing the text

In transforming a spoken piece into written form, it is essential to get to the point as quickly and concisely as possible. Avoid the use of jargon, and don't let cuteness or cleverness cloud the message. Other useful tips in converting an oral presentation into written form may include the following:

- Write once, then edit, and then rewrite.
- Be precise and clear.
- Use language carefully and exactly.

- Watch for words, terms, and phrases that can be misinterpreted or interpreted in more than one way, and rewrite to eliminate possible misunderstandings.
- Maintain the same reference terminology throughout.
- Develop a linear sequence and stick to it; do not backtrack.

Editing and revision

No matter how well a piece has been written, it can always benefit from ruthless editing. It often helps to put the text aside for a while before reviewing and editing it. A little distance gives you a fresh perspective on your work. It may also help to let others read the piece. Does it make sense to them? What do they find confusing, enlightening, redundant? Comments and feedback can help focus the piece. Another useful trick is to read the text aloud. The change from the written to the spoken word literally calls attention to areas that need editing and rewriting.

We have all used written instructions to assemble a child's toy, follow a recipe, or figure out how a computer program works. Sometimes we have been successful, but more often than not, we have felt confused and frustrated. The techniques described above will help eliminate confusion and frustration and contribute to a successful transformation of an oral presentation for publication.

SOURCE: Jerry Di Vecchio, "Transforming an Oral Presentation for Publication," *Library Administration & Management* 12 (Summer 1998): 138–39.

How to improve library literature

by Barbara L. Floyd and John C. Phillips

HOW MIGHT THE QUALITY of library literature be improved? The authors have six suggestions.—*GME.*

Release time. Library administrators must take an interest in improving the profession's literature by providing release time to their faculty members to conduct research. Because publishing is weighted heavily in personnel decisions, libraries should have written policies that specify release time for librarians to conduct research. It is not enough to grant an occasional day. High-quality scholarship requires sustained efforts, with sufficient time to develop ideas, think through methodologies, and write and revise. It cannot— and should not—be done in competition with other daily job responsibilities.

A survey we conducted in 1996 showed that many libraries where librarians have faculty status have neglected an important facet of ACRL's *Statement on Faculty Status of College and University Librarians,* issued in 1972. The statement reads: "Faculty status entails for librarians the same rights and responsibilities as for other members of the faculty. They should have corresponding entitlement to rank, promotion, tenure, compensation, leaves, and research funds." Most universities seem to have neglected this important point. Our survey revealed that few libraries have research leave policies.

A 1990 study conducted by librarians at Auraria Library, in Denver, reported on policies instituted there to assist faculty with research. Among the most important factors in successful research and publication at Auraria was the opportunity to take release time for extended periods. Other policies of that library that have resulted in an increase in publishing include: giving priority for travel funds to those presenting papers at conferences; allocating money to faculty members for research support services; and developing a research center where information on scholarly publishing (such as publication guidelines) is collected and available. All these policies promote the production of scholarly works by library faculty, and should be seriously considered by library administrators if publishing is to continue to be important to library faculty careers and the profession as a whole.

Evaluating quality. If publications are to be a part of a librarian's personnel review, their quality also must be evaluated. An assessment of quality should include, among other things, the reputation of the journal, the relevance of the chosen topic to the profession, the pertinence of the work to the faculty member's role in the library, whether or not the work is seminal, the significance of the findings, and whether the article fills a void in the body of knowledge. Methods for judging publications similar to those used by some other colleges (outside peer review, for example) should be applied to library publications. It is not enough to simply count the number of publications.

Qualified authors. Because librarianship is becoming so specialized, those who publish should have the appropriate background knowledge of the subject area, including professional experiences related to that area. Editorial board members should try to judge the qualifications of persons contributing manuscripts, even in a blind review process. A rigorous manuscript review process, for example, should ferret out those whose methodology and results reveal a lack of expertise in the area they write about. And those who evaluate the quality of publications during personnel evaluations must also take into consideration the qualifications of the author. Once accepted, editorial staffs should check articles for factual errors prior to publication.

Opening up the process. The library profession should take a renewed interest in its scholarship and strive to increase the number of persons engaged in the publishing process. Methods to open up the publishing process to greater numbers might include: shortening tenures for editors; finding more democratic ways to select editors and editorial board members; finding ways

---

Top 10 library journals for sending unsolicited manuscripts

The titles are based on a 1994 survey and represent the percent of unsolicited manuscripts accepted.

Music Reference Services Quarterly	100%
Rare Books & Manuscripts Librarianship	100%
Microform Review	~100%
International Journal of Micrographics & Optical Technology	90%
Judaica Librarianship	90%
Library & Archival Security	85%
Voice of Youth Advocates	85%
Against the Grain	83%
Library Resources & Technical Services	83%
Serials Review	80%

SOURCE: Barbara J. Via, "Publishing in the Journal Literature of Library and Information Science," *College & Research Libraries* 57 (July 1996): 365–76.

to identify new authors; demanding quality and accuracy in the literature; and accepting more manuscripts with controversial subjects. As readers, we must turn a critical eye to what we read in the literature, and if articles are poor in quality or inaccurate, we must voice our concerns. More of us must also be willing to offer our own manuscripts for publication, especially if we have not published before, and aim for the highest quality in those manuscripts. Longevity may have its merits, but editors may want to consider imposing term limits on themselves as one way to avoid stagnation and open up the publishing process.

Student training. We urge library schools to teach students research methodology and writing skills, if they are not currently doing so. These skills provide students with the foundation upon which to engage in research and publication in their professional careers. For librarians with faculty status, the ability to research and publish is essential to succeeding in academe.

Publishing outside the field. One of the most interesting suggestions the authors received from those surveyed was one that encouraged librarians to publish outside the field of librarianship. The authors agree with the respondent who felt librarians should apply their knowledge to other academic fields. This would demonstrate to others that librarians can publish on a par with their teaching colleagues, and it would improve the image of librarians. Publishing in other fields in which one has some expertise would do much to elevate the status of librarians, enabling others to see that librarians have an important role to play in the advancement of scholarship.

SOURCE: Barbara L. Floyd and John C. Phillips, "A Question of Quality: How Authors and Editors Perceive Library Literature," *College & Research Libraries* 58 (January 1997): 81–93.

Pleasing the editorial gods

by Art Plotnik

And the LORD had respect unto Abel and to his offering; but unto Cain and to his offering He had not respect. —*Genesis 4:4–5*

AS THE GATEKEEPERS OF PUBLISHING, editors seem as gods to mere authors. A manuscript is offered, and the author waits for a sign. And waits. And waits. Give me a sign, O Editor! And finally the Word comes down: "Thou hast pleased us. Contract to follow." Or, "We cannot use thy offering at the present time."

Aspiring authors rarely meet editors, and so they imagine a race of deities in the mist of the publishing empyrean. Wrathful and capricious, these higher beings decree which authorlings shall be raised from obscurity and which consigned to the hell of the unpublished.

Higher beings? *Au contraire!* Most book and magazine editors serve as minions to the real gods: the publishing brass. The only mist that enshrouds them is their cold sweat as they run to killer meetings. They labor in suburban office plazas or in midtown warrens with flimsy partitions and locked bathrooms. Surely no deity needs keys to take a whiz—or works 60 hours a week for chump change. Ergo, editors are not gods at all, but mere godlets at best.

The godlets appear in many forms, depending on the size and nature of their publications. In small operations, a few editors do it all: plan the program, acquire manuscripts, edit the text, write marketing copy, and kick author ass.

Magazine editors tend to be the most capricious godlets, and any one of them can twist the fate of your manuscript. The assistant editor tells you, "Yeah, let's see the thing"; the associate editor reads it, votes yes; the managing editor concurs; the copy editor tightens the prose; the senior editor tears it apart; the chief editor postpones publication; the production editor saves the file; the editorial assistant loses it.

Short deadlines make magazine editors shrill and subject to mood swings. Because they can transform a publication so quickly, some actually view themselves as gods—especially the chief editors. They can be puckish as well: One New York editor likes to show off his private manuscript collection—most of the articles sent to him over the last two or three years, unacknowledged and jammed into a case behind his desk. "Something for a rainy day," he says.

Book editors, those who review proposals and acquire manuscripts ("projects"), are generally less wroth. They look tired, more oppressed than angered by their countless deadlines and assignments. They spend too much time on proposals that go nowhere and projects they may never see to fruition. Occasionally a good sales report or literary honor yields a buzz; then it's back to the gloom of overload.

Literary agents, who are gatekeeping godlets themselves, help reduce the number of hopeless submissions. Still, most editors face armadas of manuscripts to battle far into the night, when real gods should be out cavorting as bulls or showers of gold.

Book editors are decent humanists who probably would be merciful to authors if time allowed and they got points for it. They would read unsolicited manuscripts; they would answer calls, letters, and e-mail from authors; they would offer advice, criticism, and consolation, what the hell. But book editors are not hired to succor the multitudes; they are paid to turn words into revenue and please the Number Gods who run the show.

If editors are less than gods, why should writers quake before them? Because editors, lowly though they may be, still guard the gates of Paradise and wield a few thunderbolts. Editors can cut a writer off cold, or support a writer throughout the publishing decision, or help make a writer a star, or, in some instances, make a writer a better writer. Editors can launch writers into nirvana with one phrase ("Loved your book . . .") or dementia with another (". . . we've got a little problem").

Until authors achieve their own godhead as bankable brand names—or land an almighty agent—they must learn to please the editorial godlets. Knowing that editors are in fact quasimortals who can be swayed and even fooled gives one some courage; but courage alone will not win the day, any more than a stupendous manuscript will automatically find its champion. One must learn how to beg for editorial favor.

The art of supplication

In my career as a writer I have knelt before many an editorial godlet, even as I've decreed the fate of writers from my own editorial roosts. From these perspectives I have observed the art of supplication: how writers can curry favor or at least avoid an editor's wrath. As a minor godlet, then, as well as an author with a butt full of thunderbolts, I offer the following advice.

An editor bases her (or his) first evaluation of a proposal more on instinct than divine justice. Like a clam sorting tidal microbes, the editor performs a food/nonfood dichotomy on incoming materials. To an editor, food is something that readers will eat up. Fresh, bite-sized, and pungent—the editor knows it when she sees it.

Nonfood reveals itself in a number of ways: too big, too small, wrong look, funny smell. Never must a writer offer anything that signals nonfood: aging or nonstandard paper; ancient typewriting or dot-matrix printouts; misspellings in the cover letter; the wrong publisher in the address; shaky handwriting, cartooned happy faces, list of school publications; old clippings; personal snapshots; home-brewed (amateur-looking) graphics; an account of how friends adored the manuscript; quote marks around "slangy" words; or signs of paranoia and rage.

The Red Pony.

Drawn by Marjorie.

Just what, you protest, do any of these signals have to do with literary merit? Intrinsically, nothing; but an editor, unable even to skim every submission, has to play the odds. The odds say that most people who cannot spell have not undergone the discipline that makes for saleable writing; they say that writers who include such extraneous items as snapshots are rank amateurs who just don't get it. Editors reject amateurism outright, just as they close themselves off to the pathetic:

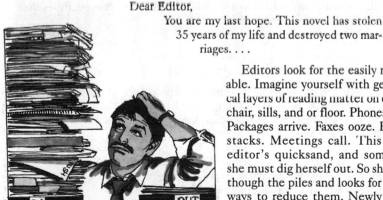

Dear Editor,
You are my last hope. This novel has stolen 35 years of my life and destroyed two marriages. . . .

Editors look for the easily rejectable. Imagine yourself with geological layers of reading matter on desks, chair, sills, and or floor. Phones ring. Packages arrive. Faxes ooze. E-mail stacks. Meetings call. This is an editor's quicksand, and somehow she must dig herself out. So she sifts though the piles and looks for quick ways to reduce them. Newly arriving materials meet a natural resistance against taking on more work. This is not callousness; this is survival. And callousness, too.

The writer's challenge: Don't help the editor resist you.

Obstacles writers create

Editors often work on impulse: Something hits them at just the right time and they decide to pursue it—until they encounter the first obstacle. Writers create obstacles with woeful presentation packages. For example, they often fail to provide contact numbers—telephone, e-mail, etc.—which belong on each piece of the presentation package. As a harried editor, I had little patience with cute letterheads—Old Ink Well Road, Weasel Run, Pa.—and no numbers.

Some writers withhold phone numbers as if they'd die if ever an editor called. In fact, editors favor the telephone (or e-mail) because it's fast and doesn't require the careful wording of a letter or fax—just as long as they, the editors and not the authors, do the dial-up.

One way to clam up an editor is to phone in proposals. "You got a few minutes? I got this idea. . . ." Editors receive a great many such calls, some of them spitefully transferred from another editor. Phoned-in proposals offend the godlets. They lack organization, they can't be passed around for evaluation, they demand attention in the middle of other obligations. Half the breathless proposals by phone never make it to paper. "Send a query," most editors will say and cut the conversation there. Writers may safely telephone editors to ask which staff member should receive their proposal. Editors don't mind a call they can handle with three or four words, such as "try Suzie Doaks" or "send it to me," though you don't have to give your own name; no one will ask.

It is better to address a specific individual than to write "Dear Editor," and a good bet to use the editor's first name: "Dear Susan" (not "Suzie"). It gets a sliver more attention and won't hurt. If on the phone the editor said "send it to me," then write: "Thanks for agreeing to review my query [or proposal or manuscript]." Maybe the editor didn't quite agree; but she won't remember and she'll feel obligated to read one more paragraph. And that paragraph, the grabber, should wake the dead. Say just about anything that will get attention, if it's not too sick. All rules for breaking into publication boil down to one: Get attention.

> Dear Susan,
> Thanks for agreeing to review my proposal.
> I lost my virginity at age eight.

Later you can explain that you meant figuratively, or according to some cult you intend to expose. If you've got one hell of a marketable idea and can deliver, editors will accept the opening hype. Don't squeeze out your cards; show your ace as quickly and as clearly as possible. You can't ask an overloaded editor to read a complicated proposal for no obvious reason, or to deduce, guess, or extrapolate what is special about your offering.

How many writers put these and far stranger demands upon the busy godlets! By the end of a rough day, what editors would most appreciate from authors is a note that says, "Please find nothing enclosed, nothing to read or do. I ask nothing." Instead, in comes a megascript with this letter (a composite of letters I've received over the years):

> Dear Editor,
>
> Herewith is the manuscript I described, in part, in my queries of June 23 and October 27, to which one of your staff responded, though I have misplaced that correspondence. Perhaps you could check your files.
>
> You'll note that parts 1 and 3 of the mss are in typescript; part two is on the enclosed disk in a CP/M Wordstar format that needs a simple conversion to whatever you have in-house.
>
> Several footnotes were added after part 1 was typed, so please add three digits to each superior number after footnote 5, and one digit to the total after the original footnote 9, so that superior numbers match with the list of footnotes.
>
> Actually, part 1 is more or less a rough draft. Perhaps you'd look it over with an eye toward what should be dropped and what developed and how. Should you need some author background, you'll find it in *Who's Who in the Fort Wayne Business Community* (Fort Wayne Chamber of Commerce, 1953). Please see that 25% of my fee goes to the Hoosier Horticultural Preservation Society. . . .

Each week editors face such clueless innocents, whom they zap like gnats in a bug light. As well as being annoying, such naive demands signal that the accompanying manuscript will ask all and give little. The presentation package should make one demand only and an implicit one at that: Begin reading. The rest should follow naturally.

The limits of humility

Scores of writers' guides provide instructions for manuscript submission. Writers must review and observe these fundamental rules, even as they master the subtleties in dealing with editors. Can the basic rules be broken? Yes, if your name is, say, Iris Murdoch and you've published two dozen successful novels. Murdoch writes her manuscripts in longhand, and, without making copies, delivers them personally to her publisher. How many authors could walk in with a paper sack of deeply philosophical fiction and demand it be published as written, without a change? Approximately one. Most other writers must be proper supplicants and follow the rules. Supplication is begging, let's face it—please read my manuscript, please see its merits! But kneeling before editors does not mean self-effacement. Editors are already negatively poised when apologetic writers start mewling and puking about their inadequacies.

> Dear Susan,
>
> Forgive my using your first name; I was advised to do so, but I probably shouldn't listen to all those tips. I'm so sorry to trouble you with this manuscript, which is overly long and probably gushier than the kind of thing you usually want. Blame it on my total ignorance of publishing. I set my story in Des Moines, the only big city I know. It was probably dumb of me not to use New York just because I've never been there. I could change the setting as well as the main character, who was based on myself. Telling my story seemed like a good idea; but when I finished I realized, who'd want to read about me?

"Right," says the editor. "Next!" Somehow this rebuff surprises the apologist, who was only fishing for kindly reassurance and expecting this response: "Trouble? You little minx, are you kidding? Your work is what publishing is all about! Overlong? Gushy? Another worldly collision between Eco and Allende is what we're calling it along Publishers Row! We not only lived to read each page, but we want you here, now, signing contracts!" Funny, that letter never comes.

SOURCE: Art Plotnik, "Pleasing the Editorial Gods," *Lumpen,* December 1996, pp. 69–71. Reprinted with permission.

How to convert a dissertation into a book

A MANUSCRIPT DESIGNED to communicate mastery of the research process to an examining committee frequently fails to satisfy the requirements of a publisher. Authors submitting theses and dissertations to a publisher may anticipate requests for extensive modifications of their manuscript if it is accepted for publication. Indeed, some effort at revision prior to submission will enhance the likelihood of acceptance.

A book is addressed to an audience that is very different from the audience to whom a thesis, dissertation, or other research report is addressed. These differences include level of interest, prior knowledge of the subject, and objectives in reading the work. Major revisions are usually necessary, even to the most effective works.

Revisions that are often required include deletions, reorganization, and the writing of additional material. Some examples:

- The style of a dissertation frequently requires the repetition of material from section to section. In many cases this redundancy can be eliminated. Tables often should be deleted or converted into an explanatory narrative.
- Many of the fine points concerning prior research or methodology on the subject should be placed in appendices or footnotes.
- Abstractions must be carefully related to the concrete world through more extensive interpretation than would be necessary in a dissertation or thesis.

SOURCE: College & Research Libraries News, April 1986, p. 277.

MATERIALS
CHAPTER FOUR

"I was reading the dictionary. I thought it was a poem about everything."

—Steven Wright

BOOKS

How to identify a first edition
by Bill McBride

Edition, printing, impression

AN EDITION IS the number of books printed before a certain percentage of the contents is revised. A **printing** is the number of copies produced when the printing plates or type are on the press. An **impression** is the same thing as a printing.

To the book collector, a **first edition** means a copy from the first printing of the first edition. To the publisher, a first edition may mean any copy of a title before it was substantially revised.

When a book says on the copyright page, "First and second printings before publication," it means that before the book was actually released for sale (published), orders from booksellers exceeded the quantity of the first printing and the book had to be reprinted. Such a copy is not a book collector's first edition.

For a publisher-by-publisher guide to identifying first editions, see my *Pocket Guide to the Identification of First Editions* (5th ed., 1994), available from McBride/Publisher, 585 Prospect Ave., West Hartford, CT 06105 (www.jumpingfrog.com).

Numbers and letters

Since the late 1940s, some publishers have adopted a new method of identifying their first editions. A series of letters (abcde) or numbers (12345, or 98765, or 135798642, etc.) appears somewhere on the copyright page. If the "a" or the "1" is present, the copy in hand is from the first printing of the first edition. If this method were used by all publishers, there would be few identification problems.

Some questions have been raised about numbers and letters when they are used in conjunction with "first edition" or "first printing." A copyright page might show "First Edition B C D E" or "First Printing 23456789." These are usually first editions because on second printings, the words are removed, leaving the letters or numbers only.

Unfortunately, some publishers have used the system of numbers and letters in conjunction with "First Edition," but leave "First Edition" on the copyright page and remove the number "1" or letter "a" to indicate the second printing.

Issue, state, and point

To the book collector, **issue** means an intermediary copy within the first printing of a first edition. **State** is synonymous with issue. A **point of issue** is a difference that exists among copies of the first printing, thus creating two or more states of the first printing.

The difference may be in the text (spelling error, punctuation change, incorrect text placement, inserted advertisements, colors of printing inks or binding cloths, size of book or page, or the imprint of the publisher). In the case of multiple errors, three or more issues may exist as some errors are corrected and others are not. Multiple points are much more common in books of the 19th century. Because the first-edition identification method is not changed to reflect the alteration during the first printing, copies can look identical unless the existence and location of a point is known. My companion guide, *Points of Issue*, lists 1,500 books in the 19th and 20th centuries with identifying points.

Sleuthing first editions

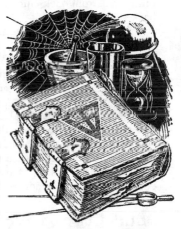

Dust jackets and author biographies, publisher's ads, and copyright information all may contain clues. If a biographical sketch of the author printed on the dust jacket mentions other works, check to see when they were published. If they followed the work in hand, then the book isn't likely a first. A dust jacket may say "second printing" when the copyright page may not. Ads for books by other authors can also help pinpoint a date. The address of a publisher may be a significant thing in itself—if a zip code is included in the address, the book must have been published no earlier than July 1, 1963, the date the codes were introduced to the public.

Determining a first edition is more often than not a reverse investigation. You are actually trying to determine if the book is a second or later printing. If you find no evidence that the book is a later printing, then you have a first.

Identifying book-club editions

Many titles of 20th-century fiction and nonfiction were published in book-club editions. These editions often resemble the true first trade editions. Here are some ways to identify book-club editions:

1. **No price** on the dust jacket. Recently, a few publishers have printed dust jackets without prices so that individual retail booksellers can affix their own price stickers. This is confounding to the collector, but typically the book-club versions are lighter, smaller, and do not carry the standard first-edition identifier on the copyright page. An exception: University publishers usually do not print prices on their dust jackets.

2. **"Book Club Edition"** printed on the dust jacket's lower inner front flap. If this portion of the jacket is cut off, be wary and look further.

3. **Back cover debossing** at the bottom near the spine. A debossed (indented) star, circle, dot, crown, or other geometric device, colored or uncolored, indicates a book-club edition, even when all other first-edition indica-

tors check out. This practice began about 1947, primarily by the Book-of-the-Month Club. Occasionally, the debossed symbol is found at the top of the back cover or somewhere in between the bottom and top edges of the back cover along the spine. Do not confuse this debossed book-club symbol with the frequently found debossed publisher's logotype or ISBN number; these *do not* denote book-club editions. Also, special exceptions to the debossing rule are several James Michener titles from 1980 to 1985 (*The Covenant, Poland, Space*) that have a debossing on the back cover, but are correct firsts if "first edition" appears on the copyright page.

4. **"A Selection of the Book-of-the-Month Club"** printed on the dust jacket where the price is usually printed (upper front dust jacket flap). This practice was common in the 1960s and early 1970s. In the later 1970s and up, the same phrase was used as a promotional line on the jacket, and you may need to compare book-club editions side by side with trade editions to determine firsts from book-club editions, especially if there is no debossing on the back cover.

5. **Reprints from original plates.** Many books printed by such publishers as A. L. Burt, Grosset & Dunlap, Tower Books, The Book League, The Literary Guild, Garden City, Walter J. Black, and others, often used the printing plates of the true first edition and neglected to alter the copyright page. Thus, some books may appear to be first editions, when in fact they are actually reprints by another company.

6. **Switched dust jackets: a caution.** Some book-club editions so closely resemble true first editions that the mere substitution of a second trade edition dust jacket for the book-club jacket can fool even veteran collectors and dealers. It is therefore wise to check *all* points of book-club identification before purchase or sale. Many of these books are termed *false firsts,* book-club editions that masquerade as true firsts.

British Commonwealth countries

Before the adoption of the International Copyright Convention of 1957, many British Commonwealth publishers were notoriously inconsistent in identifying their firsts. Since then, most have adopted the form "First published in (year)" or simply list only second and later printings, not first printings.

First paperback editions

In recent years, considerable interest has arisen in first paperback editions of 20th-century literature. First paperbacks sometimes contain new prefatory material by the author, a noted editor, annotator, or bibliographer. In some cases, a title appears in paperback before it does in hardback (early Kurt Vonnegut, Louis L'Amour, and Dean Koontz titles are good examples). Special movie or stage editions are often printed when a book is made into a movie or play. These editions are frequently illustrated inside or on the covers with scenes from the production. Additional material by the author may also be included. First and special paperback editions are as much a part of an author's bibliography as are true firsts.

SOURCE: Bill McBride, comp., *A Pocket Guide to the Identification of First Editions* (Hartford, Ct.: The author, 5th ed., 1995). Reprinted with permission.

The parts of a book

FRONT MATTER (preliminaries, prelims), usually numbered with lower-case roman numerals:

i	Bastard title (false title, first half title) or series title
ii	Ad card, series title, series list, frontispiece, or blank
iii	Title page (may be a double-page spread)
iv	Copyright page (includes copyright notice, printing history, country where printed, ISBN, CIP data [or notice that this appears on the last page of the book]; may also include publisher's address, copublishing information, acknowledgments, credits, permissions, dedication, epigraph, or colophon)
v	Dedication or epigraph (or table of contents)
vi	Blank
vii	Table of Contents opening page
recto or verso	List of Illustrations opening page
recto or verso	List of Tables opening page (may be run in after list of illustrations or begun on a new page)
recto	Foreword opening page
recto	Preface opening page
recto	Acknowledgments opening page (may be run in after preface or begun on a new page)
recto or verso	Other front matter (list of contributors, list of abbreviations, chronology, translator's note, note on orthography, etc.)
recto	Introduction opening page (if not part of main text)

TEXT, numbered with arabic numerals that continue through the back matter:

1	Half title (second half title) or part title; the half title may be numbered as part of the front matter and is usually omitted if there is a part title
2	Blank
3	Chapter 1 (opening page of main text); if the half title is omitted or numbered with the front matter and there is no part title, text may begin on page 1

BACK MATTER (end matter), usually opening recto unless there are space constraints:

recto	Appendix opening page; if there are several appendixes, each one usually starts on a new page, recto or verso
recto or verso	Notes opening page
recto or verso	Glossary opening page
recto or verso	Bibliography opening page
recto or verso	Index opening page
last recto or verso	Colophon and CIP data (if not on copyright page)

SOURCE: Richard Eckersley, et al., *Glossary of Typesetting Terms* (Chicago: University of Chicago Press, 1994). pp. 121–22. Reprinted with permission.

Secret manuals

by Bill Katz

MANUALS AND HANDBOOKS OF MAGIC and mystery date back to the Mesopotamians and Egyptians. In a sense, *The Book of the Dead* is a handbook, and the *Epic of Gilgamesh* suggests numerous magical processes in an effort to defeat death. Ritual magic, along with the necessary handbooks, is a study in itself, but the utilitarian ends of many magic recipes (from medicine to agriculture) encouraged such titles. These can be found through Greek and Roman literature as well as a part of the development of Christianity.

A group of medieval manuals and handbooks were widely copied, yet considered secret. They were circulated extensively among those familiar with Latin and encouraged the idea that the world was full of marvels and secrets open only to the select few. Such works were well known to astrologers and to alchemists, as well as to those involved with black magic.

An example was *Secretum secretorum (Secret of Secrets),* which apparently derived from a 10th-century Arab compilation. Today, the more than 600 extant copies indicate that it circulated widely, at least among scholars. The handbook was a type of encyclopedia that covered numerous topics from crafts and politics to medicine. The *Secreta Alberti (Secrets of Albert)* was a later compilation that covered secrets to be found in the careful analysis of animals, plants, and other natural items. The handbook included some 200 formulas and recipes. An idea of why it was looked to for black magic may be gained by listing a few of its subjects, each of which offered a method of response: "To know

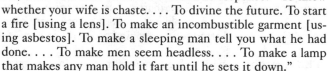

whether your wife is chaste. . . . To divine the future. To start a fire [using a lens]. To make an incombustible garment [using asbestos]. To make a sleeping man tell you what he had done. . . . To make men seem headless. . . . To make a lamp that makes any man hold it fart until he sets it down."

The advent of printing dispelled some of the mystery of these books, many of which were given wider circulation in translated, printed editions. The suggested "Secrets Revealed" content for a handbook or manual, particularly in the 16th and early 17th centuries, became a sure key to a bestseller. The ready reference works may have revealed mysteries and secrets, but, more important, they gave useful, quite workable formulas for everything from removing stains and other household hints to curing diseases and making perfumes and cosmetics. A whole group of "professors of secrets" developed, particularly in Germany and Italy, who were on the fringes of the university and made a living translating and publishing the Latin Medieval secret books.

In exploring the history of the secret books, William Eamon goes a step further and claims they set the stage for the 17th-century scientific revolution. The handbooks of secrets, he asserts, wed secrets, learning, scientists, doctors, and craftspeople in one common interest. The notion of experiment, scientific reasoning, and related matters were fostered by these reference works, out of which came the Royal Society in the mid-17th century. Furthermore, thanks to people like Francis Bacon (1561–1626), the whole notion of a select group having access to scientific secrets (i.e., secret manuals) was questionable. The Royal Society made all its proceedings public. Popular knowledge of the science was probably greater in the late Tudor and the Stuart periods than ever before or since.

SOURCE: Bill Katz, *Cuneiform to Computer: A History of Reference Sources* (Lanham, Md.: Scarecrow Press, 1998), pp. 138–39. Reprinted with permission.

Outstanding reference sources

EACH YEAR THE ALA's Reference and User Services Association's Reference Sources Committee examines hundreds of reference works to identify those that are essential for small and medium-sized public or academic libraries. The following are their picks for 1997 through 1999, incorporating reference sources published between 1996 and 1998.

The Arts

Baker's Biographical Dictionary of Twentieth-Century Classical Musicians, ed. Laura Kuhn and Nicolas Slonimsky (Schirmer, 1997).
Dictionary of Art, ed. Jane Turner (Grove's Dictionaries, 1996).
Dictionary of Women Artists, ed. Delia Gaze (Fitzroy Dearborn, 1997).

Encyclopedia of Aesthetics, ed. Michael Kelly (Oxford University, 1998).
Encyclopedia of Comparative Iconography: Themes Depicted in Works of Art, ed. Helen E. Roberts (Fitzroy Dearborn, 1998).
Encyclopedia of Interior Design, by Johanna Banham (Fitzroy Dearborn, 1997).
Garland Encyclopedia of World Music, ed. Bruno Nettl and Ruth Stone (Garland, 1997–1998).
International Encyclopedia of Dance, ed. Selma Jeanne Cohen (Oxford University, 1998).
Music Festivals from Bach to Blues: A Traveler's Guide, by Tom Clynes (Visible Ink, 1996).

Business and Economics

Business Cycles and Depressions: An Encyclopedia, ed. David Glasner (Garland, 1997).
Encyclopedia of Emerging Industries, ed. Jane A. Malonis and Holly M. Selden (Gale, 1998).
Encyclopedia of Housing, ed. William Van Vliet (Sage, 1998).
Handbook of North American Industry: NAFTA and the Economies of Its Member Nations, by John Cremeans (Bernan, 1998).
Handbook of U.S. Labor Statistics: Employment Earnings, Prices, Productivity and Other Labor Data, ed. Eva E. Jacobs (Bernan, 1997).

The Environment

American Nature Writers, ed. John Elder (Scribner, 1996).

Biographical Dictionary of American and Canadian Naturalists and Environmentalists, ed. Keir B. Sterling and others (Greenwood, 1997).

Encyclopedia of Animal Rights and Animal Welfare, ed. Marc Berkoff and Carron Meaney (Greenwood, 1998).

Macmillan Encyclopedia of the Environment, ed. Stephen R. Kellert (Macmillan Reference Library USA, 1997).

Natural Resources, ed. Mark S. Coyne and Craig W. Allin (Salem Press, 1998).

Toxic Waste Sites: An Encyclopedia of Endangered America, by Mark Crawford (ABC-Clio, 1997).

History and Culture

ABC-Clio World History Companion to the Industrial Revolution, ed. Peter N. Stearns and John H. Hinshaw (ABC-Clio, 1996).

American Eras: Development of a Nation, 1783–1815, ed. Robert J. Allison; *American Eras: Civil War and Reconstruction, 1850–1877,* ed. Thomas J. Brown; *American Eras: Development of the Industrial United States, 1879–1899,* ed. Vincent Tompkins (Gale, 1997).

Ancestral Trails: The Complete Guide to British Genealogy and Family History, by Mark D. Herber (Genealogical, 1998).

The Civil War in Books: An Analytical Bibliography, by David J. Eicher (University of Illinois, 1997).

Columbia Gazetteer of the World, ed. Saul B. Cohen (Columbia University, 1998).

Encyclopedia of Africa South of the Sahara, ed. John Middleton (Scribners, 1997).

Encyclopedia of Latin American History and Culture, ed. Barbara A. Tenenbaum (Scribner, 1996).

Encyclopedia of the McCarthy Era, by William K. Klingaman (Facts on File, 1996).

Encyclopedia of the Vietnam War, ed. Stanley I. Kutler (Scribner, 1996).

Encyclopedia of the Vietnam War: A Political, Social, and Military History, ed. Spencer T. Tucker (ABC-Clio, 1998).

Encyclopedia of U.S. Foreign Relations, ed. Bruce V. Jentleson and Thomas G. Paterson (Oxford University, 1997).

Encyclopedia of World Sport from Ancient Times to the Present, ed. Davis Levinson and Karen Christensen (ABC-Clio, 1997).

Handbook to Life in Ancient Greece, by Leslie Adkins and Roy A. Adkins (Facts on File, 1997).

Historical Atlas of the Holocaust (Macmillan Historical Museum, 1996).

Historical Encyclopedia of World Slavery, ed. Junius P. Rodriguez (ABC-Clio, 1997).

Medieval England: An Encyclopedia, ed. Paul E. Szarmach (Garland, 1998).

Nations without States: A Historical Dictionary of Contemporary National Movements, by James Minahan (Greenwood, 1996).

Printed Sources: A Guide to Published Genealogical Records, ed. Kory L. Meyerink (Ancestry, 1998).

Law

American Justice, ed. Joseph M. Bessette (Salem, 1996).

Congressional Universe (fee-based subscription service, online at www.lexis-nexis.com/congcomp/, Congressional Information Service, 1998).

Encyclopedia of American Prisons, ed. Marilyn D. McShane and Frank P. Williams III (Garland, 1996).

Encyclopedia of Constitutional Amendments: Proposed Amendments and Amending Issues, 1789–1995, by John R. Vile (ABC-Clio, 1996).

Facts about the Congress, by Stephen G. Christianson (H. W. Wilson, 1996).
Facts about the Supreme Court, by Lisa Paddock (H. W. Wilson, 1996).
The FBI: A Comprehensive Reference Guide, ed. Athan G. Theoharis, et al. (Oryx, 1998).
International Encyclopedia of Public Policy and Administration, ed. Jay M. Shafritz (Westview, 1998).
Murder Cases of the Twentieth Century, by David K. Frasier (McFarland, 1996).

Literature

African Writers, ed. C. Brian Cox (Scribner's, 1997).
Bartlett's Roget's Thesaurus, ed. Elizabeth Wear Paitha, et al. (Little, Brown, 1996).
Encyclopedia of Fantasy, ed. John Clute and John Grant (St. Martin's, 1997).
Encyclopedia of Folklore and Literature, ed. Mary Ellen Brown and Bruce A. Rosenberg (ABC-Clio, 1998).
Encyclopedia of Latin American Literature, ed. Verity Smith (Fitzroy Dearborn, 1997).
Encyclopedia of the Essay, ed. Tracy Chevalier (Fitzroy Dearborn, 1997).
Latin for the Illiterati, by Jon R. Stone (Routledge, 1996).
Oxford Companion to African American Literature, ed. William L. Andrews, et al. (Oxford University, 1997).
Reference Guide to Russian Literature, ed. Neil Cornwell (Fitzroy Dearborn, 1998).

Religion

The Cambridge Companion to the Bible, ed. Howard Clark Kee, et al. (Cambridge University, 1997).
Directory of Saints, by Annette Sandoval (Dutton, 1996).
Encyclopedia of American Catholic History, ed. Michael Glazier and Thomas J. Shelley (Liturgical, 1997).
Encyclopedia of Sacred Places, by Norbert C. Brockman (ABC-Clio, 1997).
Encyclopedia of Women and World Religion, ed. Serenity Young (Macmillan Library Reference, 1998).
Routledge Encyclopedia of Philosophy, ed. Edward Craig (Routledge, 1998).

Science, Health, and Technology

AIDS Dictionary, by Sarah B. Watstein and Karen Chandler (Facts on File, 1998).
American Horticultural Society A–Z Encyclopedia of Garden Plants, ed. Christopher Brickell and Judith D. Zuk (DK, 1997).
Dirr's Hardy Trees and Shrubs: An Illustrated Encyclopedia, by Michael A. Dirr (Timber Press, 1997).
Dinosaurs: The Encyclopedia, by Donald F. Glut (McFarland, 1997).
E-Blast: A Guide to the Web's Top Sites, by the editors of *Encyclopaedia Britannica* (formerly online at www.eblast.com, 1997–1999).
Encyclopedia of Climate and Weather, ed. Stephen H. Schneider (Oxford University, 1996).
Encyclopedia of Earth Sciences, ed. E. Julius Dasch (Macmillan, 1996).
Encyclopedia of Medicinal Plants, by Andrew Chevallier (DK, 1996).
Encyclopedia of Mental Health, ed. Howard S. Friedman (Academic, 1998).

Encyclopedia of the Cat, by Bruce Fogle (DK, 1997).

Gale Encyclopedia of Native American Tribes, ed. Sharon Malinowski and Anna Sheets (Gale, 1998).

Harvard Guide to Women's Health, by Karen J. Carlson and others (Harvard University, 1996).

Instruments of Science: An Historical Encyclopedia, ed. Robert Bud and Deborah Jean Warner (Garland, 1998).

The NASA Atlas of the Solar System, by Ronald Greeley and Raymond Batson (Cambridge University, 1997).

Notable Mathematicians: From Ancient Times to the Present, ed. Robin V. Young and Zoran Minderovic (Gale, 1998).

Ultimate Visual Dictionary of Science (DK, 1998).

Weather America, ed. Alfred N. Garwood (Toucan Valley, 1996).

Social Issues and Diversity

The ABC-Clio Companion to the Native American Rights Movement, by Mark Grossman (ABC-Clio, 1997).

American Folklore, ed. Jan Harold Brunvand (Garland, 1996).

American Sign Language Handshape Dictionary, by Richard A. Tennant and Marianne Gluszak Brown (Gallaudet, 1998).

Censorship, ed. Lawrence Amey, et al. (Salem, 1997).

Encyclopedia of African-American Culture and History, ed. Jack Salzman, David Lionel Smith, and Cornel West (Macmillan, 1996).

Encyclopedia of Cultural Anthropology, ed. David Levinson and Melvin Ember (Henry Holt, 1996).

Encyclopedia of Education, by Harlow G. Unger (Facts on File, 1996).

Encyclopedia of Urban America: The Cities and Suburbs, ed. Neil Larry Shumsky (ABC-Clio, 1998).

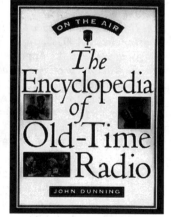

Folklore: An Encyclopedia of Beliefs, Customs, Tales, Music, and Art, ed. Thomas Green (ABC-Clio, 1997).

Growing Up in America, Rickie Sanders and Mark T. Mattson (Macmillan Library Reference, 1998).

On the Air: The Encyclopedia of Old-time Radio, by John Dunning (Oxford, 1998).

Protest, Power, and Change: An Encyclopedia of Nonviolent Action from ACT-UP to Women's Suffrage, ed. Roger S. Powers and William B. Vogele (Garland, 1997).

St. James Gay and Lesbian Almanac, ed. Neil Schlager (St. James Press, 1998).

Voices of Multicultural America: Notable Speeches Delivered by African, Asian, Hispanic and Native Americans, 1790–1995, ed. Deborah Gillan Straub (Gale, 1996).

Women and the Military, by Victoria Sherrow (ABC-Clio, 1996).

Women's Issues, ed. Margaret McFadden (Salem, 1997).

Worldmark Encyclopedia of Cultures and Daily Life, ed. Timothy L. Gall (Gale, 1998).

SOURCE: Reference Sources Committee, ALA Reference and User Services Association.

Notable books, 1998–1999

THE FOLLOWING BOOKS were chosen for their significant contribution to the expansion of knowledge or for the pleasure they can provide to adult readers. Each year the Notable Books Council of the ALA Reference and User Services Association makes the selections, based on the criteria of wide general appeal and literary merit. More information on the books can be found by consulting *Booklist, Choice,* or other review journals.

Fiction

Alvarez, Julia. *Yo!* (Algonquin, 1997).
Anderson, Scott. *Triage* (Scribner, 1998).
Anthony, Patricia. *Flanders* (Ace, 1998).
Atwood, Margaret. *Alias Grace* (Doubleday, 1996).
Barrett, Andrea. *The Voyage of the Narwhal* (Norton, 1998).
Borges, Jorge Luis. *Collected Fictions* (Viking, 1998).
Byers, Michael. *The Coast of Good Intentions* (Houghton/Mariner, 1998).
Choy, Wayson. *The Jade Peony* (Picador USA, 1997).
Danticat, Edwidge. *The Farming of Bones* (Soho, 1998).
Deane, Seamus. *Reading in the Dark* (Knopf, 1997).
Frazier, Charles. *Cold Mountain* (Atlantic Monthly, 1997).
Garcia, Cristina. *Aguero Sisters* (Knopf, 1997).
Hornby, Nick. *About a Boy* (Penguin/Riverhead, 1998).
McDermott, Alice. *Charming Billy* (Farrar, 1998).
Moore, Lorrie. *Birds of America* (Knopf, 1998).
Murakami, Haruki. *The Wind-Up Bird Chronicle* (Knopf, 1997).
Perota, Tom. *The Wishbones* (Putnam, 1997).
Roth, Philip. *I Married a Communist* (Houghton Mifflin, 1998).
Smith, Lee. *News of the Spirit* (Putnam, 1997).
Stollman, Aryeh Lev. *The Far Euphrates* (Riverhead/Putnam, 1997).
Vakil, Ardashir. *Beach Boy* (Scribner, 1998).
Yamanaka, Lois-Ann. *Blu's Hanging* (Farrar Straus Giroux, 1997).

Poetry

Doty, Mark. *Sweet Machine* (HarperFlamingo, 1998).
Hall, Donald. *Without* (Houghton Mifflin, 1998).
Hughes, Ted. *Tales from Ovid* (Farrar, 1998).
Lindsay, Sarah. *Primate Behavior* (Grove Atlantic, 1997).
Matthews, William. *After All: Last Poems* (Houghton Mifflin, 1998).
Piercy, Marge. *What Are Big Girls Made Of?* (Knopf, 1997).
Walcott, Derek. *The Bounty* (Farrar Straus Giroux, 1996).

Nonfiction

Ackroyd, Peter. *The Life of Thomas More* (Doubleday, 1998).
Alvarez, Walter. *T. Rex and the Crater of Doom* (Princeton, 1997).
Berg, A. Scott. *Lindbergh* (Putnam, 1998).
Bragg, Rick. *All Over But the Shoutin'* (Pantheon, 1997).
Branch, Taylor. *Pillar of Fire: America in the King Years, 1963–65* (Simon & Schuster, 1998).
Chernow, Ron. *Titan: The Life of John D. Rockefeller Sr.* (Random, 1998).

Clapp, Nicholas. *The Road to Ubar: Finding the Atlantis of the Sands* (Houghton Mifflin, 1998).

Ehrenreich, Barbara. *Blood Rites: Origins & History of the Passions of War* (Metropolitan/Henry Holt, 1997).

Figes, Orlando. *A People's Tragedy: A History of the Russian Revolution* (Viking, 1997).

Fouts, Roger; with Stephen Tukel Mills. *Next of Kin: What Chimpanzees Have Taught Me About Who We Are* (Morrow, 1997).

Fraser, Kennedy. *Ornament and Silence: Essays on Women's Lives* (Knopf, 1996).

Gorney, Cynthia. *Articles of Faith: A Frontline History of the Abortion Wars* (Simon & Schuster, 1998).

Hochschild, Adam. *King Leopold's Ghost: A Story of Greed, Terror, and Heroism in Colonial Africa* (Houghton Mifflin, 1998).

Junger, Sebastian. *The Perfect Storm: A True Story of Men Against the Sea* (Norton, 1997).

Kinder, Gary. *Ship of Gold in the Deep Blue Sea* (Atlantic Monthly, 1998).

Krakauer, Jon. *Into Thin Air: A Personal Account of the Mt. Everest Disaster* (Villard, 1997).

Maier, Pauline. *American Scripture: Making the Declaration of Independence* (Knopf, 1997).

Nasar, Sylvia. *A Beautiful Mind* (Simon & Schuster, 1998).

Raban, Jonathan. *Bad Land: An American Romance* (Pantheon, 1996).

Solomon, Deborah. *Utopia Parkway: The Life and Work of Joseph Cornell* (Farrar, 1997).

Suskind, Ron. *A Hope in the Unseen: An American Odyssey from the Inner City to the Ivy League* (Broadway, 1998).

Winchester, Simon. *The River at the Center of the World: A Journey Up the Yangtze and Back in Chinese Time* (Holt, 1996).

SOURCE: Notable Books Council, ALA Reference and User Services Association.

Modern dictionaries

by Bill Katz

WEBSTER SET THE PATTERN, modified to be sure by those who took over his work; but today's dictionary is not that much different from the 19th-century titles. Even a cursory look at Kenneth Kister's *Best Dictionaries for Adults and Young People: A Comparative Guide* (Oryx, 1992) will indicate both the number of dictionaries available today and the numerous publishers who make them possible. While Merriam-Webster's unabridged work goes unchallenged as the largest of the group, Kister reviews 300 English language dictionaries "of which 132 are for adults, ranging from the largest works . . . to very small pocket dictionaries that contain only a few thousand words." Another 168 entries focus on dictionaries for young people.

While the late 18th and 19th centuries had forms of abridged dictionaries, it was not until the 1930s in the United States that the now popular desk or college dictionary became popular. Pioneered by Edward Thorndike, the dictionary with 150,000 to 180,000 words was soon taken on by all major publishers such as Clarence Barnhard's *American College Dictionary* (1947) and the best-selling 10th edition of G&C Merriam.

In the 1930s, Thorndike also pioneered the children's dictionary. His series of Thorndike-Century titles was based on the simple principle of including only those words likely to be found by the average child in reading matter. For example, in 1944 Thorndike compiled *The Teacher's Word Book of 30,000 Words*. The number of words was dictated by his research, both as a lexicographer and psychologist, into the frequency of their occurrence in a large group of books, newspapers, magazines, etc., suitable for younger readers. Today a whole range of dictionaries is available for elementary through high school. Arguments continue about limiting vocabulary by age or by reading matter. Saul Landau says, "It is not self evident that a dictionary or any other book for children should avoid using words that challenge the reader to add a new word to his vocabulary."

Today's dictionaries show two major lines of change and development. The most obvious is the new technology that allows one to search a dictionary online or on CD-ROM, e.g., the second edition of the *Oxford English Dictionary* as well as countless desk and college dictionaries available as separates or parts of computer software. This permits everything from comparing etymologies to automatically correcting spelling errors. The more expensive dictionaries, such as the 1993 enlarged *American Heritage Dictionary*, reflect a second line that emphasizes combining a dictionary with an encyclopedia. Here everything from locations of universities and colleges to maps and historical documents may be located. The public has the freedom of selecting only one basic reference work while the publisher has the advantage of charging more. This carries on a tradition of many centuries and today is just as debatable as the first time the combination was made. As noted, American publishers tend to stress the encyclopedic aspects of the dictionary and, thanks to the advent of CD-ROMs and multimedia information sources, these aspects are more likely to grow than to diminish.

The Random House *Dictionary of the English Language* raised outside matter to about 20% of the entire work. A great success, this helped to make it the first dictionary in the 20th century to make the bestseller list. When Webster's was purchased by the Britannica, encyclopedic material (deleted much earlier) returned in the popular college editions, if not in the unabridged work. The result of the inclusion of such things as manuals of style, atlases, historical events, biographical data, etc., in a dictionary is twofold. First, it increases the price of the volume and, second, as most  people keep a dictionary for generations, the basic information soon is dated. The latter problem may be solved with frequent publication of CD-ROMs and/or online access to the dictionary-encyclopedia, but this remains for the future to determine.

Looking back over the 3,000–4,000 years of dictionary history, it is remarkable how little the basic form has changed. The first Sumerian dictionary and today's modern American one are both tributes to literacy and the delights of the spoken and written word. There is little more to say, other than to ask the perennial reference desk question, "Just how many words are there in the English language?" Estimates vary, particularly if neologisms, slang, scientific vocabulary, etc., are included. Webster's *Third New International Dictionary* contains some 450,000 words, but if all the English vocabulary from the beginning was included, the estimate would be from 5.5 to 6 million words.

After centuries, how many words are really used by the average individual? No one knows, but in general the figure ranges from under 1,000 to an average of about 30,000. Shakespeare employed a maximum of 30,000 words, and according to D. R. Tallantire, "even our most prolific and admired writers seldom exhibit more . . . in a lifetime of writing." Of course, words known but not used far exceed the 30,000 employed in writing. Still, the 30,000 represents less than 10% of extant English words, but they "account for more than 90% of the words appearing on any page of literature we care to examine. . . . 10% of the vocabulary of English covers 90% of the text of all volumes of literature in our libraries." The exception is technical writing. These tend to be words used once or twice and lost in the ocean of technological change.

Fortunately for dictionary publishers, from the beginning to this day, language is in constant flux and change, if only in subtle definitions, and the changes are enough to guarantee a new edition next week. Of dictionaries, someone once said, there is no end. Whether you agree or not, of new editions of dictionaries there never will be an end.

SOURCE: Bill Katz, *Cuneiform to Computer: A History of Reference Sources* (Lanham, Md.: Scarecrow Press, 1998), pp. 192–94. Reprinted with permission.

Coretta Scott King Awards

THE CORETTA SCOTT KING AWARD is presented annually by the Coretta Scott King Task Force of the ALA Social Responsibilities Round Table. Recipients are African-American authors and illustrators whose distinguished books promote an understanding and appreciation of the culture and contribution of all people to the realization of the "American dream." The award commemorates the life and work of Martin Luther King Jr., and honors his widow, Coretta Scott King, for her courage and determination in continuing the work for peace and world brotherhood.

The award was founded in 1969 by Glyndon Flynt Greer, a distinguished African-American school librarian, and it became an official ALA unit award in 1982. The following are the award-winning authors and illustrators since 1970.

Authors

1999—Angela Johnson, *Heaven* (Simon & Schuster, 1998).
1998—Sharon M. Draper, *Forged by Fire* (Atheneum, 1997).
1997—Walter Dean Myers, *Slam* (Scholastic, 1996).
1996—Virginia Hamilton, *Her Stories* (Scholastic/Blue Sky, 1995).
1995—Patricia and Fredrick McKissack, *Christmas in the Big House, Christmas in the Quarters* (Scholastic, 1994).
1994—Angela Johnson, *Toning the Sweep* (Orchard Books, 1993).
1993—Patricia C. McKissack, *The Dark-Thirty: Southern Tales of the Supernatural* (Knopf, 1992).
1992—Walter Dean Myers, *Now Is Your Time* (HarperCollins, 1991).
1991—Mildred D. Taylor, *The Road to Memphis* (Dial, 1990).
1990—Patricia and Fredrick McKissack, *A Long Hard Journey: The Story of the Pullman Porter* (Walker, 1989).

1989—Walter Dean Myers, *Fallen Angels* (Scholastic, 1988).
1988—Mildred D. Taylor, *The Friendship* (Dial, 1987).
1987—Mildred Pitts Walter, *Justin and the Best Biscuits in the World* (Lothrop, 1986).
1986—Virginia Hamilton, *The People Could Fly: American Black Folktales* (Knopf, 1985).
1985—Walter Dean Myers, *Motown and Didi* (Viking, 1984).
1984—Lucille Clifton, *Everett Anderson's Goodbye* (Holt, 1983).
1983—Virginia Hamilton, *Sweet Whispers, Brother Rush* (Philomel, 1982).
1982—Mildred D. Taylor, *Let the Circle Be Unbroken* (Dial, 1981).
1981—Sidney Poitier, *This Life* (Knopf, 1980).
1980—Walter Dean Myers, *The Young Landlords* (Viking, 1979).
1979—Ossie Davis, *Escape to Freedom: A Play about Young Frederick Douglass* (Viking, 1977).
1978—Eloise Greenfield, *Africa Dream* (Crowell, 1977).
1977—James Haskins, *The Story of Stevie Wonder* (Lothrop, 1976).
1976—Pearl Bailey, *Duey's Tale* (Harcourt, 1975).
1975—Dorothy Robinson, *The Legend of Africania* (Johnson, 1974).
1974—Sharon Bell Mathis, *Ray Charles* (Crowell, 1973).
1973—Alfred Duckett, *I Never Had It Made: The Autobiography of Jackie Robinson* (Putnam, 1972).
1972—Elton C. Fax, *17 Black Artists* (Dodd, 1971).
1971—Charlemae Rollins, *Black Troubadour: Langston Hughes* (Rand McNally, 1970).
1970—Lillie Patterson, *Dr. Martin Luther King, Jr., Man of Peace* (Garrard, 1969).

Illustrators

1999—Michele Wood, for *i see the rhythm*, by Toyomi Igus (Children's Book Press, 1998).
1998—Javaka Steptoe, for *In Daddy's Arms I Am Tall: African Americans Celebrating Fathers*, by Alan Schroeder (Lee & Low, 1997).
1997—Jerry Pinkney, for *Minty: A Story of Young Harriet Tubman*, by Alan Schroeder (Dial Books, 1996).
1996—Tom Feelings, *The Middle Passage: White Ships Black Cargo* (Dial Books, 1995).
1995—James Ransome, for *The Creation*, by James Weldon Johnson (Holiday House, 1994).
1994—Tom Feelings, for *Soul Looks Back in Wonder*, edited by Phyllis Fogelman (Dial Books, 1993).
1993—Kathleen Atkins Wilson, for *The Origin of Life on Earth: An African Creation Myth*, retold by David A. Anderson/SANKOFA (Sight Productions, 1992).
1992—Faith Ringgold, for *Tar Beach* (Crown, 1991).
1991—Leo and Diane Dillon, for *Aida*, by Leontyne Price (HBJ, 1990).
1990—Jan Spivey Gilchrist, for *Nathaniel Talking*, by Eloise Greenfield (Black Butterfly, 1988).
1989—Jerry Pinkney, for *Mirandy and Brother Wind*, by Patricia C. McKissack (Knopf, 1988).

1988—John Steptoe, for *Mufaro's Beautiful Daughters* (Lothrop, 1987).

1987—Jerry Pinkney, for *Half a Moon and One Whole Star*, by Crescent Dragonwagon (Macmillan, 1986).

1986—Jerry Pinkney, for *The Patchwork Quilt*, by Valerie Flournoy (Dial, 1985).

1984—Pat Cummings, for *My Mama Needs Me*, by Mildred Pitts Walter (Lothrop, 1983).

1983—Peter Magubane, for *Black Child* (Knopf, 1982).

1982—John Steptoe, for *Mother Crocodile: An Uncle Amadou Tale from Senegal*, translated by Rosa Guy (Delacorte, 1981).

1981—Ashley Bryan, for *Beat the Story Drum Pum-Pum* (Atheneum, 1980).

1980—Carole Byard, for *Cornrows*, by Camille Yarbrough (Coward-McCann, 1979).

1979—Tom Feelings, for *Something on My Mind*, by Nikki Grimes (Dial, 1978).

1974—George Ford, for *Ray Charles*, by Sharon Bell Mathis (Crowell, 1973).

SOURCE: ALA Social Responsibilities Round Table.

The symbolism of books

by Ad de Vries

DE VRIES'S DICTIONARY offers definitions and examples of the symbolic meanings of words beyond their literal definitions, using classical and literary sources. This is what he offers for books.—*GME.*

1. *Wisdom.*
   a. "Written inside and out": esoteric and exoteric knowledge, like a double-edged sword in the mouth.
   b. "The" book is the Bible; e.g., a "book-oath" (*2 Henry IV*, II, i: "I put thee now to thy book-oath. Deny it, if thou canst").
   c. The Bible. Old Testament: destiny, dignity, law. New Testament: divine knowledge.
2. *Secret knowledge.*
   a. Prospero talking of his book of magic: "And deeper than did ever plummet sound / I'll drown my book" (*Tempest*, V, i).
   b. The Book of Thoth (or the Book of the Writer: of Hermes-Thoth, Hermes Trismegistus) was put into a layer of boxes: gold into silver, into ivory and ebony, into iron. Thrown into the Nile, it promises the finder vast knowledge and power.
   c. The future: "a little scroll" is the future of the Church (*Revelation* 10:2), as opposed to the big scroll of the future of the world.
3. *Life.* The Book of Life, in which all people's names (or only those of the Just) are mentioned: *Exodus* 32:32; *Psalms* 69:28; *Isaiah* 4:3; *Revelation* 3:5.
4. *The Book of Remembrance* (*Malachi* 3:16).
5. *Facial expression.*
   a. "Your face, my Thane, is as a book where men / May read strange matters" (*Macbeth*, I, v).
   b. Book of praises = beautiful; a common Elizabethan conceit; e.g., "Her face the book of praises, where is read / Nothing but curious pleasures" (*Pericles*, I, i).

6. *Magic.* "Books are not seldom talismans and spells" (Cowper, "The Task: VI. The Winter Walk at Noon").
7. *The edification of nature.*
   a. "Finds tongues in trees, books in the running brooks" (*As You Like It*, II, i).
   b. Related to creative "weaving": all things crystallized within the divine omniscience.
8. *Beech tree.* The earliest runes were written on beech tablets.
9. *Combinations.*
   a. Open book: Christ is the light of the world and the Book of Life.
   b. Closed book: in the hands of God; divine mystery.
   c. Devil's book: playing cards.
   d. Little book: see 2.c.
   e. Red book: a book listing all persons in state office (originally a peerage list).
   f. Bell, book, and candle: Probably since the 8th century, a person could be excommunicated "by bell, book, and candle." These were the words from the closing formula: "Do to the book, quench the candle, ring the bell." The words have been also explained: bell = publicizing, book = authority of the presiding bishop, candle = the possibility of the ban to be lifted by repentance.

SOURCE: Ad de Vries, *Dictionary of Symbols and Imagery* (Amsterdam: North-Holland, 1974), p. 59. Reprinted with permission from Elsevier Science.

Libraries, literacy, and LC's Center for the Book

by John Y. Cole

A 1999 AMERICAN LIBRARY ASSOCIATION BRO-CHURE, *21st Century Literacy,* highlighted ALA's activities in literacy, noting that literacy has been adopted as one of five "key action areas" that will help librarians fulfill our mission "of providing the highest quality library and information services for all people." As a long-time ALA member and the first (and only) director of the Center for the Book in the Library of Congress, I applaud the brochure and the effort. The Center for the Book supports this ALA mission, defined as "helping children and adults develop skills they need to fully participate in an information society—whether it's learning to read or exploring the Internet." In support of the mission, it may be useful to know why and how the center, which was established in 1977, became an early and enthusiastic promoter of the library-literacy connection.

BOOKS GIVE US WINGS

THE CENTER FOR THE BOOK
LIBRARY OF CONGRESS

The Center for the Book was established by law in 1977 at the urging of Librarian of Congress Daniel J. Boorstin, who was eager for LC to become actively involved in promoting books and reading. The center's roots are in the activities of two predecessor organizations that had strong library connections: the National Book Committee (1954–1974), which was supported by the publishing community, and the U.S. Government Advisory Committee on International Book and Library Programs (1962–1977), supported by the State Department. Over a dozen people closely associated with these organizations became valued members of the Center for the Book's first national advisory board.

The Center for the Book has several advantages over its predecessors. Its creation was supported by the U.S. Congress and endorsed by the president. It has the authority of a government agency and enjoys the prestige of being part of LC. Moreover, it is not wholly dependent on federal funding. LC supports our four staff positions, but all program and project funds must come from elsewhere: individual, corporate, or foundation gifts or grants, or funds from other federal agencies. Thus it has a practical, project-oriented character tailored to specific activities that others are willing to support. By its nature and because of its small size, it must serve as a catalyst, a source of ideas, and a forum and not as an administrator of major programs or long-term projects. It is small and flexible, two desirable traits in the fragile and always-changing community of the book.

The Center for the Book's established purpose was to stimulate public interest in books and reading and to encourage the study of the role of books and reading in society. From the beginning libraries were involved in the center's projects. The library partnership became more concrete in the mid-1980s when, in response to interest from libraries around the country, we began the current system of affiliated state centers. The first applications for state center status came from libraries and today most of the state centers are housed in either state libraries or public libraries.

In 1987, when James H. Billington became Librarian of Congress, we officially changed the first part of the Center for the Book's mission statement to stimulating public interest in "books, reading, and libraries." Today the state affiliate program (there are 36 and the number is growing) and a partnership program that includes more than 50 national educational organizations, including the ALA, are the keys to the center's success.

Reading promotion, which includes combating illiteracy (the inability to read) and aliteracy (the lack of motivation to read), is at the heart of the Center for the Book's program. Our role (and challenge) was defined for us in 1984 by Boorstin, in his summary of the center's "Books in Our Future" study. He said: "Our democracy is built on books and reading. This tradition is now threatened by the twin menaces of illiteracy and aliteracy. We must enlist new technologies with cautious enthusiasm in a national commitment to keep the Culture of the Book alive. What we do about books and reading in the next decades will crucially affect our citizens' opportunities for enlightenment and self-improvement, their ability to share in the wisdom and delights of civilization, and their capacity for intelligent self-government." The center's national reading promotion campaigns (beginning with The Year of the Reader in 1987), its partnership programs aimed at combating illiteracy and aliteracy, and its use of all technologies and media to promote reading were shaped by this broad Boorstin definition of literacy.

Boorstin's and ALA's views of literacy are complementary. Each contains a phrase that probably would not be used by the other (Boorstin's "culture of the book" and ALA's "information literacy"), but the overall emphasis in each is the value of reading to society as well as to the individual, the importance of lifelong learning, and the need to make creative use of new technologies. The ALA brochure of course adds a new element by bringing libraries and librarians into the picture: "Libraries are places for people of all ages and abilities to want to read and learn."

The Center for the Book has worked closely with ALA in several literacy promotion projects. The Association for Library Service to Children (ALSC) was a major partner in the center's Library–Museum–Head Start partnership project. With funding from Head Start, between 1992 and 1997 the project gave hundreds of Head Start teachers hands-on instruction in involving libraries and museums that serve children in Head Start projects. In 1998, with Virginia Mathews as project coordinator, the Center for the Book succeeded ALA as the administrator of the Viburnum Foundation's Family Literacy Project. In 1999, the Viburnum Foundation offered small grants totaling $120,000 directly to 40 small rural libraries in seven Southern states.

Whenever possible, connections are made with the state centers in each state. Mother Goose Asks "Why?," a family science and literature project administered by the Vermont Center for the Book, introduces science into the lives of young children and their parents through good literature. A library-based program that reaches into 14 states and the District of Columbia, it was funded by a $1.5-million grant from the National Science Foundation.

Finally, ALA and the Center for the Book are continuing another kind of project that highlights libraries and literacy: national photography contests. The first, A Nation of Readers, promoted National Library Week in 1985. In 1991, the contest and subsequent traveling exhibition marked the Year of the Lifetime Reader. The 1999 contest, Beyond Words: Celebrating America's Libraries, was also an LC Bicentennial Project. The grand prize photograph, taken by 18-year old Kristen Baker of Liverpool, N.Y., featured three young children using a computer—with books in the background—at the Liverpool Public Library. The image and its title, "Inquiring Minds," epitomize the library-literacy connection.

SOURCE: Special report by John Y. Cole for *The Whole Library Handbook 3.*

Federal regional depository libraries

THE FRAMEWORK OF THE PRESENT depository library program was established in 1857 when a resolution was passed directing that printed documents be circulated to the public through official sources. In 1859, the statutory authority and responsibility to distribute all books printed or purchased for the use of the Federal Government were given to the Secretary of the Interior, except those for the special use of the Congress or the executive departments.

In 1860, Congress established the Government Printing Office to serve its printing and binding needs as well as the needs of the Executive Branch. The

Printing Act of 1895 relocated the Superintendent of Public Documents from the Department of Interior to the Government Printing Office. Today, this position continues to be an important function of the Government Printing Office in disseminating federal information to the public through both the depository library program and publications sales program.

Congress established the Depository Library Program based upon three principles:

1. with certain specified exceptions, all government publications shall be made available to depository libraries;

2. depository libraries shall be located in each state and congressional district in order to make government publications widely available; and

3. these government publications shall be available for the free use of the general public.

Libraries in the following list are regional depository libraries that receive all publications of the Depository Library Program. There are also selective depositories that receive a portion of the U.S. publications available.—*GME.*

Alabama—Auburn University at Montgomery Library, 7300 University Drive, Montgomery, AL 36124-4023; (334) 244-3650; fax (334) 244-3720; (aumnicat.aum.edu/departments/govdocs/govDocs.htm).

University of Alabama, Amelia Gayle Gorgas Library, Capstone Drive, Tuscaloosa, AL 35487-0266; (205) 348-6047; fax (205) 348-0760; (www.lib.ua.edu/gorgas/govdocs.htm).

Arizona—Arizona Dept. of Library, Archives and Public Records, Research Division, 1700 West Washington, Phoenix, AZ 85007; (602) 542-3701; fax (602) 542-4400; (www.dlapr.lib.az.us/research/c-fedage.htm).

Arkansas—Arkansas State Library, One Capitol Mall, Little Rock, AR 72201-1081; (501) 682-2869; fax (501) 682-1532.

California—California State Library, Government Publications, 4201 Sierra Point Drive, Sacramento, CA 95834-0001; (916) 654-0069; fax (916) 653-6114.

Colorado—University of Colorado, Boulder, Norlin Library, Macky Drive, Boulder, CO 80309-0184; (303) 492-8834; fax (303) 492-1881; (www-libraries.colorado.edu/ps/gov/frontpage.htm).

Denver Public Library, 10 West 14th Avenue Parkway, Denver, CO 80204-2731; (303) 640-6220; fax (303) 640-6228; (www.denver.lib.co.us/dpl/govpubs/govpub.html).

Connecticut—Connecticut State Library, 231 Capitol Avenue, Hartford, CT 06106; (860) 566-2587; fax (860) 566-8866; (www.cslnet.ctstateu.edu/gis.htm).

Florida—University of Florida, George A. Smathers Library, Gainesville, FL 32611-2048; (352) 392-0367; fax (352) 392-3357; (web.uflib.ufl.edu/docs/).

Georgia—University of Georgia, Main Library, 265 Jackson Street, Athens, GA 30602; (706) 542-3251; fax (706) 542-4144; (www.libs.uga.edu/govdocs/govdocs.html).

Hawaii—University of Hawaii, Manoa, Hamilton Library, 2550 The Mall, Honolulu, HI 96822-2274; (808) 956-8230; fax (808) 956-5968; (www2.hawaii.edu/~govdocs/).

Idaho—University of Idaho, Library, Rayburn Street, Moscow, ID 83844-2353; (208) 885-6344; fax (208) 885-6817; (www.lib.uidaho.edu/govdoc/).

Illinois—Illinois State Library, 300 South Second Street, Springfield, IL 62701-1796; (217) 782-7596; fax:(217) 524-0041; (www.library.sos.state.il.us/isl/depos/depos.html).

Indiana—Indiana State Library, 140 North Senate Avenue, Indianapolis, IN 46204-2296; (317) 232-3679; fax (317) 232-3728.

Iowa—University of Iowa, University Libraries, Washington & Madison Streets, Iowa City, IA 52242-1420; (319) 335-5926; fax (319) 335-5900; (www.lib.uiowa.edu/govpubs/).

Kansas—University of Kansas, Government Documents & Map Library, 6001 Malott Hall, Lawrence, KS 66045-2800; (785) 864-4660; fax (785) 864-5154; (www.ukans.edu/cwis/units/kulib/docs/govdocs.html).

Kentucky—University of Kentucky, William T. Young Library, 1000 University Drive, Lexington, KY 40506-0456; (606) 257-0500, ext. 2170; fax (606) 257-0508; (www.uky.edu/Libraries/deprds.html).

Louisiana—Louisiana State University, Troy H. Middleton Library, Baton Rouge, LA 70803-3312; (504) 388-8875; fax (504) 388-5723; (www.lib.lsu.edu/govdocs/).

Louisiana Tech University, Prescott Memorial Library, Everett Street, Ruston, LA 71272-0046; (318) 257-4962; fax (318) 257-2447.

Maine—University of Maine, Raymond H. Fogler Library, Orono, ME 04469-5729; (207) 581-1673; fax (207) 581-1653; (libraries.maine.edu/orogovdoc).

Maryland—University of Maryland, College Park, McKeldin Library, College Park, MD 20742-7011; (301) 405-9165; fax (301) 314-7111; www.lib.umd.edu/UMCP/GOV/govt_docs.html.

Massachusetts—Boston Public Library, 700 Boylston Street, Boston, MA 02116-2813; (617) 536-5400, ext. 226; fax (617) 536-7758; www.bpl.org/WWW/govdocs/govdocs.html.

Michigan—Detroit Public Library, 5201 Woodward Avenue, Detroit, MI 48202-4007; (313) 833-1440; fax (313) 833-0156.

Library of Michigan, 717 West Allegan Street, Lansing, MI 48909-7507; (517) 373-1300; fax (517) 373-9438; (www.libofmich.lib.mi.us/services/fedgov.html).

Minnesota—University of Minnesota, Government Publications Library, 309 19th Avenue South, Minneapolis, MN 55455-0414; (612) 624-5073; fax (612) 626-9353; (www.lib.umn.edu/gov/).

Mississippi—University of Mississippi, J.D. Williams Library, University, MS 38677-9793; (601) 232-5857; fax (601) 232-7465; (www.olemiss.edu/govinfo/).

Missouri—University of Missouri, Columbia, Ellis Library, Lowry Mall, Columbia, MO 65201-5149; (573) 882-6733; fax (573) 882-8044; (www.missouri.edu/~govdocs/).

Montana—University of Montana, Mansfield Library, Missoula, MT 59812-1195; (406) 243-6700; fax (406) 243-2060; (www.lib.umt.edu/dept/gov/gov.htm).

Nebraska—University of Nebraska, Lincoln, Don L. Love Memorial Library, 13th & R Streets, Lincoln, NE 68588-0410; (402) 472-4473; fax (402) 472-5131; (www.unl.edu/fedldocs/docs1.htm).

Nevada—University of Nevada, Reno, University Library, 1664 North Virginia Street, Reno, NV 89557-0044; (775) 784-6500, ext. 257; fax (775) 784-4398; (www.library.unr.edu/~bgic/).

New Jersey—Newark Public Library, 5 Washington Street, Newark, NJ 07101-

0630; (973) 733-7815; fax (973) 733-5648; (www.npl.org/Pages/Collections/govdocs.html).

New Mexico—University of New Mexico, Zimmerman Library, Albuquerque, NM 87131-1466; (505) 277-5441; fax (505) 277-4097; (www.unm.edu/~govref/govinfo.html).

New Mexico State Library, 1209 Camino Carlos Rey, Santa Fe, NM 87505-9860; (505) 476-9702; fax:(505) 476-9701.

New York—New York State Library, Cultural Education Center, Empire State Plaza, Albany, NY 12230-0001; (518) 474-5355; fax (518) 474-5786; (www.nysl.nysed.gov/feddep.htm).

North Carolina—University of North Carolina, Chapel Hill, Walter Royal Davis Library, Chapel Hill, NC 27514-8890; (919) 962-1151; fax (919) 962-5537; (metalab.unc.edu/reference/docs/feddocs.html).

North Dakota—North Dakota State University Libraries, 1201 Albrecht Boulevard, Fargo, ND 58105-5599; (701) 231-8886; fax (701) 231-7138; (www.lib.ndsu.nodak.edu/govdocs/).

University of North Dakota, Chester Fritz Library, Centennial & University Avenue, Grand Forks, ND 58202; (701) 777-3316; fax (701) 777-4811; (www.und.nodak.edu/dept/library/Collections/Govdocs/govdocs.htm).

Ohio—State Library of Ohio, 65 South Front Street, Columbus, OH 43215-4163; (614) 644-7051; fax (614) 752-9178; (winslo.state.oh.us/slogovt.html).

Oklahoma—Oklahoma Department of Libraries, U.S. Government Information, 200 Northeast 18th Street, Oklahoma City, OK 73105-3298; (405) 522-3335; fax (405) 525-7804; (www.odl.state.ok.us/usinfo/).

Oklahoma State University, Edmon Low Library, Stillwater, OK 74078-1071; (405) 744-6546; fax (405) 744-5183; (www.library.okstate.edu/dept/govdocs/).

Oregon—Portland State University, Branford Price Millar Library, 951 SW Hall, Portland, OR 97207-1151; (503) 725-4123; fax (503) 725-4524; (www.lib.pdx.edu/resources/govdocs/).

Pennsylvania—State Library of Pennsylvania, Law/Government Publications, Walnut Street & Commonwealth Avenue, Harrisburg, PA 17105-1601; (717) 787-3752; fax (717) 783-7015.

South Carolina—Clemson University, Robert Muldrow Cooper Library, Palmetto Boulevard, Clemson, SC 29634-3001; (864) 656-5174; fax (864) 656-3025.

University of South Carolina, Thomas Cooper Library, Greene and Sumter Streets, Columbia, SC 29208; (803) 777-4841; fax (803) 777-9503.

Tennessee—University of Memphis, McWherter Library, Zach Curlin Drive, Memphis, TN 38152-1000; (901) 678-2206; fax (901) 678-8218; (www.lib.memphis.edu/gpo/unclesam.htm).

Texas—Texas State Library & Archives Commission, 1201 Brazos Street, Austin, TX 78711-2927; (512) 463-5455; fax (512) 463-5436.

Texas Tech University, Library, 18th & Boston, Lubbock, TX 79409-0002; (806) 742-2268; fax (806) 742-1332; (www.lib.ttu.edu/gov_docs/).

Utah—Utah State University, Merrill Library, University Hill, Logan, UT 84321; (435) 797-2684; fax (435) 797-2880; (www.usu.edu/~library/About/gov.html).

Virginia—University of Virginia, Alderman Library, University Avenue & McCormick Road, Charlottesville, VA 22903-2498; (804) 924-3133; fax (804) 924-1431; (www.lib.virginia.edu/govdocs/).

The federal government has a tradition of compiling and printing collections of important documents, such as the *American State Papers* and *Foreign Relations of the United States*. Efforts to systematically preserve and release materials resulted in the expansion of the depository library system, and the establishment of the National Archives and presidential libraries. Despite these encouraging ventures, the general trend was for agencies to control their records and the information continued within.

Since World War II, scholarly and journalistic circles pointed out numerous abuses. Both civilian and military agencies cited national security reasons to deny outsiders access to materials. A "when in doubt, classify it" mindset took hold in the bureaucracy.

Moreover, some privileged outsiders were allowed to view records denied to others. A 20-year campaign led by press organizations and Congressman John E. Moss, U.S. congressman from California 1953–1978, patiently and adroitly maneuvered around major opposition in the executive and legislative branches. The result was President Lyndon Johnson's signing Public Law 89-487, the Freedom of Information Act (5 U.S.C. 552) on July 4, 1966.

Despite its rather grand name, the Freedom of Information Act (FOIA) and its subsequent modifications do not guarantee the automatic release of all federal records. First of all, it covers only the executive branch; Congress and the federal judiciary make their own rules. Secondly, this legislation has accepted the principle of executive control over information, though FOIA gives "any person" a means to challenge that control for specifically identified records. Thirdly, there are a number of major exemptions to the law (see sidebar on the following page). Finally, FOIA provides no meaningful penalty for individuals or agencies that do not follow its provisions. Nor does it provide any rewards.

Further FOIA fluctuations

The subsequent story of FOIA is one of ebb and flow, depending both on the administration in power and the practices of individual government agencies. The original act required an executive order on security classification, but Johnson never issued one. Richard Nixon filled in this gap in 1972 with his Executive Order 11652, which established levels of classification based on the potential damage to national security resulting from unauthorized release of information. Moreover, Nixon set in place automatic declassification for most documents. Truly important documents are protected, but lesser material can be released to the public. Nixon did have an ulterior motive: He wanted his predecessors' embarrassing documents publicized to deflect Watergate criticism.

In 1974, a post-Watergate Congress passed a strengthened FOIA over the veto of President Gerald Ford. The next change was Jimmy Carter's June 1978 Executive Order 12065, which was based on the premise that there should be as little classification as possible.

Washington—Washington State Library, Joel M. Pritchard Library, 415 15th Street SW, Olympia, WA 98504-2460; (360) 704-5227; fax (360) 586-7575.

West Virginia—West Virginia University, Charles C. Wise Library, 1549 University Avenue, Morgantown, WV 26506-6069; (304) 293-4040; fax (304) 293-6923; (www.libraries.wvu.edu/govdocs/).

Wisconsin—State Historical Society of Wisconsin, Library, 816 State Street, Madison, WI 53706-1488; (608) 264-6525; fax (608) 264-6520; (www.shsw.wisc.edu/library/govpub/).

Milwaukee Public Library, 814 West Wisconsin Avenue, Milwaukee, WI 53233-2385; (414) 286-3073; fax (414) 286-2126.

SOURCE: U.S. Government Printing Office, www.access.gpo.gov/su_docs/dpos/adpos003.html.

Federal archives and records

THE NATIONAL ARCHIVES AND RECORDS ADMINISTRATION (NARA) establishes policies and procedures for managing and preserving the permanently valuable records of the U.S. government. It was established in 1985 as an independent agency to replace the National Archives and Records Service, which was an office of the General Services Administration. NARA makes original records available for use by researchers, answers requests for information, and provides copies of documents for a fee. The office also publishes the daily *Federal Register*, the *Code of Federal Regulations*, the *U.S. Government Manual*, and many other public documents.

How to locate an unpublished government record

If the record is 25 years old or less, contact the originating agency or the clerk's office in the case of a federal court. If the record is older than 25 years, contact the appropriate regional archive (see list on the next page). In either instance, the office should be able to identify the best way for you to gain access to the record. If the record is classified, you have the option of issuing a Freedom of Information Act request to the appropriate federal agency.

National archives offices

The National Archives in Washington receives records from cabinet offices, the Supreme Court, other courts, activities abroad, and agency headquarters offices in the District of Columbia. The National Archives regional offices receive the records of all federal agencies and courts in the regions they serve. Roughly 3% of all Federal records are eventually retained in the National Archives offices. The other 97% are destroyed after 3–75 years, according to schedules set by statute and by negotiation with the agencies. When records are transferred to the National Archives, they become public property and are usually accessible to researchers, although they are subject to certain restrictions, including privacy or national security.

In January 1994 a new National Archives facility opened to researchers and the general public in College Park, Maryland. The new building represents six years of planning and construction and is the largest and most technologically advanced archives facility in the world.

The main National Archives building, which was completed in 1937, reached its records storage capacity of approximately 900,000 cubic feet in the late 1960s. To alleviate the space shortage, more than 500,000 cubic feet of archival records were stored in leased or government-owned space in the Washington area since 1970.

The College Park facility was designed to consolidate all of these scattered sites and to serve as an archives for the 21st century, protecting and preserving historical materials for future generations. It has the most advanced pollution and environmental controls; 520 miles of high-density mobile shelving for storing records; nine sophisticated preservation and conservation laboratories; and extensive research facilities. The total record storage capacity is approximately 2 million cubic

Archives in College Park

feet, and the building is designed so that additional storage units can be added on as needed.

National Archives, 700 Pennsylvania Ave., N.W., Washington, DC 20408; (202) 501-5400; inquire@nara.gov; (www.nara.gov/nara/dc/a1_info.html).

National Archives at College Park, 8601 Adelphi Rd., College Park, MD 20740-6001; (301) 713-6800; inquire@arch2.nara.gov; (www.nara.gov/nara/dc/a2_info.html).

National Archives—Central Plains Region (Kansas City), 2312 E. Bannister Road, Kansas City, MO 64131-3011; (816) 926-6272; fax (816) 926-6982; archives@kansascity.nara.gov; (www.nara.gov/regional/kansas.html).

National Archives—Central Plains Region (Lee's Summit), 200 Space Center Drive, Lee's Summit, MO 64064-1182; (816) 478-7079; fax (816) 478-7625; center@kccave.nara.gov; (www.nara.gov/regional/leesumit.html).

National Archives—Great Lakes Region (Chicago), 7358 S. Pulaski Rd., Chicago, IL 60629-5898; (773) 581-7816; fax (312) 353-1294; archives@chicago.nara.gov; (www.nara.gov/regional/chicago.html).

National Archives—Great Lakes Region (Dayton), 3150 Springboro Rd., Dayton, OH 45439-1883; (937) 225-2852; fax (937) 225-7236; center@dayton.nara.gov; (www.nara.gov/regional/dayton.html).

National Archives—Mid-Atlantic Region (Center City Philadelphia), 900 Market Street, Philadelphia, PA 19107-4249; (215) 597-3000; fax (215) 597-2303; archives@philarch.nara.gov; (www.nara.gov/regional/philacc.html).

National Archives—Mid-Atlantic Region (Northeast Philadelphia), 14700 Townsend Road, Philadelphia, PA 19154-1096; (215) 671-9027; fax (215) 671-8001; center@philfrc.nara.gov; (www.nara.gov/regional/philane.html).

National Archives—Northeast Region (Boston), 380 Trapelo Road, Waltham, MA 02452-6399; (781) 647-8104; fax (781) 647-8088; archives@waltham.nara.gov; (www.nara.gov/regional/boston.html).

National Archives—Northeast Region (New York City), 201 Varick Street, New York, NY 10014-4811; (212) 337-1300; fax (212) 337-1306; archives@newyork.nara.gov; (www.nara.gov/regional/newyork.html).

National Archives—Northeast Region (Pittsfield), 10 Conte Dr., Pittsfield, MA 01201-8230; (413) 445-6885; fax (413) 445-7599; archives@pittsfield.nara.gov; (www.nara.gov/regional/pittsfie.html).

National Archives—Pacific Alaska Region (Anchorage), 654 W. Third Ave., Room 012, Anchorage, AK 99501-2145; (907) 271-2443; fax (907) 271-2442; archives@alaska.nara.gov; (www.nara.gov/regional/anchorag.html).

National Archives—Pacific Alaska Region (Seattle), 6125 Sand Point Way, NE, Seattle, WA 98115-7999; (206) 526-6501; fax (206) 526-6575; archives@seattle.nara.gov; (www.nara.gov/regional/seattle.html).

National Archives—Pacific Region (Laguna Niguel), 24000 Avila Road, Laguna Niguel, CA 92677-3497; (949) 360-2641; fax (949) 360-2624; archives@laguna.nara.gov; (www.nara.gov/regional/laguna.html).

National Archives—Pacific Region (San Francisco), 1000 Commodore Drive, San Bruno, CA 94066-2350; (650) 876-9009; fax (650) 876-9233; center@sanbruno.nara.gov; (www.nara.gov/regional/sanfranc.html).

National Archives—Rocky Mountain Region, Building 48, Denver Federal Center, P.O. Box 25307, Denver, CO 80225-0307; (303) 236-0804; fax (303) 236-9297; center@denver.nara.gov; (www.nara.gov/regional/denver.html).

National Archives—Southeast Region, 1557 St. Joseph Ave., East Point, GA 30344-2593; (404) 763-7477; fax (404) 763-7059; center@atlanta.nara.gov; (www.nara.gov/regional/atlanta.html).

National Archives—Southwest Region, 501 W. Felix St., Building 1, Fort Worth, TX 76115-3405; (817) 334-5525; fax (817) 334-5621; archives@ftworth.nara.gov; (www.nara.gov/regional/ftworth.html).

National Archives—Washington National Records Center, 4205 Suitland Rd., Suitland, MD 20746-8001; (301) 457-7000; fax (301) 457-7117; center@suitland.nara.gov; (www.nara.gov/records/wnrc.html).

National Personnel Records Center, Civilian Personnel Records, 111 Winnebago St., St. Louis, MO 63118-4199; fax (314) 425-5719; center@cpr.nara.gov; (www.nara.gov/regional/cpr.html).

National Personnel Records Center, Military Personnel Records, 9700 Page Ave., St. Louis, MO 63132-5100; fax (314) 538-4175; center@stlouis.nara.gov; (www.nara.gov/regional/mpr.html).

SOURCE: National Archives–Great Lakes Region; www.nara.gov.

Freedom of information

by Michael E. Unsworth

THE CONCEPT OF FREEDOM OF INFORMATION is as old as our republic. Thomas Jefferson originally thought that officials and bureaucrats, knowing that their actions would eventually be seen by the citizenry, will conduct themselves appropriately in the public's interest. Unfortunately, this concept was never implemented, since Jefferson as president followed George Washington's practice of letting agencies have complete control of their records and treating presidential papers as personal property.

Another milestone in restricting public access to government information took place under President Woodrow Wilson, who established the concept of national security as a rationale to restrict access to government information during World War I. For the next 50 years, official restrictions became tighter on taxpayer-financed information.

On the other hand, the concept of public availability never died completely.

Material exempted from FOIA

Documents can be withheld from public scrutiny if they:

1. Are security-classified under the terms of a presidential executive order;
2. Relate solely to internal personnel practices or the rules of an agency;
3. Are exempt from disclosure under other federal legislation;
4. Are considered to be confidential business information, such as trade secrets or confidential financial data;
5. Deal with inter-agency or intra-agency communications that formed part of the decision-making process.
6. Permit a "clearly unwarranted" invasion of personal privacy;
7. Contain information about investigative matters that would interfere with law enforcement, deprive a person of a fair trial, cause an invasion of privacy, expose the identity of a confidential source, disclose investigative techniques, or endanger lives of law enforcement personnel;
8. Concern information about financial institutions gathered by agencies that regulate or supervise such institutions;
9. Reveal wells of a geological or geophysical nature such as oil.

Despite the overall positive tone of Carter's and Nixon's orders, a 1979 General Accounting Office study found that agencies routinely abused their provisions.

Ronald Reagan's April 1982 Executive Order 12356 reversed his predecessor's actions. Agencies were required to classify as much information as possible and at the most restrictive level with no automatic declassification. Subsequent legislation tightened access. Finally, the federal courts further restricted FOIA. The result of these actions was a dramatic increase in permanently classified records. Dissatisfaction with this state of affairs came not only from scholars and journalists, but even such stalwarts of the military-industrial complex as *Aviation Week and Space Technology*, which decried the continuing classification of Cold War projects.

Bill Clinton had to play a delicate balancing act with freedom of information. Elected with promises to mitigate the harsher aspects of the Reagan-Bush years, he also had to avoid antagonizing a distrusting national-security establishment and its Republican allies. Thus, his Executive Order 12958 on security classification was issued in 1995 after heated bureaucratic infighting.

On the face of things, Clinton returned to Nixon's and Carter's precepts with an interesting twist: He wanted to make it more expensive for agencies to maintain classification than to declassify. Though Clinton liberalized many of the draconian aspects of Reagan's policy, the philosophies and past practices of individual agencies still make the exercise of FOIA a formidable task.

In 1996, FOIA entered the computer age when Congress passed the Electronic Freedom of Information Act (P.L. 104-231). It extended freedom of information and access to electronic records. Still to be determined is the impact of rapid obsolescence of different generations of electronic records. Outdated technology, as well as agency obstructionism, will continue as a barrier to public access.

Are such massive classifications really necessary? The standard governmental line is that restricting access shields sources, often a foreign government or a covert intelligence operative (formerly known as a spy). But critics say that, in many cases, the real reason for keeping material secret is to avoid embarrassment. Also, many government officials complain that the current restrictive classification environment makes it difficult to perform realistic planning.

How to file a FOIA request

First of all, you have to determine the involvement of a federal agency in a past action. Then you have to identify a specific document. The degree of specificity depends on the amount of material your initial research uncovers. You must then send a written request to the agency.

Upon receipt, the agency has 10 working days to reply. Generally, this is an acknowledgement of receipt, a standard description of the agency's backlog, and a plea for patience. At some point, the agency's FOIA office decides if the request is "reasonable," which means there is sufficient information to identify the material and that the agency has the ability to make it available. The agency can assess a fee on a cost-recovery basis, but this can be waived if you can prove that the release of information is in the public's interest. Therefore you should make such a claim in your preliminary request.

Eventually you will receive a response from the agency. In some cases, such as my first FBI request, all the material was provided. In all too many cases, material is withheld. The agency is required to report on the number of pages reviewed, the number of pages "withheld in their entirety," and their location in specified files.

At this point, the main virtue of FOIA comes into play. You can now challenge the agency's classification decision by appealing, a legal option that earlier researchers and scholars lacked. The initial step is appealing to the agency. If the appeal is denied, then you can appeal in federal court. Here is where the downside of FOIA reveals itself: You must be prepared to pay for legal talent and to wait. My initial FBI denial (on Japanese balloon-bomb incidents during World War II), first appealed in August 1984, is still unresolved.

Clinton's executive order established an additional step in the appeal process. After agency denial, you can now appeal to the Interagency Security Classification Appeals Board, which is composed of senior officials from the National Archives, the Department of Justice, and other agencies.

What happens when records are released?

The federal government does not maintain a centralized registry of declassified documents. On the one hand, the lack of such a registry is a waste of taxpayer money—agencies could waste time examining already declassified documents. On the other hand, if such a registry had existed under the Reagan administration, it would have been even simpler to implement its policy of reclassification of declassified documents.

Some agencies, like the FBI, maintain actual and now virtual reading rooms of declassified documents. The CIA, on the other hand, has released printed collections of documents. Not surprisingly, the agency chooses what materials to include. Sometimes material is released after lengthy court challenges in which the final settlement required some form of public access.

The public sector has been the most active in making declassified information available. Many microfilm companies took advantage of declassifications by publishing individual collections. Chadwyck-Healey has entered into a partnership with the non-profit National Security Archive (www.seas.gwu.edu/nsarchive/), which was initially established to be a repository for reporters' declassified documents. The archive, currently located at George Washington University's Gelman Library, has issued thematic sets of microfilmed material (the Cuban Missile Crisis, Iran-Contra, and others).

What can be done to improve FOIA?

A simple action would be to have a specific period after which almost all documents would be declassified. Some critics call for legislation that would level true penalties on agencies and bureaucrats who cause unwarranted delays to conceal illegal acts, inefficiencies, or administrative errors. Others propose rewards: funds for better internal organization and record retrieval, career incentives and extensive training, and retention of fee money. In 1997, the Commission on Protecting and Reducing Governmental Secrecy recommended legislation that would incorporate a philosophy of disclosure into the classification process.

Even if such steps were taken, some agencies might still be nimble enough to utilize every loophole and delaying tactic. Bureaucracies like the Internal Revenue Service would continue to routinely disregard laws and regulations.

The old adage about eternal vigilance being necessary to safeguard freedom is doubly true with freedom of information. Thanks to the diligence of interested individuals and groups, important information about the government's activities has seen the light of day.

SOURCE: Michael E. Unsworth, "Freedom of Information: Its Ebb and Flow," *American Libraries* 30 (June/July 1999): 82–85.

Census records and forms, 1800–1920
by Dahrl Elizabeth Moore

THE U.S. FEDERAL CENSUS has been taken every 10 years since 1790. Its purpose originally was to allocate taxes and representation in Congress among the several states according to their populations.

This group of records is probably the most used group of records by genealogists. Finding an ancestor in a census will establish that person in place and time. The first censuses, from 1790 to 1840, enumerated only the head of the household, with other members of the household indicated in respective sex and age groups only by check marks. The U.S. Department of Commerce and Labor's Bureau of the Census has published *Heads of Families at the First Census of the United States Taken in the Year 1790* (Washington, D.C.: GPO, 1908). The following states' records have been printed in book form: Connecticut, Maine, Maryland, Massachusetts, New Hampshire, New York, North Carolina, Pennsylvania, Rhode Island, South Carolina, Vermont, and Virginia. The records for Delaware, Georgia, Kentucky, New Jersey, and Tennessee were destroyed.

Many tax lists and militia lists have been published, and these can be used in place of the destroyed schedules. Check published lists of books and periodical indexes for these, especially in the area of interest. There was little uniformity in the method of recording the first few census schedules. The early census takers used whatever paper was available. The census forms now printed for those years were taken from lists of information wanted. In 1830 the government printed the first formal forms for use by all census takers. This served the purpose of Congress for a few years, but as time went on, everyone realized more information was needed.

Then in 1850, every member of the household was recorded in the census, a true enumeration of the population. Although the previous returns could have some genealogical value for researchers, it is these later schedules that are of great importance.

Note that the 1920 form is the latest mentioned. A 72-year moratorium precludes releasing census information prior to that date to protect the privacy of the living. The release of the 1930 census returns, therefore, will take place in the year 2002. The National Archives has microfilmed all these schedules, and they are available at the archives and branches as well as all the Mormon Family History Centers. You do not have to belong to the church to use their records, and you are most welcome there. The centers are staffed by volunteers, and open hours are limited so check before going. Many large libraries and genealogical centers also have copies of some of the films as well as printed indexes for the 1850–1890 years.

There were also special census schedules taken from 1850 to 1880. They detailed manufacturing, agriculture, industry, and mortality. Also, many states

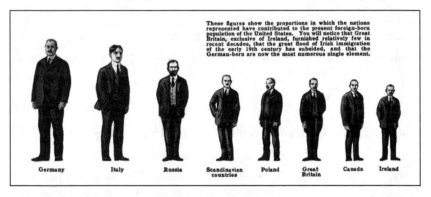

These figures show the proportions in which the nations represented have contributed to the present foreign-born population of the United States. You will notice that Great Britain, exclusive of Ireland, furnished relatively few in recent decades, that the great flood of Irish immigration of the early 19th century has subsided, and that the German-born are now the most numerous single element.

Germany   Italy   Russia   Scandinavian countries   Poland   Great Britain   Canada   Ireland

scheduled censuses in the five-year periods between the federal census (e.g., 1885). There were also census schedules for the territories out West before they became states. The 1890 census was pretty much destroyed by fire and is not available for research except for a few states. There was also a special census of the Union Civil War veterans and veterans' widows taken in 1890, and part of this survived that fire.

Soundex

For the 1880, 1900, 1910, and 1920 years, a special index was created for these schedules called Soundex. This system grouped all surnames by sound. The 1880 Soundex included only those families with children under 10 years of age, so you would have to look at the entire census, reel by reel, if a name is not included in the Soundex. Names are coded by writing the first letter of the surname and then using numbers for the remaining letters. Vowels, *y*, *w*, and *h* are crossed out of the name. Thus, *Moore* would be *M,* cross out the two *o*'s, change the *r* to 6, and cross out the *e,* and you have M 600. The surname must be an initial letter and three numbers—no more, no less. The table that governs this follows:

> 1 = b, p, f, v
> 2 = c, s, k, g, j, q, x, z
> 3 = d, t
> 4 = l
> 5 = m, n
> 6 = r
> Other examples: Lee   = L 000
>   Smith = S 530
>   Gardiner = G 635

Double consonants in a name (such as the double *o* in the name Moore) are given one number. See Bradley Steuart's *Soundex Reference Guide* (Bountiful, Utah: Precision Indexing, 1990) for a fuller explanation of this system as well as a listing of hundreds of names with their codes.

Using census records

To use the census, you must know the county of the state or the ward in larger cities such as New York. Counties changed boundaries as states grew, so it can sometimes be problematic locating the ancestor from one census year to another. See William Thorndale and William Dollarhide's *Map Guide to the U.S. Federal Censuses, 1790–1920* (Baltimore, Md.: Genealogical Publishing Co., 1987), which gives not only all these changes in map form for each of the census years, but also a bit of the history of the census taking, with all kinds of hints on using the census itself.

Some cautions in using the census must be considered. The handwriting, for one thing, can be very confusing. Some entries are very clear, but others need a lot of guessing to decipher. Moreover, we are not sure just who gave the information. It could be the family themselves, a neighbor, a child, or the census taker, who found an empty house the first time he or she came by and might have taken a guess if he or she knew the family. Check out Richard H. Saldana, ed., *A Practical Guide to the "MISTEAKS" Made in Census Indexes* (Bountiful, Utah: Precision Indexing, 1987) for further insight on this topic.

When using the census schedules, be sure to record all information, starting with the top of the page: state, county, township or other county division, ward of a city, enumeration district, date the census was taken, name of the census taker, street name, house number, family number, and so forth. Be sure to scan up and down the page where your family is located to note all those who are neighbors. A census taker usually worked one side of the street, then crossed over and did the other side; so it is important to note families on both sides of the street. They might also be family or in-laws. In spite of these limitations, the census enumeration schedules are a vital part of genealogical research. By locating a person in the census, you can find names of all persons in that household, relationship to head of household, or children you might not have known existed. Check to see if any holdings of the enumerated census (from 1850 on) are available in your area, and make note of them for your patrons. From 1790 to 1840, only the head of household was enumerated, or named. From 1850 on, all persons living at that address—whether it was a house, boardinghouse, nunnery, house of prostitution, and so forth—had to be named. This is what is referred to as "the enumerated census." Many genealogical societies have some reels of the census, usually of their state or of the area, such as the Southeast, New England, and so forth.

Other censuses

One of the first censuses taken was in England in 1086, after the conquest by William the Conqueror in 1066. He wanted to know the extent of the country he had just conquered. This is called the *Domesday Book*. Check *Encyclopedia Britannica* for details of this work.

The first modern-day census in England and Wales took place in 1801, and like the early censuses in the United States, it does not give much genealogical information. The census in England took place every 10 years, as it has in the United States, though one year later. The first census to give more information was in 1841, when all persons in the household were named. Even so, it only gave the name, sex, occupation, and whether they were born in the same county. The 1851 English census is of much more value for genealogists, with a great deal of valuable information to be found. These census records are also available for viewing in the Mormon Family History Centers, as are Canada's records. There is a 100-year privacy rule in the United Kingdom, and the latest census available for study is for 1891.

There was also an Ecclesiastical Census of 1851. All denominations were expected to take a census of places of worship. Information on this census included the date of consecration or erection, totals in attendance at the various services on March 1851, and average attendances for the previous year. These records are housed in the Public Record Office (PRO), Ruskin Avenue, Kew, Richmond, Surrey, TW9 4DU, United Kingdom; (www.pro.gov.uk). The PRO is the repository of the national archives for the United Kingdom, and the records span from the 11th century to the present. Though not of much value for names, they can be of value in tracing the churches that existed in a particular district. That could give clues as to what church your ancestor might have attended at that particular time as well as when these houses of worship were erected. Using this census, you can check the parish registers and perhaps find the names and relationships you are searching for.

SOURCE: Dahrl Elizabeth Moore, *The Librarian's Genealogy Notebook* (Chicago: American Library Association, 1998), pp. 19–22.

United Nations document symbols

A SYMBOL IS A COMBINATION OF NUMBERS and letters which serves as a unique identifier for a United Nations document. It generally does not give any significant indication of the subject of a document. All language versions of a document carry the same symbol. The first component usually reflects the parent organ issuing the document or to which the document is being submitted:

A/–	General Assembly
S/–	Security Council
E/–	Economic and Social Council
ST/–	Secretariat

The Dag Hammarskjöld Library at the United Nations in New York City.

Some exceptions occur in the case of bodies for which a special series symbol has been created not reflecting the parent organ. For example:

CRC/C/–	Committee on the Rights of the Child
DP/–	United Nations Development Programme
TD/–	United Nations Conference on Trade and Development
UNEP/–	United Nations Environment Programme

Secondary and tertiary components indicate subsidiary bodies:

–/AC. . . ./–	Ad hoc committee
–/C. . . ./–	Standing/permanent/main committee
–/CN. . . ./–	Commission
–/CONF. . . ./–	Conference
–/GC. . . ./–	Governing council
–/PC/. . . ./–	Preparatory committee
–/SC. . . ./–	Subcommittee
–/Sub. . . ./–	Subcommission
–/WG. . . ./–	Working group

Special components reflect the nature of the document:

–/INF/–	Information series (e.g., lists of participants)
–/L. . . .	Limited distribution (i.e., generally draft documents)
–/NGO/–	Statements by nongovernmental organizations
–/PET/–	Petitions
–/PRST/–	Statements by the President of the Security Council
–/PV. . . .	Verbatim records of meetings (i.e., *proces-verbaux*)
–/R. . . .	Restricted distribution
–/RES/–	Resolutions
–/SR. . . .	Summary records of meetings
–/WP. . . .	Working papers

The final component, appearing as a suffix to a symbol, reflects modifications to the original text:

–/Add. . . .	Addendum
–/Amend. . . .	Alteration, by decision of a competent authority, of a portion of an adopted formal text
–/Corr. . . .	Corrigendum (which may not apply to all language versions)

4

–/Rev. . . .	Revision (replacing texts previously issued)
–/Summary	Summarized version
–/–*	Reissuance of a document for technical reasons

Examples:

A/52/1. General Assembly, 52nd session, document no. 1.

A/CONF.151/PC/INF.8. General Assembly, United Nations Conference on Environment and Development, Preparatory Committee, information series, document no. 8.

E/CN.4/Sub.2/AC.2/1987/WP.4/Add.1. Economic and Social Council, Commission on Human Rights, Subcommission on Prevention of Discrimination and Protection of Minorities, Working Group on Contemporary Forms of Slavery, year: 1987, working paper no. 4, addendum no. 1.

UNEP/GC.18/29/Corr.1. United Nations Environment Programme, Governing Council, 18th session, document no. 29, corrigendum no. 1.

As of the 31st session (1976), the General Assembly began to incorporate the session number into the symbols of its documents (e.g., A/31/99). Similarily in 1978, the Economic and Social Council began incorporating the year into the symbols of its documents (e.g., E/1978/99); the Security Council began doing the same in 1994 (e.g., S/1994/99), with the exception of resolutions and meeting records.

The following publications are helpful in identifying committees, commissions, etc., by their document series symbols—and vice versa:

ST/LIB/SER.B/5/Rev.3. *United Nations Document Series Symbols, 1946–1977* (New York: United Nations, 1978). (Sales No.: 79.I.3) (Bibliographical Series/Dag Hammarskjöld Library; No. 5/Rev.3).

ST/LIB/SER.B/5/Rev.3/Add.1. *United Nations Document Series Symbols, 1978–1984* (New York: United Nations, 1986). (Sales No.: 85.I.21) (Bibliographical Series/Dag Hammarskjöld Library; No. 5/Rev.3/Add.1).

ST/LIB/SER.B/5/Rev.5. *United Nations Document Series Symbols, 1946–1996* (New York: United Nations, 1998). (Sales No.: 98.I.6) (Bibliographical Series/Dag Hammarskjöld Library; No. 5/Rev.5).

The same material (including updates) is contained in the "Documentation Series" database on UNBIS Plus on CD-ROM. This database allows keyword searches on a word or words in the name of a UN body, conference or publication series. Further options include subject keyword searching as well as retrieval by documentation series.

Researchers who have mastered the basics of UN documentation and are ready to tackle some more intricate aspects should consult *United Nations Documentation: A Brief Guide* (ST/LIB/34/Rev.2 + Corr.1-2. New York: United Nations, 1994), which is an excellent handbook not only for unraveling the complexities of documentation but also for providing guidance in the organization and maintenance of a documents collection.

Sales numbers

Sales publications constitute a highly selective category of publications of general/broad interest which the United Nations offers for sale in order to give them the widest possible distribution outside the UN system; they are identified by sales numbers. A sales number is a combination of letters and numbers (both arabic and roman). The first component (a letter) indicates the language of the publication; the second (two arabic numerals) indicates the year of publication; the third (roman numerals), the subject of the publication or the issuing body in some instances. The final component (an arabic numeral) is nothing more than a sequential number which has no special meaning.

Example: E.95.XIII.12 = *World Urbanization Prospects: The 1994 Revision* (i.e., an English-language title published in 1995 relating to demography).

The United Nations Sales Section disseminates official documents, publications, and electronic products of the United Nations and its agencies on demand. It also supplies documents from the Optical Disk System (ODS) in printed or electronic format to customers who do not have a subscription to the system. Information about the service and rates can be obtained by calling (212) 963-8302 or (800) 253-9646; fax: (212)-963-3489; publications@ un.org.

Official records

Official Records, always identified as such on the title page, constitute the primary documents submitted to or issued by major UN organs at a given session or during a particular year. They consist of meeting records; resolutions; reports of major organs, committees and commissions as well as the budget and financial reports (each issued as a separately numbered "Supplement" and comprehensively listed in UN-I-QUE); and reprints of other important documents (issued sessionally as "Annexes" and organized by agenda item number in the case of the General Assembly or quarterly "Supplements" listed by document symbol in the case of the Security Council). Official Records are also produced for some of the major conferences (e.g., Third United Nations Conference on the Law of the Sea).

Highly specialized Indexes, the Indexes to Proceedings, are available to facilitate the work of researchers attempting to identify both masthead documents and Official Records of the General Assembly, Security Council, Economic and Social Council and Trusteeship Council.

SOURCE: United Nations Dag Hammarskjöld Library, www.un.org/Depts/dhl/rcsguide/. Reprinted with permission.

SPECIAL COLLECTIONS

Pricing scarce and rare books and manuscripts

by Allen and Patricia Ahearn

HOW ARE RARE OR SCARCE ITEMS PRICED? Not easily.

There was a comedian back in the 1950s named Brother David Gardner. When someone would say, "Let's do that again," Brother Dave would say,

"You can't do anything again. You can do something similar." Well, if a book or manuscript is truly rare or unique, you will not be able to find anything exactly comparable to base your price on, so you must find something similar.

In order to provide a complete picture of the process of pricing, we must consult all the sources, though some of these may not be helpful in many cases. It is relatively easy to arrive at a price or, at least, a price range for most collected books because copies are bought and sold fairly regularly throughout the year. It does, however, become much more difficult to arrive at a price as one explores the pricing of the unique item, such as a great association copy of a book, a unique manuscript, or even a perfect copy of a relatively common book.

The prices paid by dealers and, in turn, the new prices they set on the books or manuscripts they sell are a factor of the individual dealer's sense of the real market price based on his or her own knowledge and readings of the auction records, other dealers' catalogs, and price guides.

To show how a price is set for a modern first edition, for example, let us look at Larry McMurtry's *Lonesome Dove* (New York: Simon and Schuster, 1985), a title published in a fairly large first printing of 42,000 copies at the publication price of $18.95. A nice copy started out on the market in 1985 at $25. It sold easily. The price moved to $40, then to $50, $75, $100, $125, $150, and, finally, to $175. We had continued to sell the book at $150, but at $175 we had no orders. Now this is a snapshot of a period of a few years. We eventually sold the $175 copy and now the book may sell for more if in mint condition, but the point is that the marketplace set the price. The dealers, of course, could not continue buying *Lonesome Dove* at $10 or $15, but paid more for each successive copy. The scouts or other sellers demanded a higher price at the wholesale level as time went on, which also had a great deal to do with the higher prices charged at the retail level.

The foregoing is a relatively common process in the marketplace and is easy to understand and follow; however, there is a tendency in some cases in recent years to jump straight to the higher value. In other words, a book which was in high demand, such as Tom Clancy's *The Hunt for Red October,* moved from $50 to $ 100 to $650 to $750, almost overnight. A dealer (or dealers) decided the book was truly scarce and would sell at the higher level. In this case they appear to have been right, even though the first printing was 30,000 copies, of which 15,000 copies went to libraries. The book continues to sell at the higher level. Whether it will continue to sell at this level in future years is anyone's guess.

But now let us consider the uncorrected proof of *The Hunt for Red October.* The proof in paper wrappers had a proof dust jacket which was different from the dust jacket used on the first edition. A copy in dust jacket was offered for $3,500. A Clancy collector, who wanted the proof but was not willing to pay more than $2,000, had asked us to find him one. Eventually, we purchased the copy that had been priced at $3,500 at a lower price and sold it to our collector for $1,850. This is not to say that the $3,500 price was too high. We have heard of only three copies being offered on the market, so it is a rare item. We do not know what the others sold for, but we believe the price we sold our copy for influenced the asking price of the other two copies.

So it is clear that the buyers—the market—really set the prices in these three examples. In the last example, the seller could have held out for the $3,500, and perhaps our customer would have eventually paid it; or someone else may have come along and bought it for $3,500. We will never know.

There are three types of published value guides that are used to determine prices.

1. Price guides based on dealer catalog entries. The most common price guides are those that report the prices asked for books in dealer catalogs. The oldest and largest of these is the *Bookman's Price Index,* which is published by Gale Research twice a year and is up to 46 volumes (and does include a section on association copies). There are others, including Edward Zempel's *Book Prices Used and Rare* (Spoon River Press); the series edited by Michael Cole under the title *International Rare Book Prices* (Picaflow Ltd.); and many others that are general or specific, such as Shelly and Richard Morrison's annual price guides to *Western Americana* and *Texiana* (Morrison Books).

These are the most useful for finding the relatively common collected books. Occasionally, one may be lucky and find an item very close to the one being priced or being offered. Although it is not certain whether an item actually sold for the price asked (more on that below), if one finds multiple entries by different dealers year after year, it can be assumed that the prices are in the ballpark.

The problems with these guides are that:

a. It is not at all certain a book sold for the price asked. This can be overcome if one calls the dealer and asks if the item was sold, which may not always be possible.

b. The price may be so out of date that it really is not relevant to today's market, even if it did sell. And the market on certain types of books and manuscripts changes rapidly.

c. These guides can report only on books that have appeared on the market; rare books either do not show up often (we *are* talking about *rare* books) or, more realistically, they are sold without ever being cataloged.

So it is recommended that you start with one of these guides because it is just possible that something similar has been cataloged recently; but keep in mind that they may not prove very useful.

2. Auction records. In the United States, the *American Book Prices Current* is published annually by Bancroft-Parkman (with index volumes published every four years). There are comparable publications in Europe and elsewhere. The chances of finding a price for a comparable rare book, association copy, or manuscript in the auction records would be greater than in the dealer catalog price guides, but in the auction records the prices for the same title will vary greatly, which may reflect condition of each book, or, more likely, who showed up to bid that day. It should be understood that auctions are where many dealers buy books for stock. Therefore, many of the auction prices may represent wholesale rather than retail prices. In some cases, the auction prices may represent forced sales and resulting low prices, while in some cases, when the auction has received high visibility, the prices paid may be significantly higher than retail. A recent example of a price that was highly inflated was Henry

James's *The Ambassadors*, which sold for $5,000 at auction, yet the buyer could have found five or more copies in comparable condition on dealers' shelves for $500 to $750.

The point is that auction prices require the knowledge of a dealer, a rare book librarian, or a collector of the particular author to be interpreted properly.

Another point worth noting is that the index volumes provide little or no description of condition; and the annual volumes are not much better. When using the auction records, it is always best to check the index first and then go back to the annual volumes, and then to the actual auction catalog (if it is available) and read the complete description.

The problems with the auction records are similar to the price guide problems in that they can report only what is put at auction; the prices may be out of date. Their advantage over price guides based on dealer catalog entries is that you know the auction prices that were actually paid. Remember, auction houses charge a premium to the buyer and the seller, so find out if the price included the premium(s).

3. Price guides prepared by individuals. These are price guides that express the opinion (we hope an informed one) of the compiler(s) of the guides. The prices are based on their experience buying and selling books, as well as their own abilities to interpret auction prices and other dealer catalog prices.

The most commonly used guide at present is our *Collected Books: The Guide to Values* (Putnam, 1998), which lists estimated prices for about 15,000 books. We have also compiled *Book Collecting: A Comprehensive Guide* (Putnam, 1995), which lists values for authors' first books; and individual *Author Price Guides* which include all the American and English first editions by a particular author, with points for identification of first editions and values.

One of the reasons for the popularity of these guides is that they contain bibliographical information useful in determining if a particular book in hand is a first edition (or a first state or issue within a first edition).

There are similar works such as Joseph Connolly's *Collecting Modern First Editions* (Studio Vista, 1972) and Tom Broadfoot's *Civil War Books: A Priced Checklist with Advice* (Broadfoot, 1996). These books represent their authors' opinions of what they would price a copy of the individual book if they were cataloging it the day the guide was prepared.

The problem with these guides is that the prices are only as good as the knowledge of their authors. The tendency is to price relatively common books high and scarce or rare books low. This is reasonable: The common books are cataloged often and the expense of the cataloging makes it difficult to price a book under $25. Also, if the book was published at $25, it is hard to value it at, say, $5, which in fact is the price you might find it at in your local bookstore. On the other hand, if one is attempting to come up with a price for a fine copy of Faulkner's *Soldier's Pay* in a dust jacket, and no copy in this condition has been on the market in ten years—at least none that the author is aware of—what price do you put into the guide? You list a price based on the last price, perhaps 10 years old, which you can find, tempered by the prices you know a few inferior copies have brought on the market in recent years. This may or may not be a reasonable price estimate, but the odds are that it will be low, particularly if there is a pent-up demand for the book.

A standard comment on price guides is that they are out of date as soon as they are published. Actually, we do not find this to be true. Most collected books tend to stay at a certain level for a year or two; and most prices do not get really out of date until three or four years go by. What people are commenting on are the "hot" authors or books that they have heard so much about and find the price guides very low compared to current prices. Did anyone project Cormac McCarthy's *The Orchard Keeper* as a $2,000 book before *All the Pretty Horses?* Was it obvious in 1990 that Hemingway's *For Whom the Bell Tolls* and *The Old Man and the Sea* would be selling for $500 to $600 in 1994?

First, on McCarthy, no one could have known *The Orchard Keeper* would reach such heights. Of course, the $2,000 was in a catalog and will eventually appear in a price guide; and we will have to ask if it actually sold. Although, in the case of McCarthy, it probably did. Now, as to Hemingway, if one were astute enough in 1990 to realize that after the October 1987 stock market crash (perhaps coincidentally), the price of "high spots" of collected books would go up faster than the prices of other collected books, then you could have foreseen that *For Whom the Bell Tolls* and *The Old Man and the Sea* would go up from about $100 to $150 in 1990 to $500 to $600 in 1994, while *Across the River and into the Trees* would go up from $100 to only $150.

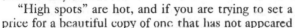
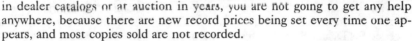

"High spots" are hot, and if you are trying to set a price for a beautiful copy of one that has not appeared in dealer catalogs or at auction in years, you are not going to get any help anywhere, because there are new record prices being set every time one appears, and most copies sold are not recorded.

As a final note on price guides and auction records, it should be said that users of these reference works have their own way of interpreting the prices. A number of people have told us they always use our guides: some use half our values; some use three-quarters of them; some double our prices; and some believe that our prices are for very good copies and that fine copies would be twice as much and mint copies would be three times as much.

A local bookstore owner who buys our guides told us he got a copy of a certain book and, if it had not been for our guides, he would have priced it at $10. As it was, he found the book listed in our guide for $150 so he priced it at $60. We bought it.

For auction records, one can usually assume that the retail price for a comparable copy of a book would be 50% to 100% higher than the auction price, but as we mentioned above, there are many instances where this rule of thumb would be way off the mark.

Other considerations

Prices paid. Obviously the amount the dealer paid for an item will influence the price he or she asks. This comes up quite often when dealers are handling unusual if not unique items; and it can cause concern on the part of the buyers when it is obvious that a book priced at $x appears in another dealer's catalog or is offered to the buyer at $2x or $3x. In this case, the buyer is aware of the cost to the dealer—and may believe the "profit" is too high, but it must be realized that the dealer bought the book because he or she believed the first dealer underpriced it. The price may be "high," but time will tell if it is too high. One of our esteemed colleagues, when asked if a book is really worth the price he has on it, always responds, "Not yet." This means a buyer must legitimize the price. If no buyer comes along, the dealer has two choices: maintain the price or lower it. Although small, the antiquarian book field is a marketplace, and supply and demand factors do apply.

Consignor's desired price. It is not uncommon for an unusual or unique item to be on consignment with a dealer. In this case, the price being asked may simply be the price the consignor has set plus a nominal profit for the dealer. The dealer may believe the price is high but is aware that the consignor will not sell the item for less; therefore, the price is set.

We recall a case in which a library that had a comprehensive collection of a certain author's works, including manuscripts and letters, was offered an important collection of letters for a high five-figure amount. The librarian felt the price was too high. The dealer had the letters on consignment. Eventually, the letters were offered to another university at the same price and the second university purchased them. Again, if no other buyer had been willing to buy the letters, the price would have been lowered or the letters would have been taken off the market.

Individual dealer "experience." It seems that a book becomes more attractive and thus more valuable once it is owned. There is clearly a psychological aspect to pricing books. If Dealer A has a book and Dealer B is interested in it, Dealer B will often exclaim about the high price Dealer A wants, how common the book is, the obvious defects that make it only a marginally collectible book, and so on. But having gotten Dealer A down as low as he possibly can and purchased the book, Dealer B becomes transfixed with the beauty and rarity of the volume. A price is not set immediately as time is needed for Dealer B to absorb the aura of the volume and determine a "fair" price for this now "priceless" tome.

HIPPO
CRATIS AC GA-
leni libri alienot, ex recognitio
ne Francisci Rabelæsi, medici
omnibus numeris absolutissi-
mi: quorum elenchum se
quens pagella indi
cabit.
Hæc medicæ fons est exundantissimus artis.
Hinc mage ni sapias pigra lacuna, bibe.

VIRTVTE DVCE.   COMITE FORT.

Apud Gryphium L...d.
1554

I remember a knowledgeable dealer seeing a second edition, albeit the first illustrated edition, of a very famous book. He told the dealer who owned it that it was nicely bound but only a second edition, after all, and perhaps worth as much as $300. The other dealer, who had not priced the book yet, listened to the sage advice of the first dealer and priced it $750. The first dealer bought the book immediately and returned to his shop. After some deliberation, he priced it at $1,250. A third dealer came in and asked how anyone could price a second edition of this book at over $1,000! After much discussion, the third dealer bought the book. This dealer went to some lengths to check on previous prices and came up with nothing of any use from any of the price guides available. He then checked all the major libraries in the United States, England, and France, and he discovered that none of them had a copy. He priced the book at $10,000, and he ultimately sold it at something approaching this amount. As a footnote, the second dealer proclaimed that the third dealer and his customer were both fools.

There is another story about how dealers' prices are set which might also prove educational. One day a dealer on a trip spied a book he believed was truly rare. The book was priced at $17,500 and was included in a catalog just mailed by the shop. The dealer asked for and received a dealer discount and left the shop with the book. He was aware that the local university did not have a copy of the book and decided to go over and offer the book to the librarian. He offered it at $24,000. The librarian had just received the catalog from the shop where the book had been purchased and realized that this was the same copy offered in the catalog at $17,500. The librarian mentioned that she had seen the book for $17,500. The dealer responded that he had bought the book and believed it was much scarcer than the catalog price would indicate and had repriced it at $24,000, which he believed was a much more realistic price. The librarian told him that she thought $17,500 was a fair price and she would be willing to pay that amount for it. The dealer said he owned the book now and felt his price was fair, and then left. He went home and did more research. He learned that the Library of Congress did not have a copy and decided that it was even scarcer than he had originally thought. He made an appointment with the rare book librarian at the Library of Congress and at their meeting, offered the book for $28,000. The LC librarian had also seen the catalog and stated the price was much too high, implying that the dealer was price gouging and making too high a profit. No deal was made. The dealer was upset that the librarian believed the book was overpriced, but he was becoming more convinced that it was scarcer than he had thought. He decided to offer it to a Midwestern university on his way to California the next week. He did offer it, at $34,000, and he sold it.

We must admit we are not sure that all the details of these stories are accurate, but we know that these scenarios have played out before and will play out again.

Summary

Most dealers do not want to sell a customer an item at a very high price when another copy may turn up on the market at a much lower price within a few years. However, when a dealer is faced with placing a price on a unique item, there is no possibility that another copy will come on the market. The problem is, what is comparable to the item? If it is a great association copy inscribed by Ernest Hemingway, what have other Hemingway association copies brought? If it is a manuscript by a prominent author, what have other manuscripts by that author brought? If none has been sold, what have the manuscripts of authors with comparable reputations sold for? There is always some comparison to be made, but many times the comparisons may be tenuous.

Another approach is to have an independent appraisal of the item, but this presents a problem if the appraisal is very high or very low. We were called in once to reappraise a collection because the owners refused to sell the material at the original appraised value. We did our own appraisal of the material and honestly thought the original appraisal had been ludicrously low. The owner and university were able to work out a price, probably somewhere between the two appraisals, although we were never told the final result. It must be added, though, that there are different kinds of, and reasons for, appraisals— for insurance purposes, for tax or estate purposes, to help the owner know what to ask for the collection if she or he were to sell it, to inform a potential buyer of the value of an item or a collection, and so on—and these factors will influence the appraiser's final figures. It would seem reasonable when contemplating the purchase of an expensive collection or item to have one, or perhaps even two, independent appraisals of the value to assure that the price is within reason.

The truly rare or unique item, if demand is high, can be priced as high as the seller wants, but the seller must find a buyer in order to legitimize the price. Even the fact that a book sells for a certain amount does not necessarily mean that another copy will sell for the same amount. The first book may have found the only buyer in the marketplace willing to pay that much. Also, a high price on one copy may bring other copies into the market, thus increasing the supply and lowering the value. The market is constantly changing with new hypermodern authors coming into fashion and record prices being set every week or so, it seems. All the materials and expertise available should be used in making a purchasing decision.

SOURCE: Allen and Patricia Ahearn, "Pricing Scarce and Rare Books and Manuscripts," *Rare Books & Manuscripts Librarianship* 9, no.1 (1994): 31–38.

Unfamiliar genres

MANY RARE BOOK LIBRARIES maintain files of certain genres or categories in their collections. These files are especially useful when a researcher cares more about the genre than the author, title, or topic. Here are some odd ones.

Allusion books—collections of contemporary allusions to a famous author.
Analects—literary fragments or gleanings.
Artillery election sermons—annual public orations delivered to state militia gatherings, focusing on military and defense concerns.
Bibelots—unusually small books.
Bills of mortality—official statements, issued periodically, on births and deaths in a district.
Block books—books printed from engraved blocks of wood, 1460–1480.
Cadastral maps—maps drawn on a large scale to show land ownership for tax purposes.
Captivity narratives—colonial and postcolonial women's accounts of their capture by Indians and assimilation into their culture.
Celestial atlases—atlases containing astronomical maps.
Chrestomathies—collections of excerpts and choice selections, especially from a foreign language.
Corantos—single-folio, double-sided newspapers, 1620s.
Costeriana—fragments of books, allegedly printed before 1473 by Laurens Janszoon Coster of Haarlem.
Epitomes—abridged works that retain the essential matter of the original.
Farces—light, dramatic compositions in a satirical or humorous vein.
Fast day proclamations—annual Congressional or special Presidential proclamations for days of fasting and thanksgiving during and after the Revolutionary War.
Fourth of July sermons—July 4 orations delivered to community gatherings following the Revolution, typically chronicling God's hand in those events.
Fraternity rituals—books of secret rituals conducted by campus greek organizations.
Gray literature—semipublished material, such as reports, internal documents, and theses.

Habilitationsschriften—German probationary treatises containing the results of original research submitted to a university.

Hornbooks—16th-century children's primers. They consisted of a thin sheet of vellum or paper mounted on an oblong piece of wood and covered with transparent horn. The wooden frame had a handle by which it was hung from a child's girdle. The sheet bore the alphabet, the vowels in a line followed by the vowels combined with consonants in tabular form, numerals, and prayers.

Imaginary voyages—fictional and fanciful travel stories.

Jestbooks—books containing jokes and witty sayings.

Letterbooks—books in which correspondence was copied, resulting in a facsimile copy.

Livres à vignettes—18th-century books illustrated by vignette copperplate engravings.

Mazarinades—anonymous political pamphlets written 1648–1651 for and against French Cardinal and Prime Minister Jules Mazarin.

Newscarriers' addresses—verses in broadside or pamphlet format presented at the start of a new year by newspaper carriers (and sometimes by other tradespeople) to request a gratuity.

Palimpsests—manuscripts in which a second writing has been superimposed upon the original text, which has been totally or partially obliterated.

Palm leaf books, or Ola books—sacred manuscripts made in south Asia from strips of young leaves of the Talipat or Palmyra palm cut into strips and secured between two wooden boards. An iron stylus was used for writing, and the leaf's surface was smeared with oil and charcoal for clarity.

Pasquinades—anonymous, satirical, antipapist poems posted on the Pasquino statue (an ancient sculpture depicting Patroclus and Menelaus) in Rome in the 16th century. The name Pasquino was given later to this statue and was probably that of a craftsman with a ready tongue who had his shop nearby.

Penny dreadfuls—morbidly sensational children's story books, cheaply published.

Promptbooks—copies of a play used by a prompter, showing actions, cues, props, costumes, scenery, and lighting.

Psalters—Books of Psalms in which the psalms are arranged for use in a religious service.

Pustakas—Indonesian books consisting of long strips of tree bark, dealing with magic, medicine, or law. Written in a brilliant ink on long strips of writing material, pustakas were folded concertina-fashion and tied together with a string of woven rushes.

Robinsonades—works describing an individual's or a community's survival without the aid of civilization, as on a deserted island.

Romans à clef—novels in which one or more characters are based on real people but given fictitious names.

Rutters—Renaissance books of sailing directions used as navigation aids.

Samizdat—forbidden or unpublishable books or periodicals circulated clandestinely.

Spirit communications—works channeled by spiritualistic or New Age mediums and allegedly authored by disembodied entities.

Success manuals—didactic, book-length works of nonfiction that promised to show men how to find success in life; written in the United States between 1870 and 1910 by ministers, educators, and publicists.

Three-deckers—late 19th-century novels published in three volumes.

Yellowbacks—cheap popular novels published in shiny yellow paper covers with a picture on the front.

SOURCE: ALA Rare Books and Manuscripts Section, Standards Committee, *Genre Terms: A Thesaurus for Use in Rare Book and Special Collections Cataloguing* (1983); Ray Prytherch, *Harrod's Librarians' Glossary* (Gower, 8th ed., 1995).

Atlases and globes

by Bill Katz

AN ATLAS IS DEFINED SIMPLY as a bound collection of maps, usually with an index of place names. Depending on how elaborate the publication, various amounts of related geographical materials from photographs and charts to encyclopedic texts will be included. The expansion of geographical skills and knowledge during the 16th century resulted in the rapid growth of wall maps of the world (few of which are extant) and more important the development of the atlas, usually constructed from collections of sheet maps.

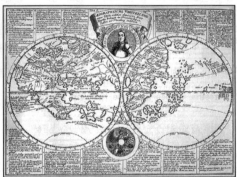

Martin Behaim (c. 1436–1507) of Nuremberg is credited with the construction of the first known extant terrestrial globe in 1492 (left), and this was the beginning of a minor industry from that time onward. Behaim's globe was constructed from a wooden sphere to which was pasted painted parchment map sections in six colors by another artist. Featuring more than 1,000 place names, it was completed in 1492 about the time Columbus set sail. The globe particularly is of interest because it shows the world Columbus must have envisioned before his voyage . . . including the contemporary view that the Atlantic separated the west coast of Europe from the eastern side of Asia.

Ptolemy was put to rest in the mid-16th century by one of the world's most famous cartographers, Abraham Ortelius. In 1570 his history-making *Theatrum Orbis Terrarum* (Theatre of the World) appeared in Antwerp. In Latin and a half-dozen European languages it went through 40 editions before it ceased being the primary atlas of the period in about 1624. In the first edition there were 53 maps, and in the last 166. The period of cartographic incunabula, characterized by a slavish following of old doctrines and strongly influenced by Ptolemy, was closed. The new period trusted the knowledge of the earth to firsthand exploration and scientific investigation rather than to the ancient classics.

As a trained engraver, Ortelius derived his authority from others, but his distinctive artistic style marked maps from that point forward. Ortelius gained additional fame when appointed geographer to King Philip II of Spain in 1575. He is particularly remembered by librarians for his pioneering work in the collecting and selling of maps and atlases. Ortelius can be said to be the first to show a considered interest in the collection and the preservation of maps. He lived in various places throughout Europe and at each place he purchased and sold maps.

The first time anyone used the term "atlas" in the title of a collection of maps was in 1585 when Mercator published his *Atlas sive Cosmographicae*. He followed the lead of Lafreri and prefaced his collection with an engraving of Atlas holding up the world. Mercator's atlas was built around the modern notion of the form. He not only wished to include maps, but a good deal of text. The publication came out in parts, with the first section appearing in 1585, the second in 1589, and four months after Mercator's death, the complete work in 1595. The atlas became a best-seller of sorts, and other mapmakers in and out of Holland recognized the importance of the atlas form.

Before the growth of nationalism, the 16th-century cartographers demonstrated a remarkable objectivity. John Hale wrote, "Neither atlases or maps showed a Europe biased towards the West. Devoid of indications of national frontiers until late in the [16th century], they were not devised to be read politically. And the busily even spread of town names did not suggest that western Europe had any greater weight of economic vitality than eastern Europe."

The atlas as a form captured the interest and imagination of people, and it became the dominant layperson's cartographic format. Some describe the 17th century as the age of atlases, primarily because not only were there numerous new works, but publishers had learned from Ortelius and Mercator how engraved plates might be used over and over again for various editions—thus improving profits, if not always the reliability of the atlas. Jodocus Hondius, for example, purchased the plates of the Mercator atlas and until 1637 published 40 different editions. While he did add descriptive texts, the maps themselves were little changed from the original 1595 work. (Ortelius's *Theatrum* continued to be printed until 1612, but then disappeared.)

A serious rival to the Mercator-Hondius atlas appeared in the person of Willem Blaeu (1571–1638). After studying astronomy, Blaeu took up the construction of scientific instruments in Amsterdam. From this he was led to an interest in maps, and in 1604 published the first of a series of maps of individual countries. He became famous for a world map which was published in 20 sheets and formed a map eight feet across. (Only one example is extant.) He turned to atlases and in 1608 published the first atlas for seamen, updating this in 1623. By 1630, using plates from the Hondius family, he issued his first general atlas. This was the beginning of what was to become the *Atlas Major* or *Grand Atlas* of 600 maps in 11 to 12 folio volumes—a work carried on by Blaeu's and his family and published in several languages between 1662 and 1663.

Not only was the Blaeu atlas one of a kind, but it became one of the most expensive books of any type published in the 17th century. Today individual maps from the volumes are sold at high prices because the Blaeu effort represents the height of the decorated map/atlas. Each map was colored by hand and the margins had massive decorations from figures of the gods to natural history and astronomical signs. Then as now they are considered as much works of arts as accurate maps. And they were accurate in that the Blaeu atlas represented almost everything known about the world in the 17th century, includ-

---

Top 15 research libraries holding alternative press titles

by Rita A. Marinko and Kristin H. Gerhard

The following libraries held the largest percentage of periodicals listed in the *Alternative Press Index* for 1996.

New York Public Library	72%	Indiana University	54%
University of Connecticut	71	University of Colorado at Boulder	52
Library of Congress	67	University of Iowa	52
University of California, Los Angeles	66	Temple University	51
University of Michigan	65	University of Maryland	51
Michigan State University	64	University of California, San Diego	48
Harvard University	60	University of Pittsburgh	48
University of Wisconsin, Madison	58		

SOURCE: Rita A. Marinko and Kristin H. Gerhard, "Representations of the Alternative Press in Academic Library Collections," *College & Research Libraries* 59 (July 1998): 363–71.

---

ing a relatively true depiction of China. Given the success of the atlas, a great number of other publishers entered the field. The engraved maps of this period, although rarely up to the quality or interest of Ortelius-Mercator-Blaeu continue to fascinate collectors and often make up a fascinating part of a library's rare book collections.

Until the mid-18th century printed atlases were too bulky, and much too expensive for the average person. An ingenious French geographer, Bruze de la Martiniere, published the answer in a pocket atlas of France in 1734. Thereafter, relatively inexpensive pocket atlases were common, often being little more than reductions of the larger, more ornamental titles.

John Ogilby (1600–1676) spent most of his life as a publisher of Greek classics, but in his late 60's he turned to map and atlas publishing. By 1675 he produced the first road map in the forms of strips (similar to the American Automobile Association's trip guides) on separate pages. The route could be followed, in the same scale, from strip to strip.

SOURCE: Bill Katz, *Cuneiform to Computer: A History of Reference Sources* (Lanham, Md.: Scarecrow Press, 1998), pp. 234–36.

MULTIMEDIA

Notable multimedia for children, 1999

THE NOTABLE CHILDREN'S Videos, Recordings, and Computer Software list is compiled annually by three committees of the ALA Association for Library Service to Children to highlight multimedia materials. These are their selections for 1999.

Videos

Chrysanthemum (Weston Woods). Chrysanthemum thinks her name is perfect, until she is teased at school. Meryl Streep narrates Kevin Henkes' award-winning picture book. Ages 3–10.

Dance Lexie, Dance (Tim Loane). 12-year-old Laura, an Irish Protestant girl, yearns to be a Riverdancer. Her newly widowed father, Lexie, rethinks his parental role to help his daughter and comes to terms with the loss of his wife. Ages 8–12.

Elmopalooza! (Children's Television Workshop). The Sesame Street Muppets and their musical guests join in a cross-cultural original musical extravaganza. All ages.

The First Christmas (billy budd Films). The nativity story using Clay Animation characters is narrated by Christopher Plummer. Christmas carols, including "Silent Night" and "O Little Town of Bethlehem," enhance the story. Ages 5 and up.

Good Night, Gorilla (Weston Woods). A precocious gorilla tiptoes behind a sleepy, unobservant zookeeper unlocking each animal's cage. The parade of animals follows the zookeeper home for a good night's sleep. Brahms's Lullaby accompanies this delightful video based on the 1994 Peggy Rathman book. Ages 4–8.

Kristen's Fairy House (Great White Dog). During a vacation on a wooded island, a young girl and her aunt blend the wonders of the real world with the imaginative and creative. The fairy house built by the girl becomes inhabited by woodland creatures. The woman is motivated to create an illustrated book on the basis of the girl's journey into the land of fairies. Ages 7–11.

Land Snails and Their Life Cycle (Klaudiusz Jankowski Productions). This lyrically beautiful video is a comprehensive study of the life cycle of land snails. Utilizing spectacular photography. Ages 9 and up.

Oceans in Motion (National Geographic). Catch a wave and learn all about the ocean with tour guide/professional surfer, "Wingnut" Weaver. Dazzling photography and creative animation illustrate the phenomena of currents, seismic activity, tides and waves. Ages 7 and up.

Sheep Crossing (Great White Dog). This video explores the world of sheep and wool while following children as they prepare their sheep for fair competition. Meet a newborn lamb and working border collies. The background music has an upbeat tempo. Beautiful New England scenery add to the viewer's sensual experience. All ages.

Smoking: Truth or Dare (Arnold Shapiro). This live-action informational video graphically illustrates the consequences of smoking and chewing tobacco for today's young people. Ages 10 and up.

Recordings

Autumnsongs. Performed by John McCutcheon (Rounder Records).

Back on Broadway. Performed by the Broadway Kids (Lightyear Entertainment).

Ben's Trumpet. Performed by Charles Turner and jazz musicians (Live Oak Media).

The Best Christmas Pageant Ever. Performed by C. J. Critt (Recorded Books).

Chrysanthemum. Performed by Meryl Streep (Weston Woods).

Door in the Wall. Performed by Roger Rees (Bantam Doubleday Dell).

Eleanor Roosevelt. Performed by Barbara Caruso (Recorded Books).

Elmopalooza! Performed by Sesame Street characters and various artists (Sony Wonder).

40 Winks. Performed by Jessica Harper (Alacazam).
Freak the Mighty. Performed by Elden Henson (Listening Library).
The Gardener. Performed by Bonnie Kelly-Young (Live Oak Media).
The Great Fire. Performed by John McDonough (Recorded Books).
if fish could sing . . . Performed by Teresa Doyle (Bedlam).
In My Hometown. Performed by Tom Chapin (Sony Wonder).
Jacob Have I Loved. Performed by Christina Moore (Recorded Books).
Jazz-A-Ma-Tazz. Performed by Hayes Greenfield and others (Baby Music
   Boom).
John Henry. Performed by Samuel L. Jackson (Weston Woods).
Joyful Noise. Performed by B. Caruso, J. McDonough, C. Moore, and J.
   Woodman (Recorded Books).
Leon's Story. Performed by Graham Brown (Recorded Books).
Moorchild. Performed by Virginia Leishman (Recorded Books).
Norwegian Tales of Enchantment. Performed by Judith Simundson
   (Makoche).
Rascal. Performed by Jim Weiss (Listening Library).
Rudy and the Roller Skate. Performed by Dan Keding (Turtle Creek).
Running Out of Time. Performed by Kimberly Schraf (Listening Library).
Sarny: A Life Remembered. Performed by Lynne Thigpen (Recorded Books).
The Silver Chair. BBC Radio Dramatization (Bantam Doubleday Dell).
Swingin' in the Rain. Performed by Maria Muldaur (Music for Little People).
Under the Green Corn Moon: Native American Lullabies. Performed by
   various Native American artists (Silver Wave).
Under the Mango Tree: Stories from Spanish Speaking Countries. Per-
   formed by Elida Guardia Bonet (Zarati).
World Tales, Live at Bennington College. Performed by Tim Jennings and
   Leanne Ponder (Eastern Coyote).

Computer software

Carmen Sandiego Math Detective by Broderbund Software. Win 95/Power
Macintosh. This new Carmen Sandiego adventure is packed with over 400
word problems, three levels of difficulty, and an illustrated glossary of terms.
With an innovative and easy-to-use interface, this software enables users to
play the role of double agent as they explore the worlds of geometry, linear
math, and other number concepts. Ages 9 and up.

Dr. Seuss Kindergarten by Broderbund Software. Win 95/98. Follow Gerald
McGrew as he collects different animals for his zoo through 250 activities
that teach phonics, measurement, and other math and language related skills.
Children can listen to over 50 Dr. Seuss characters such as Sneeches and
Barbaloots who talk to them in rhyme as the activities are introduced. Graphically interesting games make for an enjoyable and educational experience for
children. Ages 4–6.

Dr. Seuss Preschool by Broderbund Software. Win 95/98. Horton, Yertle,
and other Dr. Seuss characters lead children through interactive games that
teach letter recognition, counting, and other essential prereading skills. Smooth
integration of animation and sound makes for a seamless presentation that
only enhances the concepts presented. This engaging software will delight
and educate children. Ages 4–6.

Encarta 99 by Microsoft. Win95/98 (Mac version available by Web download). This redesigned interface enables users to move between 40,000 encyclopedia articles and other original source documents with links to over 15,000 hand-selected Web sites. There is full-text indexing, and authority is given for both text and pictorial entries. Extensive cross-referencing allows users to explore related photos, illustrations, videos, animations, and audioclips. Updates are available online.

SOURCE: ALA Association for Library Service to Children.

Selected videos
for young adults, 1999

THESE VIDEOS FOR young adults were chosen by a committee of the Young Adult Library Services Association on the basis of young-adult appeal, technical quality, subject content, and use for youths aged 12–18.

American Civil Liberties Union: A History (Films for the Humanities and Sciences). This colorful mix of video documentary follows the ACLU from its creation by its colorful founder Roger Baldwin in 1920 to its defenses of Vietnam War protestors in the 1960s and of the rights of Nazis to march in Skokie, Illinois, in the 1980s.

The Band (University of California Extension, Center for Media & Independent Learning). From band camp to the prom, a filmmaker chronicles a year in the life of his 16-year-old son, a member of the high school band, and his relationships with his other classmates. The result is a candid, humorous, and realistic film which deals with young love, divorce, anorexia, and dealing with the death of a son and sibling.

Cancelled Lives: Letters from the Inside; Substance Abuse (Bureau for At-Risk Youth). Authentic, personal letters written by incarcerated juveniles and adults to family and friends tell how they deal with the painful feelings of loneliness and regret. Well-known actors read the letters which convey the shattering consequences of committing crimes, abusing drugs, and participating in gang activities.

Creatures Fantastic: Creatures of the Night (DK Publishing). Vampires, monsters, ghosts. What's behind the allure and the fear of things that go bump in the night? This video offers a rich visual panorama through the dramatic recreation of tales ranging from ancient myth to modern urban legend.

In the Mix: Live by the Gun, Die by the Gun (In the Mix/Castle Works). Through interviews with victims, former gang members, and professionals, this edition of the national PBS series for teens explores the consequences of carrying guns as well as giving alternative ways of handling anger and explosive situations.

Internet Searching Skills (Library Video Company). A comprehensive video guide for students on searching the World Wide Web. Includes step-by step strategies explaining how to access, research, and evaluate the vast resources of the Internet.

Magnificent Fish: Forgotten Giants (Video Project). Sharks, tunas, swordfish, and other billfish are some of the most fascinating fish in the sea—sometimes swimming from the U.S. to the coast of Africa. Yet they are in danger of becoming extinct due to overfishing and overpopulation. Peter Benchley, the author of *Jaws*, is the host.

Reviving Ophelia: Saving the Selves of Adolescent Girls (Media Education Foundation). An interview with Mary Pipher, the author of the best-selling book of the same title, discusses the challenges facing today's teens, especially girls. Clips from *Clueless, Buffy the Vampire Slayer,* and magazine and TV ads show the role of media and popular culture in shaping their image of their bodies and self-worth.

Rights from the Heart, Part 3 (National Film Board of Canada). A collection of seven animated shorts from around the world covering various aspects of human rights, including child labor abuse and loss of innocence.

Veronica's Story (University of California Extension, Center for Media & Independent Learning). In this visually stunning and powerful short film, Veronica writes poignantly of trying to reach out to her uncaring mother and of being attacked by her mother's boyfriend.

SOURCE: ALA Young Adult Library Services Association.

CHILDREN'S
MATERIALS

Nasty as they want to be

by Tanya Elder

HAVE YOU EVER HAD A BAD DAY? Have you ever wanted to throttle someone? Kids have bad days also. Fights on the playground, arguments with brothers and sisters, everyday pressures. They suffer as much as we do. But sometimes, like adults, kids are nasty just to be nasty. They talk back, confront you, and in our branch, get into yelling matches with each other (and sometimes the staff). This takes its toll upon the overstressed librarian. One

day, I was in the children's room by myself, with (it seemed) hundreds of kids. I asked them to be quiet. And of course, they were, for a split second. I guess I was having a bad day, and when the noise welled up again, I lost it. And I wound up kicking everyone out.

Now, when I first started, I looked down upon the idea of kicking kids out. "Where would they go?" "They won't come back." "They will think I'm mean." But after talking to several seasoned librarians, I have found that sometimes getting kids out of the library when behavior is out of control is the only solution. Usually the rule is that you warn two to three times, and if the behavior has not changed, out they go. Always, however, say, "Let's try again tomorrow." You may get parents who do not appreciate this at times, but when parents come in, talk gently to them, and explain to them why their child has been kicked out. Most parents are on your side. They do not want their kids acting up. I try and keep lots of open communication between the parents and myself, but to tell you truthfully, you may not see many parents.

I will admit that I have occasionally been nasty to some of my kids. It's never been intentional on my part, but a reaction to something they have said, their behavior, or attitude. I must explain what I mean by nasty. Often, in my mind, stern and nasty can be synonymous. I am not accustomed to being stern. So my mind automatically associates stern as in the above definition as "sharply unpleasant." I *feel* a sharp, unpleasant pain every time I firmly demand that a child sit down because he's acting up. At the same time, I *feel* a "sharply unpleasant" pain every time that child acts up.

Do not go overboard in your firmness. The library is still that place of wonderful imagination. Imagination does not flow freely under pressure. It's not easy to avoid going overboard. With all the pressures from children, other staff, administration, and the public, it's easy to shut down. I recommend that children's librarians take a couple of days off every three months. (I don't know if your branch system will allow this, but I find it helpful.) You have to get away from the stress. You have to energize your quickly depleted batteries so that new ideas will be able to flow. You must avoid burnout. I do not have statistics to prove this, but I have heard that there is a high percentage of turnover of children's librarians who suffer from burnout. Here are some other stresses that make your job delightful.

Stress, stress, stress

There are many false assumptions about the profession of librarianship. These assumptions range from "the job is easy" to "they only read books all day." But on the whole, children's librarians have many duties. We weed collections, conduct storytimes, order books, make signs, organize and maintain displays, and straighten books. We manage our room, evaluate the impact of our programs, actively participate in community outreach, assist teachers with their curriculum, fill out reports, and handle latchkey children. Oh, and we answer reference questions.

One of the problems that I find is that when you are in a two-librarian agency, every time you start concentrated work on a project, someone takes that moment to ask a reference question. While this is part of my job, it does break up the consistency of work. And if you wind up as the branch supervisor when she\he is on vacation, your reference and work load has doubled. Let's now explore three additional pressures that are added to the job.

The numbers game

Imagine it's your first summer reading program, and you are asked by administration to double your branch's number of kids from the previous summer. The previous summer there were 250 kids signed up for the program, and so far, you already have 375 signed at the end of July. You think this is pretty good, but you are asked to sign up at least 200 more children by the middle of August.

Imagine your circulation has risen by 20% in the six months you have been at the branch. You are asked to raise it an additional 35%.

Imagine you conduct 10–15 preschool and school-aged storytimes per month for an approximate total of 200–300 children. Can you physically raise that number to a steady twenty storytimes per month, if asked? Numbers, numbers, numbers. Without numbers, libraries do not get money, so the higher the number of children participating, joining, and checking out is calculated directly into cold, hard cash. Of course, if you have a high number of children participating, joining, and checking out, you must be doing something good!

The productivity game

Programs, storytimes, reference, reports, and summer reading programs. These do not sound like much, when compared with high-pressure corporate jobs, but combined, these pressures can take their toll. Most branches in Philadelphia have two librarians, a circulation staff of between three to five, and one guard. Unless you are highly organized (and organization is not my forte), work tends to pile up. And don't forget that those reference questions can take you away from other work for anywhere from 30 seconds to 20 minutes.

Follow the librarian

It's 2:45, and you know that in 15 minutes you will be overwhelmed by the 3:00 crowd. You have gotten all of your work out of the way and are prepared to tackle the onslaught. Children come barreling in. You ask them how was their day, and they tell you about who pushed who in the lunchroom, or what they learned in math. More kids come in. Then more. Let's play a little game. It's called "Follow the Librarian." Because you are the only one on the children's side, if people don't follow you, many times you can lose track of them.

Not all of those who are following you need information. A group of children can be following you for any number of reasons, including: " She hit me," "How do you spell 'degree'?" "The computer's not working," and "Can you help me with my homework?" In light of the fact that you are being bombarded at this moment, it's usually the time when a fight, argument, or mass running around happens.

A great book under 50 pages

As a librarian, you hope to pass on your love of the written word to others. With some kids, you can pull out any book from the shelves that *you* like, and some kid will at least try it. But others may not be good readers, or do not like to read. Still others expect and demand that you find the "World's Greatest Novel," as long as it's under 50 pages. Many times, kids ask for paperbacks that are thin because the book report is due tomorrow and they are just now getting around to doing it.

A little added note: There are many children who would like you to do their homework for them. For example, they have a project due on Brazil. You look at the assignment sheet, and realize that all the information can be found in the *World Book Encyclopedia* or *Information Please Almanac*. So you pull these out, show them where the information is, and ask them if this is what they are looking for. They say yes. The child comes up to you five minutes later and asks you what the capital of Brazil is. You point to the spot where the print says "Capital." Five minutes later, the same child comes up to you and asks what the population of Brazil is. You point to the print that says "Population," and so forth, and so on.

Doing the work of eleven

In the heyday of West Oak Lane, there were three librarians and a support staff of eleven. Hours of operation were longer, but each librarian had specific duties. Now there are only two librarians and a support staff of five. If you are working in a large branch system, you too may find yourself doing a double work load. So if you feel that your work never ends, don't worry, the summer reading program is just around the corner.

In a large branch system, you may not get an enormous amount of support from the central offices. And sometimes, you feel as if you are all alone. My branch supervisor once told me something that I feel is apropos. Sometimes you feel as if you are a mom-and-pop neighborhood convenience store, a lone building on a dark corner, just trying to survive and make a little profit.

4

Alchemy

In my short career as a children's librarian, I have found that I have had to calm my state of mind, overcome my sense of sadness regarding today's youth, and constantly renew my sense of challenge and optimism. It's not easy, but sometimes, events happen that make the salad really tasty.

Alchemy is the process of turning lead into gold. Parents, teachers, librarians, social workers, foster parents, and others are in the business of turning the basic lead of a child into dazzling gold. The influence and impact of children's librarians on children are tremendous. We have a role to play like that of no other social institution. We have the power to open, explore, and expand the imagination.

"Peter King" is a child that comes into my branch frequently. Peter is constantly disruptive, ill-mannered, and impertinent, however, he is incredibly intelligent. I have had to kick Peter out more times than I can count. One day I asked Peter why he was so rude. He told me he was disruptive because he needed "a good beating and no one was around to do it." He went on to tell me that his father had died two years before, and he and his sister were being raised by their mother. I told him I wouldn't give him the "good beating he deserved," but if we started to work together things could be different.

Peter is one of those kids who has to have a report sent home about his behavior and work habits every day. His grades in these two areas were consistent C's (except for one day when he erased a D he had gotten and substituted an A in its place). One day, Peter checked out *Willie Wonka and the Chocolate Factory*. I told him it had been one of my favorite movies growing up. When he came back into the branch the next day, I asked him how he liked the movie. He said it was great but he didn't understand why Willie Wonka gave Charlie the chocolate factory after he messed up. I told him Charlie had had the courage to admit his wrong to Wonka and give back the Everlasting Gobstopper. We then went on to a discussion about some people getting along better in life by being truthful and good, and such. Peter came into the library about four days afterward and proudly showed me his behavior report. The preceding four days were all marked with B's or B-pluses for behavior and work habits. I didn't ask if Willie Wonka had anything to do with it, and I've had to kick Peter out a few times since then, but who knows? Maybe the process of alchemy has begun.

SOURCE: Tanya Elder, "Hip v. Nice v. Traditional v. Nasty v. Aaaarrrggghhh!" in Teresa Y. Neely and Khafre K. Abif, eds., *In Our Own Voices: The Changing Face of Librarianship* (Lanham, Md.: Scarecrow Press, 1996), pp. 282–304. Reprinted with permission.

Programs for babies

by Kathleen M. Flatow

SINCE CHILDREN'S SERVICES were introduced in American public libraries in the 1890s, services extended to this segment of the population have continuously increased. Now, 100 years later, children's services are an important part of library operations and a new trend is developing. That trend is the extension of public library services to the youngest members of the community—babies.

Increasingly, libraries are offering programs that focus on children two years of age or younger. It is happening locally, nationally and even internationally as libraries expand services to their youngest customers. Programs take various forms, too. They include packets for newborns and their parents, lapsit and storytime programs, reading programs, bibliographies (a form of reader's services for the very young) and educational programs for parents that will ultimately benefit their babies.

Libraries are focusing on this age group for a number of reasons. First of all, it is good public relations for the library. Second, some maintain that such programs promote literacy, help develop reading skills and encourage a love of reading that the child will carry with him or her through life. Finally, these programs are said to promote the general welfare of the community as a whole by reaching underserved populations, such as teenage parents, and teaching them nurturing skills that directly benefit their babies.

Whatever the reason, many libraries are embracing these "baby" programs. However, many other libraries still do not offer children's programs to those under the age of two, although such programming may be under consideration. Recently, I called the children's departments of 21 libraries in the north

and northwest suburbs of Chicago to find out if they offered any programming for this age group. Of these libraries, 12 offered some sort of programming for the very young. These programs ranged from "Teddy Bear Time" for infants to two-and-a-half-year-olds at Park Ridge Public Library, to infant inclusion in family storytimes at various other libraries. Babies are welcome to participate in the "Read to Me" program at Indian Trails Library and to attend drop-in craft programs at quite a few libraries. Attendance with a caregiver, usually a parent, is always mandatory. Of those libraries that offer a lapsit-type program on a regular basis, the most popular program appeared to be one called "First Step" offered once a month. Arlington Heights, Fremont, and Highland Park libraries all offer this lapsit program with age of entry beginning at 12 or 18 months, depending on the library. Very few libraries I contacted offered a structured program for babies under the age of 12 months.

In 21 contacts, I only encountered one negative reaction to the idea of programs for children under the age of two, and that may have just been a personal opinion and not the library's official stand. That librarian said that even two-year-olds do not sit still, and she could not see the point of programming for those under this age. Contrary to this attitude, most libraries stressed that even if they do not have formal programming for babies, they try to make their children's areas "baby friendly" with puzzles and plenty of board books.

In addition, other libraries do offer packets to parents of newborns. Highland Park Library does this with its "Welcome to the World" packet, which is distributed to newborns and their parents at Highland Park Hospital. The packet includes information about the library, a board book, and simple puzzles.

Some libraries in this group also offer occasional programming aimed at providing a positive library experience for the baby or toddler and his or her caregiver. These programs include songs, stories, fingerplays, and simple activities that the child and parent can do together.

Overall, I was impressed by the enthusiasm expressed by the librarians I talked to. A librarian at Cook Memorial Library noted that they got requests for programs for this age group all the time and are evaluating the possibility of adding such programs in response to this demand. Grayslake Library noted that they are contemplating a program that encourages parents to register their babies and toddlers for library cards. They hope to stimulate interest in the program by offering a free board book for those who register. Baby programs are a service that's in demand, as noted by a librarian at Barrington Area Public Library, which offered its first lapsit programming in 1997.

Public library programming for babies is popular and seems to fit a need in many communities. As a public-relations tool, these programs bring people into the library where they can become aware of the many services the public library has to offer parents as well as the children who are the initial focus of the programs. Whether the program is a lapsit storytime, a gift packet for newborns and their parents, or something as passive as a bibliography of library board books, it is a way for the library to open its doors to people who might otherwise be unaware of all the services libraries offer. Promoting reading and literacy is an important goal, and baby programs may be one way libraries can instill a love of reading in our children. This cannot be measured in any objective way, but it is an admirable goal. More significantly, though, these programs can help to bring whole families into the library. They help them to connect with other families and community resources, and they bring them into the library to introduce them to the wealth of resources and information the public library can offer.

SOURCE: Kathleen M. Flatow, "Programs for Babies in Public Libraries," *Illinois Libraries* 79 (Summer 1997): 107–9. Reprinted with permission.

Newbery Medal winners

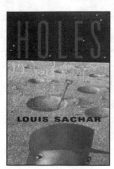

THE NEWBERY MEDAL, named for 18th-century British bookseller John Newbery, is awarded annually by the ALA Association for Library Service to Children to the author of the most distinguished contribution to American literature for children. Here are the award winners since the award's inception in 1922.

1999—Louis Sachar, *Holes* (Farrar Straus Giroux, 1998)
1998—Karen Hesse, *Out of the Dust* (Scholastic, 1997).
1997—E. L. Konigsburg, *The View from Saturday* (Jean Karl/ Atheneum, 1996).
1996—Karen Cushman, *The Midwife's Apprentice* (Clarion, 1995).
1995—Sharon Creech, *Walk Two Moons* (HarperCollins, 1994).
1994—Lois Lowry, *The Giver* (Houghton, 1993).
1993—Cynthia Rylant, *Missing May* (Jackson/Orchard, 1992).
1992—Phyllis Reynolds Naylor, *Shiloh* (Atheneum, 1991).
1991—Jerry Spinelli, *Maniac Magee* (Little, Brown, 1990).

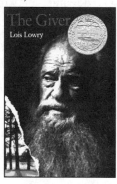

1990—Lois Lowry, *Number the Stars* (Houghton, 1989).
1989—Paul Fleischman, *Joyful Noise: Poems for Two Voices* (Harper, 1988).
1988—Russell Freedman, *Lincoln: A Photobiography* (Clarion, 1987).
1987—Sid Fleischman, *The Whipping Boy* (Greenwillow, 1986).
1986—Patricia MacLachlan, *Sarah, Plain and Tall* (Harper, 1985).
1985—Robin McKinley, *The Hero and the Crown* (Greenwillow, 1984).
1984—Beverly Cleary, *Dear Mr. Henshaw* (Morrow, 1983).
1983—Cynthia Voigt, *Dicey's Song* (Atheneum, 1982).
1982—Nancy Willard, *A Visit to William Blake's Inn: Poems for Innocent and Experienced Travelers* (Harcourt, 1981).
1981—Katherine Paterson, *Jacob Have I Loved* (Crowell, 1980).
1980—Joan W. Blos, *A Gathering of Days: A New England Girl's Journal, 1830–1832* (Scribner, 1979).
1979—Ellen Raskin, *The Westing Game* (Dutton, 1978).
1978—Katherine Paterson, *Bridge to Terabithia* (Crowell, 1977).
1977—Mildred D. Taylor, *Roll of Thunder, Hear My Cry* (Dial, 1976).
1976—Susan Cooper, *The Grey King* (McElderry/Atheneum, 1975).
1975—Virginia Hamilton, *M. C. Higgins, the Great* (Macmillan, 1974).
1974—Paula Fox, *The Slave Dancer* (Bradbury, 1973).
1973—Jean Craighead George, *Julie of the Wolves* (Harper, 1972).
1972—Robert C. O'Brien, *Mrs. Frisby and the Rats of NIMH* (Atheneum, 1971).
1971—Betsy Byars, *Summer of the Swans* (Viking, 1970).
1970—William H. Armstrong, *Sounder* (Harper, 1969).
1969—Lloyd Alexander, *The High King* (Holt, 1968).
1968—E. L. Konigsburg, *From the Mixed-Up Files of Mrs. Basil E. Frankweiler* (Atheneum, 1967).
1967—Irene Hunt, *Up a Road Slowly* (Follett, 1966).

1966—Elizabeth Borton de Trevino, *I, Juan de Pareja* (Farrar, 1965).
1965—Maia Wojciechowska, *Shadow of a Bull* (Atheneum, 1964).
1964—Emily Neville, *It's Like This, Cat* (Harper, 1963).
1963—Madeleine L'Engle, *A Wrinkle in Time* (Farrar, 1962).
1962—Elizabeth George Speare, *The Bronze Bow* (Houghton, 1961).
1961—Scott O'Dell, *Island of the Blue Dolphins* (Houghton, 1960).
1960—Joseph Krumgold, *Onion John* (Crowell, 1959).
1959—Elizabeth George Speare, *The Witch of Blackbird Pond* (Houghton, 1958).
1958—Harold Keith, *Rifles for Watie* (Crowell, 1957).
1957—Virginia Sorenson, *Miracles on Maple Hill* (Harcourt, 1956).
1956—Jean Lee Latham, *Carry On, Mr. Bowditch* (Houghton, 1955).
1955—Meindert DeJong, *The Wheel on the School* (Harper, 1954).
1954—Joseph Krumgold, *. . . And Now Miguel* (Crowell, 1953).
1953—Ann Nolan Clark, *Secret of the Andes* (Viking, 1952).
1952—Eleanor Estes, *Ginger Pye* (Harcourt, 1951).
1951—Elizabeth Yates, *Amos Fortune, Free Man* (Dutton, 1950).
1950—Marguerite de Angeli, *The Door in the Wall* (Doubleday, 1949).
1949—Marguerite Henry, *King of the Wind* (Rand McNally, 1948).
1948—William Pène du Bois, *The Twenty-One Balloons* (Viking, 1947).
1947—Carolyn Sherwin Bailey, *Miss Hickory* (Viking, 1946).
1946—Lois Lenski, *Strawberry Girl* (Lippincott, 1945).
1945—Robert Lawson, *Rabbit Hill* (Viking, 1944).
1944—Esther Forbes, *Johnny Tremain* (Houghton, 1943).
1943—Elizabeth Janet Gray, *Adam of the Road* (Viking, 1942).
1942—Walter Edmonds, *The Matchlock Gun* (Dodd, 1941).
1941—Armstrong Sperry, *Call It Courage* (Macmillan, 1940).
1940—James Daugherty, *Daniel Boone* (Viking, 1939).
1939—Elizabeth Enright, *Thimble Summer* (Rinehart, 1938).
1938—Kate Seredy, *The White Stag* (Viking, 1937).
1937—Ruth Sawyer, *Roller Skates* (Viking, 1936).
1936—Carol Ryrie Brink, *Caddie Woodlawn* (Macmillan, 1935).
1935—Monica Shannon, *Dobry* (Viking, 1934).
1934—Cornelia Meigs, *Invincible Louisa: The Story of the Author of Little Women* (Little, Brown, 1933).
1933—Elizabeth Lewis, *Young Fu of the Upper Yangtze* (Winston, 1932).
1932—Laura Adams Armer, *Waterless Mountain* (Longmans, 1931).
1931—Elizabeth Coatsworth, *The Cat Who Went to Heaven* (Macmillan, 1930).
1930—Rachel Field, *Hitty, Her First Hundred Years* (Macmillan, 1929).
1929—Eric P. Kelly, *The Trumpeter of Krakow* (Macmillan, 1928).
1928—Dhan Gopal Mukerji, *Gay Neck, the Story of a Pigeon* (Dutton, 1927).
1927—Will James, *Smoky, the Cowhorse* (Scribner, 1926).
1926—Arthur Bowie Chrisman, *Shen of the Sea* (Dutton, 1925).
1925—Charles Finger, *Tales from Silver Lands* (Doubleday, 1924).
1924—Charles Hawes, *The Dark Frigate* (Atlantic/Little, 1923).
1923—Hugh Lofting, *The Voyages of Doctor Dolittle* (Lippincott, 1922).
1922—Hendrik Willem van Loon, *The Story of Mankind* (Liveright, 1921).

SOURCE: ALA Association for Library Service to Children.

Caldecott Medal winners

SNOWFLAKE BENTLEY

Jacqueline Briggs Martin *Illustrated by* Mary Azarian

THE CALDECOTT MEDAL, named in honor of 19th-century English illustrator Randolph Caldecott, is awarded annually by the ALA Association for Library Service to Children to the artist of the most distinguished American picture book for children. Here are the award winners since the award's inception in 1938.

1999—Jacqueline Briggs Martin, *Snowflake Bentley* (Houghton Mifflin, 1998); illustrated by Mary Azarian.

1998—Paul O. Zelinsky, *Rapunzel* (Dutton, 1997).

1997—David Wisniewski, *Golem* (Clarion, 1996).

1996—Peggy Rathmann, *Officer Buckle and Gloria* (Putnam, 1995).

1995—Eve Bunting, *Smoky Night* (Harcourt, 1994); illustrated by David Diaz.

1994—Allen Say, *Grandfather's Journey* (Harcourt, 1993).

1993—Emily Arnold McCully, *Mirette on the High Wire* (Putnam, 1992).

1992—David Wiesner, *Tuesday* (Clarion, 1991).

1991—David Macaulay, *Black and White* (Houghton, 1990).

1990—Ed Young, *Lon Po Po: A Red-Riding Hood Story from China* (Philomel, 1989).

1989—Karen Ackerman, *Song and Dance Man* (Knopf, 1988); illustrated by Stephen Gammell.

1988—Jane Yolen, *Owl Moon* (Philomel, 1987); illustrated by John Schoenherr.

1987—Arthur Yorinks, *Hey, Al* (Farrar, 1986); illustrated by Richard Egielski.

1986—Chris Van Allsburg, *The Polar Express* (Houghton, 1985).

1985—Margaret Hodges, *Saint George and the Dragon* (Little, Brown, 1984); illustrated by Trina Schart Hyman.

1984—Alice and Martin Provensen, *The Glorious Flight: Across the Channel with Louis Bleriot* (Viking, 1983).

1983—Blaise Cendrars, *Shadow* (Scribner, 1982); illustrated by Marcia Brown.

1982—Chris Van Allsburg, *Jumanji* (Houghton, 1981).

1981—Arnold Lobel, *Fables* (Harper, 1980).

1980—Donald Hall, *Ox-Cart Man* (Viking, 1979); illustrated by Barbara Cooney.

1979—Paul Goble, *The Girl Who Loved Wild Horses* (Bradbury, 1978).

1978—Peter Spier, *Noah's Ark* (Doubleday, 1977).

1977—Margaret Musgrove, *Ashanti to Zulu: African Traditions* (Dial, 1976); illustrated by Leo and Diane Dillon.

1976—Verna Aardema, *Why Mosquitoes Buzz in People's Ears* (Dial, 1975); illustrated by Leo and Diane Dillon.

1975—Gerald McDermott, *Arrow to the Sun* (Viking, 1974).

1974—Harve Zemach, *Duffy and the Devil* (Farrar, 1973); illustrated by Margot Zemach.

1973—Lafcadio Hearn, retold by Arlene Mosel, *The Funny Little Woman* (Dutton, 1972); illustrated by Blair Lent.

1972—Nonny Hogrogian, *One Fine Day* (Macmillan, 1971).

1971—Gail E. Haley, *A Story A Story* (Atheneum, 1970).

1970—William Steig, *Sylvester and the Magic Pebble* (Windmill, 1969).

1969—Arthur Ransome, *The Fool of the World and the Flying Ship* (Farrar, 1968); illustrated by Uri Shulevitz.

1968—Barbara Emberley, *Drummer Hoff* (Prentice-Hall, 1967); illustrated by Ed Emberley.

1967—Evaline Ness, *Sam, Bangs & Moonshine* (Holt, 1966).

1966—Sorche Nic Leodhas, pseud. [Leclair Alger], *Always Room for One More* (Holt, 1965); illustrated by Nonny Hogrogian.

1965—Beatrice Schenk de Regniers, *May I Bring a Friend?* (Atheneum, 1964); illustrated by Beni Montresor.

1964—Maurice Sendak, *Where the Wild Things Are* (Harper, 1963).

1963—Ezra Jack Keats, *The Snowy Day* (Viking, 1962).

1962—Marcia Brown, *Once a Mouse* (Scribner, 1961).

1961—Ruth Robbins, *Baboushka and the Three Kings* (Parnassus, 1960); illustrated by Nicolas Sidjakov.

1960—Marie Hall Ets and Aurora Labastida, *Nine Days to Christmas* (Viking, 1959); illustrated by Marie Hall Ets.

1959—Barbara Cooney, *Chanticleer and the Fox* (Crowell, 1958).

1958—Robert McCloskey, *Time of Wonder* (Viking, 1957).

1957—Janice Udry, *A Tree Is Nice* (Harper, 1956); illustrated by Marc Simont.

1956—John Langstaff, *Frog Went A-Courtin'* (Harcourt, 1955); illustrated by Feodor Rojankovsky.

1955— Charles Perrault, *Cinderella, or the Little Glass Slipper* (Scribner, 1954); illustrated by Marcia Brown.

1954—Ludwig Bemelmans, *Madeline's Rescue* (Viking, 1953).

1953—Lynd Ward, *The Biggest Bear* (Houghton, 1952.)

1952—Will, pseud. [William Lipkind], *Finders Keepers* (Harcourt, 1951); illustrated by Nicolas, pseud. [Nicholas Mordvinoff].

1951—Katherine Milhous, *The Egg Tree* (Scribner, 1950).

1950—Leo Politi, *Song of the Swallows* (Scribner, 1949).

1949—Berta and Elmer Hader, *The Big Snow* (Macmillan, 1948).

1948—Alvin Tresselt, *White Snow, Bright Snow* (Lothrop, 1947); illustrated by Roger Duvoisin.

1947—Golden MacDonald, pseud. [Margaret Wise Brown], *The Little Island* (Doubleday, 1946); illustrated by Leonard Weisgard.

1946—Maude and Miska Petersham, *The Rooster Crows* (Macmillan, 1945).

1945—Rachel Field, *Prayer for a Child* (Macmillan, 1944); illustrated by Elizabeth Orton Jones.

1944— James Thurber, *Many Moons* (Harcourt, 1943); illustrated by Louis Slobodkin.

1943—Virginia Lee Burton, *The Little House* (Houghton, 1942).

1942—Robert McCloskey, *Make Way for Ducklings* (Viking, 1941).

1941—Robert Lawson, *They Were Strong and Good* (Viking, 1940).

1940—Ingri and Edgar Parin d'Aulaire, *Abraham Lincoln* (Doubleday, 1939).

1939—Thomas Handforth, *Mei Li* (Doubleday, 1938).

1938—Helen Dean Fish, *Animals of the Bible: A Picture Book* (Lippincott, 1937); illustrated by Dorothy P. Lathrop.

SOURCE: ALA Association for Library Service to Children.

Batchelder Award winners

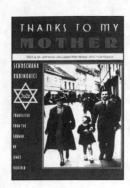

THE MILDRED L. BATCHELDER AWARD is given each year to an American publisher for the most outstanding children's book originally published in a foreign language or in another country. The ALA Association for Library Service to Children gives the award to encourage American publishers to seek out superior children's books abroad and to promote communication between the peoples of the world. The award is named for Mildred L. Batchelder, a children's librarian whose work over three decades has had an international influence. Here are the award winners since the award's inception in 1968.

1999—Schoschana Rabinovici, *Thanks to My Mother* (Dial, 1998); translated from the German by James Skofield.

1998—Josef Holub, *The Robber and Me* (Henry Holt, 1996); edited by Mark Aronson and translated from the German by Elizabeth D. Crawford.

1997—Kazumi Yumoto, *The Friends* (Farrar Straus Giroux, 1996); translated from the Japanese by Cathy Hirano.

1996—Uri Orlev, *The Lady with the Hat* (Houghton, 1995); translated from Hebrew by Hillel Halkin.

1995—Bjarne Reuter, *The Boys from St. Petri* (Dutton, 1994); translated from Danish by Anthea Bell.

1994—Pilar Molina Llorente, *The Apprentice* (Farrar, Straus and Giroux, 1993); translated by Robin Longshaw.

1993—no award presented.

1992—Uri Orlev, *The Man from the Other Side* (Houghton Mifflin, 1991); translated from the Hebrew by Hillel Halkin.

1991—Rafik Schami, A *Hand Full of Stars* (Dutton, 1990); translated from the German by Rika Lesser.

1990—Bjarne Reuter, *Buster's World* (Dutton, 1989); translated from the Danish by Anthea Bell.

1989—Peter Härtling, *Crutches* (Lothrop, 1988); translated from the German by Elizabeth D. Crawford.

1988—Ulf Nilsson, If *You Didn't Have Me* (McElderry, 1987); translated from the Swedish by George Blecher and Lone Thygesen-Blecher.

1987—Rudolph Frank, *No Hero for the Kaiser* (Lothrop, 1986); translated from the German by Patricia Crampton.

1986—Christophe Gallaz and Roberto Innocenti, *Rose Blanche* (Creative Education, 1986); translated from the French by Martha Coventry and Richard Graglia.

1985—Uri Orlev, *The Island on Bird Street* (Houghton, 1984); translated from the Hebrew by Hillel Halkin.

1984—Astrid Lindgren, *Ronia, the Robber's Daughter* (Viking, 1983); translated from the Swedish by Patricia Crampton.

1983—Toshi Maruki, *Hiroshima No Pika* (Lothrop, 1982); translated from the Japanese through the Kurita-Bando Literary Agency.

1982—Harry Kullman Jr., *The Battle Horse* (Bradbury, 1981); translated from the Swedish by George Blecher and Lone Thygesen-Blecher.

1981—Els Pelgrom, *The Winter When Time Was Frozen* (Morrow, 1980); translated from Dutch by Maryka and Raphael Rudnik.

1980—Alki Zei, *The Sound of the Dragon's Feet* (Dutton, 1979); translated from the Greek by Edward Fenton.

1979—Two awards: Jörg Steiner, *Rabbit Island* (Harcourt, 1978); translated from the German by Ann Conrad Lammers. Christine Nöstlinger, *Konrad* (Watts, 1977); translated from the German by Anthea Bell.

1978—no award presented.

1977—Cecil Bødker, *The Leopard* (Atheneum, 1977); translated from the Danish by Gunnar Poulsen.

1976—Ruth Hürlimann,The *Cat and the Mouse Who Shared a House* (Walck, 1974); translated from the German by Anthea Bell.

1975—Aleksandr Linevskii, *An Old Tale Carved out of Stone* (Crown, 1973); translated from the Russian by Maria Polushkin.

1974—Alki Zei, *Petros' War* (Dutton, 1972); translated from the Greek by Edward Fenton.

1973—S. R. van Iterson, *Pulga* (Morrow, 1971); translated from the Dutch by Alexander and Alison Gode.

1972—Hans Peter Richter, *Friedrich* (Holt, 1970); translated from the German by Edite Kroll.

1971—Hans Baumann, *In the Land of Ur: The Discovery of Ancient Mesopotamia* (Pantheon, 1969); translated from the German by Stella Humphries.

1970—Alki Zei, *Wildcat under Glass* (Holt, 1968); translated from the Greek by Edward Fenton.

1969—Babbis Friis-Baastad, *Don't Take Teddy* (Scribner, 1967); translated from the Norwegian by Lise Sømme McKinnon.

1968—Erich Kästner, *The Little Man* (Knopf, 1966); translated from the German by James Kirkup.

SOURCE: ALA Association for Library Service to Children.

Top ten children's books featuring libraries or librarians

by Norman D. Stevens

THERE ARE NOW WELL OVER 100 children's books that feature libraries or librarians, many of them of relatively recent origin. Some are excellent, most are reasonably good, and a few are mediocre. In "Books about Us for Kids," *American Libraries* 27 (October 1996): 52–53, I commented on a number of those books, especially in the context of our image, stereotypical portrayals, and related issues. There are now, fortunately, a considerable number of books that present our profession in its best light. These are my 10 favorite picture books.

1. Cari Best, *Red Light, Green Light, Mama and Me* (Orchard, 1995). Niki Daly, illus. A charming presentation of a young girl accompanying her mother to her work at a large public library, this is an excellent introduction to the idea of librarianship as a rewarding career. This is a great recruiting tool. Catch them young!

2. Barbara Cooney, *Miss Rumphius* (Viking, 1982). Miss

Rumphius is an attractive spinster librarian—without glasses—who helps people find the books they want, travels to exotic places, but finds fame by planting lupines everywhere to make the world more beautiful. Librarians can make an impact in many ways.

3. Carmen Agra Deedy, *The Library Dragon* (Peachtree, 1994). Michael P. White, illus. Miss Lotta Scales, a real library dragon with blue plastic glasses covered with rhinestones, is hired by a school library to reduce inventory damage and loss. Miss Scales terrifies everyone as she keeps *her* books on the shelves in pristine condition. A near-sighted student penetrates and finally turns Miss Scales back into a real, and welcoming, librarian. Even the fiercest of librarians may have a warm heart.

4. Jo Furtado, *Sorry Miss Folio!* (Kane/Miller, 1992). Frédéric Joos, illus. Miss Folio, a modern librarian with wire-rim glasses, has to put up with a year of monthly excuses from a young boy who hasn't returned his library book. In a happy ending the book is wrapped up and delivered to her as a Christmas present from Santa Claus. Librarians have to be patient and forgiving.

5. Nancy Smiler Levinson, *Clara and the Bookwagon* (Harper & Row, 1988). Carolyn Croll, illus. One of the few children's books that deal with library history, this a fictional account of Mary Titcomb and America's first traveling bookwagon in Hagerstown, Maryland. This is a reminder of the measures librarians have had to take to make sure that books are available to everyone.

6. Pat Mora, *Tomás and the Library Lady* (Knopf, 1997). Raul Colón, illus. This is the true story of how a welcoming librarian in Iowa introduced a migrant Mexican family's son, Tomás Rivera (who went on to become chancellor of the University of California at Riverside), to the world of books, reading, and libraries. Best of all, there is also a Spanish edition, *Tomás y la Señora de la Biblioteca*. Librarians with a positive attitude can have a real impact on the life of a patron.

7. Ann Sanders, *The Library Mice* (Ariel, 1962). Eugene Fern, illus. What would a library be without mice and a cat? This is a retelling of the fable of belling the cat to create a "world [library] in which mice can be free!" Preservation librarians and library cats may object to that premise, but I like the mice. Books can be fun to read even when they don't have a message.

8. Sarah Stewart, *The Library* (Farrar Straus Giroux, 1995). David Small, illus. Elizabeth Brown is such a voracious reader and an accumulator of books, that eventually she has to open her own public library. This positive portrayal of another spinster librarian also reflects the way in which a number of public libraries came into existence. A positive image plus some history make it a winner.

9. Colin Thompson, *How to Live Forever* (Knopf, 1996). Peter and his cat Brian search an enormous library at night for the book called *How to Live Forever*. What they discover, as they wander past thousands of books, is that, like Midas, you don't necessarily want what you ask for. The wonderful images of books, and of buildings and other objects made of books, make Thompson's work a visual pleasure.

10. Suzanne Williams, *Library Lil* (Dial, 1997). Steven Kellogg, illus. An avid reader from the day she was born,

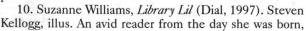

Lil grows up to be a librarian who, when there is a power failure, converts the whole town to library users. Then she puts down Bust-'em Up Bill, and his motorcycle gang, and enlists them as library helpers. A powerful woman, not a 90-pound weakling, Lil demonstrates that librarianship is indeed made up of "a thousand disparate dazzlers." This is another excellent recruiting tool.

SOURCE: Special report by Norman Stevens for *The Whole Library Handbook 3.*

YOUNG ADULT
MATERIALS

Top 10 best books for young adults, 1997–1999

4

EACH YEAR THE ALA Young Adult Library Services Association compiles a list of 10 titles that have potential appeal to young adults and exhibit either high literary standards or technical accuracy. The following list encompasses 30 titles from 1997–1999.

Bartoletti, Susan Campbell. *Growing Up in Coal Country* (Houghton Mifflin, 1996).

Bauer, Joan. *Rules of the Road* (Putnam, 1998).

Bernstein, Sara Tuvel. *Seamstress* (Putnam, 1997).

Bloor, Edward. *Tangerine* (Harcourt Brace, 1997).

Blum, Joshua, Bob Holman, and Mark Pellington. *The United States of Poetry* (Abrams, 1996).

Colman, Penny. *Corpses, Coffins, and Crypts* (Holt, 1997).

Cormier, Robert. *Tenderness* (Delacorte, 1997).

Farmer, Nancy. *A Girl Named Disaster* (Orchard, 1996).

Ferris, Jean. *Love Among the Walnuts* (Harcourt Brace, 1998).

Gilstrap, John. *Nathan's Run* (HarperCollins, 1996).

Glenn, Mel. *Who Killed Mr. Chippendale? A Mystery in Poems* (Lodestar, 1996).

Haddix, Margaret. *Among the Hidden* (Simon & Schuster, 1998).

Hesse, Karen. *Out of the Dust* (Scholastic, 1997).

Hobbs, Will. *Far North* (Morrow, 1996).

Holt, Kimberly Willis. *My Louisiana Sky* (Holt, 1998).

Klause, Annette Curtis. *Blood and Chocolate* (Bantam, 1997).

Krakauer, Jon. *Into Thin Air* (G. K. Hall, 1997).

Lobel, Anita. *No Pretty Pictures: A Child of War* (Greenwillow, 1998).

McDonald, Joyce. *Swallowing Stones* (Bantam, 1997).

Mikaelsen, Ben. *Petey* (Hyperion, 1998).

Myers, Walter Dean. *Harlem* (Scholastic, 1997).

Myers, Walter Dean. *One More River to Cross: An African American Photograph Album* (Harcourt Brace, 1995).

Pullman, Philip. *The Golden Compass* (Knopf, 1996).
Reynolds, Marjorie. *Starlite Drive-In* (Morrow, 1997).
Rowling, J. K. *Harry Potter and the Sorcerer's Stone* (Scholastic, 1998).
Sachar, Louis. *Holes* (Farrar Straus Giroux, 1998).
Thomas, Rob. *Rats Saw God* (Simon & Schuster, 1996).
Wallace, Rich. *Wrestling Sturbridge* (Knopf, 1996).
Wilkomirski, Binjamin. *Fragments* (Schocken, 1996).
Woodson, Jacqueline. *If You Come Softly* (Putnam, 1998).

SOURCE: ALA Young Adult Library Services Association.

Top 10 best books for reluctant readers, 1997–1999

WHAT BOOKS MAKE GREAT READING? Books with exciting stories and interesting characters—books about real-life heroes and fantastic adventures—books that tell you how to fix up your car and help you deal with day-to-day problems. The following books are recommended by the ALA Young Adult Library Services Association's Recommended Books for the Reluctant Young Adult Reader Committee for young adults who, for whatever reason, do not like to read. All titles are sixth-grade reading level or below, demonstrate simplicity of plot or organization of information, contain short sentences and short paragraphs, and have uncomplicated dialogue and vocabulary. The following list encompasses 30 titles from 1997–1999.

Alten, Steve. *Meg: A Novel of Deep Terror* (Doubleday, 1997).
Arnoldi, Katherine. *The Amazing "True" Story of a Teenage Single Mom* (Hyperion, 1998).
Bode, Janet, and Stanley Mack. *Hard Time: A Real Life Look at Juvenile Crime and Violence* (Delacorte, 1996).
Braillier, Jess M., and Planet Dexter, eds. *"Whaddaya Doin' in There?" A Bathroom Companion (for Kids)* (Penguin, 1996).
Coville, Bruce. *William Shakespeare's A Midsummer Night's Dream* (Dial, 1996).
Fogle, Bruce. *Dog Breed Handbook* Series (DK, 1996–97).
Fogle, Bruce. *Encyclopedia of the Cat* (DK, 1997).

Ganeri, Anita. *Inside the Body* (DK, 1996).
Greenfield, Lauren. *Fast Forward: Growing Up in the Shadow of Hollywood* (Knopf, 1997).
Hamilton, Jake. *Special Effects in Film and Television* (DK, 1998).
Hesser, Terry Spencer. *Kissing Doorknobs* (Delacorte, 1998).
Kehret, Peg. *Small Steps: The Year I Got Polio* (Whit-man, 1996).
King, Martin Luther Jr. and Coretta Scott King. *I Have a Dream* (Scholastic, 1997).
Klause, Annette Curtis. *Blood and Chocolate* (Bantam, 1997).
Lauber, Patricia. *Hurricanes: Earth's Mightiest Storms* (Scholastic, 1996).

Melton, H. Keith. *The Ultimate Spy Book* (DK, 1996).
Paulsen, Gary. *Brian's Winter* (Delacorte, 1996).
Pratt, Jane. *Beyond Beauty* (Clarkson Potter, 1997).
Reynolds, David West. *Star Wars: Incredible Cross-Sections* (DK, 1998).
Reynolds, David West. *Star Wars: The Visual Dictionary* (DK, 1998).
Shusterman, Neal. *Dark Side of Nowhere* (Little, Brown, 1997).
Silverstein, Shel. *Falling Up* (HarperCollins, 1996).
Sleator, William. *The Boxes* (Dutton, 1998).
Smith, Roland. *Sasquatch* (Hyperion, 1998).
Snedden, Robert. *Yuck! A Big Book of Little Horrors* (Simon & Schuster, 1996).
Soto, Gary. *Buried Onions* (Harcourt Brace, 1997).
Squires, K. M. *NSYNC: The Official Book* (Bantam Doubleday Dell, 1998).
Vande Velde, Vivian. *Curses, Inc.* (Harcourt Brace, 1997).
Werlin, Nancy. *The Killer's Cousin* (Delacorte, 1998).
Willson, Quentin. *Classic American Cars* (DK, 1997).

SOURCE: ALA Young Adult Library Services Association.

Starting a youth participation program

by Caroline A. Caywood

YOUNG ADULTS CAN DO MUCH MORE than most of us expect. They can select books, plan programs, tell stories, create policy. Few young adults, however, can do these things without preparation. Behind successful programs are supportive librarians who have recruited, trained, or assisted the young participants. If youth participation is to be successfully incorporated into libraries, adults and experienced youth must commit time, skill, and energy to making it work. Since all three are in short supply in most libraries, here are some ways in which those resources might best be invested.

Getting started

Over the years, many excellent youth programs have been stillborn or short-lived, while others have flourished. What makes the difference? The

National Commission on Resources for Youth, after observing the programs that seem to work best and listening to the experiences of program developers, has developed guidelines for planning new programs. Most of these guidelines are based on common sense—but experience tells us that the predictable hurdles and complications faced by all new programs can be minimizcd when common sense is used during project planning rather than after the fact. Involve young adults from the very beginning.

1. **Find out what already exists.** Perhaps other community agencies and schools are conducting youth participation programs. Be aware of the potential help or resistance other projects represent. Investigate the programs of the local schools, YM/YWCAs, recreation departments, or other agencies prior to developing a plan.

2. **Assess and define the need for the project.** Do a survey of how many people may need the planned service or opportunity and how many young adults (and adults) will participate. This information is helpful not only when planning the project, but also in convincing administrators to support it.

3. **Limit goals.** Be realistic. Can goals be accomplished within the time available? What staff and other resources will reliably be available? Too many programs begin with the intention of solving every problem in sight and deliver only a fraction of what was originally planned. It is preferable to start with fewer goals and expand gradually than to dream big and end small or extinct.

4. **When setting up a community project, ensure it is perceived appropriately by the community involved.** Whenever possible, members of the community should be involved in an advisory role from the beginning. In a library program, this might mean drawing advisors from the Friends of the Library, the trustees, volunteers, parents, or other interested patrons. In addition to engendering good public relations, this can be helpful in planning your project. You may learn of new resources, other projects, and people to assist you. You will also build a base of support for your project.

5. **Check out financial resources carefully.** Financial support takes work to obtain, but some librarians have received grants from private foundations or local businesses. Many are also ingenious in creating money-saving solutions. Existing delivery systems can be used to get youth-produced newsletters to local schools; vocational-school printing departments may print several thousand copies as part of their training. Even a physical setting can be created at low cost.

6. **After choosing specific goals, weigh all possible approaches.** Before deciding on exactly how to accomplish the project's goals, consider alternative possibilities. If youth are to be involved in producing a newsletter, will it include only book reviews, or poetry, or stories and news as well? How often will it be produced? Will it be topical or a more random collection? Will participants also investigate careers in writing or journalism? Interested or experienced young adults can contact existing advisory groups to compare how others have approached a project. Or they can simply provide their opinions. In any case, the advantages and disadvantages of each approach must be weighed before deciding on a plan, and the young adults who will be affected can be helpful in the process.

7. **Set up sound evaluation procedures.** Keep careful records of all par-

ticipants and activities, including formal and informal feedback from youth and adults who participate. Compare goals with actual accomplishments; are the goals being met? Evaluation can improve a program, demonstrate to administrators and community the effectiveness of the program, and help obtain additional financial support. Use of entertaining or moving quotes and anecdotes, appropriate photographs, and impressive statistics can be invaluable in public relations.

Recruitment

Many librarians say that an important first step in establishing youth participation is to create a young adult department that is comfortable and attractive to youth, with posters, magazines, recordings, computers, and comfortable furniture.

Incentives can also help in recruitment. Although they are unlikely to provide salaries or stipends, libraries can offer training, contact with community leaders, certificates of merit, school credit, or work experience that can be added to a resume. They can offer avid readers "first crack" at new books or a chance to help select those books; aspiring writers might get a chance to produce a newsletter.

It is essential that recruitment continue once the project is under way, so that the group will continue to expand and not remain limited to a few "stars." Turnover is inevitable, but ongoing recruitment ensures that new members continue to operate the project as older members leave. Plan programs for nonreaders as well as readers. Encouraging nonreaders to join the project can bring new and sometimes unusual ideas to group planning. Experienced teens can help to train new members: This "serial leadership" also enhances the self-esteem and reinforces the learning of the more experienced young adult.

Training

Training for *both* teens and adults is essential to the success of any library youth participation project. On a practical level, once you've assembled a group of interested young adults, you need to help them gain the skills necessary to the project's success. And you will also need to help other librarians and adult staff gain skills in working effectively with youth.

Training is also essential on a broader level. You may find both youth and adults resistant to or skeptical of the project. Despite their need for challenge and responsibility, many young adults believe that they are not capable of making real contributions and that, in any case, the library or the community will not respond to their efforts. Adults often share this skepticism. Information about successful youth participation programs may be useful in encouraging both groups.

The keys to training are: for adults, the knowledge of how young adults are best able to learn; for youth, the knowledge that they will be able to apply what they learn in real situations.

The first step in the training process is *orientation*. For the young adults involved, this means helping them understand the overall functions and services of the library, as well as how their effort will fit into the library's organization. Their collective responsibilities should be carefully defined, as well as overall goals and schedules for the project. This applies to project planning as well as implementation and evaluation.

Orientation for librarians and other adult staff should include a full explanation of the plans for a youth participation project. This will help staff members to understand what the young adults will be doing and what they, as adults, may be asked to do. Their suggestions and involvement may also prove useful and should be invited. In addition, an opportunity to talk with members of successful projects can be very useful. This kind of session could be offered at a citywide or regional librarian's meeting. Training for either group does not necessarily mean attending classes. Although some subjects may best be taught through formal lecture, most people learn by doing.

They can begin with defined tasks like writing short items for a newsletter, presenting a brief book review or doing research. They may need to learn, through practice and role-playing, how to conduct effective phone conversations or how to introduce a speaker. All jobs, no matter how basic, can provide learning opportunities and make valuable contributions to the project. Some formal learning may be needed, however, to help the group to improve communication and decision-making skills. The librarian shouldn't hesitate to call on experts to provide such training.

It is important that young adults do a wide variety of tasks and to move on to progressively more sophisticated tasks. Good work on basic tasks should be rewarded by more responsible and challenging assignments.

Similarly, taking young adults to conferences and library meetings gives them a first-hand view of the concerns and needs of libraries. With some advance planning, teenagers are usually welcome at local book review meetings, regional or state library association conferences, or issue-oriented workshops. Librarians can take an "over-the-shoulder" approach at such meetings, thinking out loud to explain to the youth why they make certain decisions or do things in certain ways. After the meeting, they can follow up by discussing with the teens what happened and why. These discussions can enhance the basic training the youth have received in decision-making or problem-solving skills. At the national level young adults are welcome to attend YALSA meetings and programs.

Some librarians find it more effective for young adults to discover their own strategies for setting goals, negotiating, or problem solving. They give teens total responsibility for some aspect of a project. Although they have adult support, the young adults must work out whatever problems arise. This approach requires restraint on the part of librarians or other adults, since there may be negative consequences if the young adults fail to take all contingencies into account. If young adults fail to confirm a workshop date with one of the speakers, for instance, that speaker may not show up.

In one library, young adults were completely responsible for the computer area. They wrote a proposal to the library board to get funding for computers. They decided on a policy and schedule for use. Young adults served as managers and were responsible for opening the area, locking it up, and for upkeep of the computers. They provided training and decided who could use the computers and with what amount of supervision. Theft or damage of the computers was also the youths' responsibility. The adults who worked with them, however, demonstrated their respect by refraining from intervention.

SOURCE: Caroline A. Caywood, ed., *Youth Participation in School and Public Libraries: It Works* (Chicago: ALA Young Adult Library Services Association, 1995), pp. 6–10.

OPERATIONS
CHAPTER FIVE

"The old man was peering intently at the shelves. 'I'll have to admit that he's a very competent scholar.'

'Isn't he just a librarian?' Garion asked, 'somebody who looks after books?'

'That's where all the rest of scholarship starts, Garion. All the books in the world won't help you if they're just piled up in a heap.'"

—David Eddings, *King of the Murgos* (1998)

BIBLIOGRAPHY

A protohistory of bibliography

by Bill Katz

BIBLIOGRAPHY IS A COMPARATIVELY RECENT reference tool. There is little sight of it until the 17th–18th centuries. At the same time, from the Romans through the Middle Ages to the Renaissance, aspects of bibliography appear. Catalogs aside, such as those employed at the library in Alexandria and probably in numerous private collections, the consensus is that the first shadow of a genuine bibliography is Galen's *De libris propriis liber* (A Book about My Own Books). The former gladiator/physician, who lived from about 129 to 199 A.D., gained fame as the court physician in the Rome of Marcus Aurelius. Considered a fine teacher, he published numerous books on medical theory and practice, and is remembered today for his knowledge of anatomy and physiology. He was second only to Aristotle in influencing science during the Middle Ages and early Renaissance, and considerably more current than the Greek philosopher. Galen's 2d-century bibliography was an effort to list his library, which he classified. Some 500 titles are under such broad headings as anatomical works, Hippocratic writings, grammar and rhetoric, etc.

The majority of early manuscript and print bibliographies, roughly from the 5th through the 15th centuries, were far less systematic. The lists of the works of theologians are faulty and incomplete, if not downright inaccurate. The primary purpose was to spread the faith, to spread propaganda. Each bibliographer slavishly copied the work of his predecessors, errors and all. (The circle was finally broken by Tritheim with his impressive listing of 1494.)

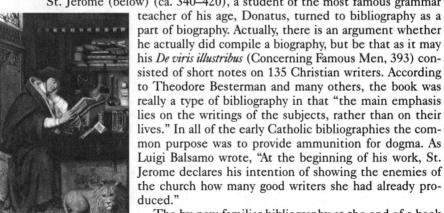

St. Jerome (below) (ca. 340–420), a student of the most famous grammar teacher of his age, Donatus, turned to bibliography as a part of biography. Actually, there is an argument whether he actually did compile a biography, but be that as it may his *De viris illustribus* (Concerning Famous Men, 393) consisted of short notes on 135 Christian writers. According to Theodore Besterman and many others, the book was really a type of bibliography in that "the main emphasis lies on the writings of the subjects, rather than on their lives." In all of the early Catholic bibliographies the common purpose was to provide ammunition for dogma. As Luigi Balsamo wrote, "At the beginning of his work, St. Jerome declares his intention of showing the enemies of the church how many good writers she had already produced."

The by-now familiar bibliography at the end of a book appeared first in Venerable Bede's (ca. 673–735) *Ecclesiastical History of the English People* (731). Some 40 works Bede considered of importance to his history are listed in a rough classified fashion as "*Notitia de se ipso et de libris suis.*" These include his and other works. They are the earliest bibliography at the end of a history, or for that matter, any form of book.

Bibliography in the Middle Ages

In most of the surviving documents of the Middle Ages the closest claim to the present meaning of bibliography is found in numerous lists or inventories of books made by private collectors as well as by monastic and cathedral schools. Most are incomplete, even in the listing or description of a specific title.

Employing the metaphor of an elaborate garden, Richard Fournival of Amiens nicely categorized knowledge by garden plots. He then moved his plots into his library where the analogy crystallized into a catalog and floor plan for his books. According to L. D. Reynolds and N. G. Wilson, his *Biblionomia* (ca. 1250) is not "the imaginary projection of a bibliophile, but the actual catalogue of Fournival's own carefully collected library. It must have contained about 300 volumes and in size and range could challenge the monastic and cathedral libraries of his day."

Near the close of the 13th century, the Franciscans (probably at Oxford) compiled the *Registrum Angliae de libris doctorum et auctorum veterum*. This is a list of works, by about 100 authors, found in cathedral and monastic libraries in England and southern Scotland. A systematic method was employed for the listings. The author came first, then his titles, and names of the libraries where the works were found. The most popular author was St. Jerome. His *Epistolae* was found in 39 libraries.

John Boston of Bury (fl. ca. 1410) was the father of the idea of a union catalog. His *Catalogus & scriptorum ecclesiae*, unlike other listings from the 17th century to the early 15th century, recorded titles in not one or two, but 195 English monasteries. Arranged alphabetically by authors, each entry includes the special interests of the 700 or so authors. Where John found a book in a monastery he recorded it after the author's name with an identification number peculiar to the individual library. Unfortunately, author names are listed without titles. Authors and titles appear, but without any reference to a library. Apparently John copied other sources and was not too methodical about what he found where. "Nevertheless, he clearly is entitled to all the credit of having initiated a type of catalogue," according to Besterman.

The shortage of books during the early Middle Ages—an average monastery would have no more than 10 to 50 individual titles—accounts for limited interest in bibliography. Systematic lists appeared only when: 1) there was a book trade where knowledge of both new and older titles was imperative for business; and 2) there was active production of both new and older titles, i.e., for the most part after the wide spread of printing in the late 15th and early 16th centuries. Until formal bibliography appeared, individuals from scholars to publishers depended primarily upon a network of informants and communication by travelers, augmented by book fairs.

By the late Middle Ages, the book trade gradually developed in the university communities. In order to ensure accurate, copied texts the universities established rules for the *stationarii* (booksellers), including notification to the public of what was available. Publishers provided a list of books, but as distribution was limited (as were potential customers), the lists were limited in both terms of distribution and size.

Richard de Bury (1286–1345), bishop of Durham, was among the first book collectors of the late Middle Ages. He is best known as the author of the famous *Philobiblon* (The Love of Books), a treatise on the joy of collecting

published in 1344 and printed in 1473. As an English ambassador in Europe he had the opportunity to examine and buy manuscripts from both private and clerical sources. Also he had books copied for him, largely from deteriorated exemplars. In 1313 he met a fellow collector at Avignon. This was Francesco Petrarch (left) (1304–1374), considered to be the father of the Renaissance. United by a love of books, if not theology, the two collectors recognized how each could help in the rebirth of knowledge. The younger Petrarch enlisted not only the help of de Bury, but friends through Europe in the endless quest for books.

Petrarch's and de Bury's humanist culture, with reliance on discovering older books, developed a third bookseller's market, outside of the traditional academic and ecclesiastic markets. Individuals now became involved with collection, with building personal libraries. They sought out books across Europe and became an important source of income for a growing number of equally independent booksellers. "Ideal" libraries, neither too small nor too large, were the focus of lists or bibliographies to be used by collectors and booksellers. The lists rarely numbered more than 100 to 200 titles. An example: Angelo Decembrio's *Politia literaria* (ca. 1450). The work was among the first bibliographic humanistic texts. The listed books are described in conversations among scholars who are instructed on how to select and arrange the titles.

Advent of printing and bibliography

With the advent of printing—with the ability in one day to publish more copies of a work than could be hand copied in a year—there arose a need to get adequate information on books available to a wider public than the university or monastic community. Luigi Balsamo wrote: "New tools for providing information came into being: prospectuses, handbills, and bulletins of works published or in preparation gradually were transformed into true catalogs." In Germany, the fatherland of the book trade, the beginnings of bibliography may be found in "the hand lists, or posters, announcing one or more books, similar to those employed earlier by copyists, that were fastened to the doorposts of churches. . . . In university towns these lists were attached to the doors of the university," according to A. Growoll. One of the earliest is the 1469 list by Johann Mentel of Strassburg. By the 16th century these modest broadsides had developed into printer/publisher catalogs which were distributed at book fairs.

A few publishers listed their books, e.g. Swenyheym and Pannartz's *Registrum librorum impressorum,* Rome, 1470. More substantial catalogs came later from Estienne, Aldus, Plantin, and major publishers throughout Europe. For example, Aldus's 1498 *Libri graeci impressi* was a single sheet of classical titles. By 1513 the list had grown to five pages. Aldus unwittingly may have been the first publisher to issue a publisher's catalog with information on not only books published, but information about those to be issued. While not considered standard bibliographies, these early publisher catalogs at least served a major purpose. They let the public know what books were available, if only from one printer.

The first substantial bibliography, after the invention of printing, followed the pattern established by St. Jerome, Isidore of Seville, and other early scholars. Its focus was on authors acceptable to the Church. In 1494, at Basel, the Abbot of Sponheim, Johann Tritheim (right) (1452–1516) published his *Liber de scriptoribus ecclesiasticis* (Books about Ecclesiastical Writers). The volume ran to over 300 pages and included information on over 1,000 authors, most of whom were associated with the Church. The bibliography was a combination of biographical data and a listing of the particular author's work. The "bio-bibliography" or author catalog was a familiar format, but Tritheim harnessed the printing press to expand it considerably. The bibliography

contained representative samples of Europe's monasteries and printer/publishers. After each author's biographical sketch, Tritheim included in chronological order the author's basic writings. In all, around 7,000 books are listed. An alphabetical index of authors was added. Besterman commented, "The contrast between the feeble theological bibliographies of the manuscript age and this first attempt in the printing era is very striking."

Tritheim established, too, the bibliography as a standard reference work. Though he was not the first to compile a bibliography, he was the first to recognize its potential importance as well as the first to stress an alphabetical index of main chronological listings. Tritheim gained his training in the Benedictine monastery of Sponheim. A brilliant scholar, he became the head of the monastery in 1483. He was 21 years old and had just finished his 15-month novitiate. One of his earliest efforts was to reorganize and catalog the monastic library. He became an avid collector; and the initial 48 volumes in the library grew to over 2,000 books and manuscripts under his supervision. As he became more involved with bibliography, he was called upon by other monastic communities for assistance, and from this possibly arose the idea for the compilation of his then massive listing of ecclesiastical writers.

Tritheim compiled other bibliographies: *Catalogus illustrium viorum Germaniae* (Mainz, 1495)—a list of over 2,000 works by more than 300 writers arranged in chronological order, again with an alphabetical index. In 1492 he finished the *De origine, progressu et laudibus Ordinis Carmelitarum*, which lists the works of 75 Carmelite Order writers. Published in Mainz in 1494, this really was little more than excerpts from his original *Liber de scriptoribus*.

Not far behind the more ambitious bibliographies were the bibliographies

of individual authors, often compiled by themselves. Erasmus (left) was among the first writers to construct his own auto-bibliography, *Catalogus omnium Erasmi Roterodami lucubrationum* (Basel, 1523). A year later he revised the listing which was in narrative, chronological form. A table indicated the classification of his works as he would have them arranged in a complete edition. In this matter he closely followed the pattern of Galen, some 1300 years before. In 1544 Jerome Cardan (1501–1576) listed his writings, *De libris propriis*, at the end of his edition of *De sapientia*. Each work is numbered in the margin. What is remarkable about the bibliography is that it was published when Cardan was only 43, and long before he had published his more important works—works that were never included, as there was no update of the original bibliography. Cardan (right), an astrologer, mathematician, and physician, gained fame as the first person to accurately describe typhus fever and as the author of an equally famous work on algebra, *Ars magna*.

Until well into the 16th century the majority of public, private, and institutional libraries had relatively small collections, developed for the most part from earlier monastic and lay holdings. As there were no more than a few hundred books, the problems of bibliography were negligible, as, of course, were any difficulties of arrangement and classification. Catalogs were hardly needed, either. The few books were easily found, as they were shelved according to subjects. Theology usually came first, with medicine and law following and so on. Books tended to be arranged by size rather than by author.

It was a century where bibliography was the extension of humanism. Bibliographers were interested primarily in authors and their texts, not in the books themselves. "The author continued to receive the interest of the compilers," wrote Louise Malclés, "but gradually the time came when the author was sacrificed to the complete and technical description of the book . . . But a long period was required for this transformation."

SOURCE: Bill Katz, *Cuneiform to Computer: A History of Reference Sources* (Lanham, Md.: Scarecrow Press, 1998), pp. 310–14. Reprinted with permission.

How to prepare a bibliography

THE BIBLIOGRAPHY COMMITTEE of the ALA Reference and User Services Association (RUSA) has prepared these guidelines intended for bibliographers, publishers, and evaluators. They are concerned with the quality and character of the elements included in a bibliography; the purpose and place of a given bibliography vis-a-vis other available resources; and its accessibility, availability, durability, and readability. The elements of a good bibliography are the same whether they are produced online or printed on paper.

Purpose

The bibliography should fill a significant need in order to justify its compilation. The subject should fit into the general scheme of available bibliographical sources, without unnecessary duplication. If similar bibliographies exist, they should be reviewed and the unique contribution of this new one should be stated explicitly. The subject should be clearly stated in the title and defined in a preliminary statement.

Scope

Scope should be clearly defined. The work should strive for completeness within its stated limitations (period, geographical area, form, language, library holdings, best books only, intended audience, etc.). Formats, where different, should be identified and each described appropriately.

Methodology

Sources consulted and information on the method of compilation should be provided.

The compiler should work with the bibliographic units. A bibliographic unit is any entity in a bibliography: book, chapters of a book, journal articles, reports, manuscripts, sound and video recordings, computer programs or print-outs, films, charts, etc. All items not personally examined by the compiler should be so identified.

Organization

Principles of organization. The organization of material should be suitable for the subject. The main arrangement should make it possible to use the bibliography from at least one approach without consulting the index. Multiple means of access should be provided. Means of access include both the meaningful arrangement of materials and the indexes to those materials. The scheme for a classified bibliography should be logical and easy for users to understand.

Necessary components. Every bibliography should have a statement of scope and purpose. An explanation of how to use the bibliography should be given. Every bibliography should have a key to all abbreviations used. A table of contents should be provided.

An index or indexes should be provided. Indexes should be sufficiently detailed to provide acceptable levels of recall and precision. Terminology should be appropriate to both subject and intended users. Cross-references should be adequate for normal reference purposes. Multiple indexes should be provided if required for complete access to the materials.

Desirable features. Entry numbers for bibliographic units should be considered. Location of copies of bibliographical units, if not readily available, is helpful.

Annotations and notes

These may be at one of three levels:

1. Informative notes, used chiefly when the nature or reason for inclusion of a title is not clear. Use of this minimal level of description should be limited to those bibliographies that approach comprehensiveness for the area they are covering.

2. Descriptive annotations should give enough of the contents to enable users to decide whether they want to read the original. Any bibliography designated as annotated should have annotations at least at this level.

3. Critical evaluations should be discriminating and should be written by someone knowledgeable in the field. They should assess the value of each item in its relationship to other works in the area. Any bibliography designated critical or evaluative should have annotations at this level. In each case the annotations or notes should be succinct, informative, and on a suitable level for the intended users. If the author has drawn upon another source for the annotation, that source should be appropriately acknowledged.

Bibliographic form

There should be sufficient information to identify the bibliographic unit easily for the purpose of the bibliography and needs of the intended user. The bibliographic form should follow a recognized standard. Examples of these standards include, but are not limited to, those described in the *Chicago Manual of Style,* the *MLA Style Manual,* and the *Publication Manual of the American Psychological Association.*

The bibliographic form should be followed consistently.

Timeliness

Retrospective bibliographies should keep the time lag between closing the bibliography and its publication to a minimum. Introductory material should make it clear at what point the bibliography was closed. Those bibliographies intended to be current should be issued as closely as possible after the publication of the bibliographical units listed.

Accuracy

Citations should be correct and free from typographical errors. Information provided in annotations and elsewhere should be factually accurate and grammatically correct. Provision for corrections after publication should be considered.

Format

Format and typeface should be clear and appropriate. The volume should be sturdy enough to withstand anticipated use. The bibliography should be designed to keep its price within the means of potential users without sacrificing important features that facilitate its use. Cumulation of ongoing bibliographies is strongly recommended.

Distribution

Published bibliographies should be properly advertised and distributed. Notice of the bibliography should be sent to a standard national bibliography.

SOURCE: "Guidelines for the Preparation of a Bibliography," *RQ* 32 (Winter 1992): 194–96.

How information retrieval started

by Gary Forsythe

THE PAPYRUS SCROLL used by the ancient Greeks and Romans was not the most efficient way of storing information in a written form and of retrieving it. Yet, as Greek and Roman scholars began to write large works that were compilations of data of various sorts, they found it useful to devise various means of organizing the material to make locating certain passages easier for the reader. Here are a few examples of what they did.

Tables of contents

Pliny the Elder (died 79 A.D.) wrote a massive work called *The Natural History* in 37 books. It was a kind of encyclopedia that comprised information on a wide range of subjects. In order to make it a bit more user-friendly, the entire first book of the work is nothing more than a gigantic table of contents in which he lists, book by book, the various subjects discussed. He even appended to each list of items for each book his list of Greek and Roman authors used in compiling the information for that book. He indicates in the very end of his preface to the entire work that this practice was first employed in Latin literature by Valerius Soranus, who lived during the last part of the second century B.C. and the first part of the first century B.C. Pliny's statement that Soranus was the first in Latin literature to do this indicates that it must have already been practiced by Greek writers.

Alphabetization

One method of information organization which we take for granted nowadays, namely alphabetization, was possibly first devised by Greek scholars of the 3d century B.C. at the library of Alexandria in Egypt in order to help them organize the growing numbers of Greek literary works. The subject of alphabetization and its use in classical antiquity was treated by Lloyd Daly in *Contributions to a History of Alphabetization in Antiquity and the Middle Ages* (Brussels: Latomus, 1967).

Hierarchies of information

There are a few other ancient works which employed arranging material under headings in order to make the writing more user-friendly and easier to consult.

Valerius Maximus wrote *Facta et Dicta Memorabilia*, a collection of memorable deeds and sayings, in about 30 A.D. The work is divided into nine books, and each book is subdivided into chapters, and each chapter has its own heading, and all entries within that chapter contain anecdotes taken from ancient literature and history that illustrate that theme.

Sextus Julius Frontinus, superintendent of the water-supply system in Rome in 97 A.D., wrote *Strategemata* in four books. Each book concerns itself with a

---

The six librarians of Alexandria

The Great Library of Alexandria, founded during the reign of Ptolemy I (ca. 367–282 B.C.), eventually contained some 700,000 manuscripts. The first six chief librarians were:

1. Zenodotus of Ephesus, librarian 284–260 B.C.
2. Apollonius of Rhodes, librarian 260–247 B.C.
3. Eratosthenes, librarian 247–194 B.C.
4. Aristophanes of Byzantium, librarian 194–180 B.C.
5. Apollonius the Classifier, librarian 180–153 B.C.
6. Aristarchos of Samothrace, librarian 153–145 B.C.

SOURCE: David Matz, *Ancient World Lists and Numbers* (Jefferson, N.C.: McFarland, 1995), p. 40.

specific area of warfare. Each book is then subdivided into chapters that each address one specific aspect of its major theme. Each chapter has a heading to clue the reader, and the chapter itself consists of brief extracts taken from historical works that illustrate the practical application of the topic.

Finally, Aulus Gellius wrote a work entitled *The Attic Nights* ca. 160 A.D. in 20 books. The work is a crazy-quilt assortment of items on Greek and Roman history, philosophy, grammar, rhetoric, and antiquarian material in general. Since the work was composed with no real order but as the various topics occurred to the author, each chapter of every book concerns an isolated subject, and this subject is clearly spelled out in a title heading that stands at the beginning of the chapter. A reader could therefore skim through a book and locate the subject by glancing over the titles of the chapters.

Interested in more? A brief but good discussion of the problems of ancient scholarship posed by the use of the papyrus scroll can be found in *Varro the Scholar*, by Jens Erik Skydsgaard (Copenhagen: Analecta Romana Instituti Danici series, 1968), pp. 101–16; Leila Avrin, *Scribes, Script, and Books: The Book Arts from Antiquity to the Renaissance* (Chicago: American Library Association, 1991); and Bill Katz, *Cuneiform to Computer: A History of Reference Sources* (Lanham, Md.: Scarecrow, 1998).

SOURCE: American Society of Indexers (www.asindexing.org/history.htm).

Ancient book indexes

by Hans Wellisch

IN ANCIENT ROME, when used in relation to literary works, the term "index" was used for the little slip attached to papyrus scrolls on which the title of the work (and sometimes also the name of the author) was written so that each scroll on the shelves could be easily identified without having to pull them out for inspection, "*ut [librarioli] sumant membranulam, ex qua indices fiant, quos vos Graeci . . . sillybus appelatis*" (so that [the copyists] may take some bits of parchment to make title slips from them, which you Greeks call *sillybus*) (Cicero, *Atticus*, 4.41.1). From this developed the usage of index for the title of books: "*Sunt duo libelli diverso titulo, alteri 'gladius,' alteri 'pugio' index erat*" (There are two books with different titles, one called *The sword,* the other having the title *The dagger*) (Suetonius, *Caligula*, 49.3). Those two books, by the way, were what we would call today "hit lists" of people whom Caligula wished to have assassinated shortly before that same fate befell him. At about the same time, in the first century A.D., the meaning of the word was extended from "title" to a table of contents or a list of chapters (sometimes with a brief abstract of their contents) and hence to a bibliographical list or catalog.

However, indexes in the modern sense, giving exact locations of names and subjects in a book, were not compiled in antiquity, and only a very few seem to have been made before the age of printing. There are several reasons for this. First, as long as books were written in the form of scrolls, there were neither page nor leaf numbers nor line counts (as we have them now for classical texts). Also, even had there been such numerical indicators, it would have been impractical to append an index giving exact references, because in order for a reader to consult the index, the scroll would have to be unrolled to the very end and then rolled back to the relevant page. (Whoever has had to read a book available only on microfilm, the modern successor of the papyrus scroll, will have experienced how difficult and inconvenient it is to go from the index to the text.) Second, even though popular works  were written in many copies (sometimes up to several hundreds), no two of them would be exactly the same, so that an index could at best have been made to chapters or paragraphs, but not to exact pages. Yet such a division of texts was rarely done (the one we have now for classical texts is mostly the work of medieval and Renaissance scholars). Only the invention of printing around 1450 made it possible to produce identical copies of books in large numbers, so that soon afterwards the first indexes began to be compiled, especially those to books of reference, such as herbals.

Index entries were not always alphabetized by considering every letter in a word from beginning to end, as people are wont to do today. Most early indexes were arranged only by the first letter of the first word, the rest being left in no particular order at all. Gradually, alphabetization advanced to an arrangement by the first syllable, that is, the first two or three letters, the rest of an entry still being left unordered. Only a very few indexes compiled in the 16th and early 17th centuries had fully alphabetized entries, but by the 18th century, full alphabetization became the rule.

SOURCE: © Hans Wellisch, *Indexing from A to Z* (New York: H.W. Wilson, 1996), pp. 136, 164–66. Reprinted with permission.

Early modern book indexes

by Bill Katz

IN HIS ANALYSIS OF the *Nuremberg Chronicle* (1493), Francis Witty gives an example of typical individual book indexing in the early years of printing: "Most of the index entries (the index is in the front) were taken verbatim from the text and sometimes not entered under what would seem the proper keyword; e.g., the statement about the invention of printing in Germany is entered under *Ars imprimendi libros* with no entry at all under any form of [printing] . . . Alphabetization . . . is rough—not ordinarily past the first syllable."

Prior to the 18th century, indexes, such as they were, represented the work of the author of the book being analyzed. By early 1700 London's Grub Street was not only the home of hack writers but of underpaid indexers. By 1762 Oliver Goldsmith in his *Citizen of the World* dismissed indexers as pretentious, generally ignorant, and fair targets for mockery. He describes an "author" as someone who "writes indexes to perfection."

The lack of adequate book indexing drove Thomas Jefferson to index his own works. Exactly how many books he analyzed is unknown, because many of his personal titles were lost in a fire. Of the surviving books, three have short indexes, of which two are inscribed on the end pages and the third is a separate sheet bound with the book. In his personal papers will be found an extensive although incomplete index to Benjamin Barton's *Elements of Botany* (Philadelphia, 1803). The index was probably made during Jefferson's second term as president. He favored it because of his fondness for American science in general and botany in particular. He had 36 volumes about botany in his library—but none had an index. Why, then, did Jefferson bother to index this

5

book? He was an inveterate indexer, and as the subject interested him, it was a delight to turn to Barton. Also, he was compulsive to a point where "he carried a notebook with him constantly and recorded in it every cent he received or spent . . . for more than sixty years." (*American Heritage,* July/August 1991, p. 88.)

Today most book indexes are arranged alphabetically, although the arrangement can differ from chronological to numerical. In the early indexes little or no attention was given to alphabetical order. The entries might be placed under the major letters of the alphabet, but after that the entries would be in haphazard order. While printers and publishers did attempt to be consistent, there was no really accepted arrangement until Diderot's *Encyclopedia* set the pattern in the mid-18th century. Entries followed a strict alphabetical order—an order which until this day dictates most arrangement.

Book indexing improved, too, during the 19th century. Indexes were necessary for multiple volumes in a reference work such as the 22-volume, seventh edition *Encyclopaedia Britannica* (Edinburgh, 1827–1842). As Robert Collison noted, "The index was an astonishing achievement of detail and conciseness, as well as a masterpiece of clarity and layout."

Turning to the five-volume index to the Yale edition of *Horace Walpole's Correspondence* (vols. 44–48, *Complete Index,* New Haven, Conn.: Yale University Press, 1983), a critic observed this may be the last "such compendious guide for which the compilers did all their work by hand and mind, the last such big index innocent of the microsecond-fast electronic fingers, files, and fitness of the processor."

SOURCE: Bill Katz, *Cuneiform to Computer: A History of Reference Sources* (Lanham, Md.: Scarecrow Press, 1998), pp. 333–34. Reprinted with permission.

Z39.50: The making of a standard

by Diane Mayo and Sandra Nelson

THE Z39.50 STANDARD was originally proposed in 1984 to provide a standard way of querying multiple bibliographic databases. Since then, it has gone through 3 versions—in 1988 (ver. 1), 1992 (ver. 2), and 1995 (ver. 3). Version 2 also incorporated and became compatible with an ISO standard (10162/3) called Search and Retrieve. Version 3 is administered by the Z39.50 Maintenance Agency at the Library of Congress.—*GME.*

Z39.50 is the American National Standards Institute's *Information Retrieval Service Definition and Protocol Specifications for Library Applications.* This means that the American National Standards Institute (ANSI) has published a standard that defines how two computers can communicate with each other for the purposes of one computer retrieving information from the other. With Z39.50, the how of the communication is defined, not what type of information can be retrieved. That distinction is an important one.

Although Z39.50 is generally thought of in the library world as a way to retrieve bibliographic data, the standard was not intended to be limited to just bibliographic data. It is an information-retrieval standard and, indeed, after years of being used primarily as a way to retrieve online catalog records from different integrated library systems, there are now systems available to be searched using Z39.50 clients that are not bibliographic systems at all. The U.S. government, for example, is using the Z39.50 standard as the basis for its Government Information Locator System (GILS), and museums are experimenting with it in a project on the computer exchange of museum information. Solinet has tested it as a way to retrieve information from community information files. Additional tests and experiments are developing in libraries and in other industries as well.

The Z39.50 standard existed for several years before it was actually implemented. The first serious implementation of the standard was developed in the early 1990s to make it possible for the users of one integrated vendor's online catalog to search the database of another vendor's online catalog. Based on the experience of trying to make version 1 of the Z39.50 standard work in a real-world application, version 2 was drafted and adopted in 1992. Version 2 is the form of the Z39.50 standard most library vendors initially adopted. Some, but not all, vendors incorporated some of the features of version 3 when it was approved in 1995. The primary difference between versions 2 and 3, from a public library's perspective, is that version 3 included the transfer of status information from a Z39.50 server to a Z39.50 client. This meant that the standard not only supported finding out if another library had the title in its catalog, it also let the user know if a copy of that title was available for loan.

As it has been implemented to date, Z39.50 is designed as a network application. The various Z39.50 servers and clients available use the TCP/IP protocol to communicate between networked computers. For all practical purposes, databases accessible through Z39.50 and the users who are trying to search them must both be on the same network or be connected to the Internet.

Online catalogs and Z39.50

As integrated system vendors developed online public access catalogs (OPACs) with differing user interfaces, libraries sought ways to make it possible for patrons to search multiple catalogs without having to master multiple interfaces. The Z39.50 standard was one way to accomplish that objective. Z39.50 client software integrated into a vendor's OPAC gives an online catalog user the opportunity to search other databases from within the library's own catalog user interface. By choosing a prompt for "other databases," the OPAC user initiates a Z39.50 search without even realizing it. To the user, the other databases look just like the library's own database.

A Z39.50 implementation is a classic client/server application. Client software is usually available from a library's own integrated system vendor and is embedded into the vendor's online catalog client or user interface. If the vendor's OPAC is running on dumb terminals, the Z39.50 client software usually runs on the library's integrated system server. If the vendor has a graphical user interface (GUI) online catalog client, the Z39.50 client may run either as a part of the vendor's GUI or on the library's server.

There are also third-party Z39.50 clients—SeaChange's BookWhere? (www.bookwhere.com) is an example—which run as stand-alone PC applications independent of an integrated system. These have their own user interfaces, which, again, are the same regardless of what systems are being searched.

The Z39.50 server is the software a Z39.50 client communicates with. The server must be developed by each integrated system or database vendor to run with its own online catalog or database. A Z39.50 server is a piece of software that translates between a vendor's internal database structure and the Z39.50 standard. The standard defines a wide variety of searches it can support, but each vendor needs to link the standard's search options to specific elements of the vendor's own database and indexes. For example, the standard defines 12 separate types of title searches that can be performed. For a vendor with only one title index, these 12 types of searches must be linked to that one index to provide reasonably complete title access.

Because the client and the server are developed by separate vendors, it is entirely possible for a library to implement only half of the Z39.50 client/ server applications. A library may contract with its integrated system vendor for a Z39.50 server, which it will make available for other libraries to search, without ever adding the client functionality to its own OPAC screens. A library without an integrated system database, or with an integrated system that is not linked to the Internet, may choose to purchase only Z39.50 client software to search other libraries' databases. Just remember, you can buy clients from a number of sources, but the server has to come from the vendor who provided your database.

Cataloging and Z39.50

Although linking OPACs was the first large-scale implementation of Z39.50, it is not the only library application in which Z39.50 has proven useful. If a Z39.50 server is programmed to do so, it can send an entire MARC record to the client to satisfy a request. Suppliers of cataloging records from the Library of Congress to commercial vendors such as the Library Corporation and Marcive have taken advantage of this feature to develop new ways for libraries to capture MARC records in machine-readable form.

Vendors of integrated systems are also incorporating Z39.50 client functions into their technical services client software as they develop GUI clients for their systems.

Interlibrary loan and Z39.50

When the Z39.50 version 3 standard was expanded to include status information in the responses to inquiries, many libraries began to see Z39.50 as a potential vehicle for interlibrary loan transactions. Several vendors are basing commercial interlibrary loan applications on Z39.50's ability to search multiple databases simultaneously with a single search request, report on the status of materials, and retrieve a full MARC record. Although Z39.50 itself doesn't include any standards for managing the request and tracking functions of an interlibrary loan transaction, it can be combined with another set of standards (ISO 10160/10161) to develop a fully functioning interlibrary loan application.

The Web and Z39.50

As discussed earlier, the primary impetus for the first application of Z39.50 was to make it possible to search different OPACs with a single user interface. Shortly after the first Z39.50 implementation, the World Wide Web burst onto the scene, and everyone's assumptions about user interfaces were changed forever. OPAC vendors began to develop Web interfaces for their catalogs, and the perceived problems of multiple user interfaces were greatly reduced by widespread adoption of Web OPACs.

However, every database vendor didn't develop a Web interface, and Z39.50 was never meant to be only a bibliographic record retrieval tool. It is meant to be a system-independent way to search databases. As the Web became the dominant user interface for all kinds of applications, another Z39.50-based product was born: the Web-to-Z39.50 gateway. This gateway is actually a piece of software that links a Z39.50 server to a Web server. Users with Web browsers connect to the Web server side of the gateway and use a Web interface to construct their search requests. The Web server interacts with the Z39.50 server to execute a Z39.50 search and receive the responses. The Web server then formats the responses as Web pages and delivers them to the inquiring browser. This makes it possible for users to query Z39.50 databases without needing to load and run Z39.50 client software.

The most important point to keep in mind is that Z39.50 services involve two separate applications: the Z39.50 server and the Z39.50 client. If you want to offer your online catalog to other libraries to be searched through Z39.50, you need to get the Z39.50 server software from your integrated system vendor. If you want to search other libraries' Z39.50 databases, or any of a number of other Z39.50-compliant databases, you need Z39.50 client software. Remember, too, that Z39.50 is a network application. You need access to the Internet to use either the server or the client features effectively.

SOURCE: Diane Mayo and Sandra Nelson, *Wired for the Future: Developing Your Library Technology Plan* (Chicago: American Library Association, 1999), pp. 183–87.

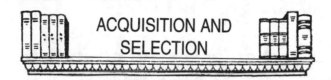

ACQUISITION AND SELECTION

Principles of acquisitions practice

IN ALL ACQUISITIONS TRANSACTIONS, a librarian:

1. gives first consideration to the objectives and policies of his or her institution;

2. strives to obtain the maximum value of each dollar of expenditure;

3. grants all competing vendors equal consideration insofar as the established policies of his or her library permit, and regards each transaction on its own merits;

4. subscribes to and works for honesty, truth, and fairness in buying and selling, and denounces all forms and manifestations of bribery;

5. declines personal gifts and gratuities;

6. uses only by consent original ideas and designs devised by one vendor for competitive purchasing purposes;

7. accords a prompt and courteous reception insofar as conditions permit to all who call on legitimate business missions;

8. fosters and promotes fair, ethical, and legal trade practices;

9. avoids sharp practice;

10. strives consistently for knowledge of the publishing and bookselling industry;

11. strives to establish practical and efficient methods for the conduct of his/her office;

12. counsels and assists fellow acquisitions librarians in the performance of their duties, whenever occasion permits.

SOURCE: Statement on Principles and Standards of Acquisitions Practice (Chicago: ALA Association for Library Collections and Technical Services, 1994).

Most highly regarded publishers

A SURVEY OF ACADEMIC LIBRARIES taken in 1994–1995 rated publishers of academic books by the quality of their publications. Here are the top 20:

1. Harvard	11. Wiley
2. Cambridge	12. CRC
3. Oxford	13. Kluwer
4. Stanford	14. Academic
5. National Academy	15. Oklahoma
6. Brookings	16. Routledge
7. Springer-Verlag	17. Knopf
8. Blackwell	18. Farrar, Straus
9. Smithsonian	19. Norton
10. Elsevier	20. Basic

SOURCE: Paul Metz and John Stemmer, "A Reputational Study of Academic Publishers," *College & Research Libraries* 57 (May 1996): 234–47.

Collection assessment statistics
by Debra E. Kachel

THERE ARE A NUMBER OF STATISTICS, comparisons, and professional evaluations that can describe and analyze the contents of a library collection. Seldom are all of them implemented, due to the time element. However, many statistical data can be easily obtained from reports that automated circulation systems produce. Sites without automation should elicit student or parent volunteers who, with a few directions, can assist with data collection. Full descriptions of these techniques are found in the author's *Collection Assessment and Management for School Libraries* (Greenwood, 1997).

Collection-centered techniques

Number of copies or items and percentage of collection. Most circulation systems generate reports that total the number of copies within Dewey classification ranges (000s to 900s) and call number prefixes (REF, F, B, etc.). Most also calculate the percentage each classification range represents in the total collection. These numbers are tabulated based on copies or bar codes used, not by number of titles. In a nonautomated environment, a school library media specialist can measure shelflist cards based on 90–100 titles per inch to determine the number of titles within specific call numbers.

Number of copies or items added per year and rate of growth. Most automated systems can either generate a report by acquisition date or a preassigned category number set up to show how many items were added during a school year. The school library media specialist must create a category called "New Materials 1999–2000" and scan the bar codes of each new title into that category number throughout the school year as materials are processed. If annual acquisitions data by classification number are maintained for two or more years, the rate of growth can be calculated. The percentage of growth is sometimes easier to understand than the raw number of acquisitions.

Age of materials. The most useful way to express how old or recent a collection is, is the *median age*. Some circulation software can compute average age for specific call number ranges, but not median age. Due to the size of most collections, only a sampling should be undertaken. If the collection is over 500 items, a systematic random sampling would provide the best results.

Circulation statistics. Most libraries collect some circulation statistics by call number, whether manually or by computer. In an automated environment, statistics are readily available. In small, nonautomated libraries without full-time staff, the school library media specialist may decide to sample circulation. For example, collect circulation statistics two Mondays, two Tuesdays, two Wednesdays, and so on for the rest of the week, randomly throughout the semester. Find the average daily circulation and multiply this by the number of school days the library is open.

Items per student. There are several different ways to calculate items or copies per student—by format (30 books per student, 3 videos per student); by subject (12 items per student in the 300s, all formats); or by format per subject (9 books per student in the 500s, 0.5 videos per student in the 500s). These statistics are meaningful to budget managers and curriculum coordinators and offer a way to compare the equity of resources across a district with schools of varying sizes.

Visual inspection. Visual inspection is a subjective, yet qualitative, method for evaluating a collection. A team of students, teachers, or other community "experts" who have some knowledge of the subject area being assessed scans the shelves, cabinets, and other storage areas where materials on the subject are located, and the school library media specialist records the team's collective comments.

Comparison to recommended lists. A frequently taught technique for collection analysis is to compare the library collection to the items in recommending sources like H. W. Wilson's *Senior High School Library Catalog* or Brodart's *The Elementary School Library Collection*. While such tools are an excellent way to build or develop a collection, having a high percentage of what appears on these lists does not mean that the collection matches the needs of the students and the curriculum in the school.

User-centered techniques

Circulation statistics. Most automated circulation systems generate reports of titles with the annual and monthly circulation indicated per title or per category. The category method allows the school library media specialist to combine a variety of sources, regardless of call number, and track their use. It is also possible to track the circulation of various types of patrons, such as student, teacher, or community. Most systems can also generate a list of the most circulated items, which may indicate that duplicate copies are needed.

Percent of relative use (PRU). This is the percentage of use that a certain call number range receives based on the percentage of items in the collection being studied. The formula is as follows:

$$\frac{\text{Percentage of circulation for the collection}}{\text{Percentage of the collection it represents}} \times 100$$

Dewey divisions calculated above 100% are defined as used, and those below as underused.

In-house use studies. Some materials are used heavily in the library because they do not circulate, such as reference and reserve materials and the most recent issues of magazines. To evaluate their use, have students and staff return them to a designated place on a special cart or section of the circulation desk. Use statistics cannot demonstrate the quality of the resources or whether the students or teachers actually used the information they found.

Interlibrary loan and document delivery statistics. Most circulation systems now affordable to school libraries do not include ILL-tracking software, thus requiring manual record-keeping. It is important to document ILL requests because the documentation will (1) detail what you do not own that students and teachers specifically want; (2) highlight unique resources in your collection that other libraries borrow; (3) verify your compliance with the copyright law and guidelines; and (4) demonstrate responsibility in the care of other libraries' resources. Regardless of what type of material is being requested, how the transaction is tracked, or which library or document delivery service fills the request, if the demand for the material is repeated over time or has a high correlation to curriculum content, attempts should be made to acquire the requested items or material for the local library.

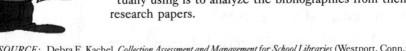

User-satisfaction surveys. A short, well-developed questionnaire, checklist, or survey can be used to gather information about the usability, quality, and availability of resources. To design the survey tool, the school library media specialist must first develop a purpose and focus for the survey, then decide who to survey and how. Questions or statements should first be field-tested with a small group of students or teachers to expose ambiguous questions.

Citation checking. Another way to ascertain if the materials students find are sources that they are actually using is to analyze the bibliographies from their research papers.

SOURCE: Debra E. Kachel, *Collection Assessment and Management for School Libraries* (Westport, Conn.: Greenwood, 1997), pp. 20–37. Reprinted with permission.

SERIALS

Shaping a serials specialist

by Linda Meiseles and Connie Foster

FROM: The Desk of a Serials Librarian

TO: Education Professionals and Information Specialists

Log in to a dynamic career! The dynamic nature of serials information requires a serials librarian, a specialist who combines in-depth knowledge, practical experience, and managerial competence with technical, financial, and philosophical expertise.

A serials librarian works most often in an academic, public, medical, government, or corporate library. Career options also may include subscription agencies, systems vendors, publishers and database producers.

Password: Change

Variety of formats, publication patterns, title changes, and price increases are a few of the many sides of serials. Serials are complex, constantly changing publications that are intellectually challenging to process, interpret, and access.

Password: Knowledge

A serials librarian completes a master's degree in library and information studies from an accredited program. Specific serials courses are very rare. Much learning occurs on the job and through continuing education opportunities.

Knowledge also means:

- familiarity with and use of standards such as ANSI, NISO, EDI, X12, AACR2, MARC;
- learning about budgets, developing collections, methods of access to serials information, preservation—everything related to librarianship in general and serials in particular;
- learning and using multiple automated processes, library systems, information databases and systems.

A serials specialist needs to understand and value interrelationships in a library environment, the university, or other workplace communities.

Password: Skills

A serials librarian must communicate effectively, explain, negotiate, discuss, train, persuade, and listen.

This career demands the ability to understand the complexities of serials and simplify patron access. Title changes, incorrect numbering, mergers present challenges that shout: Enjoy puzzles and problem solving!

A few additional skills include:

- staying current with a broad base of professional literature from librarianship, computer and information science, business and management, and subject disciplines;
- exercising good judgment and paying close attention to details;
- practicing fiscal responsibility with allocations that consume a disproportionate share of a library's budget.

Passwords: Think, plan, envision

By anticipating reporting needs and the best way to structure data within a system or by devising a new system, the serials specialist demonstrates initiative, leadership, and commitment to service. Additional forecasts include:

- expect a decrease in but not demise of print journals;
- initiate ways to manage the multiplying electronic products and gateways to infinite information;
- determine best sources for ordering materials for your collection;
- work well as a team with your colleagues in acquisitions, cataloging, public services, and interlibrary lending, as well as with vendors and publishers, as we all seek to provide the best and most timely resources at reasonable costs.

Password: Professional involvement

Bob Moawad, a motivational speaker, said, "When you're green, you grow. When you're ripe, you rot." Growth means:

- network (join and become actively involved in NASIG and other professional organizations);
- publish, serve on committees, present papers or join in panel discussions and forums to focus on critical issues;
- use electronic listservs as a way to discuss issues, trends, and practical concerns affecting serials librarians in the world of scholarly communication;
- seek and create leadership opportunities through professional involvement.

Security caution

Create strong links with other participants in the serials information chain. Be open to exciting opportunities to redefine your career and maintain the essential goal of providing information access to users. Your passwords will change periodically. This safeguard, which implies flexibility, will allow you to stay logged on now and for the coming decades.

SOURCE: North American Serials Interest Group, Continuing Education Committee, www.nasig.org/public/Shaping.Specialist.html. Reprinted with permission.

Cataloging in Publication (CIP)

THE CATALOGING IN PUBLICATION (CIP) program prepares prepublication cataloging records for those books most likely to be widely acquired by the nation's libraries. These records (CIP data) are printed in the book and greatly facilitate cataloging activities for libraries. They are also distributed prior to the books' publication in machine-readable form via the MARC (MAchine Readable Cataloging) tapes, alerting libraries and other bibliographic services around the world to forthcoming titles.

The CIP program began in 1971 as a special project, funded in part by grants from the Council on Library Resources and the National Endowment for the Humanities. It is now fully supported by Library of Congress appropriations and is administered by the Cataloging in Publication Division.

Publishers participating in this program submit a manuscript or galley of a forthcoming title to the CIP Division. This prepublication information is forwarded to the cataloging divisions where it proceeds through various cataloging stages, including descriptive cataloging, subject analysis, and the assignment of full Library of Congress and Dewey decimal classification numbers. At the end of the cataloging process, the record is forwarded to the CIP Division where the publisher's copy is prepared and sent to the publisher to be printed on the copyright page of the book. Meanwhile, the MARC version of the record is distributed to the library community, worldwide, where it appears in a variety of publications, bibliographic vendor services, and national and regional bibliographic networks.

Review your CIP data immediately upon receipt. If you have questions concerning its meaning or accuracy, write or call your CIP Publisher Liaison as soon as possible so that your concerns can be addressed well before your printing date.

After reviewing your CIP data, instruct the appropriate staff in your house to print the data on the copyright page of your publication exactly as it was supplied to you, observing all capitalization, spacing, and punctuation, and maintaining the same overall format and left margins. The Library of Congress subscribes to the conventions of International Standard Bibliographic Description which allow librarians to decipher a catalog record regardless of language. For example, the title is separated from any "other title information" (whether a subtitle or a phrase in apposition) by a [space]: [space]. It is therefore important that your data be printed according to the same conventions.

CIP elements

The format of CIP data and an explanation of its elements are given below, with the numbers keyed to the sample card on the next page. The full catalog record is distributed to MARC subscribers in machine-readable format.

    1. Main entry. Often the first named author on the title page.

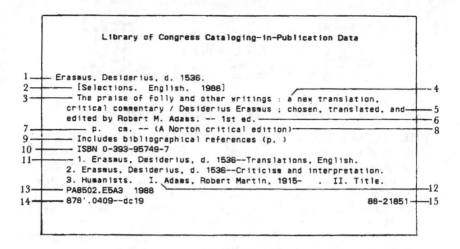

```
                    Library of Congress Cataloging-in-Publication Data

1 ───── Erasmus, Desiderius, d. 1536.
2 ─────     [Selections.  English.  1988]                                          ── 4
3 ─────     The praise of folly and other writings : a new translation,
               critical commentary / Desiderius Erasmus ; chosen, translated, and── 5
               edited by Robert M. Adams. -- 1st ed. ─────────────────────────────── 6
7 ─────        p.   cm. -- (A Norton critical edition)───────────────────────────── 8
9 ─────     Includes bibliographical references (p. )
10 ─────    ISBN 0-393-95749-7
11 ─────    1. Erasmus, Desiderius, d. 1536--Translations, English.
               2. Erasmus, Desiderius, d. 1536--Criticism and interpretation.
               3. Humanists.   I. Adams, Robert Martin, 1915-   . II. Title.
13 ───── PA8502.E5A3  1988                                                          ── 12
14 ───── 878'.0409--dc19                                              88-21851 ───── 15
```

2. Uniform title. In the example, the uniform title brings together in the catalog various English language collections of selected works by Erasmus.

3. Title.

4. Parallel title and/or other title information, including subtitle.

5. Statement of responsibility. The author statement as it appears on your title page is transcribed according to the provisions of the *Anglo-American Cataloguing Rules,* Second Edition.

6. Edition statement.

7. Physical description. This area will be updated in the Library of Congress automated database upon receipt of the published book to reflect the number of pages, illustrations, size in centimeters, and accompanying materials. Librarians expect to see "p. cm." in a CIP record; please do not alter it.

8. Series statement, including the International Standard Serial Number (ISSN) if it appears in the book.

9. Notes. In addition to notes concerning bibliographical references, this area may contain information concerning previous editions, etc. For books selected for the Library's Annotated Card program, it may also include a summary for juvenile readers.

10. ISBN. If you wish to record additional ISBNs, please add them below the CIP data.

11. Subject headings (each preceded by an arabic numeral). There will be access in library catalogs under these headings.

12. Added entries (each preceded by a roman numeral). "Title" and "Series" mean that access will be provided in library catalogs for this book by the book title and series title. Persons, especially joint authors and editors, often appear as added entries.

13. Library of Congress classification number.

14. Dewey decimal classification number. The annotation, dc 19, tells librarians that the number was assigned from the 19th edition of the *Decimal Classification.* Please do not delete this information.

15. Library of Congress card catalog number.

SOURCE: Library of Congress Cataloging in Publication Division, *CIP Publishers Manual* (Washington, D.C.: Library of Congress, 1994), pp. 1, 12–16.

Preassigned LC card numbers

A LIBRARY OF CONGRESS CATALOG CARD NUMBER is a unique identification number that the Library of Congress assigns to the catalog record created for each book in its cataloged collections. Librarians use it to locate a specific Library of Congress catalog record in the national databases and to order catalog cards from the Library of Congress or from commercial suppliers. The Library of Congress assigns this number while the book is being cataloged. Under certain circumstances, however, a card number can be assigned before the book is published through the Preassigned Card Number Program.

The purpose of the Preassigned Card Number (PCN) program is to enable the Library of Congress to assign card numbers in advance of publication to those titles that may be added to the Library's collections. The publisher prints the card number in the book and thereby facilitates cataloging and other book processing activities. The PCN is a control number. It links the book to any record which the Library of Congress, other libraries, bibliographic utilities, or book vendors may create.

Publishers participating in the program complete a Preassigned Card Number Application form for each title for which a preassigned card number is requested. Based on the information provided by the publisher, library staff preassign a card number to each eligible title. Upon receiving the number, the publisher prints it on the back of the title page (i.e., the copyright page) in the following manner:

Library of Congress Catalog Card Number: 97-65432

Only U.S. book publishers are eligible to participate in the PCN program. These publishers must list a U.S. place of publication on the title page or copyright page of their books and maintain an editorial office in the U.S. capable of answering substantive bibliographic questions. All forthcoming monographs that will be published in the United States and that are not included in the categories listed below are eligible for the PCN program. Card numbers are preassigned to materials which are most likely to be selected and cataloged by the Library of Congress for its own collections. The following are ineligible:

- Books that are already published.
- Books that do not list a U.S. city as place of publication on the title page or copyright page.
- Books for which Cataloging in Publication data has been (or will be) requested.
- Serials.
- Government documents.
- Items under 50 pages with the exception of genealogies and children's literature.
- Textbooks below the college level.
- Items not intended for wide distribution to libraries.
- Religious instructional materials.
- Expendable educational materials.
- Transitory or consumable materials.
- Translations except Spanish.
- Mass market paperbacks.

- Single articles reprinted from periodicals and other serials.
- Audiovisual materials including mixed media and computer software.
- Music scores.
- Most microforms.

To obtain Library of Congress card numbers for your forthcoming books, you must first complete the Application to Participate (lcweb2.loc.gov/pcn/pcn007.html) and obtain an account number and password. The account number and password will provide you access to the appropriate form for requesting Library of Congress card numbers.

PCN policy is to provide only one account number for each participating publisher. Particularly large houses may warrant exception to this policy. Those houses should contact their publisher liaison for further guidance upon establishing their first account.

SOURCE: The Library of Congress, lcweb2.loc.gov/pcn/.

MARC records

by Virginia M. Berringer

IN THE LATE 1950s, the Library of Congress began to investigate the possibility of automating some of its massive cataloging and records maintenance processes. By the fall of 1966, a pilot project was in place and LC began distribution of bibliographic records for English-language monographs to test the feasibility of distributing bibliographic data in machine-readable format to other libraries.

This project, supported by a grant from the Council on Library Resources, was called MARC, an acronym for *MA*chine-*R*eadable *C*ataloging. The pilot project, involving LC and 16 participating libraries, resulted in the introduction of the first of the MARC formats, the MARC format for books. This was followed during the 1970s by the introduction of individual MARC formats for serials, scores, sound recordings, audiovisual materials, maps, manuscripts, and machine-readable data files, each using the same basic structure as the format for printed monographs but including identifiers for the unique features of materials in each category.

This arbitrary division of library materials based upon publication format made it impossible to adequately record information for many types of materials, such as serials issued in nonprint formats, publications that combine materials in various formats (such as interactive multimedia packages), and print materials accompanied by computer disks, sound recordings, or videos. To rectify these problems and improve access to all data, format integration was initiated and by January 1996 had successfully been adopted, resulting in the elimination of a number of redundant fields and the validation of all tags for use in describing any materials for which they are applicable.

In the 30+ years since the introduction of MARC for English-language monograph records at LC, MARC has become an international framework for recording, storing, indexing, retrieving, manipulating, and sharing bibliographic data among libraries in nearly every part of the world. It is the basis for huge international databases, such as OCLC and RLIN, and the storage medium for the holdings of libraries in small communities and schools. MARC is everywhere, and has appeared in many variations as other countries have developed systems to fit their own cataloging and communications needs and practices. Unfortunately, the proliferation of distinctive national MARC formats makes it difficult or even impossible for systems designed to store and interpret one format to make sense of records stored according to another set of codes. The development of the ISO 2709 standard has increased the compatibility of developing formats, and there are numerous projects now under way to decrease communication difficulties between national formats.

In addition to the USMARC format for bibliographic records developed primarily by the Library of Congress, USMARC formats have been developed for authority records, holdings records, classification, and community information.

MARC structure for recording information

A MARC bibliographic record involves three elements: the record structure, the content designation, and the data content.

The record begins with information traditionally found in a library catalog. This includes descriptive elements, such as title, edition, publication information, physical description, and notes. These elements as well as access points (series, main and added entries, subject headings, and classification) are defined by national and international standards, including *AACR2*, the ISBDs, *Library of Congress Subject Headings, Sears List of Subject Headings,* and the Dewey and the Library of Congress classification schedules. This information, providing description of and access to library material, is defined in the *USMARC Format for Bibliographic Data* as the data content of the record.

Each element of bibliographic information in the data content is then assigned an identifying code that enables a computer to identify, store, and manipulate it as determined by its programming. This system of content designation is defined in the USMARC format for each category of data to be recorded.

The content of the record and its content designations are fitted into the structure of the record. The record structure for USMARC is based on the American National Standard for Bibliographic Information Interchange (ANSI Z39.2).

The appearance of online displays or output of bibliographic information varies greatly from one system to the next. Just as in typing a catalog card, system designers can determine which information goes where and how much information to include in a display. Thus, a library may choose to display only a few elements of the bibliographic record in its circulation or acquisitions functions, while displaying the full record to patrons. This is achievable because each element is defined by a unique combination of coding in the MARC record.

In the MARC record, data is grouped into several areas. Most of the data in the *leader* is created by the computer when the record is written to the storage medium. The *directory,* which makes it possible for the computer to locate information in the record by recording the exact location of each element within the record, is also automatically generated.

The *variable fields* are where the data recorded by the cataloging agency reside. There are two types of variable fields: variable control fields and variable data fields. Each variable field is identified by a three-digit numerical tag. These tags are grouped into blocks of fields containing related types of information. The first digit of the tag group identifies the type of data to be found in those fields:

0XX Control information, identification and classification numbers, etc.
1XX Main entries
2XX Titles and title paragraph (title, edition, imprint)
3XX Physical description, etc.
4XX Series statements
5XX Notes
6XX Subject access fields
7XX Added entries other than subject or series; linking fields
8XX Series added entries, etc.
9XX Reserved for local implementation

Within each tag group are often coding conventions that are repeated wherever similar data are recorded. For example, tag 100 indicates a personal name main entry. A personal name used as a subject heading is tagged 600, and a personal name as an added entry would be tagged 700. Fields that contain uniform titles will have 30 as the final two digits of the tag.

The *variable control fields* are numbered 001 through 009. Each of these fields contains either a single piece of information (such as field 001), or the record number, or information in coded form from a list of codes defined for each element in each field. Each element in a coded variable control field is identified by its position in the field. For example, the 007 field contains detailed physical description data for nonprint materials and microforms. The first position in this field represents the general type of media. If the first code is "m," the field describes a motion picture. If it is "s," it describes a sound recording. Each character in the rest of the field provides additional specific information about the item, including its specific type, size, color characteristics, sound characteristics, recording characteristics, and so on, each represented by a single letter of the alphabet as defined for that specific position in that specific field.

For a VHS videorecording, the 007 field might look like this:

007 vf cbahos

This gibberish describes the item as: a videorecording (v), on videotape (f), in color (c), in VHS format (b), with sound (a), on the videotape (h), which is ¾-inch wide (o), in stereo (s).

Additional elements in this field would enable the cataloger to specify sound characteristics, archival factors such as base materials, and so forth. Other variable control fields provide information on the source of the cataloging record, accompanying material, language, audience, dates of publication or production, and other data that can be used to identify the material being cataloged and facilitate its retrieval.

The *variable data fields* contain the information most commonly associated with a catalog record, transcribed or recorded in full-text format. A record will contain as many variable data fields as are necessary to describe the item, each identified by the three-digit tag defined for that type of data. Many of the variable field tags may be repeated as often as necessary to record the data required, as a bibliographic record will often include more than one occur-

Figure 1. Example of a MARC record.

B21542302   Last updated: 02-12-97   Created 02-12-97   Revision: 1

01 LANG: eng	03 LOCATION: bc	05 BIB LVL: m	07 SUPPRESS: –
02 SKIP: 0	04 CAT DA: 02-12-97	06 MAT TYPE: a	08 COUNTRY: nyu

09	001		32856299
10	003		OCoLC
11	005		19970212172252.0
12	008		950629s1995 nyua j 001 Obeng pam a
13	010		95034387 /AC
14	020		0872263177
15	040		DLC | cDLC
16	041	1	eng | hita
17	049		AKRR
18	050	00	ND653.R4 | bP3913 1995
19	082	00	759.9492 | 220
20	100	1	Pescio, Claudio
21	240	10	Rembrandt e l'Olanda del XVII secolo. | 1English
22	245	10	Rembrandt and seventeenth-century Holland / | cClaudio Pescio ; illustrated by Sergio ; [English translation, Simon Knight]
23	246	1	| iSubtitle on cover: | athe Dutch nation and its painters
24	246	3	Rembrandt and 17th-century Holland
25	260		New York : | bP. Bedrick Books, | c1995
26	300		64 p. : bcol. ill. ; | c36 cm
27	490	1	Masters of art
28	500		Includes index
29	520		Examines the life and art of Rembrandt against the historical, political, and religious background of the period
30	600	10	Rembrandt Harmenszoon van Rijn, | d1606–1669 | xJuvenile literature
31	600	11	Rembrandt Harmenszoon van Rijn | d1606–1669
32	650	0	Painters | zNetherlands | xBiography | xJuvenile literature
33	650	1	Artists
34	650	1	Painting, Dutch
35	650	1	Art appreciation
36	651	0	Netherlands | xCivilization | y17th century | xJuvenile literature
37	651	0	Netherlands | xSocial life and customs | xJuvenile literature
38	651	1	Netherlands | xCivilization | y17th century
39	700	1	Rembrandt Harmenszoon van Rijn, | d1606–1669\
40	700	0	S [226] ergio
41	830	0	Masters of art (Peter Bedrick Books)

rence of a specific type of information, such as subject headings, series, added entries, notes, and so on.

In addition to the tag for identifying the content of a field, the MARC format also includes two indicator positions at the beginning of each variable data field. These allow for additional instructions to the computer regarding storage, indexing, or display of the content of the field. If these indicators are

Figure 2. Another example of a MARC record.

B21542363   Last updated: 02-12-97   Created 02-12-97   Revision: 1

| 01 | LANG: eng | 03 LOCATION: bc | 05 BIB LVL: m | 07 SUPPRESS: – |
| 02 | SKIP: 0 | 04 CAT DA: 02-12-97 | 06 MAT TYPE: a | 08 COUNTRY: cau |

```
09   001          32924645
10   003          OCoLC
11   005          19970212174659.0
12   008          950726s1996  caua  j  000 0beng cam a
13   010          95032105 /AC
14   019          34883437
15   020          0152012672
16   040          DLC | cDLC
17   043          n-us——
18   049          AKRR
19   050     00   GV1061.15 R83 | bK78 1996
20   082     00   796.42 / 092 | aB | 220
21   100     1    Krull, Kathleen
22   245     10   Wilma unlimited : | bhow Wilma Rudolph became
                  the world's fastest woman / | cKathleen Krull ;
                  illustrated by David Diaz
23   250          1st ed
24   260          San Diego : | bHarcourt Brace, | cc1996
25   300          1 v. (unpaged) : | bcol. ill. ; | c23 x 29 cm
26   520          A biography of the African-American woman who
                  overcame crippling polio as a child to become the first
                  woman to win three gold medals in track in a single
                  Olympics
27   600     10   Rudolph, Wilma, | d1940– | xJuvenile literature
28   600     11   Rudolph, Wilma | d1940–
29   650     0    Runners (Sports) | zUnited States | xBiography |
30   650     1    Track and field athletics
31   650     1    Afro-Americans | xBiography
32   650     1    Women | xBiography
33   700     1    Diaz, David, | eill
```

not needed for a specific field, they are defined as blank. One common use of an indicator is to specify how many characters should be skipped at the beginning of a title field to avoid indexing under an article such as "The" (four nonfiling characters, including the space before the next word) or "An" (three nonfiling characters). Indicators can also be used to control printing or display features, such as automatic printing of notes or creation of access points from coded fields.

Within the variable fields, text that may require special manipulation, indexing, or display instructions are separated by subfield codes. These are two-character codes, defined for each tag, composed of a delimiter (|) and a letter or number. For example, in an entry for a personal name, dates are separated from the name portion of the entry by a delimiter and the letter *d*. This makes it possible to write programming to manipulate and display data in a manner that makes sense, separating the name portion of the heading from other elements. For example, the heading for Rembrandt used as a main entry would look like this in the MARC record:

100 10 Rembrandt Harmenszoon van Rijn, | d 1606–1669.

As with tags, subfield codes are usually the same for where the same type of information is used for a different purpose in the record. Providing subject access for a book on Rembrandt would require a field tagged 600:

600 10 Rembrandt Harmenszoon van Rijn, | d 1606–1669.

Learning to create and use MARC bibliographic records is an important step in opening your library to the world. The information included in the record comes from the same sources catalogers have always used to provide access to their collections. Information is transcribed from the material being cataloged according to current cataloging rules and standards. Access points are selected, subject headings assigned, and a classification determined—all using the same resources used for creating manual records. Recording this data in a MARC record requires only a knowledge of the basic structure of a MARC record, access to appropriate software, and a copy of the format documentation.

Creation of the bibliographic record using MARC coding is only the beginning. Once a database of MARC records is created, it may be used to provide access to bibliographic materials through the generation of printed card or book catalogs, or computer output microforms, in addition to online and other forms of electronic catalogs. The records can also be contributed to shared bibliographic databases where they may be used by thousands of libraries and their patrons. MARC records generate the catalog cards vendors supply, and the cards libraries purchase from the Library of Congress or from a bibliographic utility. MARC records make it possible for students of all ages to access information quickly and accurately. Figures 1 and 2 show examples of MARC records.

SOURCE: Virginia M. Berringer, "MARC and ISBD: Vital Links between Students and Library Materials," in Sharon Zuiderveld, ed., *Cataloging Correctly for Kids: An Introduction to the Tools* (Chicago: American Library Association, 1998), pp. 82–89.

Fun with AACR2: Arabic names

THE ANGLO-AMERICAN CATALOGUING RULES have uses beyond the immediate needs of catalogers. I often turn to the section on people's names (chapter 22) to find out how non-English, historical, or compound surnames should be alphabetized in an index or bibliography. (See the first *Whole Library Handbook* for articles and prepositions in surnames.) Rules for sacred scriptures and liturgical works (chapter 25) and the appendixes on capitalization, abbreviations, and numerals are similarly fascinating and most instructive. The following sections offer advice on Arabic names and errors.—*GME.*

22.22B1. Entry element. Enter a name made up of a number of elements under the element or combination of elements by which the person is best known. Determine this from reference sources. When there is insufficient evidence available, enter under the first element. Refer from any part of the name not used as entry element if there is reason to believe that the person's name may be sought under that part.

22.22C. Essential elements. If the entry element is not the given name (ism) or a patronymic derived from the name of the father (a name usually following the given name and compounded with *ibn*), include these names unless they are not customarily used in the name by which the person is known. Include an additional name, descriptive epithet, or term of honor that is treated as part of the name if it aids in identifying the individual. Generally omit other elements of the name, particularly patronymics derived from anyone other than the father.

22.22D. Order of elements.

22.22D1. When the elements of the name are determined, place the best-known element or combination of elements first. Give the other elements in the following order: khiṭāb, kunyah, ism, patronymic, any other name. Insert a comma after the entry element unless it's the first part of the name.

KHIṬĀB (honorific compound of which the last part is typically *al-Dīn*)
    Rashīd al-Dīn Ṭabīb
    Ṣadr al-Dīn al-Qūnawī, Muḥammad ibn Isḥāq
KUNYAH (typically a compound with *Abū* as the first word)
    Abū al-Barakāt Hibat Allāh ibn 'Alī
    Abū Ḥayyān al-Tawḥīdī, 'Alī ibn Muḥammad
ISM (given name)
    'Alī ibn Abī Ṭālib, *Caliph*
    Bashshār ibn Burd
    Mālik ibn Anas
PATRONYMIC (typically a compound with *Ibn* as the first word)
    Ibn Hishām, 'Abd al-Mālik
    Ibn Ḥazm, 'Alī ibn Aḥmad
OTHER NAMES
Laqab (descriptive epithet)
    al-Jāḥiz, 'Amr ibn Baḥr
    Abū Shāmah, 'Abd al-Raḥmān ibn Ismā'īl
Nisbah (proper adjective ending in *ī*, indicating origin, residence, or other circumstances)
    al-Bukhārī, Muḥammad ibn Ismā'īl
    Māzandarānī, 'Abd Allāh ibn Muḥammad
Takhalluṣ (pen name)
    Qā'ānī, Ḥabib Allāh Shīrāzī
    'Ibrat, Zafar Ḥasan

Fun with AACR2: Errors

1.0F. In an area where transcription from the item is required, transcribe an inaccuracy or a misspelled word as it appears in the item. Follow such an inaccuracy either by *[sic]* or by *i.e.* and the correction within square brackets.

The wolrd [sic] of television
The Paul Anthony Buck [i.e. Brick] lectures
What your child really wants to know about sex, and why / by Will[i]am A. Block

1.4F2. Give the date as found in the item even if it is known to be incorrect. If a date is known to be incorrect, add the correct date.

, 1697 [i.e. 1967]

If necessary, explain any discrepancy in a note.

, 1963 [i.e. 1971] *Note:* Originally issued as a sound disc in 1963; issued as a cassette in 1971.

2.5B4. If the number printed on the last page or leaf of a sequence does not represent the total number of pages or leaves in that sequence, let it stand uncorrected unless it gives a completely false impression of the extent of the item, as, for instance, when only alternate pages are numbered or when the number on the last page of leaf of the sequence is misprinted. Supply corrections in such cases in square brackets.

48 [i e. 96] p.

329 [i.e. 392] p.

1.8B4. If an ISBN number is known to be incorrectly printed in the item, give the correct number if it can be readily ascertained and add *(corrected)* to it.

ISBN 0-340-16427-1 (corrected)

3.3.B2. Optional addition for cartographic materials. Give additional scale information that is found on the item if the statement on the item is in error or contains errors.

Scale 1:59,403,960. "Along meridians only, 1 inch = 936 statute miles"

Scale [ca. 1:90,000] not "1 inch to the mile"

21.4C1. If responsibility for a work is known to be erroneously or fictitiously attributed to a person, enter under the actual personal author or under title if the actual personal author is not known. Make an added entry under the heading for the person to whom the authorship is attributed, unless he or she is not a real person.

The autobiography of Alice B. Toklas
(The life of Gertrude Stein written by herself as though it were an autobiography of her secretary, Alice B. Toklas)
Main entry under the heading for Stein
Added entry under the heading for Toklas

The hums of Pooh / by Winnie the Pooh
(Written by A. A. Milne)
Main entry under the heading for Milne

The adventure of the peerless peer / by John H. Watson ; edited by Philip José Farmer
(Written by Farmer as if by the fictitious Dr. Watson)
Main entry under Farmer

21.4C2. If responsibility for a work is known to be erroneously or fictitiously attributed to a corporate body, enter the work under the actual personal author, or under the actual corporate body responsible if the work falls into one of the categories given in 21.1B2, or under title if the actual author or responsible corporate body is unknown. Make an added entry under the heading for the corporate body to which responsibility is attributed, unless it is not a real body.

SOURCE: Michael Gorman and Paul Winkler, eds., *Anglo-American Cataloguing Rules*, 2d ed. (Chicago: American Library Association, 1988).

Why we do not need an AACR3

by Michael Gorman

LET ME START BY EXPLAINING that the name *Anglo-American Cataloguing Rules,* Second Edition (AACR2) (ALA, 1978) is a misnomer. The name stemmed from the limited scope of the project as envisaged in the early 1970s—essentially to harmonize the British and North American texts of the 1967 AACR and to incorporate the International Standard Bibliographic Description for monographs, ISBD(M), without changing the structure or principles of the rules. By the time it became evident that those modest aims had been transmuted by the forces of history and an entirely new code was aborning, it became politically necessary to preserve the pretense of continuity. Anyone who doubts that political decision need only look at the hysteria that gave rise to the War of AACR2 and imagine the response of the craven and reactionary had an entirely new name been rubbed in their faces!

Why would a completely new name have been more truthful and desirable? Among other reasons, the 1967 AACR had much more in common with ALA 1949 (the "red book") and the *Rules for Descriptive Cataloging in the Library of Congress* (the "green book" of 1949) than it did with AACR2. In fact, whole chunks of the green book were incorporated into the North American text of AACR 1967. Taking the broad view, one can see three eras of English-language cataloging codes. The first is that of the 19th-century single-author codes, those of Panizzi, Cutter, Jewett, and so on. The second is that of the 20th-century pre-Lubetzky case-law codes drawn up by committees. (This era ran from the Anglo-American rules of 1908 through the 1967 AACR.) The third—that of the post-Lubetzky, post-ISBD codes—began with AACR2. Revisionist historians could allege that the 1967 code was, at least, the precursor to that era if not actually the first code in it, but that is not a supportable position when one takes into account that Seymour Lubetzky resigned (or was pushed?) from the editorship of the 1967 code precisely because it was not to be allowed to embody his ideas.

AACR2 provided an infinitely expandable framework (in both description and access) to accommodate new media and media yet unborn and has, hence, eliminated the need for "new" AACRs to deal with the problems such new media may pose.

The context of AACR2

Some have said that a need exists for radical, structural change to AACR2. Others, myself included, believe that a need does exist for some change, but that the change should be gradual, evolutionary, and within the structures and principles of AACR2. If we are to evaluate the need for change and the nature of the change, it is imperative that we understand the real-world context of the cataloging rules. That context is: the need for standardization because of cooperation and copy cataloging; the emerging importance of the authority control concept as central to electronic bibliographic systems; other standards; and, in North America, the Library of Congress Rule Interpretations (LCRIs).

Most of these factors and influences are self-explanatory, but I would like to add a comment or two about "other standards" and the LCRIs. The other standards I am referring to are principally the ISBDs and MARC in its various manifestations. The former are our bridge to the catalogers of the world; their significance in the context of the ideal of Universal Bibliographic Control cannot be underestimated. MARC is also of great international significance, for good and ill, and I have long given up on my youthful dreams of seeing MARC thoroughly overhauled to create a format fully in tune with current systems. Like Thomas Carlyle's acquaintance who said she accepted the Universe—to which he replied, "By God, ma'am, you'd better!"—we must accept MARC, warts and all, but applaud all those who are seeking to modify its applications to conform to modern electronic bibliographic control systems. When it comes to LCRIs, we are as pious Catholics looking to the Church for guidance and our Vatican is LC. Like those religious folk, we complain when the word from on high is complicated or not to our liking. This is not LC's fault. They produce LCRIs because we ask them to, and I am sure they would be happy to get out of the interpretive business. In short, I have seen the enemy and he is us, and until cataloging matures to the point when we can distinguish between necessary and foolish consistency, the LCRIs will be always with us.

What do the AACR3 folks want?

I have read all the many statements from the American cataloging community that call for change and, in effect if not always overtly, an AACR3. There seem to be four major areas of need and complaint. They are: simplification, flexibility, the perceived need for strategic planning, and the creation of master records for multiple versions.

Simplification is a very slippery word in the context of cataloging. Do the people who ask for it want simpler rules? It can be argued that the wording of AACR2 is more direct and understandable than that of any previous code. Is the structure of AACR2 too complicated? It is true that AACR2 is far more structured than previous codes, but that structure, once understood, is a benefit, not a barrier, to use. Are there too many rules? Here we may be on to something. There are too many rules for two distinct reasons. Various "special interests" insisted on loading up the rules with descriptive elaboration that is too detailed for the general cataloger and not detailed enough for the specialist. The other reason for the superfluity of rules is that there are many hangovers from previous codes that were retained for political reasons. Perhaps the true demand of the "simplifiers" is for minimal records without all that tedious authority control. That kind of simplification of cataloging practice runs counter to the very notion of a code of cataloging rules and should be resisted at all costs.

Flexibility is a basic attribute of AACR2. There has never been a code that was so accommodating to new cataloging problems (because it is based on principle) and to new forms of communication (because of the general ISBD descriptive structure). Perhaps someone could explain the nature of the "flexibility" requested and reassure us all that it is not another code word for abandoning standards and good cataloging practice.

Strategic planning as applied to cataloging is one of the more bizarre notions currently being floated. It is clearly inapplicable to bibliographic standards and represents yet another example of the misappropriation of business management techniques and jargon and the attempt to apply them in areas to which they have no relevance. Strategic planning presupposes the need for change and is set up to create change. In this instance, it is yet another example of a solution in search of a problem.

Last, there has been some spectacularly misguided and misinformed discussion of the need to create "master records" for works that are manifested in many different physical forms. It is hard for me to believe that this notion has been put about by people who are catalogers. Let me spell it out. Descriptions are of physical objects (and, nowadays, of defined assemblages of electronic data). It is literally impossible to have a single description of two or more different physical objects and/or electronic assemblages. Once the material has been described, the cataloger looks at the manifestation in the light of the work (an intellectual construct that, by its nature, cannot be described) in order to assign access points (including uniform titles) and create authority files. This process, which should be understood by anyone who has taken Cataloging 101, clearly demonstrates that the idea of a "master record" for several manifestations of the same work is cataloging nonsense.

If not AACR3, what?

Some things could and should be done to improve AACR2 without changing its structure or principles.

1. We should get rid of all the "special" case-law rules (for example, the numerous special rules dealing with religious materials and laws).

2. We should prune descriptive rules of their over-elaboration in particular cases—those that are insufficient for the specialist cataloger and too detailed for the general cataloger (for example, in the rules for incunabula and maps). The needs of the specialist cataloger and special collections could be catered to by specialist manuals created by the relevant cataloging bodies and overseen and certified as true interpretations of AACR2 by the Joint Steering Committee.

3. We should resolve the issue of "unpublished" items (texts, video, sound, etc.) in a completely uniform manner across the chapters in Part I.

4. We should develop new or revised chapters of Part I to accommodate new media (especially electronic media, including those accessible only remotely).

5. We should study access issues for new media (especially electronic) with a view to seeing how the general rules hold up or need elaboration, without creating new case-law rules.

6. We should review Part II with the authority record concept in mind (including addressing the main-entry issue).

7. We should resolve the microform issue, not only by persuading LC to drop its "interpretation" that directly contradicts the letter and the spirit of the rule, but also by avoiding a similar debacle over the question of parallel print and electronic texts.

8. We should do a comprehensive review of the examples with a view to amending those that are no longer relevant and adding examples for new media.

9. We should create a consolidation of the unified MARC format and AACR2 and bear in mind the possibility of a principle-based subject term code to be added to create a complete cataloger's resource.

10. We should ask LC to review and curtail the LCRI program (for example, have them cease issuing rule interpretations not concerned with important questions of access).

AACR2 represents not just a major achievement in the Anglo-American cataloguing tradition, but also a beacon of a new age of global cataloging. We should celebrate and consolidate what we have wrought and work toward making an ever-improving AACR2 the basis for international cooperation devoted to attaining Universal Bibliographic Control.

SOURCE: Michael Gorman, "AACR3? Not!" in Brian E. C. Schottlaender ed., *The Future of the Descriptive Cataloging Rules* (Chicago: American Library Association, 1998), pp. 19–29.

A history of the card catalog

by Sandy Brooks

ALTHOUGH BIBLIOGRAPHIC CONTROL is seemingly taken for granted in today's libraries, there was a time when the catalog of a library's holdings may have been just a printed inventory list, or even a list existing only in the memory of the librarian. Before cataloging codes were developed, books might be arranged by size or color or in accession order on the shelves. Over time, as the size of libraries grew, the idea of a simple inventory list of holdings gave way to a need for fast and accurate retrieval of specific items. Retrieval issues have shaped both the development of cataloging codes as well as the physical format of the library catalog.

Different types of catalogs

Prior to the rise in popularity of the card catalog in the mid-1800s, the most common form of library catalog was the manuscript catalog. This was a handwritten list of a library's holdings usually bound into a book format; larger libraries would sometimes have a printed edition, but this was an unusual event. All early catalogs were finding aids reserved for use by the librarians and were rarely used by patrons.

While the card catalog was preeminent from the mid-19th through the mid-20th centuries, the printed book catalog had a brief resurgence of popularity in the mid-1900s. Advances in offset printing made it feasible and cost effective to simply print in book form copies of all the cards in the card catalog for a collection. This was done on a huge scale in 1955 in the United States with the *National Union Catalog* and again in the 1970s with the publishing of the *National Union Catalog, Pre 1956 Imprints.* At this time, though, new formats were quickly emerging. Microphotography made it possible to miniaturize card or book catalogs and make them available on microfilm or microfiche. Also, computer technologies were marching ahead, and MARC (MAchine Readable Cataloging) formats were being devised, which would eventually overtake cards as the most desirable form of library catalog.

The earliest card catalog

In November 1789, the French revolutionary government decreed that all property of religious houses was to be forfeit to the state; this included substantial library holdings. There was some discussion in the government as to what to do with these books—should they be sold to pay off government debts, or redistributed to meet the informational needs of the emerging democracy?

Card catalog, Deutsche Bücherei, Leipzig.

When it was pointed out that the sale of the materials would not amount to much, the government magnanimously decided to use the books to set up a system of public libraries. Each of the newly formed governmental districts would prepare an inventory of all seized materials in its purview and forward these inventories to a central location (Paris), where a national bibliography would be compiled. This national list would then be used to locate items within the country, redistribute materials as needed, and control duplication.

The next step was to devise a set of instructions to be used in each district for drawing up an inventory. Thus, when the information arrived in Paris it would be in a standard form that could be easily compiled. This set of instructions came to be known as the "French Cataloging Code of 1791" (*Library Quarterly* 61 (Jan. 1991): 1–14). The code has been praised for its clarity, brevity, and simplicity. (It had to be all these things, since the people making the inventories were most likely not librarians and perhaps not even scholars.)

The instructions began with an admonishment not to try to rearrange the physical items in the often disheveled libraries, other than to pick books up off the floor and put them on a shelf, and to attempt to gather volumes of a set together. Next the library workers were to count the number of books in the library and cut up sufficient paper slips to put one in each title. Starting at the upper left and moving to the lower right, numbered slips were then inserted protruding out of each book. With these preliminary steps done, the written bibliographic work could begin.

Since playing cards of the time were blank on the back, abundant, and fairly standard in size, inventory takers were instructed to write down the bibliographic information for each title on the back of a single playing card. (An ace or deuce was to be chosen for books which were likely to have a long bibliographic record so the notes could be continued onto the face of the card). Each card was divided into three distinct sections: The top was to be left blank for notations from the commission overseeing the project; the center held the bibliographic data; and the bottom section was basically a holdings statement that listed the district and library where the title was held. The physical description of each item was quite detailed to help indicate the value of a particular item and as an aid in recognizing the best example of each work.

Once all the cards were written up, the bibliographic data was copied into a book which would remain in that library as a local inventory list. The cards were alphabetized and strung together in packets, then shipped off to Paris. There the cards were compared for duplication, notated as to multiple locations, and interfiled, creating a national shelf list.

Of course, not all districts followed the rules properly, or at all. Some curators sent book catalogs to Paris instead of the cards requested; some districts did nothing. Estimates vary as to the actual number of books in these district libraries at the time, but it is thought that only about a third of them were ever cataloged and reported to Paris. This amounted to over one million cards representing three million volumes. While the idea of a complete national union catalog was eventually abandoned, the three-year program did result in the redistribution of millions of books throughout the nation's libraries, and in the foundation of a national library.

Why playing cards?

The literature does not give a definitive answer as to why playing cards were chosen as catalog cards in the French project. It has been speculated that paper may have been in short supply due to the war, forcing the planners to search out other options. Also, the cards were sturdy and so could stand some shipping and handling. There is some evidence to suggest that organizing catalogs with playing cards may have been common in France at this time, and the French cataloging code was merely the first enumeration of the practice. The convenient blank backs of playing cards had also been known to be used for other alternative purposes, such as marriage and death certificates, note-taking, and business cards.

The idea of cards or slips for a library catalog was not entirely original. As early as 1548 it was proposed that slips could be used for recording bibliographic data, which could then be pasted down or otherwise affixed in proper order in a book catalog. The Vatican library used such a slip catalog in the late 17th century, and other book catalogs throughout history were constructed this way. The French catalog was novel in that the "slips" (cards) would not then be affixed into a book format but would remain in card format. The cards were considered merely a librarian's tool, however, and not a public form of catalog. That idea would come more than a half century later.

The 19th century and beyond

The card catalog is often thought to be an American innovation, but it has been shown that the French claim that honor. Before 1853, few American libraries were using card catalogs. When the first convention of librarians was held in the United States in 1853, Charles Coffin Jewett of the Smithsonian Institution talked up his idea for a national catalog following the model of his library's card catalog. The idea must have sounded good to other librarians, for by the time of the first ALA conference in 1876 the card catalog was becoming commonplace. By 1893, it was the dominant form of catalog. (Many libraries had actually maintained "slip catalogs" for years, which documented new acquisitions to be integrated into the next edition of the book catalog. These slip catalogs formed the foundation of the new card catalogs.)

Several events occurred in 1876 that encouraged this new form of catalog. The American Library Association was formed and librarians were united in discussions about the merits of the card catalog. The planned publication of the *American Library Journal* was announced, and examples of catalog cards were solicited for printing in the journal in the hopes of starting some sort of cooperative cataloging venture. Also, the Li-

Charles Coffin Jewett

brary Bureau was formed, which would eventually standardize the catalog card and be one of the first groups to attempt mass printing of cards.

Methods of card production

Catalog cards were produced in basically four ways—by writing the information by hand, by typing, by cutting and pasting preprinted bibliographic citations onto cards, or by machine printing, either in-house or bought from a vendor. In 1893, most libraries were still producing handwritten cards, although the typewriter had been invented years earlier. (Many libraries did not feel comfortable with the new technology of the typewriter until the 1920s.) Cards were written in a special "library hand" that slanted backwards to save precious space on the card and was meant to closely resemble type. The Library of Congress used handwritten cards or printed slips from catalogs pasted onto cards until 1898. It was not until the Library of Congress began printing cards, first in 1898 for American copyrighted books, and then in 1901 when the service became available to all libraries, that cooperative cataloging became a fixture in the library profession.

The death of the card catalog?

Despite its many advantages, the disadvantages of the card catalog have come back to haunt librarians. When card catalogs were initiated in the 1800s, the grand sizes to which library collections (and thus card catalogs) would grow could not have been foreseen. As early as 1904 librarians were beginning to complain about the size of the card catalog. In his 1938 *Library Quarterly* article "The Possibility of Discarding the Card Catalog," Freemont Rider railed at the drawbacks of the monstrosity and pleaded for new technology to remedy the situation. He saw the primary problem of the card catalog as fourfold: Multiple copies could not be easily made, filing costs were high and grew proportionately as the catalog grew, the physical bulk was enormous, and it was awkward to use. The upkeep on card catalogs became such a tremendous time-consumer that librarians had little time to prepare finding lists, subject guides, or other retrieval aids for patrons. It was also criticized for keeping libraries ignorant of each others' holdings.

Some libraries began printing their catalogs on microfiche to get around these issues, including the Library of Congress and the Bibliothèque Nationale. In the late 1980s the ongoing *National Union Catalog* went to microfiche as well. The 1980s and 1990s saw many libraries retrospectively converting their holdings to electronic formats. Card catalogs were being frozen or closed at a rate that alarmed some who feared valuable information and history were being lost forever in the conversion process. Early in 1996 a plea went out on Autocat (the cataloger's Internet discussion list) to locate a suitable specimen of a card catalog for preservation in a museum setting.

While the card catalog filled an important niche in the library for over a century, it has been overtaken in popularity by the online catalog, although many smaller libraries will likely continue to use it for years to come. From its humble beginnings on playing cards in France to its new virtual life as encrypted MARC code, the card catalog has earned an honorable place in the history of libraries and information retrieval.

SOURCE: Special report by Sandy Brooks for *The Whole Library Handbook 3.*

Cost analysis of acquisitions and cataloging

by the ALCTS Technical Services Costs Committee

THE PURPOSE OF THIS GUIDE is to help the technical processing manager determine the unit cost for any acquisitions or cataloging function. To arrive at this figure one needs access to pertinent budget information and production statistics. Using this data, one can calculate the unit cost for the output of any technical processing function (e.g., the cost to catalog a title) or sequence of functions (e.g., the cost for each volume added).

When determining costs, it is important to consider all cost factors, e.g., salaries and wages, supplies, equipment (leases or amortized costs), maintenance or service contracts. The cost analysis worksheet on page 316 can be used to determine the unit cost of any acquisitions or cataloging function. The following paragraphs explain how to use this form step-by-step.

1. Define the function to be measured, such as copy cataloging or serials check-in. The actual activities that make up a function will vary from one library to another, but be sure to identify all the steps that are considered part of the function locally.   [For a list of sample variables, see the original article.—*GME*]

2. Next, determine the unit of measure and the number of units produced on an annual basis. This frequently is an output measure; for example, the output of copy cataloging is titles cataloged. The unit cost for copy cataloging would be the average cost incurred to catalog a title. The number of units produced can be determined from production statistics. If one wishes to determine a unit cost for all of technical processing, the usual unit of measure would be a volume. Items 2a and 2b explain two methods for arriving at the number of volumes to be used in such a calculation.

3. Determine labor cost for the function being measured. This figure should include the costs for benefits, time in meetings, etc. The actual costs may be available from budget information. If not, step 3a can be used to calculate average cost per hour for the involved staff, and step 3b multiplies the average cost per hour by the total number of hours devoted to the function to arrive at the labor cost for the function.

4. Identify annual costs for supplies and operating expenses for the function in question. The list of sample variables can be used as a guide in determining these.

5. If equipment is needed to perform the function being measured, its cost should be included here. The cost of most equipment will need to be amortized for this purpose; it may be necessary to consult with someone in the organization to determine how such costs are calculated locally. The cost of leasing and maintenance agreements should be included in section 4 above.

6. It is important to decide whether overhead (utilities, space, etc.) should be included in the calculation of unit cost and, if so, whether a percentage of the overhead for a larger unit should be included as well. If it is decided to include these costs, it may be necessary to consult with someone else in the organization to determine the appropriate formula for calculating them.

7. Total all of the identified costs for the function as a whole: lines 3–6 (or 3–5 if overhead costs are not applicable). Divide this amount by the num-

ber of units recorded on line 2. The result is the unit cost for the measure of the function (e.g., the cost to copy catalog a title, check in a serial issue, or the aggregate cost of processing a volume).

SOURCE: ALCTS Technical Services Costs Committee, "Guide to Cost Analysis of Acquisitions and Cataloging in Libraries," *ALCTS Newsletter 2*, no. 5 (1991): 49–52.

Cost analysis worksheet

1. Function(s) to measure: _____

2. Unit of measure: _____

   If analyzing processing cost in the aggregate, the two most common approaches for determining volume content are:

   a. total expenditure of book funds divided by the average (mean) purchase price per volume PLUS the number of gift volumes processed.

   OR

   b. total number of volumes received via order and gift PLUS the number of periodical volumes bound and added to collection.

3. Labor cost (wages and benefits): $ _____

   a. $\dfrac{\text{annual wages + benefits of all staff involved}}{\text{total annual hours paid for all staff involved}}$ = average cost per hour

   b. $\begin{array}{c}\text{Average cost}\\\text{per hour}\end{array}$ x $\begin{array}{c}\text{Hours paid for the}\\\text{particular function}\end{array}$ = labor cost for the function

4. Cost of supplies and operations related to these functions: $ _____

5. Cost of equipment related to the functions: $ _____

   (It is better to amortize large purchases. If you have no guidelines, a common standard is to amortize over 3 years any purchase exceeding $500.)

6. OVERHEAD (optional):
   a. Include overhead of processing unit?   If yes: $ _____
   b. Include overhead of library?   If yes: $ _____
   c. Include overhead of parent organization?   If yes: $ _____
   d. TOTAL OVERHEAD (Add line 6a + 6b + 6c): $ _____

   In most cases, overhead costs do not extend beyond the library.

7. Total costs:
   a. TOTAL COST PER MEASURE: $ _____
   (Add lines 3 + 4 + 5 + 6d)

   b. TOTAL COST PER UNIT OF MEASURE: $ _____
   (Divide line 7a by line 2)

What is a reproduction?

A REPRODUCTION IS AN ITEM that is a copy of another item and is intended to function as a substitute for that item. The copy may be in a different physical format from the original. Reproduction is a mechanical rather than an intellectual process. Due to the particular mechanical process used to create it, physical characteristics of the reproduction, such as color, image resolution, or sound fidelity may differ from those of the original. Reproductions are usually made for such reasons as the original's limited availability, remote location, poor condition, high cost, or restricted utility.

The following examples are reproductions:
1. Microfilm of a text, produced for preservation purposes.
2. Published microfilm reproduction.
3. On-demand macroreproduction (such as a photocopy).
4. Macroreproduction that includes a different chief source of information (chief source for the reproduction is a *data sheet* on the leaf before the reproduced *title page* of the original).
5. Black-and-white microfilm of a book that includes color illustrations.
6. Photocopy (printout) of an original microfiche; reproduction agency unknown.
7. Computer file produced by optical scanning of a printed original, and a printout from the computer file.
8. Photocopy and microfiche of a map.
9. Photocopy of a map that has been reduced from the size and scale of the original.
10. Black-and-white microfiche reproduction of a series of color maps.
11. Microform copy of an archival collection of personal papers.
12. Microfilm copy of a piece of music.
13. Tape dub of a 33 ⅓-rpm sound recording.
14. Video reproduction of a 35mm film reproduced for preservation purposes.
15. Photoreproduction of a graphic item.
16. Copy negative and microreproduction of an original photographic negative.
17. Remote-access computer file, reproduced on disks.
18. Microreproductions of a current serial.
19. Reproductions of a serial which has ceased publication.
20. Microfiche reproduction with a variant title on the fiche header.
21. Printout of a serial issued electronically.
22. Complex serial reproduction, including reproductions of partial runs with mixed paper and microform holdings.

The following items are *not* reproductions:
1. Hardcover and paperback issues of the same book with no significant bibliographic differences.
2. A monograph simultaneously issued in the United States and the United Kingdom by two different publishers.
3. A book issued both in conventional-sized type and large print.
4. A Braille edition of a book.
5. An annotated version of a novel.
6. Published music, whether full-sized or reduced, that appears to have

been printed from the same metal or photographic plates as an earlier edition.

7. A microfilm of a manuscript collection that contains significant omissions, additions, or alterations from the original.

8. A microfilm consisting of manuscript scores collected from various sources.

9. A full score and a set of parts for a string quartet.

10. A sound recording issued on LP, CD, and cassette.

11. An LP issued in both monaural and stereo.

12. An LP reissued as a CD.

13. A computer application package issued on both 3 ½- and 5 ¼-inch disks.

14. A computerized version of an encyclopedia originally published in paper form with search software added.

15. A journal published simultaneously in printed and electronic format.

16. A museum reproduction of an art original.

17. A video issued in both Beta and VHS.

SOURCE: Guidelines for Bibliographic Description of Reproductions (Chicago: ALA Association for Library Collections and Technical Services, 1995).

Dewey Decimal Classification:
The hundred divisions

MOST LIBRARY USERS KNOW the general structure of Melvil Dewey's decimal classification. First published in 1876, the Dewey Decimal Classification divides knowledge into ten main classes, with further subdivisions. Here is an outline of its 100 major subdivisions.

000 Generalities

000 The book, computer science
010 Bibliography
020 Library and information sciences
030 General encyclopedic works
040 [not assigned]
050 General serial publications
060 General organizations and museology
070 News media, journalism, publishing
080 General collections
090 Manuscripts and rare books

100 Philosophy, paranormal phenomena, psychology

110 Metaphysics
120 Epistemology, causation, humankind

130   Paranormal phenomena
140   Specific philosophical schools
150   Psychology
160   Logic
170   Ethics (moral philosophy)
180   Ancient, medieval, Oriental philosophy
190   Modern Western philosophy

ARISTOTLE.—Museo Visconti.

200 Religion

210   Philosophy and theory of religion
220   Bible
230   Christianity, Christian theology
240   Christian moral and devotional theology
250   Christian orders and local church
260   Christian social and ecclesiastical theology
270   History of Christianity and Christian church
280   Christian denominations and sects
290   Comparative religion and other religions

300 Social sciences

310   General statistics
320   Political science
330   Economics
340   Law
350   Public administration and military science
360   Social problems and services, associations
370   Education
380   Commerce, communications, transportation
390   Customs, etiquette, folklore

5

400 Language

410   Linguistics
420   English and Old English
430   Germanic languages
440   French and Romance languages
450   Italian, Romanian, Rhaeto-Romanic languages
460   Spanish and Portuguese languages
470   Classical and medieval Latin languages
480   Hellenic languages
490   Other languages

500 Natural sciences and mathematics

510   Mathematics
520   Astronomy and allied sciences
530   Physics
540   Chemistry and allied sciences
550   Earth sciences
560   Paleontology, paleozoology

570 Life sciences, biology
580 Plants
590 Animals

600 Technology and applied sciences

610 Medical sciences, medicine
620 Engineering and allied operations
630 Agriculture and related technologies
640 Home economics and family living
650 Management and auxiliary services
660 Chemical engineering
670 Manufacturing
680 Manufacture of products for specific uses
690 Buildings

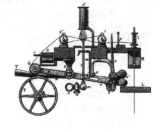

700 The arts; fine and decorative arts

710 Civic and landscape art
720 Architecture
730 Plastic arts, sculpture
740 Drawing and decorative arts
750 Painting and paintings
760 Graphic arts, printmaking and prints
770 Photography and photographs
780 Music
790 Recreational and performing arts

800 Literature and rhetoric

810 American literature in English
820 English and Old English literature
830 German literature
840 Romance literature
850 Italian and Romanian literature
860 Spanish and Portuguese literature
870 Latin literature
880 Classical Greek literature
890 Literatures of other languages

900 Geography and history

910 Geography and travel
920 Biography, genealogy, insignia
930 History of ancient world to ca. 499
940 General history of Europe
950 General history of Asia
960 General history of Africa
970 General history of North America
980 General history of South America
990 General history of other areas

SOURCE: Dewey Decimal Classification Summaries, DDC 21 (Albany, N.Y.: Forest Press, 1996).

LC classification outline

THE LC CLASSIFICATION was developed and used at the Library of Congress beginning in 1899. It has become the system of choice for many large research libraries. This list gives the scope for most one- or two-letter designators, which may serve as an aid in learning the classification schedules in more detail.

A (General works)

AC	Collections, series, collected works
AE	Encyclopedias (general)
AG	Dictionaries and other general reference books
AI	Indexes (general)
AM	Museums (general), collectors and collecting
AN	Newspapers
AP	Periodicals (general)
AS	Academies and learned societies (general)
AY	Yearbooks, almanacs, directories
AZ	History of scholarship and learning

B (Philosophy, psychology, religion)

B	Philosophy (general)
BC	Logic
BD	Speculative philosophy
BF	Psychology, parapsychology, occult sciences
BH	Aesthetics
BJ	Ethics, social usages, etiquette
BL	Religions, mythology, rationalism
BM	Judaism
BP	Islam, Baha'ism, theosophy
BQ	Buddhism
BR	Christianity
BS	The Bible
BT	Doctrinal theology
BV	Practical theology
BX	Christian denominations

5

C (Auxiliary sciences of history)

C	Auxiliary sciences of history (general)
CB	History of civilization
CC	Archaeology (general)
CD	Diplomatics, archives, seals
CE	Calendars, technical chronology
CJ	Numismatics, coins, medals
CN	Inscriptions, epigraphy
CR	Heraldry, chivalry
CS	Genealogy
CT	Biography (general)

D (History, general and outside the Americas)

D   History (general)
DA   Great Britain, Ireland
DAW   Central Europe
DB   Austria, Liechtenstein, Hungary, Czech Republic, Slovakia
DC   France, Andorra, Monaco
DD   Germany
DE   The Mediterranean region, the Greco-Roman world
DF   Greece
DG   Italy
DH   Belgium, Luxembourg
DJ   Netherlands
DK   Russia, former Soviet republics, Poland
DL   Scandinavia
DP   Spain, Portugal
DQ   Switzerland
DR   Balkan states
DS   Asia
DT   Africa
DU   Australia, Oceania
DX   Gypsies

E–F (History, America)

E   Indians, United States (general)
F   U.S. local history, Canada, Mexico, Central and South America

G (Geography, anthropology, recreation)

G   Voyages and travels, atlases, maps
GA   Mathematical geography, cartography
GB   Physical geography
GC   Oceanography
GE   Environmental sciences
GF   Human geography
GN   Anthropology
GR   Folklore
GT   Manners and customs
GV   Recreation, sports, games, leisure, physical
       education

H (Social sciences)

H   Social sciences (general)
HA   Statistics, data
HB   Economic theory, demography
HC   Economic history and conditions (by region or country)
HD   Production, land use, agriculture, industry, labor, special industries
HE   Transportation, traffic, shipping, communication
HF   Commerce, business, accounting
HG   Finance, money, banking, stocks, insurance

HJ   Public finance, taxation, public credit
HM   Sociology (general and theoretical)
HN   Social history, social problems, social reform
HQ   Sex, the family, marriage, women, feminism
HS   Societies (secret, benevolent), clubs
HT   Cities, communities, classes, race relations
HV   Emergency management, social service, welfare,
      social protection, criminology
HX   Socialism, communism, utopias, anarchism

J (Political science)

J   General legislative and executive papers
JA   Collections and general works
JC   Political theory, theory of the state
JF   Political institutions and public
      administration
JK   United States government (federal and state)
JL   America outside the United States
JN   Europe
JQ   Asia, Africa, Australia, Oceania
JS   Local and municipal government
JV   Colonization, emigration, immigration
JX   International law (no longer used)
JZ   International relations

K (Law)

K   Law (general), jurisprudence, comparative law, conflict of laws
KD–KDK   United Kingdom and Ireland
KDZ   America, North America
KE–KEZ   Canada
KF–KFZ   United States
KG–KGZ   Mexico, Central America, Caribbean
KH–KHW   South America
KJ–KKZ   Europe
KL   Ancient Orient
KLA–KLW   Eurasia
KM–KPZ   Asia
KQ–KTZ   Africa
KU–KWX   Pacific area
KWX   Antarctica
KZ   Law of nations
KZA   Law of the sea
KZD   Law of outer space

L (Education)

L   Education (general)
LA   History of education
LB   Theory, teaching, teacher training, higher
      education, school administration

LC	Forms, social aspects, religious education, other types, special classes, adult education
LD	United States
LE	America, except United States
LF	Europe
LG	Asia, Africa, Oceania
LH	College and school magazines and newspapers
LJ	Student fraternities and societies
LT	Multi-subject textbooks

M (Music)

M	Music
ML	Literature of music
MT	Musical instruction and study

N (Fine arts)

N	Visual arts (general)
NA	Architecture
NB	Sculpture
NC	Drawing, design, illustration
ND	Painting
NE	Print media
NK	Decorative arts, applied arts, antiques, other arts
NX	Arts in general

P (Language and literature)

P	Philology and linguistics (general)
PA	Classical languages and literature
PB	General European languages, Celtic
PC	Romance languages
PD	Old Germanic, Scandinavian
PE	English
PF	Dutch, Flemish, Friesian, German
PG	Slavic, Baltic, Albanian
PH	Finno-Ugric, Basque
PJ	Egyptian, Libyan, Berber, Cushitic, Semitic languages
PK	Indo-Iranian, Armenian, Caucasian
PL	East Asian, African, Oceanic languages
PM	Inuit, American Indian, artificial languages
PN	Literary history and collections, drama, journalism
PQ	Romance literatures
PR	English literature
PS	American literature
PT	Germanic literature
PZ	Juvenile belles lettres, miscellaneous literature

Q (Science)

Q	Science (general), information theory
QA	Mathematics
QB	Astronomy
QC	Physics
QD	Chemistry
QE	Geology, paleontology
QH	Natural history, biology
QK	Botany
QL	Zoology
QM	Human anatomy
QP	Physiology, animal biochemistry, experimental pharmacology
QR	Microbiology, immunology

R (Medicine)

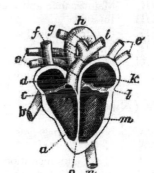

R	Medicine (general)
RA	Regulation, public health
RB	Pathology
RC	Internal medicine, medical practice
RD	Surgery
RE	Ophthalmology
RF	Otorhinolaryngology
RG	Gynecology and obstetrics
RJ	Pediatrics
RK	Dentistry
RL	Dermatology
RM	Therapeutics, pharmacology
RS	Pharmacy and materia medica
RT	Nursing
RV	Eclectic medicine
RX	Homeopathy
RZ	Alternative systems of medicine

S (Agriculture)

S	Agriculture (general), education, melioration
SB	Plant culture, pest control, diseases
SD	Forestry
SF	Animal culture, pets, veterinary medicine
SH	Aquaculture, fisheries, angling
SK	Hunting, wildlife management

T (Technology)

T	Technology (general), engineering (industrial), patents
TA	Engineering (general), civil engineering (general)
TC	Hydraulic and ocean engineering
TD	Environmental technology, sanitary engineering
TE	Highway engineering, roads and pavements

TF	Railroad engineering
TG	Bridge engineering
TH	Building construction
TJ	Mechanical engineering and machinery
TK	Electrical engineering, electronics, nuclear power
TL	Motor vehicles, aircraft, astronautics, UFOs
TN	Mining engineering, metallurgy
TP	Chemical technology
TR	Photography
TS	Manufactures
TT	Handcrafts, arts and crafts
TX	Home economics, hospitality industry

U (Military science)

U	Military science (general)
UA	Armies
UB	Military administration
UC	Maintenance and transportation
UD	Infantry
UE	Cavalry, armored and mechanized calvary
UF	Artillery
UG	Military engineering, air forces, air warfare
UH	Other military services

V (Naval science)

V	Naval science (general)
VA	Navies
VB	Naval administration
VC	Naval maintenance
VD	Naval seamen
VE	Marines
VF	Naval ordnance
VG	Minor services of navies
VK	Navigation, merchant marine
VM	Naval engineering, shipbuilding, diving

Z (Bibliography, library science)

Z	Books in general
Z 4–8	History of books and bookmaking
Z 40–115.5	Writing, paleography
Z 116–659	Printing, binding, the book trade, copyright, censorship
Z 662–1000.5	Libraries, library science, information science
Z 1001–8999	Bibliography
ZA	Information resources

SOURCE: Library of Congress.

Bliss Bibliographic Classification

THE BIBLIOGRAPHIC CLASSIFICATION (BC) was originally devised by Henry Evelyn Bliss and was first published in four volumes in the USA between 1940 and 1953. Bliss stated that one of the purposes of the Classification was to "demonstrate that a coherent and comprehensive system, based on the logical principles of classification and consistent with the systems of science and education, may be available to services in libraries," to provide an "adaptable, efficient and economical classification, notation and index."

On the formation of the Bliss Classification Association (BCA) in 1967, it was suggested that a new and completely revised edition of the full BC should be made available. The new, revised edition was initiated by Jack Mills and was to be produced in parts, comprising one or two subjects per volume. The first volumes were published in 1977.

2–9	Generalia, phenomena, information science and technology
A–AL	Philosophy, logic
AM–AX	Mathematics, probability, statistics
AY	General science
B	Physics, engineering
C	Chemistry, chemical engineering
D	Space and earth sciences
E	Biology
F	Botany
G	Zoology
GR	Agriculture
GU	Veterinary science
GY	Ecology
H	Physical anthropology, human biology
I	Psychology, psychiatry
J	Education
K	Social sciences, sociology, social anthropology
L O	History, archaeology, biography, travel
P	Religion, occult, morals and ethics
Q	Social welfare, criminology
R	Politics, public administration
S	Law
T	Economics, management of economic enterprises
U–V	Technology
W	Recreation, arts, music
X–Y	Language, literature

SOURCE: Bliss Classification Association.

Other classification schemes

Thomas Jefferson's catalogue (lcweb.loc.gov/exhibits/treasures/trm055.html).
Universal Decimal Classification (zeus.slais.ucl.ac.uk/udc/).
Colon Classification (developed by S. R. Ranganathan in the 1930s).
National Library of Medicine (www.nlm.nih.gov/pubs/factsheets/nlmclassif.html).
Expansive Classification (developed by Charles Ami Cutter in the 1890s).
Superintendent of Documents Classification (www.du.edu/~ttyler/exsudoc.htm).
London Classification of Business Studies (begun 1970 by the London Business School).

REFERENCE

Important dates in the history of reference sources

by Bill Katz

1792 B.C.—The *Code of Hammurabi* in Babylon is one of the first government documents.

652–660 B.C.—Babylonian almanac appears.

287–212 B.C.—Archimedes introduces one of the first handbooks, his *Verba filiorum*, a mathematical work.

58 B.C.—Varro's *Disciplinae*, an early encyclopedia, appears.

23–79 A.D.—Pliny the Elder perfects his 37-volume encyclopedia, *Historia naturalis*.

129–189—Galen writes the first bibliography, *De libris propriis liber.*

354—Earliest extant calendar-almanac.

959—*Suidas* (Fortress), a Greek lexicon, published.

1002—Aelfric completes his grammar *Vocabularium* at Eynsham, near Oxford.

1455—Johannes Gutenberg prints the first Latin Bible (right).

1457—First printed almanac.

1470—First printed bibliography, a catalog of Sweynheym and Pannartz that lists books printed from 1463 to 1470.

1497—First English almanac.

1524—First published geographical manual.

1527—Castiglione publishes one of the first etiquette books, *Il Cortegiano* (The Courtier).

1570—Ortelius publishes the first atlas, *Theatrum Orbis Terrarum.*

1657—*L'encyclopedie des beaux esprits,* believed to be the first reference book with "encyclopedia" in the title.

1665—*Journal des Scavans* appears, a weekly in French that lists books selectively and presents critical reviews.

1665—The first English journal, *Philosophical Transactions of the Royal Society,* begins as a voice of new science.

1721—Daniel Jablonski publishes the first short encyclopedia, *Allgemeines Lexikon,* in Danzig.

1795—First American atlas published by Matthew Carey.

1820—John Murray begins publishing travel guides, the *Red Books.*

1901—*Reader's Guide* launched as the first general periodical index for laypeople.

1907—First issue of *Chemical Abstracts,* the first modern abstracting service.

SOURCE: Bill Katz, *Cuneiform to Computer: A History of Reference Sources* (Lanham, Md.: Scarecrow Press, 1998), pp. 381–87. Reprinted with permission.

Guidelines for behavioral performance

MOST OF THE LITERATURE on the evaluation of reference services has been concerned with the factual accuracy of librarian responses to user queries. Many studies have been conducted to determine if patrons are receiving "correct" information from librarians. As has been well-reported in the reference literature, we collectively succeed according to this measure of service quality only slightly more than one-half of the time. However, these studies do not take into account the complex librarian/patron interaction during the reference process.

Reference performance cannot be measured solely by the accuracy of an answer to a factual question. In many cases, the librarian serves as a research consultant who provides guidance and advice on search strategy and process, rather than providing a specific answer to a factual question. In cases such as this, the success of the transaction is measured not by the information conveyed, but by the positive or negative impact of the patron/librarian interaction. In this type of transaction, the positive or negative behavior of the librarian (as observed by the patron) becomes a significant factor in perceived success or failure.

These guidelines are intended to be used to assist in the training, development, and/or evaluation of librarians and staff who provide information services directly to library users. They are designed primarily to deal with instances in which the patron and the librarian are working face to face. While many of the guidelines also apply to other all reference transactions, some will need to be adapted for remote users and persons with special needs.

Approachability

In order to have a successful reference transaction, the patron must be able to identify that a reference librarian is available to provide assistance and also must feel comfortable in going to that librarian for help. Approachability behaviors set the tone for the entire communication process between the librarian and the patron. The initial verbal and nonverbal responses of the librarian will influence the depth and level of the interaction between the librarian and the patron. At this stage in the process, the behaviors exhibited by the librarian should serve to welcome the patron and to place him/her at ease. The librarian's role in the communications process is to make the patron feel comfortable in a situation which may be perceived as intimidating, risky, confusing, and overwhelming. To be approachable, the librarian:

- is poised and ready to engage approaching patrons and is not engrossed in reading, filing, chatting with colleagues, or other activities that detract from availability to the patron;
- establishes initial eye contact with the patron;
- acknowledges the presence of the patron through smiling and/or open body language;
- acknowledges the patron through the use of a friendly greeting to initiate conversation and/or by standing up, moving forward, or moving closer to the patron;
- acknowledges others waiting for service;
- remains visible to patrons as much as possible;

- roves through the reference area offering assistance whenever possible.

Interest

A successful librarian must demonstrate a high degree of interest in the reference transaction.

While not every query will contain stimulating intellectual challenges, the librarian should be interested in each patron's informational needs and should be committed to providing the most effective assistance. Librarians who demonstrate a high level of interest in the inquiries of their patrons will generate a higher level of satisfaction among users. To demonstrate interest, the librarian:

- faces the patron when speaking and listening;
- maintains or reestablishes eye contact with the patron throughout the transaction;
- establishes a physical distance which appears to be comfortable to the patron, based upon the patron's verbal and nonverbal responses;
- signals an understanding of the patron's needs through verbal or nonverbal confirmation, such as nodding of the head or brief comments or questions;
- appears unhurried during the reference transaction;
- focuses his/her attention on the patron.

Listening and inquiring

The reference interview is the heart of the reference transaction and is crucial to the success of the process. The librarian must be effective in identifying the patron's information needs and must do so in a manner that keeps the patron at ease. Strong listening and questioning skills are necessary for a positive interaction. As a good communicator, the librarian:

- uses a tone of voice appropriate to the nature of the transaction;
- communicates in a receptive, cordial, and encouraging manner;
- allows the patron to state fully his/her information need in his/her own words before responding;
- rephrases the patron's question or request and asks for confirmation to ensure that it is understood;
- uses open-ended questioning techniques to encourage the patron to expand on the request or present additional information. Some examples of such questions include:
  Please tell me more about your topic.
  What additional information can you give me?
  How much information do you need?
- uses closed and/or clarifying questions to refine the search query. Some examples of clarifying questions are:
  What have you already found?
  What type of information do you need (books, articles, etc.)?
  Do you need current or historical information?
- seeks to clarify confusing terminology and avoids excessive jargon;

- uses terminology that is understandable to the patron;
- maintains objectivity and does not interject value judgments about subject matter or the nature of the question into the transaction.

Searching

The search process is the portion of the transaction in which behavior and accuracy intersect.

Without an effective search, the desired information is unlikely to be found. Yet many of the aspects of searching that lead to accurate results are still dependent on the behavior of the librarian. As an effective searcher, the librarian:

- constructs a competent and complete search strategy;
- breaks the query into specific facets;
- identifies other qualifiers of the query that may limit results, such as date, language, comprehensiveness, etc.;
- selects search terms that are most related to the information desired;
- searches under the most limiting aspects of the query first;
- verifies spelling and other possible factual errors in the original query;
- identifies sources appropriate to the patron's need that have the highest probability of containing information relevant to the patron's query;
- consults guides, databases, or other librarians for assistance when he/she cannot independently identify sources to answer the query;
- discusses the search strategy with the patron;
- encourages the patron to contribute ideas;
- explains the search sequence to the patron;
- attempts to conduct the search within the patron's allotted time frame;
- accompanies the patron (at least in the initial stages of the search process);
- explains how to use sources when the patron shows an interest;
- works with the patron to narrow or broaden the topic when too little or too much information is identified;
- asks the patron if additional information is needed after an initial result is found;
- recognizes when to refer a patron to a more appropriate library, librarian, or other resource person.

Follow-up

The reference transaction does not end when the librarian walks away from the patron. The librarian is responsible for determining if the patron is satisfied with the results of the search and is also responsible for referring the patrons to other sources, even when those sources are not available in the local library. For successful follow-up, the librarian:

- asks the patron if the question has been completely answered;
- encourages the patron to return to the reference service point;

- returns to the patron after the patron has had time to study the information source(s);
- consults other librarians when additional subject expertise is needed;
- makes arrangements, when appropriate, with the patron to research a question even after the patron has left the library;
- tries to ensure that the patron will get appropriate service after a referral by providing accurate information to the other department, library, or organization about the question, the amount of information required, and sources already consulted;
- facilitates the process of referring a patron to another library or information agency through activities such as calling ahead, providing direction and instructions, and providing the library and the patron with as much information as possible;
- refers the patron to other sources or institutions when the query cannot be answered to the satisfaction of the patron.

SOURCE: Guidelines for Behavioral Performance of Reference and Information Services Professionals (Chicago: ALA Reference and User Services Association, 1997).

Explaining electronic information resources to users

by the ALA Reference and User Services Association

THESE GUIDELINES are intended to assist information services librarians who provide and publicize new electronic information resources to users and potential users. For purposes of this document, electronic information resources include but are not limited to online search services, compact disc search services, Internet sites, World Wide Web products, online public access catalogs/systems, electronic texts, multimedia, and other sources of information that users may directly access in an electronic format.

This document offers practical guidance to library staff who are concerned with strategies for implementation, policy, procedure, education, or direct provision of electronic information resources. Though intended for all types of libraries, not every statement will apply to a particular library or type of library. Accordingly, this checklist contains suggestions and recommendations that may be adapted to local library environments.

Planning, policy, and procedure

After selection of a new electronic resource, the library staff should determine a schedule for provision of the resource for the users. Planning for this schedule should take into consideration every aspect of these guidelines and may include a time period during which the service is available in a testing/orientation mode for library staff who will be involved in the direct provision of service.

The library should determine which staff will be involved and what their specific responsibilities and assignments will be in the implementation of the electronic resource.

The library should examine existing procedures and policies to determine whether they apply to the new service and, if necessary, develop new policies and procedures.

For electronic-resources licensing agreements or specific restrictions on use, the library should determine which staff have oversight responsibility for observance of any limitations on use.

Information service providers should also conduct planning for staff education, user education, publicity, and evaluation and assessment of the service.

Staff education

The level of proficiency in the use of the new electronic information resource should be established for each information service provider, including full-time and part-time staff, involved in assisting users with the service.

Some staff may be designated as specialists who will acquire an in-depth knowledge of the service. Others may be designated as generalists who will need a basic or adequate familiarity with the service. A timetable for achieving the required level of competence should also be established.

Staff orientation and training for the new service should include accommodation for various learning styles and may involve a combination of hands-on practice, system tutorials, peer instruction, outside trainers, and/or study of appropriate manuals or other documentation.

User education/instruction

Library staff should determine the level of need for formal and informal user instruction for a new electronic information resource.

Library staff should also determine the extent to which the service should be incorporated into existing user instruction sessions and programs and the extent to which new instructional sessions or methods would be helpful.

Planning for user instruction should accommodate various learning styles and may include a combination of point of use instruction for individuals, group instruction, peer assistance, system tutorials, documentation, and/or signage.

In whatever forms it takes, user education should include provisions for assessment and evaluation.

Publicity

Responsibility for publicity should be clearly assigned.

All library staff who interact with users should be fully briefed and informed about publicity efforts prior to the implementation of those efforts.

Publicity should incorporate a variety of communication modes and formats including print and electronic ones.

Publicity may take a variety of forms, including but not limited to press releases, signage, announcements/letters to the potential user community, special events, exhibits, and presentations.

Assessment and evaluation

Responsibility for assessment and evaluation should be clearly assigned.

The library should conduct an initial evaluation and subsequent regular evaluations to determine the effectiveness of the electronic resource in meeting information needs of the user community.

Adjustments in the provision of service for an electronic resource should be based on sound evaluation and assessment techniques, including but not limited to the collection of statistical data and surveys of user/staff satisfaction with the resource.

SOURCE: Guidelines for the Introduction of Electronic Information Resources to Users (Chicago: ALA Reference and User Services Association, 1997); www.ala.org/rusa/electron.html.

Bizarre reference questions

THESE REAL QUESTIONS asked by patrons at public libraries appeared as a 1999 thread in the PUBLIB discussion list:

"I need a picture of Jesus." "Do you mean an artist's take on what he may have looked like?" "No, no. I need a photograph."

"I need a copy of my ex-husband's credit report. Just punch it up on your computer there."

I had a patron ask me today for a video of "the actual crucifixion of Christ" (her words). All of our Hollywood movies depicting the crucifixion were checked out, but she seemed happy with a book on the famous passion play held in Öberammergau, Germany.

"What way do grapes grow the best? North–south or east–west?" [Another PUBLIB subscriber said that in southeastern Ohio it should be east–west, to permit prevailing westerly winds to dry the fungus-prone grapes.]

I got asked for Mu'ammar Qadhafi's phone number. (This was around the time when the Navy shot down two Libyan fighters.) I suggested that the patrons call Tripoli information, which I found out they actually did. (Here is what I think Qadhafi's answering machine would say: "Hi, this is Mu'ammar. I'm not in, but if you leave your name and target at the sound of the explosion, I will get back to you.")

A young man wanted to know where the volcano is located in our little town of Rochester, New Hampshire. He said his teacher told him about it.

"Do men chew tobacco so that when they kiss women they can drug them with tobacco juice?"

"What do you call the stringy parts that peel away from the inside of the banana peel?" [Another PUBLIB subscriber came up with the answer: "rags."]

"You know how you can make yourself go into other people's dreams? Can you tell me how to do that?" Our dream dictionaries didn't cover that one!

"My neighbor put a 'wonderful' statue out in the trash. If I can just fix it up . . . Can you direct me to a statue repair place?" The patron wanted to glue arms on a Venus di Milo replica. She liked the shade of green it had been painted, though.

A high school student asked if we had a copy of "The Wrath of Grapes." I said, "By John Steinbeck?" She said yes, and I told her where to find it. A few weeks later, I saw a poster at a friend's house entitled "The Wrath of Grapes"— it was for the United Farm Workers.

A high-school student and her mother wanted a video of a Shakespeare play with "the original cast." Neither mother nor daughter was willing to accept that this was simply not possible, and we ended up with the daughter on the floor throwing a tantrum.

Me: "Can I help you?" Patron: "I need some cocaine." Me: "I do too. Now what can I help you with?"

A woman came up to the desk, leaned over, and in a very hushed whisper asked, "You know those 'R' books? Do you have to be 21 to read them?" It took me a few seconds to figure out that she was referring to the Reference Collection.

Someone just asked our circulation staff, who this year have the privilege of being next to the tax forms: "Where are the forms that are already filled out?"

I recently had a young man ask for a video on the chemical process to turn cocaine into crack. He swore it was for chemistry class.

I once had a patron ask for a picture of Michelangelo's Pietà. He didn't like the one I found because the statue was all one color—marble. He needed to know the colors, because he was having it tattooed on his back. I told him that nuns always said that the Blessed Mother's favorite color was blue; and he went away happy.

"I need you to convert grams to micrograms for me so I know how much of my medicine I can take. No, you can't call me back—I'm calling from a phone booth."

Many years ago one of our staff had a request for instructions on making a birch-bark canoe, insisting that a book wouldn't do— only the name of an "Indian chief" who would be willing to teach her.

A man wanted to know if Jacques Cousteau was in an insane asylum. (This was in 1990.) His friend said that Cousteau had found the entrance to hell when he heard moaning and gnashing of teeth through his undersea microphone and had gone insane. Then the man told me he didn't believe it, because he had heard the entrance to hell was in Peru.

SOURCE: PUBLIB discussion list, 1999.

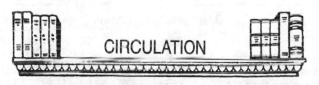

CIRCULATION

Circulation and spending: Up in 1995–97

by Lisa A. Wright

CONTINUING A THREE-YEAR UPSWING, in 1997 the index of American public library circulation was 116, a 5% increase from the 1996 circulation index of 110.

The index of expenditures rose 7% from 138 in 1996 to 147 in 1997. In constant 1990 dollars, this measure was 120 in 1997, a 4% increase from 115 in 1996.

The index values are based on figures reported annually by a sample of 112 libraries representative of all United States public libraries serving popula-

Annual indexes for a sample of American public libraries, 1990–1997: Medians (with 1980 = 100)

	1988	'89	'90	'91	'92	'93	'94	'95	'96	'97
Libraries	53	51	112	112	112	112	112	112	112	112
Circulation	98	100	100	106	110	108	107	109	110	116
Expenditures	88	90	100	106	113	119	123	131	138	147
Exp., in 1990 $	97	94	100	102	105	108	108	112	115	120

Circulation percentages: Medians

	1992	'93	'94	'95	'96	'97
Libraries	87	89	94	95	100	105
Adult	63	63	63	63	64	63
Juvenile	37	37	37	37	36	37

Expenditure percentages: Medians

	1992	'93	'94	'95	'96	'97
Libraries	112	112	112	112	112	112
Salaries	66	67	66	65	66	65
Materials	14	14	15	15	15	16
Other	18	17	19	18	18	19

Annual indexes for circulation and expenditure categories: Medians

	1988	'89	'90	'91	'92	'93	'94	'95	'96	'97
Adult circulation	91	92	100	105	109	112	109	113	116	118
Juvenile circulation	83	92	100	106	110	106	107	109	115	112
Salary exp.	82	88	100	108	117	123	128	135	141	143
Material exp.	91	101	100	106	109	112	115	126	134	139
Other exp.	90	89	100	101	100	106	114	115	123	140

Other measures: Medians

	1992	'93	'94	'95	'96	'97
Circulation per capita	5.4	5.4	5.4	5.6	6.0	6.2
Expenditures per capita	$14.60	$15.34	$15.99	$17.36	$19.17	$20.55
Expenditures per circulation	$2.55	$2.76	$2.93	$2.97	$3.13	$3.17
Material expenditures per capita	$2.08	$2.22	$2.38	$2.73	$2.93	$3.04

tions of over 25,000. The sample was taken from all public libraries serving populations of over 25,000 and is proportionally stratified according to rates of change in circulation and expenditures from 1989 to 1992 as determined from *Public Libraries in the United States,* published by the National Center for Education Statistics in 1989 and 1992.

The index scores are computed by dividing the library's reported 1997 circulation and expenditure totals by its corresponding 1990 figures and multiplying by 100. The resulting scores are ranked from highest to lowest, and the median score is the index value. The index of spending in 1990 dollars is calculated by dividing the expenditure index in each year by the Consumer Price Index (annual average for all urban consumers) converted to a 1990 base.

Adult and juvenile circulation

One hundred and five public libraries, comprising 94% of the sample, reported adult and juvenile circulation figures for 1997. Only 83 libraries reporting both the 1990 and 1997 juvenile and adult circulation figures were used to calculate the adult and juvenile indexes.

The adult circulation index increased 2% from 116 in 1996 to 118 in 1997. The juvenile circulation index decreased by 3% from 115 in 1996 to 112 in 1997. The distribution of circulation by adult and juvenile has remained fairly stable since 1992. In 1997 the circulation breakdown was 63% adult and 37% juvenile.

Annual expenditures

The index value for salary expenditures increased by 1% from 141 in 1996 to 143 in 1997. The index value for material expenditures increased by 4% from 134 in 1996 to 139 in 1997. Meanwhile, the index for "other" expenditures increased from 123 to 140, up 14% from 1996. The percentage distribution of operating expenditures in 1997 was salaries at 65% of total operating expenditures, "other" expenditures at 19%, and materials at 16%.

Circulation per capita increased from 6.0 in 1996 to 6.2 in 1997. Expenditures per item circulated also increased from $3.13 in 1996 to $3.17 in 1997. Expenditures per capita increased by 7% from $19.17 per capita in 1996 to $20.55 per capita in 1997. Material expenditures per capita increased 4% from 1996 to 1997 from $2.93 to $3.04. The 1990 census population figures were used in calculating the per-capita statistics.

SOURCE: Lisa A. Wright, "Public Library Circulation Increases As Spending Increases," *American Libraries* 29 (October 1998): 74–75.

Excuses for overdue books

by Will Manley

WHY ARE LIBRARIANS SO OBSESSED with delinquent borrowers?

The main reason, according to Dr. Wolfgang Lipkind, consulting behavioral psychologist for the Blackstone Institute of Library Studies, is that librarians as a group are very honest. In fact, his research indicates that next to Roman Catholic nuns, librarians are the most honest professional group in America. Librarians, because they are so truthful, find it exceedingly difficult to tolerate patron lies. On the other hand, chronically delinquent borrowers are one of the most dishonest study cohorts that Lipkind has ever researched. The clash between the two groups is, therefore, almost inevitable.

Lipkind's scholarly research is nicely complemented by the "real world" writings of Wilma W. Wilson, the self-proclaimed "circ clerk in tennis shoes." In her article "Overdues, Lies, and Library Patrons," she gives the following list of lies that she has been told at the circulation desk of her library:

Lies that overdue borrowers tell

1. I had a visitation from an angel and he told me that this book was demonic and that I should keep it checked out indefinitely so that no one could read it and be corrupted by it.

2. My wife is on the verge of a nervous breakdown and this book was the only thing that was keeping her sane.

3. On my way home from the library I was abducted by aliens. They didn't return me (and my library book) to earth for three months.

4. I took my book on vacation two months ago. Unfortunately the airlines lost my luggage and the book was in the luggage. They just found it yesterday.

5. I thought that the president should read this book so I sent it to him. He didn't return it until last week. He wrote that he was sorry that the book was late but that he needed it to help him with his economic policy.

6. I am toilet training my two-year-old son, and he refuses to get on the toilet unless I read him this book.

7. My house is haunted and this book is the only thing I've found that is effective in warding off evil spirits.

8. When I checked this book out, some crazy college student followed me out of the library, pointed a gun at me, and grabbed the book from me. He said he needed it desperately for a class and that he would return it when he was finished with it. I didn't get it back for six months.

9. I went into the hospital for a gall bladder operation and took the book with me for something to read during my stay. My roommate, a terminal cancer patient, took a fancy to the book and so I let him read. He liked the book so much that I didn't have the heart to ask for it back when my stay in the hospital was over. He died last week and the book was finally returned to me by his brother.

10. I kept this book out so long because I knew that I am the only person in the community smart enough to understand it.

SOURCE: Will Manley, *The Manley Art of Librarianship* (Jefferson, N.C.: McFarland, 1993), pp. 130–31. Reprinted with permission.

INTERLIBRARY LOAN

National interlibrary loan code for the United States

INTERLIBRARY LOAN IS ESSENTIAL to the vitality of libraries of all types and sizes and is a means by which a wider range of materials can be made available to users. In the interests of providing quality service, libraries have an obligation to obtain materials to meet the informational needs of users when local resources do not meet those needs.

Interlibrary loan has been described as an adjunct to, not a substitute for, collection development in individual libraries. Changes in the last decade have brought increasing availability of materials in alternative formats, an abundance of verification and location information, and a shift in the very nature of interlibrary cooperation. Interlibrary borrowing is an integral element of collection development for all libraries, not an ancillary option.

The effectiveness of a national resource sharing system depends upon the responsible distribution of borrowing and lending. Libraries of all types and sizes should be willing to share their resources liberally so that a relatively few libraries are not overburdened. Libraries must be willing to lend if they wish to borrow.

This code is designed to regulate lending and borrowing relations between libraries. It is not the intent of this code to prescribe the nature of interlibrary cooperation within formally established networks and consortia, or to regulate the purchase of materials from document suppliers. However, this code may be used as a model for development of state, regional, or local interlibrary loan codes.

This code provides general guidelines for the requesting and supplying of materials between libraries.

Definition. Interlibrary loan is the process by which a library requests materials from, or supplies materials to, another library.

Purpose. The purpose of interlibrary loan as defined by this code is to obtain, upon request of a library user, materials not available in the user's local library.

Scope. Interlibrary loan is a mutual relationship and libraries should be willing to supply materials as freely as they request materials. Any materials, regardless of format, may be requested from another library. The supplying library determines whether the material can be provided.

Responsibilities of the requesting library. The requesting library:

- should establish and maintain an interlibrary loan policy for its borrowers and make it available;
- should process requests in a timely fashion;
- should identify libraries that own and might provide the requested materials;
- should check the policies of potential suppliers for special instructions, restrictions, and information on charges prior to sending a request;
- is responsible for all authorized charges imposed by the supplying library;
- should send requests for materials for which locations cannot be identified to libraries that might provide the requested materials and be accompanied by the statement "cannot locate"—the original source of the reference should be cited or a copy of the citation provided;
- should avoid sending the burden of its requests to a few libraries—major resource libraries should be used as a last resort;
- should transmit all interlibrary loan requests in standard bibliographic format in accordance with the protocols of the electronic network or transmission system used (in the absence of an electronically generated form, the American Library Association Interlibrary Loan request form should be used);
- must ensure compliance with U.S. copyright law and its accompanying guidelines; copyright compliance must be determined for each copy request before it is transmitted, and a copyright compliance

statement must be included on each copy request; copyright files should be maintained as directed in the CONTU Guidelines;

- is responsible for borrowed materials from the time they leave the supplying library until they have been returned and received by the supplying library; if damage or loss occurs, the requesting library is responsible for compensation or replacement, in accordance with the preference of the supplying library;
- is responsible for honoring due dates and enforcing all use restrictions specified by the supplying library;
- should request a renewal before the item is due; if the supplying library does not respond, the requesting library may assume that the renewal has been granted for the same length of time as the original loan;
- should return materials by the due date and respond immediately if the item has been recalled by the supplying library;
- should package materials to prevent damage in shipping, and comply with special instructions stated by the supplying library;
- is responsible for following the provisions of this code; continued disregard for any provision may be reason for suspension of borrowing privileges by a supplying library.

Responsibilities of the supplying library. The supplying library:

- should establish and maintain an interlibrary loan policy, make it available in paper and/or electronic format, and provide it upon request;
- should process requests within the timeline established by the electronic network; requests not transmitted electronically should be handled in a similar time frame;
- should include a copy of the original request, or information sufficient to identify the request, with each item;
- should state any conditions and/or restrictions on use of the materials lent and specify any special return packaging or shipping requirements;
- should state the due date or duration of the loan on the request form or on the material;
- should package the items to prevent damage in shipping; should notify the requesting library promptly when unable to fill a request, and if possible, state the reason the request cannot be filled; should respond promptly to requests for renewals; if the supplying library does not respond, the borrowing library may assume that the renewal has been granted for the same length as the original loan period;
- may recall materials at any time; may suspend service to any requesting library which fails to comply with the provisions of this code.

SOURCE: "National Interlibrary Loan Code for the United States," *RQ* 33, no.4 (Summer 1994): 477–79.

Note: Information on the ISO interlibrary loan protocol (ISO 10160 and ISO 10161) is maintained on the Interlibrary Loan Application Standards Maintenance Agency Site (www.nlc-bnc.ca/iso/ill/).

Loaning rare and unique materials

THESE GUIDELINES ARE INTENDED for use by libraries, museums, public archives, historical agencies, and other cultural repositories in order to facilitate the interinstitutional loan for research use of special collections, including books, manuscripts, archives, and graphics.

Basic assumptions underlying these guidelines are:

1. Interinstitutional loan from special collections for research use is strongly encouraged but must be conducted in a manner that ensures responsible care and effectively safeguards items from loss or damage.

2. The decision to lend an item rests with the individual exercising curatorial responsibility for that item. Such decisions should reflect an item-by-item consideration rather than broad categorical responses.

3. It is not expected that items of significant rarity or monetary value or items in fragile condition will normally be lent for research purposes.

4. Although personal familiarity and/or direct communications with curatorial staff at other institutions can facilitate the lending process, the loan of materials should not depend solely on personal contacts but should rest on well-defined interinstitutional commitments.

5. A borrowing institution must meet significant criteria in order to provide appropriate conditions for housing and use of rare and unique materials.

Responsibilities of borrowing institutions

Institutional prerequisites for borrowing. The borrowing institution must: provide a secure reading room under constant surveillance to ensure the safety of the materials during use; have a special collections program, including staff assigned to and trained in the care and handling of special collections; provide secure storage for borrowed items during the loan period; provide storage under environmental conditions that meet accepted standards for housing special collections.

Guidelines for initiating a loan request. Requests for the loan of materials from noncirculating special collections must indicate that the borrowing institution meets the institutional criteria specified above and that the borrowing institution subscribes to the principles expressed in these guidelines.

Loan requests should normally be routed through the respective interlibrary lending (ILL) departments.

Every effort should be made to locate requested material in a general collection before submitting a request to a special collection of noncirculating materials. When a circulating copy cannot be located, that fact should be noted when requesting the item from a noncirculating collection.

Patrons should be encouraged to travel to other institutions for on-site access when their research involves long-term use or large quantities of material, or when distance presents no extraordinary hardship for them.

The borrowing institution should describe the requested material fully. Standard bibliographic sources should be used to verify each request. When a request

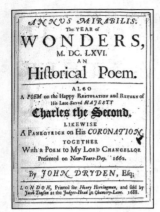

cannot be verified in these sources, full information regarding the original source of citation should be submitted.

In addition to full bibliographic description, it is desirable that requests include RLIN, OCLC, or other bibliographic utility record identification number and the call number for each item, and, whenever possible, requests should include the name of the special collection or department from which the item is being requested.

The request should indicate whether or not another edition, version, or form of material (photocopy, microform, or photograph) can be substituted for the one specified.

Guidelines for handling materials on loan. No copies of borrowed materials should be made without the explicit permission of the lending institution.

If copying is permitted by the lending institution, it should be done by special collections staff at the borrowing institution and in compliance with U.S. copyright law. The borrowing institution may, however, decline to make copies in any case and refer the patron directly to the lending institution to negotiate arrangements for copying.

The borrowing institution must comply with the loan period established by the lending institution. Unless otherwise specified by the lending institution, the loan period will be 30 days. Renewal of a loan should only be requested under unusual circumstance, and renewal requests should be submitted in a timely fashion.

The borrowing institution must abide by and administer any special conditions governing the handling and use of borrowed materials as specified by the lending institution.

If a borrowing institution fails to comply with the conditions of a loan, including proper care and packaging of borrowed items, that institution can expect that future requests to borrow special collections materials will be denied.

Responsibilities of lending institutions

Institutions receiving requests should be as generous as possible, consonant with their responsibilities both to preserve and to make accessible to their on-site user community the materials in their care.

Requests should be considered on a case-by-case basis by the individual with curatorial responsibility for the requested material.

Response to a request for the loan of special collections materials should be made within five working days.

It is the responsibility of the lending institution to indicate any special conditions governing the use of loaned materials, clearly stating any restrictions or limitations on research use, citation, publication, or other forms of dissemination.

Lending institutions reserve the right to limit the volume of material lent and the loan period. The normal loan period for special collections is 30 days.

If it is determined that a request can best be fulfilled by photocopying, lending institutions are expected to provide photocopies at a cost comparable to the standard rate within the lending institution.

Unless the lending institution so stipulates, it will not be necessary for the borrowing institution to return photocopies from special collections. If the lending institution does wish the return of photocopies, the copies should be clearly marked as loans.

Refusals either to lend or copy a requested item should include a specific reason (fragile paper, tight binding, too large to ship safely, etc.). That an item is part of a special collection is not a sufficient reason.

It is assumed that the lending institution will lend rare material at a cost comparable to the standard ILL fee charged by that institution for the loan of general library material. If the costs of shipping and insurance exceed the ILL fee, the lending institution may require additional payment. Before the material is sent, however, the lending institution must notify the borrowing institution of any additional charges and secure the borrowing institution's agreement to pay prior to sending the material.

Liability and transport for borrowed materials

The safety of borrowed materials is the responsibility of the borrowing institution from the time the material leaves the lending institution until it is returned to the lending institution.

The lending institution is responsible for packing the borrowed material so as to ensure its return in the condition in which it was sent. The borrowing institution is responsible for returning the material in the same condition as received, using the same, or equivalent, packing material.

If damage or loss occurs at any time after the material leaves the lending institution, the borrowing institution must meet all costs of repair, replacement, or appropriate compensation, in accordance with the preference of the lending institution.

The lending institution has the option of specifying alternative methods of delivery. These methods may include a different system of transportation, insurance, and special wrapping instructions. The borrowing institution can specify that the material be delivered directly to its special collections department. The lending institution can specify that the material be returned directly to the special collections department.

If alternative methods are to be employed, delivery specifications must be communicated to the borrowing institution, which must agree to return the material in the manner specified.

Verification of transfer and delivery must be made through the respective ILL department, regardless of method of delivery.

The borrowing institution will normally assume the costs of all fees associated with the loan.

SOURCE: Guidelines for the Loan of Rare and Unique Materials (Chicago: ALA Association of College and Research Libraries, 1993).

PRESERVATION

Preservation glossary

by Craig A. Tuttle

Acids belong to a class of chemicals that have different strengths and properties but which all have a pH value of below 7.0. Acids will accelerate the deterioration of paper and photographs.

Acid-free. A term used for materials that have a pH value of 7.1 or higher.

Acid migration. The transfer of acidity from one document or photograph to another either through physical contact or acidic vapors.

Alkalines belong to a class of chemicals that have different strengths and properties but which all have a pH value of 7.1 or higher. Alkalines are used to neutralize the acids in paper.

Archival-quality/Conservation-quality. Terms used to indicate that a material is chemically stable and, therefore, has a stronger resistance to adverse environmental conditions.

Calcium carbonate. A colorless or white alkaline chemical that is used as a buffer in paper and storage boxes to inhibit the formation and migration of acids.

Cellulose. The principal component of wood and plants, cellulose is the fibrous material used in the manufacture of paper.

Chemical pulping. A process that involves cooking wood fiber in a chemical solution to dissolve lignin and other wood-based impurities.

Chemical stability. The ability of certain chemical bonds to resist changes in their composition when exposed to other chemicals. Paper and photographs that are chemically stable are more resistant to deterioration.

Conservation. The use of certain procedures, techniques, and materials to chemically stabilize and physically strengthen paper and photographs.

Deacidification. A treatment used to neutralize the acids in paper by applying a mild alkaline solution. Deacidification, however, does not reverse the damage caused by acids prior to its application.

Encapsulation. A technique used to enclose an item between two sheets of polyester (mylar) plastic using double-sided, pH-balanced tape to seal all the edges. Encapsulation protects the item from pollutants, fungi, and excessive handling. The technique can easily be undone without damage to the enclosed item.

Environment. The external influences which chemically alter the composition of paper and photographs and, thus, accelerate their deterioration.

Hygroscopic. The ability of a material such as paper or photographs to absorb or release moisture in response to the relative humidity.

Lamination. An inherently destructive process that reinforces paper through enclosure between two sheets of chemically unstable plastic by sealing it with heat or acidic adhesives.

Basic preservation do's and whys for parents and students

Make sure your hands are clean. Dirt is hard to remove. An unattractive book seems less deserving of careful handling.

Gently set the crease in when you open the book. The book will open better and the binding will remain flexible and not crack.

When reading aloud, cup the book in your palm instead of doubling back the cover. The cover will stay attached to the book.

Use a slip of paper to mark a page. Objects, such as pencils, are too bulky and split the binding. Paper clips tear the pages and rust. Folded page corners break off.

Mark a book and close it when you stop reading. Don't flop it face down or set an object on top of it. The binding will crack, and the pages can become soiled.

Keep pens and markers away from books. It's too easy to accidentally mark the book and very hard to remove the marks.

Take notes on paper instead of underlining or highlighting in a library book. What is important to you may not be important to the next reader. It is very hard to read a book that someone else has marked up.

Keep books away from pets. A puppy can destroy a book in just a few minutes. Some books are made with glues that have attractive scents, and even well-behaved dogs can forget their manners. Chewed books are hard to repair.

Keep books away from babies and toddlers. Give them durable board books instead. Babies like to chew on books. Toddlers have difficulty turning pages without tearing them and will use any handy crayon or marker to adorn books. Make sure that small children have books strong enough to withstand their attention.

Leave repairs to the experts. Adhesive tape turns brown with age and stains the paper. Libraries have special repair methods that last a long time. *Never* use duct tape or electrical tape or any other household materials to repair a library book. You will cause even more damage.

Use a photocopier when you want to keep something from a library book or magazine. Torn-out pages take time and money to replace, and the binding of the book is weakened by page loss. Often more pages are loosened and will fall out soon.

Keep food and drink away from books. This includes water and coffee cups. Books are easily soiled and food residue attracts vermin.

Keep books dry in wet weather. Have a plastic bag available. Don't read library books in the bathtub. Wet books quickly become mildewed. Mildew spreads through books like the plague and presents a serious health risk to some people.

Use bookends. When books lean, their bindings are torqued and weakened. A book that is not shelved properly can pull itself out of its binding.

If books are too tall to stand upright, shelve them so their spine is down. If the spine is shelved up, the textblock hangs unsupported and will tear itself out of the binding.

Photocopy gently. Don't smash the binding onto the glass. A smashed binding can break, and the pages may fall out.

Keep books away from open windows and heaters. Books are sensitive to humidity and heat and their life span can be shortened by exposure to environmental extremes.

To transport lots of books, use a box or book truck. Books are heavy and often slippery. When they fall, their bindings can break.

Grasp the book by the middle of the spine, not the head cap, to remove it from the shelf. The head cap will tear and the spine may come off.

SOURCE: Normandy Simons Helmer, "Selling Preservation in School Libraries," in Jeanne M. Drewes and Julie A. Page, *Promoting Preservation Awareness in Libraries* (Westport, Conn.: Greenwood, 1997), pp. 133–34. Reprinted with permission.

5

Lignin. An organic bonding material found in wood fiber. The acidic properties of lignin have a deteriorating effect on paper and photographs.

Mechanical pulping (groundwood pulp). A process that involves grinding wood into short-length fibers. Mechanically pulped paper retains most of its wood-based impurities and processing chemicals and, therefore, tends to be weak and chemically unstable.

Methyl cellulose. A pH-balanced powder that dissolves in water to form a nontoxic paste that can be used as an adhesive.

Paper molds. Wooden frames fitted with tightly woven screens which are used to form individual sheets of paper.

pH scale. A scale that uses numbers from 0 to 14 to measure the level of acidity or alkalinity in paper and photographs. Each number from 6.9 to 0 indicate tenfold increases in *acidity* while the numbers from 7.1 to 14 indicate the same increase in *alkalinity*. A pH level of 7 is neutral.

Polyester (mylar) plastic. A chemically stable, durable, and transparent plastic that is used to encapsulate or enclose documents and photographic materials.

Polyethylene plastic. A chemically stable, transparent plastic used to enclose documents and photographic materials.

Polypropylene plastic. This type of plastic is chemically stable, resists heat, and is stiffer than polyethylene. It is used to enclose documents and photographic materials.

Preservation. The various methods used to maintain paper, photographs, and other materials in either their original form or by copying them onto another format such as microfilm.

Relative humidity. The percentage of moisture in the air relative to the maximum amount the air can hold at that temperature.

Sizing. A process in the manufacture of paper that uses alum rosin or other chemicals to permit the application of ink.

Temperature. A standard measurement used to determine the degree of hotness or coldness in an environment.

Ultraviolet (UV) radiation. A short-wave light spectrum that alters the chemical composition of paper and photographs.

SOURCE: Craig A. Tuttle, *An Ounce of Preservation: A Guide to the Care of Papers and Photographs* (Highland City, Fla.: Rainbow Books, 1995), pp. 91–93. Reprinted with permission.

Evaluating mass deacidification

by Henk J. Porck

THE ROLE AND MERITS of mass deacidification in preservation of library and archival materials have received a great deal of attention in the last decade. Several crucial issues have induced heated discussions; various, sometimes contradicting views have been put forward in the specialist literature and elsewhere and caused considerable confusion. The primary points of controversy relate to:

1. the necessity of preselection of materials to be treated;
2. the actual contribution of deacidification to the permanence of paper;
3. the reluctance of institutions to make use of available mass deacidification methods; and

4. the place of mass deacidification within the whole field of (mass) preservation activities.

These four aspects, presented in the form of questions, are discussed on the basis of the relevant data on five mass deacidification systems (Battelle, Bookkeeper, DEZ, FMC, and Wei T'o). In addition, the opinions of a number of experts, who have been asked for their comments on the basis of a questionnaire, have been incorporated.

1. Which materials will actually benefit from mass deacidification, and which materials have to be excluded from treatment? There appears to be a general consensus on the type of paper that benefits most from deacidification: paper that is acidic, such as alum-rosin-sized and groundwood-containing paper, paper produced under acidic conditions, and paper of all types which has become acidic through pollution. If such papers are still strong enough to be used, then mass deacidification can be expected to prolong their useful life. However, if they are already brittle or very weak, deacidification alone cannot be expected to recover their usefulness.

The idea that brittle paper should not be mass deacidified is contradicted by some research indicating that deacidification of such materials can significantly slow down their rate of degradation. It would be preferable to reformat all brittle paper as soon as possible, but the reality is that funding limitations and logistics simply do not allow this. From this perspective, by reducing further degradation, mass deacidification could buy precious time for the preservation of brittle materials.

A preselection step appears to be unavoidable for all mass-deacidification systems. Preselection criteria depend upon the strength and weaknesses (limitations) of the respective deacidification process. The serious problems specific materials present when treated by a particular process argue strongly for their exclusion from treatment by careful preselection. In general, the materials that have received most attention in this respect include coated paper, (writing) inks, dyestuffs, oversized (thick) books, leather, parchment, and synthetic bindings. Although efforts to refine the techniques used in the individual processes have of course focused on these specific problems, and improvements in the treatment process have often been realized in the course of time, this is not the place to judge the significance of these improvements and the benefits they may provide.

A type of paper to which insufficient attention has been given so far is pigment-coated paper for printing, which is found in many books and increasingly so today; not much is known about the special problems these papers might pose in mass-deacidification processes.

Modern papers in general will hopefully not create similar problems in the future if they are made to one of the new standards for permanence. It should be mentioned in this connection that there seems little point in indiscriminately treating any new acquisition, even when it has obviously been printed on nonacidic paper. It has been said that we will have to select out and avoid treating materials printed on alkaline and permanent papers. The argument "if it does not do any good, it does not do any harm either" may in fact not apply to the deacidification of weakly acidic and nonacidic paper. This problem may lie with the high alkalinity that can be reached by treatment, especially with liquid-phase deacidification systems. There are serious concerns about the long-term effects of the resulting high-pH values on the chemical and mechanical stability of these papers, and this issue deserves further investigation.

2. What is the real quantitative contribution of deacidification to the permanence of paper? With all five mass-deacidification processes, treatment has a positive effect on the permanence of paper in the long term. With the use of accelerated aging tests in combination with paper-strength measurements, degradation of treated paper is slowed down compared with untreated reference papers.

On the other hand, despite this *long-term* positive effect, often a loss of paper strength is caused as a *direct*, immediate result of deacidification, an effect that varies in magnitude with the different mass-deacidification systems. Questions with regard to the practical consequences of this reduction in mechanical stability, and the amount of time it will take to reach the turning point when the treated paper will have a better performance than the untreated, cannot yet be answered.

The *quantitative* assessment of the increase in useful lifetime that can actually be achieved by the treatment is also a complex issue and is primarily connected with the reliability of artificial aging tests. Although the real prognostic value of these tests is often seriously doubted (for instance because standard accelerated aging experiments do not take into account several factors that will have an influence in practice, such as air pollutants and use), it must be emphasized that these tests are at the moment the best measure available of how papers deteriorate under certain conditions.

The extant differences in requirements and specifications established for (mass) deacidification processes lead to confusion and to misinterpretation of research results. Therefore, for the sake of a reliable and useful evaluation of the impact of deacidification on paper permanence, there is an urgent need for standardization of both evaluation criteria and test methods, and for further research into the translation of artificial aging into practice.

3. Is it justified to wait for an ideal mass deacidification method or can/must we start now? None of the existing methods conforms to the requirements of an ideal mass deacidification process, as it has been shown convincingly that each system has both its strengths and weaknesses. Besides the safety and environmental risks connected with some of the deacidification agents and/or the solvents used, the limitations, more or less severe for the different systems and the different materials treated, vary from nonhomogeneous deacidification to side-effects hazardous to the paper and/or bookbinding material, including discolorations, color changes, staining, Newton rings, odor, bleeding of inks, dyestuffs and adhesives, and morphological changes (bubbling, cockling, change of "feel"). Optimization efforts focus on these limitations, and test studies have often been carried out over a period of years on plant units which have gradually evolved from the prototype to the pilot stage. As research reports on the efficiency and effectiveness of the mass deacidification processes do not always accurately indicate the precise stage of development of the system under study, research results cannot be always interpreted reliably.

If there is some reluctance with libraries and archival institutions to apply mass deacidification, this cannot be explained only by the fact that there is no ideal method or by lack of money. Perhaps an additional problem is introducing into a library community what is essentially a chemical-engineering process. However, a wait-and-see policy cannot be recommended, as it has been shown that this will inevitably cause companies to withdraw and give up work on systems for the commercial market, which eventually might result in the undesirable situation that further development of promising techniques will no longer be possible at all.

Many of the current objections to mass-deacidification techniques in fact lose their validity once it is generally agreed that any mass process should be applied only to nonunique objects of low intrinsic value. If the preselection process screens out the intrinsically valuable materials, which should be treated individually, the problems reported for mass deacidification systems can be considered minor compared to the benefits. The time lost in worrying about these minor problems may represent a substantial portion of the lifetime of many of the materials to which the treatment could be applied.

Taking into account the specific nature of their collections and the financial and organizational conditions, institutions should be able to decide—on the basis of existing knowledge about possibilities and limitations of the currently available mass deacidification techniques—which of the systems optimally fits their needs and to what extent they could make use of its service. Regular and independently performed tests and quality control of the treated materials will remain an essential requisite.

4. What is the place of mass deacidification in the whole field of (mass) preservation activities? The current application of mass deacidification techniques in practice shows clearly that the process is no longer considered as a panacea. In general, institutions using mass deacidification treatment also take other mass preservation measures, such as creating optimal storage conditions and microfilming.

Mass deacidification can be considered to a large extent as a "preventive preservation" measure, which should become integrated into an institution's preservation culture and should be viewed primarily as a complementary preservation option in a balanced institutional preservation program. However, within the framework of preservation of library and archival materials, mass deacidification will have an essential place, as it is evident that, given the costs and time involved, single-sheet deacidification cannot cope with the enormous amount of acid paper from the 19th and 20th centuries. Mass deacidification is a relatively inexpensive method to preserve the large amount of normal books published in the time of acidic paper production.

Besides environmental control, mass deacidification can be qualified as the one mass process that can be used on a huge number of objects that can be confidently assumed to have a specific problem in common: acid.

SOURCE: Henk J. Porck, *Mass Deacidification: An Update on Possibilities and Limitations* (Amsterdam: European Commission on Preservation and Access, 1996), pp. 42–45. Reprinted with permission.

Videotape preservation glossary

Blocking. The sticking together or adhesion of successive windings in a tape pack. Blocking can result from deterioration of the binder, storage of tape reels at high temperatures, and/or excessive tape pack stresses.

Capstan crease. Wrinkles or creases pressed into the tape by the capstan/pinch roller assembly.

Chroma level (low). Produces pastel, washed-out color.

Chroma level (high). Produces heavy, saturated colors.

Chroma noise. Colors appear to be moving on screen. In color areas of picture, usually most noticeable in highly saturated reds.

Cinch. Interlayer slippage of magnetic tape in roll form, resulting in buckling of some strands of tape. The tape will in many cases fold over itself, causing permanent vertical creases in the tape. Also, if not fixed, will cause increased dropouts.

Cinching. The wrinkling or folding over of tape on itself in a loose tape pack. Normally occurs when a loose tape pack is stopped suddenly, causing outer tape layers to slip past inner layers, which in turn causes a buckling of tape in the region of slip. Results in large dropouts or high error rates.

Control track. A synchronizing signal on the edge of the videotape that provides a reference for tracking control and tape speed. Control tracks which are heavy dropouts or which are improperly recorded may cause tracking errors or picture jumps.

Crease. A tape deformity that may cause horizontal or vertical lines in the playback picture.

Crosstalk. An undesired signal interfering with the desired signal. Can result in several types of picture distortion, mistracking, and/or noisy picture.

Curvature error. A change in track shape that results in a bowed or S-shaped track. This becomes a problem if the playback head is not able to follow the track closely enough to capture the information.

Dropout. Brief signal loss caused by a tape-head clog, defect in the tape, debris, or other feature that causes an increase in the head-to-tape spacing. A dropout can also be caused by missing magnetic material. A video dropout generally appears as a white spot or streak on the video monitor. When several video dropouts occur per frame, the TV monitor will appear snowy. The frequent appearance of dropouts on playback is an indication that the tape or recorder is contaminated with debris and/or that the tape binder is deteriorating.

Echo. A wave that has been reflected at one or more points in the transmission medium. Echoes may be leading or lagging the primary signal and appear in the picture monitor as reflections or double images commonly called "ghosts."

Edge curl. Usually occurs on the outside one-16th inch of the videotape. If the tape is sufficiently deformed it will not make proper tape contact with the playback heads. An upper curl (audio edge) crease may affect sound quality. A lower curl (control track) may result in poor picture quality.

Edge damage. Physical distortion of the top or bottom edge of the magnetic tape, usually caused by pack problems such as popped strands or stepping. Affects audio and control track, sometimes preventing playback.

Flagging. A horizontal displacement of upper portion of a picture. Also called skewing.

Flutter. Very short rapid variations in tape speed that may result in a jumpy or jittery picture.

Foldover. Tape that has folded over, resulting in the oxide surface facing away from the heads.

Generational loss. Degradation caused by tape copying.

Glitch. A form of low-frequency interference, appearing as a narrow horizontal bar moving vertically through the picture.

Head clogging. The accumulation of debris on one or more heads usually causing poor picture clarity during playback. Clogging of the playback head with debris causes dropouts.

Hydrolysis. The chemical process in which scission of a chemical bond occurs via reaction with water. The polyester chemical bonds in tape binder polymers are subject to hydrolysis, producing alcohol and acid end groups. Hydrolysis is a reversible reaction, meaning that the alcohol and acid groups can react with each other to produce a polyester bond and water as a byproduct. In practice, however, a severely degraded tape binder layer will never fully reconstruct back to its original integrity when placed in a very low-humidity environment.

Luminance. This is the portion of the video signal that contains the black-and-white information. Luminance indicates the amount of light intensity in a picture that is perceived by the eye as brightness.

Mistracking. The phenomenon that occurs when the path followed by the read head of the recorder does not correspond to the location of the recorded track on the magnetic tape. Mistracking can occur in both longitudinal and helical-scan recording systems. The read head must capture a given percentage of the track in order to produce a playback signal. If the head is too far off the track, record information will not be played back.

Noise. Any unwanted signal present in the total signal.

Pack slip. A lateral slip of select tape windings causing high or low spots (when viewed with tape reel lying flat on one side) in an otherwise smooth tape pack. Pack slip can cause subsequent edge damage when the tape is played, as it will unwind unevenly and may make contact with the tape reel flange.

Physical damage. Any distortion of the magnetic tape that prevents proper head-to-tape contact is therefore detrimental to the tape playback. These distortions can include edge damage, wrinkles, cinches, and tape stretch.

Playback demagnetization. A loss of magnetization and thus a degradation of recorded information caused by repeated playing of a recorded tape.

Popped strand. A strand of tape protruding from the edge of a wound tape pack.

Print through. The condition where low-frequency signals on one tape winding imprint themselves on the immediately adjacent tape windings. It is most noticeable on audio recordings where a ghost of the recording can be heard slightly before the playback of the actual recording. Print through is worse heading outward through a tape pack.

Roll. A lack of vertical synchronization that causes the video picture to move upward or downward.

Scratching. Gouging of the magnetic layer or base as the tape passes through a machine. Video tape scratches will cause a loss of head-to-tape contact and appear as a solid line on your screen.

Shedding. A condition in which the oxide, which forms the recording surface of a videotape, has begun to separate from the base. Loose oxide may clog video heads, causing a loss of picture.

Signal-to-noise ratio (S/N). Expressed in decibels (dBs), this term describes a ratio or difference of wanted audible or visual information (signal) versus unwanted information experienced by distorted sounds and pictures (noise). Comparatively high decibel numbers mean better sound or visual images.

Skew. A bending of picture at top or bottom of television screen caused by the changing of the video track angles on the tape from the time of recording to the time of playback. This can occur as a result of poor tension regulation by the VCR or by ambient conditions which affect the tape.

Snow. White flashes appearing in the video image caused by random noise and/or loss of magnetic particles.

Squeal. Can be caused by a build-up of debris on a guide or head. Sometimes a cleaning of the offending surface will eliminate the squeal. Squeal is also caused by the tape having poor lubrication or losing its lubrication with age. A solution is to overcoat a tape with a lubricant solution, which will eliminate the squeal so a copy can be made.

Stepping. Unsmooth packing, with transversally mispositioned sections.

Stick slip. The process in which (1) the tape sticks to the recording head because of high friction; (2) the tape tension builds because the tape is not moving at the head; (3) the tape tension reaches a critical level, causing the tape to release from and briefly slip past the read head at high speed; (4) the tape slows to normal speed and once again sticks to the recording head; (5) this process is repeated indefinitely. Characterized by jittery movement of the tape in the transport and/or audible squealing of the tape.

Sticky shed. The gummy deposits left on tape-path guides and heads after a sticky tape has been played. The phenomenon whereby a tape binder has deteriorated to such a degree that it lacks sufficient cohesive strength so that the magnetic coating sheds on playback. The shedding of particles by the tape as a result of binder deterioration that causes dropouts on VHS tapes.

Sticky tape. Tape characterized by a soft, gummy, or tacky tape surface. Tape that has experienced a significant level of hydrolysis so that the magnetic coating is softer than normal. Tape characterized by resinous or oily deposits on the surface of the magnetic tape.

Time-base error. A variation in the synchronizing signals. When time-base errors are large enough, they may cause skewing or flagging distortion of the video picture.

Tracking loss. Evidenced by picture breakup or loss of video in segments of the picture.

Trapezoidal error. A change in the angle of a recorded helical scan track. Can result in mistracking.

Video signal-to-noise ratio. An indication of the amount of noise in a black-and-white picture.

Vinegar syndrome. Characteristic of the decomposition of acetate-based magnetic tape where acetic acid is a substantial byproduct that gives the tape a vinegar-like odor. After the onset of the vinegar syndrome, acetate tape backings degrade at an accelerated rate—the hydrolysis of the acetate is catalyzed further by the presence of acetic acid byproduct.

Windowing. Interlayer slippage or magnetic tape in roll form, resulting in buckling of some strands of tape. The tape will in many cases fold over itself, causing permanent vertical creases in the tape. Also, if not fixed, will cause increased dropouts.

Wrinkle. A physical deformity of the videotape. Any creases or wrinkles in the videotape may produce dropouts or loss of picture information upon playback.

SOURCE: Bay Area Video Coalition (1996). Reprinted with permission.

Caring for photographic collections

by Debbie Hess Norris

KEEP PHOTOGRAPHIC MATERIALS at proper environmental conditions. Relative humidity is the single most important factor in preserving most photographic materials. Relative humidity levels above 60% will accelerate deterioration. Low and fluctuating humidity may also damage them. Conditions of around 68° F. and 30–40% relative humidity are appropriate and easiest to maintain in enclosed areas, such as an interior closet or an air-conditioned room—not in an attic or basement. High temperatures and high relative humidity levels will accelerate deterioration.

Temperature, not relative humidity, is the controlling factor in the stability of contemporary color photographs. Storage at low temperatures (40° F. or below) is recommended.

Atmospheric pollutants, particularly sulfur compounds, will cause black-and-white images to fade and discolor. Gas by-products given off by fresh paint fumes, plywood, deteriorated cardboard, and many cleaning supplies may cause accelerated image deterioration. Storage in nonacidic containers is recommended.

Exposure to visible and ultraviolet (UV) light is potentially damaging to photographs. Light can cause embrittlement, yellowing, and color fading in prints and hand-colored surfaces. Extended display of photographs is not recommended; however if they must be displayed, use UV-filtering plastic or glass in framing. Exposure of color slides to the light in the projector should be kept to a minimum. Use duplicate slides instead.

Handling photographic materials

If photographs are handled improperly, they can suffer disastrous damage, including tears, cracks, losses, abrasions, fingerprints, and stains. Avoid touching fragile photographic materials; salts in human perspiration may damage surfaces. Wear clean cotton gloves if possible when handling negatives and prints.

Storage of photographic materials

House photos in protective enclosures to keep out gritty dirt and dust which can abrade images, retain moisture, and deposit contaminants. Avoid and/or remove materials such as acidic paper or cardboard, polyvinyl chloride (PVC) plastic, rubber bands, paper clips, and pressure-sensitive tapes and rubber cement. Suitable storage materials should be made of plastic or paper, and free of sulfur, acids, and peroxides.

Paper enclosures must be acid-free, lignin-free, and in either buffered (pH 8.5) and unbuffered stock. Storage materials must pass the ANSI Photographic Activity Test (PAT) which is noted in suppliers' catalogs. Buffered paper enclosures are recommended for brittle prints that have been mounted onto poor-quality secondary mounts and deteriorated film-base negatives. Buffered enclosures are not recommended for contemporary color materials. Paper enclosures are opaque, thus preventing unnecessary light exposure; porous; easy to label in pencil; and relatively inexpensive.

Suitable plastic enclosures are uncoated polyester film, uncoated cellulose triacetate, polyethylene, and polypropylene. Note: Photographic emulsions may stick to the slick plastic surface at high relative humidity (RH); the RH must remain below 80%—else do not use plastic enclosures. Plastic enclosures must not be used for glass plate, nitrate, or acetate-based negatives.

Prints of historic value should be matted with acid-free rag or museum board for protection. Adhesives should not touch the print. Matting should be done by an experienced framer or under the direction of a trained conservator.

Store all prints and negatives that are matted or placed in paper or plastic enclosures in acid-free boxes. If possible, keep negatives separate from print materials. Store color transparencies/slides in acid-free or metal boxes with a baked-on enamel finish or in polypropylene slide pages. Commonly available PVC slide pages, easily identified by their strong plastic odor, should never be used because of their extreme chemical reactivity.

Place early miniature-cased photographs, including daguerreotypes, ambrotypes, and tintypes, carefully into acid-free paper envelopes and house

Approximate time in years to significant dye fading in color photographic materials

Temperature	Relative Humidity						
	20%	30%	40%	50%	60%	70%	80%
30° F. (−1° C.)	8000	3500	1500	800	600	450	350
35° F. (2° C.)	4500	2000	1000	600	350	300	250
40° F. (4° C.)	3000	1500	700	350	250	200	175
45° F. (7° C.)	1750	900	450	250	175	125	100
50° F. (10° C.)	1000	600	300	175	125	90	80
55° F. (13° C.)	700	350	200	125	80	60	50
60° F. (16° C.)	450	250	125	80	60	45	35
65° F. (18° C.)	300	150	90	50	40	30	25
70° F. (21° C.)	180	100	60	40	25	20	18
75° F. (24° C.)	125	70	40	25	19	15	12
80° F. (27° C.)	80	50	30	19	14	11	9
85° F. (29° C.)	50	30	20	13	10	8	6
90° F. (32° C.)	35	20	14	10	7	6	5
95° F. (35° C.)	25	15	10	7	5	4	3
100° F. (38° C.)	15	11	7	5	4	3	2
105° F. (41° C.)	10	7	5	4	3	2	2
110° F. (43° C.)	7	5	4	3	2	2	1
115° F. (46° C.)	5	4	3	2	2	1	1
120° F. (49° C.)	3	3	2	1	1	1	1

Each value in the table represents the approximate time for 30% density loss if new, contemporary color photos are kept in the dark at the specified conditions of temperature and relative humidity (RH). Older color images require significantly colder temperatures than contemporary ones because they are more unstable to begin with and may be significantly deteriorated already.

SOURCE: James M. Reilly, *Storage Guide for Color Photographic Materials* (Albany: New York State Library, 1998), p. 20. Reprinted with permission.

flat; keep loose tintypes in polyester sleeves, or, if flaking is present, in paper enclosures.

Storage of family photographs in albums is often desirable, and many commercially available albums utilize archival-quality materials. Avoid albums constructed of highly colored pages. Never use commercially available magnetic or "no stick" albums for the storage of contemporary or historic photographic prints in black-and-white or color. These materials will deteriorate quite quickly over time.

SOURCE: Library of Congress Preservation Directorate (lcweb.loc.gov/preserv/care/photo.html).

Drying water-damaged collections

Safety precautions

Wear protective gloves (latex or plastic) and long sleeves. If mold is present, wear a respirator. Some mold species are toxic; if any health effects are observed, contact a doctor and/or mycologist. When cleaning items with dry mold, make sure there is adequate ventilation that draws the mold spores away from you, i.e. a vacuum cleaner. Wash your hands after handling materials with mold.

Air-drying

Absorb excess moisture using a clean sponge, paper, or bath towels, etc. Do not blot on hand-written ink or fragile surfaces. Do not use printed newsprint for blotting; ink can transfer. Use fans to provide maximum air circulation but do not aim fans directly at the drying materials.

Air-drying paper documents, maps, posters, etc.

Paper is very fragile when wet and must be handled with care. Provide adequate support. Blot excess water off the documents.

Do not attempt to separate individual items while very wet. You may leave them in stacks no higher than ¼" to dry. If pages can be separated safely, they can be interleaved using absorbent or separating materials (i.e., wax paper). Change interleaving materials until item is dry.

Clean, unrusted window screens, stacked with bricks or wood blocks between them, will provide a drying surface with maximum air circulation. If drying items on a hard surface, cover the area with absorbent materials and change when wet.

When items are almost dry, place them between protective sheets such as unprinted newsprint and put a light weight on them to flatten. (If the item is too wet when placed under weights, you may create a microenvironment for mold.)

Air-drying framed items

Place the frame glass-side down and remove the backing materials. Carefully remove object and air-dry. If the object is stuck to the glass, do not remove; instead dry frame with object inside, glass-side down on a flat surface.

Air-drying books

Fan books open and stand on top or bottom edge; never stand them on the front edge. Stand books on driest edge first to provide support. As the book dries, turn it upside-down to the opposite edge every few hours.

Place a sheet of wax paper larger than the pages between the front and back cover and adjacent page before standing on edges. Replace the interleaving as it becomes saturated.

When the book is no longer wet, but still cool to the touch, close and place on a solid surface with a slight weight to keep distortion to a minimum. Check frequently to ensure that no mold is growing.

Air-drying photographic materials

Some historical photographs are very sensitive to water damage and may not be recoverable. Most prints, negatives, and color slides can be air-dried. The emulsion (picture or image) side should be face up. Avoid touching the front surface of wet or damp photographic prints or negatives. (The emulsion side often appears less glossy on negatives and color slides.) To speed drying time, dry items on a clothesline using wooden or nonabrasive plastic clothespins. If the photographs or negatives are stuck together or the emulsion is damaged, contact a photographic conservator or your local historical society or museum for advice.

If photographic materials are covered with mud or dirt and are still wet, they may be gently rinsed in a bucket of cold, clean water, or a light stream of cold water, and then dried. Contact a photographic conservator. Do not freeze them unless advised to do so by a conservator.

Recovery of water-damaged collections with mold

Active mold looks either fuzzy or slimy. Do not attempt to remove active mold. Dormant mold is dry and powdery. See safety precautions above for handling mold.

Stop mold outbreaks by improving environmental conditions. Humidity levels should be as low as possible below 75%. Use a dehumidifier. Low temperatures—below 68° F.—are recommended.

Short exposure to sunlight and circulating air outdoors may help to dry moldy items more rapidly. (There may be light damage; use this treatment only with materials where damage is acceptable.)

When the mold has become dormant through drying it can be removed, using a vacuum cleaner and/or a soft brush. After vacuuming, dispose of bag. Clean brushes to prevent spreading the mold spores. Safety precautions are particularly important in this stage.

Water damage to materials may be irreversible. The treatment of items of high monetary, historic, or sentimental value should be referred to a conservator. The Foundation of the American Institute for Conservation (FAIC) maintains a referral service of conservators who will be able to provide more information about treatment of items in private collections. Contact the FAIC office: FAIC, 1717 K Street, N.W., Suite 301, Washington, DC 20006; (202) 452-9545; fax: (202) 452-9328; infoaic@aol.com; (palimpsest.stanford.edu/aic/). Provide a complete description of the object you wish to have treated, the type of conservation service you require, the geographic area in which you prefer to have the work done, and your regular mailing address.

SOURCE: Library of Congress Preservation Directorate (lcweb.loc.gov/preserv/emerg/dry.html).

Disaster preparedness Web sites

Baltimore Academic Libraries Consortium (disaster.lib.msu.edu/disaster/). Provides a searchable database of resources. While the majority of the resources are from the Washington/Baltimore area, contributions from any area are welcome.

Colorado Preservation Alliance (www.aclin.org/other/libraries/cpa/). Offers rapid advice on various disasters. Besides the statewide action plan, there are full-text publications on various preservation techniques and resource lists.

CoOL—Conservation OnLine: Resources for Conservation Professionals (palimpsest.stanford.edu). Probably the best resource for conservation and preservation information. Links to many other agencies, as well as a directory for locating people involved with conservation or allied professions.

Extension Disaster Education Network (www.agctr.lsu.edu/eden/). A collaborative multistate effort designed to provide access to resources on disaster preparedness, recovery, and mitigation.

Federal Emergency Management Agency (www.fema.gov/pte/prep.htm). Detailed information on proper response to natural and technological disasters, including tips for individuals and families.

Iowa Conservation and Preservation Consortium (www.neirls.org/flood_recovery/flood_cover.html). Flood Recovery Booklet, a compilation of useful information.

National Task Force on Emergency Response (www.heritagepreservation.org/programs/taskfer.htm). A partnership of 29 federal agencies, national service organizations (including the American Library Association), and private institutions. It has two major goals: safeguarding America's cultural heritage from the damaging effects of natural disasters and other emergencies; and using its expertise to help the general public recover from disasters.

Northeast Document Conservation Center (www.nedcc.org/disaster.htm). Emergency assistance for institutions and individuals with damaged paper-based collections.

SOLINET Preservation Field Service Program (www.solinet.net/presvtn/disaster/disastsv.htm). Emergency disaster assistance to individuals and institutions.

University of Illinois Cooperative Extension Service (www.ag.uiuc.edu/~disaster/prep.html). Preparing for a disaster, responding to a disaster, and providing assistance to disaster victims.

SOURCE: ALA Association for Library Collections and Technical Services, Disaster Preparedness Clearinghouse, www.ala.org/alcts/publications/disaster.html.

The role of FEMA

by Michael Trinkley

THE FEDERAL EMERGENCY MANAGEMENT AGENCY (FEMA) is self-described as "responsible for a wide range of emergency planning and response activities. It works with state and local governments to help communities and citizens plan for emergencies of all types including natural disasters, technological emergencies, and nuclear attack. It also coordinates federal aid for presidentially declared disasters, helps reduce the nation's fire losses through fire prevention programs and coordinates the National Flood Insurance Program" (FEMA Publication 180, *Are You Ready for the Next Disaster?*, June 1989).

In spite of these lofty goals, FEMA has been almost universally criticized. Typical are the comments by Ed Devlin, a veteran disaster recovery planner, in the October, November, and December 1992 *Disaster Recovery Journal*: "FEMA is receiving heavy criticism again, similar to the criticism following Hurricane Hugo. FEMA was accused of inefficiency and poor coordination with other agencies following Hugo's South Carolina strike in 1989. Despite procedural changes, neither FEMA nor President Bush directed armed forces to deliver all the aid they were prepared to send until four days after the hurricane struck."

The goal here is not to bash FEMA, but to remind you that any plan prepared on the assumption and expectation of outside assistance, especially governmental assistance, is unrealistic. Governmental procedures work slowly, while your recovery of irreplaceable (or at least costly) library, museum, and archival materials must be coordinated quickly.

Still, it is good to know about FEMA and what may come your way, and what probably won't. First, it is important to realize that FEMA is not a first responder—that is the responsibility of the state and local governments. Furthermore, FEMA can't step in to coordinate without being invited. Technically, the governor of the affected state requests federal assistance by petitioning the president through FEMA. The state governor, in the petition for federal support, must assume all non-federal costs. Local governments can't request FEMA assistance—only the state's governor can do this. If the proper procedures aren't followed, or if the state has a confused or dual emergency system, aid will most likely be delayed.

It's important to understand that emergency recovery efforts begin at the local or state level. Some states invest heavily in preparing for disasters and helping citizens recover. Other states do very little. For example, the South Carolina legislature provides less than 10 cents per capita for the state's Emergency Preparedness Division. In contrast, California's Office of Emergency Services spends 96.5 cents per capita. Moreover, South Carolina's emergency preparedness budget has been cut, receiving only a little more than $300,000 in 1993, while the same office in North Carolina was funded at a level of over $2 million. It's important to understand how well equipped your state agency is to handle a disaster like a hurricane.

When FEMA is involved, it will determine the type of assistance that is necessary and establish a field office. The governor, in turn, appoints a representative called the state coordinating officer, who serves as the contact between FEMA and state or local agencies. The governor and FEMA then execute an agreement that details the types and length of assistance. Afterwards the state usually conducts briefings for different parties on the types of aid that are available.

Public Library, Defiance, Ohio. "Flood 1913."

In addition to the most advertised FEMA programs, it will also assist state and local governments and some nonprofit organizations in the removal of debris and the restoration of services. Many buildings owned by public or nonprofit organizations qualify for disaster assistance to repair the damage to the structure and cover some of the costs of conserving damaged objects. FEMA may also fund emergency protective measures for the preservation of life and property, and the repair of infrastructure (roads, bridges, water control facilities, and public utilities). For most of these the federal government pays 75%, while the state government must pick up the remaining 25%.

Many institutions are surprised to learn that FEMA will pay for only "the minimum steps which are both necessary and feasible to place the items back on display without restoring them to their predisaster condition," and that FEMA will not pay for collections damaged beyond recovery. Of equal importance, FEMA regulations stipulate that the work must be accomplished following the guidelines of the American Institute for Conservation of Historic and Artistic Work's Code of Ethics and Standards of Practice (which has clear ramifications regarding the preparation of treatment proposals, and techniques used—few local "furniture restorers" would qualify, for example).

FEMA's regulations indicate that any nonprofit organization (i.e., having an IRS tax exemption under Section 501c, d, or e) having certain categories of unreimbursed expenses associated with a declared disaster may be eligible for reimbursement of the expenses, provided the organization is "providing essential services of a governmental nature to the general public." Traditionally, most museums, libraries, zoos, and similar organizations have qualified.

To be eligible for the funds, the work must also be associated with disaster, be within a designated disaster area, and be the legal responsibility of the organization applying. Types of eligible work include emergency protective measures, debris removal, road work, water control facility work, and repair or restoration of damaged buildings.

Keep in mind that FEMA will typically pay for repair or replacement, whichever is less. This means that institutions may receive funds for replacement of a historic building, rather than the larger sum needed to restore it. FEMA will allow, however, their funds to be combined with other funds to allow restoration rather than replacement.

The request for funds (a FEMA Notice of Interest in Applying for Federal Disaster Assistance, FEMA Form 90-49) typically must be submitted to the Governor's Appointed Representative within 30 days following the designation of the county as an official disaster area. Organizations in affected areas designated for federal assistance can normally begin the process by calling

5

(800) 462-9029 or (800) 462-7585 (TDD) for the hearing and speech impaired, during announced calling hours. Those calling should be prepared to provide basic information about their organization, insurance coverage, and any other information to help substantiate losses.

A team will inspect every damage site, preparing damage survey reports to give recommended scopes of work and estimated costs following FEMA eligibility criteria. These are submitted to the FEMA regional director for approval and, once approved, are funded, with the state managing the finances.

As many from Hurricanes Hugo and Andrew can attest, assistance to historic properties, museums, and libraries can be a long time in coming and the paperwork can be mind-boggling. There is also a potential that differences in opinion will occur over the necessity of repair or the type of repair. Often reimbursement for repairs will come exceedingly slowly. Institutions would do well to understand the nature of the problems working with both federal and state agencies.

Like many federal agencies, FEMA offers many types of assistance, but you have to know about the programs to make adequate use of them. One example is FEMA's Hazard Mitigation Grant Program, which will pay up to 50% of the cost of a structural restoration project which incorporates future hazard mitigation. Another program offers grants for minimal repairs to make damaged homes habitable (which may be useful to your staff). There are also FEMA grants administered by the state to provide funding to meet serious disaster-related needs not covered by insurance or other aid programs. There are even unemployment payments up to 24 weeks for workers who temporarily lose jobs because of the disaster and who do not qualify for state benefits, such as self-employed individuals.

To maximize the benefits of FEMA, the first step occurs before the disaster—you should contact the state agency responsible for coordinating with FEMA (typically the Governor's office) and request information on the types of programs your institution might be eligible for in the event of a disaster.

You should also request information on FEMA accounting procedures. For example, institutions during Hurricane Hugo recovery discovered that FEMA required they maintain very accurate records of staff clean-up time and would pay for a maximum number of hours per day. Find out all of the details before the disaster, so you can incorporate this information into your planning.

SOURCE: Michael Trinkley, *Hurricane! Surviving the Big One: A Primer for Libraries, Museums, and Archives* (Chicora Foundation and Southeastern Library Network, 1998), pp. 79–81.

SECURITY

Marking rare books

MUCH THOUGHTFUL DISCUSSION has taken place on the appropriateness of permanently marking books, manuscripts, and other special collections materials. Failure to mark compromises security. Cases of theft show that clear identification of stolen material is vital if material, once recovered, is to be returned to its rightful owner. The following guidelines will aid libraries and other institutions in marking their materials and provide as consistent and uniform a practice as possible.

Even the most conservative marking program is going to result in permanent alteration of materials. Choices concerning marking are likely to depend heavily on aesthetic judgment balanced against the need to secure materials from theft and to assist in their identification and recovery. Each repository will have to balance those competing needs. The ACRL Rare Books and Manuscripts Section's Security Committee recommends that libraries and other institutions use marking as part of their overall security procedures and that they attempt to strike a balance between the implications for deterrence (visibility, permanence) and the integrity of the documents (both physical and aesthetic).

General recommendations

That markings be of two types—those readily visible to the casual observer, and those hidden and difficult to detect. Readily visible marks are intended to deter potential thieves; hidden marks are intended to assist in the recovery of stolen materials. If only one type of mark is to be used, it should be of the readily visible type. The size should be kept to a minimum (ca. 5-point type size for lettering).

That readily visible marks be made in an approved form of permanent ink. Visible marks should be all but impossible to remove and should never consist of just a bookplate. Although not the only form of a visible mark, ink is perhaps the best medium for this purpose, so long as the ink meets current standards for permanence and conservation. There is still controversy surrounding which inks are best suited for this purpose, so a recommendation cannot go beyond urging those in charge of marking programs to be current on the latest developments in this field.

That marks that are hidden or difficult to detect never be the only or primary types of marking. Hidden marks should never be used as the only form of marking, because they are worthless in alerting others, such as booksellers, that material has been stolen. Hidden marks are intended only as supplements to visible marks.

That visible marks be placed so that they will cause significant damage to the aesthetic and commercial value of the item if they are removed. Much controversy has surrounded the placement of visible marks. Given the varying nature of special collections materials and the varying nature of beliefs and sentiments concerning what is proper placement for a visible mark, it is probably futile to overly prescribe placement of marks. It is recommended, however, that no position for a mark be rejected outright. Some repositories might, for example, be comfortable stamping the verso of a title page or the image area of a map; others might reject those options. But no matter where the visible mark is placed, it should not be in a position that it can be removed without leaving quite obvious evidence of its former presence.

That marks be placed directly on the material itself and not on an associated part from which the material may be separated. Marks placed only on a front pastedown in a book, on a portfolio that holds prints, or on some type of backing material are rendered useless if that element is separated from the item. Especially in the case of flat items, such as maps and broadsides, it is important that the marks be applied before any backing procedure is done.

That all marks unequivocally and clearly identify the repository. Marks should not be generic (e.g., "Rare Book Room," "Special Collections," "University Library") but should rather make plain the repository to which they refer. It is recommended that visible marking consist of the repository's Library of Congress symbol. If a repository lacks such a symbol, the Library of Congress will supply one upon request. If the Library of Congress symbol is not used, then the name of the repository should be used, being careful that no confusion arises among repositories with similar or identical names.

SOURCE: ALA Association of College & Research Libraries, *Guidelines for the Security of Rare Book, Manuscript, and Other Special Collections* (Chicago: American Library Association, 1999).

Don't get taken

by Sara Behrman

LIBRARIANS WHO NEED HELP reviewing internal controls may be able to get it from the government auditor, city or county attorney, police department, state library agency, and numerous articles and books, particularly chapter eight of the *Pennsylvania Public Library Accounting Manual,* which deals with internal controls. This manual has a series of excellent internal control questionnaires (for both large and small libraries) that are designed to help identify a library's points of vulnerability.

In addition to establishing strong internal controls, take the following steps:

- Limit the handling of cash and access to inventory.
- Bond employees who are entrusted with large amounts of cash.
- Write and enforce strict policies, with zero tolerance for theft.
- Weed out potential thieves with preventative measures such as a thorough screening of every job applicant. Check references, verify education claims, and, as warranted by the position applied for, run criminal history checks.
- Limit access to the building to essential staff, and discourage arrangements that allow employees to be alone in the building before or after hours.
- Apply loan policies and security measures equally to staff and patrons.
- Establish a security committee to review practices and to recommend safeguards.

SOURCE: Sara Behrman, "When Trust Isn't Enough," *American Libraries* 29 (May 1998): 75.

SPECIAL USERS
CHAPTER SIX

"My mother and my father were illiterate immigrants from Russia. When I was a child they were constantly amazed that I could go to a building and take a book on any subject. They couldn't believe this access to knowledge we have here in America. They couldn't believe that it was free."

—Kirk Douglas

ETHNIC GROUPS

Celebrating annual
African-American events

by Gerald V. Holmes

AFRICAN-AMERICAN HISTORY MONTH is a time for librarians and faculty to focus on various ways to promote the resources and services available to faculty and students in libraries. Although resources on this topic are important to educators at all levels of learning, this article focuses only on higher education. Alfred Young explains that

> . . . during the month of February of each year, colleges and universities, elementary and secondary schools, churches, civic and social organizations throughout the country sponsor activities which highlight the achievements and contributions made by Afro-Americans. . . . the primary purpose of these activities is to instill within Afro-Americans a sense of pride and accomplishment and to inform the general public of Black America's glorious past. (*Negro History Bulletin* 43 (1980): 6-8)

African-American History Month can also serve as a motivational time to help prepare future African Americans to be scholars and leaders in our society. It is a time when African Americans can learn from the past while they prepare themselves for the future.

One way to do this is to take advantage of the many resources available in an academic library. In 1926 Dr. Carter G. Woodson founded "Negro History Week" which later became "Black History Month." He also founded the Association for the Study of Afro-American Life and History and wrote the book *Mis-education of the Negro*, which states

> . . . the scholars under discussion all shared a common goal, namely, to provide for Negro youth access to historical information and education which would be "true" and thus nullify or diminish the false and belittling propaganda type of history which had been handed to them by whites. This, it was felt, would build up the black child's self and race knowledge as well as his self-respect. In a larger sense they expected that their publications would at least partly fill the unjustifiable void in American History and its antecedents, reveal the existing distortions of actual facts, and constitute a service to the entire of historical and social science writing and understanding.

Some of the ways that libraries can help to promote the availability of this information include:

• assisting African Americans who want to study their heritage;

- assisting patrons from other cultures who want to research topics related to African-American culture;
- seeking support for special programs on African-American history;
- identifying ways to better serve African Americans.

In addition to African-American History Month, other annual African-American events include Kwanza (December 20–January 1) and Martin Luther King Jr. Day (third Monday in January). Libraries play a key role in providing significant information on African-American history and biographical information on noted African Americans. In the past, African Americans did not always have access to these collections, but this has changed. We are reminded by Hill that

> . . . programs and services were developed to reach the nontraditional library users, resulting in greater access to information for Blacks and other minorities. . . . Remember, libraries did not always serve all people. Before the mid-1800's, libraries were mostly for scholars, university students, and the rich. Years of struggle by progressive librarians eventually changed this narrow role of libraries, and made them the open, vital information centers they are today. (Levirn Hill, "Why We Need More Black Librarians," *ABBWA Journal* 4 (1992): 29–30)

Not only are libraries now open to all people and the resources they contain are available to anyone who needs them, members of the ALA, especially the Black Caucus of ALA (BCALA), have played a leadership role in recruiting African Americans to the library profession and supporting initiatives to develop library collections in the area of African-American history.

Four ways to celebrate African-American events include presenting: (1) annual displays and exhibits; Associated Publishers produces a kit that focuses on a yearly theme—the theme for the 1996 kit was "African-American Women Yesterday, Today, and Tomorrow"; (2) lectures that invite faculty, campus administrators, city or state officials, and visiting scholars to participate; (3) group readings that can be organized similar to the brown-bag luncheon book-talk format where each luncheon focuses on the specifics of a particular author or book; and (4) multimedia presentations that include videos featuring African-American themes.

In 1990 the African-American Read-In Chain, held every first Sunday or Monday in February until the year 2000, was organized. First sponsored by the Black Caucus of the National Council of Teachers of English (NCTE), the local organizers are asked to assemble programs that highlight readings worldwide. In 1995, at the University of Cincinnati, a video series was aired on a closed-circuit library cable broadcast system for educational purposes. Also in 1995, a similar program format at the Shrine of the Black Madonna Bookstore & Cultural Center in Houston sponsored a weekly series of multimedia presentations which included *AFRICA: Center of the World, African Holocaust & Diaspora, Harlem Renaissance,* and *The Black Power Movement.* Ideas like these are just a few ways that the library can creatively honor outstanding African Americans.

Summary

Celebrating annual African-American events at a time to focus on what libraries have available to support African-American students as they pursue their education. It is also a time to focus on how librarians and faculty can help African-American students sharpen their skills in library use in order to better prepare them for their chosen careers. In the past, libraries did not always open their doors to all races. For many libraries, as well as college and university campuses, celebrating the accomplishments of African Americans is a new challenge.

Today's library is a challenging resource for most students who desire to learn the intricate details of library research. Students and faculty should he aware that technology is constantly changing and everyone in the university or college community is learning by accommodating to change on a day-to-day basis. From the incoming freshmen to post-doctoral students, African Americans should not be overwhelmed with the vast amount of information that is available to them when enrolling at a new university or college. Librarians should be eager to help these new students become comfortable using the library and its resources to support their entire academic career, and they should provide a strong foundation to prepare students for the future. African-American students should not leave the academic environment without being library literate. To prepare for lifelong learning requires that students continue to acquire new skills, pursue career opportunities, enhance their potential for career advancement, and invest time to develop library research skills.

SOURCE: Gerald V. Holmes, "Celebrating Annual African-American Events," *College & Research Libraries News* 57 (February 1996): 93–96.

Spanish library phrases

by Patricia Promis and Maria Segura Hoopes

THESE ARE BASIC STRUCTURES that can be used to build dialogues, followed by lists of terms to fill in the phrase according to specific needs. Optional terms are provided when more than one is appropriate:

Directional questions

—¿Dónde está / ¿Dónde queda . . . ?	Where is . . . ?
—¿Cuál es? / ¿Cuáles son . . . ?	Which is . . . ?
—¿Quién es? / ¿Quiénes son . . . ?	Who is . . . who are . . . ?
(el) afilalápices	pencil sharpener
(el) ascensor / elevador	elevator
(el) asiento	seat
(el) autor / (la) autora	author / authoress
(el) baño / lavatorio	bathroom / rest room
(la) biblioteca de ciencias / central	SEL / Main
(el) buzón para libros	bookdrop
(el) cajón	drawer
(la) central	main
(el) clip	paper clip

(el) edificio	building
(la) editorial	publisher
(la) entrada	entrance
(el) escritorio	desk
(el) estante / (la) estantería	bookshelf
(la) fotocopiadora	copier
(la) grapadora / corchetera	stapler
(el) guión / manuscrito / original	manuscript
(el) letrero	sign
(la) librería	bookstore
(el) manual	handbook
(la) máquina para cambiar billetes	change machine
(la) mesa	table
(el) mesón / mostrador	counter
(el) mesón de préstamos	loan desk
(el) papelero	wastebasket
(el) perforador	hole puncher
(el) poste / pilar	pillar
(la) puerta	door
(la) referencia recíproca	cross reference
(el) reloj	clock / watch
(la) sala de lectura	reading room
(la) sala de objetos perdidos	lost & found
(la) sala de préstamos interbibliotecas	interlibrary loan
(la) sala de reservas	reserve book room
(la) salida	exit
(la) sección multas	fines office
(la) silla	chair
(la) sucursal	branch
(la) ventana	window

—¿Puede repetir la pregunta más despacio, por favor?
—Would you please repeat the question more slowly?

Directional answers

—El / la ... queda / está	The ... is ...
a la derecha de	to the right of ...
a la izquierda de	to the left of ...
derecho al fondo	straight ahead
cerca de	close to
lejos de	far from
arriba	up or above
abajo	down or under
junto a	next to
al lado de	next to
al norte de	north of ...
al sur de	south of ...
al este de	east of ...
al oeste de	west of ...
en la planta baja / subterráneo	in the basement

primer piso	first floor
segundo piso	second floor
tercer piso	third floor
cuarto piso	fourth floor
quinto piso	fifth floor
sala de clases	classroom
vestíbulo	lobby

The reference interview

Question:
—I need information about . . .
—Busco / necesito / quiero información / material sobre . . .

—I'm doing research on . . .
—Estoy haciendo una investigación sobre . . .

Response:
—Are you looking for information in Spanish
    or English?
—¿Quiere información en inglés o en español?

Follow-up questions:
—Can you read English?
—¿Puede leer en inglés?

—Do you need books or articles or both?
—¿Necesita libros, artículos o ambos?

—Are you looking for current material?
—¿Necesita información publicada recientemente?

To look for books:
—You look for books by subject in the subject catalog.
—Monografías o libros sobre el tema. se buscan en el fichero de materias.

—You can also look for books in the online catalog. Follow the instructions
    screen by screen.
—Usted también puede consultar el catálogo computarizado. Siga paso a
    paso las instrucciones que aparecen el la pantalla.

by subject	por materia / tema
by author	por autor / autor corporativo
by title	por títuilo

To look for articles:
—You look for articles in the appropriate indexes.
—Articulos publicados en revistas se buscan en los indices correspondientes.

—How do you look . . .
—¿Cómo se buscan?

—For example [looking at an index], this is a citation for one article.
—Por ejemplo, esta cita corresponde a un artículo.

—This is the title of the article.
—Este es el título del artículo.

—This is the author.
—Este es el autor.

—Here, in italics, is the title of the journal.
—Aquí, en cursiva, está el título de la revista.

—This is an abbreviation for the title of the journal.
—Esta es la abreviatura del título, de la revista.

—This is an acronym.
—Esta es una sigla.

—If you need really current articles, which will usually be in English, you can do a computer search.
—Si Usted necesita artículos más nuevos, que generalmente estarán en inglés, puede hacer una búsqueda computarizada.

—I'd like to do a computerized literature search on . . .
—Necesito / quiero / ?puedo? hacer una búsqueda computarizada de material / literatura en / sobre.

Internet

(los) anexos	attachments
(el) navegador	browser
Dicho sea de paso	BTW
(los) rincones para charlar	chat rooms
(el) correo-e, or correo electronico	e-mail
(las) preguntas hechas con frecuencia	FAQ
flamear	to flame
En mi humilde opinión	IMHO
(las) listas de correo	mailing lists
(el) mouse	mouse
(la) Red	the Net
(los) grupos de discusiones	newsgroups
Lee el maldito manual!	RTFM
(la) pantalla	screen
(el) servidor	server
surfear	to surf
(el) localizador universal de recursos	URL
(la) Telaraña Mundial	World Wide Web

SOURCE: Patricia Promis and Maria Segura Hoopes, *¿Habla Español? Practical Spanish for the Reference Desk* (ALA Reference and Adult Services Division, 1991), pp. 3–6; www.civila.com/ desenredada/glosario.html.

Tribal library internships

by Bonnie Biggs

DEVELOPING INTERNSHIPS in tribal libraries can provide life-changing experiences for students entering the profession. The student benefits by experiencing a degree of cultural immersion and by contributing to the operational goals of the tribal library. Most importantly, the student gains a proper perspective of libraries and how they differ; in particular, how tribal libraries serve as social gathering places as well as centers for the oral transmission of knowledge and mythology.

Interested in developing a similar project in your library's service area? Here are some things to consider:

Is there an MLS degree-granting institution in your service area? If there is, you'll want to find out if the curriculum includes internship opportunities, and if so, how the supervisory role is defined. Other than the tribal library manager, someone will need to assume overall responsibility and be the liaison between the library school and the tribal library.

Is there an Indian reservation or sizable Indian population in your library's service area? If so, you'll want to make contact with the governing body, likely a tribal council, to determine if there is a tribal library. You will want to connect with the tribal library staff and tribal council to determine their interest in an intern program. You will want to spend most of your time, perhaps several visits, listening.

Ask yourself why you and your institution would want to pursue this kind of program in the first place. Beyond altruism, does your library hold a strong commitment to community outreach? Are there compelling, mission-based reasons for engaging in projects that center on multicultural issues? Is there someone within the library whose job description or research focus naturally links them to this kind of activity? If so, will the administration support the time commitment required to develop and oversee an intern program?

SOURCE: Bonnie Biggs, "The Tribal Library Project: Interns, American Indians, and Library Services," *College & Research Libraries News* 59 (April 1998): 259–62.

THE IMPAIRED

Glossary of terms for service to the blind and physically impaired

THE MEANING OF TERMS varies in practice. This glossary is not intended to establish standard definitions, but to explain usage in libraries serving persons with disabilities.

Access. Freedom or ability to obtain or make use of.

Accessories. Equipment used with talking book and cassette machines.

Braille. A system devised by Louis Braille of embossing or transcribing for the blind in which the characters are represented by raised dots. It is graded according to the number of contractions used. *Grade 1*—Letter by letter; no contractions. *Grade 1 1/2*—Slightly contracted, no longer used in braille production. *Grade 2*—Moderately contracted; now known as English Braille American Edition; used for virtually all braille production in the United States. *Grade 3*—Highly contracted, used by some students and professionals for note taking. *Jumbo*—Enlarged dots and increased spacing; used by some persons who experience tactile difficulties.

Conventional print. Material printed in less than 14-point type.

Demonstration collection. Library materials and sound reproduction equipment furnished by a network library to agencies whose clientele might include persons with disabilities. They are a vehicle for raising public awareness and advertising availability of services.

Large type. Material printed in 14-point or larger type.

LC/NLS. Library of Congress National Library Service for the Blind and Physically Handicapped.

Limited-production material. Titles produced by LC/NLS in a small number of copies to provide supplementary titles to meet special demand. Such titles are not duplicated generally for the network, but copies can be reproduced when the need arises.

Locally produced materials. Those items produced in special formats by regional or subregional libraries emphasizing user demand and titles of local significance.

Machine lending agency (MLA). An agency designated by LC/NLS to receive, issue, and control the inventory of specially designed record players, cassette machines, and accessories essential to the provision of service.

Outreach services. Library and information programs that seek out potential patrons, particularly those who do not or cannot make use of traditional library services or materials. Examples include bookmobile service, service to people who are homebound, books by mail, service to hospitals and institutions, and home visits.

Radio reading service. Use of a radio station to transmit newspapers, articles, current books, and materials not available to persons unable to use conventional print. This service may be provided on a commercial or public service station, or more commonly, on a side band licensed by a Subsidiary Communication Authorization (SCA).

Regional library. A library for blind and physically handicapped individuals which is administered by a state library agency, public library, or agency for the blind. It must be designated by LC/NLS to administer services to the residents of a specific geographic area, typically a state. Usually provides direct services to patrons.

Sublending agency (SLA). An agency designated by a machine lending agency (MLA) to receive, issue, and control the inventory of specially designed record players, cassette machines, and accessories essential to the provision of service.

Subregional library. A department or unit of a library agency which provides service to the blind and physically handicapped residents of a specified area of the regional library's total service area. Designation requires approval of LC/NLS, the regional library, and the state library agency.

Talking book. A recording of print material on disc or cassette tape produced for exclusive use of blind and physically handicapped readers. Formats were introduced by LC/NLS in the following order:

33 ⅓—A title recorded on disc at 33 ⅓ revolutions per minute.

TB—A title recorded on disc at 16 ⅔ revolutions per minute.

RD—A title recorded on disc at 8 ⅓ revolutions per minute.

CB—A title recorded on a cassette at 1 ⅞ inches per second on two tracks of the tape.

RC—A title recorded on a cassette at 1 ⁵⁄₁₆ inches per second on two or four tracks of the tape.

FD—A very thin vinyl disc recorded at 8 ⅓ revolutions per minute.

SOURCE: Revised Standards and Guidelines of Service for the Library of Congress Network of Libraries for the Blind and Physically Handicapped (ALA Association of Specialized and Cooperative Library Agencies, 1995).

Test your learning disabilities I.Q.

Multiple choice
1. About what percent of Americans have learning disabilities?
       a. 1%   b. 15%   c. 25%   d. 45%
2. What percent of students with identified learning disabilities drop out of school? Note: This does not include those who are never identified and drop out.
       a. 15%   b. 25%   c. 35%   d. 45%
3. When the learning disabilities of young criminal offenders are addressed, what is their recidivism rate?
       a. 2%   b. 12%   c. 32%   d. 62%
4. Undetected or untreated learning disabilities have been found in what percent of adults with severe literacy problems?
       a. 10%   b. 30%   c. 60%   d. 90%

True or false?
5. Learning disabilities are neurobiological disorders.
6. Being a "slow learner" is an indicator of learning disabilities.
7. Learning disabilities run in families.
8. People have learning disabilities all of their lives.
9. People with learning disabilities are generally of normal or above average intelligence.
10. Deficits in reading skills are the most common forms of learning disabilities.
11. People with learning disabilities can learn to compensate for their conditions.

Answers: 1.b. 15%; 2.c. 35%; 3.a. 2%; 4.c. 60%; 5, 7, 8, 9, 10, 11 are all true; 6 is false.

So how'd you do on the LD I.Q. test? If you did really well, congratulations! You're one of a minority of people with good basic knowledge about learning disabilities (LD). If you didn't do very well, you're like most Americans. In a 1995 Roper poll, an overwhelming majority of respondents incorrectly identified a number of conditions, including mental retardation, as being associated with learning disabilities. Seeing the correct answers to the quiz, you can guess how all of this might affect you personally and professionally.

SOURCE: Audrey J. Gorman, "The 15% Solution: Libraries and Learning Disabilities," *American Libraries* 27 (January 1997): 52–54.

Library service to the deaf

THE GUIDELINES THAT FOLLOW are meant to inform librarians about the library needs of the deaf community. They apply to all types of libraries, including public, school, and academic, as well as special libraries serving government, commerce and industry, the arts, the military, hospitals, prisons, and other institutions. They are statements of general principles and, as such, contain no quantitative prescriptions. They are, however, meant to serve both as an encouragement to make services accessible for deaf persons and as a means to assess the completeness and quality of such services.

As these guidelines are national in scope, the District of Columbia, the 50 states, and U.S. territories should apply these guidelines to their existing services. Additionally, this document should serve as a guide to the development of state guidelines for library and information services to the deaf community. In the absence of local guidelines, these guidelines should apply.

Refer to the original ASCLA document for commentary on each guideline.

Personnel

1. Responsibility for the development, implementation, and operation of library and information services to the deaf community should be assigned to a librarian holding the degrees, certification, and/or training required to achieve professional status.

2. Library staff should receive training focusing on the issues involved in providing services to the deaf community.

3. When selecting staff to be involved with the provision of services to deaf people, libraries should attempt to employ persons who have, or are likely to be able to obtain, credibility within the deaf community.

4. Schools of librarianship should integrate into their curricula training in the provision of services to the deaf community. Such courses should also constitute a part of their continuing education programs for all levels of library staff.

5. Libraries having responsibilities at the state level, or where applicable, at an appropriate regional or local level, should establish a unit responsible for provision of advisory and consultation services to all libraries within their geographical boundaries in order to assist them in the provision of services to the death community.

6. Each state library association should establish a group within its structure to focus on the provision of library services to the deaf community.

Communication

1. All library staff should receive training in how to interact effectively with deaf people.

2. A text telephone (TTY) should be available at each main service point, for example, at each telephone reference desk in each library. TTYs must be provided for use by deaf staff members and at least one TTY should be available in each library for public use.

3. Telephones for use by library patrons or staff should be equipped with amplification.

4. Libraries should have communication aids such as assistive listening systems and equipment which can be used to support computer-assisted real-time captioning or computer-assisted note taking. These services should be available for meetings and programs upon request.

5. Libraries with television viewing facilities should provide closed-caption decoders.

6. Libraries should offer to provide sign language or oral interpreters, computer-assisted real-time captioning, or computer-assisted note-taking services for all library-sponsored programs upon request.

7. Libraries should install visible warning signals in order to alert deaf people to problems and emergencies.

Collections

1. Library collection development policies should encourage collection of materials related to hearing disabilities and deaf culture which will be of interest to both deaf and hearing patrons, thus addressing the unique needs of members of the deaf community.

2. Visual nonprint materials should form an integral part of any library's collections acquired in support of services to the deaf community. Collection development policies should encourage the acquisition of videos that support audible information with closed or open captions. In all cases, librarians should inquire about the presence of captions on any video before purchase.

3. Libraries should assemble and maintain a collection of videocassettes in sign language.

4. Libraries should collect, maintain, and offer information about educational options, referral agencies, and programs serving deaf people in a wholly unbiased fashion.

5. Libraries should assemble and provide access to a collection of high-interest, low-reading-level materials of interest to deaf readers.

Services

1. All of the library's collections, services, and programs should be made accessible to members of the deaf community.

2. Libraries should be able to provide information on local literacy programs that are accessible to deaf nonreaders. Libraries should ensure that library-sponsored literacy programs meet the needs of deaf individuals.

3. Members of the deaf community, as defined in these guidelines, should be involved in the design and development of the library's services to deaf people, including the development of services and collections, and establishment of advisory committees, service organizations, and networks.

4. Libraries should offer programs conducted in sign language.

Program marketing

1. Libraries should aggressively market their programs and services to the deaf community.

2. All library publicity should provide for access to deaf people.

SOURCE: Guidelines for Library and Information Services for the American Deaf Community (Chicago: ALA Association of Specialized and Cooperative Library Agencies, 1996).

Library services to older adults

INTEGRATE LIBRARY SERVICE to older adults into the overall library plan, budget and service program. It is essential for the leaders and policy makers of the library to understand that service for older adults is not a fad; that the need and demand for library services will only increase; that the received wisdom about older adults and libraries no longer holds; and that nothing short of a total moral and financial commitment to library services for older adults will meet the needs and demands of the present and future older library user.

Acknowledge the changing needs of older adults in the library's strategic planning and evaluation process.

Incorporate funding for materials and services for older adults in the library's operating budget.

Actively seek supplemental funding for programs and services to older adults.

Provide access to library buildings, materials, programs, and services for older adults. Older adults may have reduced visual, physical, or aural acuity. The Americans with Disabilities Act (ADA) of 1990 provides basic guidelines for access to buildings and services for people with disabilities. Knowledge of the community, attention to local populations and end-users should further guide library staff and administrators in the provision of appropriate services and programs.

Ensure easy access to library buildings by older adults.

Provide lighting, signage, and furniture compatible with older adults' needs.

Permit older adults to access information through its provision in a variety of materials and formats.

Promote the purchase and use of assistive technology devices for older adults to easily access library materials and programs.

Provide service for older adults who are unable to visit the library easily.

Treat all older adults with respect at every service point. All library users, regardless of age, benefit when staff emphasizes customer service in their work with the public. Training opportunities which focus on cultural awareness and an avoidance of aging and cultural stereotypes will enhance staff attitudes and communication skills.

Promote better working skills and communication with older adults or people of all ages through continuous staff education.

Integrate library services to older adults with those offered to other user populations.

Assure that services for older adults embrace cultural diversity and economic differences.

Utilize the experience and expertise of older adults. Older adults have valuable and long-established connections within the community that can enhance the library's performance, its place in the community, and its ability to offer additional programs. Proactive recruitment, development and inclusion of older adults bring the intergenerational role of library service full circle.

Recruit older adults to serve as program resources and volunteers.

Promote the employment of older adults as professional and support staff members.

Encourage older adults to serve as liaisons to the community.

Develop opportunities for intergenerational activities.

Provide and promote information and resources on aging. Today's library collection extends beyond the traditional print and audiovisual materials to electronic and Internet resources on aging. The library's role extends beyond gathering resources to keeping them current and actively seeking means to publicize and promote them. Library staff and administrators should position the library as a primary access point to information on retirement planning, health issues, second career opportunities, etc. to aid caregivers, family members, professionals and older adults themselves.

Develop collections to reflect the information needs of older adults.

Act as a clearinghouse for information and resources on aging for older adults, their families, caregivers, and professionals.

Incorporate technology resources and access to online and Internet services and information into library collections.

Provide library services appropriate to the needs of older adults. The explosion of accessible information and of service expectations by the public in recent years has changed the focus of library services and programs. From assisting older adults to develop new library skills to remain independent and skillful library users, to providing traditional informational or recreational programs for seniors, libraries should provide a community setting for older adult programming. Library initiated outreach services, home delivery, and remote access to collections benefit more than just one population and help all users increase or maintain independence in using the library.

Provide programming to meet the needs and interests of older adults and family members.

Train older adults to become self-sufficient library users.

Provide older adults with access to or training in technology.

Develop programming and services to meet the needs of older adults unable to visit the library.

Publicize services and programs for older adults.

Collaborate with community agencies and groups serving older adults. Library programs and services for older adults should not replicate those of other agencies, but can complement and support them. Investigate possible joint programs for older adults. Identify resources the library can provide to assist professionals who work with older adults. Contact local American Association of Retired Persons chapters, senior centers, Meals on Wheels, Area Agencies on Aging and literacy programs. Identify continuing education programs offered by area academic institutions that appeal to older adults. Day care centers and groups working with children provide opportunities for intergenerational activities. Not only can your library assist these groups but they can help to promote what you have available and they may be able to tap funding sources not usually open to libraries alone.

Identify community organizations and groups of and for older adults.

Identify roles for library and agency staff in meeting the goals of collaborative organizations.

Partner with local organizations for library programs and delivery of services.

Work with existing agencies and educational institutions to promote lifelong learning.

SOURCE: Library Services to Older Adults Guidelines (Chicago: ALA Reference and User Services Association, 1999).

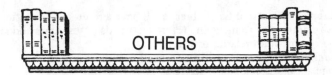

OTHERS

Juvenile correctional libraries: Collections and facilities

THE MATERIALS IN THE JUVENILE CORRECTIONAL LIBRARY shall be selected to meet the educational, informational, recreational, career/ vocational, and personal needs of its users.

To ensure that the materials meet these needs, the library shall have a printed statement of policy that defines the principles, purposes, and criteria to be considered in the selection and maintenance of library materials. These criteria should specify items defined by the facility as contraband. The *Library Bill of Rights*, *"Free Access to Libraries for Minors"* shall be incorporated in this policy. This policy shall apply to gifts as well as to purchased items. The collection policy statement shall include a procedure to be followed in the event of an objection to an item in the collection. The policy shall also include guidelines for the regular discarding and replacement of outdated, unused, and worn materials.

Standard library materials selection publications shall be used to ensure the quality of the collection. An effort shall be made to acquire award-winning or otherwise notable materials.

The library collection shall reflect the needs, abilities, and current interests of the resident population. Print materials shall be at the reading levels of the resident population. Ethnic and non-English language materials shall reflect resident population demographics. Print materials may consist mainly of paperbacks. Items in heavy demand shall be provided in multiple copies.

The library collection shall include materials that support the school curriculum. Faculty and staff recommendations shall be considered when selecting library materials that support the curriculum.

The collection shall include legal reference materials which satisfy user needs and court mandates.

The collection shall include materials which assist residents in developing positive survival skills and in preparing for successful transition back to the community.

The collection shall also include titles popular among teenagers, and high interest low-vocabulary materials to assist in the development and improvement of reading skills. Formal or informal user surveys should be conducted at least annually to determine reading interests, reading levels, ethnic diversity, etc.

Computer software: A minimum collection of 25 programs. Other materials as appropriate: Games: puzzles, kits, art objects, realia, comic books, etc. Equipment: The library shall have sufficient equipment to meet the needs of its users to utilize the media collection.

6

Reference collection: Each library shall have a reference collection of sufficient size and scope to meet the reference needs of residents and staff and to support curriculum-related research.

The minimum reference collection shall include:

- One set of encyclopedias less than 5 years old;
- Two current general almanacs;
- Twelve dictionaries (including foreign languages, quotations, biographical dictionaries, and other dictionaries on appropriate subjects);
- Two world atlases and one road atlas;
- One current local telephone book;
- One medical encyclopedia;
- One current world record book;
- One GED study guide;
- One current college directory and one current vocational/technical school directory.

Facilities

Short-term facility: In the case of short-term facilities, the on-site library shall consist of an extended deposit collection placed in the day room and shall be accessible during day room times.

Long-term facility: The library shall be functional in design and inviting in appearance.

Good lighting, acoustical treatment, carpeting, and temperature control necessary for the comfort of library users and preservation of the materials collection shall be basic requirements of the library.

The library shall be centrally located in order to provide maximum security and utilization by all residents and staff.

The library shall be close to educational facilities with ready access from living quarters and offices.

The library shall be in a place which at all times can be properly monitored by, and is readily accessible to, security staff.

The library shall be a secure, separate, lockable area and shall be used only under the supervision of the librarian or other qualified staff trained by the librarian.

The size of the library shall allow for sufficient space for carrels, tables, chairs, equipment, library materials, and for the comfortable and efficient use of the library's resources.

Space shall be assigned to adequately house legal reference materials.

The reading room shall seat a minimum of 10% of the population each day (allowing 25 square feet per person), but never fewer square feet than needed to accommodate the largest class.

In addition to the collection, the library space shall include ample provisions for reading activities, conferences, individual and group viewing and listening, staff library materials, locked storage for materials and equipment, an administrative office, and work room.

Furnishings and equipment: The furnishings and equipment for the library shall contribute to the effectiveness of the library program and provide a comfortable and inviting environment.

Furniture shall be selected for attractiveness, durability, comfort, and ease of maintenance, and must meet the facility's fire code standards.

The types of machinery and equipment will vary depending upon the service program of the institution and library. Basic to all libraries are a typewriter, a computer, a printer, a photocopier, and a telephone. Computer technology shall be incorporated in library operations, collections, and services.

Electrical outlets adequate for the operation of equipment and machinery shall be provided.

SOURCE: *Library Standards for Juvenile Justice Correctional Facilities* (Chicago: ALA Association of Specialized and Cooperative Library Agencies, 1999).

Library services for the poor

THE AMERICAN LIBRARY ASSOCIATION PROMOTES equal access to information for all persons, and recognizes the urgent need to respond to the increasing number of poor children, adults, and families in America. These people are affected by a combination of limitations, including illiteracy, illness, social isolation, homelessness, hunger, and discrimination, which hamper the effectiveness of traditional library services. Therefore, it is crucial that libraries recognize their role in enabling poor people to participate fully in a democratic society, by utilizing a wide variety of available resources and strategies. Concrete programs of training and development are needed to sensitize and prepare library staff to identify poor people's needs and deliver relevant services. And within the American Library Association the coordinating mechanisms for programs and activities dealing with poor people in various divisions, offices, and units should be strengthened, and support for low-income liaison activities should be enhanced.

Policy objectives

The American Library Association shall implement these objectives by:

1. Promoting the removal of all barriers to library and information services, particularly fees and overdue charges.

2. Promoting the publication, production, purchase, and ready accessibility of print and nonprint materials that honestly address the issues of poverty and homelessness, that deal with poor people in a respectful way, and that are of practical use to low-income patrons.

3. Promoting full, stable, and ongoing funding for existing legislation programs in support of low-income services, and for proactive library programs that reach beyond traditional service sites to poor children, adults, and families.

4. Promoting training opportunities for librarians, in order to teach effective techniques for generating public funding to upgrade library services to poor people.

5. Promoting the incorporation of low-income programs and services into regular library budgets in all types of libraries, rather than the tendency to support these projects solely with "soft money" like private or federal grants.

6. Promoting equity in funding adequate library services for poor people in terms of materials, facilities, and equipment.

7. Promoting supplemental support for library resources for and about low-income populations by urging local, state, and federal governments, and the private sector, to provide adequate funding.

8. Promoting increased public awareness—through programs, displays, bibliographies, and publicity—of the importance of poverty-related library resources and services in all segments of society.

9. Promoting the determination of output measures through the encouragement of community needs assessments, giving special emphasis to assessing the needs of low-income people and involving both antipoverty advocates and poor people themselves in such assessments.

10. Promoting direct representation of poor people and antipoverty advocates through appointment to local boards and creation of local advisory committees on service to low-income people, such appointments to include library-paid transportation and stipends.

11. Promoting training to sensitize library staff to issues affecting poor people and to attitudinal and other barriers that hinder poor people's use of libraries.

12. Promoting networking and cooperation between libraries and other agencies, organizations, and advocacy groups in order to develop programs and services that effectively reach poor people.

Ten reasons why . . .

. . . A Person Who Works with People Who Are Homeless Would Use a Library

1. Government reports
2. Legislation, rights, laws
3. Funding sources and information
4. Demographic information
5. Instructional materials
6. Current events in the field
7. Latest research in the field
8. Maps, phone books, directories
9. Subject searches and reference questions
10. Special programs

. . . A Person Who Is Homeless Would Use a Library

1. Community information and referral services
2. Regional guides and newspapers
3. Job search/career guidance
4. Quiet study environment
5. Educational/vocational courses information
6. Programs for children
7. Literacy/ESL tutoring
8. New reader/foreign language materials
9. Adult programs
10. Audiovisual materials

SOURCE: Joshua Cohen, "10 Reasons Why . . . ," in Karen M. Venturella, ed., *Poor People and Library Services* (McFarland, 1998), pp. 123–24.

13. Promoting the implementation of an expanded federal low-income housing program, national health insurance, full-employment policy; living minimum wage and welfare payments, affordable day care, and programs likely to reduce, if not eliminate, poverty itself.

14. Promoting among library staff the collection of food and clothing donations, volunteering personal time to anti-poverty activities and contributing money to direct-aid organizations.

15. Promoting related efforts concerning minorities and women, since these groups are disproportionately represented among poor people.

SOURCE: ALA Handbook of Organization 1998/1999; approved by ALA Council, June 1990.

Best of times, worst of times
by Will Manley

YOU DON'T READ THAT MUCH about the homeless these days. It's not that the homeless no longer exist, it's just that people have very little sympathy for them anymore. When the unemployment rate sinks beneath 4% and the annual economic growth rate climbs above 4%, it's not surprising to see the sympathy rate hit rock bottom.

Don't get me wrong. Americans are the most forgiving, most understanding, and most sympathetic people on the planet. We are famous for coming to the aid of people and countries all over the world who need our help. We give our money, our time, our prayers, and even our lives to assist those who, through no fault of their own, are down and out.

For years, the inner-city homeless have been seen in that light as blameless victims of impersonal and sometimes cruel economic forces beyond their control. In our current robust economic times, however, the prevailing perspective is that any American who really needs a job can find one. It's no coincidence that welfare reform has taken place in this economic climate. As a result, sympathy for the homeless has pretty much dried up. While you don't often hear them referred to in polite company by the old pejorative terms of "bums" or "hobos," you are now beginning to hear the word "slacker" more often than ever before.

Clearly the homeless have hit hard times. That's because the old-fashioned Puritan work ethic is still the value that we Americans, liberal and conservative alike, cherish most. Even President Clinton, with all his legal and personal problems, is given the benefit of the doubt by the vast majority of Americans because he works hard and is doing a good job.

You can say many things about librarians. We suffer from stereotypical images that we will never shake (and that by the way is the real reason why we are trying to expunge all derivations of the word "library" from the English language); but it is my experience that despite our rather forbidding image, we librarians, more than any other occupational group, personify those two strong American values of sympathy and hard work. What we accomplish every day with a scarcity of resources to serve the least of our brethren is truly amazing.

Yes, libraries are among the places that the homeless habitually inhabit, and yes, the homeless can be the bane of our existence; but despite the inconveniences that they create, we librarians are consistently in the forefront of championing their needs and securing their rights even in the best of economic times.

Unlike the well-dressed people, who at night and on the weekends descend upon the civilized amenities of big-city cultural districts, we do not have the luxury of whining self-righteously about the unpleasantness of having to lay eyes upon ill-kempt slackers looking for a handout. "Want a tip?" I recently saw a tuxedoed young yuppie exclaim to a bedraggled panhandler who had just opened his limousine door outside a glittering Broadway theater, "I'll give you a tip—GET A JOB!"

No, we librarians cannot simply wave away the homeless with righteous indignation. We have to live with them all day, every day. They are an intrinsic part of our world and we know something about them that the rest of America is unwilling to admit. The homeless will always be with us. Even in the best of times there are significant numbers of people who, because of physical or mental illnesses, simply cannot get and hold a job. It is not their fault.

The irony, of course, is that for a street person the best of times is the worst of times precisely because people do self-righteously turn their backs on them. Here's where we librarians have a special role to play. It is our job to put America back in touch with its best instinct—helping those who need help. I know we've got problems of our own with new technological paradigms to adapt to, but don't people come before paradigms? We've gotten so obsessed with machines that we've forgotten about flesh and blood. While the debate will rage on and on over the next few years about the desirability of eliminating the word "library" from the vernacular in favor of something more technocratic, I will stubbornly cling to the title "librarian" because for me a librarian is someone who cares about people.

If you don't buy any of that, consider this: When we help the homeless, we help ourselves.

SOURCE: Will Manley, "Best of Times; Worst of Times," *American Libraries* 29 (May 1998): 128.

PROMOTION

CHAPTER SEVEN

"How much do you think we spend altogether on our libraries, public or private, as compared with what we spend on our horses? . . . If public libraries were half so costly as public dinners . . . even foolish men and women might sometimes suspect there was good in reading."

—John Ruskin, *Sesame and Lilies* (1865)

PROMOTION

ALA initiatives

by Joyce Kelly

EACH YEAR FOR MANY DECADES, the American Library Association has sponsored important activities that help promote libraries and literacy issues nationwide.

National Library Week

National Library Week is a national holiday for libraries—a special time to celebrate the contributions of all types of libraries and librarians. Even in the mid-1950s, Americans were spending considerably more time watching television and listening to the radio than they were curling up with a good book. Reading was on the decline. In an effort to make reading a national priority, ALA and the American Book Publishers Council formed the National Book Committee in 1954. This nonprofit committee worked through a number of goals, encouraging people to do more leisurely reading, improve their incomes and health, and develop strong and happy family lives.

In 1957, the committee developed a plan for a National Library Week, based on the premise that if people were motivated to read, they would use and support libraries.

With the cooperation of ALA and the Advertising Council, the first National Library Week was observed March 16–22, 1958, with the theme "Wake Up and Read!" The following year, it was again observed and ALA Council voted to continue it as an annual celebration. When the National Book Committee disbanded in 1974, ALA became the sole sponsor of National Library Week.

How you observe National Library Week at your library depends, in part, on the theme. For example, in 1998 there was a dual theme: "Kids Connect @

the Library" and "Global Reach, Local Touch." One recommended activity was to celebrate America's diversity. Libraries reached out to community and campus groups reflecting other cultures and celebrated that diversity with speakers, exhibits, films, fairs, and other special performances during National Library Week and throughout the year. In 1999, the theme was "Read! Learn! Connect! @ the Library." These are some recommended ways to celebrate that will work regardless of what the theme might be.

Post a National Library Week message on your Web site. Something as simple as "Happy National Library Week" could suffice, or it could be something more elaborate. Whether simple or lively, the message is sure to be noticed by someone.

Hang posters in the library, but also ask local

businesses to display National Library Week posters and give away bookmarks. Order National Library Week promotional items through the ALA
Graphics catalog, which features banners, posters,
T-shirts, and bookmarks.

Host a roundtable discussion with local news
media, college presidents, legislators, and representatives from social, religious, or other groups.
Discuss whatever key issues are facing libraries nationally and in your community.

Invite local officials and legislators for a special National Library Week tour or program to
highlight the many ways your library serves its
constituents. Invite the public to meet their
elected representatives and share what the library
means to them. Invite the media and publish
photos in your library newsletter or annual report.

**Showcase a variety of your best library re-
sources.** Many libraries are fortunate enough to have materials
that will include something for everyone, regardless of your patron's age, race,
socioeconomic status, gender, sexual orientation, religion, culture, or interests.

Remind new parents that it's never too late to start raising a reader.
Provide an ALA "Born to Read" T-shirt and you could have a newspaper photo
opportunity.

Reach out to low-income and at-risk families (and others who might not
be visiting the library on a regular basis). Work with housing developments to
offer National Library Week parties, door prizes, storytelling, and refreshments
in community rooms. Sign up residents for library cards.

Invite celebrities to attend your National Library Week functions. This
often is a long shot, but there are many occasions when famous people accept
an invitation. It's worth a try; celebrities bring out the crowds and attract
media coverage for your programs. Plan for this a year or more in advance:
Most celebrities have jam-packed schedules.

National Library Weeks to 2007

2001, April 1–7	2005, April 10–16
2002, April 14–20	2006, April 2–8
2003, April 6–12	2007, April 15–21
2004, April 18–24	

Library Card Sign-up Month

September is the time when libraries across the country remind parents that
a library card is the most important school supply of all. Library Card Sign-up
Month came from a 1987 national campaign to combat illiteracy. With support
from the Reader's Digest Foundation, ALA and the National Commission on
Libraries launched the campaign with the theme "The best gift you'll ever

SIGN-UP FOR A LIBRARY CARD

give your child . . . a library card."

Hundreds of thousands of children (and adults) received library cards during the first year of the national campaign, more than 100,000 in the state of West Virginia alone. The New York Public Library signed up more than 60,000 patrons during the first six weeks of the campaign. The Louisville (Ky.) Public Library signed up more than 50,000 card-carrying readers. In other parts of Kentucky, a total of 11,777 new borrowers were registered by 58 libraries—the result of a special promotion by the Kentucky Library Association.

Despite the success of the first campaign, the need is ongoing. While library use is high all across the nation, a 1998 Gallup poll revealed that 66% of American adults held library cards. Library Card Sign-up Month is an opportunity to encourage everyone to get that very valuable resource in hand.

Rally around the library. Launch your campaign with a pep rally on the library lawn. Explain that the drive is part of a national effort to improve literacy. Make it a local media event with banners flying. Invite the local school bands. Have local dignitaries talk about what the library card means to them. Have them take a turn at the registration table. To get things kicked off, make your own crowd. Arrange to bus in students and spread the word that the rally will be a big event. Ask service organizations to donate free refreshments. Have special prize drawings.

Have local vendors "card" kids. Ask local merchants to provide a discount on movies, food, music CDs, books and other products when a child shows his or her library card during the month of September.

Issue baby's first library card. Get names of new parents and babies from the county clerk. Send a note of congratulations with a library brochure and an invitation to come to the library and pick up a free gift (perhaps a book donated by a local bookstore). Include a library card made out in the baby's name and a book list of recommended titles for parents and babies.

Go where the action is. If you aren't getting the traffic you'd like to have in your library, go to prenatal classes, daycare centers, parent groups, churches, malls, citizenship classes, grocery stores, amusement parks, sporting events, school, and the workplace.

At work. Offer to do book talks and other special lunch-hour programs for employees of local businesses and factories. Show them firsthand what the library has to offer and sign them up for cards. Ask local businesses to sponsor billboard or bus signs with the theme of Library Card Sign-up Month.

Banned Books Week

Banned Books Week—Celebrating the Freedom to Read is held each year during the last week of September. It has been observed since 1981 to remind Americans not to take this precious democratic freedom to read for granted. Firmly rooted in the First Amendment, the rights of free speech and freedom of the press require continual vigilance.

Organize a reading and discussion series of books that have been banned or challenged.

Cosponsor an essay contest with the state library association, a local school, or a community group.

Use bumper stickers. "Book banning burns me up!" is a popular one.

Wear T-shirts with clever messages. Bookmarks, posters, and other items are available through the ALA Office for Intellectual Freedom.

Alert the media. Ask the student or community newspaper to devote an issue to Banned Books Week.

Stage a mock trial or moot court. Put a banned book on trial and have students argue for and against the book. Select a jury that has not read the book. For mock trial materials and technical assistance, contact the Constitutional Rights Foundation (www.crf-usa.org); Street Law (www.streetlaw.org); and the Center for Civic Education (www.civiced.org).

Create a radio spot. Improve the spot with music! Ask the radio station's technician, engineer, or disc jockey to help you select music and dub it into the radio spot.

Teen Read Week

This national literacy initiative is aimed at kids roughly 12–18 years old, their parents, and other concerned adults. The goals are to motivate kids to read and to remind parents and educators to encourage older as well as younger children to read for enjoyment.

The ALA Young Adult Library Services Association notes that the number of teenagers who can read but choose not to is growing. Kids who don't read lose their reading skills and reading scores drop. Despite those alarming findings, few if any efforts are being made to focus literacy efforts on this critical age group. In 1998, YALSA launched Teen Read Week, an annual event held in October.

Plan a community-wide celebration of Teen Read Week in cooperation with schools and youth service organizations.

Sponsor a "Teen Read Contest." Invite students aged 12–17 to submit their ideas for a national advertising campaign to motivate teens to read. Provide local prizes.

Display posters and bookmarks. They are available in the ALA Graphics Catalog.

Invite a popular author to speak with teens. Ask the Friends of the Library to underwrite the expenses.

Hold workshops for parents on "Turning teens into readers" to give them tips and resources they can use at home.

Ask local radio stations to air a public service announcement you create.

Gather testimonials and photos of teen readers. Ask their permission to publish them in the community and/or school newspaper.

Plan a teen reading camp during the summer.

More information about these ALA-sponsored activities is available from the ALA Public Information Office, 50 E. Huron St., Chicago, IL 60611 (www.ala.org/events/).

SOURCE: ALA Public Information Office.

50 things to do with a library card

ONE GOOD WAY to promote your library is to make a list of the activities, services, and research that a library card offers, then distribute it in places where it will provoke interest. The following list was produced by the Greater Bay Area Library Council.

1. Scare yourself with a mystery.
2. Learn how to lower your taxes.
3. Reserve a book.
4. Trace a friend in an out-of-state telephone book.
5. Prepare for your job interview.
6. Pick up a book on cassette and listen to it in your car as you drive home.
7. Read a large-print book without wearing your glasses.
8. Check out the latest jazz CD by Chick Corea.
9. Spruce up the house with the latest books on interior design.
10. Borrow Hawaiian music for your luau.
11. Get a schedule of classes for local colleges.
12. Discuss what you've read in a book discussion group.
13. Attend a Sunday musicale in the library.
14. Find out about library service to homebound individuals.
15. Look up your new credentials in a medical directory.
16. Find out what was happening in Newport Beach in 1940.
17. Check out a legal question in *California Code Annotated*.
18. Call for a quote on what AT&T stock did today.
19. Look in *Who's Who in America* to see if your boss made it into the book.
20. Learn how to plan a drought-resistant garden.
21. Trek to another planet in a science-fiction novel.
22. Find out where to send a consumer complaint.
23. Learn how to clean ink stains from a marble counter.
24. Head for the nautical collection if your boat springs a leak.
25. Call the Reference Desk to find out who said, "To err is human, to forgive divine." Did you bet it was Shakespeare? It wasn't.
26. Get some local demographic information for the business report you're writing.
27. Spend a couple of nostalgic hours looking at back issues of *Life* magazine.
28. Decide which VCR to buy with the help of consumer guides.

29. Check the financial standing of your bank or savings and loan.
30. Borrow a set of audiocassettes that teach you how to speak French.
31. Get information about potential new customers for your business from *Dun & Bradstreet's* Million Dollar Directory.
32. Enjoy changing exhibits.
33. Take home Bach, Beethoven, and Brahms.
34. Entertain your preschooler with a book and a read-along audiocassette.
35. Join others for a brown-bag lunch and hear a stimulating speaker.
36. Volunteer as a literacy tutor.
37. Learn who won the America's Cup in 1901.

38. Let the children choose an armload of read-aloud stories.
39. Ask for information about how to start a business.
40. Get tax forms and tax filing information.
41. Get a list of materials that help improve reading skills.
42. Make photocopies; some libraries even have a color copier.
43. Get an interlibrary loan from a library in another city—it's done quickly by computer.
44. Enroll your child in the library's summer reading program.
45. Check on an out-of-town lawyer in *Martindale's*.
46. Ask a staff member to give a talk to your service organization.
47. Look in *Standard & Poor's* and *Moody's* directories for information on a potential investment.
48. Check out a video on boating safety.
49. For a leaky faucet, you might look up a book on how to do your own plumbing.
50. Learn what's happening at City Hall by checking the City Council agenda before a meeting.

SOURCE: Greater Bay Area Library Council, www.gbalc.org/50ways.htm.

Try these eight winning promotional ideas

by Nancy H. Marshall

IF YOU HAVE RUN OUT of ideas to promote your library, consider trying a few of these public relations activities from past John Cotton Dana contest participants, or borrow other winning entries from the ALA headquarters library. To borrow materials, submit an ALA-accredited interlibrary loan form to the ALA Library and Research Center, 50 E. Huron St., Chicago, IL 60611.

1. Sponsor a cultural or ethnic festival that features library materials, staff, and services.

2. Develop a program with a catchy theme to convince state legislators to invest more money in library services and fund new technology to help all citizens get ready for the 21st century.

3. Raise funds for the library with a celebrity roast or other special event.

4. Promote anything new—a library building, remodeling project, or dedication anniversary.

5. Introduce with great fanfare library automation projects, new services, special acquisitions.

6. Take statewide approaches to such issues as literacy and involve schools, government offices, businesses, and community leaders.

7. Prepare eye-catching exhibits that display library materials, issues, or hot topics. Use multimedia to enhance the presentation.

8. Involve your users, Friends, and trustees in fundraising and promotional events, and remember to have fun in your PR efforts.

SOURCE: Nancy H. Marshall, "Libraries and Athletics at Texas A&M: A Winning Team," *College & Research Libraries News* 57 (October 1996): 576–79.

ALA poster celebrities, characters, illustrators, and authors

MANY CELEBRITIES have appeared on American Library Association posters advocating reading and literacy. For the first time, here is a comprehensive list of poster personalities through 1999. Items marked with an asterisk are no longer available from ALA Graphics.

Celebrities

Muhammad Ali
Tim Allen
Wally Amos*
Alec Baldwin
Antonio Banderas
Mikhail Baryshnikov*
Kim Basinger
Ruben Blades*
Michael Bolton
David Bowie*
George Burns*
Barbara Bush*
Nicolas Cage
Kirk Cameron*
Diahann Carroll*
Rachel Carson
Michael Chang*
Cesar Chávez
The Chicago Bulls (Scottie Pippen, John Paxson, Phil Jackson)*

Anna Chlumsky*
Sandra Cisneros*
Glenn Close*
Phil Collins*
Sean Connery
David Copperfield
Bill Cosby
Courteney Cox
Cindy Crawford
McCauley Culkin*
Adam Curry*
Geena Davis
Melvil Dewey
Matt Dillon*
Frederick Douglass
Janet Evans*
Fabio
Harrison Ford
Michael J. Fox*
Morgan Freeman
Gandhi*
Bill Gates
Mel Gibson
Danny Glover
Whoopi Goldberg
John Goodman*
Graham Greene
Goldie Hawn*
Grant Hill
Zora Neale Hurston
William Hurt*
Lee Iococca*
Bo Jackson*
Peter Jennings*
Samuel Johnson*
Jackie Joyner-Kersee*
Michael Keaton
John F. Kennedy
Martin Luther King Jr.
Stephen King*
KRS-One*
Emeril Lagasse

Lassie
Joey, Anthony, and Matthew
    Lawrence
Spike Lee
Jay Leno
Sugar Ray Leonard*
LL Cool J
Rebecca Lobo
Loretta Lynn*
Malcolm X
Dan Marino*
Branford Marsalis*
Steve Martin*
Marlee Matlin
Terry McMillan*
Golda Meir*
Bette Midler
Toni Morrison*
Eric Namesnik*
Paul Newman*
Brandy Norwood
Bill Nye, the Science Guy*
Rosie O'Donnell
Edward James Olmos
Olsen Twins
Shaquille O'Neal
Michelle Pfeiffer
Elvis Presley
Keshia Knight Pulliam*
Aileen Quinn*
Phylicia Rashad*

R.E.M.
Eleanor Roosevelt*
Roseanne*
Margaret Sanger*
Rob Schneider
Andrew Shue
Jimmy Smits
Patrick Stewart
Sting*
Isiah Thomas*
Barbara Walters
Denzel Washington
Jesse White Tumbling Team*
Billy Dee Williams*
Oprah Winfrey
Kristi Yamaguchi

Characters

Alice in Wonderland*
American Girls: Kirsten*
American Girls: Molly*
American Girls: Samantha*
Animalia: Lazy Lions
Barbie
Barney
Buffy the Vampire Slayer cast*
Bugs Bunny
The California Raisins*
The Cat in the Hat
Curious George*
Curly*
Disney: Beauty and the Beast*
Disney: Doug
Disney: Donald Duck
Disney: Gargoyles*
Disney: Goofy

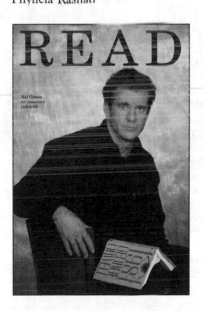

READ

The Cat in the Hat
for America's Libraries

Disney: Mickey Mouse
Disney: Pinocchio*
Disney: Recess TV
Disney: Winnie the Pooh
Doctor Quinn, Medicine Woman cast
E.T.*
The Flintstones
Garfield
Goliath*
Goosebumps*
Gulliver
Hercules
Hare Whodini*
Jughead*
The Little Engine That Could
Little Women*
Magic School Bus*
Matilda
Miss Spider
Muppets: Cleopigtra*
Muppets: Kermit and Miss Piggy
   (Librarian)*
Muppets: Miss Piggy and Kermit
   (Building a Nation of Readers)
Muppets: Muppet Babies*
Muppets: Zoe
The Old Woman Who Loved to Read
Paddington Bear*
Peter Rabbit

Pippi Longstocking*
Power Rangers
Puzzle Place Kids
Ralph S. Mouse*
Ramona*
Rugrats
Sesame Street: Big Bird
Sesame Street: Zoe
The Simpsons
Snoopy*
Star Trek cast
Star Trek Voyager cast
Star Wars: C-3PO
Star Wars: Chewbacca
Star Wars: Darth Vader
Star Wars: R2-D2
Star Wars: Yoda
Stellaluna
Storytime: Kino
Superman*
Sylvia*
Waldo
Wee Pals*
Wild Things*
Xena
Xena: Gabrielle

Illustrators

Chris Van Allsberg*
Graeme Base
Quentin Blake
Janell Cannon
Rafael López Castro*
Raul Colón
Jim Davis
Leo and Diane Dillon
Dr. Seuss
Sally Martin de Gastelum
Anne Geddes
Edward Gorey
George and Doris Hauman
Nicole Hollander*
Doug Keith
Kiki
David Kirk
Robert McCloskey*
Dean Morrissey
Jerry Pinkney*
Patricia Polacco*
Beatrix Potter
Mitchell Robles

Synthia Saint James
Richard Scarry
Maurice Sendak
Ken Skalski
David Small
James Stevenson*
R. L. Stine*
Alan Tiegreen*
Kristin Nelson Tinker
Morrie Turner*
William Wegman*
David Wiesner
John Winch

Authors

Lewis Carroll*
Beverly Cleary
Roald Dahl
Rita Dove
Wade and Cheryl Willis Hudson
A. A. Milne
Pat Mora
Watty Piper
Sara Stewart

SOURCE: ALA Graphics.

Advice for library advocates

1. A significant advocacy effort requires a significant time commitment. It consumes a part of every day, and simply becomes part of your job.

2. If you have promised people something in exchange for their support, be sure to deliver, or your next effort will fail.

3. If you make customer service a primary focus of your mission, support will follow.

4. To achieve success, every board and staff member—from administrators to front-line employees—must fully understand, and be personally committed to, the library's advocacy efforts.

5. Always be prepared for misinformed do-gooders to insert themselves into your campaign and make it more difficult.

SOURCE: William R. Gordon, "How Your Grassroots Garden Grows," *American Libraries* 28 (August 1997): 33.

The U.S. national library symbol

THE NATIONAL LIBRARY SYMBOL was launched at the 1982 ALA Annual Conference for use by libraries throughout the United States in promoting awareness of their services. Originally developed by the Western Maryland Public Libraries, this symbol was recommended for national use by an ALA presidential task force.

Its purpose is to increase public awareness of libraries through widespread use on library directional signs and promotional materials. The symbol was designed primarily for use on exterior library signs appearing on streets, highways, campuses, and buildings; but it can also be used by individual libraries on newsletters, posters, booklists, library cards, bookmarks, letterhead, and other promotional materials.

The impetus for adopting a national library symbol developed from a recommendation of the 1979 White House Conference on Library and Information Services, which suggested "adopting a library symbol for the Nation" as one way to increase public awareness.

The symbol triggers recognition of a library through a graphic representation that people instantly associate with libraries—the book and reader. It does not attempt to capture the essence of the modern library or represent the range of its resources. This would be

impossible to do in a clean, easily recognized image. Once the public is cued to the presence of a library by the basic symbol, additional symbols, signs, and promotional materials can be used to further educate users about the full range of library resources. A standard shade of blue (PMS 285) is used as the background color on directional and building signs.

SOURCE: ALA Public Information Office.

Library newsletter tips
by Phil Bradbury

Use good-sized body type. 10-point type is acceptable, 11 or 12 points is most legible. Above all, resist the temptation to "get more material in" by using a too-small type size. You gain space and lose your reader; a poor bargain. You can use a smaller type size for sidebars. A border and a slightly different format help them stand apart from the regular text and maintain its readibility.

Use graphics sparingly. A lot of newsletter editors went ga-ga over the plethora of computer clip art available, and have dressed up their pages with a wild clutter of cuts, inserts, and other odd elements. To be on the safe side, if you are not sure what you are doing, use no more than one or two graphic elements to a column or page.

Use only one or two styles of typeface in either heads or text and stick with them. Avoid esoteric or fancy type styles—if you are tempted to try these intriguing possibilities, indulge yourself only in a special, separate piece of printed publicity.

Write less and say more. Pare down overlong sentences and paragraphs. Then edit again. Keep your items of news and information as short and punchy as possible.

Organize your material. Present it in some logical order, preferably with identifying heads or sections so that the reader can scan quickly for items of interest. Once the order is established, be as consistent as possible in later issues.

SOURCE: Phil Bradbury, "Mind Your Newsletter P's & Q's," *Library PR News*, no. 103 (January/February 1997): 4.

What to do when the media calls

1. Ask questions. Determine the name and type of publication or station. Find out what the story is about, the reporter's angle, and when the deadline is. If you do not feel qualified to address the issue or are uncomfortable with the approach, say so. Suggest other angles or sources of information.

2. Be clear about who you represent—yourself, your library, or a library association.

3. Be prepared to answer the standard "Who–What–Where–When–How and Why" questions. Have supporting facts and examples available.

4. Beware of manipulation. Some reporters may ask leading questions (something like "Would you say . . ." followed by an idea for your agreement). Make your own statement.

5. Think first. Don't be pressured into responding. Never give incorrect information. If you don't know an answer or need more time, tell the reporter that you'll call back at a given time.

6. Pause before answering questions. Think about what you want to say and the best way to say it. Never repeat a negative. Keep comments positive.

7. Be brief and to the point. This is especially important with broadcast media when you only have 20 seconds to respond.

8. Never say "no comment." Maintain an open, positive attitude. If you are waiting for direction from your board or need time to study the issue, say so.

9. Offer quotes, facts and statistics to support your issue and enhance the reporter's story.

10. Alert the ALA Public Information Office if there is an issue or incident that you feel merits comment, research, or additional briefing material from ALA.

SOURCE: ALA Public Information Office.

Ten keys to acting effectively within the local political structure

1. Know where the library stands. What are its principles, its goals, and its objectives.
2. Know what can be compromised and what cannot.
3. Know the circumstances of your community.
4. Know what are the basic policy thrusts of the local government administration. What do they consider important?
5. Get to know the people who drive local government administration policy.
6. Know the rules and regulations governing the local municipality
7. Present defensible budgets to the administration.
8. Give accurate information and responses.
9. Develop public pressure as a method of supporting library aims.
10. Don't be too slow or too quick to take political action: Timing is everything.

SOURCE: Edwin Beckerman, *Politics and the American Public Library* (Lanham, Md.: Scarecrow Press, 1996), pp. 93–98. Reprinted with permission.

FUNDRAISING

How to organize a Friends foundation

THE PRIMARY REASON to form a foundation is to create a funding source separate and distinct from the regulations and restrictions that apply to any governmental institution. The foundation can establish its own rules and buy equipment or provide services for the library without regard to competitive bidding, committee approvals, etc. The library Friends group and the library foundation are clearly separate groups. The foundation is usually formed when larger amounts of money are needed than can be raised by the Friends group, and these funds can then be invested until they are disbursed.

1. Contact a lawyer to develop documents pertaining to foundations, such as articles of incorporation and bylaws (necessary for limited liability), and to obtain federal and state tax-exempt status.

2. Select a steering committee or board of directors that will reflect your community and the needs of your library. Define your needs and mission statement with this group.

3. It is usually helpful to have lawyers, bankers, public relations, and marketing people, as well as high-profile community and corporate leaders, serve on the full board.

4. It is often necessary to hire a director for the foundation with fund-development experience. Disbursement of the funds is normally decided between the foundation board and the library director.

5. Monies raised are often best looked after and invested by bank trust companies or other money managers. A survey of your community will help you determine where to place your funds.

6. Opportunities abound for fundraising. The Friends of Libraries U.S.A. *News Update* and its office can provide many ideas. The foundation is an excellent vehicle to promote a deferred-giving program.

7. Be sure to involve elected officials, library trustees, and other interested parties in the development of the foundation.

8. Develop a long-range plan for the foundation, and periodically reevaluate it with your foundation board of directors and the librarian.

9. Maintain a liaison to the Friends of the Library and to the trustees to keep open lines of communication.

SOURCE: Friends of Libraries U.S.A. (www.folusa.com).

Foundations, corporations, and planned giving

by Victoria Steele and Stephen D. Elder

THIS SECTION INTRODUCES THE RUDIMENTS of raising money from corporations and foundations, and from planned-giving prospects. It aims to provide you with enough information to direct these aspects of your fundraising program without overwhelming you with needlessly detailed data. Our remarks are primarily addressed to the university setting, though many of the principles discussed are generalizable to other library settings.

Today, in central development offices of universities, there are fundraisers who specialize in corporations and foundations, and there are other fundraisers who specialize in planned giving. Together, these areas involve certain technical complexities for the professional fundraiser. However, for the library director, the basic issues they raise and the basic approaches they require differ

little from those described previously in connection with raising funds from individuals.

In all three of these areas of development, the most effective way to begin raising funds is to cultivate relationships with the specialists in your university so that the library benefits from their expertise and contacts. These relationships should be ongoing, and you should maintain them in the way that you would a relationship with a colleague whose professional goodwill you have come to rely on. That this goodwill is necessary becomes apparent when you consider that, of all the voluntary support going to higher education in 1990, less than 1% was designated to libraries. It is important for librarians to stay visible and pursue relationships with central development staff so that the library is not forgotten in favor of more traditional, high-profile areas.

Public vs. private funds

In general, government dollars are the hardest to raise. The applications for government grants usually require enormous amounts of work, and the awards are often relatively small. Relative to its financial yield, the securing of government money receives a disproportionate amount of attention from librarians, both in practice and in the library development literature. Perhaps this is so because librarians feel comfortable with government grant applications which, in comparison to face-to-face fundraising, seem to be relatively clear-cut processes.

As a result, librarians tend to be knowledgeable about and good at grant applications. When they need help, they can find it both in the literature and from the agency to which they are applying. We assume that your library will, as a matter of course, be engaged in pursuing such grants, and we wish you success. However, your librarians should handle the application processes, or you should engage a grant writer on a consulting basis. Coordinate these activities with your development staff, but do not assign them to it. *Government grants are not where the money is.* Individuals are your best prospects.

Foundations and corporations as giving organizations

The key to unlocking giving from foundations and corporations is contained in this simple statement: *the same principles that apply to raising money from individuals apply to raising money from foundations and corporations.*

All of us regularly read about large foundation or corporate gifts to libraries, and we think, "I want one too!" With vexation and a touch of envy, we find ourselves asking, "Why aren't we doing something about approaching this or that organization?" The answer is that foundation and corporate gifts are not the "open-to-all-comers, all-it-takes-is-a-good-proposal" affairs we sometimes imagine them to be.

In fact, large corporate and foundation gifts often are the result of a process that is almost identical to the one for individual givers and rarely the result of an impersonal grant-application process. Behind every large foundation or corporation gift to a library is a unique story. These stories almost invariably involve individuals who, as heads of corporations or foundations, have become committed to a library exactly in the manner that individual prospects do, but with the added dynamic of their organizational affiliations. And these stories have implications for you as a unique institution: Just as it is not realistic for you to consider approaching individuals who are committed to other institutions, so it is not realistic for you to hope to duplicate another library's success story in terms of its foundation or, corporate gifts.

But it is possible to create your own success story by keeping the following points in mind.

1. Individuals—not corporations and foundations—are your best prospects. Relative to overall giving in this country, corporate and foundation gifts account for a small percentage of the philanthropic pie, roughly 10% annually. Your energies should be focused on your best prospects, and these are individuals. Do not forget this if and when you decide to launch out in search of corporate and foundation support. That said, corporations and foundations tend to be supportive of education and educational institutions. Indeed, corporate and foundation giving amounted to 42% of all voluntary support for higher education in 1989 and in 1990. But, of the voluntary support for current operations designated to academic libraries in 1990, about 50% came from individuals, about 40% came from foundations, and only 10% came from corporations.

In some libraries, support from foundations and corporations may exceed these percentages, but when this happens it is because individuals with access to foundation or corporation money become committed to the library's cause.

2. Identify and cultivate key individuals within corporations and foundations. The most effective strategy is to identify individuals within important foundations and corporations who have some tie to your institution and, having done this, to cultivate them. In essence, you need a friend at court. A good relationship with such a friend will allow you to build a partnership with his organization. Once you have a partnership, you can then work together with people in the organization to develop a successful proposal. Just as with individual prospects, you build incremental commitment by sharing drafts of the proposal. By the time the final proposal is submitted, you should have a clear idea of the likelihood of your success.

Unfortunately, many people adopt a strategy of identifying *possibly* sympathetic foundations or corporations rather than *already* sympathetic individuals, and of proceeding from there. Generally, this strategy works only when, at some stage in the process, you also identify a volunteer who knows someone at the particular organization and who can intercede on your behalf. The worst way to go about raising money from foundations and corporations is simply to read about them and send them proposals out of the blue with no champion to back them within the organization.

3. Work with the central development office. One of the most productive things you can do if you want to bring in corporate and foundation dollars is to cultivate the central development staff responsible for this area in your university. Build relationships with them. If they understand and adopt your goals and if they like and respect you personally, they will work on your behalf. They will know, for example, which volunteers have ties to which foundations and companies. They will have well-established relationships within various organizations and will be creative in coming up with ideas and approaches. If they do not like you, however, they will not be helpful. As one central development staffer in foundation and corporation gifts remarked, "they will simply ignore you."

Foundations. In light of the previous discussion, it should be no surprise that some of the largest foundation gifts going to libraries today are being awarded without any formal applications or proposals. In these cases, individual trustees feel a deep personal commitment to a library and serve as its advocate within the foundation. This is not to deny that foundation funds can be secured through formal channels, especially small- to medium-sized gifts, but the fact remains that your most promising potential funders are those foundations to which your organization has a tie in the form of a relationship with an individual.

Nevertheless, every library wants to go to Pew, Mellon, Kresge, Keck, and the other big national foundations. Every library hopes that it can, by filling

---

Quotable facts about library funding

Americans go to school, public, and academic libraries three times as often as they go to movies.

Reference librarians in the nation's public and academic libraries answer more than seven million questions weekly. Standing single file, the line of questioners would stretch from Boston to San Francisco.

Federal spending on libraries totals only 54 cents per person—less than two postage stamps.

A 1998 poll conducted by Gallup for the American Library Association found that nearly all respondents expect libraries to be needed in the future, despite the increased availability of information via computer.

Public libraries

There are more public libraries than McDonald's—a total of 15,994, including branches.

Americans spend more on potato chips and snack foods than on public libraries ($5.2 billion).

Americans check out an average of six books a year. They spend about $21 a year in taxes for the public library—less than the cost of one bestseller.

Public libraries are the number one point of online access for people without Internet connections at home, school, or work.

School libraries

Research shows the highest achieving students attend schools with good library media centers.

Americans spend five times as much money on home video games ($4.8 billion) as they do on school library materials for their children.

School library media centers spend an average of $8.50 per child for books—about half the average cost of a hardcover book.

Students visit school library media centers almost 2.3 billion times during the school year—more than twice the number of visits to state and national parks.

Academic libraries

Academic librarians answer about 112 million reference questions each year—three times the attendance at college football games.

College libraries receive less than three cents of every dollar spent on higher education.

If the cost of gas had risen as fast as the cost of academic library materials since 1980, it would cost $5.69 a gallon to put fuel in your car.

SOURCE: Quotable Facts About America's Libraries (Chicago: ALA Public Information Office, 1998).

---

out an application, land a grant from these philanthropic heavyweights. Such ambitions will likely meet, however, with some formidable obstacles. Assuming you do not have a contact within any of these foundations, you will have several additional challenges beyond the fact of going in cold. For one thing, it may be difficult to get clearance from within your own organization to make the approach. For another thing, it may be difficult to establish relationships within the ranks of program officers and directors of big foundations because they tend to have heavy work loads and a high rate of turnover. Finally, many foundations will consider only the institution's highest funding priority, and all too often this is something other than the library.

Corporations. There are two levels of corporate giving: a level of large corporate grants and partnerships and a lower level at which, in some companies and firms, managers above a certain rank are given an allocation for charity that they may dispense as they wish. People with access to these latter funds can be excellent candidates for upper-level Friends memberships or purchasers of tables at your gala. However, they are not sources of large corporate gifts.

Some libraries have tried to attract corporate gifts through the formation of corporate Friends groups.

Such programs entail considerable planning and marketing, but they have not met with much success. This is not surprising. Corporate giving accounts for a mere 10% of all giving to academic libraries; and just a few major gifts will account for 90% of total giving. Hence, using an annual-fund approach to reach corporate sponsors is to marry the least successful fundraising approach for libraries with the least responsive target group.

Fee-based services are another method that some libraries have begun to use with the idea of raising money. However, in 1992, most of them were barely breaking even, let alone turning a profit. And those that were making money were only producing very modest amounts of income.

A much more productive approach to corporate fundraising is to look for opportunities for creative partnerships. Corporate gifts, it is well known, reflect a kind of enlightened self-interest on the part of a company. Rarely do companies give away money simply to be altruistic. Usually they are generous because there is something in it for them. To be successful in this arena, you must be prepared to think in terms of forming partnerships—of making mutually satisfying, yet ethical, business deals.

What are some examples of creative deal making? These might include working with a major furniture manufacturer to develop new workstations, working with a major publisher to develop and test electronic publishing, or working with a major computer company to design library applications. Such partnerships often result in in-kind gifts from corporations. Outright cash gifts usually come about only after these business-like partnerships have been successfully forged.

Planned giving

Planned, or deferred, giving is a broad term encompassing a variety of financial arrangements in which a donor gives an asset, such as stocks, real estate, books, manuscripts, photographs, or some other appreciated asset, to a nonprofit organization or institution, but still reaps benefits from the gift as long as she lives. In essence, the institution agrees to assume the burden of investing or managing the asset, while the donor enjoys a tax break and receives regular payments from the recipient organization. The following are some general recommendations with respect to planned giving.

1. Cultivate relationships with the planned-giving development people in your university just as you would with the corporate and foundation people.

Cooperative relations with the planned-giving office can result in big gifts to the library. Many times planned-giving donors approach the university without fixed ideas about where their gift should go; the planned-giving professional is in a prime position to guide that decision. Since this area is highly technical, the advanced discussions of a planned gift are now handled mostly by specialists, many with legal or tax backgrounds. When you get to this point, such specialists will help you with the details and logistics of the gift.

The planned-giving office also will help you with efforts to identify planned-giving prospects. For example, they may arrange luncheons or seminars on estate planning or they may sponsor similar events in order to present the concept of planned gifts to people who have been identified as prospects for gifts of this type. Your development officer will see that the people you have identified as planned-giving prospects are invited to these events. If you can persuade the planned-giving people to present the library as an attractive giving opportunity at these gatherings, they can be excellent agents for directing planned-giving candidates to the library.

To impress the planned-giving people with your own seriousness, it might be well to offer to host one of these events in the library. You should also try to involve the planned-giving staff in discussions of your prospects. Finally, read the brochures of the planned-giving office, which usually are not technical and can give you an overview, from the prospect's point of view, of what that office can accomplish.

2. Learn how to recognize a prospect who might benefit from a planned gift. The ideal planned-giving prospect has no heirs, is in his or her late sixties or early seventies, and has been involved in your organization in some way. Also, a married couple in the same age group with no heirs can be good planned-giving prospects. People without heirs naturally think of leaving their assets to a nonprofit organization. People with heirs also think about their estates, and sometimes consider making gifts to nonprofit institutions; but they tend, out of ignorance, not to realize that if they leave their estate entirely to heirs it will be taxed so heavily that their deaths will primarily benefit the government.

The maxim "charity begins at home" may be relevant in more ways than one to your efforts to benefit from planned giving. Many people in your own university and in your own library will fit the profile of the ideal planned-giving candidate. Faculty and emeriti faculty, for instance, understand the value and importance of the library. Moreover, it is common, unfortunately, for faculty members to harbor grievances against their departments and thus come to see the library as their campus "home." Emeriti faculty members sometimes require extra attention and patience, but some of them have amassed surprising wealth, and many of them have valuable collections of art and books. Even scholars of modest means frequently own property. In some parts of the country, real estate values have skyrocketed to such an extent that the gift of any property will translate into a major gift.

Your university may be able to provide you with a list of retired professors (and, perhaps, those about to retire). Review the list with people in the administration who know the faculty and work with the planned-giving experts on your campus to contact, cultivate, and solicit them. Analogous approaches can be considered with regard to members of your own staff. For obvious reasons, however, pursuing such gifts may be problematic, and we advise discretion if you elect to do so.

3. Keep planned giving in front of your supporters. Whenever possible— at events, in newsletters, and in brochures—encourage your audience to think of the library when they think about estate planning. Obviously, this must be done with sensitivity and tact. Because they are nonthreatening, newsletters are good vehicles for describing planned gifts. Another good technique is to involve, perhaps on your Friends' board, attorneys and accountants who can work with their clients to direct planned gifts to your library.

Because they require so much work in advance, planned gifts tend to be unusually well-considered. For this reason, they tend to be given to institutions to which the giver feels a strong tie. Unfortunately, it is the rare university alumnus who thinks about the library when considering a gift to his alma mater. Usually, donors think first of the school or program they attended. For this reason, the library should be as visible as possible among the planned-giving staff and before prospects. It also helps if the library is an institutional priority.

4. Understand the motivations behind a planned gift. One of the major motivations behind establishing trusts is the avoidance of estate taxes. Estate taxes are a concern these days for a surprisingly large number of people, being, as they are at present, levied on net assets of more than $600,000 for an individual and $1.2 million for a married couple. The equity in a house, plus other assets, such as stocks or a business, often exceed these amounts. In addition, many people have taken advantage of tax-deferred employee savings plans. Thanks to the effect of compounding interest in those savings plans, the accumulation of assets by the American public is growing dramatically.

Two types of deferred gifts. There are many different types of planned or deferred gifts, so many, in fact, that you will want to work with planned-giving professionals whenever the possibility of a gift arises. Therefore, rather than offer a technical description of planned-giving vehicles, this section describes a simple model for thinking about types of planned gifts.

One of the most common is the *charitable remainder trust.* Charitable remainder trusts may be structured in several ways, but they basically involve the donor's giving an asset and receiving regular payments equaling a certain percentage of the value of the asset. Another type of planned gift, less popular now, is the *charitable lead trust,* in which an institution receives the income from the donor's asset for an agreed-upon period, after which the asset is transferred to the donor's heirs. Both arrangements can reduce gift and estate taxes and provide a charitable deduction for the donor.

The following tree-and-fruit analogy helps clarify the difference between these two deferred-giving instruments.

Charitable remainder trust = The donor gives the tree and keeps the fruit.

Charitable lead trust = The donor gives the fruit and keeps the tree.

Even though the charitable lead trust is not used much now, the fruit-and-tree analogy can be a useful tool for explaining the basics of a planned gift to a prospect.

The planned-giving call. When you initially broach the idea of a planned gift with someone, you say something like this: "Planned giving allows you to change the situation (you delicately avoid saying 'of your death' at this point) from one of involuntary taxation, where the bulk of your assets goes to Uncle Sam, to one of voluntary giving, where the bulk can go to the library." And then you can use the tree-and-fruit analogy to give the person a rough idea of how a planned gift works. While talking with the person, try to find out as much as possible about his personal situation, and then suggest, if appropriate, that you introduce her to "an expert from the Development Office."

You will probably accompany the expert on the first call. This call should be handled much as you would handle any other development call. There are, however, two important but very sensitive pieces of information you need to know about planned-giving prospects: their overall wealth and their age. The planned-giving officer will probably lead into the discussion by raising the question of the prospect's goals. Do they want to leave something to their children? Do they need income now? Would they like to give you their property but retain a place to live for their lifetime? Because the value of a person's estate is critical in terms of taxation (in 1991, $1.2 million for a couple resulted in a 43% tax; $600,000 for a single person resulted in a 37% tax; and a $2.5 million estate was taxed at 55%), your colleague will be trying to get a sense of the person's net worth. "What do you own?" is one way of putting the question. The prospect's age is also very important information because the IRS will determine tax deductions on the basis of life expectancy. Asking people their age directly can sometimes be difficult. One technique for dealing with this is to suggest a range ("Are you over 65?") or to ask when they were born.

At this early stage, you will keep things very simple during the giving-information part of the meeting. You will explain how you can help the prospect accomplish his goals, you will promote your institution and your cause, and lastly you will lay the groundwork for a later visit. After this first call, you can probably turn things over to the planned giving officer, who will continue to nurture discussion. When things have progressed sufficiently, the planned-giving officer will suggest a meeting with the prospect's attorney or accountant to begin to draw up an agreement.

Appreciated assets. A donation of appreciated assets can produce a double tax benefit for the donor when the contribution is structured so that the appreciated value of the assets escapes taxation. For example, Mr. and Mrs. Donor own securities worth $ 100,000 that they purchased for $20,000. (Assume they are in the 35% tax bracket: 28% federal, and 7% state.)

The wrong way to do it. If the securities are sold, the $80,000 of appreciation will result in a capital gains tax of 35%: $28,000. The net proceeds of $72,000 ($100,000 less $28,000), if contributed, would save taxes of $25,200 ($72,000 × 35%). The end result is that the Donors would pay tax of $2,800 ($28,000 less $25,200, or, if you prefer, 35% of the $8,000 differential between $80,000 and $72,000) and the nonprofit organization would receive $72,000.

The right way to do it. A better way to structure the gift would be for the Donors to give the appreciated securities to the organization outright. The capital gains, in this case, would not be taxed. The full fair-market value of the gift would be allowed as a charitable deduction. The Donors would also get a charitable deduction of $35,000 ($100,000 × 35%) when they filed their next tax return. The end result is a double tax savings, in which the Donors would avoid capital gains taxes of $28,000 on the $80,000 of appreciation and would get a $35,000 tax break because of the charitable deduction, for a total tax savings of $63,000. In addition, the library would receive the full $100,000.

This example also applies to other kinds of assets, such as real estate, antiques, and other items of value. It is possible to treat a collection of books, manuscripts, photographs, or other library materials as an appreciated asset. These items receive a full fair-market-value deduction if their use is related to the purposes of the university. This is good to know because often (especially in special collections) older people will come to you asking you to buy their collections. The valuable ones frequently carry price tags that make them out of the question as far as a purchase is concerned. In these cases, a planned gift can provide a win-win outcome for both the collectors and library.

How much should I emphasize planned giving? Though planned-giving prospects are abundant in and around universities, planned gifts themselves are not as abundant as the prospect pool might suggest. There are several reasons for this. From the point of view of the prospect, planned gifts can seem complicated; they seem too complicated for most people after about age 75. Another drawback from prospects' perspectives is that planned gifts sometimes involve more talking and more effort than wills, with the result that the prospects spend more time on the uncomfortable subject of their demise.

There are also some impediments from the development side. Most planned gifts take a huge amount of effort. It is not unusual for such a gift to require 18–24 months and 13–18 visits. Generally, the only planned gifts that go fast are the ones that come from people who are financially sophisticated and already understand the benefits that can be realized by this type of gift, especially through the avoidance of capital gains taxes.

Some planned-giving professionals will tell you that the biggest gifts are made in people's wills, and that you should spend at least as much time encouraging this form of giving as you do the more complicated kinds of planned gifts. As it is undeniably true that many of your biggest gifts will be testamentary, you should emphasize this form of giving as much as discretion and good taste allow.

The best advice is to not overemphasize planned giving in your program, but to know a viable planned-giving prospect when you see one. Above all, remember that planned giving and fundraising from corporations and foundations all reflect the uniqueness of your situation. The types of gifts that come to your organization will reflect its own unique support base.

SOURCE: Victoria Steele and Stephen D. Elder, *Becoming a Fundraiser: The Principles and Practice of Library Development* (Chicago: American Library Association, 1992). pp. 103–11.

How to say thanks

by Adam Corson-Finnerty and Laura Blanchard

THERE IS A FUNDRAISING SAW that goes like this: A donor can never be thanked too often, or by too many people.

People sometimes ask us if we think that Web recognition can substitute for print and plaque recognition. The short answer is no. Our contention is that Web recognition should be in addition to other forms of stewardship.

The Penn Library recently received a spectacular gift for the complete renovation of our information processing center (cataloging and acquisitions), as well as for the creation of an electronic training classroom. We have so far thanked the donor couple in the following ways:

1. Many phone calls, letters, and personal visits to say "thanks."

2. Special mention by the university provost at a symposium that the donor couple attended, and a round of applause.

3. A special event at the sites, showing them off in mid-construction, which involved speeches, souvenir hard hats, and free food and drink. Lovely color photos from this event were sent to the donors.

4. A nicely designed Web site that has the donors' picture, a quote from the alumni half of the couple, an artist's conception of the spaces, a description of the spaces and what they will accomplish, a link to the new donor-named Directorship of Information Processing, with a picture and grateful quote from the recipient; a link to the information Processing Center site (now renamed for the donor) with tons of library information, including reviews of new books.

5. A related press release that the donor reviewed and approved.

6. A thank-you lunch in New York for friends, family, and colleagues of the donor. Each person received a packet containing printed pages from the Web site. (And, by the way, additional gifts came in from this group, in honor of the donors.)

7. A gala ribbon-cutting dedication event on Alumni Day, with other donors in attendance, and the president expressing her gratitude on behalf of the entire university community

8. An extensive article, with pictures, and based on personal interviews, in our *Planned Giving Newsletter,* which will go out to thousands of alumni.

9. Two handsome plaques, with language approved by the donors, as well as their name being etched in glass at the entrance to both facilities.

And perhaps other things that we dream up along the way

Note that the Web site was just one of the things we did by way of saying thanks. But also note that a Web site is a "living" entity that can still evolve and that will continue to be shared with the donor, and other prospective donors, as the years go by.

SOURCE: Adam Corson-Finnerty and Laura Blanchard, *Fundraising and Friend-Raising on the Web* (Chicago: American Library Association, 1998), pp. 17–18.

Federal funding from LSCA to LSTA

by Gwen Gregory

YOU MAY BE SURPRISED to hear that some state libraries in the United States get a third of their total budget from the federal government, most of it in the form of grants.

The federal government has supported library services with grants since the Library Services Act (LSA) took effect in 1956. The Library Services and Construction Act (LSCA) succeeded LSA in 1964. Both LSA and LSCA granted funds to the state library agencies to promote library services, especially to the underserved, and to build libraries.

Throughout the 1990s, librarians and ALA lobbied for changes to LSCA because they felt that some of its original goals had been accomplished, and federal aid should be redirected to meeting new needs, such as providing electronic access to information. Finally, in 1996 Congress made major changes in our government's information policy by enacting the Library Services and Technology Act (LSTA).

How is it different?

LSTA continues to funnel federal money through the state libraries, which then distribute it to local libraries. So how is LSTA different from the good old LSCA we had grown to love? First, LSTA administration has moved to a new federal agency. Second, there are several changes in how funds may be used. Third, LSTA is for use by all types of libraries, not just public libraries as was the case with LSCA.

The Institute for Museum and Library Services (IMLS) administers the LSTA program (www.imls.fed.us). The merger of the Institute for Museum Studies with the Department of Education's former Office of Library Programs (OLP) created this new federal agency, part of the National Foundation on the Arts and Humanities. Many of the staff from the OLP moved to the IMLS, and new staff members have been hired since the move. When I visited with them last year, IMLS staffers were positive about LSTA and how it will support libraries. Jane Heiser, IMLS director of state library programs, observed that "LSTA allows a state to prioritize and target on its own. The states like this; they lobbied for it."

The second major change is that LSTA itself has new priorities. Two main goals of LSTA are electronic networking (including resource sharing) and targeting the underserved. Previously, federal funds were available for construction of library buildings; now the emphasis has shifted to building the technological infrastructure to use electronic information. Programs in this category might include setting up electronic networks between libraries or shared access to Web-based research sources. Providing service to "underserved rural and urban populations and to those with difficulty using libraries" is the second goal. Programs of this type include literacy efforts, creation of new libraries, and bookmobiles. States are allowed to divide their LSTA funds between the two objectives to meet their needs, and can spend funds centrally or give subgrants to individual libraries or consortia.

The inclusion of all types of libraries in the LSTA program is the third major change. In previous years, LSCA was devoted to the promotion and development of public libraries. Now LSTA expands availability to all libraries. This means that the state libraries, as the LSTA administering agencies, will be working with all libraries to develop and carry out LSTA programs. School, academic, and special libraries can now receive LSTA funds and take part in LSTA programs. This new emphasis should promote integration and cooperation between types of libraries. As librarians, we know that a wide variety of library resources is available in any given community. Just imagine what a patron who is interested in cooking could find in different types of libraries. An elementary school library will have picture cookbooks for children. A public library will have popular adult cookbooks as well. An academic library will have treatises on the history of food and cooking. The special library at the local hospital will have materials on cooking for those with particular illnesses.

A patron may visit any one of these libraries and really want information available at one of the others. How can librarians get patrons the information they need? In a given community, residents will likely patronize several libraries depending on their information needs

at that time. The library community as a whole can better serve its patrons by helping them find the resource they need regardless of the type of library in which it is housed. LSTA promotes multitype library cooperation, which in turn supports integration of all our libraries into one comprehensive source of information. For example, a consortium of local libraries could use LSTA funding to create an electronic union catalog so that all members could see what items the others have.

Of all the types of libraries mentioned here, school libraries are by far the most numerous. However, they often lack the most basic materials and staff. For example, the Massachusetts LSTA plan points out that in that state there are 1,689 school library media centers, compared to 370 public libraries. Of the 1,689, 40% were not staffed by a librarian and 18% were not staffed by a librarian or an aide.

State libraries recognize that serving these libraries may be a formidable task. Heiser said that "Including school libraries is the largest current challenge; state plans have to address this issue." States are working toward this goal. Massachusetts is committed to creating a grant program for school libraries by 2002. Missy Lodge of the State Library of Ohio commented that "much of the state library's emphasis with LSTA will be working with school libraries. We are taking the opportunity afforded by LSTA to strengthen our connection to school library programs in Ohio." LSTA will strengthen school libraries by promoting cooperation.

In order to find out more about the transition to LSTA, I sent a mail survey to LSTA coordinators at the state libraries in the summer of 1998. I received responses from 88% of recipients. I also conducted in-depth case studies of several states' LSTA programs and found a number of common issues. Compared to their LSCA programs, most states have increased emphasis on computer-related topics such as the Internet, computer training, and networking. Eighty-three percent of state libraries report that their local libraries are in favor of this increased emphasis on technology. The state libraries also place more emphasis on cooperation between libraries. However, they report less emphasis on other areas, including literacy, serving the underserved, and acquisitions.

How does it stack up?

How does the IMLS stack up to the old OLP? The state libraries compare the IMLS favorably. Eighty percent felt that the IMLS was easier to work with. LSTA coordinators especially appreciated the reduction in the amount of paperwork required. Roy Bird of the Kansas State Library remarked, "Our staff are extremely pleased with the IMLS. Their responses and helpfulness have been a refreshing change, allowing us to concentrate on what is important: using federal funds to help libraries provide the best possible service."

In order to meet the goals of LSTA the state libraries are setting up grant programs and working out the details of what their libraries need and want from LSTA. State libraries were required to submit a five-year plan in 1997 detailing how they will use LSTA funds. As anticipated, the states are developing a wide variety of programs using LSTA funds. Some states are using LSTA funds to buy statewide access to online database services such as UMI's ProQuest Direct. Others are developing a wide variety of subgrant programs to channel funds to individual libraries for information literacy, computer training, preservation, establishment of new public libraries in unserved areas, and establishment of library consortia.

The first LSTA funds were distributed in December 1997. Grant amounts are determined by a population-based formula, with the states required to contribute matching funds. Grants disbursed in December 1998 varied from $14,263,331 for California to $66,792 for American Samoa. The total allocation for state grants in 1998 was $135,366,938.

The first years of LSTA will constitute a major transition for libraries. "The LSTA program is a much cleaner, clearer, simpler and more focused program than LSCA, resulting in fewer rules and regulations," says Peg Branson of the Wisconsin State Library. The states are getting accustomed to their new freedom. Many state libraries will be learning more about the different types of libraries and their needs. State libraries will be designing innovative projects and making grants to individual libraries. School, academic, and special libraries will be working with public and state libraries to create multitype projects.

LSTA provides librarians with a great opportunity to share their specialized knowledge with colleagues in other types of libraries. We can also better serve our own patrons by providing easier access to more information. In your state, ask the state library agency to find out about local LSTA programs and grants and about how your library can participate.

SOURCE: Gwen Gregory, "From Construction to Technology: An Update on Federal Funding," *American Libraries* 30 (June/July 1999): 22–23.

TECHNOLOGY
CHAPTER EIGHT

"There was a new library in the Civic Centre. It was so new it didn't even have librarians. It had Assistant Information Officers."

—Terry Pratchett, *Johnny and the Dead* (1993)

LOW TECHNOLOGY

Eyeglasses

by Frederick G. Kilgour

THE INVENTION, IN THE LATTER HALF OF THE 1280s, of eye-glasses intended primarily for reading probably increased reading by as much as 60%. Eyeglasses extended reading capability an average of 15 years beyond the age of 45, a time by which most people would have lost the near vision required to read a printed page. Ninety-five percent of people currently older than 45 use eyeglasses for reading or other close work. George Minois recorded the life expectancy of English males born between 1276 and 1300 as 14.7 years at age 45 and constructed a table of population data from Périgueux, France, that enabled me to calculate the life expectancy at the end of the 14th century as 14.45 years at age 45. If one assumes that people began the serious use of books at age 20 and continued to 45, eyeglasses would have increased reading time by 15 years, or 60%.

Edward Rosen, author of the most thorough study of the origin of eyeglasses (*Journal of the History of Medicine and Allied Sciences* 2 (1956)), dated "the invention shortly

Woman using a lorgnette

after 1286" and concluded that although the inventor was unknown, "Pisa has a better claim on him than any other locality." Rosen also assembled early references to eyeglasses: two references in the rules of a Venetian guild in 1300 and 1301; the price in Bolognese *soldi* of "eyeglasses with case" in 1316; a 1322 listing in an inventory of the belongings of a deceased Florentine bishop; and a Tuscan merchant's 1339 complaint listing "one pair of eyeglasses" among goods purchased in Florence and stolen from him. In the 1360s Petrarch wrote that his keen sight "left me when I was over 60 years of age, so that to my annoyance I had to seek the help of eyeglasses," and Guy de Chauliac, surgeon at Montpellier, wrote in his oft-published *Chirurgia Magna*, "if these things do not avail, recourse must be had to spectacles of glass or beryl."

Further evidence of growth in the use of eyeglasses is the establishment of the Venetian guild of eyeglass makers in 1320. Six decades later, London imported eyeglasses, mostly from the Low Countries, at the rate of 384 pairs per month over the period from July 1 to September 29, 1384. A century later, the rate was 480 per month over the period from November 8, 1480, to July 21, 1481.

The earliest artistic depiction of eyeglasses is in a posthumous portrait of Hugh de Saint-Cher, the originator of concordances, painted as a fresco by Tommaso da Modena in 1312 on a wall in a monastery in Treviso. Hugh never wore spectacles, for he died more than 20 years before their invention, but Tommaso apparently thought that a man of Hugh's age would have needed to wear them to read. The painting is sufficiently detailed to enable one to see the structure of the eyeglasses, which are two hand-magnifying glasses held together at the ends of the handles by a rivet. The only knowledge of these devices was derived from such paintings until 1913, when "two complete rivetted spectacles as well as fragments of such" were discovered under the planks between the rows of choir stalls in a convent in Weinhausen, Germany. Analysis of these eyeglasses revealed many equivalents with eyeglasses in paintings. Horst Appuhn reports that "the general dating of the 14th and 15th centuries is given for the spectacles." Two decades after the Weinhausen find, excavations in a refuse dump at the Trig Lane archaeological site in the City of London uncovered another "Pair of rivetted Spectacles . . . dated by a variety of techniques to 1440 or the years immediately thereafter, [making them] the earliest spectacle frames . . . of known date."

SOURCE: © Frederick G. Kilgour, *The Evolution of the Book* (New York: Oxford University, 1998), pp. 77–78. Reprinted with permission.

Compact disc maintenance and repair

by Samuel M. Goldwasser

PROPER CARE OF A CD PLAYER does not require much. Following the recommendations below will assure peak performance and long life, and minimize repairs.

- Locate the CD player in a cool location. While the CD player is not a significant heat producer, keeping it cool will reduce wear and tear on the internal components and assure a long trouble-free life.
- Don't locate CD players in dusty locations or areas of high (tobacco) smoke or cooking grease vapors. I cannot force you to quit smoking, but it is amazing how much disgusting, difficult-to-remove brown grime is deposited on sensitive electronic equipment in short order from this habit.
- Make sure all audio connections are tight and secure to minimize intermittent or noisy sound.
- Finally, store CDs away from heat. The polycarbonate plastic used to mold CDs is quite sturdy, but high temperatures will eventually take their toll. Return them to their jewel cases or other protective container when not being played.

Preventive maintenance

You no doubt have heard that a CD should be cleaned and checked periodically. "Purchase our extended warranty," says the salesperson, "because CD players are very delicate and require periodic alignment." For the most part, this is nonsense. CD players, despite the astonishing precision of the optical pickup, are remarkably robust. Optical alignment is virtually never needed for a component CD player and is rarely required even for portable or automotive units. In fact, modern CD players often don't even have any of these adjustments—the components of the optical pickup are aligned at the factory and then fixed in place with hardening sealer.

An occasional internal inspection and cleaning is not a bad idea, but not nearly as important as for a VCR. Realistically, you are not going to do any of this anyway. So, sit back and enjoy the music but be aware of the types of symptoms that would be indications of the need for cleaning or other preventive or corrective maintenance—erratic loading, need to convince the CD player to cooperate and play a disc, audio noise, skipping, sticking, and taking longer than usual to recognize a disc or complete a search.

CD lens-cleaning discs

Every CD or stereo-equipment department and discount store—even sidewalk vendors—carries CD lens-cleaning discs. Are they of any value? Can they cause damage?

I generally don't consider CD lens-cleaning discs to be of much value for preventive maintenance since they may just move the crud around. However, for pure non-greasy dust (no tobacco smoke and no cooking grease), they probably do not hurt and may do a good enough job to put off a proper cleaning for a while longer. However, since there are absolutely no standards for these things, it is possible for a really poorly designed cleaning disc to damage the lens. In addition, if it doesn't look like a CD to the optical pickup or disc-in sensor, the lens-cleaning disc may not even spin. So, the drawer closes, the drawer opens, and nothing has been accomplished!

CD protection and handling

Although CDs are considerably more tolerant of abuse than LPs, some precautions are still needed to assure long life. Also, despite the fact that only one side is played, serious damage to either side can cause problems during play or render the CD totally useless.

It is important that the label side be protected from major scratches that could penetrate to the information layer. Even with the sophisticated error correction used on the CD, damage to this layer, especially if it runs parallel to the tracks, can make the CD unusable.

The CD is read by focusing a laser beam through the bottom 1.2-millimeter of polycarbonate. As a result of the design of the optical system used in the pickup, at the bottom surface the beam diameter is about 1 millimeter, and thus small scratches appear out of focus and in many cases are ignored and do not cause problems.

At the pitted information layer, the beam diameter has been reduced to under 2 micrometers. Still, scratches running parallel to the tracks are more problematic and can cause the optical pickup to get stuck repeating a track, jumping forward or back a few seconds, or creating noise or other problems on readout. In severe cases, the CD may be unusable, especially if the damage is in the directory area.

This is why the recommended procedure for cleaning a CD is to use soap and water (no harsh solvents which may damage the polycarbonate or resin overcoat) and clean in a radial direction (center to edge, *not* in the direction of the tracks as you would with an LP). While on the subject of CD care, CDs should always be returned to their original containers for storage and not left out on the counter where they may be scratched.

If there is a need to put one down for a moment, the label side is probably preferable since minor scratches have no effect on performance so long as they do not penetrate to the storage layer below (in which case the CD is probably history). Protectors are available to prevent damage to the label side of the disc. Personally, I think this is taking care to an excessive level but, hey, if you use your CDs as frisbies, go for it!

CD cleaning

You do not need a fancy CD cleaning machine. Use a soft cloth, tissue, or paper towel moistened with water and mild detergent if needed. Wipe from center to edge, *not* in a circular motion as recommended for an LP. *Never* use any strong solvents. Even stubborn spots will eventually yield to your persistence. Washing under running water is fine as well.

Gently dry with a lint free cloth. Do not rub or use a dry cloth to clean, as any dirt particles will result in scratches. Polycarbonate is tough, but don't expect it to survive everything. Very fine scratches are not usually a problem, but why press your luck?

Should I really worry about cleaning my CDs?

Something that not everyone is aware of is the multilevel error-handling technology in a CD player. A dirty CD may not produce instantly obvious audio problems but can nonetheless result in less than optimal audio performance.

Very severe errors—long bursts—will result in audible degradation including noise and/or muting of the sound. Even this may not always be detectable depending on musical context.

Shorter runs of errors will result in the player interpolating between what it thinks are good samples. This isn't perfect but will probably not be detected upon casual listening. Errors within the correcting capability of the CIRC code will result in perfect reconstruction. Not all players implement all possible error-handling strategies.

Therefore, it is quite possible for CD cleaning to result in better sound. However, a CD that is obviously clean will not benefit and excessive cleaning or improper cleaning will introduce fine (or not so fine) scratches that can eventually cause problems.

Can a dirty CD or dirty lens damage my player?

So the droid in the CD store warned you that dirty CDs could do irreparable harm to your CD player, your stereo, your disposition, etc. "Buy our $19.95 Super-Laseriffic CD cleaning kit."

The claim made at one major chain was that dirt or dust on the laser eye would cause heat buildup that would burn out the mechanism. This is different from a dirty disc. The cleaner he was pushing was a little brush attached to a CD that brushed off the lens as it played.

This is total rubbish. The power of a CD laser is less than one milliwatt and is not concentrated at the lens. Those cleaning CDs with the little brushes are next to useless on anything but the smallest amount of dry dust. There are a lot of suckers out there. Save your money.

The worst that can happen is the CD will not play properly. There may be audible noise, it may fail to track properly, abort at random times, or not even be recognized. The electronics will not melt down.

It is just about impossible for a dirty CD to do any damage to the player. A dirty lens will only result in disc recognition or play problems similar to those caused by a dirty CD. The laser will not catch fire. The only way damage could occur is if you loaded a cracked CD and the crack caught on the lens.

Can a CD player damage CDs?

The perhaps unexpected answer is a definite "yes," even though everyone has heard about the virtues of non-contact laser playback. There are several ways that a broken or poorly designed or manufactured player can result in scratched discs:

1. If the lens moves too high while attempting to focus and the mechanical stop does not prevent it from hitting the disc, scratches can occur. On some players, the objective lens can easily go this high if focus is not found on the first pass. Note that in most cases, the lens will not suffer since it is protected by a raised ridge which is what actually scratches the disc.

2. Mechanical misalignment of the spindle motor or plastic cabinet parts can result in the disc touching the bottom or top of the disc compartment and this can leave scratches. This could be the result of poor or cheap design, shoddy manufacturing, or damage from a fall or other abuse.

3. If the control logic gets confused, it may allow you to eject a disc while it is still spinning and not fully supported by the spindle platter. A dirty disc that resulted in failure of the CLV servo to lock can result in a disc speed runaway condition with some players. If the drawer is then opened too soon, the disc will still be spinning because the controller has no way of knowing its present status and will not have provided enough reverse torque to stop the spindle motor—or too much and it will be spinning in reverse.

The likelihood of any of these is increased with dirty, smudged, warped, or previously damaged discs.

Minor scratches may not result in a serious problem and there are products to polish them—I don't know how well they work. However, if these scratches can be proven to be a direct consequence of a defective player still under warranty, you should try to get some compensation from the manufacturer for any seriously damaged and now unplayable CDs.

Repairing a scratched CD

So your five-year-old decided that your favorite CD would make a nice frisbee—didn't really know much about aerodynamics, did he? Now it sounds like a poor excuse for a 78 rpm record. What to do?

There seem to be about as many ways of fixing scratches on CDs as producing them in the first place. However, they fall into three classes of technique:

1. Mild abrasives: plastic or furniture polish, Brasso metal polish, toothpaste. These will totally remove minor scratches.

2. Fillers: Turtle wax, car wax, furniture wax. Apply over the whole disc and buff out with a lint-free cloth. Filling larger scratches should be fairly effective but the disc will be more prone to damage in the future due to the soft wax.

3. Blowtorch: At least one person who claims to have worked for several years in used CD stores swears by this technique. Supposedly, he uses a pencil-type pocket butane torch and with great dexterity fuses the surface layer of the readout side of the disc so that all of those scratches and unsightly blemishes—well—melt away. Obviously, there are dangers in using fire on plastic and this is likely a last resort. I would assume that you are rolling with hysterical laughter at this point. In any case, I would not take this approach too seriously.

As with cleaning a CD, when applying or rubbing any of these materials, wipe from the center to the outside edge. A CD player can generally track across scratches that are perpendicular to its path reasonably well, but not those that run parallel to the tracks.

A mild abrasive will actually remove the scratch entirely if it is minor enough. This is probably more effective where the surface has been scuffed or abraded rather than deeply scratched.

Wax-like materials will fill in the space where the scratch is if the abrasive was not successful. Even deep scratches may succumb to this approach.

A combination of methods 1 and 2 may be most effective.

Exorbitantly priced versions of these materials are available specifically marketed for repair of CDs. However, the common abrasives and waxes should work about as well.

I cannot comment on the use of the blowtorch or how many years of practice is required to get your CD repair license with this technique. However, I am highly skeptical that this works at all and suspect that destruction of the CD is the most likely outcome—totally melting, warping, or cracking or shattering from the thermal stress. In other words, I don't recommend trying the blowtorch approach unless you have a stack of AOL or MSN CDs to sacrifice and you have sufficient accident insurance!

An alternative to CD home repair are companies specializing in this service. A couple of these are: AuralTech CD (www.nsynch.com/~auraltech/) and CD Repairman (www.cdrepairman.com). I do not have information as to their effectiveness or cost. However, if you have an irreplaceable CD that someone used as a skateboard, one of these may be worth considering.

Repairing top-side problems on CDs

If scratches penetrate to the information layer, all bets may be off. Much of the optical-system compliance with respect to damage depends on the short depth of focus assuring that surface scratches "on the bottom" will be out of focus and ignored. This is not possible with damage to the pits. Even though the CIRC code should be able to deal with thousands of bad bits, such damage can confuse the tracking servos to the point where the disc will be unusable.

What if the aluminum (or gold) reflective layer has come

off with no damage to the plastic underneath? First of all, I don't know how this could occur unless you were attempting to clean them with a strong solvent. Any physical damage which removed the mirror coating will also damage the pits and recoating will be useless.

Some discs may still work on some players or drives without the aluminum coating. However, this isn't that likely. How to replace it? Ideally, vacuum deposition is needed. The problem isn't only the reflectance but the microstructure—the original coating was vacuum-deposited to conform to the pits and lands of the information layer. It is perfectly uniform below the resolution of the laser beam. Modeling (silver- or gold-colored) paint is amorphous and rough at these feature sizes and floppy disc write-protect stickers or other adhesive-backed reflective films don't even come close to contacting the information layer consistently. Mirror paint may work but is a long shot.

SOURCE: Samuel M. Goldwasser, *Notes on the Troubleshooting and Repair of Compact Disc Players and CD-ROM Drives,* chapter 4, at plop.phys.cwru.edu/repairfaq/REPAIR/F_cdfaq2.html, version 2.86, © 1998. Reprinted with permission.

COMPUTERS

What are digital libraries?

by Donald J. Waters

THE MEANING OF THE TERM "digital library" is less transparent than one might expect. The words conjure up images of cutting-edge computer and information-science research. They are invoked to describe what some assert to be radically new kinds of practices for the management and use of information. And they are used to replace earlier references to "electronic" and "virtual" libraries.

The partner institutions in the Digital Library Federation (DLF) realized in the course of developing their program that they needed a common understanding of what digital libraries are if they were to achieve the goal of effectively federating them. So they crafted the following definition, with the understanding that it might well undergo revision as they worked together:

> Digital libraries are organizations that provide the resources, including the specialized staff, to select, structure, offer intellectual access to, interpret, distribute, preserve the integrity of, and ensure the persistence over time of collections of digital works so that they are readily and economically available for use by a defined community or set of communities.

This is a full definition by any measure, and a good working definition because it is broad enough to comprehend other uses of the term. Those other definitions focus on one or more of the features included in the DLF definition, while ignoring or de-emphasizing the rest. For example, the term "digital library" may refer simply to the notion of "collection," without reference

---

Digital Library Federation

The Digital Library Federation (originally known as the National Digital Library Federation) exists under the organizational umbrella of the Council on Library and Information Resources (CLIR), which also incorporates the Commission on Preservation and Access. The Director of the Federation is Donald J. Waters.

The Digital Library Federation (DLF) was founded in 1995 to establish the conditions for creating, maintaining, expanding, and preserving a distributed collection of digital materials accessible to scholars, students, and a wider public.

The founding members are 12 university research libraries and the Library of Congress, the National Archives and Records Administration, the New York Public Library, and the Commission on Preservation and Access. The university libraries are California/Berkeley, Columbia, Cornell, Emory, Harvard, Michigan, Pennsylvania State, Princeton, Southern California, Stanford, Tennessee/Knoxville, and Yale.

Other university libraries have since joined the Federation, among them Chicago, North Carolina State, Indiana, Minnesota, and Pennsylvania, and the California Digital Library. Participating institutions have a seat on the steering committee and the opportunity to join with other participants in a variety of projects and other initiatives designed to develop digital library capabilities.

The Research Libraries Group (RLG) and the Online Computer Library Center (OCLC) are formal allies of the Federation. A senior officer of each organization sits on the DLF Steering Committee "with voice, but without vote."

SOURCE: Council on Library and Information Resources, www.clir.org/diglib/dlforg.htm

---

to its organization, intellectual accessibility, or service attributes. This is the particular sense that seems to be in play when we hear the World Wide Web described as a digital library. But the words might refer as well to the organization underlying the collection, or, even more specifically, to the computer-based system in which the collection resides. The latter sense is most clearly in use in the National Science Foundation's Digital Library Initiative. Yet again, institutions may be characterized as digital libraries to distinguish them from digital archives when the intent is to call attention to the differences in the nature of their collections.

The DLF's definition of "digital library" does more than simply enumerate features. It serves in addition as the basis for the DLF's perspective on the scope of digital libraries and on the functional requirements for their development.

SOURCE: Donald Waters, "What Are Digital Libraries?" Council on Library and Information Resources, *CLIR Issues*, no. 4 (July/August 1998): 1, 5. Reprinted with permission.

8

Rural computer lingo

Log on. Makin' the wood stove hotter.

Log off. Don't add any more wood.

Monitor. Keep an eye on the wood stove.

Download. Gettin' the firewood off the pickup.

Megahertz. When yer not careful downloadin'. (Watch th' toes!)

Floppy disk. Whatcha get from pilin' too much firewood.

Disk operating system. The equipment the Doc uses when you have a floppy disk.

RAM. The hydraulic thingy that makes the woodsplitter work.
Hard drive. Gettin' home in mud season.
Prompt. What you wish the mail was in mud season.
Windows. What to shut when it's 30 below.
Screen. What you need for black-fly season.
Byte. What black flies do.
Chip. What to munch on.
Microchip. What's left in the bag when the chips are gone.
Modem. What you did to the hay fields.
Dot Matrix. John Matrix's wife.
Printer. Someone who can't write in cursive.
Laptop. Where little kids feel comfy.
Keyboard. Where you hang your keys.
Software. Them plastic eating utensils.
Pentium II. One of them fancy imported cars.
Mouse. What eats the horses' grain in the barn.
Mainframe. The part of the barn that holds the roof up.
Enter. C'mon in!
Digital. Like those numbers that flip on your alarm clock.
Program. What's on the TV when there's reception.
CD-ROM. The place in the bank where they sell retirement accounts.

SOURCE: *News-Notes* (North Central Iowa Regional Library), October 1997; reprinted in *The Unabashed Librarian*, no. 106 (1998), p. 32.

Time spent using computers

by Joyce K. Thornton

THIS TABLE SHOWS the average percentage of the work week that the staff of ARL libraries spent using computers, as determined by a 1996 survey.

83%	Computer staff (computer support specialists, database managers, programmers, system heads)
58%	Nonlibrarian professionals (administrative assistants, executive assistants, newsletter editors, development officers)
45%	Library assistants, library technicians, library specialists
42%	Secretaries
40%	Nonadministrative librarians
37%	General staff (clerks, photocopy staff, mailroom clerks)
33%	Library administration (directors, archivists, department heads)

SOURCE: Joyce K. Thornton, "Carpal Tunnel Syndrome in ARL Libraries," *College & Research Libraries* 58 (January 1997): 9–18.

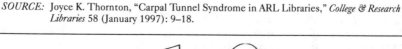

Technology in Public Libraries

U.S. public libraries serving a population of 100,000 or more turned increasingly to Internet, OPACs (online public access catalogs), and CD-ROM services for their patrons from 1995 to 1998. According to the ALA Public Library Association's annual surveys, the following percentages of this group of 461 libraries offered these services each year:

Service	1995	1996	1997	1998
OPACs for their collections	87.3%	90.5%	95.4%	95.9%
Regional or statewide networked OPACs	37.1	43.5	48.8	49.0
Commercial databases on OPACs	29.0	44.3	49.6	59.0
Internet access for library staff	68.3	93.5	98.1	99.4
Internet access for patrons, with staff intermediaries	28.2	52.4	65.1	65.0
Internet access for patrons, direct	23.3	49.4	75.3	85.4
Internet accounts for patrons	4.3	6.5	8.0	7.2
Local information databases (community, news, etc.)	60.7	61.3	70.2	72.5
Support to a freenet	18.7	25.0	22.3	18.7
Computers for patron use inside the library	60.7	61.9	70.0	70.5
Software for patron use inside the library	53.4	54.2	61.4	64.7
Commercial database searches, by staff intermediaries	70.5	67.9	70.8	71.1
Commercial database searches, by patrons	8.1	13.1	26.3	33.3
CD-ROM products for patron use inside the library	93.2	94.3	96.0	95.9
Library information faxed to patrons	59.9	67.3	67.8	70.0
Fax machine for patron use	17.3	19.3	18.5	18.2
Computers for patron use outside the library	0.5	1.2	1.1	1.1
Software for patron use outside the library	17.3	20.5	24.7	29.5
CD-ROM products for patron use outside the library	9.8	24.1	30.9	47.9
Remote access to OPAC	69.6	74.1	80.2	81.5
Remote access to other information (CD-ROM, etc.)	19.8	27.7	33.5	38.8
Remote access to the Internet	16.3	25.3	30.3	31.1
Databases searchable with single-search software	16.5	23.8	27.9	36.1
Automated attendant for first telephone contact	26.6	33.9	34.9	43.0
Voice mail for service and information requests	23.6	34.2	35.7	40.8
Telephone services for the deaf (TDD)	73.4	72.0	74.0	70.8

SOURCE: ALA Public Library Association, ALA Office for Research and Statistics, and University of Illinois Library Research Center, August 1998.

8

The ten commandments of computer ethics

1. Thou shalt not use a computer to harm other people.
2. Thou shalt not interfere with other people's computer work.
3. Thou shalt not snoop around in other people's computer files.
4. Thou shalt not use a computer to steal.
5. Thou shalt not use a computer to bear false witness.
6. Thou shalt not copy or use proprietary software for which you have not paid.
7. Thou shalt not use other people's computer resources without authorization or proper compensation.
8. Thou shalt not appropriate other people's intellectual output.
9. Thou shalt think about the social consequences of the program you are writing or the system you are designing.
10. Thou shalt always use a computer in ways that ensure consideration and respect for your fellow humans.

SOURCE: Computer Ethics Institute, Washington, D.C. Reprinted with permission.

THE INTERNET

Can schools and libraries help the poor catch up?

by The Benton Foundation

TRADITIONALLY, WE HAVE LOOKED TO SCHOOLS and libraries to help eliminate disparities in access to information resources. Unfortunately, through no fault of their own, many of these institutions mirror the technology gap rather than mitigate it.

Despite considerable progress, schools in low-income communities have fewer computers and modems than schools serving wealthier districts. According to *Computers and Classrooms: The Status of Technology in U.S. Schools,* a 1998 study by the Educational Testing Service (ETS), minority and poor students had significantly less access to computers in their classes than more affluent children. Schools with minority enrollment greater than 90% had a student-to-computer ratio of 17 to 1, compared to the national average of 10 to 1. For computers with advanced graphics and interactive video capabilities, the discrepancies were even bigger. While 62% of schools in high-income areas had Internet access in 1995, just 31% of schools serving low-income populations had access, according to the Department of Education's 1996 report, *Getting America's Students Ready for the Twenty-First Century.* ETS's later study found that the number of schools with Internet access rose markedly in 1996, but the gap remained: 75% of schools in high-income areas and just 55% in low-income areas had Internet access. "The kids with the most needs are getting the least access," an ETS researcher told the *Washington Post.*

Insufficient hardware or network connections aren't the only and may not even be the biggest problems for schools in poorer communities. Because of inadequate teacher training, these schools may not be using the computers they have in ways that have the greatest long-term benefits for students. All too often, they use computers for rote learning or drill exercises. In wealthy schools, on the other hand, where there generally is more money for curriculum development and teacher training, computers tend to be used more for complex learning activities, analysis, and writing skills that command higher wages in today's economy.

As Delia Neuman at the Maryland College of Information Services put it in a 1990 study that remains one of the few academic analyses of the issue, "economically disadvantaged students, who often use the computer for remediation and basic skills, learn to do what the computer tells them, while more affluent students . . . learn to tell the computer what to do." (The Benton Foundation explores the educational role of computer networking in its report, *The Learning Connection: Schools in the Information Age*, 1998.)

Libraries, meanwhile, are working to reduce inequality in access to new technologies, but they lack resources to do the whole job. According to Richard Kreig, public libraries in the city of Chicago had just one computer for every 20,000 residents they served in 1995, while libraries in the city's suburbs had one for every 13,000 residents. Krieg asserts that the discrepancy would be even greater if figures were available to compare the number of computers available in libraries in low-income sections of Chicago to those at suburban libraries.

Internet access is also spread unevenly among libraries, with the greatest disparity between libraries in urban/suburban and rural areas. While 72.3% of all public libraries had some type of Internet connection in the spring of 1997, library systems serving populations of 25,000 and above had a better than 90% connectivity rate, according to the *1997 National Survey of U.S. Public Libraries and the Internet*. Those serving populations of 5,000 or less had a connectivity rate of around 56%. Even among libraries that are connected, Internet access for patrons varies widely.

There is a direct link between the wealth of a library's neighborhood and the ability of that library to serve its neighborhood information needs, argues the Urban Libraries Council's Joey Rodger. "Ninety percent of library funding is local," she says. "Where there are many, many poor people, the local library has less capacity to serve them."

SOURCE: Benton Foundation, *Losing Ground Bit by Bit: Low-Income Communities in the Information Age* (Washington, D.C.: Benton Foundation, 1998), www.benton.org/Library/Low-Income/. Reprinted with permission.

Greatly exaggerated death of the library

by Arlene Rodda Quaratiello

AS A LIBRARIAN, there are a number of television commercials that irritate me. One was that Packard Bell ad that portrayed libraries as "forbidding, hostile places" (*American Libraries* 27 (December 1996): 17). Another was the commercial in which a woman poses the following question to her computer: "How many rooms are in the Vatican?" The computer immediately responds with a video clip of a game show host asking this same question to three contestants, one of whom, to the delight of the woman at home, answers it correctly.

Librarians know that finding information is not as easy as these commercials and the media in general would lead one to believe. The promise of quick information might sell computers, but it's far from being a reality. One of the challenges academic librarians face is convincing impressionable students, who are bombarded with misleading messages, that the World Wide Web is not all it's cracked up to be, that it's not possible for them to do all their research in their dorm rooms, even if they do have the best computers, and that the library is still a vital institution at the heart of the college campus.

Desk Set: A more realistic picture

In contrast to current media images is one of my favorite movies, *Desk Set* (1957), starring Katharine Hepburn as Bunny Watson, a librarian at a television station, and Spencer Tracy as Richard Sumner, a consultant who is hired to make the station more efficient by installing EMMARAC (Electro-Magnetic Memory And Research Arithmetical Calculator). Although this movie was made more than 40 years ago, its themes are surprisingly relevant to the issues of information retrieval that concern us today, not only in special libraries but in all libraries.

In the film's climactic scene, Sumner's assistant Miss Warriner has arrived to operate the newly installed Emmy (as the computer is affectionately nicknamed) while Bunny and her staff have just received pink slips. As the phone begins to ring, Bunny and the others, believing themselves fired, refuse to answer it, so Miss Warriner picks it up in frustration. The caller needs to know if the king of the African Watusi tribe drives a car. Miss Warriner types in the question, "Does the king of the Watusis drive a car?" After emitting a series of dramatic blips and boops, Emmy spits out reviews of a fictional adventure film about the Watusis, which hardly provide an answer to the question. Meanwhile, the phone keeps ringing, and neither Sumner nor Miss Warriner is able to answer any questions accurately. Bunny and her crew decide to strut their stuff, springing into action to answer every question without Emmy's help.

After a messenger delivers a pink slip to Sumner, and the president of the station calls to complain that he too has gotten one, it becomes apparent that another computer recently installed in the payroll department has malfunctioned, firing everyone by mistake. After reassuring the librarians that they haven't been fired, Sumner informs Bunny that Emmy was never intended to replace the library staff, but to assist them with tedious questions, allowing them more time to perform complex research. Bunny decides to give the computer a chance, asking, "How heavy is the earth?" to which Emmy replies, "With or without people?"

Technology as a tool

I appreciate *Desk Set* because, aside from its assertion that noncomputerized sources can sometimes be the best sources of information, it supports the idea that technology is merely a tool and cannot replace the expertise of librarians. Computers cannot think like human beings, who have the ability to pose questions in the appropriate context. To offer a real-life example, I tried to find information about *Desk Set* on the Web. My initial AltaVista search did not employ any advanced techniques, so I retrieved useless ads for phones and desk organizers (I should have known better). When I used the search statement + "desk set" +lang, however, I found a small set of highly relevant sites because this search statement only retrieved those sites which contained both "desk set" (as a phrase) and "lang" (the last name of the director of the film).

The reality is that most students that I encounter rely on simple searches. They don't use Boolean logic. They probably don't realize that most Web search engines insert "or" between the words they enter. In general, they haven't got a clue that AltaVista searches the complete text of sites, while Lycos restricts its search to the most significant parts. Many don't know that searching the Web differs from searching a periodical index accessed via the Web. The media have given them the impression that computers are brilliant machines that will read their minds and give them exactly what they need with little effort on their part.

The reality is that computers are quite dumb; librarians are therefore indispensable as intermediaries. A July 14, 1996, *Boston Globe Magazine* article even referred to librarians as "the astronauts of cyberspace." I heartily agree. As the novelty of the Web begins to wear off and students realize that finding information is not as easy as ads for computers make it seem, I hope that they emerge from their dorm rooms and realize that there will always be a need for libraries and librarians. Perhaps the information they need might even be found in a book.

SOURCE: Arlene Rodda Quaratiello, "Greatly Exaggerated Death of the Library," *College & Research Libraries News* 58 (October 1997): 625–26.

Nine rules for creating Web graphics

by Susan Jurist

NO MATTER HOW MANY WORDS a picture may save you, putting pictures on a Web page does more than save typing; it creates a look and an attitude that says who you are and what you will be delivering. In essence, putting images on a Web page is creating an advertisement that says "look at me, I'm worth looking at."

Watch shoppers in a supermarket. Despite the lower-priced generic items, how many shoppers actually buy the simply packaged nonbrands? Not that many, when you see how many more advertised, creatively packaged items are on the shelf and paid for at the cash register.

Now you are probably thinking that a library is not the same as a box of laundry detergent, and you are right, but the current generation uses the Web to decide everything from what movie to see to what school to go to. Students will look at a university's Web page to decide if it would be an exciting place to spend the next four years. As librarians, we want those same students to look at the information we are making available, but first we have to get them to see that there is information. They will stop at an arresting Web page—they won't read yards of plain text.

GPO Gate University of California

You can have a great-looking Web page whether or not you have a computer artist on staff, although those of you with some art background will have an easier time than those without it. Some of the most elegant and efficient Web pages have minimal graphics. One of my favorite Web designs is one I did for GPO Gate (above)—it's simple, yet looks good. The real impact comes from the font, Hiroshige, as much as it does from the design of the Capitol.

Creating sharp graphics for the Web—sharp in the sense of "grabs your attention," as well as the traditional sharp vs. fuzzy distinction—can be done. It takes time and patience—if you have talent, that will help—and following the top nine rules comes first.

1. Design for the average user. The average user is looking at a 14"-monitor and is using the Netscape browser. Unless you have a special audience in mind, don't design for the highest, or lowest, common denominator. Go average and you should be safe for most users.

The average user is using either a PC or a Mac. If you use only one system, and most of us do, always remember the other exists and the other is different.

2. Smaller is better. Period. The "why" should be obvious but, given some of the existing Web designs, it must not be. The first reason is that smaller loads faster. Even if you are sitting at a very fast PC connected by ethernet to a T3 line, waiting for a large graphic to load is not fun. If some of your intended audience are sitting at home in front of not-very-fast machines connected by a 14.4-baud modem, they are going to be more than bored, and they are not going to wait to see what you have to show them.

Smaller is also better because the average user is sitting in front of that 14" screen. Yes, some of us doing the designing are using 17" or 20" screens, but we are the minority. You don't want to design a graphic that takes up so much screen real estate that essential information is off the screen, or design one that can't be fully seen without scrolling.

On the previous page is the home page for the University of California–San Diego Web site. A professional designer worked on the look and feel, but two of us then worked for one full week to take the designer's ideas and fit them on one screen. It wasn't easy, but it was worth the effort.

Smaller for a digital image does not mean just two-dimensional size; also involved are file format, bit-depth, and type of image.

3. You are now designing for a computer screen, not the printed page. Printed 8.5 × 11″ pages are usually designed for a "portrait" view in which the height is greater than the width. Computer screens, on the other hand, are "landscape"—the width is greater than the height. So stop thinking vertically and start thinking horizontally. The first screen someone comes to on a Web page is the most essential. If that doesn't grab them, they won't scroll down to see what else you are offering.

4. You have to stop thinking in terms of inches (or cm for the metrically oriented). From now on, you have to start thinking in pixels, the dots of light that make up an image on a screen. The average screen has a resolution of 640 × 480 pixels, and that should be your new frame of reference. But you don't have the whole screen as your canvas. Both the browser and the operating system take up screen real estate too. With Netscape, assuming you have the square buttons for home, etc., and the location bar, the overhead is 124 pixels in height and 21 pixels in width. That means the maximum any image should be is 619 × 356. But since the Netscape browser defaults to an opening size of approximately 600 pixels, my rule of thumb (the one I use now, don't look at my earlier efforts) is to create images no larger than 600 × 400. For banners across the top of the page, my goal is 500 × 100 or less.

5. You have two format choices for graphics files—gif and jpeg—and choosing which to use isn't that difficult if you consider the following:

File type	in-line	bit depth	image type	transparent
.gif	yes	2–8	flat areas of color	yes
.jpeg	yes, but	24	photographic	no

In-line images are those that appear on the screen with html-generated text. All browsers can display gif in-line images, and most, but not all, can display jpeg in-line images. Jpeg in-line images will crash some browsers, and that should be taken into consideration.

Bit-depth refers literally to how many bits each pixel has to describe a color; 2-bit images are black and white, an 8-bit image can describe up to 256 colors (or shades of gray), and 24-bit images can display millions of colors.

In the real (analog) world, the eye (and color film) can see millions of colors. If you have a color photograph or a color painting, you would want millions of colors for your file as well.

But our friend the average user has a monitor that can show only 8-bit color. When an 8-bit monitor displays a 24-bit image (or when you change a 24-bit image to 8-bit), the software "dithers" the 256 allowable colors to approximate the colors it can't show you. The dithering is a pattern, or random pattern, that combines two or more colors to simulate a third and can be quite distracting. The original image looks smooth, but the dithered one has obvious noise that would be distracting if it were, for example, the sky in a photograph.

All Net browser software will dither a 24-bit image for an 8-bit system, but they won't do as good a job as graphics software like Adobe Photoshop. In the past, I used only 8-bit gif images on my Web pages so I could control the dithering and palette transformation. Now, as more people are getting higher-end systems, I use jpeg for images with a large color range that are the primary focus of a Web page.

The overall characteristics of your image should also affect your choice of file types. The gif compression algorithm works best with flat areas of color. A gif file of an image with a lot of dithering will be larger than a GIF file of flat colors. A jpeg compression of a photographic-quality image would be much smaller. For example, a gif file of a color gradient is 26K, while the corresponding jpeg file is only 17K; but a gif file of the same size, filled with flat color, is 17K as well. Remember that for loading times, smaller really is better.

Jpeg, on the other hand, is not the best for images with flat areas of color or high contrast. The jpeg compression algorithm tends to leave "artifacts" (small areas of off-color pixels) that become obvious in high-contrast, linear pictures.

The final, and often deciding reason to use gif inline images is if you need the effect of transparency where the background or background colors show through (used most often on decorative text, like in the GPO Gate banner). The jpeg format does not support transparency.

6. Color is not color is not color. You've created this gorgeous color scheme for your Web pages on your PC. The color is subtle but still high-concept; the combinations make your heart sing. You recommend the URL to everyone you know. One of your friends is on a Mac and tells you it's the gaudiest thing she's ever seen. Another friend, who has a PC, says the colors all clash. Are they wrong? No. Every system displays colors differently. Not only are Mac system colors (the default 256-color palette) different from the PC system colors, but most of the browsers have default palettes that are different from both (and from each other). You cannot guarantee that the colors you see are the colors someone else sees. Even when using defined "safe" colors—colors that are *supposed* to be the same on both platforms—you can get into trouble.

The best thing to do is to put some Web pages up and then look at them on both a Mac and a PC. If you have access to different browsers, you might want to check them too, but it isn't worth getting an America Online account just to see how something looks on it.

7. An image is an image, but it may not save any words at all. There are times to use images and icons and there are times not to use them. Although there are literally thousands of free icons available for the taking on the Web, that doesn't mean you should. Almost every iconic button in use on the Web has words next to it explaining what it is. Which is not to say you should never use decorative buttons, arrows, bullets, etc., but use them with care, and ask yourself first if this image is worth waiting for. Sometimes it is and sometimes it isn't. It's definitely a judgment call, and one that often separates the good pages from the bad.

And remember, if you are going to use images as buttons, this is a good time to consider the user who is on a Lynx browser with a VT100 connection and can't see the pictures at all. Can that user still navigate your page without them?

8. There is one thing you can do to make your image appear to take less time to load than it really does (because we both know you are going to ignore my guidelines and make images that are too big anyway) and that is in the html statement for in-line graphics. If you know the size *in pixels* of your image and you add that information, the text will be able to load more quickly because the browser will know how much space it has to leave for each picture. For example, <img width=300 height=75 src="chaco.gif">

9. You will need good graphics software. This last rule is so important I almost put it first. Any image that you create online, copy from a Photo-CD, or scan in on a consumer-level scanner ($20,000 or less) will benefit from simple modification with good software. And good does *not* mean the paint software that comes with Windows. My favorite application, and one I cannot recommend highly enough, is Adobe Photoshop, but there are other software packages with similar functionality that you can choose from. Basically you want software that will let you modify and correct digital images as well as create images from scratch. You should be able to type text in it and be able to save files in either jpeg or gif formats. Some software now has built-in features for creating transparent images and interlaced gifs (the images that come up in several passes, gradually getting sharper), though there is shareware available that will do those conversions as well.

Whatever package you choose, take the time to learn and use it. There is nothing that will replace experience, and there is no shortcut you can take to get there. A person without an art background but with a good understanding of the software can make better graphics than someone who knows art but doesn't know the digital brush from the digital pencil. Good luck.

Further reading. I've seen one book that explains Web graphics well: *Designing Web Graphics: How to Prepare Images and Media for the Web*, by Lynda Weinman (3d ed., New Riders, 1999).

SOURCE: Susan Jurist, "Top Ten Rules for Creating Graphics for the Web," *College & Research Libraries News* 57 (July/August 1996): 418–21.

Teaching Web evaluation
by Jim Kapoun

OVER THE LAST YEAR, I have noticed (in my undergraduate library instruction classes) that faculty members are demanding more Web usage from their students. In fact, some faculty members may exclude most print resources in favor of Web pages. If you are an instructional librarian, you know that the Web, in its ever-changing formats, is seemingly here to stay.

I have discovered that most undergraduate librarians (including myself) regard the Web as another tool to use in the arsenal of research materials. However, some of the students and faculty members who attend my instruction classes take on a different view, especially the traditional-aged undergraduate college student. Their view is: "Web pages must be the correct source because it is the most current and easiest to access form of information."

The assumption is not true, of course, but it is an almost impossible task to refute. Students seem to gravitate to the Web first and grudgingly consult paper materials afterwards. This report is not about the merits of the Web over paper; it is about trying to provide accurate ways for undergraduate students to evaluate Web resources for their research.

8

Five criteria for Web evaluation

When teaching the Web to students, I include a section on evaluation. I pattern my Web evaluation lecture like a librarian who evaluates print items for inclusion into a library collection. I base Web evaluation on five criteria that I

use for print evaluation: accuracy, authority, objectivity, currency, and coverage. To develop this model I had to first acknowledge that most students today tend to conduct research with speed rather than accuracy and rarely evaluate resources. So the criteria I present must be digestible and almost transparent to the student. In other words, the student must be trained to evaluate a Web document like second nature.

In the evaluation lecture, I present at least two but no more then four Web sites on a relevant subject for the class. One or more will be labeled a "good" Web site and at least one site will be labeled a "poor" Web site. I distribute a sheet of criteria (see below) and have the students quickly evaluate the pages presented. You cannot get bogged down with details; the goal is to provide the student a quick but comprehensive set of criteria to draw conclusions as to the Web pages' quality. In some classes, outside practice assignments are helpful to enforce this skill.

In time I have noticed that some students who have been to my classes are evaluating Web pages on their own and without the aid of the handout; they just do it. The success of this teaching component is patience and practice by the student.

Evaluation of Web documents

1. Accuracy of Web Documents

Who wrote the page and can you contact him or her?
What is the purpose of the document and why was it produced?
Is this person qualified to write this document?

2. Authority of Web Documents

Who published the document and is it separate from the "Webmaster?"
Check the domain of the document; what institution publishes it?
Does the publisher list his or her qualifications?

3. Objectivity of Web Documents

What goals/objectives does this page meet?
How detailed is the information?
What opinions (if any) are expressed by the author?

How to interpret the basics

1. Accuracy

Make sure author provides e-mail or a contact address/phone number.

2. Authority

Know the distinction between author and Webmaster.
What credentials are listed for the author(s)?
Where is the document published? Check URL domain.

3. Objectivity

Determine if page is a mask for advertising; if so, information might be biased.
View any Web page as you would an infomercial on television. Ask yourself why was this written and for whom?

4. Currency of Web Documents

When was it produced?
When was it updated?

How up-to-date are the links (if any)?

5. Coverage of the Web Documents

Are the links (if any) evaluated and do they complement the documents' theme?
Is it all images or a balance of text and images?
Is the information presented cited correctly?

4. Currency

How many dead links are on the page?
Are the links current or updated regularly?
Is the information on the page outdated?

5. Coverage

If page requires special software to view the information, how much are you missing if you don't have the software?
Is it free, or is there a fee to obtain the information?
Is there an option for text only, or frames, or a suggested browser for better viewing?

Putting it all together

Accuracy. If your page lists the author and institution that published the page and provides a way of contacting him/her, and . . .

Authority. If your page lists the author credentials and its domain is preferred (.edu, .gov, org, or net), and . . .

Objectivity. If your page provides accurate information with limited advertising and is objective in presenting the information, and . . .

Currency. If your page is current and updated regularly (as stated on the page) and the links (if any) are also up-to-date, and . . .

Coverage. If you can view the information properly—not limited to fees, browser technology, or software requirements, then . . .

You may have a higher-quality Web page that could be of value to your research.

SOURCE: Jim Kapoun, "Teaching Undergrads Web Evaluation," *College & Research Libraries News* 59 (July/August 1998): 522–23.

Notable Web sites for children, 1999

THE NOTABLE CHILDREN'S WEB SITES Committee of the ALA Association for Library Service to Children started recommending Web sites on an annual basis in 1998. The sites are selected based on excellence of the material, clarity of design and purpose, ease of navigation, and interest to children from preschool to 14.

At the Tomb of Tutankhamen (www.nationalgeographic.com/egypt/). The *National Geographic*'s Web site is one of the best educational resources we know. It has a "you-are-there" look at the unearthing of the boy pharaoh's tomb, done in the style of the original *National Geographic* article.

Audrey Wood's Web site (www.audreywood.com). Author/illustrator Wood and her husband Don have created an interactive look into the many books they've created. A great site for the Woods's many fans.

Bill Nye the Science Guy's Nye Labs Online (www.nyelabs.com/ flash_go.html). Science fans and those who might not be will get a jolt out of Bill Nye and his whimsical science lessons.

8

FunBrain.com (www.funbrain.com). Great fun! These learning games are divided into age categories and are the Internet's more advanced cousin to old-fashioned flash cards.

Kids' Castle (www.kidscastle.si.edu). The Smithsonian Institution's site for kids is full of interactive looks at many of the museum's treasures and educational program. But it's bright, colorful, and lots of fun as well.

Kinetic City Cyber Club (www.kineticcity.com). Join the Cyber Club Members from their radio show as they travel the world in a tireless quest for truth, justice, and the perfect deep-dish pizza (and tell us a little about physics, energy, and similar topics along the way).

The Moonlit Road (www.themoonlitroad.com/welcome001.html). If you like storytelling, especially ghost stories, check out this site. Creepy stories of the South can be heard with Shockwave or Real Audio capabilities. Attached info about Southern culture is also great fun to read.

National Zoo (Washington, D.C.) (www.si.edu/natzoo/). If you like animals and you like Web cams, you'll love this look at our nation's zoo in the Capital. If you tune in at 11:30 a.m., you can watch them feed the elephants!

Redwall: the Brian Jacques Home Page (www.redwall.org/dave/

jacques.html). Updated and improved, the Redwall site has audio files, photos, and basically everything a fan of Brian Jacques's Redwall series would want to know about the author and his works.

Salem (www.nationalgeographic.com/features/97/salem/). Want to know more about the witchcraft trials at Salem? Try this site! You are there . . . and have been accused of being a witch. A powerful and intense (and very interactive) history lesson.

SchoolHouse Rock (genxtvland.simplenet.com/SchoolHouseRock/index-hi.shtml). Young people of all ages enjoy this Grammar Rock, Multiplication Rock, and Science Rock—learn the lyrics to your favorite S.R. songs and hear some of them, too!

UNICEF Voices of Youth (www.unicef.org/voy/). Sponsored by the United Nations Children's Fund, this site is a gathering place for children and educators to learn more about young people all over the world.

Yuckiest Site on the Internet (www.nj.com/yucky/). Young people who love yucky things will pay a visit to this site to learn about the gross and cool things in their bodies, about worms, roaches, and lots more.

Zoom Dinosaurs (www.zoomdinosaurs.com). An "interactive online hypertextbook" about dinosaurs, this commercial site is a good one to be used by younger children, their parents, and their teachers.

SOURCE: ALA Association for Library Service to Children.

Building Web sites
for kids and young adults

by Walter Minkel and Roxanne Hsu Feldman

IF AND WHEN THE WEB is fully indexed, it should be easy to find appropriate Web sites on any topic for students from ages 8 to 18. Until that remote time, youth librarians may have to create their own Web pages that bring together links to useful sites. Here are some tips on how to construct them.—*GME.*

All pages in the directory should look and function in a similar way, and all pages should be clear. The National Cathedral School Internet Database (www.ncs.cathedral.org/library/upper/ncsid/) has a beautifully clear and simple design with lots of content and lots of white space. Place your content into a centered 1 × 1 table with a width of perhaps 85% or 90% of the screen to give the page some margins.

Go easy on the graphics and colors. No, you don't need to stick with only black type on a white background, but you should use a minimum of graphics. Avoid loud colors, background art that makes the text difficult to read, and (please!) animated gifs. Use the fun stuff on your children's area home page and your directory of "fun and games" links—not in your YPWRC (Young Person's Web-Reference Collection).

Your directory site should be easy to navigate. A rule to follow that goes back to the beginnings of Web design in 1994 is that everything on your site should be no more than three clicks from everything else. Have a clear table of contents and don't nest pages more than three levels deeper than the table of contents. For example, if you want to break your animals list into separate pages, don't have a second table of contents appear on a separate page when your site visitor clicks on "animals" in your main table of contents. If you look at the animals page in the Multnomah County Library Homework Center (www.multnomah.lib.or.us/lib/homework/animhc.html), you will see that the animals sites are all on one long page. You can reach each section, say the invertebrates section, of that long page easily by clicking on the list of sections at the top of the animals page. No site link in the Homework Center is more than two clicks from the main table of contents; the same is true of the links in the National Cathedral School's Internet Database.

Place the sites and sections in each page into alphabetical order by title. Many of the homework-help pages out there are jumbled in no particular order. This may sound nitpicky, but we have argued this point with other librarians who feel that, "Hey, it's the Web; people don't expect things to be in alphabetical order." Believe us, people using a library wonder what's going on if things aren't in alphabetical order. You may feel that kids don't care. Well, aren't we trying to set a good example of organizing information for students? It also shows pride in what you're doing.

When typing titles, use the title that's on the page, not the title you wish were on the page. Many sites out there have titles that are less than

clear, particularly pages dealing with topics like the arts, literature, and poetry. All librarians know that there are certainly books with titles we wish we could change, too. For example, HarperCollins's Big Busy House (www. harperchildrens.com) needs some explanation; it's a site of news and activities based on the publisher's books for children. If a site's title is less than clear, describe its content particularly well in an annotation.

Annotate every site. Few YPWRCs annotate their sites; this is both amazing and sad. When you're doing readers' advisory work with users, don't you

(since you can't have read every book in the collection) and they like it better when you can hand them an annotated booklist? The role of the library in the age of the Web, once again, should be to add value to the resources out there by locating them, collecting them, organizing them, and *describing* them. There are at least ten astronomy sites out there, for example, suitable for kids. Why should a particular student or teacher use one of them over another? You should be telling them why.

Watch for those "slip through the cracks" sites. Most sites on the Web that are suitable for young people will fit pretty clearly into a standard group of topic headings. However, an occasional site that you want your clients to find will be hard to classify. Look, for example, at Professor Bubble's Official Bubble Homepage (bubbles.org). It's a science site *and* a fun site; where should you list it? If you decide to put it under science, where would you put it if your science page is broken into the following subtopics: astronomy, biology, chemistry, earth sciences, physics, science experiments, and weather? Dewey classifies "bubbles" as a topic under physics. Will young people find it there? You might want to list it on your fun sites page as well. Don't be hesitant to list a page in two locations.

Look particularly for sites that do what other media in your collection can't, and note their special capabilities in your annotations. When we do Web instruction in schools or for classes visiting the library, we often show them two sites. One is the Egyptian Hieroglyphics site (www2.torstar.com/ rom/egypt/). Here you can go to a hieroglyphics translator page where you can type anything you want, click a button, and have it translated into hieroglyphics in a matter of seconds. The other page we often show is the U.S. Census Bureau's Pop Clocks page (www.census.gov/ftp/pub/main/www/popclock. html). Here you can see the current estimated population of the United States and of the world. We ask students to memorize the last few numbers of the population, wait thirty seconds, and hit the reload or refresh button again. "Whoa!" many of the students say when they see how much the populations have grown in such a short time. No book or audiotape can do these things. However, remember (and stress to your young users) that the Web doesn't have everything, despite what is shown in the TV commercials. The Web is only *one* information source, alongside books and other media.

Check your spelling and grammar before putting your pages online. Nothing is more embarrassing than a site from a public or school library that contains misspellings, misplaced apostrophes, and grammatical errors. For better or worse, the public expects the work of librarians to be grammatically perfect. Be sure to have someone who is not involved in the site—and has an editor's eye—read over the text of your pages.

Check your pages once they're online, on a variety of computers, monitors, and browsers. Remember that everyone's equipment is not the same as yours.

- If you have a 17″ monitor, remember that many computer users have 15″ monitors, and vice versa. The monitor size definitely will affect the appearance of your pages, as will the screen settings on your monitor (for example, 640 × 480 versus 800 × 600 resolution).
- If you're a Windows PC user, how does your site look on a Mac (and vice versa)?
- How does the site look under older versions of America Online's browser, which many AOL subscribers are still using?
- If you're using Internet Explorer, how does the page look in Netscape? Even if you upgrade your browser whenever a new version comes out, remember that most people don't. Remember that there are still folks out there who use the text-only browser Lynx or turn off the image loading to speed things up.
- Do all of your graphics include "alts" (text tags that describe graphics), so that text-only users will be able to understand and use your page?

Don't use frames, sound, or animation for directories of links. Young people who have grown up with electronic media are often easily distracted by anything that flashes, makes noise, or moves. Frames are not good for library sites because our goal is to reach as many users as we can, and frames make it harder to find the URLs of linked sites, to see an entire linked page, and to print without confusion. Keep your pages as simple and clear as possible. You don't want users to *stay* on your page; you want them to pass through your page to the materials they're seeking. You also don't want someone using an older browser to be unable to load your reference links because the page also contains a file their version of the browser can't handle.

SOURCE: Walter Minkel and Roxanne Hsu Feldman, *Delivering Web Reference Services to Young People* (Chicago: American Library Association, 1998), pp. 57–60.

Filtering software in libraries

by the ALA Intellectual Freedom Committee

ON JUNE 26, 1997, the United States Supreme Court issued a sweeping reaffirmation of core First Amendment principles and held that communications over the Internet deserve the highest level of constitutional protection.

The Court's most fundamental holding is that communications on the Internet deserve the same level of constitutional protection as books, magazines, newspapers, and speakers on a street corner soapbox. The Court found that the Internet "constitutes a vast platform from which to address and hear from a worldwide audience of millions of readers, viewers, researchers, and buyers," and that "any person with a phone line can become a town crier with a voice that resonates farther than it could from any soapbox."

For libraries, the most critical holding of the Supreme Court is that libraries that make content available on the Internet can continue to do so with the same constitutional protections that apply to the books on libraries' shelves.

The Court's conclusion that "the vast democratic fora of the Internet" merit full constitutional protection will also serve to protect libraries that provide their patrons with access to the Internet. The Court recognized the importance of enabling individuals to receive speech from the entire world and to speak to the entire world. Libraries provide those opportunities to many who would not otherwise have them. The Supreme Court's decision will protect that access.

The use in libraries of software filters which block constitutionally protected speech is inconsistent with the United States Constitution and federal law and may lead to legal exposure for the library and its governing authorities. The American Library Association affirms that the use of filtering software by libraries to block access to constitutionally protected speech violates the Library Bill of Rights.

What is blocking/ filtering software?

Blocking/filtering software is a mechanism used to:
- restrict access to Internet content, based on an internal database of the product, or;
- restrict access to Internet content through a database maintained external to the product itself, or;
- restrict access to Internet content to certain ratings assigned to those sites by a third party, or;
- restrict access to Internet content by scanning content, based on a keyword, phrase or text string, or;
- restrict access to Internet content based on the source of the information.

Problems with blocking/filtering software

Publicly supported libraries are governmental institutions subject to the First Amendment, which forbids them from restricting information based on viewpoint or content discrimination.

Libraries are places of inclusion rather than exclusion. Current blocking/filtering software prevents not only access to what some may consider "objectionable" material, but also blocks information protected by the First Amendment. The result is that legal and useful material will inevitably be blocked. Examples of sites that have been blocked by popular commercial blocking/filtering products include those on breast cancer, AIDS, women's rights, and animal rights.

- Filters can impose the producer's viewpoint on the community.
- Producers do not generally reveal what is being blocked, or provide methods for users to reach sites that were inadvertently blocked.
- Criteria used to block content are vaguely defined and subjectively applied.
- The vast majority of Internet sites are informative and useful. Blocking/filtering software often blocks access to materials it is not designed to block.

- Most blocking/filtering software is designed for the home market. Filters are intended to respond to the preferences of parents making decisions for their own children. Libraries are responsible for serving a broad and diverse community with different preferences and views. Blocking Internet sites is antithetical to library missions because it requires the library to limit information access.
- In a library setting, filtering today is a one-size-fits-all "solution," which cannot adapt to the varying ages and maturity levels of individual users.
- One role of librarians is to advise and assist users in selecting information resources. Parents and only parents have the right and responsibility to restrict their own children's access—and only their own children's access—to library resources, including the Internet. Librarians do not serve *in loco parentis*.
- Library use of blocking/filtering software creates an implied contract with parents that their children *will not be able* to access material on the Internet that they do not wish their children read or view. Libraries will be unable to fulfill this implied contract, due to the technological limitations of the software, thus exposing themselves to possible legal liability and litigation.
- Laws prohibiting the production or distribution of child pornography and obscenity apply to the Internet. These laws provide protection for libraries and their users.

How can your library promote Internet access?

Educate yourself, your staff, library board, governing bodies, community leaders, parents, elected officials, etc., about the Internet and how best to take advantage of the wealth of information available. For examples of what other libraries have done, contact the ALA Public Information Office at pio@ala.org.

Uphold the First Amendment by establishing and implementing written guidelines and policies on Internet use in your library in keeping with your library's overall policies on access to library materials. See the Library Bill of Rights on pp. 456–57 and its Interpretation on Access to Electronic Information, Services, and Networks at www.ala.org/alaorg/oif/electacc.html.

Promote Internet use by facilitating user access to Web sites that satisfy user interest and needs.

Create and promote library Web pages designed both for general use and for use by children. These pages should point to sites that have been reviewed by library staff.

Consider using privacy screens or arranging terminals away from public view to protect a user's confidentiality.

Provide information and training for parents and minors that reminds users of time, place, and manner restrictions on Internet use.

Establish and implement user behavior policies.

For more information on this topic, contact ALA's Office for Intellectual Freedom at (800) 545-2433, ext. 2433; or oif@ala.org.

SOURCE: Statement on Library Use of Filtering Software (Chicago: ALA Intellectual Freedom Committee, 1997).

Developing real-world Internet policies

by Karen Hyman

I STARTED SPEAKING TO LIBRARY GROUPS about Internet policies in the summer of 1995. Sex on the Internet was so hot that a term paper by a Carnegie Mellon University undergraduate named Marty Rimm drove O. J. Simpson off the cover of *Time* magazine, and so scarce that Rimm had to troll the adult bulletin-board services and alt.sex news groups to find the goods. Newspapers speculated that the nut case of the day might have used the Internet. Filtering software news was SurfWatch blocking the Gay and Lesbian Square Dance Page. The Communications Decency Act was still a gleam in Senator Exon's eye. The few libraries offering public access to the Internet received flattering, gee-whiz press coverage. When the local television station grilled me over kids looking at "dirty pictures" at the library, it was noteworthy enough for an ALA video. My 1995 message to library groups was: The raunch level is overhyped. Filtering is a sledgehammer solution. Instead, educate yourself and your board. Develop an Internet policy that you can articulate and defend. Be ready for bad press, because it's coming.

Today, the number of online picture galleries and virtual sex clubs on the Yahoo list swells at the same rate as the Dow. Every nut case has his own Web page. Filtering software has become more flexible and risen to the level of an intellectual-freedom litmus test. The CDA has come and gone and come again and gone again. Every publication from the *New York Times* to the *Shopper's Guide* has done a "smut at the library" story.

If you need evidence that you're on the edge of the unknown, reflect on the recent past and project that amount of change into the near future. Two years and 5,000 miles later, my 1997 message to the troops was: Every choice is flawed and don't trust anyone who tells you anything different.

Reality check

How are libraries actually dealing with the Internet? The truth is in the variety of policies and practices:

- Open access; "use at your own risk."
- Parents advised or required to supervise their children at the library.
- Parental permission forms, ranging from "no permission" equals "no Internet access" to "no permission for Internet access" equals "no access to the library at all."
- Furniture and/or screens to prevent overviews.
- Terminals in highly visible locations.
- Stand-up terminals only.
- Signups/time limits.
- User agreements ("I promise not to look at anything that may be reasonably construed to be offensive . . . ").
- Filtering at all or some terminals by blocking keywords and categories. These are determined by the vendor, or they are vendor catego-

ries selected by the library, or URLs determined by the library (i.e., proxy servers, protocol sniffers). Access may also be limited to sites chosen by the library.

- Staff monitoring of access to "pornographic" or "sexually explicit" or "sexually suggestive" sites. Offenders are asked to change the screen, leave the terminal, not use the Internet again at the library, leave the library, or leave the library and not come back.
- No graphical interface to the Internet.
- Minimal or no public Internet access.
- A plethora of rules that turn off pornfreaks and everybody else.

The worst choices or, what NOT to do

If choosing what to do seems hard, it's only because it is. No choice avoids the major pitfalls. The worst choices somehow manage to hit them all. The big 10:

1. Abdicate selection responsibility. From filtering online what you would or should buy in print to accepting online what you wouldn't or shouldn't.

2. Curtail access to information. How? Restricting access to the library and/or the circulating collection to adults who comply with Internet policies and children who have parental permission to use the Internet. Filtering by keyword or by categories like "extremist" that block online the kinds of materials that are within selection policies. Limiting access to a few thousand sites with limited search capability in the name of selection. Having fewer or no public terminals or no graphical access as a way to handle intellectual-freedom issues.

3. Provide legally obscene material to minors. Not offensive or suggestive but obscene, as in appeals to "prurient interest" with no "redeeming social value." There is no community support for providing this material in the public library at all, even though some of it may be "constitutionally protected free speech." We noticed this when we failed to purchase porn flicks and S&M pictorials for all these years. None. Not just a few because our budget was so limited.

4. Drain limited resources. Staff troll the terminals for porn sightings and nudge people to replace the privacy shield they just removed. Staff holed up in the back room programming in or programming out. Six public-access terminals with three people looking at porn, one playing a game, and two in a chat room with each other.

5. Create a PR nightmare. This is what you spent my tax money for? My kid can use the Internet on your terms or not at all? I have to sit next to this guy pulling up crotch shots? What do you mean there's nothing you can do?

6. Loss of credibility. Can you look arrogant, clueless, radical fringe, and terminally tedious all at the same time? Not a great place from which to start a defense of controversial print and online materials that are within your selection policies.

7. Loss of relevance. Now, let me see. I can sign up for half an hour no more than twice weekly, no less than 24 hours, or no more than one week in advance, and you can't provide Internet-trained staff to help me, but I should be a responsible consumer of information because the Internet contains inaccurate information. . . . Never mind.

8. Staff revolt. For some reason staff does not want to take on the role of screen police, age police, permission-form police, and collector of 10 cents a page for the network printout of the circle-jerk pictorial. Most libraries end up in the newspaper because their own staff dropped a dime on them.

9. Fear. Of making a choice, looking foolish, not being what passes for politically correct in front of our colleagues, being sued, losing our jobs, going to jail, having a dialogue with our own users and maybe finding out that they wouldn't recognize the Bill of Rights if they read it and would vote against it if they did.

10. All of the above.

Solutions (the short list)

Instead of getting trapped in the big 10:

Pick a common-sense approach and give it a try. Forget about the perfect choice because it isn't out there. See how it works out. Whatever you pick will probably change anyway. Pay attention to how you implement whatever you choose, because details count. Involve your staff and your community. Be forthright about the problems. Think for yourself and use your whole brain while you're doing it.

Focus on customer service. Provide value as an evaluator, organizer, and creator of information. Be a teacher, mentor, resource person, expert. Help people get information and get a grip on technology. Make a difference. If you're doing this now, feel good about yourself.

Keep your mind open. Learn all you can and revisit what you've learned.

Avoid accepting or repeating hearsay. Listen to someone who disagrees with you. Avoid reducing complex issues to single-issue litmus tests that demonize the "sinners" and confer sainthood too easily on the rest. Really look at and talk about all of the options, instead of passing resolutions that denounce libraries along with the deficiencies and "illegality" of products you've never seen or worked to improve.

Find common ground. We're a profession where positions on intellectual freedom run the gamut from A to B. We have a lot going for us—commitment to intellectual freedom and the experience to know what's involved and a rare and genuine concern for children's access to information. We need to follow the rules of dialogue not debate, and stop marginalizing opponents, avoiding or misrepresenting the facts that don't fit personal theories, and eschewing common ground for a win-lose mentality—all in the name of intellectual freedom.

People with important work to do can't afford a fetish for dissension. Nobody wins in a circular firing squad.

SOURCE: Karen Hyman, "Internet Policies: Managing in the Real World," *American Libraries* 28 (November 1997): 60–62.

ISSUES

CHAPTER NINE

"Experience teaches us to be most on our guard to protect liberty when the government's purpose is beneficent. The greatest dangers to liberty lurk in insidious encroachments by men of zeal, well-meaning but without understanding."

—Louis D. Brandeis, *Olmstead v. United States*, 277 U.S. 438 (1928)

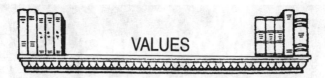

VALUES

In search of something else

by Bernard Vavrek

IN *SELLING THE INVISIBLE* (Warner Books, 1997), author Harry Beckwith theorizes that Burger King has not won "the burger wars" against McDonald's because the latter enterprise sells experiences, and not just sandwiches.

Reading this, it occurred to me that this could account for my friend Robin's having made an art form out of collecting memorabilia at the "golden arches," my children's invitations to birthday parties there, and Ronald McDonald's annual appearance in the Autumn Leaf Festival Parade through beautiful downtown Clarion, Pennsylvania. But what really piqued my interest was how such commercial "experiences" translated into the nonprofit world—in other words, the expectations users bring to their public library visits.

Are books and information really as central to all our clients' needs as we think, or are library customers also in search of something else? For that matter, are public libraries really in the information business?

In light of how rapidly library reality is changing as we apply information technology, these are crucial questions we need to articulate for all types of

---

A look at reality

How a staff member sees it:
I really would rather not work weekends and evenings.
I have so much work to do, and there never seems to be enough time in the day.
Books are appropriate in the library's collection; videos are frivolous.
It's budget time and the city council should give the library more money; after all, the library is a good thing.
I wish the customer wouldn't keep asking for things we don't have; it takes time to request materials from other libraries.
Why should we have a display of third-grade drawings? That's not what the library is for.

How a customer sees it:
If the library is not open when I can use it, I'll find information elsewhere.
I rarely ask questions of the library staff because they always seem so busy.
It would be nice if the library had videos; since they don't, I'll have to rent them at the video store.
I don't want my taxes to go up. The library isn't important in my life, so why should I have to pay more taxes?
I really need these materials; if this library can't get them, I'll try another library or order them from the bookstore.
If my child's drawing is displayed in the library, I'll stop in to see it. Otherwise, I visit the library rarely.

SOURCE: Darlene E. Weingand, *Customer Service Excellence* (Chicago: American Library Association, 1997), p. 115.

libraries. Most particularly, small and rural libraries must reexamine their roles. With 80% of all public libraries in this country serving populations of 25,000 or less, these institutions comprise the backbone of U.S. public librarianship.

After hearing my concerns, some of my Clarion University library school students helped me identify the factors driving the amazingly rapid deployment of technology in small and rural libraries. Unsurprisingly, our list

Carnegie Library, Madison, Minn., ca. 1928.

included: the romantic and practical values library users and staff members alike assign to technology, the increasing affordability of computer hardware and software, governmental automation initiatives at regional and state levels, the introduction of the universal-service discount, and the largesse of private entities such as Bell Atlantic and the Gates Library Foundation.

We also discussed the challenges facing staffers as they attempt to integrate yet another new set of skills into their professional repertoire, especially since most (albeit enthusiastic) library directors serving small communities have had no formal library education. Inevitably, we concluded, some personal relationships with library clientele must end up suffering. After all, there are only so many hours in a day, and we all know that there is no such thing as time freed up by the application of technology.

Of course, none of us were advocating a return to traditional library values at the expense of technology. But we had to acknowledge that, notwithstanding the evolutionary shift in emphasis throughout Libraryland away from the tactile world of books, there may be a less obvious set of on-site user experiences left unfulfilled by our fervent rush to the Internet—a gap filled by the laid-back ambiance of super bookstores and Internet cafes.

Here's our list of those subtler, endangered face-time experiences:

1. Community center. As the only publicly funded facility that is open daily in some small or rural communities, the public library may afford its users their only opportunity to meet each other.

It's only in public libraries that organizations and individuals are equally welcome, the former to convene important meetings and the latter to do nothing more serious than play cards, if they so desire. And in communities where public libraries are the venue for town meetings or the headquarters for local literacy services, the library as a physical presence takes on an additional significance.

Indeed, many growing communities are choosing to house their public libraries in the equivalent of reinvented town squares—facilities that also house such public-sector entities as the local governing authority, health and welfare offices, and recreation departments.

2. Recreational facility. Public libraries offer an activities and programming spectrum that runs the gamut from holiday breakfasts with Mrs. Santa Claus to arts-and-crafts classes and used-book sales.

3. Safe haven. Traditionally, patrons have viewed the public library as a venue in which they could energize themselves without having to fear for their safety. Despite the associated problems, the growing after-school influx of latchkey children into public libraries proves the trust parents, guardians, and caregivers place in the public library by the simple act of leaving their youngsters there unsupervised.

Sadly, unfortunate events in public libraries around the country are eroding this image. In particular, rural libraries in geographically remote areas need to recognize the opportunities and vulnerabilities of their unique situations.

4. Purveyor of morality and decency. The public library has historically signaled its willingness to support free expression even as it protected those who had not yet attained the age of reason from access to unwholesome information. I don't condone attempts by some to censor access to information with which they disagree, but it has occurred to me that perhaps the motivations of such people stem from their misperceptions of their libraries' mission prior to the passage of the Communications Decency Act.

5. Tender loving care. Perhaps the primary experience people look to "buy" at their public libraries is a personal relationship with a staffer. Granted, trustees don't really want to encourage the town's lonely hearts to monopolize the librarian's time. But such encounters commonly occur nonetheless.

Witness the individuals who repeatedly ask staff members what books to read next, or expect that "their" librarian will always alert them when new titles by their favorite authors become available. For that matter, why do parents and children mob child-centered activities, such as story hours, at the typical public library? Do adults really lack the time to read to their children, or do they want to experience the enthusiasm of a beloved children's librarian?

Such personal relationships also infuse a library's outreach services. Visits to people who are homebound, bookmobile stops at senior centers, and other door-to-door services are the epitome of one-to-one community activism.

Undoubtedly, the spread of information technology to small and rural community libraries will revolutionize lifelong learning in every corner of America. In our rush to get online, however, let's keep in mind the offline connections our patrons still expect us to be "selling" them after all these years.

SOURCE: Bernard Vavrek, "What Are Public Library Users Really Buying?" *American Libraries* 29 (March 1998): 42–44.

Outsourcing in perspective

by the ALA Outsourcing Task Force

OUTSOURCING OF LIBRARY SERVICES has been practiced as far back as 1828, when a Hartford, Conn., bindery published books and sold them by subscription. A number of critical events in the 20th century have shaped outsourcing issues as we see them today: the provision of catalog cards by the Library of Congress (1901); the Greenaway Plan for blanket orders of new publications (1958); the outsourcing of federal libraries (1983); and the outsourcing of cataloging at Wright State University (1993). The outsourcing of collection development in the Hawaii public libraries (1996) and the privatization of library services at Riverside County (California) Free Library (1997) are recent events that have caused professional outcry.

In 1901, the Library of Congress began providing catalog cards on a cost-recovery basis, enabling libraries to, in effect, outsource the cataloging of materials already handled by the Library of Congress. This service can be regarded as the precursor to various cooperative cataloging efforts, and to the formation of bibliographic utilities and other agencies from which cataloging can be purchased. The availability of networked bibliographic utilities further fostered the widespread practice of copy cataloging, in which minimal skill is required to attach holdings to records in such central databases as OCLC and Western Library Network (WLN).

The Greenaway Plan, initiated at the Philadelphia Free Library, was an approval plan through which librarians automatically received copies at the same time reviewers did, and selected those titles that met collection needs. The Greenaway Plan is notable in that it actually enhanced the professional nature of book selection, a key component of collection management, through commercializing a portion of library service—the receipt of review copies.

Privatization—which places control, governance, and potential profits in the for-profit sector—is a relatively new phenomenon in libraries.

In 1983, the Office of Management and Budget concluded that federal library services qualified for privatization. The stated intent of Circular A-76 (www.whitehouse.gov/OMB/circulars/a076/a076.html) was to prevent government competition with private industry. Library operations were mingled with other office and administrative services under the definition of commercial activities. Classifying federal agency libraries as commercial services met with protests from the library community. In 1985, ALA passed a resolution focused on concerns about diminution of professional skills that called the classification of library services as commercial activities "inaccurate and inappropriate" and "a major distortion of the nature and purpose of libraries." Nevertheless, many federal library services were contracted to private companies or effectively privatized. In the fall of 1998, the Department of Defense placed a moratorium on further contracting-out of general libraries; the Department of the Army placed a moratorium on contracting-out of all army libraries.

When the National Technical Information Services (NTIS), an agency of the U.S. Department of Commerce, was targeted for privatization in 1986, ALA again passed a resolution protesting this decision, expressing concerns that this action "adversely affect[s] equal and ready access to scientific and technical documentation." At that time the efforts of ALA and others were successful in avoiding privatization. Today the NTIS is a nonappropriated government agency, self-funded from the sale of products and services.

Another critical event was Wright State (Ohio) University's outsourcing of its entire cataloging operation in 1993. The cataloging department was dissolved and cataloging was contracted with OCLC. The library press closely followed the Wright State University outsourcing. A review of library literature indicates that most articles in the traditional library press were favorable, although there is anecdotal evidence of contentious discussion which is not fully documented.

9

In 1996, the Hawaii State Library out-sourced the selection and processing of Hawaii's public library collections to Baker & Taylor, a major library vendor. In Hawaii and throughout the nation, there was significant discussion and criticism of these activities, cul-minating in legislation passed by the Hawaii state legislature and signed into law by the gov-ernor in June 1997, affirming the role of local librarians in materials selection. Ultimately, the contract with Baker & Taylor was terminated and no similar contract has been pursued in that state.

In 1997, the Riverside County (Calif.) Free Library privatized library ser-vices for all 25 of its branch libraries. The county awarded the contract to Library Systems and Services (LSSI), a company with a history of managing library contracts for special and federal libraries. This was the first documented instance of privatization of an entire public library system. Press reactions were cautiously observant; there was a notable lack of professional criticism. Calabasas, Calif., followed Riverside County's example and outsourced its li-brary services with LSSI; Jersey City, N.J., initially contracted with LSSI, but the contract was voided in October 1998 by court order, citing critical errors in the original decision-making process of the Library Board.

In 1998, a library board in Loudoun County, Va., was criticized in a legal opinion for delegating the deselection of the library's electronic resources available on the Internet to a private company, through use of that company's filtering software package. In ruling that the board policy constituted uncon-stitutional "prior restraint," particularly with the lack of "sufficient standards" or "adequate procedural safeguards," the judge wrote:

> The degree to which the Policy is completely lacking in standards is demonstrated by the defendant's [the library board] willingness to entrust all preliminary blocking decisions—and, by default, the over-whelming majority of final decisions—to a private vendor.

Governance issues

Governance becomes the critical issue in reviewing the impact of outsourcing and privatization on library services. The Outsourcing Task Force repeatedly returned to issues of governance and private versus public accountability. Comparisons of consortial and commercial services help illustrate this issue.

Consortial shared services, commercial services, and networks share simi-lar objectives and often perform similar tasks and functions. All provide library services that libraries may or may not perform themselves. All may manage employees delivering these services. All may function at sites geo-graphically removed from the libraries they serve.

The locus of governance is one area where commercial services sharply diverge from not-for-profit shared services. Identifying the locus of governance involves determining to whom a concern is primarily answerable and ascer-taining for whom employees work. Commercial services are nondemocratic, while the governance of shared services is determined by the membership. The primary accountability for commercial services is to internal stakeholders or shareholders of the company, whose motives are commercial viability and profitability, not necessarily public service. There are, in some cases, different laws and applications of the law as applied to the public and private sectors. For instance, individual and public rights under the First Amendment are more readily upheld when the public sector and government action is involved.

There are great concerns that a commercial contract for total privatization of library operations in the public sector conflicts with the traditionally public nature of library governance. The Task Force believes it is critical that the governing body for the library retain its responsibility for establishing and maintaining policy and control of the product and services provided and for the policies that direct its activities.

Other important issues include the potential impact of outsourcing and privatization on "open meeting laws" and the public laws dealing with freedom of information and the confidentiality of records. Within the public sector, certain laws enable citizens to hold public agencies accountable in very specific ways. It is unclear how these laws would apply to the private sector activity for which a public agency has contracted.

Core library services

One major issue is the concern about the complete outsourcing or privatization of library materials selection, cataloging, reference service, and library management, all defined as core services in this document. These activities are taught in library and information science schools. They constitute the intellectual, abstract core of librarianship, which is part of the library education curriculum and their centrality to librarianship is reinforced by professional activity and policy. Many librarians believe that much of the essence of core services is taught and learned within library settings.

There are many routine applications for outsourcing in librarianship, and many uses for commercial services. Rarely do librarians question outsourcing or privatizing of activities not directly associated with librarianship. Indeed, librarians have traditionally employed other professionals to perform services related to librarianship that support core library services, e.g., preservation, conservation, and automation.

When core services such as cooperative cataloging or consortial collection management are outsourced to not-for-profit agencies run by and for librarians, the nature of the work remains in-house—closely associated with and accountable to the libraries that benefit from the outsourced services.

To outsource an intellectual service suggests that it is a simple commodity that can be quantified, described in a written document, and contracted to the lowest bidder. Much of the important work of librarianship is abstract and nonquantifiable. The successful practice of librarianship is closely tied to the particular characteristics of the communities served.

When core services are outsourced, they may be conducted at sites geographically remote from the libraries they serve, by agencies with separate governance and with staff with limited opportunities for professional library associations. The peer relationship is lost, as are the opportunities for informal knowledge transfer, skill-sharing, and the many innovations that result from skilled practitioners observing their communities. Loss of these intimate connections threatens to erode the corporate body of library service.

Human resources issues

Of great concern is the impact of outsourcing and privatization on the quality and professional integrity of employees. Qualified professional library staff members are critical to developing and maintaining collections responsive to the needs of serviced populations and to providing access to information. Although personnel costs are often of great concern to administrators and elected officials, the library's ability to instruct, educate, inspire, and stimulate individuals is priceless. A library manager's greatest challenge is maintaining a workforce that reflects the needs of the population served while operating within a defined budget.

Another personnel issue is the displacement of the individuals who once performed the outsourced functions. There is always a human cost associated with workforce reduction. This factor could contribute to larger profession-wide issues, impacting recruitment and retention.

Outsourcing and privatization raise other personnel supervision issues. When a servicing agency hires an individual to provide a contracted service, the local institution loses control over the function, the professional performance qualifications, and the performer of that endeavor. The library may have a work standard that differs from that applied to employees hired by the outside contractor. These disparities could raise serious issues of equitable treatment and employee morale.

Pay and benefits are potential issues in any outsourcing and privatization scenario. When outsourcing, a library gives control of compensation to the service agency and can no longer guarantee equitable pay and benefits. When the primary rationale for outsourcing an activity is cost reduction, it is doubtful that salaries and benefits of the employees of the service agency remain a concern of the library.

Outsourcing and privatization also raise issues of maintaining a competent workforce professionwide and ensuring that professional librarianship delivers promised services. Traditionally, vendors have provided quality service by hiring librarians trained in libraries, but as activities are increasingly outsourced, the number of librarians who have been trained in those activities within libraries decreases. For example, as more institutions send their materials to commercial companies for preservation, the individual libraries lose key information on preservation techniques and methods, as well as staff expertise on effective product evaluation. Vendor-employed catalogers who are professionally trained but have little or no experience with cataloging in a local setting have no opportunity to develop the kinds of insights into their work, its purposes, and uses that catalogers at the local level have. These librarians are ill-equipped to take what they know about cataloging, catalog structure, and user needs, and combine this knowledge for innovative practice, systems, and service.

Librarians must understand what their core professional activities are and maintain channels for sharing knowledge in these areas with colleagues. The profession must ask who will provide the labor pool of qualified librarians if an increasing number of libraries outsource professional activities. The profession must be assured of adequate education of librarians performing activities for vendors, so that qualified librarians can complete tasks requiring judgment and decision making both in and out of libraries. Librarians must protect standards of education, training, and professional advancement.

Management issues

Despite professional concerns, outsourcing of some core services has become an increasingly prevalent management practice. Its widespread use calls for guidance within the profession on whether to outsource and how to ensure quality control of outsourced activities. This is not to suggest that ensuring a quality product can resolve all outsourcing issues; the concerns raised above demonstrate that some problems related to outsourcing are inherent in the practice regardless of the nature of the contract. However, outsourcing has been a practice for all types of libraries, and guidance for current practice is necessary.

Before deciding to outsource any activity or service, decision makers must determine whether outsourcing will, indeed, reduce costs and maintain or improve the quality of services. If so, is it the best way to improve productivity and service delivery? Decision makers also must determine how they will maintain effective control over outsourced services and functions. With respect to human resources, libraries must weigh the effect of outsourcing on accountability, diversity, goals, and morale.

Outsourcing decisions must be made within the context of the planning process for individual libraries, which mandates a clearly articulated mission and objectives aimed at accomplishing this mission. With its mission and objectives in hand, a library can assess what impact potential outsourcing would have on service delivery. Standards of service, quality control, and accountability for the outsourced activity must be established.

Finally, evaluation of outsourcing activities is essential and should include both quantitative and qualitative measurements. Most current literature measures the impact of outsourcing in total dollar benefits to the organization, but the impact on information services delivery is usually underemphasized or poorly documented. The impact on other less tangible matters, such as morale, the development of a trained workforce, and obligations to cooperative partners is addressed even less effectively. Not all benefits or problems can be calculated in monetary terms. The California Library Association's resolution on outsourcing recognizes this and states, "The primary measure of service benefit must be effectiveness in meeting the needs of library users" (1998) (www.cla-net.org/html/policies.html).

There are assertions that the private sector can perform library and information jobs less expensively. Even if this were true, absolute dollar savings are not a sufficient and adequate measure of library services. Historically and by definition, public goods are "market failures" that are essential public services, but are not profitable enough for the marketplace to support. Planning documents central to our profession, such as Charles R. McClure, et al., *Planning and Role Setting for Public Libraries* (ALA, 1987), ignore the profitability concept entirely and focus on delivery of information services to the public.

SOURCE: ALA Outsourcing Task Force, *Outsourcing and Privatization in American Libraries* (Chicago: American Library Association, January 6, 1999), pp. 5–10.

Outsourcing newspeak

by George M. Eberhart

AS THE WORD "OUTSOURCING" takes on an increasingly negative tone, new terms like "cosourcing" have been proposed. Here is a glossary of neologisms that will no doubt be standard usage for collection developers in the 21st century.

Alohasourcing—Saying hello to outside vendors for book selection and goodbye to a relevant, accessible collection (the Hawaii model).

Flacksourcing—Using an outside PR agency to handle your press releases on outsourcing.

Geosourcing—Making sure that your vendor is located on the same continental plate as you are.

Liposourcing—Trimming the fat from vendor selection lists.

Naysourcerers—People who are against most forms of outsourcing.

Netsourcing—Abandoning real materials in favor of virtual materials on the Web.—*Norman Stevens*.

Pansourcing—Purchasing every single book that is published, and returning for a refund titles that do not circulate after one year.

Parasourcing—Relying on occult methods such as automatic writing, divination, and channeling for materials selection.

Pseudosourcing—Forming a dummy corporation from your own acquisitions staff and paying them extra to do what they do best.

Psychosourcing—Allowing insane selection decisions to be made by a vendor.

Quasisourcing—Telling the board of education that you are going to outsource, but never quite getting around to it.

Retrosourcing—Allowing a vendor to purchase older titles that would have been selected under current profiles had outsourcing been in place at the time.

Smurfsourcing—Allowing only suburban white folks to select materials.

Tyrannosourcing—Massively reengineering the acquisitions process without consulting staff.

Unsourcing—Repairing all the errors you made while outsourcing.

Weaselsourcing—Using only unscrupulous vendors.

Zombisourcing—Reviving an old approval plan that should have been buried long ago.

SOURCE: George M. Eberhart, "Outsourcing Newspeak," *American Libraries* 28 (June/July 1997): 29.

Outsourcing computer services

by Stuart Kohler

AS THE USE OF COMPUTERIZED SYSTEMS becomes more and more common in libraries of all sizes, so has the use of outside vendors, contractors, and consultants to install, implement, and maintain these systems. Acquiring systems, services, and applications may often be undertaken more cost-effectively by arranging for them with nonlibrary personnel, but once the decision to outsource is made, there are many issues that must be carefully considered. The recommendations presented here are general in nature and should not be taken to substitute for competent legal advice when drafting contractual documents.

Types of computer services

The range of possible types of services runs from a contract for a specific piece of custom software to a comprehensive contract for the provision of complete librarywide computer services. While there may be some overlap in the following list, five general categories of outside assistance in automated systems may be identified:

1. Small, custom software applications (library kiosks, pieces of computer-assisted instruction, specific database applications for newsletter or mailing list purposes, etc.).

2. Services, such as short-term on-site training sessions for library staff, long-term agreements for user or network support, subscriptions to remote databases of periodicals, or other content-specific resources. Network services might also include the installation and maintenance of a local area network, including the required hardware and software, servers, and workstations.

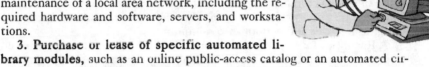

3. Purchase or lease of specific automated library modules, such as an online public-access catalog or an automated circulation system, usually to run on a personal computer.

4. Purchase or lease of an integrated library system that includes an OPAC and systems for circulation, serials, acquisitions, and other areas of library administration, usually to run on a mini or mainframe computer.

5. Comprehensive contracts for total library-wide automation, training, maintenance, upgrade, and support for all related computer systems.

Issues to consider

Potential problem areas may be divided into nine general categories:

1. Clear statement of need/clarity of contract. Not only should the statement of need explain specifically what is required, there should also be a brief summary of how the new system will improve efficiency, service, reduce costs, or other justification for undertaking the project. Build this specificity into the contract with the provider, as lack of clarity is a frequent cause of outsourcing problems.

2. Evaluate contractors/vendors. If the project is large enough, it may be appropriate to call for bids. The library is paying for expertise but also experience. Therefore the library should ask questions such as: Has the contractor done similar work elsewhere? Are references available? If it is a new area for the contractor, will the fees reflect his or her learning curve?

3. Compatibility with existing systems, hardware, and/or software. Diversifying computing platforms (Windows or Macintosh or both?) may enfranchise new sectors of the library's community, but it also adds increased levels of complexity for maintenance, troubleshooting, and perhaps future expansion of related systems.

9

4. In-house maintenance requirements/training of staff to operate new system. Who trains staff? Will the original trainees be able to train new staff hired later? Will the system be a self-contained, dedicated-use system (stand-alone) that would be easier for staff to learn and use, or will it be accomplished by adding on to an existing system? The latter may force staff to learn more about the general operation of the existing system than a dedicated-use application would. Training should also be included on backing up current data and archiving procedures for old data.

5. Scope of contract. Once the contract is turned over to the library, is there any long-term responsibility by the contractor if bugs are discovered or changes are desired? Who owns custom-written software? If the library does not obtain title to software, the consultant may realize additional profit by selling the same work again to another library, albeit with some modification. If so, the fee schedule should reflect the true value of what is being created and its true ownership. When contracting for full-text periodical databases, are there copyright restrictions?

6. Billing and completion arrangements. Will there be a single, flat fee for the completed/delivered product, or an hourly fee for its creation? For hardware or systems maintenance contracts, will service calls be billed on an hourly basis or does the contract fee cover all necessary service requests? What is the time frame for delivery of completed work or for completion of repairs? The latter may be articulated in terms of performance measurements, such as performance goals and performance minimums.

7. Remedies for unacceptable work. Unfortunately, an unscrupulous entrepreneur may attempt to maximize profits by declining to deliver exactly what was promised in absence of specific remedies specified in writing.

8. Likelihood of long-term accessibility to information such as full-text periodical databases (especially important if considering cancellation of periodical subscriptions) or long-term usefulness of the software application under consideration.

9. Acceptance testing. This is absolutely crucial and should include a reasonable testing period—not simply a demo by the consultant at turnover.

Example

As an example of the process at a conceptual level, we will consider the development of a custom piece of software to maintain the membership records of a Friends organization, following the nine issues outlined above. Although the process becomes more complex for larger projects, the procedure will remain the same in principle.

The first step is to clearly state the goals, functionality, and features of the Friends software. This particular project would have as its goal the creation of software to collect, maintain, and extract information about the Friends membership including the elements of name, address, membership type, renewal date, and a miscellaneous note section. In terms of functionality and features, the system should be easy to use, must be able to produce (printed on either paper or label stock) mailing lists (by zip code as well as last name) and renewal lists. In addition, the system must include a mail-merge function able to produce customized correspondence to the membership.

Once this information is presented to the consultant, the next step is to establish an approximate time for completion of the project and identify if new or existing hardware (computer or printer) or new software (upgrade to current database application) will be required. If the latter is true, who is responsible for making the required purchases? Establish also who enters sample data for testing purposes and the complete data for the full system. If data are to be supplied by the library, what is the required data format? Clarify title to the resulting software and also clarify how much staff training the consultant will include.

Finally, an overall fee for the project or an hourly rate should be agreed upon. If an hourly rate is selected, it may be useful to establish a maximum total charge to prevent the project from taking on a life of its own. As a precaution, discussion at this point should include remedies for undelivered or unacceptable work.

The next step is when the consultant returns with a demonstration version of the software, with an evaluation done using sample data. At this point, change orders may be necessary. Requesting changes in the way the software operates or in the pieces of information included is often a fact of life in software development. It is not necessarily evidence of poor planning or mistakes. Systems seem to have a natural gestation period, but it is essential to minimize the number of change orders and the magnitude of the changes requested. Each change from the original contract usually constitutes additional charges.

Acceptance testing with live data is usually the conclusion of the project, save for paying the consultant. At this point, the software would be turned over to the library and future responsibility for the consultant would likely occur only if bugs (such as dues payment miscalculations) show up after the acceptance testing is completed and the project accepted.

SOURCE: Stuart Kohler, "Contracting for Computer Services in Libraries," *College & Research Libraries News* 58 (June 1997): 399–401.

INTELLECTUAL
FREEDOM / ACCESS

The evolving First Amendment, 1787–2000

EVERY CHALLENGE to the First Amendment has helped shape the current interpretation of Americans' rights. This time line was developed by ALA's Office for Intellectual Freedom.

1787—The U.S. Constitution is ratified on the unwritten condition by many states that a Bill of Rights be added soon afterward.

1788—The Constitution goes into effect; nine states have ratified it, with others to follow.

1791—The First through Tenth Amendments are adopted, comprising the Bill of Rights.

1798—Fearing war with France, Congress passes the unpopular Sedition Act of 1798, curtailing First Amendment freedoms. Numerous newspaper editors (including Benjamin Bache, grandson of Benjamin Franklin and editor of Philadelphia's *Aurora*) were harassed, fined, and jailed under the Act, which expired in 1800.

1868—The Fourteenth Amendment is adopted. The due process clause of this amendment serves as the basis for the Supreme Court to restrict state actions infringing on civil and political rights. Up to this time, the free speech rights of the citizen of a state were safeguarded solely by the state's constitution and laws.

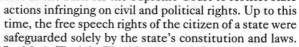

1885—Mark Twain's *The Adventures of Huckleberry Finn* is banned in Concord, Massachusetts. The book continues to be one of the most frequently challenged or banned books in the United States.

1917—The Supreme Court defines freedom of speech narrowly in the years around World War I, upholding the Espionage Act of 1917 in several cases.

1919—Supreme Court Justice Oliver Wendell Holmes announces in *Schenck v. United States* (249 U.S. 47) a "clear and present danger" test to determine whether speech is protected by the First Amendment. Using the test, the Supreme Court affirmed the wartime convictions of the defendants charged with interfering in armed forces recruitment by mailing leaflets to new recruits urging them to resist conscription.

Justice Holmes shows the intended reach of his "clear and present danger" test by dissenting in *Abrams v. United States* (250 U.S. 616), which affirmed the convictions of several Russian immigrants who distributed from an open window circulars that denounced as hypocritical President Wilson and urged workers to unite in support of the Bolshevik revolution.

1920—Roger N. Baldwin creates the American Civil Liberties Union (ACLU).

1923—Writer Upton Sinclair (right) is arrested in Los Angeles after trying to read the Bill of Rights in public at a dockworkers' strike. He is later charged with "discussing, arguing, orating, and debating certain thoughts and theories, which . . . were detrimental and in opposition to the orderly conduct of affairs of business, affecting the rights of private property. . . ."

1925—When science teacher John Scopes challenges a Tennessee law forbidding him from teaching the theory of evolution, one of the most notable trials in U.S. history follows. Though Scopes lost, his conviction was overturned later on a technicality. In 1968, the Supreme Court ruled on the same issue when it said that First Amendment freedoms were violated by requirements that only the biblical theory be taught.

The Supreme Court, in *Gitlow v. New York* (268 U.S. 652), decides that rights protected under the First Amendment are among the personal "liberties" protected by the due process clause of the Fourteenth Amendment from impairment by states. Nevertheless, the Court declined to apply Justice Holmes's "clear and present danger" test and upheld the defendant's convictions under New York statutes for publishing a manifesto advocating, advising, or teaching the overthrow of organized government by force or violence.

1931—In *Near v. Minnesota ex rel. Olson* (283 U.S. 697), the Supreme Court interprets the First and Fourteenth Amendments to forbid as "prior restraints" a lawsuit authorized by a state statute to enjoin future publication of a newspaper. The case extended the definition of "prior restraints" to include more than simply official prepublication review that involves either licensing or censoring of particular content.

The Supreme Court invalidates California's "anti-red flag" law in *Stromberg v. California* (283 U.S. 359). The Court found the California statute that made it a felony to display a red flag "as a sign, symbol, or emblem of oppression to organized government" repugnant to the Constitution.

1939—The American Library Association adopts the *Library Bill of Rights* (see pp. 456–57), the profession's basic policy statement on intellectual freedom involving library materials.

1942—In *Chaplinsky v. New Hampshire* (315 U.S. 568), the Supreme Court upholds a New Hampshire statute as a valid regulation of "fighting words," i.e., words "which by their very utterance inflict injury or tend to incite an immediate breach of peace." Fighting words, like certain other limited classes of speech, e.g., the lewd and obscene, "are no essential part of any exposition of ideas and are of such slight social value as a step to truth that any benefit that may be derived from them is clearly outweighed by the social interest in order and morality."

1943—The Bill of Rights is included for the first time in the handbooks given to immigrants to study for their citizenship tests.

1951—During the era of McCarthyism and witch-hunting, the Supreme Court weakens free-speech rights by ruling that speakers can be punished for advocating overthrow of the government, even if the likelihood of such an occurrence is remote.

1953—The Freedom to Read statement is issued by the Winchester Conference of the American Library Association and the American Publishers Council, which in 1970 would consolidate with the American Educational Publishers Institute to become the Association of American Publishers. The statement is subsequently endorsed by the American Booksellers Association, American Booksellers Foundation for Free Expression,  American Civil Liberties Union, American Federation of Teachers, AFL-CIO, Anti-Defamation League of B'Nai B'rith, Association of American University Presses, Children's Book Council, Freedom to Read Foundation, International Reading Association, Thomas Jefferson Center for the Protection of Free Expression, National Association of College Stores, National Council of Teachers of English, P.E.N.-American Center, People for the American Way, Periodical and Book Association of America, Sex Information and Education Council of the United States, Society of Professional Journalists, Women's National Book Association, and the YWCA of the USA.

1957—The appeal taken in *Roth v. United States* (354 U.S. 476) directly raises before the Supreme Court the question of whether obscenity is speech protected under either the First or Fourteenth Amendments. U.S. Justice Brennan answered that it is not, and set forth the standard for judging obscenity as "whether to the average person, applying contemporary standards, the dominant theme of the material taken as a whole appeals to the prurient interest." The "Hicklin test," which judged obscenity by the effect of isolated excerpts upon the most susceptible persons in a community, was thus rejected.

The Supreme Court in *Yates v. United States* (354 U.S. 298) draws a distinction against advocacy of an abstract doctrine such as Marxism and advocacy directed at promoting unlawful action. The decision construed certain federal statutes regulating subversive political activity to permit advocacy and teaching of the forcible overthrow of the government, even with evil intent, so long as the advocacy and teaching is divorced from any effort to instigate action.

1961—In *Scales v. United States* (367 U.S. 203) the Court further construes the  statutes at issue in *Yates v. United States,* upholding a clause that criminalizes knowing membership in any organization that advocates the overthrow of the government by force or violence. The clause presses the limits of constitutionality, the Court observed. However, "active" members who also have a "guilty knowledge and intent"—going beyond "merely an expression of sympathy with an alleged criminal enterprise . . . unaccompanied by any significant action" or "any commitment to undertake such action"—engage in illegal advocacy.

1962—The Supreme Court in *Engel v. Vitale* (370 U.S. 421) rules that public-school use of a prayer composed by state officials and recommended as part of a program for moral and spiritual training violated the First Amendment prohibition against governmental establishment of religion. The Court found irrelevant the fact that the prayer may have been denominationally neutral or that its observance by students was voluntary.

1964—In the first libel case to reach the Supreme Court, *New York Times v. Sullivan* (376 U.S. 254), the justices rule 9–0 that a public official may not recover damages for a defamatory statement, unless he can prove the statement was made with "actual malice."

1967—The American Library Association establishes the Office for Intellectual Freedom. The office's goal is to educate librarians and the general public on the importance of intellectual freedom.

1968—Upholding a federal law against burning draft cards, the Court says that incidental limitation on First Amendment freedoms is justified in some cases.

1969—Reversing the conviction of a Ku Klux Klan member, the Supreme Court in *Brandenberg v. Ohio* (395 U.S. 444) overrules its earlier decision, which had upheld criminal syndicalism statutes that proscribe advocacy of violent means to effect political and economic change. Constitutional guarantees do not permit a state to forbid such speech, except where advocacy of the use of force "is directed to inciting or producing imminent lawless action and is likely to incite or produce such action."

The Freedom to Read Foundation is created. The Foundation assists groups or individuals in litigation by securing counsel, providing funding, and participating either directly or as a "friend of the court" in important and possibly precedent-setting litigation.

1971—Efforts by the U.S. federal government to stop the publication of the "Pentagon Papers" brings to a head conflicting claims of free speech and national security. The Court ruling in *New York Times Company v. United States* (403 U.S. 713) reaffirms the heavy presumption that a "prior restraint" of free expression is constitutionally invalid. Because the government fails to meet the "heavy burden of showing justification" for such a restraint, newspapers are not enjoined from releasing the secret history of American involvement in Vietnam.

1973—Striving to remove confusions concerning a test for obscenity requiring that the material be "utterly without redeeming social value," the Supreme Court in *Miller v. California* (413 U.S. 15) reformulates the test. The Court's test, which still stands, involves three parts. First, the average person, applying contemporary community standards, finds that the work, taken as a whole, appeals to the prurient interests. Second, that the work depicts sexual conduct in a patently offensive way. Third, the work, taken as a whole, lacks serious literary, artistic, political, or scientific value.

1977—When neo-Nazi Frank Collin and his National Socialist Party of America are denied a permit to march in Skokie, a Chicago suburb with thousands of Holocaust survivors, the ACLU fights for their First Amendment rights. The protracted legal battle, concluding after the Supreme Court refuses in *Smith v. Collin* (439 U.S. 916) to reverse the proceedings, resulted in Collin eventually obtaining a permit. The party's march, however, is held in Chicago's Marquette Park.

1978—In proceedings on a complaint about an afternoon radio broadcast of comic George Carlin's seven "dirty words" monologue, the Supreme Court in *Federal Communications Commission v. Pacifica Foundation* (438 U.S. 726) upholds an FCC order as to "possible" sanctions against the radio station, which found the monologue as broadcast "indecent" but not obscene.

1979—When the *Progressive,* an alternative newspaper in Madison, Wisconsin, prepares to run a cover story that explains how to build a hydrogen bomb, the government takes quick action to prevent publication. After a seven-month showdown, the government backs down and the article runs.

1981—Banned Books Week: Celebrating the Freedom to Read is created. The week is sponsored by the American Booksellers Association, American Booksellers Foundation for Free Expression, American Library Association, American Society of Journalists and Authors, Association of American Publishers, and National Association of College Stores.  These groups sponsor this week to draw attention to the danger that exists when restraints are imposed on access to information in a free society.

1982—In *Island Trees Union Free School District No. 26 v. Pico* (457 U.S. 853), a divided Supreme Court recognizes that a board of education's discretion to remove books from junior and senior school libraries is more limited than it is with respect to classrooms and the curriculum. The plurality opinion by Justice William Brennan declares that "local school boards may not remove books from school library shelves simply because they dislike the ideas contained in those books and seek by their removal to prescribe what shall be orthodox in politics, nationalism, religion, or other matters of opinion."

The Supreme Court adds child pornography as another category of speech excluded from First Amendment protection. The ruling comes in the case *New York v. Ferber* (458 U.S. 747), when the Court upholds the constitutionality of a New York statute prohibiting persons from promoting a sexual performance by a child under the age of 16 by distributing material, which need not be legally obscene, that depicts such a performance.

1989—Burning the U.S. flag is a protected form of symbolic political speech, the Supreme Court rules in *Texas v. Johnson* (491 U.S. 397). Because a principal function of free speech is to invite dispute, any interest asserted by the state in preventing breaches of the peace from outraged onlookers is found to be insufficient to support the defendant's conviction under a Texas statute prohibiting "desecration of a venerated object."

1990—The Supreme Court in *U.S. v. Eichmann* and *U.S. v. Haggerty* (496 U.S. 310) strikes down convictions under the Flag Protection Act of 1989, passed by Congress in response to the Court's flag desecration decision that year.

The constitutionally protected right to receive obscenity, and information generally, in the privacy of one's home does not extend to child pornography, the Supreme Court rules in *Osborne v. Ohio* (495 U.S. 103). The Court finds that Ohio reasonably concluded that the state will decrease the production of child pornography, thereby protecting child victims, if it penalizes those who possess and view the product.

1997—The first Supreme Court decision regarding the Internet, *American Library Association v. U.S. Department of Justice* and *Reno v. American Civil Liberties Union* (117 S.Ct. 2329, 138 L.Ed.2d 874), strikes down provisions of the Communications Decency Act regulating "indecent" and "patently offensive" speech. Intended to protect minors, the Act is found to reduce, unconstitutionally, "the adult population (on the Internet) to reading only what is fit for children."

SOURCE: ALA Office for Intellectual Freedom.

The library bill of rights

THE AMERICAN LIBRARY ASSOCIATION affirms that all libraries are forums for information and ideas, and that the following basic policies should guide their services.

1. Books and other library resources should be provided for the interest, information, and enlightenment of all people of the community the library serves. Materials should not be excluded because of the origin, background, or views of those contributing to their creation.

2. Libraries should provide materials and information presenting all points of view on current and historical issues. Materials should not be proscribed or removed because of partisan or doctrinal disapproval.

3. Libraries should challenge censorship in the fulfillment of their responsibility to provide information and enlightenment.

4. Libraries should cooperate with all persons and groups concerned with resisting abridgment of free expression and free access to ideas.

5. A person's right to use a library should not be denied or abridged because of origin, age, background, or views.

6. Libraries which make exhibit spaces and meeting rooms available to the public they serve should make such facilities available on an equitable basis, regardless of the beliefs or affiliations of individuals or groups requesting their use.

Since 1948 when the Library Bill of Rights was first adopted, ALA Council has affirmed 16 interpretations that elaborate its provisions:

Access for children and young people to videotapes and other nonprint formats. Adopted 1989. (www.ala.org/alaorg/oif/acc_chil.html).

Access to electronic information, services, and networks. Adopted 1996. (www.ala.org/alaorg/oif/electacc.html).

Access to library resources and services regardless of gender or sexual orientation. Adopted 1993. (www.ala.org/alaorg/oif/acc_gend.html).

Access to resources and services in the school library media program. Adopted 1990. (www.ala.org/alaorg/oif/accmedia.html).

Challenged materials. Adopted 1971. (www.ala.org/alaorg/oif/chal_mat.html).

Diversity in collection development. Adopted 1982. (www.ala.org/alaorg/oif/div_coll.html).

Economic barriers to information access. Adopted 1993. (www.ala.org/alaorg/oif/econ_bar.html).

Evaluating library collections. Adopted 1973. (www.ala.org/alaorg/oif/eval_lib.html).

Exhibit spaces and bulletin boards. Adopted 1991. (www.ala.org/alaorg/oif/exh_spac.html).

Expurgation of library materials. Adopted 1973. (www.ala.org/alaorg/oif/exp_lib.html).

Free access to libraries for minors. Adopted 1972. (www.ala.org/alaorg/oif/free_min.html).

Library-initiated programs as a resource. Adopted 1982. (www.ala.org/alaorg/oif/lib_res.html).

Meeting rooms. Adopted 1991. (www.ala.org/alaorg/oif/meet_rms.html).

Restricted access to library materials. Adopted 1973. (www.ala.org/alaorg/oif/rest_mat.html).

Statement on labeling. Adopted 1951. (www.ala.org/alaorg/oif/labeling.html).

The universal right to free expression. Adopted 1991. (www.ala.org/alaorg/oif/univ_exp.html).

SOURCE: ALA Office for Intellectual Freedom.

The freedom to read

THE FREEDOM TO READ is essential to our democracy. It is continuously under attack. Private groups and public authorities in various parts of the country are working to remove books from sale, to censor textbooks, to label "controversial" books, to distribute lists of "objectionable" books or authors, and to purge libraries. These actions apparently rise from a view that our national tradition of free expression is no longer valid; that censorship and suppression are needed to avoid the subversion of politics and the corruption of morals. We, as citizens devoted to the use of books and as librarians and publishers responsible for disseminating them, wish to assert the public interest in the preservation of the freedom to read.

We are deeply concerned about these attempts at suppression. Most such attempts rest on a denial of the fundamental premise of democracy: that the ordinary citizen, by exercising critical judgment, will accept the good and reject the bad. The censors, public and private, assume that they should determine what is good and what is bad for their fellow citizens.

We trust Americans to recognize propaganda, and to reject it. We do not  believe they need the help of censors to assist them in this task. We do not believe they are prepared to sacrifice their heritage of a free press in order to be "protected" against what others think may be bad for them. We believe they still favor free enterprise in ideas and expression.

We are aware, of course, that books are not alone in being subjected to efforts at suppression. We are aware that these efforts are related to a larger pattern of pressures being brought against education, the press, films, radio, and television. The problem is not only one of actual censorship. The shadow of fear cast by these pressures leads, we suspect, to an even larger voluntary curtailment of expression by those who seek to avoid controversy.

Such pressure toward conformity is perhaps natural to a time of uneasy change and pervading fear. Especially when so many of our apprehensions are directed against an ideology, the expression of a dissident idea becomes a thing feared in itself, and we tend to move against it as against a hostile deed, with suppression.

And yet suppression is never more dangerous than in such a time of social tension. Freedom has given the United States the elasticity to endure strain. Freedom keeps open the path of novel and creative solutions, and enables change to come by choice. Every silencing of a heresy, every enforcement of an orthodoxy, diminishes the toughness and resilience of our society and leaves it the less able to deal with stress.

Now as always in our history, books are among our greatest instruments of freedom. They are almost the only means for making generally available ideas or manners of expression that can initially command only a small audience. They are the natural medium for the new idea and the untried voice from which come the original contributions to social growth. They are essential to the extended discussion which serious thought requires, and to the accumulation of knowledge and ideas into organized collections.

We believe that free communication is essential to the preservation of a free society and a creative culture. We believe that these pressures toward conformity present the danger of limiting the range and variety of inquiry and expression on which our democracy and our culture depend. We believe that every American community must jealously guard the freedom to publish and to circulate, in order to preserve its own freedom to read. We believe that publishers and librarians have a profound responsibility to give validity to that freedom to read by making it possible for the readers to choose freely from a variety of offerings.

The freedom to read is guaranteed by the Constitution. Those with faith in free people will stand firm on these constitutional guarantees of essential rights and will exercise the responsibilities that accompany these rights.

We therefore affirm these propositions:

1. It is in the public interest for publishers and librarians to make available the widest diversity of views and expressions, including those which are unorthodox or unpopular with the majority.

Creative thought is by definition new, and what is new is different. The bearer of every new thought is a rebel until that idea is refined and tested. Totalitarian systems attempt to maintain themselves in power by the ruthless suppression of any concept which challenges the established orthodoxy. The power of a democratic system to adapt to change is vastly strengthened by the freedom of its citizens to choose widely from among conflicting opinions offered freely to them. To stifle every nonconformist idea at birth would mark the end of the democratic process. Furthermore, only through the constant activity of weighing and selecting can the democratic mind attain the strength demanded by times like these. We need to know not only what we believe but why we believe it.

2. Publishers, librarians and booksellers do not need to endorse every idea or presentation contained in the books they make available. It would conflict with the public interest for them to establish their own political, moral, or aesthetic views as a standard for determining what books should be published or circulated.

Publishers and librarians serve the educational process by helping to make available knowledge and ideas required for the growth of the mind and the increase of learning. They do not foster education by imposing as mentors the patterns of their own thought. The people should have the freedom to read and consider a broader range of ideas than those that may be held by any single librarian or publisher or government or church. It is wrong that what one can read should be confined to what another thinks proper.

3. It is contrary to the public interest for publishers or librarians to determine the acceptability of a book on the basis of the personal history or political affiliations of the author.

A book should be judged as a book. No art or literature can flourish if it is to be measured by the political views or private lives of its creators. No society of free people can flourish which draws up lists of writers to whom it will not listen, whatever they may have to say.

4. There is no place in our society for efforts to coerce the taste of others, to confine adults to the reading matter deemed suitable for adolescents, or to inhibit the efforts of writers to achieve artistic expression.

To some, much of modern literature is shocking. But is not much of life itself shocking? We cut off literature at the source if we prevent writers from dealing with the stuff of life. Parents and teachers have a responsibility to prepare the young to meet the diversity of experiences in life to which they will be exposed, as they have a responsibility to help them learn to think critically for themselves. These are affirmative responsibilities, not to be discharged simply by preventing them from reading works for which they are not yet prepared. In these matters taste differs, and taste cannot be legislated; nor can machinery be devised which will suit the demands of one group without limiting the freedom of others.

5. It is not in the public interest to force a reader to accept with any book the prejudgment of a label characterizing the book or author as subversive or dangerous.

The ideal of labeling presupposes the existence of individuals or groups with wisdom to determine by authority what is good or bad for the citizen. It presupposes that individuals must be directed in making up their minds about the ideas they examine. But Americans do not need others to do their thinking for them.

6. It is the responsibility of publishers and librarians, as guardians of the people's freedom to read, to contest encroachments upon that freedom by individuals or groups seeking to impose their own standards or tastes upon the community at large.
It is inevitable in the give and take of the democratic process that the political, the moral, or the aesthetic concepts of an individual or group will occasionally collide with those of another individual or group. In a free society individuals are free to determine for themselves what they wish to read, and each group is free to determine what it will recommend to its freely associated members. But no group has the right to take the law into its own hands, and to impose its own concept of politics or morality upon other members of a democratic society. Freedom is no freedom if it is accorded only to the accepted and the inoffensive.

7. It is the responsibility of publishers and librarians to give full meaning to the freedom to read by providing books that enrich the quality and diversity of thought and expression. By the exercise of this affirmative responsibility, they can demonstrate that the answer to a bad book is a good one, the answer to a bad idea is a good one.
The freedom to read is of little consequence when expended on the trivial; it is frustrated when the reader cannot obtain matter fit for that reader's purpose. What is needed is not only the absence of restraint, but the positive provision of opportunity for the people to read the best that has been thought and said. Books are the major channel by which the intellectual inheritance is handed down, and the principal means of its testing and growth. The defense of their freedom and integrity, and the enlargement of their service to society, requires of all publishers and librarians the utmost of their faculties, and deserves of all citizens the fullest of their support.
We state these propositions neither lightly nor as easy generalizations. We here stake out a lofty claim for the value of books. We do so because we believe that they are good, possessed of enormous variety and usefulness, worthy of cherishing and keeping free. We realize that the application of these propositions may mean the dissemination of ideas and manners of expression that are repugnant to many persons. We do not state these propositions in the comfortable belief that what people read is unimportant. We believe rather that what people read is deeply important; that ideas can be dangerous; but that the suppression of ideas is fatal to a democratic society. Freedom itself is a dangerous way of life, but it is ours.

SOURCE: ALA Office for Intellectual Freedom. Adopted June 25, 1953; revised January 28, 1972, January 16, 1991, by the ALA Council and the AAP Freedom to Read Committee.

Books banned abroad, 1998–1999

Reinaldo Arenas, *Before Night Falls* [Cuba].
Aung Sang Suu Kyi, *Freedom from Fear* [Myanmar].
Siobhan Dowd, ed., *This Prison Where I Live* [Iran].
Duong Thu Huong, *Novel Without a Name* [Vietnam].
Nuruddin Farah, *Secrets* [Somalia].
Palden Gyatso, *Autobiography of a Tibetan Monk* [Tibet].
Hong Ying, *Daughters of the River* [China].
Charles R. Larson, ed., *Under African Skies* [Kenya].
Pramoedya Ananta Toer, *This Earth of Mankind* [Indonesia].
Latif Yahia, *I Was Saddam's Son* [Iraq].

Twelve new silly and illogical reasons to ban a book

The *Whole Library Handbook 2* (1995) contained the top 10 silliest reasons to ban a book (p. 427). Since then some other candidates have turned up.—*GME*

1. **It encourages suicide-induced reincarnation.** Laurence Yep's *Dragonwings* was challenged at the Apollo-Ridge schools in Kittanning, Pennsylvania, in 1992 because it might encourage children to "commit suicide because they think they can be reincarnated as something or someone else."

2. **It causes polarization.** J. D. Salinger's *Catcher in the Rye* was removed in 1997 from the curriculum of the Marysville (Calif.) Joint Unified School District for its profanity and sexual situations. The school superintendent removed it to get it "out of the way so that we didn't have that polarization over a book."

3. **It might cause Buddhism to erupt.** D. T. Suzuki's *Zen Buddhism: Selected Writings* was challenged at the Plymouth-Canton, Michigan, school system in 1987 because "this book details the teachings of the religion of Buddhism in such a way that the reader could very likely embrace its teachings and choose this as his religion."

4. **It encourages children to think independently.** Robert Cormier's *The Chocolate War* was removed from the Grosse Pointe (Mich.) School District library shelves in 1995 because it deals with "gangs, peer pressure, and learning to make your own decisions."

5. **It needlessly breaks wind.** Bruce Coville's *My Teacher Glows in the Dark* was contested in the classrooms and school libraries in Palmdale, California, in 1995 because the book includes the words "armpit farts" and "farting."

6. **It discourages learning English.** Ellen Levine's *I Hate English* was challenged by a school board member in the Queens, New York, school libraries in 1994 because "The book says what a burden it is they have to learn English. They should just learn English and don't [sic] complain about it."

7. **It's not about Texas.** Herman Melville's *Moby Dick* was banned from the advanced placement English reading list at the Lindale, Texas, schools in 1996 because it "conflicts with the values of the community."

8. **It's nutritionally incorrect.** Faith Ringgold's *Tar Beach* was challenged in the Spokane, Washington, elementary school libraries in 1994 because it stereotypes African Americans as eating fried chicken and watermelon and drinking beer at a family picnic. The book is based on memories of the author's family rooftop picnics in 1930s Harlem.

9. **It's a silly-ass book.** *Anne Frank: Diary of a Young Girl* was challenged at the Baker Middle School in Corpus Christi, Texas, in 1998. Among other reasons, parents objected to the word "ass" in the sentence: "What a silly ass I am!"

10. **Any stupid reason.** Harry Allard's *The Stupids Die* was pulled from the shelves of the Howard Miller Library in Zeeland, Michigan, in 1998 for review because a parent complained: "Once you allow 'stupid' as a word to call people, who knows what they'll come up with?"

11. **It might lead to harder stuff.** Maurice Sendak's *In the Night Kitchen* was challenged at the Elk River, Minnesota, schools in 1992 because reading the book could "lay the foundation for future use of pornography."

12. **It has talking and smoking animals.** Lewis Carroll's *Alice's Adventures in Wonderland* was banned in China in 1931 because "animals should not use human language, and that it was disastrous to put animals and human beings on the same level." William Steig's *The Amazing Bone* was challenged at the West Amwell schools in Lambertville, New Jersey, in 1986 because of "the use of tobacco by the animals."

What you should do if you are served with a subpoena

by Theresa Chmara

YOU ARE A LIBRARIAN APPROACHED by a police officer and served with a subpoena, compelling you to produce patron records identifying the names of all patrons who have borrowed books on childbearing in the last nine months. Farfetched? Impossible? Unfortunately, it is neither of those things. It happened several years ago. Fortunately, the librarian, with the assistance of the city attorney and the support and cooperation of her library board, was able to convince a court that the subpoena should be "quashed," a legal term meaning that she did not need to comply with the subpoena request.

What should you do if you are served with a subpoena requesting information about patron records or if you are simply asked to supply such information without a subpoena request? Whether the request comes from a law-enforcement authority or a private individual or group involved in litigation, you should take the same steps. As an initial matter, inform the requester that you cannot comply without consulting with an attorney. A subpoena generally does not require an immediate response, but rather provides a response date some time in the future.

Although the response time may only be days away and a requester may otherwise demand immediate compliance, you should never provide patron borrowing information without consulting an attorney. There are important reasons why you must exercise caution.

First, many states have specific statutes that protect patron borrowing information and designate such information as confidential. In those states, it is a statutory violation to produce identifiable patron information to persons other than library employees engaged in their regular library duties, unless there is a court order compelling the library to produce such information. A subpoena is not a court order. Although it will have a court caption and appear to be an official court document, it is, in fact, issued at the request of an attorney or law-enforcement officer and is not reviewed by a judge prior to issuance.

Increasingly, libraries are also maintaining video collections for patron use. It is a violation of federal law to produce information related to borrowing of videos. The Video Privacy Protection Act prohibits the disclosure of information about video use. This federal law applies in every state.

Second, producing patron borrowing information is harmful to First Amendment concerns, whether or not a state particularly designates such information as confidential. Release of patron borrowing information impacts First Amendment concerns. If patrons believed that their reading material would be subject to public scrutiny, the exercise of their First Amendment rights would be chilled. Patrons would refrain from reading material on controversial issues or sensitive topics if they believed that their choice of reading material could become the subject of public exposure and scrutiny. Your library should develop a confidentiality policy concerning patron borrowing information and publicize that policy to your patrons.

Third, the request may be overly broad and burdensome to the resources of the library. Irrespective of First Amendment concerns and statutory provisions, a subpoena may be quashed if it is unduly burdensome. Law enforcement officials may be conducting legitimate investigations, but the breadth and scope of their requests may trample important First Amendment rights without a compelling need for the requested information. Only a court can conduct the necessary balancing test to determine if there is a sufficiently compelling need for the information to justify the production of confidential patron borrowing information. The library should be involved in those court proceedings to fully apprise the court of the important First Amendment rights at stake if disclosure is permitted.

For example, in the case requesting patron information regarding books on childbearing, law enforcement officials were conducting a legitimate inquiry into a child abandonment case. There was, however, no reason to believe that the person who had abandoned a newborn baby had borrowed books from the library on childbearing prior to committing the criminal act. There was every reason to believe that people who had committed no crimes and borrowed books on childbearing would be subjected to interrogation based simply on their choice of reading material. The law enforcement officials were engaged in a fishing expedition. Recognizing the important First Amendment rights at stake and the failure of the law enforcement officials to demonstrate a compelling need for the information, the court in that case concluded that the librarian was not required to comply with the subpoena.

In some cases, law enforcement officials may have a legitimate need for patron borrowing information. In those cases, the court will issue a "court order" requiring the library to produce such information. A library should consult an attorney even if it receives a court order to determine the propriety of an appeal. If the library has not been involved in the proceedings before the court, it is likely that the judge would not have had a complete presentation of the important First Amendment issues. However, the library and librarian would not be violating any statutory protection of patron borrowing information by releasing information pursuant to a court order.

In the absence of a court order requiring a librarian to produce such confidential information, the librarian must maintain the confidentiality of patron borrowing information to protect the First Amendment rights at stake in such a situation and to comply with any applicable state or federal protections of such information. If you are confronted with a request for patron borrowing information, always seek legal advice.

SOURCE: Freedom to Read Foundation News 23, no. 2 (1998).

The fee-or-free debate

DECIDING WHETHER TO CHARGE USER FEES for access to certain library services, especially access to computers and the Internet, is a frequent debate in public and academic libraries. Charging fees goes against the grain of many librarians' natural instinct to provide free service. The following point-counterpoint was first developed by the National Commission on Libraries and Information Science in 1985, but the issues are still relevant.—*GME.*

Pro-fee arguments

1. Charging fees increases recognition of the value and importance of library services.

2. Fees encourage efficient use of public resources. Those who benefit from a given service should pay for its associated costs. An efficient pricing system allows the consumer the flexibility to choose from a variety of public goods and services and pay an amount that is in proportion to the amount consumed.

3. Fees promote service levels based on need and demand. The willingness of the public to pay for a service is a good indication of the public's demand for the service.

4. Fees encourage management improvements. Examples of such improvements include increased productivity, better time management, better organization and control, and the establishment of a management plan based on staffing, equipment, and available resources. Accurate financial control is an ongoing responsibility for the departments that administer fee-based facilities.

5. Fees limit waste and overconsumption. Setting a fee can lessen inefficient or wasted use of public facilities. Fees have a rationing effect on user consumption. Indeed, a pricing plan may be structured to limit "peak load" situations or encourage use in off hours.

6. Fees enhance investment in ongoing maintenance and repair of public facilities. Fees improve the level of facility maintenance in providing revenue dedicated to maintaining the service.

7. Fees encourage a better understanding of the financial limitations of the local government. Pricing public facilities indicates that there are financial limits to what government can provide.

8. Premium service should be provided only to those willing to pay a premium. Users should be given the choice of having these services. These are services not traditionally provided by the library.

9. The tradition of charging for services is part of American culture. Users pay fees for other public resources and services such as bridges, highways, museums and parks.

10. Fees control growth of and lower demand for service. If service demand is greater than capacity to meet that demand, fees help to discourage "frivolous" use of services.

11. Escalating service costs make user fees a necessity. Information has economic value. "Free" access to information is not the same as "without charge." Adopting a no-fee policy forces substantial limits to service. "Free" services are unrealistic in times of tight budgets.

12. Most library users can afford to pay a fee. The public library serves a relatively young, educated, middle-income segment of the population. Low-income persons make limited use of the library. A fee-based library would relieve the poor of the tax burden associated with the free library.

13. Without fees, public and academic libraries could not serve the larger community or nonresidents. Fees for nonresidents are equitable since this group does not pay the taxes levied on residents. Fees for nonstudents are equitable because this group pays no tuition.

14. Fees cover only a small portion of the total costs of service provision.

15. Fees for most services are simple and inexpensive to collect.

16. Local policy may require libraries to charge for services.

Anti-fee arguments

1. Library services are a public good. Free access is a fundamental right of each citizen.

2. The American tradition of free library service is damaged by charging fees. Fees are the beginning of the end of free library services.

3. Fees are illegal. (In some states, laws prohibit the charging of fees in some municipal or other public agencies. Lawyers need to be consulted.)

4. Fees are discriminatory. Only those who can afford to pay may use special services. Fees negate equal access to information. They discriminate against those users who either lack the resources to pay for services, or are unwilling to pay for services. An individual's access to information will be based on ability to pay rather than need.

5. Fees represent a form of double taxation. Users are charged first by taxes to operate public services and then by charges for special services.

6. Libraries will place emphasis on revenue-generating services. Libraries will shift from nonrevenue producing services to those which generate revenue, even if the nonrevenue services are vital to a part of society which cannot afford the fee.

7. Fees will have the long-term effect of reducing public support for libraries.

8. Fees might not be used to support library services. Revenues received from fees may be returned to the general revenue fund and allocated for nonlibrary uses.

9. The social benefits of library services are difficult to measure, therefore a fee cannot be efficiently assigned. Fees charged have been set by tradition and habit and not out of any analysis of market demands or costs.

10. It is difficult to define special and basic services and to distinguish between them. Should citizens be expected to pay extra for better fire department equipment, or additional police security assistance? Services once viewed as special are now viewed as basic.

11. Private- and public-sector markets are separate and should remain separate. The private sector should charge fees, reap profits, and compete in whatever manner is appropriate. Publicly funded libraries should provide services out of their budgets and should not provide services for a fee.

12. The costs of administering and collecting fees outweighs the financial benefits of fees.

13. Most users have little need for fee-based online services. Users don't need a speedy response; they simply want an answer. Fee-based online services are really a convenience for the librarian, not the user.

14. If the service cannot be provided without a fee, the service should not be provided.

15. Improvements within library management and delivery of services would diminish the need for fees.

16. There is considerable staff resistance to fees.

17. Charging for a service subjects libraries to liability risks because of the responsibilities implicit in providing a service for a fee.

SOURCE: *The Role of Fees in Supporting Library and Information Services in Public and Academic Libraries* (Washington: National Commission on Libraries and Information Science, 1985), pp. 9–10.

PATRON BEHAVIOR

Noisy and rowdy behavior

by the Fairfax County (Va.) Public Library

DISRUPTIVE AND UNSAFE BEHAVIORS include loud talking, loud laughter, crying, screaming, using media without earphones, running, jumping, playing games (e.g., hide and seek, tag, etc.), throwing things, pushing and shoving that may result in disturbing other patrons, injury to patrons or staff, or damage to library property. These behaviors may be exhibited by children, teenagers, or adults. Patrons should be informed of policies and the consequences of not adhering to them.

Responsibility. Action is to be taken when a staff member observes noisy and rowdy behavior or receives a patron complaint that such behavior is occurring. All complaints should be treated with courtesy and sympathy. When a staff member receives a complaint, before taking action, he/she should observe and evaluate the situation. If appropriate, the staff member should suggest to the patron who complains certain alternatives, such as the use of a quieter area of the library.

First contact. Request that the individual or group change behavior using nonjudgmental, factual statements. Speak in an even tone of voice, make friendly eye contact, and avoid negative body language. You may wish to offer assistance in locating materials. No warning should be issued at this time. Communicate the situation to other staff assigned to the area.

What you might say at this time: "Have you found what you need?" "May I help you?" "You may not be aware that the sound of your voices carries and that others who are working here have complained." "Please stop running (or shoving, etc.). You may hurt yourself or others." "Please do not climb on the security gate. It is electrical equipment."

Second contact. If problem behavior continues, a warning should be issued. Restate the problem, offer alternatives, and tell them they will be asked to leave. Alternatives to consider are:

a. Suggesting that large groups sit at more than one table.
b. Suggesting moving to another location within the library or outside the library.
c. Offering an unoccupied meeting room, following the meeting room booking procedures as appropriate for discussion groups. Inform the person in charge.
d. Requesting the accompanying adult to control his/her children.

What you might say at this time: "You were asked to be quieter 15 minutes ago, and the noise level is still too high. Perhaps you could break up into smaller groups or continue your conversations outside. You need to be quieter or you will be asked to leave." "If you don't stop running, you will be asked to leave."

Third contact. The person in charge, accompanied by the staff member, may back up the person handling the situation, or take the initiative at this point. Two or more staff members should be present when dealing with a group of more than three or four people.

An example of what to say: "You have been given opportunities to quiet down (stop running, etc.) and have not done so. Now I have to ask you to leave the library."

If all contacts fail to stop inappropriate behavior and the person(s) refuse(s) to leave, they should be informed that they are trespassing and the police will be called.

Call the police on your local nonemergency number, unless the person(s)

Crisis prevention tips

by Tom R. Arterburn

The following "10 Tips for Crisis Prevention," provided by the National Crisis Prevention Institute, demonstrate the kind of training librarians are receiving to deal with episodes ranging from a student demonstrating signs of substance abuse and acting irrationally or a disruptive user exhibiting signs of a serious psychological disorder:

1. **Be empathic.** Try not to be judgmental of your client's feelings. They are real—even if not based on reality—and must be attended to.

2. **Clarify messages.** Listen to what is really being said. Ask reflective questions, and use both silence and restatements.

3. **Respect personal space.** Stand at least two to three feet from the person acting out. Encroaching on personal space tends to arouse and escalate tension.

4. **Be aware of body position.** Standing eye-to-eye or toe-to-toe sends a message of challenge. Standing one leg length away and at an angle off to the side is less likely to provoke an individual.

5. **Permit verbal venting when possible.** Allow the individual to release as much energy as possible by venting verbally. If this cannot be allowed, state directives and reasonable limits during lulls in the venting process.

6. **Set and enforce reasonable limits.** If the individual becomes belligerent, defensive, or disruptive, state limits and directives clearly and concisely.

7. **Avoid overreacting.** Remain calm, rational, and professional. How you respond will directly affect the individual.

8. **Use physical techniques as a last resort.** Use the least restrictive method of intervention possible. Employing physical techniques on an individual who is only acting out verbally can escalate the situation.

9. **Ignore challenge questions.** When the client challenges your position, training, policy, etc., redirect the individual's attention to the issue at hand. Answering these questions often fuels a power struggle.

10. **Keep your nonverbal cues nonthreatening.** Be aware of body language, movement, and tone of voice. The more an individual loses control, the less he/she listens to your actual words. More attention is paid to nonverbal cues.

SOURCE: Tom R. Arterburn, "Librarians: Caretakers or Crimefighters?" *American Libraries* 27 (August 1996): 32–34.

9

become(s) abusive or threatening. If so, call the police on 911. If necessary, other staff may be asked to make the call to the police.

Complete incident reporting form and forward to appropriate officials.

Repeated incidents by the same person or group may require special action on the part of the branch manager; i.e., building rapport with school parent-teacher groups or guidance departments. It may help to learn names and addresses of patrons involved, but do not ask for ID. A discussion with parents of children or young adults involved could be helpful also.

Call your local police community relations office to request advice and assistance.

SOURCE: Fairfax County (Va.) Public Library, *Problem Behavior Manual* (Fairfax, Va.: Fairfax County Public Library, 1990), pp. 23–26.

Ten most wanted problem patrons

by Will Manley

WHICH TYPE OF PATRON is the most troublesome for library staffers?

In an article entitled "A Rogues' Gallery: Patrons Who Drive Librarians Nuts," Erma Denkinger identifies her "ten most wanted problem patrons."

1. The Magazine Hog. This person takes possession of up to 10 current magazines at a time and then retreats to a nook or cranny in the library where he cannot be easily found. This wouldn't be too bad if the magazines in question were things like *Ceramics Monthly* or *Microbiology Today,* but the magazine hog always lays claim to fun stuff like *People, Cosmo,* and *Rolling Stone.* This is definitely a problem for patrons who do not want to have to read *Ceramics Monthly* while waiting for the magazine hog to finish with *Cosmo.* Invariably the reference librarian is called in to referee, and invariably the hog says something like, "Has the Library Board passed a rule that says I cannot take 10 magazines at once?"

2. The Coupon Clipper. Where does it say in the Library Bill of Rights that patrons have a First Amendment right to clip coupons out of magazines and newspapers? There is nothing more maddening than to be reading an absorbing article about the marital problems of the Royal Family and come to a gap in the page where a coupon for Glad sandwich bags has been clipped.

3. The CD-ROM Printer Junkie. We should have seen this coming when we installed computers and printers in our libraries for public use. Let people print for free and they'll print to their hearts' delight—not because they need the information but because there is something hypnotic about watching a printer print endlessly and tirelessly. It's almost like watching a player piano in action. Some television commercials on knowing when to say when might be really helpful here.

4. The Sleeper. Don't misunderstand this one. Sleeping in a library is fine. All the latest research shows a direct link between sleep and mental acuity. Since we obviously need sleep to think clearly, it is not difficult at all to accept sleeping as a valid library activity. Sometimes, however, sleepers

become irresponsible, specifically when they fall asleep (face down) on magazines and newspapers that other patrons want to read. From a librarian's standpoint, this presents a very ticklish situation. Do you wake the patron up and risk the wrath of a person who has been abruptly returned from dreamland or do you try to extricate the newspaper ever so gently out from under the patron's nose?

5. People with Self-Contradicting Requests. Reference librarians are steeled to finesse their way through impossible requests: Where can I buy an HO scale model of the White House? How can I get grape Kool-Aid stains out of a white carpet? Is there a method by which I can really toilet train my one year-old in 24 hours? People don't really expect you to find anything helpful in these areas; they simply hope that they'll get lucky. That is not the case, however, when someone asks for a nice, clean wholesome contemporary novel with no sex, violence, or coarse language. Good luck meeting expectations on that one. Or how about the patron who wants an easy explanation of the meaning of "quantum physics." There ought to be one, but there isn't. It's a hopelessly complex subject. You feel very stupid.

6. Ten Minutes to Closing; Ten Sources to Go. It's 8:50 on a Monday evening—ten minutes to closing and your feet hurt, your stomach is growling, your head aches. It's Miller time—time to catch the second half of Monday night football. In anticipation you begin closing out your reference statistics, signing off your computer, and straightening up the chaos on the desk in front of you. Then this twerp marches in and asks you for ten sources for a term paper he is doing on the subject of the reproductive cycle of   the   fruit fly in tropical climates.

7. 1 Know the Mysteries of the Universe and of Your Next Door Neighbor. You're a nice person. You master the little things that separate good service from exceptional service. You get to know your patrons by name. You wish them a good morning and implore them to have a good day. Some of them think you mean it. So while you're trying to do some work they talk and they talk and they talk—about the big bang theory, the failure of representative democracy, and some of the weird stuff that your next-door neighbors have been hanging on their clotheslines while you've been at work staffing the reference desk. Only the latter is of the least bit of interest to you.

8. You're a Public Servant and You Have to Eat Garbage and Like It. Isn't it time that we retire the phrase "public servant" from our conversational vernacular? Wasn't the Emancipation Proclamation signed in 1863? Apparently some people don't seem to have noticed. These are the people who when you hesitate to read them 78 different stock quotations over the phone remind you that you are their tax-supported slave.

9. You're just a Typical Bureaucrat. It's hard in this day and age to think of a more stinging insult than to call someone a "typical bureaucrat." We'd rather be called a mass murderer, because at least mass murderers get some sympathy. ("He was so misunderstood. His father beat him, his mother abused

Pyro-patron policy

by John Hebert

1. Patrons already on fire when entering the library will not be allowed to register, renew, or use research materials.
2. Patrons already in the library exhibiting signs of Spontaneous Human Combustion (SHC) will be encouraged to stand in the parking lot until arrival of fire department equipment.
3. If a flaming patron wishes to wait inside for the fire department, especially in case of inclement weather, the senior circulation desk clerk will stand by with a minimum of one fire extinguisher.
4. Flaming patrons reaching a temperature of Fahrenheit 451 or greater will be removed (carefully) from the library before they ignite the collection.
5. It is permissible for library staff to notify a flaming patron previously unaware of his/her situation by diplomatically stating: "Hey! You're on fire!"
6. In all cases of flaming or potentially conflagrated patrons, library staff will:
   a. Remain calm.
   b. Evacuate other patrons as necessary.
   c. Evacuate library staff not needed for the immediate fire-fighting effort.
   d. Notify the fire department by the most expeditious means.
   e. If deemed necessary, run in circles while screaming, "Fire!"

SOURCE: John Hebert, "Pyro-Patron Policy," *The Unabashed Librarian*, no. 106 (1998), p. 4.

him, and his teachers never gave him a chance.") But bureaucrats get nothing but ridicule (can't get a job in the private sector), calumny (doesn't do anything all day but drink coffee and read books), and blame (the reason we had a four-trillion-dollar deficit is because we have too many bureaucrats). It's the hardest thing in the world, therefore, at the end of a long, stressful day not to strangle the patron who calls you a "typical bureaucrat" when you refuse to keep the library open an extra hour so that he can finish the work he is doing in the microfilm room.

10. Back Home Our Library Had "The Texas Chain Saw Massacre" on Videotape. The most effective way to insult a library is not to say, "This library stinks," but rather to say, "This library makes the one in my hometown look like the Library of Congress." No doubt about it, librarians are real sensitive about having their libraries compared unfavorably with other libraries, especially when the comparison is made on rather dubious grounds like who's got the best collection of disgusting horror movies. But some patrons just love to rub it in when we are unable to meet their rather plebeian tastes. It's maddening to be insulted by a cultural cretin.

SOURCE: Will Manley, *The Manley Art of Librarianship* (Jefferson, N.C.: McFarland, 1993), pp. 134–36. Reprinted with permission.

Minimizing sexual harassment

by Scott F. Uhler and Rinda Y. Allison

IF LIBRARIES COULD ELIMINATE sexual harassment entirely, they would. But since that is probably impossible, the next best thing is to reduce harassment as much as possible, which will also reduce the likelihood of success of any claims of sexual harassment brought against a library. There are numerous steps that can be taken to reduce harassment and the likelihood of success of such a claim. Reaction may not be enough; certain strategic actions are also advisable.

1. Have a complete policy. While having a policy won't prevent claims, it is a critical first step in demonstrating library efforts to reduce sexual harassment. The policy should clearly state that sexual harassment of employees or patrons will not be tolerated. The following should be part of the policy:

Include a definition of sexual harassment— not only the legal definition, but also examples of what the district considers harassing behavior. Sexual assault will be prohibited, of course, but the kinds of behavior that can lead to a hostile environment should also be identified. This could include unwelcome touching or communications, sexual gestures, comments, jokes, looks, and "stalking" behavior.

Emphasize that the library has a zero tolerance level for harassing behavior. If this is a new or newly enforced portion of your policy, be certain to notify employees of that fact, along with examples of the prohibited behavior and results of violating the prohibitions.

Make it clear that harassers will be disciplined.

Provide a complaint procedure that is easy to comply with. Be certain you have at least two individuals to whom complaints may be made (preferably one male and one female).

Consider having a two-level complaint system. The choice of complaint level is entirely the victim's. An informal complaint could result in separate discussions with victim and perpetrator and raise awareness of harassment and its effects. This would be helpful when a zero-tolerance policy is first enforced. A formal complaint would lead to a full investigation and report of its outcome. Confidentiality should be emphasized. The employee does not have to face the complained-of party at the investigation level.

Make it clear that false claims will be considered harassment themselves and will subject the maker to discipline.

Make it clear that retaliation for reported harassment will also be treated as harassment.

Consider and develop the investigation procedure in advance—before you receive a complaint—which should minimally include questioning of appropriate persons, full written documentation of findings and reporting the result to the victim. Remember, the investigation process is intended to recognize the rights of both parties. An adequate investigation process is critical to properly addressing the rights of both the accuser and the accused.

Institute appropriate discipline and follow through. Discipline should be graduated according to the seriousness and number of complaints.

Conclude your policy with a statement that it is not intended to operate as a contract or alter any employee's status as an at-will employee.

2. Have a strong unofficial policy preventing sexual harassment. This means that supervisors and administrators must be committed to identifying and eradicating sexual harassment. Without their commitment, the best offi-

9

472 THE WHOLE LIBRARY HANDBOOK 3

cial policy is useless. The attitude of administrative personnel is critical to the success of the policy.

3. Disseminate the policy to employees. The sexual harassment policy should have a prominent position (by reference and summarizing or by inclusion of the whole policy) in the employee handbook, along with the complaint and investigation procedure. Emphasize the library's zero tolerance position. Be certain that employees receive copies of the policy at the beginning of each year and post a copy at the library building(s).

4. Conduct in-service training on sexual harassment prevention, recognition, and response for administrators. Administrators need to know how to avoid or respond to harassing behavior against employees or themselves. They also need to know if and when action on their part is appropriate, and if all questioned behavior should be reported under the policy. The unofficial policy against sexual harassment noted above will make it easier for employees and administrators to discuss questions among themselves without feeling that they are nit-picking or looking for trouble.

5. Conduct employee assemblies or smaller meetings. Employees need to know about harassing behavior—how not to be a part of it, and how to report it if it occurs. They need to be encouraged to ask reasonable questions and need to know of whom to ask them. They also need to know that it is not always funny to jokingly perform harassing acts and that library response may be an investigation and swift disciplinary action.

6. Screen applicants for employment. All applicants for employment, and contractors and subcontractors who will work on or about library property, should be screened to the fullest extent possible.

7. Pursue discipline against harassers. A library cannot leave action against harassers to the court. It is essential that a prompt and thorough investigation be conducted as soon as possible. Even if criminal charges are brought against a harasser, the high standard of proof in criminal charges and, therefore, the uncertainty of conviction means that an alleged harasser may be back at the library if not convicted. By that time, the information necessary for a library discipline determination will be much harder to obtain.

8. Be alert to the rights of alleged harassers. While all of the above activities are taking place, it is imperative that libraries respect the rights of persons accused of harassment regardless of the outcome of the investigation.

9. Keep careful, thorough records. Document all acts taken to address sexual harassment issues. Note in your files when and how the policy is disseminated and to whom, and when training or information sessions are held and what is covered. Keep full records of complaints received, investigations made, and actions taken. Document your responses to rumors or questions of appropriateness that are brought forward. Keep investigation files confidential to the fullest extent possible.

10. Use your policy and procedures. Having carefully worded, explicit policy that addresses all kinds of possible issues and procedures is of no use if it is not used. The point of a policy is to reduce the likelihood of sexual harassment. It cannot do that if it is not used. The protection from liability that a well-established, officially adopted policy can give will not apply if the policy is ignored (*Praprotnik v. St. Louis*, 485 US 112, 108 S.Ct. 915, 928 (1988)).

SOURCE: Scott F. Uhler and Rinda Y. Allison, "A 10-Step Program: Reducing the Likelihood of Sexual Harassment and the Possibility of Successful Sexual Harassment Lawsuits," *Illinois Libraries* 79 (Spring 1997): 64–65. Reprinted with permission.

LEGISLATION

How to communicate with policymakers

WHETHER YOU DO IT IN PERSON, by phone or letter, communication is the key to being an effective advocate. The following tips for effective communication with public officials are offered by the ALA Washington Office.

1. **Be brief.** A legislator's time is limited. So is yours.

2. **Be appreciative.** Acknowledge past support and convey thanks for current action.

3. **Be specific.** Refer to local library and district needs.

4. **Be informative.** Give reasons why a measure should be supported.

5. **Be courteous.** Ask, do not threaten or demand. Be assertive but be polite.

Personal visits. Face-to-face discussion is the most effective means of communication. It is essential to establishing a solid working relationship if you do not already know each other. Schedule a meeting when the governing body is not in session—before pressures build up. Federal legislators generally have one or more district offices. Visits there will often be more convenient than in Washington. Members of Congress return periodically during recesses and between sessions. Check with the district office for a schedule.

Constituents are always welcome. Be sure you have a firm appointment. Use the district office to make local or capitol appointments. Get to know secretaries, administrative assistants, and other staff. Call the day ahead to confirm your appointment. When paying a visit, keep the delegation—librarian, trustee, friend, or other supporter—small enough for an easy exchange of views. Leave your card and any background materials. Follow up with a written thank you and any additional information.

Telephone calls. Once you have established a relationship, telephone calls are appropriate and easy. Regular contact with staff is possible and desirable. Limit your calls to the legislator. When should you call? Call to ask support before a hearing or floor vote, to ask for help with legislative colleagues or to convey urgent local concerns. Gauge how far to pursue by the reaction you get. Remember, it is more difficult for a legislator to temporize in a conversation than by letter.

Letters. These are the fuel which powers any legislative vehicle. Letters are read. Letters elicit responses. They represent votes. Each letter-writer is deemed to represent several like-minded if less highly motivated constituents. Letters may be formal or informal, typewritten or handwritten. They should be composed by you, giving reasons for your position and giving the legislator reasons to support it. If you are asking support for a particular bill, cite it by number and author, its title or subject.

Telegrams, mailgrams, e-mail. These are fast, easy ways to communicate with policymakers when the need for action is critical. Use Western Union's nationwide toll-free telephone number, (800) 325-6000. Low rates are available. You can also send messages to Congress electronically by e-mail or other online services.

9

Tips for writing to legislators

Legislators want to hear from their constituents and to be perceived as responsive. A well-written letter lets them know you care and can provide valuable facts and feedback that helps the legislator take a well-reasoned stand.

1. **Use the correct form of address.**

2. **Identify yourself.** If you are writing as a member of your library's board of trustees, as a school librarian, or as a Friend of the library, say so.

3. **Say why you're coming forward.** Let your elected officials know you are counting on them to make sure that all libraries—public, school, and college—have adequate funds and that libraries are central to developing the information superhighway.

4. **Be specific.** If budget cuts have forced your library to reduce hours, slash book budgets, or close branches, say so.

5. **Focus on the people** who count on these services. Cite real-life stories or examples of how the library makes a difference to people in your community.

6. **Use statistics sparingly.** A few well-chosen numbers can validate your argument. Too many can overwhelm.

7. **Be brief.** A one-page letter is easier to read—and more likely to be read.

8. **Be sure to include** your return address on the letter, not just on the envelope.

9. **Compound your letter's impact** by sending copies to your senators, city councilors and members of Congress. Be sure to give a copy to your library's campaign coordinator.

10. **Be strategic in your timing.** Know the budget cycles for your local and state governing bodies. Send letters to arrive early to maximize their impact.

SOURCE: ALA Washington Office.

COPYRIGHT

Copyright basics

COPYRIGHT IS A FORM OF PROTECTION provided by the laws of the United States (Title 17, U.S. Code) to the authors of "original works of authorship," including literary, dramatic, musical, artistic, and certain other intellectual works. This protection is available to both published and unpublished works. Section 106 of the 1976 Copyright Act generally gives the owner of the copyright the exclusive right to do or authorize others to:

- reproduce the work;
- prepare derivative works;
- distribute copies of the work; and
- display or perform the work publicly.

It is illegal for anyone to violate any of the rights provided by the copyright law to the owner of copyright. These rights, however, are not unlimited.

One major limitation is the doctrine of "fair use," which is given a statutory basis in Section 107 of the act. In other instances, the limitation takes the form of a "compulsory license" under which certain limited uses of copyrighted works are permitted upon payment of specified royalties and compliance with statutory conditions.

Who can claim copyright?

Copyright protection subsists from the time the work is created in fixed form. The copyright in the work of authorship immediately becomes the property of the author who created the work. In the case of works made for hire, the employer and not the employee is considered to be the author. The authors of a joint work are co-owners of the copyright in the work, unless there is an agreement to the contrary.

Copyright in each separate contribution to a periodical or other collective work is distinct from copyright in the collective work as a whole and vests initially with the author of the contribution.

What works are protected?

Copyrightable works include the following categories:
1. literary works;
2. musical works, including any accompanying words;
3. dramatic works, including any accompanying music;
4. pantomimes and choreographic works;
5. pictorial, graphic, and sculptural works;
6. motion pictures and other audiovisual works;
7. sound recordings; and
8. architectural works.

These categories should be viewed broadly. For example, computer programs and most compilations may be registered as literary works; maps and architectural plans may be registered as graphic works.

What is not protected by copyright?

Several categories of material are generally not eligible for federal copyright protection. These include, among others:

1. Works that have not been fixed in a tangible form of expression; for example, choreographic works that have not been notated or recorded, or improvisational speeches or performances that have not been written or recorded.

2. Titles, names, short phrases, and slogans; familiar symbols or designs; mere variations of typographic ornamentation, lettering, or coloring; mere listings of ingredients or contents.

3. Ideas, procedures, methods, systems, processes, concepts, principles, discoveries, or devices (as distinguished from a description, explanation, or illustration).

4. Works consisting entirely of information that is common property and containing no original authorship; for example, standard calendars, height and weight charts, tape measures and rulers, and lists or tables taken from public documents or other common sources.

9

How to secure a copyright

No publication or registration or other action in the U.S. Copyright Office is required to secure copyright. Copyright is secured automatically when the work is created. Before 1978, federal copyright was generally secured by the act of publication with notice of copyright, assuming compliance with all other relevant statutory conditions. U.S. works in the public domain on January 1, 1978, remain in the public domain. Federal copyright could also be secured before 1978 by the act of registration in the case of certain unpublished works.

The use of a copyright notice is no longer required under U.S. law, although it is often beneficial. Because prior law did contain such a requirement, the use of notice is still relevant to the copyright status of older works.

How long copyright protection endures

Works created on or after January 1, 1978, are ordinarily given a term enduring for the author's life plus an additional 70 years after the author's death. For joint works, the term lasts for 70 years after the last surviving author's death. For anonymous or pseudonymous works, the duration is 95 years from publication, or 120 years from creation, whichever is shorter.

Works originally created before January 1, 1978, but not published or registered by that date, are computed in the same way. In no case will the term of copyright for these works expire before December 31, 2002; for works published on or before December 31, 2002, the term will not expire before December 31, 2047.

Works originally created and published or registered before January 1, 1978. Under the 1909 act, copyright was secured for a first term of 28 years from the date of publication or registration, after which it could be renewed. The 1976 Copyright Act extended the renewal term to 47 years for copyrights subsisting on January 1, 1978, making these works eligible for a term of protection of 75 years. Public Law 105-298, enacted October 27, 1998, further extended the renewal term of copyrights still subsisting by an additional 20 years, providing for a renewal term of 67 years and total protection of 95 years.

Mandatory deposit

Although a copyright registration is not required, the 1976 Copyright Act established a mandatory deposit requirement for works published in the United States. In general, the owner of copyright or the owner of the exclusive right of publication has a legal obligation to deposit in the Copyright Office, within three months of publication in the United States, two copies (or phonorecords) for the use of the Library of Congress. Failure to make the deposit can result in fines and other penalties, but does not affect copyright protection.

For general information about copyright matters, contact the Library of Congress, Copyright Office, Publications Section LM-455, 101 Independence Ave., S.E., Washington, DC 20559-6000; (202) 707-3000; fax on demand (202) 707-2600; (www.loc.gov/copyright/).

SOURCE: U.S. Copyright Office, lcweb.loc.gov/copyright/circs/circ01.pdf.

Literacy 101 for the digital age

by Carla J. Stoffle

SUCCESS IN THE NEXT CENTURY—personal, professional, civic, and economic—will depend on the ability to participate intellectually in the emerging knowledge-based society. The knowledge explosion and economic changes brought about by the rapidly expanding information and telecommunication technologies require individuals to be skilled independent learners.

Futurists expect this information explosion, along with the transformation of the economy from a manufacturing and raw-materials base, to have a dramatic impact on the workplace. For example, the average 21st-century worker may need the skills to cope with as many as seven major employment changes in his or her lifetime.

The quality of daily life and full civic functioning will be similarly affected. For instance, individuals will need the ability to decipher a bombardment of messages in a number of media and styles, ranging from advertising to political debates, statistical reports, and public policy choices.

In the past, the basic ability to read and write, coupled with physical access to print-based resources, sufficed in securing reasonable employment and full civic participation. People also knew that they would probably fare even better with better-than-basic reading and writing skills (e.g., earned their college degree).

Libraries have always considered it their mission to provide and protect physical access to information for all, regardless of socioeconomic status, age, or educational attainment. In yesterday's print-based environment, some libraries (especially public, school, and community college libraries) moved beyond shouldering responsibility for ensuring simple physical access to providing basic literacy programs—rudimentary reading and writing—to ensure people intellectual access to library resources. And participating libraries were generally successful.

Academic libraries have traditionally interpreted their educational role as teaching students the basic skills necessary to find, evaluate, and use the information and information-retrieval tools they need to complete course assignments and build lifelong learning skills. In 1989, ALA's Presidential Committee on Information Literacy dubbed such skills "information literacy," defining it as: "able to recognize when information is needed and have the ability to locate, evaluate, and use effectively the needed information. . . . Ultimately information-literate people are those who have learned how to learn. They know how to learn because they know how knowledge is organized, how to find information, and how to use information in a way that others can learn from them. They are people prepared for lifelong learning, because they can always find the information needed for any task or decision at hand."

Other writers, most notably Hannelore Rader and William Coons ("Information Literacy: One Response to the New Decades," in *The Evolving Educa-*

tional Mission of the Library, edited by Betsy Baker and M. E. Litzinger, Chicago: ALA Association of College and Research Libraries, 1992), and Lawrence McCrank ("Academic Programs for Information Literacy: Theory and Structure," *RQ,* Summer 1992) expanded the list of skills information-literate people must possess to include the ability to:

- acquire and store one's own information (e.g., skills with databases, spreadsheets, and word processing);
- recognize and articulate public-policy issues relating to information (e.g., copyright, privacy, and privatization of government information);
- engage an information professional in a collaborative fashion as a resource as much as any impersonal tool.

With the rapid expansion of the Internet and electronic information sources in the last 10 years, Coalition for Networked Information Executive Director Clifford Lynch has identified in an internal CNI document a new concept, "information technology literacy," as: "an understanding of the technology infrastructure that underpins much of today's life; an understanding of the tools technology provides and their interaction with this infrastructure; and an understanding of the legal, social, economic, and public policy issues that shape the development of the infrastructure and the applications and use of the technologies."

Although Lynch distinguishes information-technology literacy from information literacy, it is clear that they are closely related. Certainly, he identifies both as absolutely necessary to function effectively in today's society. And whether information-technology literacy is added to the definition of information literacy or the two are merged under a new umbrella name—say, basic literacy in the digital age—these are skills that every academic library instruction program should impart.

An apple for the librarian

But how can academic libraries successfully assume the responsibility for producing "information literate" graduates under this expanded definition when they have had such mixed results in developing effective instructional programs—or even convincing individual campuses that such instruction is necessary? First, academic libraries will have to switch their focus from things to people. They will have to become "teaching libraries" that not only support campus curricula and research, but practice them themselves, as Alan E. Guskin, Joseph A. Boissé, and I argued in "The Academic Library as a Teaching Library: A Role for the 1980s" *(Library Trends,* Fall 1979).

Libraries will have to make education a priority. Rather than relegating education to an adjunct activity of reference or other library programs, we'll have to reallocate considerable resources to teaching and constantly assess the effectiveness of our programs against customer needs and learning. The library must develop performance measures and identify and quantify meaningful related outcomes.

We'll also have to extend our concept of librarians' role as educators to partnering with faculty in designing individual courses and curricula. Effective learning in higher education will require the integration of the new information and telecommunication technologies in the instructional program. By aiding faculty, the library will help produce information-literate citizens, an achievement that cannot be accomplished independent of the courses and curricula of the institution.

As essential as partnering with faculty is to the success of information literacy programs, partnerships with other institutional units and professionals are equally essential. The library can no longer make it alone. There are not enough resources. Librarians must work with computing professionals, staff in the campus teaching and learning centers, remedial institution staff, and student-service professionals who create and support the learning community that must exist outside the classroom.

Librarians must also modify their concepts of how they'll teach such skills. The successful instruction programs of tomorrow will be scaleable—that is, deliverable to large numbers of students without unreasonably increasing the number of librarians deployed as teachers.

Not only will we need to use the technology effectively to deliver instruction ourselves, but we'll also need to identify how support staff can help. Librarians must change the paradigm that applies technology to "their" work and apply the technology to improving the campus educational program instead.

Librarians must learn how to be effective teachers and designers of assignments in more systematic ways than the hit-or-miss methods in vogue today. In fact, librarians of the future should be expected to attend immersion train-

---

Nine Information-literacy standards for student learning

Information literacy

The student who is information literate accesses information efficiently and effectively.
The student who is information literate evaluates information critically and competently.
The student who is information literate uses information accurately and creatively.

Independent learning

The student who is an independent learner is information literate and pursues information related to personal interests.
The student who is an independent learner is information literate and appreciates literature and other creative expressions of information.
The student who is an independent learner is information literate and strives for excellence in information seeking and knowledge generation.

Social responsibility

The student who contributes positively to the learning community and to society is information literate and recognizes the importance of information to a democratic society.
The student who contributes positively to the learning community and to society is information literate and practices ethical behavior in regard to information and information technology.
The student who contributes positively to the learning community and to society is information literate and participates effectively in groups to pursue and generate information.

SOURCE: Information Power: Building Partnerships for Learning (Chicago: American Library Association, 1998).

9

ing programs such as the initiative Cerise Oberman describes in "The Institute for Information Literacy" *(College & Research Libraries News,* October 1998) as part of their professional development. The creation of instructional internships for students, as well as for practicing librarians, needs to be a regular part of the continuing-education program of the library. Also, a basic part of librarians' performance evaluations should be focused on their teaching effectiveness.

Finally, librarians will need to find ways to continually develop their own technological skills, including an aptitude for adapting technology to the needs of customers (knowledge management). If we cannot keep up, how can we teach students to do so? Librarians must, in effect, become information literate in the broadest sense and create educational programs to ensure their skills are up to date.

Fill the breach, or else

What happens if the academic library does not step up to this educational role? Most likely, other units on campus or commercial enterprises will fill the breach, widening the gap between the information haves and have nots as instructional costs mount and academe partners with groups that do not share commitment to education as a public good, as librarians do. Also, the library may be relegated to second- or third-class status in the campus priority list.

What if no one steps up to the challenge? America's future citizen-leaders will be ill-equipped to compete effectively in the information-based global economy of the next century. The consequences for the U.S. are enormous.

Am I calling for a radical expansion of librarians' recognition of information literacy as the new foundation for basic literacy and our critical role in imparting those concepts? Yes. Is the library profession up to it? I believe so.

SOURCE: "Literacy 101 for the Digital Age," *American Libraries* 29 (December 1998): 46–48.

Making your library literacy-ready

A PRIMARY GOAL of library-based literacy programs is to help adult-literacy learners become lifelong learners by enabling them to access all of the library's resources and services. To do this, make sure that your library's mission and its plan of service actively meet the needs of adult-literacy learners. Fully integrate literacy programs into the library environment by initiative at the administrative, middle-management, and public-service levels.

The following suggested activities can help accomplish this goal:

- Establish an ongoing committee of library staff at various levels to discuss long-range literacy projects, develop grant proposals, etc.
- Consider each staff development occasion as an opportunity to present literacy-related staff training.
- Invite literacy learners to participate in the library, such as presenting bilingual children's story times, mounting displays, and printing signs.

- Invite non-literacy library staff to literacy events such as "Learners Accomplishment Day" or "International Literacy Day."
- Create displays or bulletin boards about literacy in general public areas of the library (i.e., not just in the "Literacy" room.)
- Promote literacy resources and events in library newsletters, newspaper columns, media PSAs, library annual reports, and any other publicity about the library.
- Communicate the literacy curriculum to public service staff: Explain the library skills training received by learners and how theme-based classes may impact the learners' use of library collections.
- Anticipate the impact that the learner curriculum may have on non-literacy library staff: the need for tours, special access to collections, demand for material, etc.
- Take opportunities to sensitize non-literacy library staff to adult learner issues by sharing facts about literacy, the definition of functional illiteracy, and cultural awareness of the ethnic groups served in the program.
- Take the lead in your organization's diversity training program.
- Train a librarian at each site to serve as liaison to the literacy program.
- Ensure distribution of any current literacy information and referral tools (whether library-produced or other) to each library site.
- Make library literacy program information available at each public service station in bookmark or other handout format, in English and other languages as needed.
- Consider the needs of adult learners at all planning stages for technology, for collection development and for staff training.
- Provide staff training opportunities on Adult New Reader (ANR) and ESL, collection development and usage. Invite staff to try out literacy software.
- Establish a plain-language policy for all library-produced information. Literacy staff and learners could assist in editing publicity, bibliographies, Web sites, and signage for clarity.
- Encourage learners to meet library staff. Arrange for mock reference interviews as practice for learners (the librarians will be learning something, too!)
- Encourage library staff to serve as guest speakers in literacy classes.
- Encourage library staff to become volunteer literacy tutors.

There are many opportunities to promote general literacy issues, as well as specific literacy programs to library users and the public at large. First, non-literacy library staff need to have a foundation of knowledge regarding these issues and programs. Next, the staff must take advantage of opportunities to support adult learners in becoming lifelong library users. As an example, librarians often need to spend time assessing the library skills level of their clients. Interactions will be more effective and efficient when librarians know ahead of time which resources and skills the learners have been exposed to in the literacy program. Finally, staff should integrate literacy issues into the library's overall mission and planning process.

SOURCE: Adult Literacy Program, Onondaga County (N.Y.) Public Library, for the Literacy in Libraries Across America initiative; ALA Office for Literacy and Outreach Services.

ETHICS

Ethical guidelines for special collections

by the ACRL Rare Books and Manuscripts Division

THE SPECIAL COLLECTIONS LIBRARY should develop and make public a statement of its policies regarding the acquisition and disposal of items. Collection development policies and practices must be designed to improve the quality of the collections, providing clear guidelines while remaining flexible enough to permit effective response to unexpected opportunities. While the governing body bears final responsibility for the collections, including both acquisition and disposal, writing the collection development statement and rigorously assessing the pertinence of items to the collections or the library's programs should be the responsibility of the special collections librarian in consultation with appropriate collection development staff.

Additions to the collections. Materials collected by the special collections library should be relevant to the library's purposes and activities and consistent with the collection development policy.

Particular care should be taken to ensure that records of ownership and of any conditions agreed to at the time of acquisition are maintained. For full legal and ethical protection of the library and any other parties concerned, the types of records to be maintained and the forms of instruments of conveyance and other documentation to be employed should be developed in consultation with legal counsel.

The library should retain clear and detailed records of purchase of materials and ensure that donated materials are accompanied by an appropriate document transferring title, preferably unrestricted, but with any limitations clearly described in the instrument of conveyance. It should take particular care to ensure that materials accepted "on deposit" are accompanied by clear documentation of ownership, any conditions of deposit, and the rights and responsibilities of both library and owner, and that the documentation includes agreement of ownership and provision for disposition of the materials in case of abandonment.

In the light of the particular problems of sensitivity and confidentiality which may arise in connection with oral histories and other individual testimonies, the library should make sure these are collected only under the terms of clear written agreements controlling access to and use of such materials.

Deaccession of materials from the collections. In the deaccession of rare books and manuscripts, the special collections library must weigh carefully the interests of the public for which it holds the collections in trust, the interests of the scholarly and cultural community, and the institution's own mission. The institution must consider any legal restrictions, the necessity for possession of valid title, and the donor's intent in the broadest sense.

Procedures for the deaccession or disposal of materials must be at least as rigorous as those for purchasing and should be governed by the same basic principles. The decision to dispose of library materials must be made only after full and scrupulous consideration of the public interest and the needs of researchers; the process of deaccession should be carried out in as open and public a manner as possible.

Mandatory restrictions on disposition which accompanied a donation must be observed unless it can be shown clearly by appropriate legal procedures that adherence to them is impossible or substantially detrimental to the institution. When statements of donor's preferences accompanied the acquisition, any departure from them must be carefully considered and negotiated with the donor or the donor's heirs or settled by appropriate legal procedures.

Responsibility to the needs and reputation of the library requires that, in preparing for and accomplishing any deaccession, the special collections library must take care to define and publicly state the purpose of the deaccession and the intended use of monetary or other proceeds of the deaccession, to avoid any procedure which may detract from the library's reputation for honesty and responsible conduct, and to carry out the entire process in a way which will not detract from public perception of its responsible stewardship. The following points must be taken into consideration The library must ensure that the method of deaccession will result in furthering the agreed purpose of the deaccession, whether this be monetary gain or more appropriate placement of scholarly resources.

The deaccessioning library must disclose to the potential new owner or intermediary agent any action, such as the retention of a photocopy of the material, which may affect the monetary or scholarly value of the material.

To the fullest extent possible, the library must make public information on the disposition of deaccessioned materials.

The library must not allow materials from its collections to be acquired privately by any library employee, officer, or volunteer, unless they are sold publicly and with complete disclosure of their history.

Due consideration should be given to the library community in general when disposing of items. Sales to, or exchanges between, institutions should be explored as well as disposal through the trade.

Library-donor relations

Written policies governing relationships with donors must be provided to both staff and potential donors, governing such matters as authentication, referral to appraisers, and provision of information about tax regulations concerning donations.

Advice on authenticity or market value. Potential donors and others often seek guidance on the authenticity or market value of books and manuscripts. It is proper to assist the owner of materials in the use of reference tools for these purposes, but libraries must ensure that librarians exercise due caution when offering further advice, characterizing it as informed opinion only and explicitly warning against employing it in place of professional appraisal. Caution must be exercised in giving written certification of the authenticity or authorship of specific materials beyond the ordinary nonbinding statements made in the course of cataloging or normal reference work.

Tax matters. United States Internal Revenue Service regulations prohibit librarians from acting as appraisers of materials given to their institutions. While donors may be helped to find expert appraisers and tax advisers, special collections libraries must make certain to avoid any appearance of collusion

9

with potential donors to bypass provisions of the law regarding gifts. (*Note:* Librarians from other countries should consult the appropriate legal codes of their own countries for similar restrictions which may govern the provision of information on valuation, authenticity, and the like.)

Referrals. Special collections libraries should avoid any appearance of collusion or favoritism by requiring librarians to provide, whenever possible, more than one name in referring potential donors or other inquirers to appraisers, booksellers, and other persons who may be of assistance to them.

The book trade. Libraries and the book trade share a long tradition of mutually beneficial cooperation in building collections and a common concern for their preservation. Libraries and librarians must conduct all business with booksellers and vendors in an open and ethical manner.

Libraries whose budgetary constraints require that payments for goods or services be deferred to a future time should discuss these constraints with booksellers and vendors before acquisition processes are initiated or materials are ordered "on approval." Libraries which hold materials "on approval" or under exclusive offer have a responsibility to reach acquisition decisions quickly; they should also make certain that payment procedures, to the extent that these lie within their control, are as expeditious as possible.

Libraries which choose to dispose of deaccessioned materials by sale or trade to dealers rather than by public auction should offer them to a number of dealers for bid, wherever feasible. Institutional fiduciary responsibilities must outweigh library-dealer relationships that could permit the appearance or the reality of favoritism.

Libraries should respect the property rights of booksellers whose materials they have under consideration, handling the materials carefully, not making photocopies without permission of the bookseller, and making sure that material to be returned is packed securely and returned promptly and safely.

Objectivity and authenticity

The library must be scrupulous in the observance of objectivity in its provision of information about its collections and in the accuracy of its attestations of the authenticity of its materials.

Institutional practices must be designed so that exhibitions, publications, and public information are presented honestly and objectively. The stated origin of an item or attribution of a work must reflect thorough investigation and must promptly be changed in the event of accurate challenge. Library exhibitions and publications routinely address a wide variety of social, political, artistic, or scientific issues. Exhibitions from whatever source and on any subject can be appropriate, if approached objectively and without prejudice.

Special collections libraries must take special care in the representation and identification of forgeries and facsimiles. Items known or proven to be forgeries must be clearly identified as such. Special collections libraries which knowingly acquire forgeries must do so only for use, study, and display as forgeries.

In arranging for the manufacture and sale of facsimiles, reproductions, or other commercial items adapted from items in a library's collections, all aspects of the commercial venture must be carried out in a manner that will not discredit either the integrity of the library or the intrinsic value of the original object. Care must be taken to identify reproductions permanently for what they are, to record their source and degree of completeness, and to ensure the accuracy and high quality of their manufacture.

SOURCE: Standards for Ethical Conduct for Rare Book, Manuscript, and Special Collections Librarians, with Guidelines for Institutional Practice in Support of the Standards (Chicago: ALA Association of College and Research Libraries, 1992).

ASIS professional guidelines

by the American Society for Information Science

THE AMERICAN SOCIETY FOR INFORMATION SCIENCE recognizes the plurality of uses and users of information technologies, services, systems and products as well as the diversity of goals or objectives, sometimes conflicting, among producers, vendors, mediators, and users of information systems. ASIS urges its members to be ever aware of the social, economic, cultural, and political impacts of their actions or inaction.

ASIS members have obligations to employers, clients, and system users, to the profession, and to society, to use judgment and discretion in making choices, providing equitable service, and in defending the rights of open inquiry.

Responsibilities to employers, clients, system users

- To act faithfully for their employers or clients in professional matters
- To uphold each user's, provider's, or employer's right to privacy and confidentiality and to respect whatever proprietary rights belong to them, by limiting access to, providing proper security for, and ensuring proper disposal of data about clients, patrons, or users.
- To treat all persons fairly.

Responsibility to the profession

To truthfully represent themselves and the information systems which they utilize or which they represent, by

- not knowingly making false statements or providing erroneous or misleading information informing their employers, clients, or sponsors of any circumstances that create a conflict of interest;
- not using their position beyond their authorized limits or by not using their credentials to misrepresent themselves;
- following and promoting standards of conduct in accord with the best current practices;
- undertaking their research conscientiously, in gathering, tabulating, or interpreting data; in following proper approval procedures for subjects; and in producing or disseminating their research results;
- pursuing ongoing professional development and encouraging and assisting colleagues and others to do the same; and
- adhering to principles of due process and equality of opportunity.

9

Responsibility to society

To improve the information systems with which they work or which they represent, to the best of their means and abilities by
- providing the most reliable and accurate information and acknowledging the credibility of the sources as known or unknown;
- resisting all forms of censorship, inappropriate selection and acquisitions policies, and biases in information selection, provision, and dissemination;
- making known any biases, errors, and inaccuracies found to exist and striving to correct those which can be remedied.

To promote open and equal access to information, within the scope permitted by their organizations or work, and to resist procedures that promote unlawful discriminatory practices in access to and provision of information, by
- seeking to extend public awareness and appreciation of information availability and provision as well as the role of information professionals in providing such information;
- freely reporting, publishing, or disseminating information subject to legal and proprietary restraints of producers, vendors, and employers, and the best interests of their employers or clients.

Information professionals shall engage in principled conduct, whether on their own behalf or at the request of employers, colleagues, clients, agencies, or the profession.

SOURCE: American Society for Information Science, adopted May 1992. Reprinted with permission.

Code of ethics for archivists

by the Society of American Archivists

ARCHIVISTS SELECT, PRESERVE, and make available documentary materials of long-term value that have lasting value to the organization or public that the archivist serves. Archivists perform their responsibilities in accordance with statutory authorization or institutional policy. They subscribe to a code of ethics based on sound archival principles and promote institutional and professional observance of these ethical and archival standards.

Archivists arrange transfers of records and acquire documentary materials of long-term value in accordance with their institution's purposes, stated policies, and resources. They do not compete for acquisitions when competition would endanger the integrity or safety of documentary materials of long-term value, or solicit the records of an institution that has an established archives. They cooperate to ensure the preservation of materials in repositories where they will be adequately processed and effectively utilized.

Archivists negotiating with transferring officials or owners of documentary materials of long-term value seek fair decisions based on full consideration of authority to transfer, donate, or sell; financial arrangements and benefits; copyright; plans for processing; and conditions of access. Archivists discourage unreasonable restrictions on access or use, but may accept as a condition of acquisition clearly stated restrictions of limited duration and may occasionally suggest such restrictions to protect privacy. Archivists observe faithfully all agreements made at the time of transfer or acquisition.

Archivists establish intellectual control over their holdings by describing them in finding aids and guides to facilitate internal controls and access by users of the archives.

Archivists appraise documentary materials of long-term value with impartial judgment based on thorough knowledge of their institutions' administrative requirements or acquisitions policies. They maintain and protect the arrangement of documents and information transferred to their custody to protect its authenticity.

Archivists protect the integrity of documentary materials of long-term value in their custody, guarding them against defacement, alteration, theft, and physical damage, and ensure that their evidentiary value is not impaired in the archival work of arrangement, description, preservation, and use. They cooperate with other archivists and law enforcement agencies in the apprehension and prosecution of thieves.

Archivists respect the privacy of individuals who created, or are the subjects of, documentary materials of long-term value, especially those who had no voice in the disposition of the materials. They neither reveal nor profit from information gained through work with restricted holdings.

Archivists answer courteously and with a spirit of helpfulness all reasonable inquiries about their holdings, and encourage use of them to the greatest extent compatible with institutional policies, preservation of holdings, legal considerations, individual rights, donor agreements, and judicious use of archival resources. They explain pertinent restrictions to potential users, and apply them equitably.

Archivists endeavor to inform users of parallel research by others using the same materials, and, if the individuals concerned agree, supply each name to the other party.

As members of a community of scholars, archivists may engage in research, publication, and review of the writings of other scholars. If archivists use their institution's holdings for personal research and publication, such practices should be approved by their employers and made known to others using the same holdings.

Archivists who buy and sell manuscripts personally should not compete for acquisitions with their own repositories, should inform their employers of their collecting activities, and should preserve complete records of personal acquisitions and sales.

Archivists avoid irresponsible criticism of other archivists or institutions and address complaints about professional or ethical conduct to the individual or institution concerned, or to a professional archival organization.

Archivists share knowledge and experience with other archivists through professional associations and cooperative activities and assist the professional growth of others with less training or experience. They are obligated by professional ethics to keep informed about standards of good practice and to follow the highest level possible in the administration of their institutions and collections. They have a professional responsibility to recognize the need for cooperative efforts and support the development and dissemination of professional standards and practices.

9

Archivists work for the best interests of their institutions and their profession and endeavor to reconcile any conflicts by encouraging adherence to archival standards and ethics.

SOURCE: Society of American Archivists, adopted 1992. Reprinted with permission.

GLOBAL CONCERNS

How to go global

by Barbara J. Ford

THE NEW ERA OF GLOBALIZATION demands that we reexamine our professional roles, responsibilities, and values. As librarians, we bring skills and expertise that can help our communities and communities around the world deal with new political, social, and economic realities. Here are 10 areas where libraries can lead our communities in "going global."

Celebrate America's diversity. Reach out to community or campus groups reflecting other cultures and countries and celebrate that diversity with speakers, exhibits, films, and special performances. Plan programs, slide shows, displays, and fairs around international holidays, United Nations, and world commemorative days. Invite returned Peace Corps volunteers, Library Fellows, Fulbright Scholars, or others with international expertise to speak.

Expand and diversify your library's collection of multicultural and multilingual materials. Add United Nations materials and publications to your collection. Include materials on language learning. Host reading groups with an international focus.

Get connected. The Internet provides opportunities to connect to other cultures. Check out recommended international sites on the ALA Web page (www.ala.org/GoGlobal!/sites.html). Provide Web sites of international libraries, U.N. agencies, and other bodies that promote learning about other countries, cultures, international travel, and global cooperation.

Persuade policymakers that libraries are an investment in a more literate, productive, and globally competitive nation. Invite them to your library to see how students and people of all ages are getting help with their jobs and studies. Encourage trustees and Friends to participate in state and national library legislative days.

Promote public awareness of global resources at your library during National Library Week—or any week. Contact the ALA Public Information Office for a free National Library Week tip sheet. Watch for handsome new posters, T-shirts, and other promotional items in the fall ALA Graphics catalog. Also watch the ALA Web page for monthly suggestions of multicultural celebrations and programs.

Learn more about global information issues, such as copyright, and how they affect your library and libraries around the world. Become a member of ALA's International Relations Round Table or International Relations Committee. Become active in ALA divisions with a special focus on international issues such as preservation. Indulge in free membership and newsletters of UNESCO's Network of Associated Libraries.

Connect with libraries in other countries. If your city has a sister-city program, seek sponsorship for an exchange of library staff. Work with international library colleagues to organize a conference or training program or focus your state library conference on international issues. Plan now to attend the International Federation of Library Associations and Institutions (IFLA) conference in 2001 in Boston. Contact World Wise Schools to connect with a Peace Corps volunteer.

Leave home. Join one of the ALA-organized delegations to international book fairs. Apply for a Fulbright Scholarship, overseas fellowship with the Women in Development Fellows Program, or other grants from organizations that support international librarianship. Join the Peace Corps, U.N. Volunteers, or other international volunteer organizations.

Support libraries overseas by offering books, journals, and other materials to a donation program, choosing books with multicultural themes or role models in other countries. Adopt an international library partner on your own or through IFLA. Become a resource person or correspondent with librarians or library school students abroad.

Increase your global awareness. Learn another language. Take a course in the literature, history, or culture of another country or region. Become a literacy volunteer to teach English as a second language to refugees and immigrants. Read more about the social, economic, political, health, and environmental issues affecting the world. Join a study tour abroad. Use your information skills to assist international human rights groups and promote intellectual freedom worldwide.

SOURCE: Barbara J. Ford, "How to Go Global," *American Libraries* 28 (October 1997): 35.

Organizations that donate books overseas

A SMALL NUMBER OF organizations distribute books to other countries. Many of them distribute books overseas at no cost to the donating library or person other than shipping costs to the U.S. facility. Quite a few are volunteer organizations. If you are interested in contributing books or journals, always query the organization first.—*GME.*

American Assistance for Cambodia, P.O. Box 2716, GPO, New York, NY 10116. Needs English-language medical and nursing textbooks and journals from 1990 on.

The Asia Foundation, Books for Asia, 465 California St., 14th Floor, San Francisco, CA 94104; (415) 982-4640; fax (415) 392-8863; info@ asiafoundation.org; (www.asiafoundation.org). Division of the Asia Foundation, 501(c)(3) non-profit established in 1954. Ships over 500,000 books per year to various Asian nations. Donations should be sent to the BFA Warehouse at 451 Sixth St., San Francisco, CA 94103.

Association pour la Diffusion Internationale Francophone de Livres, Ouvrages, et Revues, 5 rue de la Boule Rouge, 75009 Paris, France; +33 (1) 47 70 1083; fax +33 (1) 47 70 0769; afal@starnet.fr; (www.starnet.fr/adiflor/). Distributes French-language materials to Africa, Latin America, and Central and Eastern Europe.

Book Aid International, 39-41 Coldharbour Lane, Camberwell, London SE5 9NR, England; +44 (171) 733 3577; fax +44 (171) 978 8006; info@ bookaid.org; (www.bookaid.org). Distributes to developing countries in Africa. Books for children and young adults; fiction; general nonfiction; primary, secondary, and university textbooks less than 15 years old.

Books for Africa, 5233 Silver Maple Circle, Minneapolis, MN 55343; (612) 939-9889; fax (612) 933-6966; info@booksforafrica.org; (www.booksforafrica. org). Sends books to various countries in Africa; books should be new or barely used; textbooks should be no more than eight years old; atlases no more than five years old; encyclopedias should be the most recent edition.

Books for All, Brunhildenstrasse 34, D-80639 München, Germany; +49 (89) 172383, fax +49 (89) 260 7896. A project of the Children's Libraries Section of IFLA. Converts donations into UNESCO unit of money given to institutions in developing countries for the purchase of children's books.

Books for the Barios, Inc., Whitman Road, Suite D, Concord, CA 94518-2355; (510) 687-7701; fax (510) 687-8298; books4rp@ix.netcom.com. Distributes recent, basic medical and nursing texts to impoverished areas in the Philippines. Patient-oriented literature is especially welcome.

Books to Schools in Ghana, 385 Park Place, Brooklyn, NY 11238. Distributes books and supplies to rural primary and secondary schools in Ghana, West Africa. Books appropriate for primary and secondary school students.

Bridge to Asia, 450 Mission Street, Suite 407, San Francisco, CA 94105-2521; (415) 356-9041; fax (415) 356-9044; asianet@bridge.org; (www.bridge. org/Books.html). Accepts new or used books; no American history, foreign language, or lifestyle (i.e., diet, pop psychology) books accepted; book list not required, but would be appreciated.

Brother to Brother International, Inc., 4025 S. McClintock, Suite 210, P.O. Box 27634, Tempe, AZ 85285-7634; (602) 345-9200; fax (602) 345-2747; bbi@worldvision.org; (www.bbi.org). BBI only collects donations in Arizona.

The Brother's Brother Foundation, 1501 Reedsdale St., Suite 3005, Pittsburgh, PA 15233-2341; (412) 321-3160; fax (412) 321-3325; bbfound@aol.com; (www.brothersbrother.com/educate.htm). Distributes to developing countries, especially the Philippines, Jamaica, and Ghana. Call before sending donations. New books. Primary, secondary, and college level textbooks; professional reference and medical books. Books are donated usually at 20 copies per title ranging from 110-500 titles. BBF prefers to work with schools, organizations, etc., capable of utilizing large quantities of books—at least 20,000.

California-Indonesia Education Foundation, 2650 Ryan Road, Concord, CA 94518; (510) 682-5563; fax (510) 682-5538. Distributes medical journals and texts to universities and medical schools in Indonesia.

Canadian Organisation for Development through Education, 321 Chapel St., Ottawa, Ontario K1N 7Z2, Canada; (613) 232-3569; fax (613) 232-7435; codehq@codecan.com. Book distribution network for Africa and Belize.

Cuba-America Jewish Mission, c/o June Safran, 444 34th Street, Oakland, CA 94609; (510) 526-7173; June_B._Safran@bmug.org; (www.jewishcuba.org/cajm/cajm.html). Spanish-language literature and philosophy for all ages. Intended to revitalize Jewish life in Cuba.

Darien Book Aid Plan, Inc., 1926 Post Rd., Darien, CT 06820; (203) 655-2777; bookaid@aol.com; (www.darien.lib.ct.us/dba/). Mails books to institutions and libraries around the world; distributes through Peace Corps volunteers.

Donohue Group, Inc., 185 Silas Deane Highway, Wethersfield, CT 06109; (860) 529-2938; fax (860) 529-5849; office@dgiinc.com; (www.dgiinc.com). Sends books directly to libraries in Eastern Europe and the former Soviet Union.

International Book Bank, 815 Central Ave., Suite F, Linthicum, MD 21090; (410) 636-6895; fax (410) 636-6898; ibbusa@worldnet.att.net; (puma.dpg.devry.edu/~sslechta/). Mails books to schools, libraries, and educational institutions in selected countries in Eastern Europe.

International Book Project, Inc., 1440 Delaware Ave., Lexington, KY 40505; (606) 254-6771; fax (606) 255-5539; ibp@iglou.com. Books less than 10 years old; journals less than 5 years old. Call for donation procedures before sending. Preprimary through university-level publications including a wide variety of library books, and medical and nursing books. Distributes to needy in the U.S. and overseas (mostly overseas).

Lagos Business School, Patricia O. Idahosa, Librarian, 35 Adeola Hopewell Street, P.O. Box 73688, Victoria Island, Lagos, Nigeria; +234 (1) 262 0993; fax +234 (1) 262 0996; lbs@gacom.net. Accepts books and journal donations.

Medical Books for China International, 13021 East Florence Avenue, Sante Fe Springs, CA 90670-4505; (800) 554-2245, (562) 946-8774; fax (562) 946-0073; mbci@aagl.com; (www.aagl.com/mbcifrm.htm). Needs books, journals, audio and videotapes, and medical equipment. Distributes in the People's Republic of China. Medical books and journals from 1985 current.

Operation Bookshelf, 37 Drake Rd., Scarsdale, NY 10583; (914) 723-0024. Sends books to libraries and schools worldwide.

Philippine Library Materials Project Foundation, Fr. W. Masterson Avenue (Manresa), P.O. Box 277, Cagayan de Oro City 9000, Philippines; fax +63 (8822) 72-83-56; plmp@xu.edu.ph. Distributes English-language books and journals in the Philippines.

Polish American Congress, 5711 North Milwaukee Avenue, Chicago, IL 60646; (773) 763-9944; fax (773) 763-7114; pacchgo@interserv.com; (www.polamcon.org). Distributes textbooks to university and hospital libraries in Poland. Recent needs include medical and technical books, and English-language educational materials.

Project Handclasp, c/o Commander M. C. Tavelson, Naval Base, San Diego, CA 92132; (619) 532-1492. Uses empty cargo space on U.S. Navy ships to transport educational and humanitarian materials to Navy ports of call.

Project HOPE, International Textbook Distribution Program, Attn.: Scott

9

Crawford, Route 255, Millwood, VA 22646; (800) 544-4673; fax (540) 837-1813; scrawford@projhope.org; (www.projhope.org). Sends primarily medical and nursing texts; area of distribution is worldwide.

Sabre Foundation, Inc., 872 Massachusetts Ave., Suite 2-1, Cambridge, MA 02139; (617) 868-3510; fax (617) 868-7916; sabre@sabre.org; (www.sabre.org/BOOKS.html). Sends college- and professional-level educational materials to 18 countries in Eastern Europe, Asia, and Africa.

UNI-BOOK (Universal Book Effort), 5620 Williams Lake Rd., Deming, WA 98244; (360) 592-2382; fax (360) 592-9042. Distributes books to libraries in Africa, Asia, and the former Soviet Union.

United States Book Exchange, 2969 West 25th Street, Cleveland, OH 44113; (216) 241-6960; fax (216) 241-6966; usbe@usbe.com; (www.usbe.com). Distributes to libraries in underdeveloped countries and libraries which have severe budgetary problems in all other locations. Medicine, science, and technology, including information processing. Periodicals in all academic fields.

World Bank Volunteer Services Book Project, 1818 H St., N.W., Room NB1-105, Washington, DC 20433; (202) 473-8960; fax (202) 522-0301; wproject@worldbank.org. Distributes to developing countries. Needs new and used medical texts (less than 10 years old) and journals (less than 5 years old). Encyclopedias less than 20 years old. Fiction (paperback and hardcovers). Publications on economics and international development.

World Vision, 34834 Weyerhauser Way South, Federal Way, WA 98063-9716, (206) 815-2267. Sends books to educational programs, schools, and institutions in Africa and Latin America.

SOURCE: American Libraries 28 (October 1997):54; SLA Web site at www.sla.org/membership/irc/bkdonate.html; SUNY/Buffalo Health Sciences Library Web site at ublib.buffalo.edu/libraries/units/hsl/cms/donation.html; World Library Partnership Web site at RTPnet.org/~wlp/resource.htm.

LIBRARIANA
CHAPTER TEN

"A librarian's life is the life for me
For there's nothing at all to do, you see,
But to sit at a desk and read new books,
And admire yourself, and think of your looks.
To questioning souls one can tartly say:
'I can't be bothered with *you* to-day,
For I haven't finished this novel. See?'
A librarian's life is the life for me."

—William Fitch Smyth, "A Librarian's Life" (1910)

The –ana

by Bill Katz

A CLOSE COUSIN TO THE FLORILEGIUM and anthology, the "–ana" is often used as a noun suffix to indicate a collection of materials about a given subject or person. Two examples: *Americana* or *Scaligerana*. Today, although rarely used, it retains its original Latin meaning of a collection of information, usually around a person, place, or thing, although numerous early –anas were scattered books of facts, epigrams, quotes, etc. In the best single article on the history and development of the –ana, F. P. Wilson (*Huntington Library Quarterly*, 1940) points out that Samuel Johnson (right) believed the term came from the "last syllables of . . . titles; as Scaliger*ana*, Thuani*ana*; they are loose thoughts, or casual hints, dropped by eminent men, and collected by their friends." The –ana tends to be associated with conversation and things unpublished, but the suffix –ana was extended to include a writer's miscellaneous

papers, like the *Baconiana* of 1679, or anecdotes about somebody, like the *Addisoniana* (1803), most of which were collected from printed sources.

Some believe the earliest examples of –ana may be found in the Old Testament's *Book of Proverbs*. At any rate, the *Proverbs* served as a model for the collections of the Middle Ages. Francis Bacon (1561–1626) held that while the description "–ana" was late to the language, its roots could be traced back to the Greeks. Aristotle (384–322 B.C.) in his *Topica* (i.e., 14.105) alludes to –ana when he says, "We should select also from the written handbooks of arguments. . . . In the margin too [of the handbook or commonplace book] one should indicate the opinions of individual thinkers." Early versions of –ana could be found in the collected conversations of Epictetus (50–138) set down by his disciple Arrian in the *Encheiridion* and *Discourses;* as well as Pythagoras six centuries before (c. 582–507 B.C.). Although nothing is known of the pre-Socratic Greek philosopher's writings, knowledge of him and his ideas comes from followers. The short, instructive sayings of Cicero (106–43 B.C.) are the subject of a book by Julius Caesar. In Plutarch's *Parallel Lives* (first translated into English by Sir Thomas North (1579)), Plutarch (c. 46–120) appears to have depended upon now lost –ana.

The first successful published book of –ana probably was the 1666 issue of *Scaligeriana*, which highlighted the conversation of Joseph Scaliger (1540–1609), the Dutch historian. Here, as in –ana to follow, the reader found conversation and table-talk between Scaliger and his friends, witticisms, anecdotes, and almost anything else that brought out the personality of the scholar. The best French collection of –ana is the collected conversations and witticisms of Giles Ménage (1613–1692). The *Ménagiana* (1693) is a typical apparently uncoordinated collection of philosophical speculation, classical quotes, verse, and epigrams that was reprinted in 1789–1791 and represented several times thereafter, often in part in other works.

By the early 18th century the French –ana fell out of favor and, as F. P. Wilson points out, "they were so discredited that collectors of them preferred to disguise their wares under such titles as 'Recueils' or 'Melanges.'" Much was due to the habit of compilers of making up conversations and anecdotes; or, at best, badly copying and transcribing thoughts and words; or, at worse, putting into the person's mouth the sayings and writings of others conveniently copied from earlier –ana. Plagiarism became common. The English looked more favorably than the French upon the –ana, and by 1750 the form was widely represented.

A fine example of the –ana is to be found in the collection of writing of Robert Southey and Samuel Taylor Coleridge. First published in 1812, these short pieces were simply titled *Omniana*. The pieces, closer to essays than short comments and bits of conversation, covered everything from "Welsh names" to "A librarian" Coleridge knew. Actually, the book was more a collection of essays than –ana, but the authors were wed to the old term.

Gradually the various types of collections of wit and wisdom joined to become several well-known and continuous forms. Out of the florilegium, from the –ana, came the essay. The tradition begins with Montaigne (1580) and Francis Bacon (1597), both of whom were familiar with and used the traditional forms to build essays. A related literary work, the anthology, might be said to be an umbrella heading for all of the earlier and later collections.

Today, the essay and the anthology are drawn upon for reference answers, but 19th-century developments and changes in the earlier forms—from the –ana to collections of anecdotes—are of more immediate importance because from them came the familiar ready reference book: the book of quotations.

SOURCE: Bill Katz, *Cuneiform to Computer: A History of Reference Sources* (Lanham, Md.: Scarecrow Press, 1998), pp. 77–79. Reprinted with permission.

Famous librarians' favorite books

WHAT DO PROMINENT LIBRARIANS have to say about their favorite books? In previous editions of *The Whole Library Handbook*, library leaders have identified the publications that have given them great enjoyment or have significantly affected their professional or personal lives and philosophies. This edition adds the treasured readings of seven new individuals to the corpus. I defined the term "book" as loosely as possible, to allow them to select everything from incunabula to Web sites.—*GME.*

KHAFRE K. ABIF, Head of Children's Services, Mount Vernon (N.Y.) Public Library.

1. Joseph A. Baldwin (aka Kobi Kazembe Kalongi Kambon), *The African Personality in America: An African-Centered Framework* (1992). Listening to this Afrikan-centered scholar-professor's lectures during a course in black psychology in spring 1990 at Florida A&M University was the most profound in developing my Afrikan manhood.

2. Carter G. Woodson, *Mis-Education of the Negro* (1933). This treasured classic is just as poignant today as it was 67 years ago.

3. Alex Haley and Malcolm X, *The Autobiography of Malcolm X* (1976). His voice, philosophy, experience, and intelligence speak volumes.

4. Tony Martin, *Literary Garveyism: Garvey, Black Arts, and the Harlem Renaissance* (The New Marcus Garvey Library, no.1), (1983). The work of Marcus

10

Garvey for self-reliance and self-determination of Afrikan people throughout the diaspora set a high mark for all nationalists of this century.

5. John Mason, *Four New World Yoruba Rituals* (1985). I can never say that I have finished this book; it is a daily ritual which assists me with ancestor commemoration and the traditions of Orisha.

6. Teresa Y. Neely and Khafre K. Abif, *In Our Own Voices: The Changing Face of Librarianship* (1996). The experience of editing and writing with Teresa taught me a great deal about publishing. What a project this was! We call it the birth of a 410-page baby.

7. Virginia Hamilton, *The People Could Fly: American Black Folktales* (1985). This work evokes emotion and triumph for the memory of my family's struggle up from slavery.

8. Jacqueline Woodson, *From the Notebooks of Melanin Sun* (1995). Woodson provides us with a tool for an open discussion of issues not addressed by my community.

9. Patricia Polacco, *Chicken Sunday* (1992). This story reminds me of childhood, college breaks, and visits home. My MaDear, Barbara J. Page, has filled my life with wonderful Chicken Sundays.

10. Trish Cooke, *So Much* (1994). A "Babies In The Library" program is not complete without an impassionate and playful reading.

W. LEE HISLE, Associate Vice-President, Learning Resource Services, Austin (Tex.) Community College.

1. Harper Lee, *To Kill a Mockingbird* (1960). My first adult novel—read in the Seventh Grade. I didn't know what "rape" meant. Its lessons of loyalty, kindness, bravery in the face of adversity, and equality have stood the test of nearly 40 years. Atticus Finch for President!

2. Cormac McCarthy, *Blood Meridian: or, The Evening Redness in the West* (1985). A bloody, dark, and disturbing book set in a harsh southwestern landscape full of murderously horrific images. The good guys are terrible; the bad guys are really out there. Poetic ultraviolence where Melville, Faulkner, Peckinpah, and the Old Testament mingle in the same dust. I loved it.

3. William Faulkner, *Light in August* (1932). God, what a writer. The human quality of redemption through forgiveness crystallized in the tragic everyman, Joe Christmas. I've read this book repeatedly; it just gets stronger.

4. William Gibson, *Neuromancer* (1984). Gibson makes no apologies or explanations for his brilliantly realized cyberworld of the near future. If you don't get it, Mr. Jones, well, there isn't any help on the way. When I finished this one, I simply starting reading it again immediately. I didn't want to surface.

5. John Steinbeck, *In Dubious Battle* (1936). One summer I read all the Steinbeck I could find. This one started the onslaught and changed my politics. Workers unite!

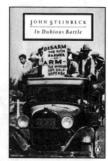

6. E. Annie Proulx, *The Shipping News* (1993). I couldn't put it down. I cried, I feared, I lived in Quoyle's skin, and finally I rose with his emergence. An incredible feat of writing that haunts the reader as it illuminates the human condition.

7. Robert Caro, *The Years of Lyndon Johnson: The Path to Power, Vol. 1* (1982). This book rooted Texas into my heart. Read "The Sad Irons" chapter and understand the soul of LBJ and his beautiful Hill Country. LBJ believed that if you do all you can do, success will surely follow. Words to live by.

8. Joseph Heller, *Catch 22* (1961). Finally, life is absurd—and hilarious.

9. Monroe C. Beardsley, *Thinking Straight: Principles of Reasoning for Readers and Writers* (1966). Ah, Logic. My first religion. This was the text in my all-time favorite academic class.

10. Robert Pirsig, *Zen and the Art of Motorcycle Maintenance: An Inquiry into Values* (1974). The pursuit of quality defined my first years as a librarian—and has shadowed every part of life since. This exploration of self and soul is a guidebook to a life worth living.

KATHLEEN DE LA PEÑA McCOOK, former Dean, School of Library and Information Science, University of South Florida, Tampa.

1. Peter Guralnick, *Last Train to Memphis* (1994). Biography of Elvis Presley's first 23 years. Stands for the legacy of the century's foremost musician—and my favorite.

2. *The Catholic Worker* (est. 1933), along with Dorothy Day, *The Long Loneliness* (1952), and William D. Miller, *A Harsh and Dreadful Love: Dorothy Day and the Catholic Worker Movement* (1970). *The Catholic Worker* and the community it fostered are guideposts for living. This legacy has been preserved at the Marquette University Archives.

3. Willa Cather, *Death Comes to the Archbishop* (1927), and Paul Horgan's *Lamy of Santa Fe* (1975). Jesuit bishop Juan Bautista Lamy of Santa Fe, civilizer of my mother's girlhood home, New Mexico, led a life of scholarly activism and faith.

4. Nelson Algren, *The Man with the Golden Arm* (1949). Willa Cather's work evokes my mother; Nelson Algren's my father, lost to the *Neon Wilderness* (1947). And what more can be said of a writer than Simone de Beauvoir was buried wearing his ring?

5. Marjory Stoneman Douglas, *The Everglades: River of Grass* (1947). My husband Bill grew up in the Florida Keys in Marathon, a community of less than 500, in the days before air conditioning. Mrs. Douglas' book evokes the Florida of Bill's youth when he camped off the Tamiami Trail in the Everglades. It is the Florida he has given to me.

6. Joyce Carol Oates, *Do With Me What You Will* (1973). All of Oates's books amaze me, but this one most of all.

7. Thomas Mann, *Joseph and His Brothers* (H.T. Lowe-Porter transl., 1974 ed.). The deep well of the past explored in the prose of thought.

8. John Kennedy Toole, *Confederacy of Dunces* (1980). I spent ten years at Louisiana State University whose press—at Walker Percy's behest—published this book after Toole took his life. It won the Pulitzer Prize and is the funniest examination of the human condition I have ever read.

9. Annie Proulx, *The Shipping News* (1993). A recent book that haunts the reader in its clarity.

10. *Social Responsibilities Round Table Newsletter,* American Library Association. Actually, all the publications and work of SRRT—especially the feminist task force that led to my first book (with Kathleen Weibel), *The Role of Women in Librarianship 1876–1976*, has provided a touchstone for professional action.

10

WILL MANLEY, Community Services, Tempe (Ariz.) Public Library.

1. Nathan H. Azrin and Richard M. Foxx, *Toilet Training in Less Than a Day* (1989). This redeemed fatherhood for me.

2. Samuel Richardson, *Clarissa* (1748). An effective soporific during a painful period of acute insomnia.

3. Henry James, *The Ambassadors* (1903). Ditto.

4. Thor Heyerdahl, *Kon-Tiki* (1950). I found within this book an autographed letter from Vice-president Nixon, which I sold for $2,000—the sale price of a predatory Rambler, my first auto.

5. The *Chicago Yellow Pages* for 1972–1973 served as prop for the northwest corner of my bed.

SPENCER G. SHAW, Professor Emeritus, School of Library and Information Science, University of Washington, Seattle.

1. *The New Testament of Our Lord and Saviour Jesus Christ; and the Psalms* (pocket-sized National Edition, 1941), and Kahlil Gibran, *The Prophet* (pocket ed., 1923). These two volumes were invaluable support for me during my period of service in World War II. I had them constantly in my possession.

2. John Gunther, *Death Be Not Proud: A Memoir* (1949). A touching tribute to a remarkable boy whose brave fight against terminal cancer while pursuing his education stirred the reader's deepest emotions.

3. James Weldon Johnson, *God's Trombones: Seven Negro Sermons in Verse* (1927), and Lorenz Graham, *How God Fix Jonah* (1946). These two books, filled with biblical stories in poetic verse, reveal the rich interpretations in African and African-American renditions. I have used these in religious education workshops, selections on radio and television, and in presentations before educational and library associations.

4. Oscar Wilde, "The Selfish Giant," in *The Complete Fairy Tales of Oscar Wilde* (1888). Among the many stories that I have shared with audiences of all ages, this particular selection with its carefully crafted elements of modern imaginative literature never fails to evoke favorable emotional responses.

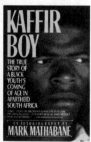

5. Mark Mathabane, *Kaffir Boy: The True Story of a Black Youth's Coming of Age in Apartheid South Africa* (1986). In this searing depiction of the inhumanity of one race against another, the indomitable will of the young protagonist propelled him from a life of imposed degradation to a life of freedom and achievement in another country.

6. Alfred Stefferud, ed., *The Wonderful World of Books* (1952). An excellent compilation of essays, exploring every facet of the subject of reading—its pleasures, importance, scope for all ages, and influence on our lives. I was privileged to submit a chapter.

7. Sarah L. and A. Elizabeth Delany, with Amy Hill Hearth, *Having Our Say: The Delany Sisters' First 100 Years* (1993). Through the insights of two remarkable, unforgettable sisters, a vital historical portrait of America—of a loving and devoted family who had the tenacity and upbringing to endure racial bias—is etched in the frank, sometimes humorous observations of these women.

PEGGY SULLIVAN, Chicago, Illinois.

1. Jane Austen, *Pride and Prejudice* (1813). Recalling that Winston Churchill is supposed to have read this during London's worst part of World War II, I

have always thought it was the almost perfect novel, the wonderful escape, and—considering the delightfully different film adaptations that have been produced—a complete cultural effect.

2. Ray Bradbury, *Dandelion Wine* (1957). This is so heartily Midwestern, yet so varied, and such a surprise from the man who made his name in science fiction. I have used it in many programs, urged others to read it, and have always found it fresh when I returned to it.

3. Richard P. Feynman, *"Surely You're Joking, Mr. Feynman"* (1985). This is as close as I get to science as a favorite. Getting some idea of why Feynman thought as he did is a great way to talk in the shoes of a genius who reveled in interests and ideas.

4. John Gunther, *Death, Be Not Proud* (1949). When I read this almost 50 years ago, soon after my father's death, it touched me. The thought of it still does.

5. Anne Morrow Lindbergh, *Gift from the Sea* (1955). Every woman probably has one book that marked her move to awareness of herself as a woman. For me, this book is it. I have probably reread it as often as I have given it as a gift—and that's a lot of gifts.

6. Margaret MacDonald, *The Storyteller's Sourcebook* (1982). I splurged to buy this, planning to use it in storytelling programs, but it has been more than that for me—an introduction to much of folk literature, a reminder of what a scholarly librarian like MacDonald can contribute, and just fun to browse and explore.

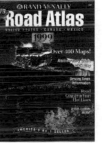

7. *Rand McNally Road Atlas*. When I replaced my 1992 edition with the 75th anniversary edition, I realized I owed a lot to this book. I've used it to make up names for case studies, to find people's home towns, to chart my own routes, to settle arguments, and sometimes just to enjoy the names on the land.

8. William Shakespeare, *The Plays* (1590–1622). No matter what edition, Shakespeare has to be on the list. I recently read every word of a student's edition of *Twelfth Night* and realized that there was so much that I had not known or appreciated before.

9. Pamela L. Travers, *Mary Poppins* (1934). How could I choose a children's book other than *Little Women*? Because *Mary Poppins* introduced me to humor and fantasy as well as to life.

10. *The World Almanac*. Used most recently to verify the longevity of popes, I have used this in a hundred ways. I discover a college I'd never heard of; I review a list of kidnappings; I play a game where we try to find the city that has a five-digit ZIP code closest to its population—and I remind myself what ZIP stands for. Love that general index!

11. Mysteries. If I could credit only one author of mysteries, I'd have to string together 13 names (in alpha order, of course): Amanda Charlotte Dick Dorothy Ellis Harry Helen James Lee Jonathan Josephine Patricia Sara Tony Burke Cornwell Cross Francis Gash Hillerman Kemelman MacInnes McLeod Paretsky Peters Sayers Tey.

ANN K. SYMONS, Librarian, Juneau Douglas High School, Alaska.

1. Michael Wilhoite, *Daddy's Roommate* (1990). The librarians in the Juneau School District purchased this book for the elementary schools. Little

did we know that we would live through a yearlong challenge by the People for Responsible Education.

2. Ann K. Symons and Charles T. Harmon, *Protecting the Right to Read: A How-to-Do-It Book for School and Public Librarians* (1996). I learned as much about intellectual freedom from writing a book as I did going through a major censorship challenge—one followed the other.

3. Lucy Jane Bledsoe, *Working Parts* (1997). A must-read literacy story. Winner of ALA's 1997 Gay, Lesbian, BiSexual Task Force Book Award for fiction.

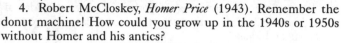

4. Robert McCloskey, *Homer Price* (1943). Remember the donut machine! How could you grow up in the 1940s or 1950s without Homer and his antics?

5. Harper Lee, *To Kill a Mockingbird* (1960). Read by every high school English student, and reread again and again.

6. Nevil Shute, *A Town Called Alice* (1949). The first adult book I read. I was sorry I went back and reread it in 1998—how politically incorrect it seemed today and how much I enjoyed taking it from the adult section of the library when I was 11. The places were so exotic and the story romantic.

7. Chris Crutcher, *Stotan!* (1986), and all of Crutcher's works. Crutcher captures the essence of adolescence in each of his powerful books. Must-reads for YAs and those who work with them.

8. Sandra W. Soule, ed., *America's Favorite Inns, B&Bs, & Small Hotels: The West Coast* (15th ed., 1997). My goal is to visit every inn pictured and described in this glorious book.

9. Richard Stevens, *Zipper the Zany: The Little Cat Who Tried to Write a Book* (1945), and Howard Baer, *China A–Z* (1946). These were my first picture books. I still have both of them although today the latter is only *China E–S*.

10. Anything by Dick Francis. I hate horses, but a friend convinced me to read Francis. I eagerly await each year's new novel—a good read to escape by.

Words beginning with "bibl–"

THE FOLLOWING LIST consists of words deriving from the Greek words *biblion* (papyrus reed) and *biblos* (book). Egypt exported papyrus for writing material to Greece and other regions through the Phoenician port of Byblos (modern Jubail, Lebanon), from which comes the root word *bibl-*, the source of both Bible and bibliography.—*GME*.

Bible, n. The sacred scripture of Christians, comprising the Old Testament and the New Testament.

bible, n. Any book or reference work accepted as authoritative, informative, and reliable.

bible, n., v.t. In TV series production, the general outline of plots and character development prepared before the first program of the season.

Bible bug, n. An insect that makes a chirping, shrilling, or clicking sound.

Bible paper, n. Thin, lightweight, bright, opaque, durable paper for Bibles or reference books. Originally made from vegetable fiber in China and Japan, though erroneously thought to come from India.

Bible style, n. A flexible, round-cornered, leather binding.

bible-tripe, n. (Northumbrian dial.) The third stomach of a ruminant, so called from the similarity of its folds to the leaves of a book.

bibleback, n. A round-shouldered person; or a pious and/or sanctimonious person.

Bibler, n. A student or reader of the Bible.

bibler, n. Six cuts on the back as punishment.

bibler, n. (Scots.) Senior boy in a school.

bibless, adj. Having no bib.

biblet, n. (Obsolete.) A book or library.

biblike, adj. Resembling a bib.

biblia abiblia, n. Books that are of no humanist interest; irrelevant materials brought together in one volume, simply to make a book.

Biblia pauperum, n. Medieval picture books containing illustrations of scriptural subjects.

Biblián, n. Town in Ecuador, northeast of Cuenca.

Bibliander, n. Greek surname of Theodor Buchmann, 1500?–1564, Swiss theologian and Oriental scholar.

biblic, adj. Biblical.

biblic, n. In medieval universities, the lowest grade of bachelor of theology.

biblical, adj. Pertaining to the Bible or the era and region in which events of the Bible took place.

biblicism, n. Adherence to the letter of the Bible.

biblicist, n. One who so adheres.

biblid, n. A bibliographic identification code established by the International Standards Organization (ISO) for contribution to serials and monographs with several authors.

bibling-rod, n. A wand with four apple twigs twisted together at the end that is used to administer a beating.

biblio, n. A bibliographical note in a book, usually on the reverse of the title page.

biblio style, n. In typography, a hanging indent.

biblioanomaly, n. Any event, behavior, condition, or discovery regarding books or libraries that does not conform to prevailing world views. Weird book stuff in general. *George Eberhart.*

bibliobibuli, n. People who read too much. *Gerald Donaldson.*

biblioblast, n. A large-scale celebration of books (e.g., BookExpo). *Norman Stevens.*

bibliocaper, n. A harebrained prank or petty crime associated with books or libraries. *George Eberhart.*

bibliocapitalism, n. Often used with the adjective "creeping." The absorption of independent bookstores by the megachains. *George Eberhart.*

bibliocat, n. A cat who lives in a library, especially one who is a member of the Library Cat Society. *Norman Stevens.*

bibliocharybdis, n. A dangerous whirlpool of books likely to drown unwary readers. *Gerald Donaldson.*

bibliochresis, n. The use of books.

bibliocide, n. Miscataloging a work so that it becomes unfindable in a library. *Sanford Berman.*

10

biblioclasm, n. Destruction of books.

biblioclast, n. A person who mutilates or destroys books.

bibliocosmetology, n. Using free haircuts to lure people into a library.

bibliocrypt, n. A place for enshrining dead books. *Norman Stevens.*

bibliodeltiologist, n. A collector of postcards that depict libraries, books, or reading. *Norman Stevens.*

bibliodemon, n. A book fiend or demon. *Gerald Donaldson.*

bibliofame, n. Renown as a bibliographer. *Norman Stevens.*

bibliofilm, n. A microfilm used to photograph the pages of valuable books.

bibliofood, n. Edible books. *Norman Stevens.*

bibliogenesis, n. Production of books.

bibliognost, n. One versed in knowledge about books.

bibliogony, n. The art of producing and publishing books.

bibliogourmand, n. An obsessive collector of cookbooks. *Norman Stevens.*

bibliograph, v.t. To put in a bibliography.

bibliograph, n. A graph of any curve that describes Bradford's law of scattering, named after science librarian Samuel Clement Bradford; or a bibliographer.

bibliographe, n. A describer of books and other literary arrangements. *Gerald Donaldson.*

bibliographee, n. The person about whom a bibliography has been written.

bibliographer, n. An expert in bibliography.

bibliographic, bibliographical, adj. Pertaining to bibliography.

bibliographic center, n. An organization, often a department of a library, that maintains a collection of reference books from which it is possible to give information concerning the availability of books.

Bibliographic Classification, n. A classification system devised by Henry Evelyn Bliss, first published in outline form in 1910, characterized by the organization of knowledge consistent with scientific and educational consensus.

bibliographic control, n. Complete bibliographic records of all bibliographic items published; standardization of bibliographic description; providing physical access through consortia, networks, or other cooperative endeavors; or providing bibliographic access through compiling and distributing union lists and subject bibliographies and through bibliographic service centers.

bibliographic coupling, n. The theory that if any two scientific papers contain a citation in common, they are bibliographically related.

bibliographic database, n. A database consisting of computer records that represent works, documents, or bibliographic items.

bibliographic description, n. Part of a catalog record that identifies the item it represents, exclusive of access points, call numbers, or other control numbers.

bibliographic identity, n. The name used on an item to identify the creator. An individual who uses more than one name on his or her works is said to have multiple bibliographic identities.

bibliographic index, n. A systematic list of writings or publications.

bibliographic information, n. The details concerning a publication that are sufficient to identify it for the purpose of ordering or locating it.

bibliographic instruction, n. An information service to a group, which is designed to teach library users how to locate information efficiently.

bibliographic item, n. A document or set of documents in any physical form, forming the basis for a single bibliographic description.

bibliographic level, n. One of three standard styles of description prescribed by AACR2R, containing varying amounts of information from the least (Level 1) to the most (Level 3).

bibliographic network, n. A network established and maintained for the sharing of bibliographic data through the use of a standard communication format and authority control.

bibliographic record, n. A record of a bibliographic item that comprises all data contained in or accommodated by a bibliographic format such as MARC.

bibliographic reference, n. A set of bibliographic elements essential to the identification of a work.

bibliographic search, n. The process of identifying a work and obtaining bibliographic data about it through a systematic search of bibliographic tools and other sources.

bibliographic service center, n. An organization that serves as a distributor of computer-based bibliographic processing services.

bibliographic unit, n. Any document, part of a document, or several documents, that are treated as a bibliographic entity.

bibliographic utility, n. An organization that maintains online bibliographic databases, enabling it to offer computer-based support to users.

bibliographic volume, n. A publication distinguishable from other publications by virtue of having its own title page, half title, cover title, or other means of establishing its separate identity.

bibliographical ghost, n. A work or edition of a work, recorded in bibliographies or otherwise mentioned, of whose existence there is no reasonable proof.

bibliographical note, n. Text set apart from the text of a document, which contains a reference to one or more works used as sources.

bibliographical organization, n. The pattern of effective arrangement achieved by means of a systematic listing of recorded knowledge.

bibliographical scatter, n. The appearance of an article on one subject in a periodical devoted primarily to another subject.

bibliographical strip, n. The contents of a part of a periodical.

bibliographical tool, n. A publication used by a bibliographer in the course of her work.

bibliographical warrant, n. The basing of book classification according to the actual groupings into which books tend to fall for use, ignoring minute classes for which there is no literature, but including composite classes for which there is a literature.

bibliographing, n. The act of consulting bibliographies.

bibliographize, v.t. To make a bibliography of.

bibliography, n. The study of books as physical objects; the art of correctly describing books; or, a list of works, documents, or bibliographic items, usually by author, subject, or place of publication.

bibliography of bibliographies, n. A bibliography that describes bibliographies.

biblioholic, n. One afflicted with biblioholism. *Tom Raabe.*

10

biblioholism, n. The habitual longing to purchase, read, store, admire, and consume books in excess. *Tom Raabe.*

bibliojape, n. A humorous variant book title, as in *Great Sexpectations. George Eberhart.*

biblioklept, n. A person who steals books.

bibliokleptomania, n. Obsessive stealing of books.

bibliolater, bibliolatrist, n. A book worshiper.

bibliolatry, n. Extravagant devotion to or dependence upon books.

bibliolestes, n. A book robber or plunderer.

bibliolite, n. Certain laminated schistose rocks, otherwise called book-stones.

bibliologist, n. One versed in bibliology.

bibliology, n. The study of books, embracing knowledge of the physical book in all its aspects, such as paper, printing, typography, illustration, and binding.

bibliomancy, n. Divination by means of a book, especially the Bible, opened at random to some verse or passage, which is then interpreted.

bibliomania, n. Excessive fondness for acquiring and possessing books.

bibliomaniac, n., adj. Characterized by bibliomania.

bibliomanian, bibliomane, n., adj. Bibliomaniac.

bibliometrics, n. The use of statistical methods in the analysis of a body of literature to reveal the historical development of subject fields and patterns of authorship, publication, and use.

biblionarcissism, n. The art of convincing others that you are more bookish than you really are. *Tom Raabe.*

biblionomy, n. The body of laws or perceived knowledge pertaining to bibliography and/or librarianship. *Norman Stevens.*

bibliopegic, adj. Related to the binding of books.

bibliopegist, bibliophegist, n. A bookbinder.

bibliopegy, n. The art of binding books.

bibliophage, bibliophagist, n. An ardent reader.

bibliophilately, n. The study of books and libraries on postage stamps. *George Eberhart.*

bibliophile, n. A person who loves or collects books.

bibliophile binding, n. A binding, usually ornate, such as one that might be used by a bibliophile.

Bibliophile de la vieille roche, n. (French.) A book collector of the old school whose interests ranged widely and who did not specialize.

bibliophile edition, n. A specially printed and bound edition of a book published for sale to bibliophiles.

Bibliophile Jacob, n. Pseudonym of Paul Lacroix, 1806–1884, French scholar.

bibliophilic bibliography, n. A listing of materials related to and for book collectors.

bibliophilism, bibliophily, n. A love of books.

bibliophobe, n. A person who hates, fears, or distrusts books.

bibliophobia, n. Dislike of books.

bibliophthor, n. A book destroyer. *Gerald Donaldson.*

bibliopoesy, n. The making of books.

bibliopole, bibliopolist, n. A bookseller, especially a dealer in rare or used books.

bibliopolic, bibliopolar, adj. Pertaining to booksellers.

bibliopolism, n. The trade or art of selling books.

bibliopoly, bibliopolery, n. The selling of books.

bibliopsychology, n. Study of authors, books, and readers, as well as their interrelationships.

biblioriptos, n. One who throws books around. *Gerald Donaldson.*

bibliort, n. Something other than a bookmark used by people to mark a place in a book-ticket stub, laundry list, etc. *Paul Dickson.*

bibliosoph, n. One who knows about books.

bibliotaph, n. A person who caches or hoards books.

bibliotaphy, n. Burying books to ensure their safekeeping. *Tom Raabe.*

bibliothec, n. A library.

bibliotheca, n. A library or collection of books; the Scriptures.

bibliothecal bibliography, n. The phase of bibliography concerned with the collection, preservation, and organization of books in libraries.

bibliothecal classification, n. A classification system devised for arranging library materials.

bibliothecary, bibliothecarian, n. A librarian.

bibliothece, n. (Old English.) The Scriptures.

bibliotheke, n. A library.

Bibliothèque bleu, n. (French.) Popular pamphlets with blue wrappers.

bibliotherapist, n. One who practices bibliotherapy.

bibliotherapy, n. The use of reading materials in a program of directed reading that is planned and conducted as an auxiliary in the treatment of mental and emotional disorders and social maladjustment.

bibliothetic, adj. Pertaining to or based on the placing or arrangement of books.

bibliotics, n. The analysis of handwriting and documents for authentication of authorship.

bibliotime, n. A season, occasion, or appointed hour for reading books. *Norman Stevens.*

bibliotrain, n. Railroad car converted into a mobile library.

Biblis, n. Town in Germany, north of Mannheim.

biblist, n. One who makes the Bible the sole rule of faith.

Byblia, n. A woman who fell in love with her brother Caunus and was changed into a fountain near Miletus. *Ovid, Metamorphoses.*

Byblos, n. Ancient Phoenician city known for exporting Egyptian papyrus; modern Jubail in Lebanon, 20 miles north of Beirut.

Weird titles

IN 1998 RUSSELL ASH and Brian Lake published a second edition of their book-length collection of odd book titles. Here are some of their weirdest.

Lord Aberdeen, *Jokes Cracked by Lord Aberdeen* (Dundee: Valentine, 1929).

Charles Elton Blanchard, *The Romance of Proctology* (Youngstown, O.: Medical Success Press, 1938).

Watson Davis, *Atomic Bombing: How to Protect Yourself* (New York: William H. Wise, 1950).

R. L. Dione, *God Drives a Flying Saucer* (London: Corgi, 1973).

Adams Farr, *The Fangs of Suet Pudding* (Gerald G. Swan, 1944).

Don Fart-inhando Puffindorst [Jonathan Swift], *The Benefit of Farting Explain'd* (London: A. Moore, 1727).

10

Geoffrey Howson, ed., *Handbook for the Limbless* (Disabled Society, 1922).

Matthew Peter King, *In Vain I Strive with Aspect Gay; or, Up All Night* [sheet music], n.d.

D. Lowe, *A Toddler's Guide to the Rubber Industry* (Leicester: De Montfort Press, 1947).

Bernarr Macfadden, *Be Married and Like It* (New York: Macfadden, 1937).

G. A. Martini, *Metabolic Changes Induced by Alcohol* (Berlin: Springer-Verlag, 1971).

Lewis Omer, *Hand Grenade Throwing As a College Sport* (New York: A. G. Spalding, 1918).

George Ryley Scott, *The Art of Faking Exhibition Poultry* (T. Werner Laurie, 1934).

William Tebb and Col. Edward Perry Vollum, *Premature Burial and How It May Be Prevented* (Swan Sonnenschein, 1896).

Mark Twain, *Oliver Twist* (Athens: Harmi-Press, 1963). Attributed to Mark Twain on the cover, but the publishers managed to credit Charles Dickens on the title page.

SOURCE: Russell Ash and Brian Lake, *Bizarre Books* (London: Pavilion, 1998).

Unusual page markers

by Sally Hogan

AT THE LIBRARY RECENTLY, I picked up a volume of famous quotations and found someone had used toilet paper as a bookmark. In my many years of borrowing library books, I have come across various items used for markers, but never toilet paper. I was curious as to what other impromptu markers I might find. Here are the results of my search: old library catalog  cards, library checkout slips, Post-It notes, a twist tie, a "to do" list, a cardboard strip, a hair pin, the feed strip from computer paper, a bookmark provided free from the library, a flyer announcing the circus that had come to town several months ago, a checkbook deposit slip, plastic wrap, an empty Sweet'n'Low packet, a gum wrapper, waxed paper, scraps of paper, an index card, a genuine store-bought bookmark, and the ribbon marker provided with the book.

Dog-earing pages was very popular, as well as turning down half the page. I also found a *Far Side* cartoon from a calendar dated October 31, and marking a page in a Bible reference book was an advertisement for the best fairs and festivals in the United States. A note card with a cheery greeting written to Mel from Carolyn marked a tomato-apricot chutney recipe. In James Thurber's *Writings and Drawings,* marking a page from "My Life and Hard Times" was a charge receipt from L. S. Ayres, the department store.

There were other unusual markers. In the *Biography of Mickey Rooney* was a list of helpful Bible verses for various concerns: When you wonder what God thinks of you, read Romans 1–3. A section in *Managing Office Romance* was marked with a paper clip. A Mylanta coupon was nestled between pages in *Extended Health Care at Home,* and a book on healthy eating contained a candy wrapper.

A piece of what looked like peppermint candy was stuck in a book on mathematics between the chapters on "Newton's Optics" and "Huygen's Treatise on Light." A torn-up résumé was in the *Art of W C. Fields*. The Professor Plum card from the Clue board game was in *Awakening from the Deep Sleep*, a book about men changing from a life driven by work, women, and addiction, to one that is based upon their feelings and desires for what will bring them happiness. A leaf marked the poem, "Sitting by a Bush in Broad Sunlight," in a collection by Robert Frost. And Willa Cather's story *Shadows on the Rock* held small rocks.

In the art, photography, history, and travel sections, I found no book markers. Nor did I find markers in the fiction, mystery, science fiction, or romance sections, which surprised me. I found no markers in the books on collecting, which didn't surprise me. Collectors as a general rule hang on to everything. The section containing the most markers was religion.

In all, I found 20 scraps of torn paper, 22 old library catalog cards, eight Post-It notes, and 24 library checkout slips. The book *Struggle Against Terrorism* had nine pages marked with scraps of torn paper, and in *Spell Crafts* 19 pages were dog-eared.

I didn't find anything of value, like money. I came close. One book contained two gift certificates each good for a meal at, of all places, the hospital. Unfortunately they had expired two days earlier.

At first I was fascinated with the checkout slips. I learned a great deal of information about people from those tiny slips. I discovered the person's full name and the date and time of day they had checked out their books. If they had any fines to pay, how much they paid. I learned what material they took home, and how many items they checked out. (One slip contained 36 titles.) I learned of the woman who is interested in cooking with chocolate, and one who is all thumbs when it comes to plumbing. I know the man who likes to draw and play the guitar, and the one who is interested in fly fishing. I know who likes to cross-stitch. And I know the people who want information on personal computers and the Internet. I know those who are looking for work, or are searching for a better position, or trying to keep the one they have. I know the name of the person who wants to understand about fatal friendships and the one who wants to be a tough-minded optimist.

At first I liked it, but as I discovered more and more slips, I started to feel there was something wrong in knowing this information about people without their awareness. I felt as though I was a voyeur, a Peeping Tom. Although I came by this information because of others' own carelessness and I really wasn't doing anything illegal, I asked myself if I would want someone to know that much about me. Would I want someone knowing what I liked to read? When I came to the library? What my interests are? No, I wouldn't. What I check out of the library is my business. It's private.

I resolved not to read any more names on the slips, not to pry into anyone's private life again. Then in a book on the Dead Sea scrolls, I found something very interesting—a library receipt for $17.63. Some person had to pay a huge fine. I couldn't keep from looking at the top of the slip to see who it was. The name on the slip was mine! Yes, on October 18 at 10:38 a.m., I paid a fine, renewed one book, and checked out five new books. I could not believe a part of my life was buried in a book about the Dead Sea scrolls, sitting on a library shelf, waiting to be discovered. I took the slip, folded it, and placed it in my

10

pocket. I felt relieved that the slip had escaped the prying eyes of some other library patron. Of course, there is the possibility that someone picked up the book, read all about me, then placed the book back on the shelf, leaving the information for another person to discover. But probably not; after all, how many years were the Dead Sea scrolls lying around before they were discovered? I think my checkout slip was in a safe place.

SOURCE: Sally Hogan, "Unusual Page Markers: A Lesson in Patron Privacy," *Public Libraries* (January/February 1999): 15.

The word "library" in 114 different languages

Afrikaans	biblioteek	Hawaiian	he waihona puke
Akan	nhomakorabea	Hindi	pustakālaya, laibrarī
Albanian	bibliothekë	Hungarian	könyvtár
Amharic	biblioteca	Icelandic	bókasafn
Arabic	khīzana,	Ilocano	bibliotéka
	ḥizâna-t kutub,	Indonesian	perpustakaan
	kutubhâna,	Irish	leabharlann
	maktaba	Italian	biblioteca
Armenian	krataran, qradun	Japanese	toshokan
Baluchi	kytabjah	Kikuyu	mabukumongañitio
Basque	liburutegi		gĩkundi
Belorussian	biblijateka	Konkani	pustakañsāl
Bengali	pustAghawr	Korean	do-sŏ-kwan
Breton	levraoueg	Kosraean	laepracri
Bulgarian	библиотéка	Kyrgyz	китепкана
Catalan	biblioteca	Lao	hohng sai muit
Cebuano	pamasahonan	Latin	bibliotheca
Chinese	túshūguǎn	Latvian	biblioteka
Cornish	lyverjy	Lithuanian	knygynas
Czech	knihovna	Malay	perpustakaan,
Danish	bibliotek		taman pustaka
Dutch	bibliotheek	Maltese	librerija
Egyptian		Manx	lioar-hasht
(ancient)	st n 3š' w	Maori	whare pukapuka
Esperanto, Ido	biblioteko	Maranao	roang a ribro
Estonian	raamatukogu	Marshallese	ḷāibrāre
Fijian	vale ni wilīvola	Mayangna	wauhtaya ûni
Finnish	kirjasto	Miao	tsev khaws-qiv
French	bibliothèque		ntawr nyeem
Frisian	bibleteek	Michif	
Fulani	móoftirde defte	(Metis)	ita lee leevz
Gaelic	leeberary		kaw-ashtayki
Georgian	bibliotek'a	Mongolian	lmkzl p'l
German	Bibliothek	Norwegian	bibliotek
Greek	βιβλιοτεκα	Occitan	bibliotèca
Hausa	lābùrārè	Panjabi	laibrerī

Pashto	kitab khāna	Tahitian	paepae buka
Persian	kutub-khánah	Tamil	pusthagasâlai
Polish	biblioteka	Tatar	китапхане
Portuguese	biblioteca	Telugu	granthaalayam
Romanian	biblioteca	Thai	(f)hawng!
Russian	библиотéка		sa-(l)moot!
Samoan	fale faitautusi	Tibetan	kun-dga-ra-ba,
Sanskrit	pustakâgāra		pe-chha-khang
Serbo-Croatian	knjižnica	Turkish	kütüphane
Slovak	knižnica	Turkmen	kitaphana
Slovene	knjižnica	Ukrainian	бібліотека
Somali	libreriya,	Ulwa	buktak ûka
	maktabad	Urdu	katabkhānā
Sotho	laebrarı,	Uzbek	кутубхона
	bokgobapuku	Vietnamese	thụ viện
Spanish	biblioteca	Wakashan	bu'gwilas
Sudovian	laiskabutan	Welsh	llyfrgell
Swahili	nyumba cha	Xhosa	indlu yeencwadi
	kuwekea vitabu,	Yiddish	bibliotek
	maktaba	Yoruba	ilé ìlùwé
Swedish	bibliotek	Zulu	iqoqo lamabhuku
Tagalog	aklatan		

American Sign Language: The right "L" hand, palm out, describes a small circle.

ASCII characters: 76,105,98,114,97,114,121

Hexadecimal: 4C,69,62,72,61,72,79

International Morse Code: • — • •   • •   — • •   • — •   • — • •   — • — —

Amharic	ቤተ ፡ መጻሕፍት	Georgian	ბიბლიოთეკა
Arabic	مكتبة، دار الكتب، مجموعة كتب؛ سلسلة كتب	Gujarati	પુસ્તકાલય
		Hebrew	סִפְרִיָּה
Armenian	գրատուն	Hindi	पुस्तकालय
Bengali	পুস্তক সমূহ	Irish	Leabarlann
Burmese	စာကြည့်တိုက်	Japanese	図書館
Chinese	图书馆	Khmer	បណ្ណាល័យ
Egyptian	𓉐𓏠𓂧𓈖𓏏𓏤𓏜		

10

Marathi	'लाइब्ररि	Telugu	గ్రంథాలయం
Panjabi	ਲਾਇਬ੍ਰੇਰੀ	Thai	ห้องสมุด
Sindhi	لائبريري	Tibetan	དཔེ་མཛོད
Sinhala	පුස්තකාලය, පොත්ගුළ	Urdu	کتب خانہ
Tamil	புத்தகசாலை	Yiddish	ביבליאָטעק
		Freemason's cipher	⌐⌐⌐⌐⌐<

Fingerspelling

Semaphore

The Molesworth Institute's
50 favorite library quotations

by Norman D. Stevens

AT HIS SPEECH AT THE OPENING of the Mitchell Library in Manchester, England, in 1911, Lord Rosebery (left) commented on the plethora of platitudes about libraries. He observed that "There is no subject except theology and politics on which so many speeches have been delivered. . . . The wise man," he went on to say, "when he has reached the age of 60 never opens a library." Lord Rosebery estimated that more than 22,000 platitudes had been uttered at Carnegie library dedications alone. No one, not even the most astute library historian, has any idea of the true number of comments, favorable and unfavorable, that have been spoken or written about the value of libraries. The research staff of the Molesworth Institute has been able to identify, with due diligence, approximately 1,000 such comments. These 50 favorite library quotations have been carefully selected to represent diverse points of view and to bring to the attention of Our Profession some of the more delightful, obscure, and valuable of the entries found in our files.

1. "The function of a great library is to store obscure books."
   —Nicholson Baker, *New Yorker*, April 4, 1994, p. 78.

2. "Human beings can lose their lives in libraries. They ought to be warned."
   —Saul Bellow, *Him With His Foot in His Mouth* (1984), p. 11.

3. "I . . . had always thought of Paradise in form and image as a library."
   —Jorge Luis Borges, *Borges: A Reader* (1981), p. 280.

4. "A library doesn't need windows. A library is a window."
   —Stewart Brand, *How Buildings Learn* (1994), p. 33.

5. "Problems of human behaviour still continue to baffle us, but at least in the library we have them properly filed."
   —Anita Brookner, *Look at Me* (1983), p. 5.

6. "People make too much fuss about the sacrosanctity of libraries."
   —Anthony Burgess, *Urgent Copy* (1973), p. 288.

7. [Libraries are] "a kind of communism which the least revolutionary among us may be proud to advocate."
   —Joseph Chamberlain, quoted in J. J. Ogle, *The Free Library* (1897), p. 52.

8. "When in doubt, go to the library."
   —Kate Charles, *A Drink of Deadly Wine* (1992), p. 116.

9. "A library . . . is . . . a quiet storage place, and what it stores is the memory of the human race. It is a place for the soft rustle of pages and the quiet stir of thoughts over the reading tables."
   —John Ciardi, *Saturday Review*, August 26, 1961, p. 24.

10. "A library . . . should be the delivery room for the birth of ideas—a place where history comes to life."
    —Norman Cousins, *ALA Bulletin*, October 1954, p. 475.

11. "The time was when a library was very much like a museum, and a librarian was a mouser in musty books . . . The time *is* when a library is a school, and the librarian is in the highest sense a teacher."
    —Melvil Dewey, *American Library Journal*, September 30, 1876, p. 6.

12. "The three most important documents a free society gives are a birth certificate, a passport, and a library card."
    —E. L. Doctorow, *New York Times*, March 27, 1994, p. 20.

13. "Old libraries have wings like attics in houses where families have lived for many generations."
    —Michael Dorris and Louise Erdrich, *The Crown of Columbus* (1991), p. 185.

14. "Is a library, then, an instrument not for distributing the truth but for delaying its appearance?"
    —Umberto Eco, *The Name of the Rose* (1983), p. 286.

15. "This is the door
    By which we enter in
    This great white marble mausoleum
    Of dead and dying thoughts."
    —James Waldo Fawcett, *Bruno's Weekly*, October 25, 1916, p. 1169.

10

16. "Libraries . . . house our dreams."

—Nikki Giovanni, *American Libraries*, May 1996, p. 56.

17. "[The library's] real virtue is . . . it preserves error as well as truth and nonsense as well as sense."

—Harry Golden [original source unidentified].

18. "When the lights go out in our libraries, the Dark Ages are coming again!"

—Mitch Hager, in G. Edward Nichols, *The Norman Williams Public Library* (1985), p. 25.

19. "Libraries will get you through times of no money better than money will get you through times of no libraries."

—Anne Herbert, *The Whole Earth Catalog* (1969).

20. "Books are the friends of the friendless, and . . . a library is the home of the homeless."

—G. S. Hilliard, "Address to the Mercantile Library Association of Boston" (1850).

21. "The free library is a living room to an ordinary citizen, a treasury to a researcher, and a chamber of horrors to a dictator."

—Bengt Hjelmqvist (1998) [personal communication].

22. "This palace is the *people's own!*"

—Oliver Wendell Holmes (right), quoted in Thomas Greenwood, *Public Libraries* (1891), p. 7.

23. "A library implies an act of faith which generations still in darkness hid sign in the night in witness of the dawn."

—Victor Hugo, "L'année Terrible," June 1871.

24. "The library was the only place in town where one could venture in search of both change of scene and intellectual stimulation. It was an interface with the outside world of ideas."

—John A. Jakle, *The American Small Town* (1982), p. 109.

25. "No place offers a more striking conviction of the vanity of human hopes than a public library."

—Samuel Johnson, *The Rambler*, March 23, 1751; included in *Yale Edition of the Works of Samuel Johnson* (1969), vol. 4, p. 201.

26. "This is a library. Kids and adventurers welcome. All others Stay Out."

—Dean Koontz, *Cold Fire* (1991), p. 384.

27. "What is a library, after all, but a place where the dead, neatly coffined in their separate volumes, continue to speak."

—Brad Leithauser, *The Norton Book of Ghost Stories* (1994), p. 13.

28. "One of the joys of historical research is the revelation of how much milk of human kindness there is in libraries."

—Walker Lewis, *Without Fear or Favor* (1965), p. [538].

29. "The existence of a library is an assertion, a proposition nailed like Luther's to the door of time."

—Archibald MacLeish [original source unidentified].

30. "There is no better way in this world to lose something forever than to misfile it in a big library."

—Norman Maclean, *Young Men and Fire* (1992), p. 147.

31. "Every library tyrannizes the act of reading, and forces the reader—the curious reader, the alert reader—to rescue the book from the category to which it has been condemned."

—Alberto Manguel, *A History of Reading* (1996), p. 199.

32. "Where else [but the library], in our noisy age, do you find posted and heeded, the immortal and healing word SILENCE?"

—Christopher Morley (left), *Saturday Review of Literature*, July 3, 1937, p. 14.

33. "In the presence of a library I am always oppressed with a sad consciousness of my own ignorance."

—Jean Paul, quoted in *Dedication of the Frederick H. Cossitt Library at North Granby, Connecticut* (1891), p. 7.

34. "Printed on the reverse is a sign of the times [NO SILENCE]. Perhaps nothing has ever hurt the image of librarianship and libraries so badly as those grim signs demanding SILENCE."

Art Plotnik, *Wilson Library Bulletin*, November 1969, [between p. 296–97].

35. "The public library is one of the few places left where one can be private."

—Lawrence Clark Powell, *Arizona Highways*, August 1960, p. 7.

36. [A library can be] "not just a lake at which powerful beasts come to drink, but also a fountain from which animating streams flow out to shyer woodland creatures."

—Lord Anthony Meredith Quinton, in *In Praise of Libraries* (1989), p. 36.

37. "Many of the greatest adventurers of our age . . . didn't travel much further than . . . a library."

—Salman Rushdie, *Imaginary Homelands* (1991), p. 225.

38. "We are the only planet, so far as we know, to have invented a communal memory stored neither in our genes or our brains. The warehouse of that memory is called a library."

—Carl Sagan [original source unidentified].

39. "If a public library is doing its job, it has something in it that offends every single person."

—Phyllis A. Salak, *American Libraries*, April 1993, p. 287.

40. "My good opinion of a town or village was based largely on the existence of two facilities for its inhabitants and visitors: public libraries and public conveniences."

—Emmanuel Shinwell, *Conflict Without Malice* (1955), p. 124.

41. "Libraries do lots of good; their reports show this."

—John C. Sickley, *Suggestions to Librarians for a More Literary Form of Report* (1918).

10

42. "As soon as there were two tablets of stone, the need for a library must have been apparent."

—Alan Taylor, *Long Overdue* (1993), p. 19.

43. "Mommy, if it were the end of the world, and everybody was getting ready to die . . . would you have to take your library books back?"

—Peggy Taylor, *The Catholic Digest*, April 1987, p. 66.

44. "There it is: that wonderful library smell. How could I have forgotten it? The *feel* of libraries—the way they look, smell, sound—lingers intensely as the memories of a fierce first love."

—Susan Allen Toth, *Reading Rooms* (1991), p. 4.

45. "A public library is the most enduring of memorials, the trustiest monument for the preservation of an event or a name or an affection; for it, and only it, is respected by wars and revolutions, and survives them."

—Mark Twain, in *Mark Twain and Fairhaven* (1894), p. 7.

46. "The death of a library, any library, suggests that the community has lost its soul."

—Kurt Vonnegut Jr., quoted in *Hartford Courant*, January 31, 1995, p. A9.

47. "A coupla months in the laboratory can save a coupla hours in the library."

—F. H. Westheimer [original source unidentified].

48. "Were this library built and the fond mother would say, 'Where is my boy tonight?' and the response should be, 'He is at the Library,' she could thank God that he is where no harm would come to him."

—Swan Wintersmith, *Elizabethtown* (Ky.) *News*, January 30, 1906.

49. "There is in the British Museum an enormous mind . . . [that] is hoarded beyond the power of any single mind to possess it."

—Virginia Woolf, *Jacob's Room* (1922), p. 107.

50. "In the beginning there was the book, and the book inspired and angered others to write books, and when the people could no longer cope with all the books they had created, they begat libraries, and the Lord said, 'I don't know what else we can do.'"

—Anonymous, from a broadside printed by the Quiet Desperation Press (1986).

Library cats

by Gary Roma

CATS IN LIBRARIES are a wonderful tradition. They perform many duties, including mousing, goodwill, promotion, and entertainment for patrons and staff. Filmmaker and comedian Gary Roma maintains a Web site (www. ironfrog.com) that, as of March1999, mapped the locations of 272 library cats—104 current, and 168 former residents. Roma also produced a documentary video in 1997, *Puss in Books: Adventures of the Library Cat*, that features many of these felines and examines the problem of patrons who are allergic to them. The following list gives the name, years of residence, and location of one library cat per state; for others, visit the Iron Frog Web site. —*GME.*

Alabama—Honey Bun, 1987–1990 (died Apr. 7, 1994), St. Margaret's School Library, Bayou La Batre.

Alaska—none.

Arizona—Boots, 1990–present, Benson Public Library.

Arkansas—Angel, 1976–1977 (died 1980), Fletcher Branch Library, Little Rock.

California—Winston, 1996–present, South County Branch Library, Arroyo Grande.

Colorado—Hemingway, 1993–present, Southern Peaks Public Library, Alamosa.

Connecticut—Emily, 1989–present, Mystic and Noank Library, Mystic.

Delaware—none.

Florida—Dewey, 1997–present, Martin County Library, Indiantown Branch.

Georgia—Tallulah, 1998–present, Douglas County Library, Douglasville.

Hawaii—Gypsy, 1998–present, Kihai Library.

Idaho—L. C. Dickens, 1993–present, Garden Valley District Library.

Illinois—Puddin', 1986–1994, Chicago Ridge Public Library.

Indiana—Pooh and Tigger, 1997–present, Beech Grove Public Library.

Iowa—Dewey Readmore Books, 1988–present, Spencer Public Library.

Kansas—Libby, 1996–present, Girard Public Library.

Kentucky—Smokey Dickens, 1996–present, Bowling Green Public Library.

Louisiana—none.

Maine—Libby, 1986–present, Walker Memorial Library, Westbrook.

Maryland—none.

Massachusetts—Melville Dewey, 1987–1994, Eastham Public Library.

Michigan—Deuce, 1982–present, Kent District Library, Caledonia.

Minnesota—O'Keefe, 1982–1996 (d. 1996), Duluth Public Library.

Mississippi—Miss Gussie and Miss Theo, 1996–present, Evans Memorial Library, Aberdeen.

Missouri—Woody, 1990s, Meramec Library, St. Louis Community College, Kirkwood.

Montana—Maizie, 1994–present, Glasgow City/County Library.

Nebraska—Goldie, 1996–present, Broken Bow Public Library.

Nevada—Baker (1983–1994, died June 28, 1994) and Taylor (1983–1997, died Dec. 19, 1997), Douglas County Public Library, Minden—perhaps the most famous library cats, thanks to posters and other ads by book distributors Baker & Taylor.

New Hampshire—Carnegie (shown on right), 1989–1995, Rochester Public Library.

New Jersey—Gimpy Cat, 1995–present, Hunterdon County Library, Flemington.

New Mexico—Ed, 1993–present, Farmington Branch Library.

New York—Bookend, 1997–present, Jervis Public Library, Rome. (SUNY/Morrisville boasts a stuffed Siberian tiger named Morris.)

North Carolina—none.

North Dakota—Cleo Boom Boom Marie, 1987–1990, Fargo Public Library.

10

Ohio—Sophie, 1998–present, Highland County District Library, Hillsboro.
Oklahoma—none.
Oregon—Smokey, 1994–present, Rogue Community College Library, Grants Pass.
Pennsylvania—Dr. Seuss, 1986–present, Bradford Area Public Library.
Rhode Island—none.
South Carolina—Webster, 1986–1987, University of South Carolina Library, Beaufort.
South Dakota—none.
Tennessee—none.
Texas—Mitzi, 1993–present, Crowley Public Library.
Utah—Libby, 1993–1995, College of Eastern Utah Library, Price.
Vermont—Pages, 1996–present, Brandon Free Public Library.
Virginia—Molly Van Wyck, 1983–1997 (died Jan. 11, 1997), Van Wyck Branch, Norfolk Public Library.
Washington—Dui, 1994–present, Kitsap Regional Library, Bremerton.
West Virginia—Dewey Decimal, 1994–present, Princeton Public Library.
Wisconsin—Maggie, 1995–present, Community Library, Salem.
Wyoming—none.

SOURCE: Gary Roma, Library Cats Map, www.ironfrog.com.

A guide to haunted libraries
by George M. Eberhart

IN THE FALL, a journalist's fancy lightly turns to thoughts of ghosts. Newspapers and magazines that haughtily refrain from printing news of the paranormal for 11 months of the year eagerly jump on the Halloween coach in October to regale their audiences with dubious tales of the preternatural.

American Libraries is no exception. However, unlike less reputable media, we go to original sources whenever possible to ascertain whether or not our spooks are spurious. And in so doing we have uncovered a hauntful of genuinely eerie events hiding amid the folktales.

Libraries are haunted?

Bleak mansions and somber castles usually spring to mind when we think of haunted places. But ghostly phenomena—whatever the cause—can manifest in well-lit, modern offices as well as crumbling Carnegies. Of course, it helps if you inadvertently build your library on top of a graveyard.

Haunted libraries fall into two types. First, there is the "building with a reputation" where a convenient murder, curse, or other tragedy has occurred. Library staff can then blame the odd noise, the occasional book falling off the shelf, or glitches in the air conditioning on the resident "scapeghost." No one reports anything too spooky, and the children's librarians have a good time with it at story hour.

Second, there are libraries where credible, responsible people observe enigmatic human shapes, hear disembodied voices, and witness other classic parapsychological events. Glib explanations about how the building must be settling ring about as hollow as those mysterious footsteps late at night on the upper floorboards. The library staff learns to live with its wraith, usually by accepting the paranormal as a normal working condition.

Both categories of haunted libraries are described here. Like a good journalist I will begin with Type One, forcing you to read through to the end to get to the good stuff. Just make sure you don't finish this article alone in bed, late at night, during a violent thunderstorm.

'Tis the curse of service

As if library directors didn't have enough to worry about, a curse would be enough to send stress levels over the line. Fortunately, the curse on Peoria (Ill.) Public Library directors seems to have lifted long ago. Uttered in 1847 by the lawyer-plagued woman who owned the land where the library now stands, the curse is said to have been responsible for the untimely deaths of three directors: The first was killed in a streetcar accident in 1915, the second died from a heart attack suffered after a heated debate at a library board meeting in 1921, and the third committed suicide in 1924 by swallowing arsenic. Since then, Peoria directors have lived long, fruitful lives.

Ruth did it

On October 11, 1947, Ruth Cochran, assistant librarian at the Umatilla County Public Library in Pendleton and president of the Eastern Oregon Library Association, suffered a cerebral hemorrhage as she was closing the building. She went to the basement to rest, but soon became too weak to move or summon help. The next day the custodian's wife found her, still conscious, and she was taken to the hospital where she died, according to the Pendleton *East Oregonian*. Ever since, spooky events in the library have been blamed on Ruth's ghost.

Harvey Thompson, a library patron who took an interest in Ruth, told me there is "something in the building that makes people nervous." Once a custodian was alone in the building painting the children's room when the intercom system buzzed repeatedly. "The folklore was that Ruth was suffering in the basement trying to summon someone," Thompson said.

The library, now called the Pendleton Public Library, moved to another location in November 1996 and Ruth's old building was converted into a city art center. Director Tom Hilliard said that he never saw or heard anything he couldn't explain: "It was an old building [a Carnegie built in 1916]. Noises turned out to be pipes expanding or a bird in the attic."

Rockin' wraith

The Cairo (Ill.) Public Library boasts of a ghost that one young library patron has dubbed Toby. Director Monica Smith told me that Toby usually hangs out in the special collections room on the second floor of this 1884 building. "I'm here a lot of times by myself at night, and I do hear many different sounds like someone walking around upstairs," Smith said. "Many times I come back and

10

find the lights on that we turned off in that room. I definitely think there is a presence here."

Former librarian Louise Ogg once saw a ghostly light rise up from behind a desk, pass slowly by her office, and disappear into the book stacks. Another staff member was with her and saw the same thing. There used to be a rocking chair in the library that made creaking noises by itself, as if someone were rocking in it. "You kinda get used to it," Smith said.

No cooking in the law library, please

About 1985 the Howard County Law Library in Ellicott City, Maryland, moved into haunted quarters, a historic home built in 1840 by Edwin Parsons Hayden. Law librarian Edy Butler said, "I've been told there are ghosts here, but I have yet to see one or hear one."

The place may be quiet now, but it wasn't in the 1970s when the Hayden House was home to the Howard County District Court. Retired Judge J. Thomas Nissel told me that his secretary used to come to work early in the morning and, together with other people, would smell eggs, toast, and bacon cooking. "They would look around," he said, "but there were no facilities for cooking breakfast at all. By the time I got there at nine or so, it was all gone."

The offices of the Department of Parole and Probation seemed to harbor the most activity. A rocking chair in the department head's office kept rocking back and forth on its own. "One fella, Mr. Howard, a probation officer, he had this ghostlike figure follow him up the stairs one evening when he came in," Judge Nissel said.

The building was gutted and renovated right before the library moved in. Perhaps this is why phenomena stopped. "Or else the ghost just doesn't like to read," quipped Butler.

Ghosts who read, succeed

The female ghost at the Bernardsville (N.J.) Public Library has been so active that the staff issued it a library card. Jean Hill, local-history-room volunteer, told me that "she was not put on our computer with the rest of us mortals, but her card is always available should she choose to use it."

Beginning in 1974, employees started seeing an apparition moving through the front rooms of the library building, which was a tavern during the Revolutionary War. The ghost is said to be that of Phyllis Parker, the innkeeper's daughter, who suffered a nervous breakdown when her British-spy boyfriend was executed. You can read the whole story in *Phyllis—The Library Ghost?*, a booklet published by the library and written by local-history-room volunteer Eileen Johnston.

The last known Phyllis sighting took place in November 1989 when a 3-year-old boy saw a lady in a long, white dress in the reading room and said hello to her.

Gray lady at large

The Willard Library staff in Evansville, Indiana, likes their resident ghost so much that they feature her on their library Web page (www.willard.lib.in.us). A "lady in gray" has been seen in this Victorian Gothic building since 1937. The specter sports a scent of perfume that is often sensed near the elevator, near the rest rooms, or in the children's room (shown at right). Occasionally staff will walk into "cold spots" in the library, which are also indicative of its presence. Former director William Goodrich told me that the lady appeared once on a security monitor placed near the rest rooms. According to current director Greg Hager, a recent visitation was on August 6, 1996, when an employee felt a cold spot and saw the apparition briefly in the special collections department.

Doorway deviltry at a museum library

The Fort Concho museum complex near San Angelo, Texas, was an active army outpost from 1867 to 1889, and it has its share of ghost stories. Lights have been reported late at night inside the museum library, housed in the former bachelor officers' barracks.

Museum librarian Evelyn Lemons told me that in early August 1997 she was sitting at the microfilm reader looking at names of people who had died at the fort. "The back door just suddenly started coming open, and when I said 'Hello,' it stopped. It's a wooden porch, so you can hear people when they walk off," she said. There was no one outside, of course. "I guess I should have looked at whose name I was on when I was looking up dead people, to find out who was coming in the back door."

Lemons recalled other brushes with the unseen when she was an educational assistant working in a different building, Officer's Quarters #9. An invisible presence locked the door on her several times. However, it used a restored 19th-century lock, not the modern deadbolt.

Chills in the LRC

Lewis and Clark Community College in Godfrey, Illinois, started life in 1838 as Monticello College. Its most revered headmistress was Harriet Haskell, the ardent feminist who directed the college from 1868 to 1912. Haskell's favorite room was said to be the chapel, which now serves as the school's learning resources center.

Stories about Haskell haunting the library have been collected by Lewis and Clark history professor Lars Hoffman. One incident in the 1970s involved

10

"a young librarian who didn't believe in ghosts. She was working at night," Hoffman told me, "there weren't many people, if any, in the library, and she felt a hand touch her on her shoulder blade. She turned around and no one was there. It so raised the hair on the back of her neck that she quickly closed the library and left."

For many years Hoffman brought his history classes to the library as a folklore lesson. Invariably one or two students, without being told beforehand, mention to him one of the two prominent cold spots in the reading room.

Just can't quit readin'

The local history room of the New Hanover County Public Library in Wilmington, North Carolina, harbors the ghost of a patron who frequented the library conducting Civil War research. Local-history librarian Beverly Tetterton told me that some mornings she has found files spread out on a reading-room table when she is certain she had put everything away the night before. Sometimes people report the sounds of pages turning—subtle rustling noises that a "librarian would recognize as the sounds of doing research."

She often finds one book, *The Papers of Zebulon Baird Vance*, left out on the table. About 1995, Tetterton related, a 10-year-old boy came into the room to investigate the ghost. "I gave him the book to look at. Later, he walked up and said, 'Do you think this has anything to do with it?' Inside this book was an envelope addressed to the person that I thought might be the ghost. I had been through that book hundreds of times and *never* seen that envelope. I could feel my hair standing straight up."

Buffy, 911

Someone should call on TV high-school protectress Buffy the Vampire Slayer to investigate the bizarre haunting at Rocky Mountain High School in Byron, Wyoming. In 1952 or 1953 school superintendent Harold Hopkinson was working late in the office when he heard footsteps coming down the hall and going up the short staircase to the library. After hearing the library door open and close twice, he heard them again and this time he got up and looked out into the hall.

"As I stood there looking," Hopkinson told me a few years ago, "those footsteps went right past me and *there was no one there*. I heard them continue down the stairs to the front door, which I heard opening. . . . I didn't dream it. There really was something walking on that old floor, which used to creak in a certain way." He said his predecessor refused to go to that part of the building after dark, and so did he for some time afterwards.

The custodial staff agrees that something is amiss. Eddie Davis, who was a maintenance man at the high school for 13 years, heard a bloodcurdling scream coming from the girl's rest room late one night in 1989. "It set my hair on end," he said. But when he cautiously went inside, there was no one there.

Another time Davis's wife, also a custodian, was retrieving some cleaning materials from the second floor when she saw a small, "smoky-looking something" in the hall. "It stunk to high heaven," she told me. "I got the feeling that thing was telling me, 'Jump out the window!' I couldn't move; I couldn't get to the door. But finally I took off and ran. I wouldn't want that to happen to me again," she whispered.

Ghosts in Green River

The spirits aren't as restless as they used to be in the Sweetwater County Library in Green River, Wyoming, but almost from the day it opened in 1980 lights went on and off for no reason and flapping sounds reverberated through the building at night. Library Director Patricia LeFaivre told me that her staff has seen dots of light dancing on the walls inside the closed art gallery room in such a way that ruled out an external light source like car headlights.

Back when the library had electric typewriters instead of computers, at least two of the machines were seen to type on their own. There was no paper loaded at the time, so if these were messages, they were lost. The staff experimented by leaving paper in the typewriters overnight, but no phantom typing occurred.

The most bizarre event occurred some years ago when the interlibrary loan librarian turned away briefly from her computer—it was a dedicated Geac terminal—and when she looked back she saw her name spelled out on the screen. "I don't think the system could have done that itself," LeFaivre explained. "It had no word processing capabilities, and at that time we didn't have e-mail. Her name appeared in quite large letters . . . with nothing else on the screen."

The library was built on top of a cemetery dating from the 1860s. Most of the graves, primarily those of Asian railroad workers, were moved in the 1920s, but a coffin turned up as recently as 1985. Paranormal activity most often takes place when maintenance crews are working on the building or the grounds.

"We've developed an interest in the haunting and keep notes in the ghost log when anything happens," LeFaivre said. "What's interesting is that when we finally accepted the ghost's existence, it seemed to quiet down—like it just wanted to be recognized."

"That would be Master Windham, sir"

Great Britain has more haunted places per square mile than any other country in the world, so it is no surprise that there are several haunted libraries there. My favorite by far is the ghost of William Windham III, an 18th-century scholar and close friend of lexicographer Samuel Johnson. Windham's spirit has been observed in the library of his family estate for the past 170 years.

David Muffon was in charge of putting the estate, Felbrigg Hall, in Norfolk, in order after it was acquired by the National Trust. In November 1972 he was working at a desk in the library when he noticed a "gentleman sitting in the armchair by the fireplace reading books. It was so natural I thought nothing about it. . . . After about 15 seconds he put the book down beside him on the table and faded away."

Muffon asked the old family butler if the house had any ghosts and was told: "Oh yes, there's the ghost of William Windham who sits in the armchair on the far side of the fireplace." For many years the butler had set out books, specifically those given to Windham by Samuel Johnson, on the table for the ghost to read.

"Rather more interesting," Muffon told me, "the next year we actually

10

found in a trunk in the attic clothing very similar to the clothing I saw the ghost wearing from the 1780 period."

Other American haunted libraries

Clayton (Calif.) Public Library. The new library's heat-activated security system goes off when no one is around, suggesting to a local ghosthunter that heat from a haunt is the cause. The clock and air conditioning also behave suspiciously.

Dover (Del.) Public Library. Not haunted, but the library's technical services department keeps a human skull in a hatbox. It allegedly belongs to a notorious 19th-century woman outlaw.

Rotunda, U.S. Capitol Building, Washington, D.C. The Library of Congress once inhabited the rooms to the west of the Rotunda. A male librarian allegedly haunts the area, looking for loot he stashed somewhere. (It was found in 1897.)

Gorin Library, Millikin University, Decatur, Illinois. A room in the basement is supposed to be haunted by a maintenance worker who was accidentally killed there.

Roy O. West Library, De Pauw University, Greencastle, Indiana. An old story has the ghost of James Whitcomb, governor of Indiana from 1843 to 1848, appearing to students who took home books that he had donated to the library.

Brucemore Mansion, Cedar Rapids, Iowa. Strange groans and laughter are heard and objects move by themselves in the library of this 1886 home.

Cedar Rapids (Iowa) Art Museum. Prior to 1985 this building housed the Cedar Rapids Public Library. An apparent case of "crisis apparition" occurred sometime in the late 1960s when a longtime patron was seen in the library by several people shortly after she had died in a fire.

Hutchinson (Kans.) Public Library (left). The ghost of Ida Day Holzapfel, head librarian from 1915 to 1925 and 1947 to 1954, has been seen and heard since her death in 1954. The stacks area in the southwest corner of the basement is notorious for its cold spots, disembodied voices, and hazy apparitions.

Thomas Jefferson Library, University of Missouri, St. Louis. Basement Level One has a reputation for spooky goings-on. Former director Dick Miller had a weird experience there on the first day of his job—phantom footsteps and a clear voice that spoke two words: "Hello, boy." The elevators go up and down frequently after hours, as noted by campus police.

Joseph Papp Public Theatre, New York City. This building housed the Astor Library in 1859 when librarian Joseph Green Cogswell allegedly met the ghost of Austin L. Sands, a wealthy insurance executive, wandering in the alcoves.

Harvey (N.Dak.) Public Library. Lights switching themselves on and chairs and book trucks that rearrange themselves are said to be caused by the ghost of a woman who was murdered in a house where the library now stands.

Hinckley (Ohio) Library. A young woman in an old-fashioned blue dress and a man with a hat have been seen in this 1845 structure. Others have felt an odd presence in the upper rooms, occasionally paper clips sail through the air, and a workman once saw a ghostly figure on the basement stairs.

Steubenville (Ohio) Public Library. The spirit of Ellen Summers Wilson, the first librarian in this 1902 Carnegie, haunts the attic where her office was located.

Linderman Library, Lehigh University, Bethlehem, Pennsylvania. A cantankerous ghost allegedly pesters students and staff. He is thought to be an elderly gentleman who frequented the library and was a general nuisance.

Easton (Pa.) Public Library. Spooky sounds and sensations are blamed on Mammy Morgan and others who were buried in a cemetery uncovered at this site when the library was built in 1903.

Gettysburg (Pa.) Borough Office Building. Formerly the Adams County Public Library, this Civil War–era building had a ghost in the 1940s and 1950s called "Gus," who would move objects, turn on the water fountain, ride the elevator, and cook food in the building.

Civil War Library and Museum, Philadelphia. Footsteps, an eerie presence, and phantom cigar smoke have been experienced here.

Historical Society of Pennsylvania, Philadelphia. A spectral typist frequently heard in a room on the third floor is said to be the ghost of cataloger Albert J. Edmunds. Voices, footsteps, shadowy forms, and an address-label machine that operated without being plugged in have been well-witnessed.

Library Hall, American Philosophical Society, Philadelphia. A cleaning lady claimed to have bumped into Ben Franklin's ghost, his arms full of books, in the 1870s or 1880s.

Heyward House, Charleston, South Carolina. James Heyward's ghost is said to walk in the library of his Charleston home. He died in a hunting accident in 1805, and his apparition is clad in a green hunting coat.

Hampton Plantation, McClellanville, South Carolina. The sounds of a man sobbing and a chair that rocks itself in the downstairs library are evidence of a ghost in this 1735 building.

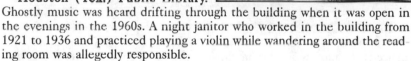

Thomas Hughes Free Public Library, Rugby, Tennessee (right). The ghost of Eduard Bertz, the librarian who organized this collection in 1881–1883, is said to have appeared to Brian Stagg in the late 1960s and given him hints on how to restore the library to its original shelf arrangement.

Houston (Tex.) Public Library. Ghostly music was heard drifting through the building when it was open in the evenings in the 1960s. A night janitor who worked in the building from 1921 to 1936 and practiced playing a violin while wandering around the reading room was allegedly responsible.

Henry Prescott Chaplin Memorial Library, Norwich University, Vermont. Now converted to classrooms, the old library building housed a male ghost who supposedly knocked books off the shelves and played tricks with the lighting.

Blandfield Mansion, Essex County, Virginia. A male figure haunts the downstairs library of this 18th-century mansion.

Edgehill, Warrenton, Virginia. The ghost of Civil War Col. William Chapman has been seen in the mansion library, and he is thought responsible

10

for opening locked doors and making loud noises late at night.

Stratford Hall, Westmoreland County, Virginia. The apparition of Revolutionary War hero Henry "Light Horse Harry" Lee has been seen at a desk in the library.

British haunted libraries

Windsor Castle, Berkshire. The castle library is said to be haunted by Queen Elizabeth I.

Bexley Library, Hall Place, Greater London. This 1537 manor house harbors the ghost of the Black Prince and his wife the Fair Maid of Kent. A White Lady is also in residence.

Blackheath Library, St. John's Park, Greater London. The library in this former vicarage is inhabited by the ghost of Elsie Marshall, who grew up in the house. Lights come on when the building is empty, and an unseen presence brushes past people at the door.

Mannington Hall, near Cromer, Norfolk. The antiquarian Augustus Jessop was examining rare books in the manor house library in 1879 when he was joined by a silent but book-loving apparition dressed in antique ecclesiastical clothing.

York Museum Library, York. In 1954 the library was disturbed by a series of paranormal incidents involving a book entitled *The Antiquities and Curiosities of the Church*. Every fourth Sunday at 8:40 p.m., an unseen hand would remove the book from its shelf and drop it to the floor. An intense cold spot would presage the event, and on at least one occasion the caretaker reported seeing the outline of an elderly man searching for a book.

SOURCE: George M. Eberhart, "Phantoms among the Folios: A Guide to Haunted Libraries," *American Libraries* 28 (October 1997): 68–71, updated with additional sources.

Buffy the Vampire Slayer's school librarian Rupert Giles

by GraceAnne A. DeCandido

I AM NOT ALONE IN THE BELIEF that the appearance of school librarian Rupert Giles on television's *Buffy the Vampire Slayer* has done more for the image of the profession than anything in the past 50 years, with the possible exception of Katharine Hepburn in *Desk Set*. Giles, this wily and attractive professional, is our hero librarian: a pop culture idol whose love of books and devotion to research hold the key to saving the universe—every week.

I know librarians who use quotations from the episodes in their e-mail sig files; even the Internet Public Library has named all of its office computers after characters in the show. For those who might inexplicably have missed it, here is a rundown of the dramatis personae in the Buffyverse from 1997 to 1999.

Giles is The Watcher: the source of training, counterintelligence, and guidance for high-school student Buffy Summers, the one of her generation chosen to be Vampire Slayer. Giles is school librarian at the high school in Sunnydale, a balmy southern California town most noted for being situated on the Hellmouth—a place where vampires, demons, and the forces of darkness gather as bees to honey.

Buffy, a small, delicate-looking blonde of superhuman strength, relies on Giles not only for adult support and coaching, but also for the research necessary to do that for which the Vampire Slayer has been chosen. In the third season, Giles was officially relieved from his Watcher duties, but he ignored that and continued as Buffy's trainer, confidant, and father-figure.

School librarian Rupert Giles and vampire slayer Buffy Summers.
Images courtesy of Warner Brothers TV

Buffy's buds (called affectionately the Slayerettes or the Scooby Gang) include the never-cool Xander; his best friend, the brilliant and fashion-impaired Willow; Xander's reluctant sweetie and later nemesis, the gorgeously shallow Cordelia; and Willow's genius (and occasional werewolf) boyfriend Oz the musician. They comprise Buffy's support group. They meet and conduct most of their research in the school library. Giles, whose collection-development policy must be an extraordinary document, has access in the stacks to a vast number of volumes on vampire and demon lore, the occult, witchcraft, spellcasting, and other rarities not usually found among copies of *Huckleberry Finn* and *Weetzie Bat*. (That got him into trouble with censors, too, as we have seen in the "Gingerbread" episode.)

Others in the cast definitely hail from the dark side. Buffy's own love (and sometimes ex-honey) is a brooding, beautiful, 243-year-old Irish vampire named Angel, who has been cursed with a conscience. There are many vampires, demons, and evil guys, some of whom make multiple appearances. The school principal is a regular bad guy; while the town mayor is an evil of monumental proportions.

Giles: our great sage and sex symbol

It is a heady experience for any profession to find itself an integral part of a wildly popular TV series. How much more so for librarians, who have been bedeviled with a poor public image since at least the 19th century. Giles moves across the stereotype in other, not necessarily positive ways—he is both male and technologically inept.

Giles is tweedy, occasionally befuddled, and very wise, with a certain amount of darkness in his own past. He dropped out of Oxford to pursue high magick, but then moved to the British Library and thence to Sunnydale when duty called. He comes from a family of Watchers, reads multiple languages, and,

10

until her untimely death, had a passionate relationship with the Romany technopagan computer instructor, Jenny Calendar.

Here is a librarian model who is elegant, deeply educated, well (if fussily) dressed, handsome, and charged with eroticism. In a world of teens where parents rarely make an appearance, he is a stable, friendly, and supportive adult. He stands by Buffy even when the powers that be require him to step down. He lives the faith that answers can be found, and most often found in the pages of a book.

Giles is icon and image for us; in him we see our quotidian struggles to provide the right information and the right data resolved into a cosmic drama with the forces of darkness, some of which are extremely attractive, by the way. We love Giles because at last we have a pop image for our uneasy relationship with dark and light, information and story, books and technology.

We mourned when—and this is as emotionally complicated as it gets—the vampire with a soul who loved Buffy murders Jenny whom Giles loved. We see Giles struggle valiantly with information sources, we can see his love of story, we can see, as Xander says, that "knowledge is the ultimate weapon" and that format is the least of our problems when there are vampires and demons about.

Giles: "I believe the subtext here is rapidly becoming text"

The librarians who follow *Buffy* find a great deal of library lore and information-seeking behavior, as well as an occasional drop of genuine wisdom, in the words of the denizens of Sunnydale.

> *Willow:* How is it you always know this stuff? You always know what's going on. I never know what's going on.
> *Giles:* Well, you weren't here from midnight until six researching it.
> —"Angel"

The plodding nature of most research cannot be eliminated, even by brilliance and magic, even when we might not want to know what it is we are seeking. It is Giles' particular gift to cast a glamour over the kind of dogged reference we practice daily. He invests the methodical search for the fact that will solve the problem at hand with a kind of fierce joy, but he never underestimates its cost in time or care.

> *Giles:* I'm sure my books and I are in for a fascinating afternoon.
> —"Phases"

> *Giles (echoing Buffy):* Get my books. Look stuff up.
> —"The Pack"

> *Willow:* I'm sure he will. He's like . . . Book Man!
> —"Passion"

Books are central. It is in books that Giles, as the Watcher, finds the images, the information, the incantation, the lore that will assist Buffy in her struggle against the Hellmouth and its universe of monsters. While Giles relies upon Willow to search the Internet for materials, like newspaper records and police logs not easily accessible in print, Giles believes that what he needs

to know for Buffy's sake lies in his many volumes at home and at work. Giles also makes that necessary leap of faith common to all good librarians: He bridges the chasm between the information as it lives in the text and the transfer of that information into a form the Slayerettes and Buffy can actually use. Sometimes that means literal translation, other times it means recasting what he reads into stories, tag lines, or aphorisms that make sense to the teens he serves. The sacredness of the book, the literal power of words, underscore the action in Buffy's world. They form the matrix and latticework for all that terrific "pow! kick! stake!" stuff that happens later.

> *Xander:* He's like SuperLibrarian. Everyone forgets, Willow, that knowledge is the ultimate weapon.
> —"Never Kill a Boy on the First Date"

> *Willy:* So, what can I do for you? Couple of drinks?
> *Xander:* Yeah. Let me get a double shot of, um . . . of information, pal.
> —"Amends"

While snide comments about Giles's profession abound, the core belief that knowledge is the answer underlies all. This is apparent from Xander's remarks, even though he and others are often cavalier about regular school assignments. There are many weapons to be had in Sunnydale. Buffy uses the classic cross and stake, among others, and Giles has an armory of medieval weaponry, most of it stored at the library. The Slayerettes have a very high level of rapier teen wit, peppered with pop-cult references and sly asides. The thirst to know, however, is at the core of it all: to know the forces of darkness, to name them, and hence to defang them; to know themselves, as they dance on the edge of maturity; to search out the specifics of how to overmaster a particular demon along with the principles of how knowledge can lead to larger truths. What a message for us to emblazon on our T-shirts and on our hearts.

> *Angel:* They're children, making up bedtime stories of friendly vampires to comfort themselves in the dark.
> *Willow:* Is that so bad? I mean the dark can get pretty dark. Sometimes you need a story.
> —"Lie to Me"

10

Willow places her hand precisely on a central truth of *Buffy*, and of librarianship. Sometimes these teens need a story to cover themselves for a lost assignment or a lost weekend. Sometimes, though, they need a story to tell themselves to get through the latest horrific vision or ghastly demise. Sometimes it is the story itself that brings both comfort and information: In the beginning of the third season, a voiceover from Jack London's *Call of the Wild* was used to great effect.

Buffy also identifies her role as a storybook hero in "Killed by Death," when she tells the child in the hospital, "We both know there are real monsters. But there are also real heroes that fight monsters. And that's me." The story enables us to see not only Buffy as a true hero, but Giles—Book Man, SuperLibrarian—as a hero also.

> *Jenny (to Giles):* The divine exists in cyberspace the same as out here.
> —"I Robot, You Jane"

Giles has definite issues with computers and online technology. He is a living metaphor for what those of us *d'un certain âge* might have gone through as the profession we thought we had joined transmuted itself into something very, very Else.

The core of librarians who got their MLS degrees 25 years ago and more are now doing things professionally that were unimaginable to the selves we were then. We came to librarianship because we loved the sound of words talking to each other, rubbing up against each other; or because the world inside a story was far more real to us than the world inside our neighborhoods; or because we loved chasing an idea around. For many of us, librarianship originally was a choice to separate ourselves from workplaces that were less humane, less involved in the drama of peoples' lives.

It came as a shock to some of us, as it does to Giles, that the glass box (the computer Jenny refers to as "the good box") could also be a tool in the search for knowing, and an increasingly indispensable tool. In "I Robot, You Jane," Giles tells Jenny, "If it's to last, then the getting of knowledge should be tangible" in the smell and texture of old volumes. In the same episode, Giles confesses to Buffy that computers fill him with "childlike terror." Jenny gently chides him for living in the Middle Ages and assures him he will enter the new century with a few years to spare. We do see him, much later, yelling at a computer that has wantonly disconnected him from the "Frisky Watchers Chat Room" ("Gingerbread").

> *Giles:* They're confiscating my books.
> *Buffy:* Giles, we need those books.
> *Giles:* Believe me, I tried to tell that to the nice man with the big gun.

> *Giles:* This is intolerable. Snyder has interfered before, but I won't take this from that twisted little homunculus.
> *Snyder:* I love the smell of desperate librarian in the morning.
> *Giles:* You get out . . . and take your marauders with you.
> *Snyder:* Oh, my. So fierce.

> *Snyder:* Just how is, um, *Blood Rites and Sacrifices* appropriate material for a public school library? Chess Club branching out?
> —"Gingerbread"

Giles knows about challenges to the school library, too. In this chilling episode, mothers turn against their own children, attempting to burn the books that the principal and the parents see as harmful, occult, or just plain weird.

There's an aborted plot to torch teens along with titles in the guise of chasing after child murderers (the ghost children turn out to be demons themselves, sent to sow discord).

> *Buffy:* You're the Watcher, I just work here.
> *Giles:* Yes. I must consult my books.
>
> —"When She Was Bad"

> *Buffy:* But, Giles, it's one thing to be a Watcher and a librarian ...
> The point is, no one blinks an eye if you wanna spend all your days
> with books.
>
> —"What's My Line (Part 1)"

Giles takes a lot of kidding because of his perceived stuffiness, his single-minded approach to problems, and his apparent lack of current awareness. However, the kidding doesn't negate how fully the Slayerettes are invested in Giles as both a mentor and a symbol of adult comfort and reassurance. He knows what his job is, so do they, and so do we.

YA reference librarian Lesley Knieriem of the South Huntington Public Library, New York, said it well in an e-mail: "Giles is appealing to librarians in that he portrays us as we like to think we are: enormously intelligent, literate, genteel, sensitive, devoted to our patrons, with a sexy, ferocious 'ripper' concealed within, only to be let out when needed to slay the demons of ignorance. Yes, he does fit many of the stereotypes: bookish, stuffy, reserved, technophobic (this last isn't any of us!). Giles embraces his stuffiness, pokes gentle fun at it, and transcends it."

> *Giles:* To forgive is an act of compassion, Buffy. It's not done because
> people deserve it. It's done because they need it.
>
> —"I Only Have Eyes For You"

We have all had supervisors who have done unforgivable things to us; we may have done a few ourselves to those we supervise. We have all had patrons who have fought their particular demons right in front of the check out desk, and we wanted to avert our eyes. Giles, given to pronouncements but rarely to exhortation, here states a truth as cleanly as any prophet. We hope it comforted Buffy; it can certainly comfort us.

> *Giles:* You mean life?
> *Buffy:* Yeah. Does it get easy?
> *Giles:* What do you want me to say?
> *Buffy:* Lie to me.
> *Giles:* Yes, it's terribly simple. The good guys are always stalwart and
> true. The bad guys are easily distinguished by the pointy horns or
> black hats. And, uh, we always defeat them and save the day. No
> one ever dies, and everybody lives happily ever after.
> *Buffy:* Liar.
>
> —"Lie To Me"

We have seen the books and materials that provide us with information and textual analysis of the bad guys can also provide us with stories wherein we conquer the demons and go forth. Giles reminds us that some days, the dragon wins. And that good and evil are rarely so separate that we can distinguish them clearly without the white light of study and analysis.

> *Giles:* You did good work tonight, Buffy.

10

Buffy: And I got a little toy surprise.
Giles: I had no idea that children en masse could be gracious.
Buffy: Every now and then, people surprise you.

—"The Prom"

Named as Class Protector during her senior prom, Buffy has a moment of solace and Giles sees the teenagers he serves in a new light. People surprise us all the time, in the questions they ask, in the way they use the answers, in their need to know, and sometimes in their gratitude.

Buffy and her friends have now graduated from high school, in a spectacular denouement that banished Angel and provided us with ample reason to wonder what Giles's next career move would be. He says Buffy no longer needs the Watcher's Council, but it is clear she still needs a librarian.

Indispensable Buffy references

Christopher Golden and Nancy Holder, with Keith R. A. DeCandido, *Buffy the Vampire Slayer: The Watcher's Guide* (Pocket/S&S, 1998).

There are many Buffy Web sites, official and not-so. For Giles groupies, however, there is nothing like Sonja Marie's The Official Giles' Appreciation Society Panters Home Page (www.geocities.com/TelevisionCity/7728/gaspers.html).

Another good site is The Buffy Cross & Stake (slayer.simplenet.com/tbcs/main.html).

SOURCE: GraceAnne A. DeCandido, "Bibliographic Good vs. Evil in *Buffy the Vampire Slayer,*" *American Libraries* 30 (September 1999): 44–47.

Bibliocapers from *American Libraries*

Defacing library materials

Talk show host Rosie O'Donnell made librarians everywhere wince when she ripped out a page of a library book and then told actress Meg Ryan to keep the book during a May 20, 1997, telecast.

Researchers from the show had borrowed the 1979 yearbook from the Bethel (Conn.) Public Library because it has Ryan's school photo. A contrite Rosie donated $1,000, the cost of replacing the valuable collector's item, to the library. Bethel Director Alice Knapp said a graduate has since donated another copy to the library, which Knapp has placed under lock and key, swearing to never lend it out again.

Document de-liver-y

A Baltimore woman was arrested for pouring raw chicken livers into the overnight drop box of an Anne Arundel County library and several mailboxes, according to the June 12, 1997, *Washington Post.* A video surveillance camera in the library caught the woman in the act. Library officials said books had been destroyed by the night deposits on several occasions.

SOURCE: American Libraries 28 (August 1997): 23.

Librarians on stage and screen

by Martin Raish, Frederick Duda, and George M. Eberhart

THE FIRST TWO EDITIONS OF the *Whole Library Handbook* included a list of librarians and library assistants in movies. This feature proved so popular among readers that it has been greatly expanded and contains many new citations. For updates, see Martin Raish's "Filmography of Librarians in Motion Pictures" (www.lib.byu.edu/dept/libsci/films/introduction.html). Raish is chair of the Department of Library Instruction and Information Literacy at Brigham Young University Libraries.—*GME.*

1917—A Wife on Trial; Mignon Anderson plays underpaid children's librarian Phyllis Narcissa who marries for money.

1919—A Very Good Young Man; A young woman turns down a marriage proposal from an assistant at the public library (Bryant Washburn) because her mother has convinced her that he is too morally faultless.

1921—The Blot; Claire Windsor as Amelia Griggs, a clerk at the public library, is saved from a life of poverty by the marriage proposal of a wealthy young man.

1921—The Lost Romance; Mayne Kelso as a librarian.

1923—Only 38; May McAvoy's husband, a clergyman, leaves her a widow with teenage twins to support. She sends them to college where she accepts a job as a librarian. To their dismay she soon sheds her old-fashioned clothes and becomes a bit wild.

1924—Lily of the Dust; Pola Negri as Lily, an innocent librarian who catches the eye of officers in a German garrison.

1932—Forbidden; Barbara Stanwyck is small-town librarian Lulu Smith. On her way to work she is taunted by local kids as "old lady four eyes," and later she declares, "I wish I owned this library. . . . I'd get an axe and smash it to a million pieces, then I'd set fire to the whole town and play a ukulele while it burned." She takes a cruise and falls for an unobtainable man, a district attorney married to a crippled woman.

1932—No Man of Her Own; Carole Lombard as Connie Randall, public librarian. This film is noted for the scene in which Clark Gable ogles Lombard's legs while she stands on a ladder to reach a book on a high shelf. His scandalous stare created quite a controversy, and prompted the founding of Hollywood's League of Decency.

1934—Imitation of Life; Fredi Washington as 19-year-old Peola Johnson, who lies to her mother about having a night job in the library (see 1959 remake below).

1936—Cain and Mabel; Clark Gable kisses his wife behind the library shelves. A fierce librarian presides.

1937—Navy Blues; Richard Purcell as Rusty, a sailor, meets a prim, drab librarian, Mary Brian as Doris, who turns into a ravishing beauty.

1938—Scandal Street; Louise Campbell as Nora Langdon, public librarian.

1938—Start Cheering; Arthur Loft as the librarian.

1939—Fast and Loose; Robert Montgomery as rare-book dealer/detective Joel Sloane tries to locate the missing books of library tycoon Ralph Morgan as Nicholas Torrent.

1939—Within the Law; Claire Du Brey as a librarian.

1940—The Philadelphia Story; Hilda Plowright as the Quaker librarian.

1941—Citizen Kane; Georgia Backus as Bertha Anderson, manuscripts librarian, Thatcher Memorial Library.

10

1941—Livet går vidare; [Swedish] Åke Claesson as the librarian.

1941—A Man Betrayed; Minerva Urecal as a librarian.

1942—Quiet Please, Murder; George Sanders as Fleg, library thief; Frank O'Connor as library guard.

1942—Unusual Occupations; [Short] Grace MacDonald plays herself as a librarian with a streetcar bookmobile.

1943—Flesh and Fantasy; Ian Wolfe as the librarian (uncredited).

1943—En Flicka för mej; [Swedish] Saga Sjöberg as a librarian.

1943—The Human Comedy; Adeline De Walt Reynolds as children's librarian.

1943—Shadow of a Doubt; Eily Malyon as librarian, Santa Rosa (Calif.) PL.

1944—It Happened Tomorrow; John Philliber as Pop Benson, a veteran newspaper librarian who befriends Dick Powell. After Pop dies, his ghost returns to give Powell copies of the next day's paper for three successive days.

1944—Lady in the Dark; Mary MacLaren as a librarian.

1945—Adventure; Greer Garson as Emily Sears, San Francisco PL.

1945—Spellbound; On the lam in New York City, Dr. Constance Peterson (Ingrid Bergman) is considered harmless by a hotel detective (Bill Goodwin) because he thinks that she looks like either a librarian or a schoolteacher.

1945—A Tree Grows in Brooklyn; Lillian Bronson as children's librarian.

1945—Wonder Man; Danny Kaye plays both Buzzy Bellew, a nightclub singer who is murdered because he witnessed a mob killing, and his twin brother, Edwin Dingle, a brilliant, bookish scholar who spends his days at the library writing with both hands. There he meets and falls in love with the beautiful young librarian Ellen Shavley (Virginia Mayo).

1946—The Big Sleep; Carole Douglas as librarian, Hollywood PL; Dorothy Malone as antiquarian bookseller.

1946—Happy Birthday; [Broadway comedy, 1946–47] Helen Hayes as public librarian Addie Bemis, a teetotaler, who finds romance in the Mecca Cocktail Bar in Newark, N.J. (Hayes won a Tony award for her performance in 1947, the first year Tonys were awarded.)

1946—It's a Wonderful Life; Donna Reed as Mary Hatch, Bedford Falls PL (in alternate life).

1947—Good News; June Allyson as Connie Lane, student library assistant, Tait College Library. She falls for the football hero, Peter Lawford, and together they sing "The French Lesson" in the college library, dancing through the stacks as she reshelves books with little attention to call numbers.

1947—So Well Remembered; [British] Martha Scott as public librarian Olivia Channing, who appears to be meek but turns out to be aggressive and ruthless. Roddy Hughes plays another librarian.

1947—The Web; Robin Raymond as the newspaper librarian.

1948—Apartment for Peggy; Crystal Reeves as a librarian.

1948—Sitting Pretty; Mary Field as a librarian.

1949—All the King's Men; The Willie Stark Library is featured in a "March of Time" style newsreel.

1950—The Asphalt Jungle; Sam Jaffe as inmate "Doc" Erwin Riedenschneider gets to work in the prison library for good behavior.

1950—Peggy; Ellen Corby as the librarian Mrs. Privet.

1951—As Young As You Feel; Carol Savage as a librarian.

1951—Katie Did It; Ann Blyth as Katherine Standish, New England librarian.

1951—The Racket; Harriet Matthews as a librarian.

1952—The Thief; Ray Milland as Allan Fields, atomic spy and library user.

1953—Pickup on South Street; Jay Loftin as the librarian (uncredited).

1953—The War of the Worlds; Sylvia Van Buren (Ann Robinson) is a library science teacher.

1954—Skuggan; [Swedish] Olav Riégo as the librarian.

1955—The Cobweb; At an exclusive psychiatric clinic, the doctors and staff are about as crazy as the patients. The clinic head, Dr. Stewart McIver (Richard Widmark), thinks that it would be good therapy for his patients to design and make new drapes for the library.

1955—Desk Set; [Broadway comedy, 1955–56] Bunny Watson (Shirley Booth) and her assistants confront automation in a radio and TV reference library (see 1957 movie version below).

1955—The Girl Rush; Kim Halliday (Rosalind Russell) was a librarian before inheriting a half-share in a Las Vegas hotel.

1955—Summertime; A classic romantic drama about an American spinster librarian/secretary (Katharine Hepburn as Jane Hudson) on holiday in Venice who has an affair with a handsome merchant.

1955—Violent Saturday; One character is a stereotypical female librarian, but she is also a purse-snatcher.

1956—The Man Who Never Was; [British] Gloria Grahame as librarian Lucy Sherwood has a pivotal role in convincing a Nazi agent of the legitimacy of a bogus allied plan to invade Greece, instead of Sicily.

1956—Storm Center; Bette Davis as Alicia Hull, public librarian; Kim Hunter as Martha Lockridge, assistant, then acting librarian; Kevin Coughlin as Freddie Slater, young adult reader and arsonist.

1957—Curse of the Demon; [British] A librarian (John Salew) at the British Museum Reading Room informs Dana Andrews as Dr. John Holden that the title *True Discoveries of the Witches and Demons* is not on the shelf.

1957—Desk Set; Katharine Hepburn as Bunny Watson, research librarian for a communications firm; Joan Blondell as Peg Costello, and Dina Merrill as Sylvia Blair, library support staff; Spencer Tracy as Richard Sumner, automation consultant.

1957—Interlude; June Allyson as Helen Banning shelves books in the American Cultural Center in Berlin.

1957—Witwer mit 5 Töchtern; [West German] Heinz Erhardt as a widowed librarian raising five daughters.

1958—Horror of Dracula; [British] An investigator is sent to Dracula's castle on the pretext of cataloging the Count's rare books and journals.

1958—Hot Spell; Elsie Weller as a librarian.

1959—The Crimson Kimono; Stafford Repp as the city librarian.

1959—The FBI Story; Jimmy Stewart as Chip Hardesty kisses a librarian (Vera Miles) in the stacks.

1959—Imitation of Life; Susan Kohner as Sarah Jane Johnson, a singer and dancer in a strip joint, who tells her mother that she has a job cataloging books in the library at night.

1959—Twilight Zone; [TV series] "Time Enough at Last" episode. Bank teller Burgess Meredith as Henry Bemis finds that the world has been destroyed in a nuclear holocaust. He decides to commit suicide until he sees a library. This is paradise to him, and he begins to organize books to read for years to come. Just as he settles down to read, his glasses slip from his face and break, trapping him in a blurry world forever.

1959—Web of Evidence; [British] Vera Miles as librarian Lena Anderson helps Paul Mathry (Van Johnson) clear his late father of murder.

1960—Bluebeard's Ten Honeymoons; [British] Milo Sperber as the librarian.

1960—Doctor in Love; [British] Sheila Hancock as a librarian.

1961—Breakfast at Tiffany's; Elvia Allman as shushing librarian, New York PL.

1961—Return to Peyton Place; Robert Sterling as Mike Rossi, school principal, is fired for refusing to remove Allison Mackenzie's (Carol Lynley's) racy novel from the school library.

10

1961—Twilight Zone; [TV series] "The Obsolete Man" episode. In a future State, librarian Romney Wordsworth (Burgess Meredith) is considered obsolete and sentenced to die. He devises a test to see if the State or the individual is stronger.

1962—Bon Voyage!; James Millhollin as the librarian.

1962—Cape Fear; Josephine Smith as a librarian.

1962—Murder, She Said; [British] Stringer Davis as Mr. Stringer, the village librarian, appears as Miss Marple's friend in this and other Margaret Rutherford interpretations of Agatha Christie's sleuth.

1962—The Music Man; Shirley Jones as Marian Paroo, librarian, River City (Iowa) PL, tries to expose Robert Preston as a con man.

1962—Only Two Can Play; [British] Peter Sellers as John Lewis, librarian, Swansea Library.

1962—Rome Adventure; Suzanne Pleshette as Prudence Bell, assistant librarian in a girls' school.

1962—Sherlock Holmes and the Deadly Necklace; [French/Italian/German] Danielle Argence as a librarian.

1962—The Tell-Tale Heart; [British] Laurence Payne as Edgar Marsh dreams he is a crippled librarian.

1962—That Touch of Mink; Honeymooners are interrupted in Al's Motel in Asbury Park, N.J., by Philip Shayne (Cary Grant), who leads Mr. Smith (John Fiedler) to believe that he had an affair with Mrs. Smith (Barbara Collentine). After Grant departs, Mr. Smith says to his wife, "You librarians live it up pretty good." Mrs. Smith later tries to convince her husband that there was no other man in her life until he walked into the library.

1963—Cleopatra; Rex Harrison as Julius Caesar, library arsonist, Alexandria, Egypt; Elizabeth Taylor as Cleopatra, intellectual freedom advocate.

1963—Spencer's Mountain; James MacArthur as Clayboy Spencer fails to negotiate a higher salary to run the local library.

1964—7 Faces of Dr. Lao; Barbara Eden as Angela Benedict, public librarian of Abalone, Ariz.

1965—The Spy Who Came in From the Cold; [British] Claire Bloom as Nan Perry, librarian and Communist; Richard Burton as Alec Leamas, library assistant and spy.

1965—You Must Be Joking! [British] James Robertson Justice as the librarian.

1966—La vita agra; [Italian] Pippo Starnazza as the librarian.

1966—The Whisperers; [British] Dame Edith Evans as Mrs. Maggie Ross, a lonely old lady who spends lots of time reading the daily papers and warming her toes in the library.

1966—You're a Big Boy Now; Peter Kastner as Bernard Chanticleer, library page, New York PL, who steals a Gutenburg Bible from the library; Rip Torn as Bernard's father, I. H. Chanticleer, rare book librarian; Karen Black as Amy and Tony Bill as Raef, library assistants.

1967—Cop-Out; Melinda Mays as a librarian.

1967—Quatermass and the Pit; [British] Noel Howlett as the abbey librarian.

1968—Leben zu zweit; [East German] Walter Lendrich as the librarian.

1968—Twisted Nerve; Hayley Mills as librarian Susan Harper.

1969—Goodbye, Columbus; Richard Benjamin as Neil Klugman, library assistant, Newark (N.J.) PL.

1969—Kes; [British] Billy Casper (David Bradley) goes to the public library to get a book on hawks, but the haughty librarian (Zoe Sutherland) sends him away because he is dirty and obviously irresponsible.

1970—The Dunwich Horror; Sandra Dee as Nancy Wagner and Donna Baccala as Elizabeth Hamilton, student assistants, Miskatonic University Library; Toby Russ as a librarian.

1970—Ha-Simla; [Israeli] Three short stories of life in Tel Aviv. The first: A girl meets a boy in a library and has to decide what to do next.

1970—Love Story; Ali MacGraw as student assistant, Radcliffe College Library.

1971—The Failing of Raymond; [Made for TV] Adrienne Marden as a librarian.

1971—Making It; Doro Merande as high school librarian Ms. Hobgood tells a student that books by D. H. Lawrence are not for general distribution.

1971—Rio das Mortes; [West German, Made for TV] Carl Amery as the librarian.

1971—They Might Be Giants; Wilbur Pabody (Jack Gilford) plays an archivist/librarian friend of Sherlock Holmes who helps him do research.

1972—Savage Messiah; [British] Alexei Jawdokimov as a library student.

1972—Z.P.G.; When Geraldine Chaplin becomes secretly pregnant, her husband accesses an automated library cubicle for information on childbirth and is immediately arrested and interrogated. The "library" has no human attendant.

1973—Soylent Green; In 2022, Detective Thorn (Charlton Heston) and Sol Roth (Edward G. Robinson) find out that librarians have all the power because they are the only ones who have information or know how to get it.

1973—Wicker Man; [British] Ingrid Pitt is the Scottish public librarian who helps an investigator research the disappearance of a young girl.

1974—Céline et Julie vont en bateau; [French] Juliet Berto is Céline, a young magician, and Dominique Labourier is Julie, a pretty, red-haired librarian. In one scene they are "spying" on each other in the library—Julie stamps cards indiscriminately and Céline tears pages out of books. Later they break into the library in the middle of the night and steal a valuable old book of magic spells they need in order to fulfill their "mission."

1974—Chinatown; Jake Gittes (Jack Nicholson) uses the county archives. The clerk (Allan Warnick) is a sullen young man who does not like his job, and only grudgingly provides assistance. Nicholson tears out part of a page from a record book by covering the noise with a cough.

1974—The Girl on the Late, Late Show; [Made for TV] Mary Ann Mobley as a librarian.

1974—Mr. Sycamore; Jean Simmons as Estelle Benbow, librarian.

1974—Norman Conquests; [Broadway play, 1974–75] Tom Courtney as Norman, a drunken librarian who spends his time trying to seduce his wife and sisters-in-law.

1974—A Pendragon legenda; [Hungarian] László Szuczvay as the librarian.

1974—Zardoz; [British] Zed (Sean Connery) finds in a forgotten library the book that helps him find the secret of Zardoz.

1975—The Girl Who Couldn't Lose; [Made for TV] An intelligent librarian (Julie Kavner as Jane Darwin) becomes a sensational game show contestant.

1975—Rollerball; Sir Ralph Richardson as an absented-minded Swiss librarian.

1976—All the President's Men; Jaye Stewart and James Murtaugh as clerks, Library of Congress; Jamie Smith Jackson and Ron Menchine as *Washington Post* librarians; Robert Redford as Bob Woodward and Dustin Hoffman as Carl Bernstein, LC researchers.

1976—Carrie; Sissy Spacek as Carrie White is in the high school library stacks when William Katt as Tommy Ross asks her to the prom.

1976—Logan's Run; Peter Ustinov as the Old Man explains what a library is to Logan (Michael York).

1976—One Summer Love; Mimi Obler as a librarian.

1977—The Remake; A middle-aged librarian (Ed Nylund) learns that he has cancer.

10

1978—American Hot Wax; Ted Schwartz as Gary the music librarian.

1978—Debbie Does Dallas; Stodgy librarian Mr. Biddle has to put up with sex in the stacks.

1978—Foul Play; Goldie Hawn as Gloria Mundy, librarian, San Francisco. Other librarians are Marilyn Sokol as a young, attractive, dark-haired man-hater; and Frances Bay as an older grey-haired woman who takes home an armful of books to read.

1978—Karate Ghostbuster; [Hong Kong] Jackie Chan plays the part of the class clown in a shaolin temple whose deadliest secret is stolen. All is lost until Jackie's character discovers the dancing blue ghosts with bright red hair who haunt the library.

1978—Movie Movie; Trish Van Devere as Betsy McGuire, public librarian.

1979—The Attic; Frances Bay as a librarian who devotes her life to caring for her disabled father.

1979—Escape From Alcatraz; Clint Eastwood as inmate Frank Morris works in the Alcatraz library.

1979—Love on the Run; [French] Daniel Mesguich as Xavier the Librarian.

1980—My Bodyguard; Dorothy Scott as a librarian.

1980—Somewhere in Time; Christopher Reeve falls in love with a girl in a photograph. A librarian (Noreen Walker) helps him find information about her.

1981—The Beyond; [Italian] Director Lucio Fulci as a librarian (uncredited).

1981—Höjdhoppar'n; [Swedish] Margareta Olsson as a librarian.

1981—House by the Cemetery; [Italian] Carlo de Mejo as an unctuous librarian helps Paolo Malco as Father do research at home.

1981—Lola; [West German] Andrea Heuer as a librarian.

1981—The Pit; [Canadian] John Auten as a library janitor, and Cindy Auten as a library clerk.

1981—Ragtime; The J. P. Morgan Library in New York City is taken over by revolutionaries; the director of the library is portrayed as a bombastic, yet cowardly, curator. John Sterland plays a library guard.

1981—This House Possessed; [Made for TV] K. Callen as the library woman, who wants to give Sheila Moore (Lisa Eilbacher) some newspaper articles.

1981—Wacko; Jacqueline Cole as a librarian.

1982—Computercide; [Made for TV] Linda Gillen as a librarian.

1982—Irezumi: Spirit of Tattoo; [Japanese] A young woman pleases her middle-aged lover by having her back covered with tattoos. He is a mild-mannered librarian who wears conservative business suits and is utterly ordinary except for his passion for tattooed skin.

1982—The Last American Virgin; Blanche Rubin as a librarian.

1982—Sophie's Choice; Meryl Streep as Sophie Zawistowska, a Polish immigrant, seeks a book by the American poet Emily Dickinson, though she pronounces the name "Emil Dickens." A prissy, surly male librarian played by John Rothman is in no mood to provide reference service and tells her there is "no American poet named Dickens."

1982—Ucna leta izumitelja Polza; [Yugoslavian] Boris Juh as the librarian.

1983—Christine; A scene early in the film portrays a confrontation between the "hero" and the school librarian (Jan Burrell) over talking. The book that Dennis (John Stockwell) pulls off the shelf in the library before asking Leigh (Alexandra Paul) out is *Christine* by Stephen King.

1983—Getting It On; Fran Taylor as a librarian.

1983—Hammett; Marilu Henner as a sexy San Francisco librarian; Liz Roberson plays a library user.

1983—Hysterical; A librarian declares, "The library is closed. All white people must leave."

1983—**The Lords of Discipline;** Helena Stevens as a librarian.

1983—**The Prodigal;** Ian Bannen plays an author in the library.

1983—**Screwballs;** [US/Canadian] Caroline Tweedle as a librarian.

1983—**Something Wicked This Way Comes;** Jason Robards Jr. as Charles Halloway, librarian, Green Town (Ill.) PL.

1984—**Cal;** [British] Helen Mirren as Marcella, an attractive widow who works in a library in Northern Ireland; J. J. Murphy as a library user.

1984—**The Element of Crime;** [Danish] Mogens Rukov as the librarian.

1984—**Footloose;** A bookburning attempt at an Iowa school library is stopped by John Lithgow as Rev. Shaw Moore.

1984—**Ghostbusters;** Alice Drummond as librarian, New York PL; John Rothman as library administrator, New York PL; Ruth Oliver as library ghost; Bill Murray as Peter Venkman, library ghost exterminator.

1984—**Ordeal by Innocence;** [British] Donald Sutherland uses the local library to look at newspapers, while the elderly lady librarian is checking in returned books.

1984—**Wet Gold;** [Made for TV] Laura (Brooke Shields) takes her friend Sampson (Burgess Meredith) to a library, where she finds an old newspaper article that substantiates his story of a lost treasure.

1985—**Agnes of God;** Victor Désy as the librarian.

1985—**The Body in the Library;** [British, Made for TV] In the small village of St. Mary Mead, Colonel and Mrs. Bantry, owner of the local manor (Gossington Hall), is shocked when one morning a young lady's body is found in the library. To find out the truth, the Bantrys call in the help of their good friend and detective Miss Jane Marple (Joan Hickson).

1985—**Brazil;** [British] This Orwellian vision of the present/future (set somewhere in the 20th century, but using technology from the 1970s) tells the story of a lowly bureaucrat (Jonathan Pryce as Sam Lowry) who is the closest thing this society has to a librarian. He grudgingly accepts a promotion from Information Storage to Information Retrieval and meets the girl of his dreams.

1985—**The Breakfast Club;** Five students (Emilio Estevez, Anthony Michael Hall, Judd Nelson, Molly Ringwald, and Ally Sheedy) undergo weekend detention in the school library. In a continuity goof, the library clock changes during the same scenes throughout the movie.

1985—**Bridge Across Time;** [Made for TV] Adrienne Barbeau as Lynn Chandler, head librarian, Lake Havasu City PL, Arizona.

1985—**Clue;** In the library, Col. Mustard's (Martin Mull) whiskey glass jumps from the table to his hand.

1985—**Defence of the Realm;** [British] Philip Whitchurch as the newspaper "cuttings" librarian.

1985—**The Empty Beach;** [Australian] Deborah Kennedy as a newspaper librarian.

1985—**Forbidden;** [West German] Guntbert Warns as the librarian.

1985—**Heaven Help Us;** Kevin Dillon as class bully Rooney asks Malcolm Denare as class nerd Caesar to help him with his homework when they meet in the stacks of St. Basil's Catholic School Library in Brooklyn.

1985—**Maxie;** Mandy Patinkin as Nick, rare book librarian, San Francisco PL; Valerie Curtin as Ophelia Sheffer, supervising librarian and sexual harasser, San Francisco PL.

1985—**My Science Project;** Linda Hoy as a librarian.

1985—**Wetherby;** [British] Dame Judi Dench as Yorkshire librarian Marcia Pilborough.

1986—**The Name of the Rose;** [Italian/French/German] Volker Prechtel as Malachia, monastery librarian, unnamed Benedictine abbey in Italy, 1327; Michael Habeck as Brother Berengar, assistant librarian.

10

1986—Off Beat; Judge Reinhold as Joe Gower, skating library assistant by day, dancer by night.

1986—Raiders of the Living Dead; Zita Johann as a librarian.

1986—Resting Place; [Made for TV] John Lithgow is assigned to help the family of a black officer who was killed in Vietnam. In looking into the officer's background he learns that when he was about eight years old the librarian wouldn't let him borrow a book because he was black. He said he would wait until she changed her mind. He stayed all day until she finally gave in and let him have the book.

1986—Traps; [Australian] Lesley Stern as a librarian.

1986—Wimps; Freshman wimp (Louie Bannano) helps quarterback woo library clerk Roxanne (Deborah Blaisdell, aka X-rated star Tracey Adams).

1987—Agent Trouble; [French] Catherine Deneuve plays middle-aged librarian Amanda Weber who decides to investigate the apparent cover-up of a mass murder.

1987—Frenchman's Farm; [Australian] Ian Leigh-Cooper as the librarian.

1987—Harry and the Hendersons; A librarian (Peggy Platt) helps people find books on Bigfoot.

1987—Ironweed; A sick and homeless woman tries to take refuge and get warm in front of a fireplace in the reference room of the public library, but a librarian (Bethel Leslie) catches her sleeping in the chair and, very nicely, tells her she is welcome to use the library, but sleeping is not allowed.

1987—Mindkiller; A shy, studious library clerk (Joe McDonald) reads about the power of the mind and develops amazing telekenitic abilities, but these eventually turn against him.

1987—Prick Up Your Ears; [British] Gary Oldman as playwright Joe Orton and his roommate Alfred Molina vandalize books in a public library, are kicked out by the librarian, and get put in jail for six months.

1987—The Rosary Murders; Sandy Broad as a librarian.

1987—Slamdance; Lin Shage as a librarian.

1987—Wings of Desire; [West German] Seven angels find solace in a large public library in Berlin.

1988—Criminal Law; Irene Kessler as Peggy, a librarian.

1988—Death of a Son; [British, Made for TV] Jon Cartwright as the reference librarian, and Eileen Nicholas as the mobile librarian.

1988—Georgia; Roy Baldwin as the librarian.

1988—The Gift; [Australian, Made for TV] Victoria Eagger as a librarian.

1988—Hidden City; [British] Cassie Stuart is a film librarian who becomes obsessed with finding a mysterious piece of film hidden by the government.

1988—The House on Carroll Street; William Duff-Griffin as the FBI librarian.

1988—Kingsajz; [Polish] The dwarf kingdom, Shuflandia, exists in the cellar of a library. Only the most obedient dwarves get the chance to grow to king size and inhabit the larger world.

1988—Martha, Ruth & Edie; [Canadian] Andrea Martin as a timid, small-town librarian who is reunited with her two crazy aunts from Hollywood at her mother's funeral.

1988—Nico the Unicorn; [Canadian] Leni Parker as a librarian.

1988—Running on Empty; Justine Johnson as a librarian.

1988—Shadows in the Storm; Thelonius Pitt (Ned Beatty) is sacked from his position as a Donne-quoting librarian because of heavy drinking.

1988—Winnie; [Made for TV] Florence Schauffler as a librarian.

1989—Chances Are; Morton Downey Jr. as Alex Finch meets the girl of his dreams (Mary Stuart Masterson as Miranda Jeffries) in the Yale University library when she is pleading with an old-fashioned librarian for relief from a fine. He tells the librarian that someone is fondling the folios, sending her in a tizzy in search of the offender. He then erases the bill from the computer and sends the girl on her way with a smile.

1989—Dr. Jekyll and Mr. Hyde; [Off-Broadway play] A psychotic killer (who never appears on stage), formerly a mild-mannered librarian, dismembers 16 ½ bodies because he suffers from quantum synaptic dualism.

1989—Happy Together; Alexandra Page (Helen Slater) roller skates around the college library's card catalog/reference area, leading to the inevitable shushes from the librarian (played by Rocky Parker, who is also listed in the movie credits as "biker's girlfriend").

1989—How I Got into College; Marlene Warfield as a librarian.

1989—Incident at Dark River; [Made for TV] Michaela Nelligan as a librarian.

1989—Indiana Jones and the Last Crusade; Indiana Jones (Harrison Ford) finds the final clue to the location of the lost chalice in a library in Venice. To do so he must break a hole through the marble floor, and coordinates his pounding with the sound of the librarian stamping books.

1989—The Lady Forgets; [Made for TV] Judith Berlin as a librarian.

1989—Major League; Rene Russo as Lynn Wells, special collections librarian, Cleveland (Ohio) PL. We are even told that she has a master's degree and a license plate that says "READ."

1989—Old Gringo; Laurel Lyle as a librarian.

1989—UHF; The manager of a small TV station hits it big with a mix of crazy programs. A vignette for the program "Conan the Librarian" features a patron asking for a book on astronomy. Conan (Roger Callard) picks him up and says threateningly, "Don't you know the Dewey Decimal Classification?" Later, Conan slices another borrower in half for returning a book late.

1990—Angel at My Table; [New Zealand] This is the true story of Alexia Keogh as Janet Frame, a repressed little girl who grew up to become New Zealand's most famous novelist and poet. As a young girl, she wins a prize at school—a free trip to the local library. She is awe-struck by her first visit to a library and wanders the stacks selecting books for her family.

1990—Awakenings; Adam Bryant as the librarian.

1990—Caroline? [Made for TV] Laura Whyte as a librarian.

1990—The Comfort of Strangers; [Italian/British] Natasha Richardson plays a character that she describes as "an American mother and librarian, . . . an intelligent, strong woman who is also vulnerable and a survivor."

1990—Flight of the Intruder; Adam Biesk as the librarian.

1990—The Handmaid's Tale; [US/German] Natasha Richardson as Kate wins a game of Scrabble. The Commander (Robert Duvall) says, "I knew you would be good at this. You used to be a librarian."

1990—I Love You to Death; Rosalie (Tracey Ullman) goes to the public library and finds her husband (Kevin Kline) cheating on her. Anthony Rapoport is the librarian.

1990—I'm Dangerous Tonight; [Made for TV] Felicia Lansbury as a librarian.

1990—Joe Versus the Volcano; Tom Hanks as Joe Banks claims to be an advertising librarian for a medical supply company.

1990—The Nasty Girl; [German] Michael Schreiniger and Beate Anna Weiser as librarians.

1990—Personals; [Made for TV] Jennifer O'Neill as Heather Moore, serial-killer reference librarian. Terrence Slater plays the library receptionist.

1990—Playroom; Olivera Viktorovic as a librarian.

1990—Sakura no sono; [Japanese] Guidance room segment filmed at Fukagawa Library, Koto-ku, Tokyo, Japan.

10

1990—Stanley & Iris; Dortha Duckworth as a Waterbury (Conn.) public librarian who shushes Robert De Niro for reading out loud.

1990—Stephen King's It; [Made for TV] Tim Reid as Mike Hanlon, librarian, Derry (Me.) PL. Megan Leitch plays a library aide.

1990—Transylvania Twist; Stefen (Angus Scrimm), a Transylvanian librarian, must collect the fine on *The Book of All Evil*, which is 200 years overdue. He confronts the heir to the book, Lord Byron Orlock (Robert Vaughn).

1990—The Two Jakes; A librarian gives Jake Gittes (Jack Nicholson) a hard time.

1990—Xiaoao jianghu; [Hong Kong] In the later years of the Ming dynasty, a kung-fu manual known as the sacred scroll is stolen from the Emperor's library, triggering a power struggle to retrieve it.

1991—Carolina Skeletons; [Made for TV] Louis Gosset Jr. plays a marine officer who returns to his home town. In trying to clear his brother's name of a murder charge, he gets the local archivist/librarian (Melissa Leo as Cassie) to help him find the trial records.

1991—Christmas on Division Street; [Made for TV] When visiting the libary for some research work, Fred Savage as Trevor Atwood meets a homeless man (Hume Cronyn) and reacts the way most act towards the homeless. With Crystal Verge as the librarian, Dwight McFee as a library guard, and Forbes Angus as a library patron.

1991—Deception: A Mother's Secret; [Made for TV] Mary Marsh as a librarian.

1991—Facklorna; [Danish, Made for TV] Mats Bergman stars as the librarian.

1991—Heading Home; [British] Janetta Wheatland (Joely Richardson) moves to London after WWII and finds a job as a librarian.

1991—Hear My Song; [US/British] A Liverpool club manager and his girlfriend are trying to put on a concert, but realize at the last minute that the musicians have no sheet music. So they dash to the local music library. Mary MacLeod as the librarian is a middle-aged, no-nonsense woman with her hair parted very straight down the middle. She says the two are in luck: The performer's music is "registered." They can have it copied and available in 10 days. But they sweet-talk her into giving them the music immediately and rush away to the concert. Our reporter says, "In about two minutes, the librarian changes from 'Keeper of the Information' to 'Bureaucratic Blocker of Access' to 'Helpful Supporter of True Love and Good Concerts.' It is a very sweet scene."

1991—Homicide; Steven Goldstein as the librarian, Charlotte Potok as the assistant librarian, and Andy Potok as the library technician.

1991—Little Secrets; Monica Walsvick as a librarian.

1991—The Old Lady Who Walked in the Sea; [French] Lara Guirao as a librarian.

1991—The Perfect Bride; [Made for TV] Robin Krieger as a librarian.

1991—Salmonberries; [German] A woman (k. d. lang) who grew up in Kotzebue, Alaska, returns to its public library to find out who her parents were. She befriends the librarian (Rosel Zech), an East German refugee who lost her husband while escaping.

1991—Sleeping with the Enemy; Julia Roberts as Sarah Burney gets a job as a library assistant in Cedar Falls, Iowa, while she hides from her abusive husband after faking her death.

1991—Stepping Out; Andrea Martin as Dorothy, a mousy librarian with allergies.

1991—La Totale!; [French] Miou-Miou plays Helene, a librarian who is bored with her life and her husband, whom she regards as a pleasant but dull man employed by the telephone company. In fact he is a top undercover secret agent.

1992—The Baltimore Waltz; [Off-Broadway play] An elementary school teacher named Anna (Cherry Jones) learns that her brother, a young San Francisco librarian named Carl (Richard Thompson) is terminally ill with AIDS.

1992—**Buried on Sunday;** [Canadian] Jean Gregson as a librarian.

1992—**A Child Lost Forever;** [Made for TV] Annie Waterman as a librarian.

1992—**Conte d'hiver;** [French] Loic (Herve Furic) is a librarian who excites Charlotte Véry's mind but whose admiration bores her a bit.

1992—**Forever Young;** While Daniel McCormich (Mel Gibson) is researching microfilm in the library, his 10-year old friend Nat Cooper (Elijah Wood) sees a girl he has a crush on. Nat says, "I'm in a library on a Saturday. She'll think I'm a geek."

1992—**The Gun in Betty Lou's Handbag;** Penelope Ann Miller as children's librarian Betty Lou Perkins confesses to murder to get the attention of her policeman husband. At her trial, the judge says: "That's Betty Lou Perkins? Hell, I don't go to the library enough." Marian Seldes as head librarian Margaret Armstrong believes that "The best effect of any book is that it be returned unmutilated to its shelf."

1992—**Hard-Boiled;** [Hong Kong] Gang hit-man/undercover cop played by Tony Leung kills an out-of-favor gang leader in a public library using a gun previously hidden in a fake volume of Shakespeare. The police inspector, played by Yun-Fat Chow, identifies the book and finds the weapon by cleverly noticing the imprint of the book in the blood on the library table. The librarian is Hoi-Shan Lai.

1992—**Little Nemo;** June Foray as a librarian.

1992—**Lorenzo's Oil;** Michaela Odone (Susan Sarandon) and her husband Augusto (Nick Nolte) search for a cure for their son's adrenoleukodystrophy (ALD) in the library of the National Library of Medicine (although actually filmed in the Library of Congress Reading Room). As Augusto examines the literature on long-chain fatty acids, Mary Pat Gleason as the reference librarian brings him a veterinary science journal article that proves helpful.

1992—**Scent of a Woman;** A timid prep school student works in the library, and when a classmate asks him to borrow a book that's on reserve, he lets the book go out overnight.

1992—**The Seventh Coin;** Mark Nelson as the librarian.

1992—**Storyville;** Ron Gural as the librarian.

1992—**Straight Talk;** Shirlee Kenyon (Dolly Parton) walks into a Chicago library and asks about a job. The ogre at the circulation desk (Susan Philpot) stares at her short, tight dress, shakes her head and says, "I don't think so."

1992—**Tale of a Vampire;** Julian Sands as a vampire becomes attracted to Suzanna Hamilton as Anne, a librarian.

1992—**Talking to Strange Men;** [British, Made for TV] Sara Griffiths as Penelope, a librarian.

1992—**Wild Card;** [Made for TV] Jane Abbott as a librarian.

1993—**Akhareen abadeh;** [Iranian] Mostafa is in charge of the mobile library, and he has to travel to many villages to distribute books among children. The last village is situated at a high altitude, and reaching the village turns out to be a hazardous trip.

1993—**Augustitango;** [Swedish] Lotta Beling as a librarian.

1993—**The Blue Kite;** [Chinese] The story of a young boy and his family in China during the 1950s and 60s. The father, Quanxin Pu as Lin Shaolong, is a librarian. Following the death of Stalin he is called, with all the librarians, to a meeting to discuss why they have not found any reactionaries among the staff. He leaves to use the toilet, and upon returning realizes that he has been chosen as the reactionary. He is sent to a collective farm for "reeducation" and soon dies there.

10

1993—Body Bags; [Made for TV] Betty Muramoto as a librarian.

1993—The Countess Alice; [British, Made for TV] Connie (Zoe Wanamaker), a childless, aging librarian who is bored with her job, puts cheap tea in Fortnum and Mason tins to keep up appearances for her mother (Wendy Hiller).

1993—Demolition Man; Lenina Huxley (Sandra Bullock) informs John Spartan (Sylvester Stallone), who had been cryogenically frozen for 36 years, about the Arnold Schwarzenegger Presidential Library, named after the first president not born in America.

1993—Ernest Rides Again; Alex Diakun as the librarian.

1993—Foreign Affairs; [Made for TV] Maggie Wells as a librarian.

1993—Genghis Cohn; [British] Heather Canning as a librarian.

1993—Heart and Souls; Harrison Winslow (Charles Grodin) is a shy librarian and aspiring singer.

1993—The Last Seal; [German] Saddek Kebir as the librarian.

1993—Morning Glory; [Made for TV] Miss Beasly (Nina Foch) is a nice small-town librarian who helps a newcomer to town (Christopher Reeve) do some research on bees. But she won't give him a library card because he can't prove residency. Later he becomes the library custodian.

1993—Philadelphia; Tom Hanks plays a gay lawyer stricken with AIDS who seeks redress for having been fired. At one point he is looking for information in the library, but the male librarian (played by Tracey Walter) is not at all helpful, or even friendly. The library is referred to as "The University of Pennsylvania Law School Library," but it's really the Furness Fine Arts Library, located a couple of blocks away.

1993—Public Access; A sleepy small town is stirred to trouble by a newcomer using the local public access cable station. He dates Rachel, the shy, young town librarian (Dina Brooks) who complains to him about an old grievance.

1993—Red Hot; [Canadian] Mara Zemdega as a Russian music librarian.

1993—The Return of Ironside; [Made for TV] Debra-Jayne Brown as a librarian.

1993—Rubdown; [Made for TV] Rochelle Swanson as a librarian.

1993—Rudy; Marie Anspaugh as a librarian.

1993—The Seventh Coin; While looking for clues to solve some old murders, a rookie police officer uses newspapers on microfilm. He asks the librarian (Mark Nelson) how to find out if one of the people mentioned is still alive. The librarian replies, "Have you tried the telephone book?"

1993—The Unnamable II: The Statement of Randolph Carter; The last half-hour of this film takes place in the Miskatonic University library where two people are chased through the stacks by the monster. They end up in the Rare Book Room where they find the missing pages of the manuscript that help them defeat the creature. A policeman also gets killed in the stacks. At one point someone says, "My God, it's gone into the stacks. You can get lost there even in the daytime."

1994—City Slickers II; Treasure hunters search for information on microfilm while other library patrons (Kenneth S. Allen and Helen Siff) shush them.

1994—A Friend of Dorothy; Bianca as a librarian.

1994—Fun; [Canadian] Cindie Northrup as a prison librarian.

1994—Getting In; Angela Jones as a librarian.

1994—I Love Trouble; Annie Meyers-Shyer as a "student librarian."

1994—Judicial Consent; Billy Wirth as Martin, a handsome (but also psychopathic) law library clerk who has an affair with a trial judge.

1994—Monkey Trouble; Julie Payne as the doofy librarian who loses her cool when a monkey pops out of Eva's (Thora Birch) backpack, but she does use her computer to quickly come up with the information requested.

1994—Necronomicon; H. P. Lovecraft (Jeffrey Combs) discovers the dreaded *Necronomicon* guarded by monks in an old library administered by the chief librarian (Tony Azito) and his attendant (Juan Fernández).

1994—The NeverEnding Story III; [US/German] Hiding from school bullies The Nasties, Bastian (Jason James Richter) finds his favorite book *The NeverEnding Story* in the library, where it is later discovered by the gang leader Slip (Jack Black). Mr. Coreander, the school librarian, is played by Freddie Jones.

1994—The Pagemaster; While seeking shelter from a storm in a mysterious library, Tyler (Macaulay Culkin) is mystically transported to an animated world of books representing Adventure, Fantasy, and Horror.

1994—Paperback Romance; [Australian] Eddie (Anthony LaPaglia) falls for Sophie (Gia Carides) after hearing her musing aloud—and erotically ("I felt him devouring me . . .")—at a public library. What he doesn't realize is that she's a romance writer trying out lines, and that the plaster cast she's wearing is meant to conceal the fact that her leg has been paralyzed since childhood by polio.

1994—Party Girl; Mary (Parker Posey) calls her librarian godmother, Sasha von Scherler as Mrs. Lindendorf, for bail money after being arrested for throwing an illegal party. To repay the loan, she begins working as a clerk in a public library (shot in the Jersey City, N.J., PL). At first she hates it ("Keith Richards would make a better librarian than me!"), but then decides to master the DDC and become a paragon of a paraprofessional. In one powerful speech, Mrs. Lindendorf remarks on how Dewey hired women as librarians because they couldn't be expected to think too much.

1994—Quiz Show; Anthony Fusco as the librarian.

1994—Separated by Murder; [Made for TV] Florence Roach as a librarian.

1994—The Shawshank Redemption; Tim Robbins as model prisoner Andrew Dufresne transforms the Shawshank Prison library into a well-stocked collection and befriends the old prison librarian (James Whitmore as Brooks Hatlin) One prisoner, holding a book as if it's the first he has ever picked up, reads the title with wonder: "*The Count of Monte Cristo*, by Alexandree Dumbass."

1994—Slaughter of the Innocents; Donna Todd as a librarian, Zakes Mokae as a library janitor.

1994—Stanley's Dragon; [British] Valerie Minifie as a librarian.

1994—With Honors; Simon (Joe Pesci), a homeless man, lives in the furnace room of Harvard's Widener Library. Patricia D. Butcher plays a librarian.

1995—Clean, Shaven; June Kelly as a librarian, and Marty Clinis and Ruth Gotheimer as patrons.

1995—O Convento; [Portuguese/French] An American professor goes to an old convent in Portugal to research his thesis that Shakespeare was born in Spain rather than in England. His wife thinks he is spending too much time with the young, beautiful librarian (Leonor Silveira as Piedade) and this eventually leads to trouble for everyone.

1995—Dangerous Minds; Jeff Feringa and Sarah Marshall as high school librarians.

1995—Discworld; [British] Features an orangutan as a librarian.

1995—The Garden; Gia Rhodes as the voice of the librarian.

1995—The Last Supper; Pamela Gien as an illiterate librarian.

1995—Mad Love; Sharon Collar as a librarian.

1995—Mimi wo sumaseba; [Japanese] A young girl, Youko Honna as Shikuzu Tsukishima, finds that all the books she chooses in the library have been previously checked out by the same boy. Later she meets a very infuriating fellow. Could it be her "friend" from the library?

10

1995—Remember Me; [Made for TV] Marcia Bennett as a librarian.

1995—Se7en; Morgan Freeman as Detective William Somerset studies monographs by Dante, Milton, and Chaucer for hints to grisly serial killings. Brad Pitt as Detective David Mills settles for the Cliff Notes versions. Somerset gets a sudden hunch that the killer has a library card. Brad Pitt as detective David Mills: "Just because the fucker's got a library card, doesn't make him Yoda." With Hawthorne James, Roscoe Davidson, and Bob Collins as library guards, and Jimmy Dale Hartsell as a library janitor.

1995—Twelve Monkeys; Portions filmed at Ridgeway Library in Philadelphia.

1996—Big Bully; Rick Moranis as David Leary comes back to teach at his old high school. As he walks down the hall to his classroom on the first day he passes the library, peers in, and sees his old librarian still sitting at her desk, just as he remembers her. He walks in, reminds her who he is, tells her how meaningful the library was in his life . . . and she pulls out an overdue slip and tells him how much he owes on a book he still has out.

1996—Black Mask; [Hong Kong] Jet Li plays Tsui Chik, a gentle, mild-mannered Hong Kong librarian who is also the superhuman superhero Black Mask. At one point he uses CD-ROMs as deadly weapons, throwing them at the enemy.

1996—Buried Secrets; [Made for TV] Nicky Guadagni as a librarian.

1996—Evil Has a Face; Bridgett Baron as a librarian.

1996—The Fragile Heart; [Made for TV] Miriam Leake as a librarian.

1996—High School High; Jon Lovitz as Richard Clark saves Tia Carrere as Victoria Chapell from attempted rape in the school library.

1996—Little Witches; Catholic girls do research on witchcraft in school library.

1996—Meeting Mr. Subian; Jennifer Hayden as a librarian.

1996—Small Faces; [Scottish] Liz Lochead as a librarian.

1996—The Substitute; Several gang members try to beat up teacher Shale (Tom Berenger) in the school library, but he manages to throw most of them out the window. He locks up all their guns in a caged office (in the library!) but soon after is shot by one kid who finds another gun. The kid then turns to shoot the librarian but she pulls a gun on him. Berenger then revives (he was wearing a bullet-proof vest) and tosses the kid out the window.

1996—Twilight Man; [Made for TV] Randall Haynes as a library guard.

1996—Wilderness; [British, Made for TV] A disturbed young librarian (Amanda Ooms as Alice White) has trouble convincing her lover that she's a werewolf. She moves to a retreat in Scotland, where she morphs permanently into a wolf.

1997—Bliss; Lois Chiles is Eva, the sexy and sane librarian, who impresses Baltazar Vincenza (Terence Stamp) with her ILL expertise.

1997–   —Buffy the Vampire Slayer; [TV series] Anthony Head as Rupert Giles, Watcher and school librarian at Sunnydale (Calif.) High School.

1997—Casper: A Spirited Beginning; [Made for Video] Edie McClurg as a librarian.

1997—Do Me a Favor; Frances Fisher as a librarian.

1997—Down with America; This film concerns a federal agent (Peter Roach), an obsessed librarian (Meri Stevens), and two people obsessed with silence in the library (Robb Sherman, Kevin Flowers).

1997—Dream with the Fishes; Beth Daly as a hospital librarian who is seen on the phone identifying Bashful as the one of the seven dwarfs who "everyone forgets" for one of the main characters who is dying in the hospital. (This scene was shot in a real medical center library. The character wears the name badge of the librarian who works there, and she is visible in the background.)

1997—First Do No Harm; [Made for TV] Barbara Stewart as a librarian.

1997—**Ice Storm;** Elena (Joan Allen) goes to an outdoor book sale at the New Canaan (Conn.) Library.

1997—**Keep the Aspidistra Flying;** [British] Joan Blackburn as a librarian.

1997—**Most Wanted;** David Basulto as library security guard.

1997–1998—**Once a Thief;** [TV series] James Allodi as Nathan Muckle, agency librarian.

1997—**187: Documented;** Harri James as a high school librarian.

1997—**Picture Perfect;** Partially filmed at the New York Public Library.

1997—**To Love, Honor, and Deceive;** Janet Sherkow as a librarian.

1997—**Wag the Dog;** Johnny Dean's (Willie Nelson's) song "Good Old Shoe" is recorded on fake album. Presidential adviser Robert De Niro orders: "Put this in the Library of Congress right away. Folk music section, 1930, right away. Get it in the stacks of the Library of Congress, now."

1997—**Welcome to Sarajevo;** Footage of Bosnian National Library burning.

1998—**Age to Age;** Dot Braun as a librarian.

1998—**The Census Taker;** Ethan Aronoff as the librarian.

1998—**City of Angels;** Seth (Nicolas Cage) is an angel who falls in love with Maggie (Meg Ryan). Seth and the other angels hang out at the library (supposed to be L.A. from the other scenery, but really the San Francisco PL) reading people's thoughts. Maggie is curious to know who left a copy of Hemingway's *A Moveable Feast* on her nightstand and she returns it to the library. She approaches a helpful but direct librarian (Sid Hillman) at a computer terminal, who tells her, "I can't tell you who checked it out, but I can tell you when."

1998—**Desperate Measures;** Randy Thompson as a library guard.

1998—**Echo;** [Made for TV] Kevin Blatch stars as the librarian.

1998—**Gods and Monsters;** Lisa Vastine as a librarian.

1998—**Half Baked;** At the end credits, the cast makes the audience aware of learning more about hemp at your local library.

1998—**I've Been Waiting for You;** [Made for TV] B. J. Harrison as a librarian.

1998—**Mercury Rising;** Barbara Alexander as a librarian.

1998—**Out of Sight;** Chuck Castlebery as a library guard.

1998—**Pleasantville;** The library becomes the most popular place in town, with teenagers lining up outside the door, eager for new ideas in color.

1998—**Rehearsals for War;** [Italian]; Lidia Koslovich as a librarian.

1998—**A Simple Plan;** Bridget Fonda as Sarah works at the local library.

1998—**Star Trek: Insurrection;** Lee Arone-Briggs is listed in the cast credits as a librarian, but there is no scene in which she appears. At one point Riker and Troi do some research about an alien race they plan to visit, and read lots of backgound information from electronic records. But the scene in which the librarian helped them find the information was cut before the film was released.

1998—**Stranger in Town;** [Canadian, Made for TV] Kris Alvarez as a librarian.

1998—**Summer of the Monkeys;** [Canadian] Beverly Cooper as a librarian.

1998—**The Sweetest Gift;** [Made for TV] Marcia Bennett as a librarian.

1998—**The Truman Show;** Library scenes filmed at the University of West Florida.

1999—**The Accountant;** [British] Portions filmed at Verwood Library, Dorset, England.

1999—**Angel's Dance;** Caroline Alexander as a librarian.

1999—**The Mummy;** Rachel Weisz as Evelyn Carnarvon, a young Egyptologist and librarian in Cairo in the 1920s. In an early scene she manages to topple all the ranges of books in the library.

SOURCE: Martin Raish; Frederick Duda; numerous contributions from readers; Internet Movie Database (us.imdb.com).

10

Marjorie Warmkessel's
10 favorite library postcards

by Marjorie M. Warmkessel

IN THE PREVIOUS TWO EDITIONS of this handbook, Billy Wilkinson made clear his difficulty in choosing only 10 favorite library postcards. There are so many worthy competitors. How does one choose? When given this same assignment, I decided to narrow the field by considering only those cards that picture people in or near the library. These cards vividly shed light on trends in our social history by showing people engaged in everyday activities and by capturing specific styles of dress and modes of transportation. In their 1980 book *A Social History of Britain in Postcards, 1870–1930,* Eric J. Evans and Jeffrey Richards write: "But the medieval historian would give his eye teeth for postcards from the peasants and nobles of his era with whatever scraps of information they might contain about the patterns of existence."

For those interested in social history from the late 19th century to the present, however, postcards provide a fascinating glimpse of patterns of existence. Many of the changes in society over the last century or so can be seen in my selection of 10 favorites. You may also notice that all of them are from states whose names fall in the first half of the alphabet. Perhaps for the next edition I will select cards from states in the second half.

Interior, Carnegie Library, Dawson, Georgia. This interior view of a Georgia public library from about 100 years ago is definitely one of my all-time favorite cards. I suspect that this scene was carefully staged; vases of fresh flowers are surrounded by books laid out on the table. Paintings and flags are hung on the walls and potted plants are positioned in strategic locations. The only human being in sight is obviously the librarian, sitting statuesquely behind a small but elevated desk. In spite of the artificiality of the scene and the sternness of the librarian, the library does look like a warm and inviting place.

Interior view, Carnegie Library, Agnes Scott College, Decatur, Georgia.
From this card we can learn a great deal about college life in the early years of the 20th century. Women wearing long pastel-colored dresses sit quietly in straight-backed chairs at long, wooden study tables. The atmosphere is very stark and serious; everything is utilitarian with no extraneous decoration.

Julia Rogers Library, Goucher College, Towson, Maryland. Another card of a library from a women's college—this one from the middle of the 20th century—shows students walking from the library, carrying books and all wearing midcalf-length skirts, sweaters, and bobby socks. Having attended Goucher College in the 1970s, I can say that at that time the library building looked pretty much the same as it does in this picture, but students dressed much differently.

JULIA ROGERS LIBRARY, GOUCHER COLLEGE,
TOWSON, BALTIMORE 4, MD.

10

Public Library, Sioux City, Iowa. This beautiful card shows people strolling in front of the library building, an imposing stone structure which was obviously the centerpiece of this part of town. Women are wearing long dresses and stylish hats, and carrying parasols; men and children are also dressed up. A horse and carriage wait just outside the entrance to the building.

Public Library, Chicago. In my collection I have dozens of postcards of the Chicago Public Library, but this is one of my favorites—I think because of the energy that it conveys to the viewer. People no longer have the luxury of strolling past the library, but are walking briskly; automobiles line the streets, seeming to be headed in every possible direction. Men and women still wear hats and most parts of their bodies are covered, but the style of clothing is simpler than was the case earlier in the century.

Welwood Murray Memorial Library, Palm Springs, California. A change in fashion is quite evident from this card. No longer do women wear long dresses or even midcalf-length skirts. These women walking past the library are dressed in colorful shorts with bare midriffs.

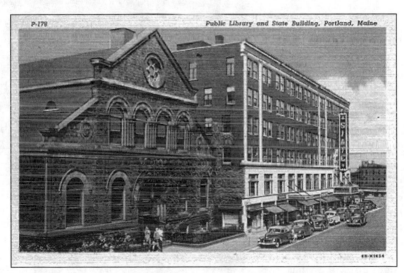

Public Library and State Building, Portland, Maine. From this card we can see that the position of the library building as one of the biggest buildings in town has changed. Though more interesting architecturally than its neighbor, it is not as large as the brick state building next door. It is difficult from this card to get a sense of the clothing styles, but it is easy to get a sense of the style of cars at the time that this picture was taken.

10

15030. Public Library, Colorado Springs, Colorado.

Public Library, Colorado Springs, Colorado. Prominent on this card is the bicycle rack in front of the library's entrance. A popular means of transportation in the early part of the 20th century, bicycles were easier to maintain than horse-drawn carriages or automobiles. A gentleman wearing a suit and hat watches another man, similarly dressed, standing near the bicycles.

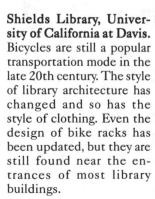

Shields Library, University of California at Davis. Bicycles are still a popular transportation mode in the late 20th century. The style of library architecture has changed and so has the style of clothing. Even the design of bike racks has been updated, but they are still found near the entrances of most library buildings.

Greetings from Albany, Georgia. I could not resist including this multiview card that includes the Carnegie Library. The selected photograph does not picture any people, cars, bicycles, or horses, but this is really one of my favorite library postcards and I think it does shed light on society of the early 20th century for a couple of reasons. First, the fact that the library is even included among a group of five views from around town is significant. Along with the library are pictures of the court house, Broad Street, St. Paul's Episcopal church, and firefighters. And this does not even begin to address the intriguing composition with the Pansy Princess (or perhaps the Goddess of Postcards) serenely staring from the center of the card. They just don't make postcards like this any more!

Greetings from
Albany, Ga.

Bibliophilately revisited

by Larry T. Nix

GEORGE EBERHART'S ARTICLE on bibliophilately, which appeared in the June 1982 issue of *American Libraries* and in the first edition of this handbook, got me hooked on collecting library-related postage stamps. Eberhart's article pointed out that libraries and librarians are not a common theme for postage stamps and that a complete collection could be assembled for a relatively modest sum. Library stamps continue to be relatively scarce, with less than 70 additional library stamps, around four a year, being issued in the past 18 years. This compares to tens of thousands of other stamps issued by postal administrations from around the world during the same period. Because library stamps are so limited in number, I'm always delighted when a new stamp

Figure 1

is issued or when I find an older stamp of which I was previously unaware. I've included a few of my favorite finds in this article, with an emphasis on items not included in the *American Libraries* article.

Figure 1. The Mercantile Library of New York was founded in 1820 as a membership library for young men working for merchants in New York City. It still survives as a membership library specializing in fiction. In 1870, the library had a collection of over 140,000 volumes, and circulated hundreds of thousands of items a year. Many of the books were sent directly to the homes of members by delivery wagon. In order to get home delivery, members prepaid for this service by purchasing delivery stamps. They would then affix these stamps to one side of a book-order form that included regular postage on the opposite side. The form was then mailed to the Mercantile Library. The Mercantile Library delivery stamp is considered to be a "local" stamp and was used from 1870 to 1875. It is listed in Scott's *Specialized Catalogue of U.S. Stamps*. A collector would not consider its purchase a modest investment.

Figure 2. A 20-cent pre-stamped postal card commemorating the 250th anniversary of the Redwood Library and Athenaeum was issued by the U.S. Postal Service in March 1999. The timing was a little off, since the library was established in 1747. The Redwood is a membership library like the New York Mercantile Library. The building in which the Redwood is housed is one of the oldest library buildings in the United States. Peter Harrison, considered to be

Figure 2

America's first architect, designed it. The postal card for the Redwood is part of the preservation series by the USPS. It was only distributed in Rhode Island, at post offices with special philatelic windows, and directly from the USPS distribution center in Kansas City, Missouri.

Figure 3

Figure 3. The building at the bottom of this stamp depicting the United Nations complex in New York City is the UN's Dag Hammarskjöld Library. The United Nations issued it in March 1968, and is only one of many stamps issued both by the UN and other countries that show the library. It holds the distinction of being the library that appears on the most different stamps. Dag Hammarskjöld, UN Secretary General from 1953 to 1961, participated in the planning of the library, but he was killed in a plane crash before its opening in 1962. Previously the library was located in an office building located on the same site. That building is depicted on the second stamp issued by the UN in 1951 and also on other stamps.

Figure 4. Although Andrew Carnegie gave grants for 2,509 library buildings throughout the English-speaking world, this is the only one that appears on a postage stamp. The Victoria (B.C.) Public Library was built in 1904 and designed by Thomas Hooper and C. Elwood Watkins in the Romanesque style of Boston architect Henry Hobson Richardson. It is currently a bank building. The Canada Postal Corp. issued the $5 stamp in February 1996. An-

Figure 4

Figure 5

drew Carnegie was honored on a United States stamp in 1960 to commemorate the 50th anniversary of the Carnegie Endowment for International Peace. I have sought unsuccessfully to get the USPS to issue a stamp depicting a Carnegie library in commemoration of the 1,679 Carnegie public library buildings in the United States.

Figure 5. India issued this stamp in December

1992 on the centennial of the birth of Dr. Shiri Shiyali Ramarit (S. R.) Ranganathan (1892–1972). Ranganathan is, of course, known by every current and former library school student for his five laws of library science (see p. 62). He is by far the most famous library educator appearing on a postage stamp. The United States has never honored a true librarian on a stamp, though Benjamin Franklin was librarian of the Library Company of Philadelphia for a brief period. Poor Melvil Dewey (1851–1931) with his flawed greatness is not likely to have a stamp commemorating the sesquicentennial of his birth, even though he is probably the most famous librarian of all time.

Figure 6

Figure 6. When the Library of Congress opened the building now known as the Jefferson building in 1897, it was proclaimed to be the most beautiful building in the world by the American public. It did not appear on a postage stamp, however, until 1982. On the other hand, France issued this stamp almost immediately in honor of the opening of the new building of the Bibliothèque Nationale de France in December 1996. The new library, designed by French architect Dominique Perrault, received criticism from the public and the staff because of its unusual design. Much of the 1.5 million-square-foot building is underground. On the four corners of the building are large towers where most of the collection is housed. These towers can be seen at the bottom left of the stamp. The controversial new British Library, which opened in 1997, may never appear on a stamp, since its number-one critic is Prince Charles.

Figure 7. The Netherlands celebrated the bicentennial of the its national library, the Koninklijke Bibliotheek (Royal Library), with this stamp in June 1998. Its collections include the largest assemblage of Dutch incunabula and books printed in the 16th century in the world. Our own national library, the Library of Congress, celebrates its bicentennial in the year 2000. A stamp was issued on April 24, 2000, in honor of this occasion.

Figure 7

Figure 8

Figure 8. This stamp issued by the Netherlands Antilles in February 1995 is unusual in several respects. First, it depicts a living person, Cedric Virginie; usually stamps depict people no longer with us. The USPS has a rule of not including anyone on a postage stamp who has not been dead for at least 10 years (with the exception of presidents). Second, it depicts a person described as a worker in a public library. Usually, ordinary people—including library workers—don't get depicted on stamps. Finally, Cedric is in a wheelchair. I know of no other library stamp depicting an individual with a disability. This stamp and one other were issued to celebrate the 50th anniversary of the Mgr. Verriet Institute for the Physically Handicapped.

Figure 9. This is one of four stamps issued by Bermuda in September 1989 to celebrate the 150th anniversary of the Bermuda Library. This stamp depicts the Hamilton Main Library. The

Figure 9

other stamps depict St. George's Old Rectory, the Sumerset Library, and the Cabinet Building. The Bermuda Library provides both national and public library services. Residents and visitors alike can freely use it. What a great place to go to check out a book in February!

Figure 10. Norway celebrated the 200th anniversary of its public libraries in October 1985 by issuing two stamps. This one depicts library users in a modern public library. The other stamp issued depicts Carl Deichman (1705–1780), who is considered the founder of the public library

Figure 10

system in Norway. We give Benjamin Franklin credit for founding in 1731 the first subscription library in America which was the predecessor of the free public library. Franklin appeared on the very first stamp issued by the United States, and has appeared on more stamps than any other American besides George Washington.

Figure 11

Figure 11. I love this 1984 stamp because it celebrates what most public libraries are primarily about—building a nation of readers. Although not specifically a library stamp, this stamp depicting Abraham Lincoln reading to his son does have library ties. The stamp design, created by Bradbury Thompson, is based on a Matthew Brady daguerreotype from the collection of the Library of Congress. Thompson also designed the Library of Congress and America's Libraries stamps that were issued in 1982. The Library of Congress is using the theme "Building a Nation of Readers" for its reading program running from 1997 to 2000. This is not surprising since John Y. Cole, director of the Center for the Book at the Library of Congress, was instrumental in promoting the adoption of both the stamp and the reading program.

My interest in collecting library-related stamps has expanded to include a variety of other items that I collectively call postal librariana. These items include:

- library-related first-day covers (envelopes that have a stamp cancelled with a first-day-of-issue postmark, often accompanied by a cachet or illustration);
- envelopes with a special library postmark and/or cachet;
- older envelopes that were mailed to and from libraries;
- envelopes with a library-related meter slogan; and
- pre-stamped postal cards with a library notice or message on the reverse.

My search for postal librariana has been interesting, educational, sometimes frustrating and therapeutic, and most of all fun. Join in the fun and get hooked on bibliophilately. To find out more about the collecting of topical stamps, covers, and related items contact the American Topical Association at P.O. Box 50820, Albuquerque, NM 87181-0820.

SOURCE: Special report by Larry Nix for *The Whole Library Handbook 3.*

Worst serial title changes, 1995–1999

1995

Worst Serial Title Change of 1995. To the *PDA Journal of Pharmaceutical Science and Technology.* Or should we say worst title changes? A little—oops, a long—history will explain. In 1946 it started as *The Bulletin of the Parenteral Drug Association.* This lasted until 1978, when it became *Journal of the Parenteral Drug Association.* In 1981 it became the *Journal of Parenteral Science and Technology.* Not satisfied with waiting so long between title changes again it became, in January 1994, *The Journal of Pharmaceutical Science and Technology,* then three issues later, *The PDA Journal of Pharmaceutical Science and Technology.* There must have been a delayed-action drug in its title that set off two changes so quickly after going so long without. Since we're in Chicago, let's hope this new title doesn't do like Michael Jordan, but stays retired for a long time to come.

User-Friendly Title Change Award. To *Interface,* which changed to *Journal of New Music Research.* In an age when serials catalogers are struggling to make sense out of electronic publications, many of which have obscure names, here is a user-friendly change that clarifies for the reader just what the publication is about.

Missing Persons Award. To *Daily Graphic.* In 1982 it changed to *People's Daily Graphic.* Last year it changed back to *Daily Graphic.* We wonder: where have all the people gone?

Holy Grail Award. To *Arthuriana.* It started as *Quondum et Futurus,* which merged with *Arthurian Interpretations* to become *Quondum et Futurus* again, but since its numbering reverted to vol. 1, no.1, it generated a new catalog record. (Do we need Numbering Changes of the Year awards now?) Last year it became *Arthuriana.* The publisher seems to be on a holy quest of its own—the perfect title. At least we can pronounce the new one.

Short and Not-So-Sweet Award. To *JADARA,* which changed from *Journal of the American Deafness and Rehabilitation Association.* The publisher's goal, as stated in the publication, is to help professionals provide better service in the field. Communicating your intent clearly is a worthy goal, but doing it by obfuscating the title is not the best approach.

Please Don't Reach Out and Touch This Title Anymore Award. To AT&T for its *800 Consumers Directory.* In 1987–88 it was called *The AT&T Toll Free 800 Directory for Consumers.* Then it changed to *AT&T Toll-Free 800 Directory (Consumer Ed.).* Now it's *The AT&T Toll-Free National 800 Directory (Consumer Ed.).* We begin wondering—are they going to do all this with an international directory also?

Snake in the Grass Award. To the Nebraska Library Commission (formerly the Nebraska Public Library Commission). Unfortunately this year we had to make it the "King" Snake in the Grass Award. In 1931 their publication started out as *The Nebraska Public Library Commission Bulletin.* Over the years it has changed to *Nebraska Public Library; Nebraska Public Library Commission [Newsletter]; Newsletter to Nebraska Librarians; Newsletter to Nebraska Librarians, Trustees and Friends; Newsletter; Overtones from the Underground; NLC Overtones; Overtones;* and finally last year to *N-Compass.* Their record speaks for itself. However, we would like to congratulate them on doing such good work in creating job security for Nebraska serials catalogers.

10

1996

Worst Serial Title Change of 1996. To *Exquisite Corpse*, which changed to simply *Corpse*, then after one issue changed back to *Exquisite Corpse*. This not-so-dead-after-all title was more than just a dead body. As the editor implied, when justifying the return to the original title, once an exquisite corpse, always an exquisite corpse. Let's hope they finally bury it.

Wasted Air Award. To the *Journal of the Air & Waste Management Association*, which changed from *Air & Waste*, which changed from *Journal of the Air & Waste Management Association*. This is a change that wastes air, words, and catalogers' patience.

Retire This Title Change Once and For All Award. To *New Choices*. It's the last in a long list of title changes: *New Choices for Retirement Living* changed from *New Choices for the Best Years*, which changed from *50 Plus*, which changed from *Retirement Living*, which changed from: *Harvest Years/Retirement Living*. Who says there isn't life after 50 (title changes, that is)?

Can't Stop Now Award. To the *New Review of Hypermedia and Multimedia*. It used to be called just *Hypermedia*. Shows you what happens when you keep going and going and . . .

Non-Specific Award. To *New Directions for Evaluation*, which changed from *New Directions for Program Evaluation*. Thanks for now putting us in the dark about what's being evaluated. **First Things First Award.** To the *Journal of Gerontology*, which split into *Journal of Gerontology. Series A, Biological Sciences and Medical Sciences;* and *Journal of Gerontology. Series B, Psychological Sciences and Social Sciences*. We're so glad they want to teach us our As and Bs. We hope they stop long before they get to *Journal of Gerontology. Series Z*.

Thinking of the Consumer Award. To the *Journal of Retail Banking Services*. It used to be merely *Journal of Retail Banking*. Good to see they're finally going to offer us a full-service title change.

No Answers Here Award. To *IEE Solutions*, which used to be *Industrial Engineering*. In our minds they didn't solve anything by coming up with this solution.

Extinct Words Award. To *Endangered Species Bulletin*, which used to be *Endangered Species Technical Bulletin*. Thank you for endangering catalogers' peace of mind by extinguishing words in your title.

Oh, So That's Who Award. To the *Journal of Adolescent & Adult Literacy*, which changed from the *Journal of Reading*. We're pleased they clarified who's doing all the reading. Next thing you know, they'll realize young children also read and—well, let's not give them any ideas.

After All Is Said and Done, He's Still Only a Jock Award. To *Coach and Athletic Director*, which changed its name from *Scholastic Coach and Athletic Director*. So it had to take them 65 volumes to realize there's very little scholastic about being a coach?

Eyes Open Finally Award. To *National Theater Critics Reviews*, which started in 1943 as *New York Theater Critics Reviews*. How could it take them 52 years to notice there's theater outside New York City?

Snake in the Grass Award. In thanks to the California School Library Association for taking us from one confusion to another by changing *CMLEA Journal* to simply *Journal*. Maybe the fact the association suffered its 14th name change in 80 years had something to do with it. Obviously with all those changes they wanted to get back to the basics.

1997

Worst Serial Title Change of 1997. To *Journal (Florida Alliance for Health, Physical Education, Recreation, Dance, and Driver Education)* for changing four times within one year. Where else but in foggy San Francisco could the awards committee recognize a title that provides so much obfuscation in so little time?

Most Politically Correct Title Change. To *Human Quest* (St. Petersburg., Fla., 1996), which dropped "Churchman's" from its title because a reader protested: "Why *The Churchman's Human Quest?* That leaves out a lot of good people." The committee was relieved that this reader didn't think *Human Quest* objectionable and insist on calling it *Huperson Quest*.

Least Affordable Title Change. To *Air Progress* (Canoga Park, Calif., 1996), changed from *Air Progress Affordable Flying*. This change was caused by the fact that the publisher had *actually thought* flying was *affordable*.

Most Unfriendly Title Change. To *Friendly Street Reader*, for its two title changes in four issues. With a Friendly Street like this, who needs a Mean Street?

It's Time for a Commercial Break, or Best Improved Title Award. To *Journal of Commerce* (New York, N.Y., 1996), formerly *Journal of Commerce and Commercial* (New York, N.Y., 1927). At last, a title change for the better.

Keep Your Hands to Yourself Award. A hands-down winner with *Getting Results for the Hands-on Manager*, which used to be *Supervisory Management*. We think management should just stick to supervising.

Mummy Award. Preserved for *Preservation* (Washington, D.C.), for changing from *Historic Preservation* (Washington, D.C.). It would help if they took their own advice and preserved their title first.

At Least They Got Their T's and Q's Right Award. To *TQS Review*, for changing from *TQS News, TQS, TQS Currents*, and *TQ News*. With initials like this, who cares about the rest of the title?

Spice of Life Award. To *Variety's On Production*, formerly *On Production* and *Post-production*. After all, variety is the spice of life.

Who Cares? Award. Shared by *Alternatives Journal* (Peterborough, Ont., formerly *Alternatives*, Waterloo, Ont.); and *Digital System Report* (was *Digital Systems Journal*) for their absolutely trivial and content-free change in title.

Big Mama Snake in the Grass Award. Won by none other than *ALA Washington News* for dropping "letter" from its former title *ALA Washington Newsletter*. Is the letter in the mail, or did they shred it?

Seven Year Itch Award. For *AALL Spectrum*, formerly *American Association of Law Libraries Newsletter* (1989); *American Association of Law Libraries Newsletter*, 1976–1989; and *American Association of Law Libraries Newsletter*, 1970–1976. The AALL seems to be suffering with a chronic scratch, since it keeps coming around every seven years just like the fabled itch.

Missing Librarian Award. Did not miss *Virginia Libraries* (Alexandria, Va.), which used to be *Virginia Librarian* (1954–1976), *Virginia Librarian Newsletter* (1977–1986), *Virginia Librarian* (Alexandria, Va., 1986). Can libraries survive without the librarian?

Karen Muller Made Us Do It Award. To *RUSA Newsletter*, changed from *RASD Newsletter*, due to the name change of the division. The award is named after ALCTS Executive Director Karen Muller, who won the Snake in the Grass Award in 1990 for changing *RTSD Newsletter* to *ALCTS Newsletter* after the division voted to change its name.

10

1998

Worst Serial Title Change of 1998. To the Royal Geographical Society of London, for being the Royal Pain in the Bib by calling the title of its magazine three different names in as many issues. The magazine began as *The Geographical Magazine* (May 1936–November 1988), changed to *Geographical* (December 1988–April 1995), then proceeded to *Geographical Magazine* (May 1995–May 1997), followed by *The Royal Geographical Society Magazine* (June 1997), and back to *Geographical* (July 1997). Not only did the title change unnecessarily and repeatedly, it always changed in the middle of the year and volume. To make things even worse, the numbering was also screwed up. One of the nominators, Jeanette Skwor, said: "I cannot think of a finer example of the spirit of this award." It was only fitting that the committee granted this prestigious award from the recipient in the U.K. capital for such a capital bibliographical crime.

Asian Crisis Award. To *Asia-Pacific Magazine* (1997), published by the Research School of Pacific and Asian Studies, Australian National University. This title continues *New Asia-Pacific Review* (1996–1997), which is the offspring of *New Asia Review* and the original *Asia-Pacific Magazine,* both having a brief lifespan.

Healthy Choice (Not) Award. To *Nutrition Forum* (Amherst, N.Y.), published by Prometheus Books, for changing back to its original title: *Nutrition Forum* (Philadelphia, Pa.), after a short life (three issues, Sept./Oct. 1996–Jan./Feb. 1997) under the name *Nutrition & Health Forum.* Do they think health has nothing to do with nutrition?

No Business Is Bad Business Award. Earned by the UCLA Anderson Forecasting Project for its *UCLA Anderson Forecast for the Nation and California,* formerly the *UCLA Business Forecast for the Nation and California.* Thanks, but no thanks, for this most notable reduction in meaningfulness of the title word.

I Want to Live, or Walking Dead Award. Belonged to *Transactions of the Faculty of Actuaries,* published by the Faculty of Actuaries in Scotland. This title is supposed to have merged with *Journal of the Institute of Actuaries* to become *British Actuarial Journal* in 1995, but guess what? It came back to haunt us with numbers 285–286 in 1997, even though the volume 3, part 4 (1997) issue of the *British Actuarial Journal* still says on its cover: "incorporating *Journal of the Institute of Actuaries* and *Transactions of the Faculty of Actuaries.*" Welcome to the serials Twilight Zone.

Most Miss-Guided Award. To Peterson's Guides for dropping the word "guide" from seven of its guide titles. Practically, all these have merged to form *Peterson's Guide to Frustration.*

Medieval Torture in the Electronic Age Award. Found its winner in the *Medieval Review,* formerly *BMMR.* This e-journal changed its title with the July 1997 issue, but carried with it all the previous issues under the old title. This weird behavior caused CONSER to come up with a brand-new solution: "Incorporating entry."

The Snake in the Grass Award, aka E-dentity Crisis Award. Presented to *UCLA Library Staff Newsweb,* an electronic newsletter published by the UCLA Library Administration Office. In its nominator's (Michael Randall) words: "After a staid and responsible publishing history of almost 33 years, the digital age wreaked havoc upon the *Library Newsletter/UCLA.* A new electronic version with the title *UCLA Library Newsweb* began publication with no. 837, on

June 17, 1997. But not having drawn its last breath, *Library Newsletter/UCLA* continued publishing until no. 839, July 25, 1997. For this three-issue overlap period, both titles published simultaneously, with slightly differing contents. Then, showing that change occurs quickly in the digital age, the title changed again, for no apparent reason and with no explanation, to *UCLA Library Staff Newsweb*, with no. 855, on March 16, 1998."

1999

Worst Serial Title Change of 1999. A tie between the *European Journal of Organic Chemistry* and the *European Journal of Inorganic Chemistry*. These two journals were formed by the merging of various parts of five separate journals of chemistry originating from the following countries: France, Belgium, Germany, Italy, and the Netherlands. We think they deserve the "Ee-yew! The EU Award," since these two were most likely to trigger a chemical imbalance in any cataloger who had to cope with these merging European Union countries.

The Congressional Shenanigans Award. To *CQ Weekly*, formerly *Congressional Quarterly Weekly*. Hey guys, we've had enough fooling around for the year without this too.

The Unwanted Preposition Award. Belongs to *Journal for Nurses in Staff Development*, formerly called *Journal of Nursing Staff Development*. These tiny particles managed to inflict much pain on catalogers, many of whom are nursing a grudge against this title.

The Less Is More (Work for Catalogers) Award. To *PAJ*, which shrank its name from *Performing Arts Journal* in both its print and online versions. This was decidedly a bad performance on their part. Bring down the curtains on this one before we start throwing eggs.

The Keep Your MITs off This Title Award. To *Technology Review: MIT's Magazine of Innovation*, formerly called *MIT's Technology Review* and *Technology Review*. We don't agree with MIT's idea of innovation—changing the title back and forth is not high technology.

The 3, 2, 1, and Stop! Award. To *News (Regional Arts and Culture Council)*, formerly *Art Notes (Portland, Ore.)* and *Technical Assistance Newsletter*. All these tiresome title changes took place within the last year. As the year went by, the titles got shorter and shorter. At this rate, the publication should disappear completely by next year (we hope).

The Snake in the Grass Award. To *School Library Media Quarterly*, which split into *Knowledge Quest* and *School Library Media Quarterly Online*. This two-faced title had a split personality problem: It couldn't decide if it wanted to be a print or an electronic publication, so it became both. Unfortunately for the catalogers, neither version kept the old title. In our opinion, this is a sure sign of media madness.

The Mini-Snake in the Grass Award. To *ALCTS Newsletter Online*, formerly *ALCTS Newsletter*. This publication ceased its paper format and went strictly electronic. While this may be great for saving the trees, it's killing the catalogers.

SOURCE: ALA Association for Library Collections and Technical Services. For earlier and later versions of these facetious awards, see (ala8.ala.org/alcts/organization/ss/worst.html).

10

American Libraries' dubious distinction awards

by Leonard Kniffel

AT *AMERICAN LIBRARIES* WE'VE ACQUIRED enough typos, silly mistakes, and snippets of wit in classified ads and other materials over the years to keep us chuckling. We hope you'll forgive our self-indulgence in sharing them with you. (Our own mistakes are not nearly so funny.)

We did not make these winners up.

The Applicant Is in the Mail Award: To Hong Kong University, which instructs that "applicants with a resume and the names and addresses of three references should be sent by mail to fax."

Best Vantage Point Award: To St. Mary's College of Maryland for appointing an agile library and information technology director who "reports directly to the provost and sits on the president's cabinet."

Beta Phi Moo Award: To NPM Advertising, which requested that we "Please send a teat sheet upon publication."

Big Is Beautiful Award: For the news release, "Johnson County Central Resource Library Opens to Heavy Patron Use."

The Boss Is in the Mail Award: To Southern Arkansas University, which asks that job applicants "send letter of application, resume, and three persons who may be contacted as references."

Crime Buster Award: To Auburn, Alabama, which advertised for a children's librarian with an "acceptable criminal background check." Candidates without criminal backgrounds automatically are presumably disqualified.

Department of Redundancy Department Award: To the Family Friendly Libraries organization, which purports to advocate for same. Hello in there. Libraries are already the family-friendliest institution in the world.

Done Wrong Award: To Roger W. Mason Jr. of Dunn Wright Products, who sent the following message: "My company is in the process of evaluating magazine classified ads for our use. Please send all information on this matter. I will be out of town for a while so please contact by mail. Please be sure to state the following: rate per word, display ads, circulation, and what type of readers subscribe (housewives, fishermen, etc.) and briefly describe magazine."

Doubting Thomas Award: To the University of Manitoba Libraries, where employment recruiters encourage applications from "members of visible minorities," H. G. Wells notwithstanding.

Dropped Drawers Award: To Nicholson Baker for the eloquent exposure of his neurotic obsession with card catalogs.

Duh Award 1996: To America Online for briefly banning the word "breast" from its cyber-airwaves in an effort to squelch obscenity.

Duh Award 1998: To be shared by all of those (you know who you are) who sent faxes or e-mail messages ending with "Please contact me if this message does not come through."

Et tu Brute Award: To Clifford Stoll for his comment in *Entertainment Weekly,* "The central lie in this movie is that if you can control computers, then you have power. Look around! Those with lots of information, like librarians, virtually have zero influence."

Euphemism Award: To the University of North Carolina/Charlotte, where "the head of information commons" is responsible for services provided on "the major patron interaction floor" of its library.

Fire Prevention Award: To Wayne State University for advertising that "all buildings, structures and vehicles at WSU are smoke-free." By all means, let us know what the secret fuel is.

A First Name Would Have Helped Award: To *Library Journal* for the headline, "Pancake Is SLA President-Elect."

Freudian Slip Award: To Mississippi State University libraries for an ad in which applications and resumés were to be sent to the "Assistant Death of Libraries." Runner-up is Western Maryland College, where the library is "automated (Dying)." Sorry, Dynix.

Get a Clue Award: To the U.S. Congress for the Communications Decency Act. Does the word Constitution mean anything to you at all?

Good Luck Award: To D. E. Shaw & Company, a global investment bank looking for "candidates who have grown an institutional library." We can't even get one to sprout.

Good Scout Award: To Anne Arundel County Public Library for telling us, "Library Prepares for Next Twenty Years."

Health Watch Award: For the news release, "Library Experiences Largest Growth Ever."

His Own Department Award: For the news release, "New York City Department for the Aging Commissioner Comes to Brooklyn Public Library."

Honest Self-Interest Award: To the librarians at Northern Michigan University, where "willingness to share chocolate" was listed with other qualifications for reference/library instruction librarian.

Hot Stuff Award: To what's his name, author of *Primary Colors,* for creating the horny librarian Ms. Baum. But we still want to know who she was based on.

Hunk Award: For the news release, "Providence College Employs Muscular Therapist."

Imodium Award: For the news release, "Book Cellar Bowels to Open for Used Book Sale."

Kama Sutra Award: To Northeast Texas Community College for not discriminating on the basis of race, religion, age, or "national original sex."

Kentucky Derby Award: To the Library of Michigan, which was looking for applicants with "experience with handicappers."

Let Me See If I Heard That Right Award: To the U.S. Postal Service for admitting that its fourth-class rate was unfair to libraries, then refusing to roll it back.

Lost in Translation Award: To Lyubov Kazachenkova, who sent an e-mail message inviting *American Libraries* to cover a conference in Russia because "I am interested in participation of real skin specialists such as your reporters."

McAggravation Award: To McDonald's and the Disney Corporation for sending countless librarians on a search for Dumbo's mother's name and other trivia. If we answer the questions, do we get the car?

Misery Loves Company Award: To Bartlett Public Library in Illinois, where applicants for the directorship are expected to "commiserate with experience."

Most Overused Nounlike Verbs Award: To ALA, for "vision," "partner,"

10

"interface," and "impact." I vision, therefore I partner. I interface, therefore I impact.

Prosperous Poltergeist Award: To West Deptford Public Library, where, according to a letter to the editor, "One of our deceased patrons used the library and our stock market course and did very well in the stock market."

Robotics Award: To the Jesuit-Strauss-McCormick Library in Chicago, where an automation librarian is expected to "install, maintain, and train staff." Plugged in or battery operated?

So There Kenneth Starr Award: To California State University/Northridge, where the senior assistant librarian unabashedly "participates in faculty affairs" and "other possible assignments depending on background and interest."

Stop the Presses Award: To the National Lighting Bureau for rushing off a news release to let us know that it is "a group that advocates quality lighting." Special recognition to NLB chair Robert V. Morse, who issued this daring assertion: "We are looking forward to promoting high-benefit lighting in new ways this year."

That Hurts Award: To the Oregon Institute of Technology, where the library director "sits on the provost's staff." Ouch.

Truth in Advertising Award: To Franklin D. Roberts, director of the Mantor Library at the University of Maine/Farmington, who acknowledged in recruiting for a new head of reference services that "a sense of humor in the face of

jackhammers is also a plus," and for pointing out that Farmington is "the home of Chester Greenwood (inventor of earmuffs)."

Whirling Dervish Award: To West Virginia University libraries for a classified ad proclaiming that "technical services librarians may be expected to rotate for at least four hours per week."

Who the Hell Are You Award: To Bev Coleman, librarian wannabe from Montana, who blabbed to the media about Unabomber Ted Kaczynski's library borrowing record.

SOURCE: American Libraries 27 (Sept. 1996): 33; and 29 (Sept. 1998): 36.

Index

support staff, 133–138
symbolism of books, 224–225
Symons, Ann K., 499–500

T
technology
    awards, 180–181
    public libraries, 419
Teen Read Week, 387
thanking donors, 404–405
theft, 362
Thornton, Joyce K., 418
titles, weird, 505–506
training
    for electronic resources, 332–334
    Web site evaluation, 427–429
travel grants, 155–160
Trinkley, Michael, 358–360
trustees, 113–114, 125–129
Turner, Kaye Y., 27–28
Tuttle, Craig A., 344–346

U
Uhler, Scott F., 470–473
United Nations documents, 240–243
unserved users, 22–23
Unsworth, Michael E., 233–237
U.S. Copyright Office, 474–476
user fees, 463–466
users, characteristics of, 19–21

V
values, 440–442
Vavrek, Bernard, 440–442
videos
    notable children's, 254–255
    preservation of, 349–352

young adult materials, 257–258
visually handicapped users, 370–372

W
Warmkessel, Marjorie, 546–551
water-damaged collections, 355–357
Waters, Donald J., 416–417
Web sites
    design, 431–433
    evaluation, 427–429
    graphics, 423–427
Wellisch, Hans, 286–287
Womack, Kay, 79–81
Woodward, Jeannette, 47–48
words
    beginning with "bibl," 508–510
    "library" in 114 languages,
      508–510
    outsourcing newspeak, 448
    rural computer lingo, 417–418
work-study programs, 135–138
Wright, Lisa A., 335–337
writing and editing, 199–208

Y
Young, Sherry E., 135–138
young adult materials
    best books, 271–273
    videos, 257–258
young adult services
    awards, 173–175
    correctional facilities, 377–379
    Friends groups, 132
    programs, 273–276
    Teen Read Week, 387

Z
Z39.50, 288–291

GEORGE M. EBERHART is a senior editor of *American Libraries* magazine for the American Library Association. From 1980 to 1990 he was editor of *College & Research Libraries News*, the news magazine of ALA's Association of College & Research Libraries division. He has also written on the subjects of UFOs, crypto-zoology, and postcard collecting. Eberhart holds a bachelor's degree in journalism from Ohio State University and an MLS from the University of Chicago.